McGRAW-HILL INDUSTRIAL ORGANIZATION
AND MANAGEMENT SERIES

L. C. MORROW, *Consulting Editor*

★ ★ ★

Industrial Organization
and Management

McGRAW-HILL
INDUSTRIAL ORGANIZATION AND MANAGEMENT SERIES

L. C. MORROW, *Consulting Editor*
Consulting Editor, Factory Management and Maintenance

Assisted by a Board of Industrial and Educational Advisers

Industrial Organization and Management

LAWRENCE L. BETHEL
Director, New Haven YMCA Junior College
Formerly Lecturer in Industrial Administration
Yale University

FRANKLIN S. ATWATER
Industrial Engineering Manager
The Fafnir Bearing Company

GEORGE H. E. SMITH
Lawyer and Economist

HARVEY A. STACKMAN, JR.
Personnel Administrator, Scovill Manufacturing Company
Instructor of Personnel Administration
New Haven YMCA Junior College

Second Edition
Third Impression

New York   Toronto   London
McGRAW-HILL BOOK COMPANY, INC.
1950

INDUSTRIAL ORGANIZATION AND MANAGEMENT

PREFACE TO THE SECOND EDITION

Special Note to Second Printing

This text was originally conceived in wartime in condition of material, production, and price controls. It was tested and extensively used in wartime management and industry training classes. Presenting the subject of industrial management in terms of basic functions, principles, and processes, the book proved itself eminently useful in the postwar transition period as the wartime sellers' market turned to a buyers' market with increasing competition. Changes and additions were made in the second edition to the text in 1950 in consideration of experiences of both wartime and peacetime operations. Profound changes in the international situation are again emphasizing defense production with accompanying economic controls. Here, then, is a text with improvements and additions, which has served through a full cycle of the economy, from defense and war production, to peace, and back again to defense production.

The aim of the first edition was to achieve balance in presenting the principles of industrial management which within itself is a field composed of many highly specialized functions. Primary emphasis was given to the interrelationship of functions and the principles governing them rather than to the technical details of each function. Many of the latter are included, but only for the purpose of illustrating the application of basic principles. Industrial experience during the war and now during a period of competition has revealed the importance of unity within the organization. The engineer, the accountant, the research technician, the salesman, the production supervisor, and the shopworker are all members of the same enterprise. Each must have understanding and appreciation of the work of the other, of the interdependence of their functions, and of the fundamental principles by which they may carry on their joint endeavors with greatest effectiveness.

Toward this end the four authors, each with a background of specialization different from the others, worked together for a period of several years in the preparation and use of the material. Each part of the material had to receive the full consideration and endorsement of all four authors.

These same emphases have been continued in the second edition. But in addition to the benefits to be derived from the joint efforts of the authors, the second edition has the advantage of improvements suggested by the many instructors who have used the book in their college groups. To these people the authors extend grateful acknowledgment. Their suggestions have focused attention on the strengths of organization and content of the first edition that should be preserved and amplified.

The second edition has grown also from an acknowledgment of a significant turn in our economy. Immediately following the Second World War we were in an upward spiral where emphasis was on higher production. By the beginning of the 1950's, however, much of the backlog of business had been absorbed and a competitive period was again upon us, with the emphases on increased quality and service with lower costs and prices. The second edition has acknowledged these emphases with the addition of sections on production processes, waste control, plant and equipment maintenance, equipment replacement, and several other sections dealing with principles of cost reduction and the complete reworking of material in sales, quality control, and physical facilities.

This edition also observes significant developments in labor and governmental influence in the management of an industrial enterprise. These are reflected particularly in a new chapter, Industrial America—Control at the Mid-Century, and in the complete revision of the section on Administration of Industrial Relations.

The methods of presentation in this edition remain the same as before. However, all illustrations and cases have been reconsidered and rewritten or substituted where necessary to make them truly illustrative of the current application of basic principles.

New bibliographies and specific references have been prepared for each chapter in order that the reader may have a guide to further reading of material appropriate to the problems of this period of industrial development.

THE AUTHORS

NEW HAVEN, CONN.
   March, 1950

PREFACE TO THE FIRST EDITION

The art of managing an industrial enterprise today is a highly complex one. Technological developments with respect to both products and production equipment, increasingly close relationships between enterprises and between entire industries, expanding governmental controls, enlarged bodies of regulations for dealing with organized groups of employees— these are only some of the ever-changing circumstances that continually complicate the task of today's industrial managers. Confronted with such mobile conditions, the field of industrial management has been both broadened in scope and subdivided as to activity. The net result has been the establishment of such specialized functions as industrial relations, methods analysis, production planning, each with its own sphere of influence and effort, yet all coordinated and integrated into a working entity known under that rather nebulous title of "the management."

Each function of industrial management is based on established principles by which the competent manager is guided, consciously or otherwise, in his particular sphere, regardless of whether his company is making paper clips or passenger airplanes or whether it has 100 or 100,000 employees. Many a successful cost accountant, for example, has moved from one type of industrial enterprise to another in an entirely different field and has applied his cost-accounting principles with equal success. In fact, any list of a half dozen or so competent industrial managers is almost certain to include one or more whose firm grasp of fundamentals has enabled him to operate successfully in different kinds of enterprises.

It is these universal principles of management with which the authors of this volume have been primarily concerned. Thus the material presented here should be of interest, first of all, to the student of industrial management in college, extension, or work-study training. For such a student, this volume should serve as an introductory text, after which he may pursue further his specialized studies of the various management functions. Second, it should assist professional engineers, lawyers, accountants, and others who in their dealing with industry must possess a working knowledge of fundamental management principles. Third, this volume may be useful to practitioners in industrial management. For this group, a review of basic management principles may be the means

vii

of gaining a better perspective—of enabling them to see the woods as well as the trees.

To serve these purposes this book depends in each chapter upon a method of presentation composed of four parts: (1) brief fundamental statements of the background and operating principles pertaining to the function in question, (2) case examples illustrating the application of principles, (3) consideration of controversial issues of the present and tentative outlook of the future, and (4) case problems and questions adapted from actual plant situations through which the reader may experience specific adaptations.

The material for this book has been developed and used by the authors in connection with their classes over a period of three years. It has grown out of the recognition of a need for text material that will make a balanced presentation—the kind of presentation that might result from personal observations and studies by men who as a group would represent divergent fields of specialization, such as finance, economics, industrial relations, production engineering, and marketing—yet who, through working together over a period of years, might be able to agree upon basic fundamentals and define basic controversies.

The authors make no claim to have originated principles new to industrial management. Those here treated are in wide use by industry. They are thoroughly tried and tested and have been found to be sound. However, the authors have presented these principles with new emphases in light of the changed circumstances accelerated particularly by the intense industrial activity of World War II. Finally, the authors believe that here considered are certain new trends, technological developments, and adaptations of principles, all of which show promise of more general adoption by industry.

On points where controversy exists they have attempted to state opposing points of view as expressed by other authors of management materials in order to stimulate thinking that may assist in the solution of these problems by the managers of industry today and tomorrow.

The authors wish to make grateful acknowledgment to the many industrial executives who have contributed illustrative and case material as well as thoughtful criticisms and suggestions for the improvement of the manuscript. Appreciation is extended also to Annette L. Atwater and Katharine Blenis for their diligent and efficient service in the assembly and arrangement of the manuscript.

LAWRENCE L. BETHEL
FRANKLIN S. ATWATER
GEORGE H. E. SMITH
HARVEY A. STACKMAN, JR.

NEW HAVEN, CONN.
March, 1945

CONTENTS

Section One

American Industry

Section Two

Organization of the Industrial Enterprise

Section Three

Operation of the Industrial Enterprise

A. Manufacturing the Product

B. Administration of Industrial Relations

C. Selling the Product

D. Managing the General Offices

Section Four

Coordination of the Industrial Enterprise

American Industry

CHAPTER I

FUNDAMENTAL CONCEPTS

THE PATTERN OF ECONOMIC ACTIVITIES

A broad simple pattern sets the framework for the economic activities of people everywhere. This pattern consists of the four major processes that make up an economic system (see Fig. 1).

First, there is the process that provides the raw materials needed in modern economy: the minerals and fuels; the grains and other vegetable and animal food products; wool, cotton, flax, and other fibers; lumber; stone, sand, and clay; leather, hides, and skins; and like commodities. This is the work of enterprises engaged in agriculture, mining, lumbering, hunting, and fishing—often called the "primary industries."

Second, there is the process by which these raw materials are manufactured or converted into different forms, *i.e.*, the manufacturing process carried on chiefly in factory enterprises. The products turned out here fall into two general classes: semimanufactures, which are partly fabricated goods passing from producer to producer for further processing, and finished goods to be sold to the ultimate consumer. Thousands of enterprises, classified in 20 industry groups, carry on the manufacturing process.[1]

[1] See first edition (p. 1, note 1) for the 20 industry groups as classified by the United States Census of Manufactures for 1940. Preliminary releases of the 1947 census are slightly different, as follows: (1) food and kindred products; (2) tobacco manufactures; (3) textile-mill products; (4) apparel and related products; (5) lumber and products, except furniture; (6) furniture and fixtures; (7) paper and allied products; (8) printing and publishing industries; (9) chemicals and allied products; (10) petroleum and coal products; (11) rubber products; (12) leather and leather products; (13) stone, clay, and glass products; (14) primary metal industries; (15) fabricated-metal products; (16) machinery (except electrical); (17) electrical machinery; (18) transportation equipment; (19) instruments and related products; (20) miscellaneous manufactures.

The third is the distributive process by which raw materials and manufactured goods are passed from producer to producer and from producers to consumers. Here are found the commercial and trading enterprises. They facilitate the passage of goods from the crude raw materials through the many stages of processing and manufacture to the ultimate consumers. In the main, their operations consist of buying and selling as middlemen, storing, sorting, grading, packaging, and moving goods about to places where they are most needed.

The fourth element—the furnishing of services in the economy—has rapidly grown to prominence in recent years. While many are thus engaged in producing and handling tangible goods, there are others who render an infinite variety of services at every point in the economic system: domestic services; financial and professional services to individuals and to business enterprises; mechanical services in factories and in the community; general public services such as transportation, communication, the furnishing of heat, light, and power, and similar services commonly classed as public utilities; and government services. Although the performance of services is not a process like agriculture and manufacturing, it is one of the four broad fields into which an economic system is divided.

Here, then, is the essence of economic life: people making goods and performing services while in turn they use the products and benefit by the services of others. The material basis of daily living is thus a cooperative cycle of making and using goods and services. All four fields of economic activity are mutually dependent parts of the larger whole, the national economy. And because the nation is not a self-sufficient economic unit, it carries this cooperative cycle beyond its borders by taking part with other nations in the international exchange of goods and services.

Division of Labor and Specialization.—The entire field of industrial activity, like the economic system as a whole, is pervaded by the principle of division of labor and its refinement, specialization. Division of labor originated in the dim recesses of the distant past, even before the beginnings of civilization lighted the pages of history enough for us to see that primitive people lived together and shared in work for their common benefit. In its simplest form, division of labor means dividing up the work by the devotion of labor either to particular activities and products, or to the minute operations required in the making of a single product. The principle is based upon differences in climate, locality, and terrain, natural resources, personal aptitudes and skills, cultural and other distinguishing features of environment and people.

It is division of labor and the consequent need for cooperation that

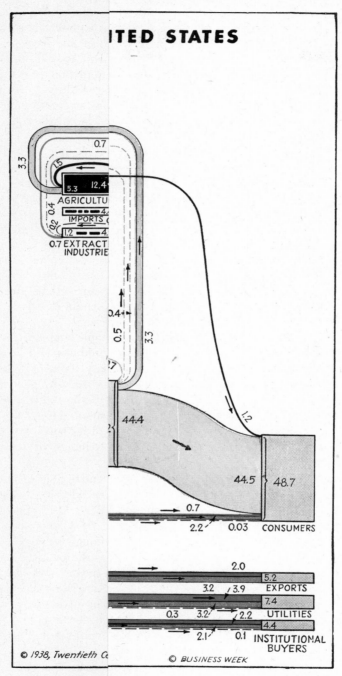

3.3

0.7

1.5

5.3   12.4

AGRICULTU

0.4   4.

IMPORTS

0.2   1.2   4.

0.7 EXTRACT
INDUSTRIE

0.4

0.5   3.3

7

44.4

1.2

44.5   48.7

0.7

2.2   0.03   CONSUMERS

2.0

5.2

3.2   3.9   EXPORTS

7.4

3.2   UTILITIES

0.3   2.2

4.4

2.1   0.1   INSTITUTIONAL
BUYERS

© 1938, Twentieth C

© BUSINESS WEEK

FIG. 1.—(Reproused from Agnew, H. E., R. B. Jenkins, and
J. C. Drury's "O

tie the many parts of a complex economy together. They account for the fact that, although there is no apparent grand plan or all-powerful, human, guiding hand to organize and control economic life, yet there is a workable coordination that unites all parts of the economic machine. The division of labor shows itself in the separation of people into the elementary occupational groups of farmers, artisans, merchants, soldiers, and the like. It also manifests itself in those territorial divisions of economy that give us great regions of the world devoted primarily to agriculture, lumbering, mining, shipbuilding, and manufacturing industries.

The world's important seaports and trading centers—Liverpool, Rotterdam, Hamburg, Copenhagen, Leningrad, Lisbon, Le Havre, Marseille, Venice, Odessa, Calcutta, Canton, Hong Kong, Shanghai, Yokohama, San Francisco, New Orleans, Philadelphia, New York, Boston, and others—reflect the world's division of labor; for it is through these great gateways of commerce that the specialized products of one region are exchanged for those of other regions.

Modern specialization begins to emerge more clearly as the division of labor is further refined. It means that land, labor, and capital are devoted to special uses or functions determined by natural conditions, man-made adaptations and contrivances, special training, and the like. Land, for example, may be put to special uses depending upon its location, soil texture, and content, or upon the prevailing climate and rainfall. Similarly, labor may be devoted to special tasks by reason of the special aptitudes, skills, and training of the worker. Buildings, tools, machines, and other capital instruments are usually constructed to perform particular operations. A business unit may concentrate its entire enterprise on making one small part of a product. It is through specialization along such lines as these that we get Irish linen, English cutlery, Belgian lace, Dresden china, Swiss watches, French wines, Spanish cork, Italian olives, Russian caviar, India's tea, oriental carpets, the spices of the tropical Pacific islands, Brazilian coffee, Argentine beef, American cigarettes, Florida oranges, Detroit automobiles, and thousands of other national, regional, and local specialties.

By specialization agriculture becomes something more exact than "farming"—something more precise even than grain farming, fiber production, plantation farming, or truck farming. Farmers specialize in wheat, buckwheat, rye, corn, barley, rice, sorghum, soybean, cotton, flax, peanuts, sugar cane or sugar beet, coffee, tea, tobacco, apples, peaches, grapes, tomatoes, celery, lettuce, and other single commodities. Animals may be raised for fibers (Australian wool), pelts (silver fox), breeding (blooded stock), transportation (Eskimo dogs, saddle and draft horses), pets, and for many special purposes, as well as for food and related products.

Specialization is carried much further in the manufacturing industries. The 20 principal industry groups are further divided into 446 separate industry classifications, and within each one there are thousands of enterprises based upon certain specialized products, parts of a product, or processes. Within the single industrial establishment there is specialization in organization and function, subdivision of activities by departments and by sections within departments, and further specialization by process and by operation until a single machine, a tool, or a worker performs a minute task exclusively.

The influence of specialization on the general economy is obvious to people in modern times. It means greater quantities of goods in less time and with less effort, wider varieties, more unusual products, better quality, increasing utilization of by-products and less waste, more efficient employment of land, labor, and capital, and generally rising standards of living. At the same time increasing specialization creates greater interdependence, a condition that operates to bind together and unify the many parts of the economic system.

Specialization itself depends upon the extent of the market and upon the smooth flow of goods between markets. If the market is not wide enough, it will not be possible for individuals, firms, or regions to devote themselves to specialized tasks in the hope of exchanging their surpluses (products in excess of their needs) for the surpluses of others. They will have to limit their specialization to provide time to engage in supplying themselves with the products they want and cannot get by the exchange of their specialized surplus goods. The growth of population and the ease of access to markets encourage specialization. More extensive, faster, and cheaper transportation, lower tariffs, and the removal of other arbitrary trade barriers tend to widen the market area and thus extend the possibilities of specialization.

But specialization has its disadvantages too. One of the greatest of these springs from the valuable function that specialization performs in unifying the economic system—the condition of dependency it creates. In days when an enterprise was highly self-sufficient—when it provided most of its own raw materials, supplied many of its own simple tools and equipment, exercised greater control over its labor supply, carried on all the processes of manufacture under its own roof, and was in direct contact with its markets—it enjoyed a position of considerable independence and stability. And the economy in which such enterprises functioned enjoyed a high degree of security from economic disruption, unemployment, and distress.

Today, because of the lengths to which specialization has been carried, each single enterprise is dependent for its success upon thousands of other enterprises over which it has no control. Let a strike or a breakdown occur in the plants making sheet steel, and the whole automobile industry is slowed down and may be brought to a standstill. This, in turn, will affect coal and iron mining, transportation, rubber, leather, textile, electrical, glass, paint, chemical, and associated industries. The circle of disruption is ever widening and leaves no part of the entire economy unaffected. As whole industries have become closely dependent upon other industries, so have thousands of enterprises within a single industry become dependent upon the smooth functioning of each and every one of their number. Finally, in the single enterprise, every department, section, process, operation, and machine is dependent upon all others. A miscalculation or disruption anywhere along the line from the policies of top management to the disposal of the finished product may easily throw the entire enterprise into confusion.

Specialization thus yields enormous benefits, but it demands a heavy price for them. The more interdependent economic life becomes, the more vulnerable it is to breaks in the chains of industries, processes, and operations. This fact has a significant meaning in the field of industrial management. The price that must be paid to secure the benefits and to avoid the dangers of specialization is scientific management and the closest cooperation throughout the whole economy. Upon management falls the burden of discovering the extent to which specialization can be carried with good rather than bad effects. It means sound organization and financing, proper selection and use of men, materials, tools, and machines, skillful coordination of all parts of the enterprise, frequent check and constant control over performance, and careful appraisal of end results. In the wider sphere of the national economy, it means too that there must be closer coordination between enterprises, between industry and industry, and among all industries for the good of the country as a whole. Scientific management within the single firm has already been carried far and is constantly being studied for further application, but there is great need for closer integration and better management in the private economy as a whole. The intensity of competition has obscured the other side of its shield—cooperation. The great challenge today to management is not only to improve the functioning of the single enterprise but to develop policies and methods by which to unify the economy as a whole and put it to the service of the community.

THE FIELD OF INDUSTRIAL ENTERPRISE

Of the four great processes that together form the framework of the economic system, we are primarily concerned with only one: the field of the manufacturing industries, or "industrial enterprise" as it is commonly called. *Guided by management, an industrial enterprise combines land, labor, and capital in variable proportions to make a producing unit*

TABLE I.—GENERAL STATISTICS FOR ALL MANUFACTURING INDUSTRIES
IN THE UNITED STATES: 1947 AND 1939 *

Item	1947	1939
Number of establishments..............	240,881	173,802
Proprietors and firm members.........	188,948	123,655
All employees:		
Average number...................	14,294,304	9,527,306
Wages and salaries.................	$39,689,527,000	$12,706,102,000
Wage earners:		
Average number...................	11,916,188	7,808,205
Wages...........................	$30,242,343,000	$ 8,997,515,000
Value added by manufacture..........	$74,425,825,000	$24,486,856,000

NOTE: Value of products and cost of materials are omitted because of the unknown and widely varying amount of duplication contained in such totals. The 1939 figures have been revised to exclude data for establishments classified as manufacturing in 1939 but classified as nonmanufacturing in 1947.
* Data for above table obtained from Bureau of Census, U.S. Department of Commerce, which is now compiling figures in the latest biennial census of manufacturing. For the official, published 1939 census figures, see the first edition of this volume.

turning out tangible goods.[2] Referred to in the periodical government census of manufactures as an "establishment," this unit may be a huge plant or factory employing many thousands of workers such as those operated by General Motors, General Electric, the International Harvester Company, and the Aluminum Company of America; or it may be a small shop with only two or three dozen employees.[3]

[2] The term "land" covers not only "standing room," *i.e.*, physical location of industrial plant, but also natural resources (natural raw materials), the character of the soil, rainfall, temperature, the earth's waters, and other features associated with land. "Labor" includes brainwork, manual work, and all the characteristics of individuals engaged in personal services. "Capital" refers chiefly to buildings, tools, machines, equipment and materials, produced by man and used in further production. In common use, capital often lumps together land, money, buildings, equipment, and materials, as being the total investment in an industrial enterprise.

[3] In general, statistics of manufacturing establishments in the government census are collected only for enterprises turning out products in excess of $5,000 total value during the year. Other qualifications touching the nature of establishments are also applied in order to confine data to manufacturing proper. See periodic reports on the "Biennial Census of Manufactures," U.S. Department of Commerce, Washington, D.C.

The Nature and Types of Industrial Production.—*The essence of industrial production is the transformation of raw materials by factory methods into things wanted by society.* Materials are brought into the plant where they are processed or manufactured into different forms, qualities, and quantities, and then shipped out of the plant either for use or further processing in other factories, or for immediate use by ultimate consumers.

Industries are divided into broad classes according to the nature of the industry, the use made of the product, and the amount of service obtained from it before it is consumed or becomes unfit for further use. Thus, industries that manufacture materials, tools, machines, and equipment for use in the operations of other factories are classed as *producer-goods industries*. Those which turn out products intended for direct use of the people in the home or generally in daily living, are *consumer-goods industries*. Many products might fall in either class depending upon who uses them and for what purpose; but in the main the distinction between the two classes is a fundamental one of the utmost importance to the single enterprise and to the economic system in general.

Of similar importance is the classification of industries on the basis of the amount of use obtained from a product before it is completely used up or destroyed. Thus we have *durable- nondurable-, and semidurable-goods industries*. If an item may be used over and over again, giving service or satisfaction over a long period of time, the item is durable. A watch, radio, automobile, and a house are consumers' durable goods. Many tools, machines, other factory equipment, warehouses, and factory buildings are producers' durable goods. If an item is used up completely in one or a few operations, it is considered nondurable. Food is an important example; fuel is another. Thousands of items fall between these two extremes and are often considered semidurable goods.

These classifications of industries based upon the use made of the products—producer and consumer goods—and upon the amount of service that can be obtained from the goods—durable, nondurable, and semidurable—hold important meaning for industrial management. The type of goods produced strongly influences the organization, finances, business policies, labor supply, production methods, marketing channels, and general prosperity of the single enterprise. And the economic system in general may be backward or progressive, may provide a low or high standard of living, and may function steadily or with fluctuations, depending upon conditions bearing upon each type of manufacture and upon the relations among the different types of goods.

Individual and Social Aspects of Industrial Enterprise.—Industrial enterprise serves two sets of interacting interests: those of the individuals and groups engaged in industry and those of society generally, or the private and the public interest. To the individual, industrial enterprise is an outlet for his energies and creative desires, a means of livelihood, and a source of profit.[4] To society it is primarily a method of producing, with the least expenditure of time and effort, the manufactured goods wanted by the people in the community. Industry has much wider meaning for society—in economic, political, cultural, and philosophical senses—but for the time being only the narrow, practical object of material gain is considered. Sometimes private and public interests serve each other. Spurred on by the hope of profits to produce more for themselves, individuals incidentally put more goods in the service of the community. On many occasions the two interests are in sharp conflict. A monopolist secures an immediate, temporary gain by restricting production and holding the price high, but his action is in direct conflict with the interests of the community which has less goods to share. Again, an individual may make a handsome profit in producing and selling narcotics or worthless patent medicines, but his gains are made at the expense of the community's welfare. Ultimately, the neglect of the social interest reacts to destroy the temporary advantages gained by the private producer who considered only his own private interest.

Industry derives its main driving forces—profit and competition—from the meaning that industry holds for individuals and for society. Individuals undertake the arduous tasks of industry because they are a means of livelihood and a source of profit to them. But when they enter the field they find other individuals similarly engaged. Opportunities for profitable enterprises are limited, at least relative to time and conditions; and so, in order to make a place for themselves, producers have to compete with others in the field. This means they have to produce more and better goods, in shorter time, and at lower prices than do their competitors. It is from this competitive striving between producers that society realizes its own objective—more and better goods for all the people with less time and effort. That is why certain governments place emphasis on maintaining competition. If competition grows weak (as it may do from many causes) or if it is nonexistent (as in private monopoly), the main driving force on which the community relies for more and better goods runs down. Some other driving force has to take its place if the community is to maintain and increase its material welfare. Government regulation and government operation of enterprises are two of the most common substitutes for competition; but, although they have ad-

---

[4] The term "profit" has several meanings. Here, it is used in the common business sense of the excess of business income over all business expenses calculated by ordinary accounting methods.

vantages to replace those lost by the failure of competition, they also bring disadvantages, many of which lead to positive harm.[5]

Industrial management has the constant task of understanding the conditions and relations between private interests and the interests of society. The single industry must be guided in harmony with both interests. Personal liberty, the security of private property rights, and the freedom permitted to individual initiative and enterprise, which are essentials of the private enterprise system, depend upon a proper understanding of and adjustment between interests of individuals and those of society. This should become clear as the influence of both interests is seen at work in every part of the process of organizing and operating an industrial enterprise.

THE GROWTH OF AMERICAN INDUSTRY

The prime factors in the growth of American industry are land settlement, the exploitation of natural resources, technological progress, expanding markets, and the freedom permitted to private economic enterprise. Together, these factors fill a period of almost three centuries, from the early colonial settlements of the seventeenth century to the Great Depression of 1929. Strongly influenced by these factors, American industry passed through some four major stages in its development to contemporary times. In the years since 1929, new and different forces joined with the old to set a fifth stage in the growth of industry. A better understanding of current industrial enterprise will be gained if these five stages are briefly traced.

Industrial Growth: Colonial Industries.—The earliest manufactures revolved wholly around the problem of subsistence in a raw unsettled country. Food and other agricultural production, lumbering, shipbuilding, and ship fitting heavily occupied the early colonists. But beside the woodsman's ax, the gun and trap of the fur gatherer, the farmer's plow, the fishing smack, and the whaler, was the household and village shop of simple craftsmen who toiled to turn out the stern necessities and the rarer luxuries demanded by a pioneering people. Industry was in the handicraft stage, carried on mainly in the household, and kept close to the job of turning crude raw materials into simple products for the immediate use of the struggling settlers. Manufacturing proper, with its division of labor, industrial capital investment, and production for the general market, did not make its appearance for more than a century after the early settlements. But the infant industries that did take hold in colonial days gained considerable impetus during the Revolution when the imports of manufactured goods from England were cut off. By the

[5] See Chaps. II and XXXI.

time Alexander Hamilton made his "Report on Manufactures," calling
for the encouragement and protection of young industries, he was able
to describe some seventeen industries "which are carried on as regular
trades and have attained to a considerable degree of maturity." They
included leather and iron products, tools and machinery, textiles, pottery,
spirits, paper, hats, oil, sugar, hardware, carriages, tobacco, and gun-
powder. These were supplemented by articles made largely in the homes
of the people—homespun textiles, knit goods, clothing, hosiery, lace,
boots and shoes, iron and copper utensils, nails, and some of the finer
specialties of cabinetmakers and silversmiths.

Industrial Growth: Exploitation of Natural Resources.—The second stage began in the later years of the Napoleonic wars when the United
States was cut off from foreign competition by its own protective legislation and by the war with England. The period thus begun extended
approximately from 1800 to 1860 and centered largely about manufactures
having to do with the settlement of the country and the exploitation of
its natural resources. Striking out from the thin Atlantic coastal strip occupied by the colonies, the pioneers fanned out to the South, West, and
North, blazing the way for others to follow. It was a movement that
was to continue through several stages of industrial growth. At intervals
for more than a century wave upon wave of settlers, gaining force through
extensive immigration, rolled ever westward, leaving in their wake those
who cut the broad prairies into quarter sections, marked out the range
lands, staked the mines, clustered in the rich river valleys, and set up
villages which in time became towns and thriving cities.

The surge of the adventurer, the needs of the settler, and the fast-grow-
ing population called into being the services of transport and communication, the construction industries, and created an ever-rising demand for
manufactured goods. The first definitely protective tariff encouraging
home manufactures was enacted in 1816, and in the same year the Second
National Bank was set up for the further development of American
sources of capital and credit. By the Constitution, free trade between
the states held the way open for a brisk commerce as the different sections
of the country were settled. Although agriculture predominated in the
economy of the nation and furnished increasing exports to Europe,
Americans turned with feverish energy to the development of all other
natural resources with which the country abounded. To the subsistence
stage, agriculture added another—that of supplying raw materials in an
increasing flow for industrial uses at home and abroad; and timber and
minerals were exploited. All during this period the link between natural
resources and manufacturing remained very close, complementing each
other. Household industries and village shops continued to be the pre-

vailing methods of conducting industrial operations but, as the period drew to a close, factory production rose in importance. The factory brought the several processes of manufacture under one roof, centralized and increased the use of power, introduced specialized tools and machines, and hired workers for fixed wages and hours. Individual proprietors and partnerships owned the greater part of these enterprises, and capital came partly from the slow process of accumulation and partly from sources abroad.

Industrial Growth: the Factory System.—The major characteristic of the third stage of industrial development is the expansion of the factory system until, by 1890, industry exceeded agriculture as the dominant economic activity of the country. The older factories expanded in size and in volume of output; large numbers of new establishments were begun and grew rapidly. The exploitation of natural resources continued unabated all through this period, but of great significance was the shift in important industries away from dependence upon agricultural raw materials and over to the minerals, particularly coal, iron, and steel. The growth of industry during this period was especially marked by technological developments: the great increase in inventions of products and processes, the wider use of steam engines as prime movers, the application of mechanical science to industrial processes, greater specialization in tools, machines, and labor, and the rapid expansion of the principle of interchangeable parts introduced successfully in America by Eli Whitney as early as 1798.

The natural increase in the home population, augmented by waves of immigrants, furnished expanding domestic markets and provided a growing labor force to meet the insatiable demand for goods. Invested capital grew enormously, and more and more of it was being generated by the rapidly increasing economic activity within the country while reliance upon foreign capital was reduced. In accumulating it and making it available to producers, a change took place in the method of organizing enterprises. The incorporated company rose in importance compared to the simpler forms of individual and partnership enterprises. This development opened up larger possibilities for the further expansion of the principle of the factory system—the integration of industrial processes and the combination of enterprises. By this time the foundation for modern industry was well laid; every field and process of manufacture was opened up, and the stream of American industrial products increased in volume and variety. Although the exportation of agricultural produce continued large, the exports of manufactures began to bulk larger—iron, steel, copper, and other metal products, agricultural implements, specialties in factory machines and tools, business machines, home wares, and many products based upon American inventions filled the holds of ships that cleared American shores for foreign ports throughout the world.

Industrial Growth: the American Industrial Revolution.—The fourth stage constitutes an industrial revolution peculiarly American. What took place between 1890 and 1930 was much more than the further growth of the factory system; it was a complete transformation of the whole field of industrial production. By the introduction of new sources of power—notably the electric dynamo and the gasoline engine—power was specialized and brought to the work instead of the work having to be taken to the power, as was largely the case with steam. A whole series of new inventions came into wide everyday use, of which the telephone, automobile, motion-picture visual and sound apparatus, radio, airplane, and automatic machine tools are the most conspicuous end products. They revolutionized communication and transportation, amounting to a conquest of time and space hitherto undreamed.

Great changes took place in production processes. By the science of time and motion studies; by the scientific arrangement of materials, machines, and processes; by the standardization of products; and by the redesign of factory buildings, the crude benchwork of the factory system was converted into the flexible assembly line of continuous mass production. Skill, precision, great power, multiple operations, and automatic controls were built into machines. The crude products of iron and steel were refined by the use of alloys, making metals lighter, more durable, and adaptable to wider uses. Other base metals—copper, brass, bronze, nickel, aluminum, and their alloys—came into wider, more specialized use. New chemical processes and products emerged from the laboratories that were rapidly being established in industry after industry.

Production was integrated and concentrated, bringing together under single management the many processes of manufacture from the raw materials to the finished products. This was obviously accompanied by greater combinations in the field of business organization. By almost every yardstick other than number of establishments, the corporation exceeded individual proprietorships and partnerships as the prevailing form of business organization. But more than that, the corporation itself, in many fields of industry, was merely a subsidiary unit in larger corporate structures such as the trust and holding company. Through outright merger and by such methods of business combination, many complementary and associated corporations were brought under one management. The largest companies in the most flourishing period of the simple factory system were dwarfed by the great industrial empires built up in the first quarter of the present century.

The World War from 1914 to 1918 intensified the entire development.

War had become a battle of national economic systems as much as it was a struggle of great armies in the field. By patriotic appeals and through the paramount power of government to command the nation's economy, production was enormously intensified, hastening and further enlarging industrial growth. So much was exported from the United States to the belligerent nations that the previous capital loans made by foreigners to America in the years before 1914 were paid and liquidated. The United States became one of the world's largest creditor nations, while the industrial and banking structure of the country supplied its own needs for capital. The whole movement of industrial transformation, business concentration, and corporate combination continued more intensively in the postwar years. It resulted in a tremendous output of material goods and in the consequent rising standards of living throughout the country. But agriculture, on the other hand, did not share in the general prosperity of the country; it never fully recovered from the depressed condition into which it had fallen in the period of adjustment at the close of World War I. Agricultural productivity remained at high levels, but the balance between agriculture and industry remained tipped against the farmer whose income decreased even as the national income rose to higher and higher levels. This, together with an accumulation of other factors which are not yet wholly agreed upon by business specialists and economists, caused the entire structure of the country to become unbalanced in 1929 and to degenerate rapidly into the greatest depression the nation had ever experienced.

Industrial Growth: Depression and War.—The fifth stage is a combination of many phases of industrial development. There is the phase extending from 1929 to 1933 in which industry, along with other fields of private enterprise, sought to make adjustments to meet and perhaps to overcome the economic collapse that swept the United States as well as other countries of the world. There had been many panics and economic breakdowns in history. In the course of its development, the United States experienced many economic crises of varying severity from a number of causes. And many countries, including the United States, suffered great economic distress in the depression of 1873. But always, at least in the United States, economic adjustments reached a new equilibrium from which the nation resumed its progress and went on to higher levels of production and material welfare.[6] But the depression beginning in 1929 did not follow the usual course. Economic adjustments of the traditional kind were tried, but it seemed impossible to carry them to the point where a new equilibrium was reached. Production was

[6] For further comment upon other business cycles, depressions, and crises in American economic history, see Chap. IV.

curtailed, costs reduced, prices lowered, excessive capitalization was squeezed out, and weak and inefficient enterprises were forced into bankruptcy. In the simpler economic activities of other times, say before 1875, these adjustments helped to bring about a new balance of economic relationships which went far toward overcoming depression and hastening the return of better times. But in the complex economy of 1930 such adjustments seemed to work the reverse. The depression became worse and more widespread; competition became more intense and destructive in the areas where competition still functioned vigorously; unemployment rose to alarming totals; and actual want and distress stalked the land.[7] Perhaps a new, workable balance would have come if these painful adjustments could have been carried deep enough and over a longer period, but people who had few resources with which to resist distress, and businessmen who were reluctant to see the empire they had built go to pieces could not wait for traditional methods to effect a cure. They demanded stronger medicine. Without thought of the deeper implications, they turned to government for relief.

Recovery and Reform.—Such conditions helped to bring about the second phase through which industrial development passed in this period. This phase lasted from 1933 to 1940. It was marked by vigorous actions of the Federal government in all fields of economic life. Government participation in economic affairs is not a new thing; it is found in varying degrees in all periods of history. What was new—or at least seemed to be new in American life—was the unprecedented scale of government operations and the peculiar directions they took when compared to the mild government intervention in private enterprise in previous years.

No field of American life was untouched. The Federal government intervened in agriculture, industry, finance, labor relations, state and local affairs, and for the health, welfare, and security of the people. Billions of dollars were spent on successive programs of "recovery and reform." In many matters during the worst period of the depression, private enterprise itself asked for government aid or readily welcomed it when it was proffered. Almost every sizable group interest in the country—farmers, investors, businessmen, workers—had some grievance or sought some relief. Feeling unable to do anything for themselves because of the magnitude of the depression, these groups turned to government and either sought positive aid for themselves or legislation directed against the unbalance and abuses in other sections of the economy that adversely affected them. An outstanding example was the demand for the loan of government funds to stave off financial collapse; and when the Recon-

---

[7] For a detailed description of the situation, see Beard and Smith, "The Future Comes: A Study of the New Deal" and "The Old Deal and the New."

struction Finance Corporation was set up to make these loans, it was enthusiastically received. Another example was the demand for "fair-trade laws" to protect business from the worst practices of competition which the depression had intensified. In this way, as well as upon the initiative of government, public intervention in economic operations came in the form of regulatory laws, investigations, schemes for planning the national economic life such as the Agricultural Adjustment Act (AAA) and the National Industrial Recovery Act (NIRA), public undertakings on a large scale, lavish subsidies, financial manipulation, and huge relief and security programs—all openly intended to bring about "a new deal." [8]

These efforts and conditions filled the period from March, 1933, to about April, 1940. The effect upon industry is not altogether clear. In general, industrial employment, output, and profits rose quickly from 1933 to 1936, slumped badly in 1937 and 1938, and began upon a slower, fluctuating rise in the remainder of the period. After much confusion and conflict the attempt to plan and regulate industrial operations through the NIRA was held to be unconstitutional by the Supreme Court, and the scheme petered out. President Franklin D. Roosevelt, many heads of Federal departments, and the more aggressive New Deal congressmen denounced the "economic royalists" among business and industrial leaders, charging that the depression and subsequent failure to achieve higher prosperity were due to their narrow vision, selfishness, and unwillingness to cooperate. Federal departments and agencies kept up a persistent attack upon monopoly conditions in industrial and business enterprise which they claimed prevented full employment, capacity output, lower prices, and a more equal distribution of wealth and income.

On the other hand, many industrial and business leaders protested against "government interference with business," denounced the "huge Federal bureaucracy," and inveighed against the "socialism of the New Deal." They criticized the government aid extended to farmers and bitterly resented the support that they claimed New Deal laws and activities gave to labor organizations and to labor's demands for more pay, shorter hours, and better working conditions. Others in business and industry openly supported the New Deal or made such adjustments as they could to the new conditions. Although critical of the Federal government on occasions and always aggressive in defense of its interests, organized labor in general was in sympathy with the directions taken by government and actively supported the New Deal.

During the 7-year period to 1940 increasing numbers of workers found places again in industry. But the New Deal found no permanent solu-

[8] The political slogan of the Franklin D. Roosevelt campaign in 1932 and successive years.

tion for unemployment. Approximately fourteen million men were out of work in 1933, and after 7 years of extraordinary effort to solve the problem some nine million remained unemployed. During the same period industrial activity increased substantially, but the problem of achieving and maintaining capacity production also remained unsolved. A huge Federal debt, chiefly for farm subsidies, public works, relief, and social security, had been created. Government regulations and activities, originally looked upon as temporary expedients to bring about reform and recovery, tended to become permanent and were expanded rather than relaxed. Labor was restless and strikes were frequent. Industrial managment and business had not become wholly reconciled to the objectives and methods of the New Deal.

National Defense and War Industry.—Affairs were in this unsatisfactory state when war broke out in Europe in September, 1939. This was soon to lead to the third phase of current industrial development: national defense activity and finally a full war economy. In the 20 months preceding Pearl Harbor, American industry followed a course which reflected the mixed feelings held by the people at large toward the war. But by the Lend-Lease Act, the destroyer deal to aid Britain, and by other manifestations in foreign policy, it soon became clear that the United States openly committed itself to aid all countries resisting Germany, Italy, and Japan. This commitment and the obvious need to strengthen its own security led to a large increase in national-defense production until the surprise attack on Pearl Harbor made the United States a full belligerent against all three Axis nations.

Although the military forces had an M-day plan for war production, industrial conversion from peacetime to war basis was slow and difficult. Some lag in conversion is inevitable in this transition because it is impossible to redirect the entire economy as required by war without time-consuming equipment changes, materials and labor shortages, production "bottlenecks," and other maladjustments arising to delay the change-over. Moreover, conversion to war production is further prolonged in democratic countries where government cannot use arbitrary force to compel a quick change-over. Thus it was that trial, error, and confusion marked the course of industry from 1940 to 1942 while industry and government worked out a satisfactory system of war production.

The production system in the war economy which finally emerged had the following characteristics: (1) outright abandonment of the production of civilian goods in many lines, especially the metals, and the subordination of all other civilian production to military preferences, (2) government-controlled production through a program of designated end-use products, supported by priorities and allocations of raw materials,

(3) man-power allocation between civilian and military requirements by the Selective Service Administration, United States employment services, and through some indirect "freezing" of civilian workers in certain industries and areas, (4) price control and rationing of consumer goods, and (5) government supervisory direction and control over all associated elements of the economy in the interests of war. The goal sought was to organize the entire industrial system into one gigantic machine geared to maximum war production with the absolute minimum of civilian supply and maintenance. This had been the meaning of total war abroad and it had to become the program at home if the United States was to fulfill the war obligations it had undertaken.

Such severe regimentation would not have been possible had it not been supported by the strong spiritual force of a free people united in war. Although the cost was staggering, the war effort proved to be eminently successful. Goods in amazing volume and variety poured forth from the American industrial machine until the scales of war were overwhelmingly tipped against the enemy. In many respects war reorganized the entire industrial system of the country, giving management new policies, ideas, methods, tools, machines, and products to work with, but it also created grave problems to be solved in the postwar world.

Reconversion to Peace and the Postwar World.—The reconversion of industry to peacetime production after V–J Day was as painful and difficult as the conversion to a war economy had been and took almost as long. Plants had to be reconditioned and refitted while a pent-up demand for peacetime goods forced a feverish pace. Returning soldiers had to be absorbed, controls tapered off, materials shortages overcome, extremes in inflation and deflation avoided, and labor-management relations had to be readjusted under the difficult conditions following in the wake of war.

Conditions in the postwar world gave little opportunity for industrial stabilization or economic equilibrium. Instead of peace, a "cold war" developed between the United States supported by its west-European allies and a militant communism spearheaded by Soviet Russia. This conflict, together with the necessity of military occupation in many areas of Europe and Asia, forced the United States to continue with unprecedented military budgets in peacetime. In addition the United States undertook to aid in the economic rehabilitation and military security of western Europe through vast loans and gifts, giving foreign nations billions of dollars in purchasing power to add to the heavy demand pressing upon American production capacity.

At home the Federal government kept its employees above the two-million level, continued and enlarged upon its public-works programs, financed an extraordinary system of loans, subsidies, and insurance protection to every sector of the economy, and projected large programs of housing and social-welfare services throughout the country with federal aid.

The combined foreign and domestic undertakings of the Federal government in the postwar years kept the federal budget well above 40 billion dollars each year to fiscal 1950 with no signs that subsequent budgets could be reduced much below that level.   This meant that the Federal government alone was collecting in taxes almost a fifth of the national income, with grave implications for the national economy and for the system of private enterprise which had prevailed in the United States until recent times. Beginning with the year 1951, defense and foreign-aid budgets rose to astronomical heights, with the end not in sight and with war a matter of touch and go.[9]

[9] Reporting on the American bill for taxes for the year 1948, the Census Bureau observed that nearly three-fourths ($40,000,000,000) of the 1948 Federal-state-local tax total of $54,500,000,000 was collected by the Federal government.   In taxes per person this worked out to Federal $274, state $53, and local governments $45.   *The New York Times*, Aug. 8, 1949.

CHAPTER II

INDUSTRIAL AMERICA—CONTROL AT THE MID–CENTURY

In the course of its development industry passed from a condition of relatively free enterprise to one in which the element of government regulation plays a strong part. At various stages in history government intervened to prevent monopoly, to preserve active competition, to eliminate evils and abuses in the capitalistic system, to conduct enterprises (such as public works) which were beyond the capacity of private enterprisers, to give aid in times of crises or to open up economic opportunities, to enforce the public interest as major changes came in technology and as modern life became more complex, and to protect the health, safety, and welfare of the worker and of the general population. Whatever activities government undertook, they were either openly declared to be permanent, or if temporary, they tended to become permanent. If they were limited in scope, they tended to expand. Among the more important questions of the day are whether government will restrict itself to setting and enforcing the rules of the game or will expand further to take over functions of management and even to conduct, on its own, enterprises formerly private (as in the expanding socialistic systems of Great Britain and western Europe). The question has become intensely practical because we live in an age of competing economic systems where the outcome is not at all clear although it is of the utmost importance to the management of private enterprise and to the general population.

The question immediately uppermost for the student of industrial management is to understand clearly how industrial enterprise is controlled today. Control implies the power to fix the objects and guiding policies of economic (and related) activities, to make the rules and regulations governing economic operations, and to determine how and to whom economic benefits are to be distributed.

Controls in the system of private free enterprise, during which the might of industrial America matured, were partly naturalistic and partly determined by general law. Incentives to produce goods and services came largely from the selfish desires of men to improve their own welfare. Freedom to engage in whatever enterprise appeared promising and to shift from job to job as opportunity arose was insured by natural conditions and by government in America. The law protected the right of contract and private ownership and the right to enjoy the rewards derived from them, but actual distributive shares depended largely upon the individual and the enterprise. The owners and later the managers determined the internal policies and operations of the enterprise and a good part of the general conditions of production as well. Competition and the price system were relied upon to regulate activity and to insure balance and equity. The consumer, exercising his free choice in the market place, was a powerful factor in the control of enterprise. With government setting and enforcing general rules, these were the main lines of control in the system which prevailed in America until government regulation and other new controlling factors expanded to their present prominence. Although the system was never perfect, it worked with amazing success, as any tests of performance could easily demonstrate.

By the mid-century mark, 1950, the outlines of new forces controlling industrial America have taken definite shape. Three powerful groups in the nation emerged to share in and to contest for further control over the industrial system: the owners and managers of private enterprise, organized labor, and the Federal government.

Modern Relation between Government and Business.—Government and business—politics and economics—have always been closely associated in fact. At certain periods in history the association has been so close as to make it appear that economic and political life are controlled by one and the same group of persons. At times, the purely political group has been so strong as to dominate the activities of economic groups. At other times the situation has been reversed; private economic groups were strong enough to dominate the governing groups, if they did not actually form the government itself. Again, there have been times when the balance was so even that each group was held to its own sphere and entered the other sphere only by consent and for limited purposes.

In the main, dominant control over American economic life was exercised by representatives of the private economy for at least a century—particularly in agriculture, manufacturing, and trade. Other sections of the economy were more strongly influenced by government. For some sixty years of this period, at least until the Civil War, the farmers and planters kept the agrarian interests uppermost. During the next forty years, as manufacturing forged ahead of agriculture in importance, promoters of business ventures and industrialists held the upper hand. They were joined, shortly before 1900, by the financiers, when the corporation became the most effective method of organizing and financing business enterprise.

Government Becomes an Active Operator in Economic Life.—But even while these private interests exercised the controlling voice in national life, government bodies (particularly the Federal government) began building a separate place for themselves in the management of economic affairs. The Federal government began a definite movement in this direction as early as 1887 with the passage of the Interstate Commerce Commission Act for the regulation of the railroads. There had been regulatory laws before this, but they were too few in number to establish a pattern or to interfere very much in the routine management of private enterprise. Regulatory laws came much faster after 1887 and covered so many phases of private economy that in time the process went beyond mere regulation and practically made government a part of management in economic enterprise. Today, the role of government as an active element sharing in control of economic operations shows itself in eight ways: (1) by intricate regulations affecting almost every field of activity, every enterprise, and every process of private economic life; (2) by control and deliberate manipulation of the banking and monetary system; (3) by the provision of an elaborate array of government services; (4) by actual participation as promoter, financier, and operator of large-scale public works and other enterprises; (5) by commodity controls, purchases, and other stabilization operations; (6) by the employment of taxation and deficit financing to transfer wealth and income from the more to the less fortunate groups in the population through loans, grants, subsidies, benefits, and social-welfare services; (7) by the control, almost exclusive in many cases, of economic relations between the United States and the rest of the world; and (8) by the political action of the executive department of government allying itself with special-interest groups to expand government powers, to influence the political behavior of voters, and to influence Congress. The combination of these activities backed by the economic power of 40-billion-dollar annual Federal government budgets and by its political influence and power to compel compliance makes government—the Federal government in particular—a powerful and active partner in the general conduct of industrial enterprise.

The degree to which government has pushed for active participation in control of economic life can be gathered from the statement of policy found in the Employment Act of 1946. Here, it was declared to be the

. . . continuing policy and responsibility of the Federal government . . . , with the assistance and cooperation of industry, agriculture, labor, and state and local governments, to coordinate and utilize all its plans, functions and resources for the purpose of creating and maintaining . . . conditions under which there will be afforded useful employment opportunities . . . for those able, willing, and seeking work, and to promote maximum employment, production and purchasing power.

The act created a Council of Economic Advisors to analyze and interpret economic developments and to appraise the programs and activities of the Federal government in relation to current trends. The Council reports to the President with recommendations of policies deemed necessary to maintain a high level of business activity and employment. The President is required to present an economic report to Congress each year (and may make other reports from time to time) which is to be reviewed by a joint Congressional committee in order to provide continuing study and coordination of government policies and programs. This law, climaxing years of expanding government participation in economic activities, certainly gives notice that the Federal government has assumed part of the responsibility for the economic welfare of the nation and intends to take an active part in attempting to assure economic stability and security.[1] Whether or not the attempt will be successful remains for the future, but under the policy set it is clear that henceforth government will take actions in the economic sphere which will have important bearing upon industrial enterprise.

Government itself is a composite of the elected representatives of the people who make the general laws, of the top departmental officials who make and execute policy within the broad mandates of law, of the thousands of lesser officials who administer the affairs and programs of bureaus, agencies, boards, commissions, and public corporations, together with the army of lawyers, accountants, professional and scientific experts, secretaries, and clerical help who staff the public offices. This range of public functionaries is found at every level of government—Federal, state, and local—together with a large body of skilled and unskilled manual workers of every trade and occupation who work in government enterprises and service government properties.[2] All of them influence in varying degrees the workings of the industrial system. What is even more significant is that, after government reaches a certain size in numbers employed and in scope of operations, it acquires powers, momentum, vested interests, and the political support of special groups (farmers, labor, etc.) which tend to

[1] When slackened business activity and rising unemployment appeared in several sections of the country in the summer of 1949, the Federal government acted under this law to provide procurement contracts and other work opportunities for distressed industries. See *The New York Times,* Aug. 10, 1949, "White House Picks 11 Areas for Federal Spending Help." Although the Federal government had taken other kinds of economic action under this law, this was the first time it acted directly to aid specific communities and industries.

[2] Census Bureau reports as of January, 1949, show that Federal, state, and local governments employed 6,083,000 persons, or one person in every ten of the country's working force. Approximately $1,340,400,000 in taxes was required to meet their pay checks for one month.

make it an independent operator following conceptions of economy of its own, and it is no longer readily controlled by the people generally or by their elected representatives.[3]

Management and the Modern Framework of Law and Government. In casting about for some method of procedure by which to relate management to the network of laws and regulations affecting industrial enterprise, certain facts offer helpful suggestions. Management, for instance, is highly specialized in relation to company operations. The top officers make policy and supervise the enterprise as a whole. The purchasing department sees to the procurement of materials and equipment. A well-defined production department guides the manufacturing operations. A sales department attends to the marketing of the product. In other words, specialized management is now essential to smooth and efficient operations. When we turn to the network of laws and regulations, we find it divided into sections that correspond roughly to the specialized functions of management and to the logical departments of company operations. There is a fairly well-defined body of law dealing with purchasing operations, with production processes, with marketing, taxation, and with employer-employee relations. This parallel of specialization, rough as it is, affords a basis for fitting the individual enterprise into the framework of law.

The following eight groups of laws and regulations outline the general legal contacts confronting the modern industrial enterprise in the course of its regular operations:

1. Laws relating to the formation and termination of industrial enterprises.
2. Laws concerning plant and equipment.
3. Laws governing the acquisition and use of materials and supplies.
4. Laws governing production operations.
5. Laws governing labor relations.
6. Laws governing the product.

[3] Examples abound but belong more properly in a text on political economy. In the first session of the 81st Congress, for example, a strong bipartisan group of Senators sought to force economies in the huge Federal budget but were unable to make much headway against the complex forces in government which resisted cuts in appropriations. It is well known in public finance that at least 40 per cent and possibly more of the Federal budget consists of "untouchable" or irreducible items because of fixed charges, prior legislation obligating the public purse, and the political impossibility of making cuts against the resistance of government bureaus and private pressure groups. See *The New York Times*, Aug. 3, 1949, "Federal Financing Worries Institute," a report by the Institute of Life Insurance, and June 29, 1949, "Budget Cut Runs into Snag." For views on the significance of growing government control see James Burnham, "The Managerial Revolution," and Frederich A. Hayek, "The Road to Serfdom."

7. Laws governing the distribution or disposal of the product.

8. Taxation laws and regulations.

It is obviously impossible in the space of a chapter to set forth the individual laws falling in each group or even to list the basic requirements of the principal laws now in operation. Not only are laws pouring from three levels of government; not only are they constantly being changed; but also voluminous regulations are being issued and many others changed daily by a large group of government administrative agencies. Administrative and court decisions also add to the difficulty of keeping abreast of the law. The relative stability of the earlier framework of law is gone; today, law is constantly changing in its broad policies and operating details. Daily study and compliance with government requirements is a necessity with every phase of an industrial enterprise. No single company official can be expected to supervise the company's legal obligations as did the company president or lawyer in days of relative stability. Government contracts have become a bulwark for many industries, but to get and hold them is a complex process.

But the company is not wholly adrift in an uncharted sea of shifting laws and regulations. Each of the company executives, through education and experience, has a working knowledge of what is permissible and legal in his field. The company should be able to rely upon its general manager, legal and accounting counsel, production and maintenance engineers, personnel manager, sales manager, traffic and shipping managers, and other specialized officers for proper guidance through the network of laws affecting each stage in the industrial enterprise. These, in turn, can find ample guidance in the publications of professional, technical, and trade associations; chambers of commerce; and government departments and agencies and in the large body of available technical literature. Many firms find it profitable to retain a firm of counselors or to subscribe to commercial publications giving current information on laws, administrative regulations and rulings, contract opportunities, and court decisions. The basic information gathered from these sources is often set up in guides or manuals in each department, kept reasonably current, and used as working tools to keep the company abreast of its responsibilities.

Organized Labor Acquires a Share in Control of Industry.—Organized labor is the third major group now sharing in the control and responsibilities of industry. It reached its present status after a painful struggle lasting many decades. While this is not the place to describe union organization or labor-management relations,[4] it can be said briefly it was not until 1890 that the union movement crystallized sufficiently to form a loose organization which became the American Federation of Labor.

[4] See Chap. XXIII.

Union membership remained small until World War I when it burgeoned, fell again in the 1920's, and then expanded enormously under the favorable legislation passed and administered by the New Deal. With the formation of mass industrial unions by the C.I.O. after 1935, union leaders more and more made use of the political power of union voters to maintain their friends in office and to help them enact laws increasing union membership, strengthening union power, and providing wide benefits for the nation's workers. World War II served to increase the powers, membership, and benefits enjoyed by organized labor.

By 1945 the union movement, consisting of the large federations and the independent unions, had organized about a third of the nation's entire labor force. In many specific industrial fields the unionization came close to 100 per cent of workers engaged and industry-wide bargaining tremendously increased union power. Through affiliation with others in the federations it became possible for a strike to cripple entire industries. And because of the interdependence of industrial operations, a strike in a single key industry such as coal or steel brought dozens of other industries to a standstill. The power of unions showed itself dramatically in 1946 when industry after industry—electrical, meat packing, steel, coal, railroad, shipping, and others—was shut down by strikes. In that year alone the nation suffered a peak of almost 5,000 strikes, and American workers directly involved lost 116 million days of pay. The single strike in rail transportation affected the nation's whole economy so seriously that President Truman himself went before a joint session of Congress and asked for a drastic law to draft rail workers into the Army. Although this was denied him by Congress, the labor situation in the country was considered serious enough for the passage of other legislation to correct abuses and to bring equity and balance into labor-management relations.[5]

Organized labor's power to exert controlling forces upon management and industry can be seen clearly when its methods of operation are examined. There are (1) labor's traditional economic power to affect industry through wage, hours, working conditions, and benefits contracts in collective bargaining and through a variety of strikes, slowdowns, boycotts, and other work stoppages, some capable of permanently damaging private enterprises and crippling the national economy; (2) the effect of mass organizations upon industrial policies, standards, and operations; (3) labor's political power through alliances with political parties, through influence on voting habits of an organized minority, and through pressures on lawmaking bodies at all levels of government; (4) labor's power to make use of laws to harass management and to compel it to yield to union

---

[5] For more comprehensive treatment of labor organization and labor laws, see Chap. XXIII.

demands; and (5) labor's social power through the effects which a well-financed and well-organized minority can create in each community and in the nation at large. When this is backed as it is by union treasuries well-filled and constantly replenished by the checkoff system for collecting dues, by the strict control exercised by union leaders over the internal affairs of unions and over union workers, and by alliances between powerful unions, it can be seen readily that neither private management nor the system of economy can function successfully without the cooperation of organized labor. *Conversely, it places upon organized labor a new and grave responsibility for the operation of industry which until recent times rarely rested upon the worker or upon labor organizations.*[6]

The Mid-century Pattern of Control over Business and Industry. Many of the controlling forces inherent in a free-enterprise system continue to function in the American economy, but they are hedged about by numerous qualifications and restrictions developed in the course of changing times. The consumer, within certain limitations, also exercises free choice to buy or not to buy, to shift his favor from seller to seller and from one product to another and thus continues to be a powerful controlling influence on all stages of the industrial process. Within the industrial process itself new forces and instruments of control are at work. The significant result of the growth of government and of organized labor is to give to each, along with management, a share in the control of industry. With some exceptions they do not sit with management and determine policies and operations, but by the powers they possess, by the privileges they enjoy, and by the activities they engage in, they strongly influence the function of management and the workings of the economic system.

SUMMARY AND BROAD PROBLEMS

Chapter I is a brief survey of American industrial progress; no further summary is necessary. Chapter II considers the problem of control over the industrial system in the light of modern trends. Both chapters recount certain significant developments worth summarizing because they illuminate future industrial problems. They are

1. The chief emphasis in the long-term growth of industry has been upon increasing the capacity to produce. While the need of greater production continues to challenge industry, a serious problem is found in the growing frequency of periods (crises and depressions) in which industry seems unable to distribute through traditional economic processes all the goods it has the capacity to produce. The question for the future seems to be to discover how to order economic conditions so that industry

---

[6] See Chap. XXIII, Joint Relations, for further discussion of these areas of responsibility.

will operate at all times at maximum efficient capacity and to find means for distributing the goods produced at that level.   Other economic systems (socialistic and communistic) claim to be solutions of this problem, but impartial observation shows that the loss in individual freedom, initiative, self-reliance, and even quantity and quality of production and other values is greater than any attainable gains in stabilization and equitable distribution of goods.   So the problem remains.

2. American industrial history discloses a persistent tendency toward integration of industrial operations.   This was the meaning of the factory system, which brought under one roof the many processes required to make a single product.   It is also the significance lying behind corporate combinations, which unified complementary industries and brought many products under one management.   The latest evidences of the same tendency took place in World War II in which "big business," so called, grew bigger and took over most of the prime contracts of the war economy.[7]   Recognition of this condition can be found in the establishment during and after the war of Congressional committees and special bureaus in the executive department to aid and protect "small" business.[8]   Here is a trend too deep-rooted to ignore.   What implications does it hold for the future?

3. Along with integration, there appears to be a progressive decline in competition at work over the long term.   While competition remains active as one of the main driving forces of economic activity, there is no denying the fact that many developments in the course of time have weakened its operation.   War, which is the only activity thus far capable of stimulating capacity production, practically eliminates competition. In the place of competition, war production is based upon government correlations of demand and supply on the assumption of maximum-capacity operations.   Price is merely a counter and not a controlling force.   But war and government control also bring with them a degree of regimentation not tolerated by the American people in time of peace.   How to maintain competition as a driving force, free of its abuses but with its guarantees of freedom of initiative and enterprise, is the challenge of the immediate future.

4. Industrial history discloses a shift in controls over industrial operations.   In early industry, control was exercised by owner-managers fol-

---

[7] A single large firm with a prime contract, of course, subcontracted out to many small firms (sometimes thousands) the production of items entering into the final product.

[8] For significant details on the current degree of "the concentration of productive facilities" see a recent report prepared by the Federal Trade Commission and sent to Congress Aug. 23, 1949.

lowing rule-of-thumb methods. With the coming of the corporation, control shifted to professional (hired) managers who gave full play to methods of scientific management. The third shift in control is marked by the participation of government in management through public economic activities, boards, commissions, and regulations. The fourth, most recent development is the rise of organized labor to a status where it strongly influences control of industry. Today, control over industrial policies, operations, and fruits of production is shared by owners and managers of enterprises, by organized labor, and by government.[9] As a result of their powers all three have become responsible to the people at large for the proper functioning of the industrial system. What are the economic, political, and social effects of this significant change in control of industry? Compare American developments with recent trends in Great Britain, Australia, and New Zealand, especially the two latter where in January, 1950, Socialist Governments were voted out of office.

5. Accompanying the participation of government in the management of private enterprise is a decided increase in the number and scope of government (public) economic undertakings. This is accompanied by an increase in government aids and services in the interests of health, education, economic security, old-age support, and general welfare of the people. Today, one person in every ten of the working force is a government worker. Taxation transfers almost one-fourth of the national income from the people who produce it over to the public treasuries to be spent by the three levels of government.

Careful consideration of these tendencies shows that each bears a close relationship to the others. Together, they seem to call for a reexamination of the function industry performs in modern economy and of the methods by which industry operates. It is the hope of the authors of this volume to make a contribution toward this end through a systematic treatment of the organization and management of an industrial enterprise.

[9] It is interesting to note that every plant today is an arm of the government for the collection of income taxes, Social Security taxes, and other imposts and otherwise assists, at considerable expense to itself, in carrying out many government regulations and activities. Where unionized, some plants serve the union as collectors of dues, and representatives of the union (shop stewards) are at hand at all times to protect the workers in their rights and privileges.

CHAPTER III

BASIC INDUSTRIAL STRUCTURES

Among the many possible ways of describing the basic industrial structures in American economy, two stand out as particularly significant: types of ownership and types of organization. In other words: Who owns the industrial enterprises of the country and how are these enterprises organized to carry on industrial operations?

TYPES OF OWNERSHIP

Ownership is a legal term. Most commonly it means the legal title to a thing, the right of possession and disposal. Applied to an industrial enterprise it means title to and possession of the assets of the enterprise, the power to determine the policies of operation, and the right to receive and dispose of the proceeds.[1] When an enterprise is so organized that individuals exercise and enjoy these rights in their own interest, the ownership is said to be *private*. If they attach to political bodies, *i.e.*, to municipal, state, or Federal governments or to any agencies created by them, the ownership is *public*. In a very few cases, the elements of ownership are divided so that private persons and public bodies share in the operation of the same enterprise. These may be said to be *mixed* business units; and although their number at the present time is small, there are indications that it may increase substantially.[2] Whereas there are thus three main types of ownership—private, public, and mixed— each one is worked out in several different forms; and it is in these forms that we see the basic structure and characteristics of industrial enterprise.

[1] Ownership, it will be seen, properly includes control over the thing owned. Since the development of the corporation, however, there is a tendency to speak of the "separation of ownership and control." By this is meant that, although all the legal rights of ownership are vested in the stockholders, practical conditions operate so as to place control over the affairs of the corporation in the hands of its officers and managers, many of whom may not even be stockholders. So substantial is this power of control that those who exercise it practically enjoy the benefits of ownership, sometimes even against the real legal owners. For a more complete discussion of this interesting development, see Berle and Means, "The Corporation and Private Property."

[2] This is an example, although not a perfect one, whereby ownership (title) of an enterprise may vest in the public, while operating control is in the hands of a private management group. See preceding note.

Forms of Private Ownership

Privately owned industrial enterprises take five basic forms: individual proprietorship, partnership, corporation, corporate combinations, and cooperative (including mutual) organizations. A given manufacturing enterprise may be organized in any one of these forms, but usually one form is more desirable than others. The choice depends upon a careful consideration of a number of factors among which are the following: who the promoters are and what ideas they hold toward the several forms of organization, the nature and size of the business to be started, the capital required and the means of procuring it, the length of time the enterprise is expected to operate, technical conditions affecting the enterprise, type of products to be manufactured, method and volume of production, kind of markets to be supplied and methods of marketing, competitive conditions in the chosen industry, methods of sharing the benefits and obligations of the enterprise, and the influence that all laws and government regulations exert upon private enterprise. In the light of these factors, each form of organizing ownership has special characteristics which make it suitable for some kinds of economic activities and not for others.

1. The Individual Proprietorship.—Where the enterprise is small, requires but little capital, and lends itself readily to control by one man, it is likely to take the form of the individual or sole proprietorship. The small machine shop, woodworking plant, printing establishment, canning factory, and hundreds of similar enterprises exist in this form of ownership. It means that a single individual promotes the enterprise; gets together the necessary land, buildings, machinery, and labor; and conducts the actual manufacturing operations in person. The enterprise need not be very small, but it is unlikely to be very large. A single enterpriser, operating in his own name, meets with certain practical difficulties in accumulating and borrowing capital. This has a tendency to restrict the scale of his operations and to limit the possibilities of rapid expansion even when conditions are favorable. Moreover, large-scale enterprises today require an increasing degree of plant specialization which, in turn, demands specialization in management. Even if the single owner succeeds in building up a competent subordinate staff, the task of over-all direction and coordination is likely to be beyond his capacity when the enterprise becomes too large. The knowledge that he is liable to creditors and all others' who acquire claims against him, to the extent of not only his business assets but also his personal property as well, has been a strong influence in persuading single enterprisers to adopt some other form of ownership under which to organize the enterprise.

That the single proprietorship has not been abandoned completely is due mainly to certain advantages that it still possesses. The ease with which an enterprise in this form may be started is one of them. To the man of ideas but of small means, it offers an open door to many opportunities. With the exception perhaps of a small license fee and compliance with a few local regulations pertaining to his operations, the single enterpriser may set up shop on his own initiative. In business for himself, he has every motive to exert his utmost efforts to the enterprise. If he hires helpers, he can supervise and work with them directly, gaining the advantage of personal contact with his men and with the operations they carry on for him. In the same manner, he gets the "feel" of the business and gets to know every phase of it thoroughly. He can make the most of opportunities through freedom of initiative and quick decision. The knowledge of his sole ownership gives him a sense of pride and satisfaction in his work and achievements, and the independence he enjoys gives him a sense of pleasure and security. These inducements, together with the fact that many enterprises by their very nature must be small, have operated to keep the number of individual proprietorships quite large even though the volume of their operations is today a small part of the industrial total.

2. The Partnership.—The need to overcome the disadvantages of the single proprietorship is, perhaps, the chief reason for the partnership form of business ownership. Here, two or more individuals join for the purpose of conducting an enterprise. Each will make some substantial contribution to the business, and their association brings to the joint enterprise a larger capital and more men skilled in plant operations and management who also have the incentive of an interest in its success.

The partnership organization is formed as easily as is the single enterprise. By an oral or written agreement,[3] the partners outline the nature of the enterprise, set forth their respective rights and obligations, determine the shares each one is to have and how the profits are to be divided, and outline any other terms and conditions affecting their joint venture. The several interests of the partners need not be equal. They may even form a "limited" partnership in which one or more partners (usually those who contribute money or patents without active participation in the enterprise) are not to be held liable for the debts or obligations of the partnership beyond what they have invested. In this case, the law usually requires certain forms of public notice. In some localities a simple certificate of copartnership must be filed before the firm is legally

[3] Where two or more individuals associate in a joint venture having the elements of a partnership in fact, courts of law usually declare a partnership to exist to protect creditors and for other purposes, even though no oral or written contract of partnership had been entered into.

authorized to do business, especially if the partnership is conducted under a name other than the true names of the partners.

The added advantages of the partnership are partly offset, however, by several serious disadvantages. Not only the assets of the partnership but also the personal property of each partner is subject to levy for the debts of the partnership. Each partner is liable to creditors for the whole debt of the firm, not merely for his proportionate share. This is an obligation imposed by law, and only limited partners may escape it in restricted situations. One partner may bind all, and each partner is responsible for the actions of his associates. Disagreements between partners often lead to delays and difficulties that may seriously endanger the enterprise. The death of a partner automatically dissolves the partnership. This is because the law construes a partnership to be a personal relationship, at an end when death takes one of the partners. But it can be readily seen that this places a great hardship on the firm which may be compelled to wind up its business, or at least disrupt it, at a most inconvenient time. These disabilities have not prevented many sound partnerships from operating, but they have strongly influenced the trend toward the corporate form of enterprise which, as we shall see, is free from many of the disadvantages affecting partnerships.

3. The Cooperative Organization.—A cooperative association has some elements of a large partnership and also many features of the corporation, although it is distinct from both. It took practical form about a century ago (1844) in Rochdale, England, where a group of people formed an association and set up a retail store for the purpose of supplying themselves with food and other merchandise at cost. It was a consumers' cooperative designed to eliminate the profit of the "middleman." In the course of time the English cooperative societies greatly enlarged their membership and branched out into the fields of wholesale enterprise, manufacturing, and the growing and production of raw material commodities. The cooperative idea spread to Europe, and large numbers of societies were formed in many countries. The movement is much less extensive in the United States.

The principal theory of the cooperative association is the elimination of profit and of the economic evils which it is believed a profit system of economy generates. Under the cooperative system, enterprises are formed to provide goods and services to members at cost. The cooperative societies may be simple associations like a large partnership or chartered organizations very much like a corporation. Members pay fees or buy shares in the association. The total amount of shares each member may buy is usually limited in the bylaws and, unlike the corporation, each member has but one vote regardless of the investment he has in the cooperative society. This is to assure economic democracy in the operation of the association and to make it impossible for one person or a small group to get control of the enterprise by acquiring a large-share interest with the accompanying larger voting power. Where the association is a small one, it may be organized just as is the partnership. Usually, the cooperative society needs and seeks a large membership; and as a matter of practical convenience in management, it is chartered as a nonprofit organization. In most states a special section of the corporate laws deals with the formation of associations of this type. When so formed, the cooperative society functions very much like a corporation with elected officers, board of directors, and periodic shareholders' meetings. In most cases, the enterprise is conducted in the same way that an ordinary profit-making company operates, but at stated intervals such profits as accrue are returned to the members in the form of dividends on the amount of shares they hold, or upon the volume of business a member brings to the enterprise.

There are many kinds of cooperative organizations. Consumers' cooperatives usually draw their membership from the general public and carry on retail trade operations such as grocery, clothing, and variety stores, gasoline stations, and similar goods and service enterprises supplying the ultimate consumer. Others, called producers' cooperatives, draw their membership chiefly from producers of grains and other farm products, livestock, fruit, milk, and dairy products. Most of these associations employ the cooperative principle chiefly to enable their members to buy supplies at wholesale, eliminating a "middleman's profit," and to market their produce collectively in conditions that will assure them the highest return. It is questionable whether these are true cooperatives, but they use the cooperative form of organization and employ many of its operating principles. Building and loan associations and certain types of credit unions are examples of the cooperative principle in the field of finance. They make it possible for people of small means to acquire a home and to borrow money for other purposes at relatively low rates of interest. Other associations provide for fire, health, life, automobile, and other forms of insurance on a cooperative basis. Many fraternal benefit associations and "mutual" insurance companies employ cooperative principles, but not all of them are cooperatives in the full sense of the word.

In Great Britain, the Scandinavian countries, and other parts of Europe, the cooperative associations engaged in manufacturing occupy a prominent place; but their number and importance in the United States are insignificant. This can be readily seen in Tables II and III.

Many reasons account for the failure of manufacturing cooperatives in the United States. Good management personnel is often lacking in the membership of these associations, and they are reluctant to call in outsiders and pay them salaries on the level that such men can get in the regular profit-making field. In many cases, management in the cooperative association is hampered in policy making and operations by the intervention of members who have a direct say in the enterprise. Many associations, also, embrace social functions in addition to their manufacturing operations, and these often place a strain on the main job of production. For these and other reasons, cooperative organizations in the United States have made little place for themselves in the field of manufacturing.

4. The Corporation.—Corporations dominate the manufacturing field in the United States. In numbers alone they barely equal the noncorporate enterprises. In the Census of Manufactures (see Tables II and III) corporations number 118,138 as against 122,743 for the total of individual ownerships, partnerships, cooperative associations, and all other noncorporate enterprises. This would seem to put the two forms of ownership, corporate and noncorporate, on a basis of comparative equality. But numbers are not the only basis for ranking the importance of the two groups in the manufacturing field. By all other yardsticks, corporations completely overshadow the noncorporate enterprises. They employed 10,647,386 out of 11,916,188 factory wage earners for the year 1947, or 89.4 per cent. In the same year corporations added by manufacture $68,418,994,000 to the value of their products out of a total added value of $74,425,825,000, or 91.9 per cent. Noncorporate enterprises employed only 10.6 per cent of the wage earners and added by manufacture only 8.1 per cent to the total value added by manufacture to products. In short, corporations have taken over the field of manufacturing. If measured by any other yardstick such as income or business assets, the result would be the same. The reasons for this dominance lie in the great advantages which the corporate business unit possesses over all other forms of organization.

The Nature of the Corporation.—The corporation is an artificial business unit. The law makes its creation possible and governs a large part of its operations. Once formed, the corporation has its own name and an independent status separate from the stockholders who compose it. It may sue or be sued in its own name, acquire real and personal property, and exercise many rights and privileges guaranteed by law to natural persons. Its term of life is usually limited by statute to a period of years, varying in length in the different states, but provisions for successive renewals practically make the corporation permanent unless voluntarily ended by its stockholders or forced by business reverses to liquidate.

TABLE II.—GENERAL STATISTICS FOR ESTABLISHMENTS CLASSIFIED BY TYPE OF OPERATION AND LEGAL ORGANIZATION: 1947*

(Money figures in thousands of dollars)

Type of operation and type of ownership	Number of establishments	All employees	Salaries and wages	Production workers	Production worker wages	Value added by manufacture
Independent single unit...........	205,668	6,286,769	$16,905,283	5,231,462	$12,456,879	$30,398,196
Central-office unit...............	35,213	8,007,535	22,784,244	6,684,726	17,785,464	44,027,629
Corporate ownership...............	118,138	12,856,299	36,574,635	10,647,386	27,635,457	68,418,994
Noncorporate ownership (individual, partnership, etc.).....	122,743	1,438,005	3,114,892	1,268,802	2,606,886	6,006,831

* Data obtained from Bureau of Census, U. S. Department of Commerce, which is now compiling figures in the latest census of business. For the official, published 1939 census figures, see Table II, page 32, 1st edition of this volume.

TABLE III.—GENERAL SUMMARY FOR NONCORPORATE FORMS OF OWNERSHIP: 1947*

(Money figures in thousands of dollars)

Type of ownership	Number of establishments	All employees	Salaries and wages	Production workers	Production worker wages	Value added by manufacture
Individual......................	69,519	585,514	$1,183,808	522,379	$1,000,983	$2,165,649
Partnership.....................	50,787	757,140	1,686,684	672,995	1,432,287	3,353,697
Other†..........................	2,437	95,351	244,400	73,428	173,616	487,485
Total.........................	122,743	1,438,005	3,114,892	1,268,802	2,606,886	6,006,831

* Data obtained from Bureau of Census, U. S. Department of Commerce, which is now compiling figures in the latest census of business. For the official, published 1939 census figures, see Table III, page 32, first edition of this volume.
† Includes cooperatives, establishments operated by estate administrators, trusteeships, receiverships, and public and quasi-public organizations.

The basic structure of the single corporation is very simple. It is composed of any number of stock- or shareholders who are the real owners of the corporation, a board of directors elected by the membership to fix the policies and conduct the business, and a group of top-ranking officers who actively manage the company's affairs. In many corporations, although not in all, there is one other group, the bondholders, people who have invested money in the business in return for a guaranteed rate of interest.

Forming the Corporation.—The corporation is usually formed by a small group of interested persons who may put up money, land, buildings, equipment, patents, and other real and personal property to get the company started. Sometimes these people merely perform the services of promoters and organizers, taking payment or stock for what they do. They decide upon the name, location, and character of the business. They usually fix the amount at which the corporation will be capitalized, and the number, value, and classes of shares that will be issued. They also determine the basic policies that are to guide the company's operations. The greater part of this information is embodied in an application for a charter in the state where the company is to have its principal place of business. Certain fees and proceedings are necessary before the state, acting usually through the Secretary of State, approves the charter and authorizes the promoters to complete their organization and commence business. When the charter is granted, the promoters have a seal made bearing the name of the corporation, which is part of its legal signature, and prepare to set up a system of corporate accounts. They then call a meeting of the stockholders of the company who elect the board of directors, approve the bylaws that define the powers and duties of officers and set forth the rules for conducting the corporation, and transact other business proper to stockholders' meetings. They may elect certain officers of the corporation, but usually the election of officers is a function of the board of directors. With organization completed and after compliance with state and Federal requirements governing the sales of stock, the books may be opened to the public for stock subscriptions, and the corporation is ready to do business.

Classes of Capital Stock.—Although there are many variations of stock ownership, they are usually grounded on two basic classes: common and preferred. The authorized capital stock of the company is divided between the two classes, and each single share is some convenient multiple of the total amount in the class. This is usually decided in accordance with the method of financing, the type of people expected to invest, and how stockholders may dispose of their shares in the financial markets. Shares thus have a stated or par value, but in many corporations the common stock may have a nominal value of $1 or be rated as no-par stock. But whether or not an original issuing value is placed upon stock, the real value depends upon the net worth of the company according to the books or as appraised in the securities markets.

Organizational Advantages of the Corporation.—One of the great advantages of the corporation is the way it meets the ownership and financing problems. By the sale of thousands of shares to many large and small investors, the corporation can get together capital of almost unlimited amount to meet the greater capital requirements of modern industrial enterprise. Single proprietorships and partnerships, not having access to the multitude of investors, do not have this capacity to expand their capitalization readily and indefinitely. The corporation also makes the ownership of enterprises extremely flexible. Investors may become part owners of a company by the simple purchase of stock, and they may dispose of their holdings just as easily. Shares of stock (ownership) are transferable without affecting the company's status or operations.

Unlike the situation with single proprietorships and partnerships, the liability of stockholders of a corporation is limited to their actual investment in the business. The knowledge that they are in no danger of loss of their real or personal property beyond the amount of their shareholdings makes people willing to share in corporate ownership; and this helps to widen the market for dealings in stocks. Of similar influence is the fact that the death of a shareholder has no effect upon the corporation; the stock simply passes into other hands while the corporation continues its business. The corporation thus avoids the great disruption that death of an owner usually works in the proprietorship and partnership. These advantages—the ease of acquiring large amounts of capital, the flexibility given to ownership, the limited liability of stockholders, and the continuance of company business regardless of the death or incapacitation of its stockholders—have given the corporation great superiority over other forms of business ownership.

Corporate Stockholders.—The ultimate control of the corporation rests in the hands of the stockholders. They exercise control through the voting power at regular or special meetings by electing the board of directors and passing upon broad policies and other phases of the business, but not all stock has voting power. In most cases the common stock has the voting power, but in recent years many corporations have been formed in which the voting power has been narrowly restricted. Common stockholders take the greatest risk in the enterprise because they have no assurance of receiving any return on their investment. They are completely dependent upon the general success of the business and draw dividends out of what is left only after the claims of creditors, bond-holders, and preferred stockholders are satisfied. But, whereas their risk is great, their residual ownership of the business often yields them great gains when the corporation proves to be highly successful. It may result in giving them large dividends and the value of their stock is greatly en-hanced. At least this is so as a general rule, but in late years the manipu-lation of securities and abuses in corporate management have cast some doubt upon the advantages of common stockholding.

Holders of preferred stock may or may not share in the control and general success of the enterprise. In most cases they do not have voting privileges. Preferred stockholders are usually people who do not wish to participate actively in the affairs of the corporation and who prefer to receive a fixed return on their investment rather than risk losses in the hope of making large gains.

Sometimes, stock dividends are paid in lieu of cash. There are many reasons for the practice. By paying in stock rather than in cash, the earnings remain in the business for expansion and other purposes. Also, by increasing the number of outstanding shares the market price of a stock is reduced, and this leads to greater activity in the securities markets for the stock. It likewise makes a high dividend from large earnings look smaller to the public which is often critical of excessive corporate earnings. It keeps the business of the corporation unattractive to competitors who might enter the field showing high profits. Increases in stock sometimes scatter the voting power of stock among so many small owners who do not bother to attend stockholders' meetings that control of the corporation may fall into the hands of a small self-interested group. Many motives, good and bad, lie behind stock dividends; and, if the advantages of the practice are to be preserved without opening the door to serious abuses, stockholders and the public must be constantly alert.

Control of the Corporation.—The real control of the corporation is in the hands of the board of directors and the officers. Stockholders who are the owners are too numerous, often too disinterested, and meet too infrequently to exercise control except in the broadest way. Moreover, it is the day-to-day conduct of the corporate business that is the most effective exercise of control, and this is the function of management. In most corporations management does a conscientious and honest job, but there has been plenty of evidence in recent years that the separation of control from ownership has opened the door to great abuses.[4]

[4] BERLE and MEANS, "The Corporation and Private Property"; RIPLEY, WILLIAM Z., "Main Street and Wall Street"; LAIDLER, HARRY W., "Concentration of Control in American Business"; see also, Proceedings of the Senate Temporary National Economic Committee (created pursuant to Pub. Res. 113, 75th Cong.), and Senate Investigation of Stock Market Practices (1933–1934).

Operational Advantages of the Corporation.—Although it has raised many serious problems in every phase of economic and social life, the corporate form of ownership and operation is an instrument of great advantage to industrial enterprise. It offers an excellent mechanism for mobilizing the large capital needed for modern industrial operations. It permits extended specialization in management, plant and equipment, factory organization, labor, and marketing. By making ownership more flexible, by placing a limit on personal liability, and by providing for almost perpetual continuance of the company without disruption through death of its owner-members, the corporation overcomes some of the most serious difficulties of proprietorships and partnerships.

Although like all other forms of economic organization the corporation is subject to corrupt use, inefficiency, and stagnation, nevertheless it is less likely than others to continue in those conditions for long because it must meet a series of powerful challenges to its vitality. It cannot operate the business in "any old fashion" as can the sole proprietor who has only himself to please. It has a direct responsibility to investors who expect and demand concrete results. It cannot direct attention away from its failures by political and emotional devices as can the managers of publicly owned enterprises. The corporation is subject to searching criticism from investors, competitors, labor, and the public. The corporation must compete actively for money capital, land, raw materials, trained managers, and labor; for efficiency in operation; and for wider markets. Even the largest and most powerful corporations, some of which seemed at times to be a law unto themselves in many things, have been overtaken and forced to give a better account of themselves. On balance, taking the good and the bad in the history and operations of corporate business units, no finer instrument exists with which to meet the complex problems of modern industrial enterprise.

5. Corporate Combinations.—The ingenuity that produced the simple corporation as a business unit did not stop with that achievement. Many of the conditions that led to the development of the corporation suggested a further step—the combining of two or more corporations. Promoters of business enterprise reasoned that, if superior advantages made the corporation a more desirable business unit than proprietorships and partnerships for many purposes, it might be possible to secure still greater advantages by a further extension of the corporate idea. And so, partly because of conditions in industrial enterprise and partly from the many motives inducing promoters to experiment with new forms of business organization, a new chapter in the history of corporate development came to be written in the last half century.

The essence of the development lies in the drawing together of two or more independent corporations and placing them, by one device or another, under the control or operation of one ownership interest. A movement in that direction had definitely set in after 1875 and has continued ever since. Twice within that period, in the years 1897–1903 and again from 1925–1929, the movement was greatly accelerated, and both world wars aided the general trend.[5] In the later period, large numbers of enterprises were linked together in great chains. Outstanding instances of consolidation occurred in the public-utility field, in motion-picture theaters, hotels, department stores, and other merchandising enterprises. Manufacturing has continued to be an attractive field for consolidations ever since the turn of the century.

A whole literature has grown up around large-scale enterprise, concentration, and corporate combinations. It explores in detail not only the extent of combinations, but also the motives that lie behind them, the methods by which they are brought about, and the political, economic, and social effects they have produced. The subject is important and interesting, but we cannot enter upon it here except in the most limited way. We are concerned with basic industrial structures, and here we may note that the combination movement has added some new methods of ownership and control to those represented in the proprietorship, partnership, and simple corporation.

The Merger.—There is nothing new, of course, in the full merger. This occurs when corporation A acquires all the assets of corporation B (and perhaps several others) and either merges them in its existing organization or forms a new corporation combining in one organization the several companies formerly independent.

Informal Methods of Corporate Association.—It is where the consolidation does not result in full merger, but retains the independent character of the enterprises being joined, that new business units make their appearance. To avoid legal penalties stemming from antitrust laws, to forestall government regulation, and for various other reasons, many informal methods have been used which amount to loose combinations but do not result in new business units. Among these are the "gentlemen's agreement," the pool, interlocking directorates, patent and other controls by which a group of companies act in unison on certain phases of their operations or by which one company controls others.

The Trust.—Desire to overcome the weaknesses in these informal combinations probably played as strong a part as did the evolution of industrial organization in finding forms for corporate combination. The first of the more formal devices was the trust. Sufficient shares of stock

[5] THORP, WILLARD L., "The Merger Movement," Part III, *Monograph* **27**, The Structure of Industry, Proceedings of the Temporary National Economic Committee, 76th Cong., 3d Sess., Washington, D.C., **1941**.

to insure the control of voting power in several companies are transferred to a board of trustees. The original stockholders receive a trust certificate giving them a proportionate share of the earnings of the stocks held in trust. They are usually large stockholders who stand to benefit most by the operations of the trust. With control over several companies in their hands, the trustees can elect boards of directors and officers who will carry out the purposes for which the trust was formed.

The Holding Company.—When public condemnation destroyed the usefulness of the trust device, promoters resorted either to the merger or to the holding company for the purpose of effecting combinations. Like the trust, the holding company was a new business unit. By permitting the combining companies to retain their identities, the holding company avoided many of the problems connected with the merger. Such a combination is also easier to form because it is done through securities manipulation. The common procedure is for the promoter to negotiate with a number of enterprises and agree upon a purchase price for each property. The holding company is then formed with sufficient capitalization to pay off all the original owners in cash or stock and to leave a surplus for the promoters and bankers. Another method is for an existing holding company to exchange its own stock for a controlling interest in the companies it seeks to combine. When acquired, the properties of the consolidated companies may be mortgaged to the public on bond issues, and the money used for the purchase of additional properties. When carried to the extreme (as many were in the late 1920's), holding companies were pyramided in several layers—a number of operating companies grouped together under one holding company; several holding companies grouped under a superholding company, and so on. And the financing arrangements in a pyramid of this kind were such that the top holding company often controlled a huge industrial empire by a proportionately insignificant money outlay on the part of the promoters and bankers.

The main objects in forming supercorporate business units are in many respects legitimate and in others illegal and socially harmful. Where the many desirable advantages of large-scale enterprise can be secured without monopoly and without frauds or abuses affecting labor, investors, and the public, the movement toward integration seems to be economically and socially desirable. The fact that many legitimate objects were achieved is perhaps the reason why supercorporations continued to increase and to flourish even though the American public held a deep-rooted antipathy to monopolies in the industrial and commercial fields. But where business units combine to exploit the investing public, restrict production, control the use of factory and business equipment, eliminate competition, share markets, regulate prices for their selfish interests, conceal profits, avoid tax laws, and pursue common labor relations against the legitimate interests of workers, the combinations run afoul of the law and are socially undesirable. It is largely against these abuses and not against legitimate large-scale enterprise that the older antitrust laws (Sherman Act of 1890, Clayton and Federal Trade Commission Acts of 1914, state blue-sky laws, and other antitrust legislation), Public Utility Holding Company Act of 1935, Securities Act of 1933, Securities Exchange Act of 1934, and similar legislation are directed.

"Big business" is still with us and has much to do with "big government" and "big labor." As far as private industry is concerned, the problem of "bigness" yields to no final solution because the line between good and bad is thin and difficult to draw. Public prosecutors and courts have spent years trying single celebrated cases, and great combinations have been broken up, but without appreciable effect on the over-all combination movement. Through the investigation and "cease and desist" technique, the Federal Trade Commission has made constructive but modest headway in recent years. Notwithstanding the imposing body of antitrust laws, court decisions, and less formal methods of dealing with undesirable combinations, it appears that whatever solution there is must be found in the further evolution of business units in which time and experience can exert influence. Meanwhile, remedies against abuses lie in eternal vigilance on the part of all concerned—investors, labor, others in the industrial field affected by a monopoly, competitors, and the government, acting in the interests of the general public.

The chief forms of private ownership of industrial enterprise, then, are the proprietorship, partnership, cooperative association, corporation, and the holding company in corporate combinations. The tendency is toward making each a specialized instrument for the accomplishment of certain purposes in industrial organization. In all of them, including the cooperative association, the element of private profit is uppermost, and any advantages to the general public are incidental. For business structures in which the public welfare is paramount, it is necessary to consider forms of public ownership.

Forms of Public Ownership

Public welfare and necessity are the chief reasons for the establishment of publicly owned enterprises by governments, although other less worthy motives such as jobs for political party supporters may play a part. This does not mean that all the people share equally in the benefits of public enterprises; some sections of the public may benefit directly and materially while others derive merely incidental benefits. Nor does it mean that public enterprises are always undertaken without expectations of profit in the ordinary business sense. Many public enterprises are operated very much like private enterprises and expect to realize a profit on their activities. But it does mean that the general public welfare is the prime consideration and that if any profits are realized they will be devoted to public rather than private interests.

In the United States public ownership proceeds on three levels of government: municipal, state, and Federal. Most of the enterprises are of the public-utility or public-service type: postal services, ship construction and operation, arsenals, printing and engraving plants, port and terminal services, toll road and bridge operations, waterworks, gas and electric plants, street railways and bus lines. These are but a few samples of a range that is rapidly growing. Aside from prison industries, operated mainly for penal and social purposes, governments have remained aloof from the field of general manufacturing until recent times. But the range of their activities has been steadily widening, at least along the fringes of industrial enterprise; and under the pressures of depressions, wars, and public indignation over abuses in private enterprise, the tendency for governments to enter the industrial field is becoming more manifest.[6]

Government activities have been conducted mainly through political agencies and instrumentalities. Even when they are economic in substance, there is a strong tendency to employ political means—laws, regulations, and recognized departments of government. If, now, the trend is toward much greater and more concrete government participation in economic activities, does government simply enlarge the usual political means, or does it adopt new forms? That it does enlarge the usual political devices is obvious from our survey of increasing government intervention in economic life. But it also adopts forms that it finds in the field of private business enterprise.

Public Corporations.—Greater use is being made of the corporate device, and it takes the form of the public corporation. This seems to be the main direction in which government organization of economic activities is likely to move in the future. But the public corporation is neither wholly public nor private in its structure. It combines elements of both; it is a mixed economic unit. Disregarding at this place the motives that bring such a unit into being, how is it promoted, how organized, how operated, and what are some of its main characteristics?

The active promoters are the political administrations and the recognized departments of government. A president, a state governor, a city mayor, a political party leader or prominent group, a secretary of the

[6] See Chap. II.

treasury or of agriculture may originate or become the spokesman for proposals to have the government undertake some economic enterprise.[7] In this way, Senator George W. Norris was the promoter (although not the only one) of the Tennessee Valley Authority. The National Resources Board in its monumental study on postwar problems offered many suggestions for the formation of new business units through a government and private business partnership. These few, but typical, samples indicate the way in which promotion proceeds in the field of public corporations. The action may originate or be supplemented by support of committees of public-spirited citizens, of large self-interested groups or blocs in the community, state, or nation, and of public opinion generally manifested in many ways.

If not originally presented in the form of legislative bills, proposals are soon placed in that form and laid before the proper lawmaking body— city council, state legislature, or Federal Congress—for consideration and debate. The bill, which may or may not be detailed,[8] usually sets forth the broad policies and scope of the public enterprise to be undertaken, outlines the form in which it is to be set up, describes its powers, designates the government agency responsible for its management, defines the sources of its property and finances, and prescribes all other basic features. The legislative bill performs a function for the public enterprise similar to the application for a corporate charter in the private economy. When passed, the act becomes the organic law of the public enterprise, serving very much as does the corporate charter in the private economy.

The forms of public enterprise at the present time seem to be in a state of change. Old forms are being enlarged or altered; new ones are being tried out; but two old forms continue to be the ones most frequently used. One is the public corporation. The statute is its organic law and may be its charter also, but usually some department head is authorized to form the public corporation by applying for a state charter in the regular manner. The people are the stockholders, acting through their legislative representatives. A board of directors is usually designated by law, as are the managing officers. Methods for appointing both are

---

[7] An intimate view of how proposals for government economic action originate and are matured may be found in Raymond Moley's "After Seven Years," which covers a period of the New Deal marked by active operations by government in the economic field.

[8] Two main schools of thought exist with reference to the relationship that ought to hold between the lawmaking body and public enterprises. One contends that all the legislature can do is to set forth the *general* conditions and policies of the public enterprise and leave the regular departments of government to work out the details and administer the enterprise. The other school would have the legislature work out the details itself and exercise active supervision over their administration.

prescribed by law. The corporate funds come from the public treasury, from the powers of the corporation that authorize it to float public loans and borrow from banks, and from the operations of the company. In other respects it has the powers of the private corporation and may be given added powers as an arm of the government. When so established, it operates very much like the private corporation. The Tennessee Valley Authority, Federal Crop Insurance Corporation, Commodity Credit Corporation, Inland Waterways Corporation, Virgin Islands Company, and the RFC are random samples of Federal public corporations formed in this way.[9] Some of these activities may be operated in something like a partnership between the Federal government and state and local bodies; others are semipartnership relationships with private enterprise such as in the industrial field occupied by the Defense Plant Corporation. These mixed business relationships are in the process of evolution at the present time and may ultimately result in a new form of business organization.

The Nonincorporated Public Enterprise.—The other principal form of public enterprise is the nonincorporated enterprise. No separate corporation is set up as such. The statute sets forth all the details of the enterprise as outlined above, but directs some regular department of government to operate it, or sets up a special agency for that purpose. Almost every department of government operates enterprises of this character either by a special division in the department or by an agency specially created, but not incorporated, for the purpose. The Supply Division, Ordnance Department, and Panama Canal organization of the War Department operate activities in this form. The Fleet Maintenance Division, Bureau of Yards and Docks, Bureau of Ordnance, and Bureau of Ships in the Navy Department are of the same type. In the Treasury Department, there are the Bureau of Engraving and Printing, Bureau of the Mint, and similar operating divisions. In the Interior Department, the Bureau of Reclamation constructs and operates irrigation projects; the Bureau of Mines operates a helium gas plant; the National Park Service supervised the Civilian Conservation Corps and conducts considerable construction work in the Park System; and the Puerto Rico Reconstruction Administration carries on a wide range of enterprises in our Caribbean possession. The entire Post Office Department is a large economic empire, and the Government Printing Office is the largest printing plant in the world.

[9] For an interesting, full report on government corporations, see Joint Committee on Reduction of Nonessential Federal Expenditures, Congress of the United States, *Document* 227, entitled "Government Corporations," 78th Cong., 2d Sess., Washington, D.C., 1944.

State and local governments use both the corporate and noncorporate forms of establishing and operating economic enterprises. In addition, all three levels of government employ many indirect forms which make them active participants in the conduct of industrial and business enterprises. It is almost certain that the changes now taking place in government with reference to public enterprises, and in the relationships between government and private enterprises, will result in the formation of many new types of industrial ownership and operation.

TYPES OF OPERATION

Ownership relates to the rights over the assets, income, and control of an industrial enterprise. To a limited extent it may also determine the main lines of operation as well. But the formation of enterprises into distinctive operational structures is really a separate branch of industrial organization. There may or may not be a connection between operating organization and ownership organization. Thus, a proprietorship or a corporation may operate a single business unit turning out a single product; or either one may function as a central office unit operating a score of different operating units turning out hundreds of products. It is the purpose of this section to describe the main forms of operating organizations.

The Independent Single Operating Unit.—Operating organizations fall into two main classes, each of which includes several subordinate forms. The smaller in importance of these two classes is the independent single unit type of establishments. It means a manufacturing unit composed of a single plant or factory. Although it may utilize many different kinds of raw materials, products, and processes in its internal operations, its operations and final product usually fall in some one industry of the 20 industry classifications of the manufacturing census. The form of ownership of these independent single units (proprietorship, partnership, corporation, etc.) plays no part in distinguishing the group. It is the character of its manufacturing operation, of its product, and of its assignment to an industry group—mainly functional operations—that determines the class. The number of establishments in this group totals 205,668 out of 240,881 manufacturing establishments of all kinds in 1947. They employ 44 per cent of the total number of wage earners in manufacturing and of the total value added to products by manufacture, they add 40.8 per cent.

The Central-office Operating Unit.—From the standpoint of operating complexity the second large group is the more important and interesting. It is the central-office type of manufacturing establishments. When two or more plants are controlled or operated by one ownership interest, the enterprise is a central-office unit. The essence is multiple-plant operation; and it is the way these plants are organized for operating purposes that is most interesting to the student of basic industrial structures. The number of establishments controlled by these central-office units in 1947 was 35,213, which is slightly less than one-sixth the number of independent single units.[10] But the central-office group employs 56 per cent of the factory wage earners and by manufacture adds 59.2 per cent to the value of products of all manufacturing establishments.

From the results of a detailed study of this class of operating units for the year 1937, we have a clear picture of the main lines of their organization.[11] In that year there were 25,699 manufacturing establishments controlled by 5,625 central offices. The average central office controlled slightly over five establishments, but the range in this respect was quite wide. A single central office, for example, operated 497 establishments. A similar range was evident in assigning the units to industry groups; two-thirds of the central offices were active in only one industry; but a single central office operated establishments in 25 different industries. Wide variations marked other characteristics of these central-office units, but it is only their functional relationships, or operating structures, that concern us here.

Horizontal Combinations.—There are two structural types of central offices. The simple central office controls establishments operating exclusively in one industry. Approximately 63 per cent of the multiple-plant units were of this type. Each enterprise brings together a number of plants engaged in the same or similar activities in one industrial field. In other words, the combination is a horizontal one. A chain of bread-baking companies, a chain of newspapers, a group of companies making concrete products, a number of glass plants, an enterprise operating several canning factories in various sections of the country, a group of plants turning out radio parts are examples of the simple horizontal combination.

The complex central office brings together two or more plants whose products fall in more than one industry classification. A combination of this type takes many forms distinguished functionally by the kind of products produced, the nature of processes employed, and the method of marketing.

Vertical Combinations.—A vertical combination, for example, performs "successive functions." Each plant or unit in the combination performs some operation in the chain of major processes from raw mate-

[10] This number represents a 3.3 per cent increase over 1939. The number of independent single units increased 37 per cent in the same period.

[11] Temporary National Economic Committee, *Monograph* 27, The Structure of Industry; Part II, The Integration of Manufacturing Operations by Walter F. Crowder.

rial to finished product. A textile plant processing cotton into yarn, weaving the yarn into cloth, and manufacturing dresses from the yard goods is a vertical combination. A company logging its own forest area, operating sawmills, running a planing and woodworking shop for dressed and fabricated wood products, and perhaps including a furniture manufactory in the group is another example. Others operate plants in a pulp-and-paper products combination, in iron and steel, in foods, leather, machinery, chemical, and miscellaneous industry groups.

Loosely, the term "vertical combination" has been applied to the automobile industry to indicate that a company may control plants manufacturing everything that goes into the automobile, but this is inaccurate. It is only when the processes are successive, when the product at each stage is passed on to another plant for the next stage of production, that we have a true vertical combination.

Combinations Based on Divergent Functions.—Another group of industrial combinations are based upon "divergent functions" such as those involved in joint products, by-products, and like processes. In the *joint product* group, the manufacture of any one of the different products might be discontinued without affecting the others produced. Examples of combinations based upon joint product manufacture are enterprises making butter and cheese from milk, a textile concern making shirts and dresses out of yard goods, combinations making different fabricated products out of steel, and companies making different paper products from pulp. Combinations in the *by-product* group depend on the main product. The by-product is incidental and usually results from the waste or excess raw material used in manufacturing the main product. The meat industry is a good example, where the animal on the hoof is turned into fresh meat, glue and gelatine, grease, soap, animal shortening, sausage casings, fertilizer, and other products in different establishments. There are a large number of industrial combinations of this kind in the food, chemical, coal, and petroleum industries. Where *like processes* are employed, there are many industrial combinations turning out varied and different products. Using cotton and wool as raw materials, the spinning mill, for example, manufactures wool yarn and cotton thread by similar processes. Printing and publishing combinations employ like processes to turn out newspapers and periodicals in one industry group, and book, music, and job printing in another industry group. Smelting plants turning out refined copper, lead, and zinc in different plants may also be grouped together in this type of combination.

Combinations Based on Convergent Functions.—A fourth group of combinations center about "convergent functions." The plants in a combination of this kind may start out with different products but, somewhere in the course of operations from raw materials to market, the different products are combined into a single product or meet in a common market. Combinations of this type may deal with *complementary products* as when one plant of a combination makes cigars and another makes boxes, the two being combined in the single box of cigars sold to the trade. A manufacturer of pins, for example, controls a printing establishment for making labels and a paper boxmaking plant, all three being integrated when the box of pins is ready for sale. The automobile industry furnishes combinations of this type, bringing together many plants manufacturing different products that go into the automobile. A further refinement of this group would show that there are combinations based upon complementary materials, complementary parts, complementary products, and complementary industries. Almost every industry in the 20 principal industry groups furnishes examples in one or more of these subgroups.

Some combinations employing convergent functions include plants dealing with *auxiliary products*. The auxiliary product is needed in the manufacture of the final product but does not add to the physical material of the finished goods. A company making ice cream, for example, may also control another plant making ice to use in its operations. A factory using considerable machinery may also operate a separate machine repair shop for its own and outside contract work. Chemical and metallurgical combinations may have a plant to manufacture chemical catalysts used in its main processes. A factory depending upon truck deliveries may set up a garage for the repair of the transportation equipment. Combinations of this type range through practically all the industry groups.

There are also combinations active where the different products or processes do not converge at any stage of the manufacture of the finished article, but meet in a *common market*. A manufacturer of electric refrigerators may set up another plant to produce electric ranges because the two products reach the same market. The food industries furnish innumerable examples where plants producing dissimilar products are combined because they meet in a common market. Typewriter plants may be combined with a factory producing carbon paper. Plants making concrete and clay products, glass, gypsum and asbestos products, cement, wallboard, and plaster, may be drawn together in one combination because all these products serve one common market, the building trades. The chemical and machinery fields hold many examples. Companies specializing in beds may add plants making bedsprings and mattresses. The desire to exploit the same market, to offer a full line of goods, to link together associated items like beds and mattresses, and many other reasons account for combinations of this type.

Combinations Based on Unrelated Functions.—Finally, there are the combinations based upon "unrelated functions." Such combinations are found in every industry, and usually there is some special circumstance that accounts for the nonfunctional grouping. The research laboratories of large companies often discover new products totally unrelated to the firm but valuable enough to induce it to set up special plants to produce and sell the discoveries. Where an existing combination has unused plant and resources, it may devote them to the production of some profitable article even though production of the article is functionally unrelated to the other products of the firm. A combination purchasing land for subsurface minerals and oil may operate a dairy company because the land purchase included a large dairy farm and creamery.

Causes of Combination.—The reasons for combinations are innumerable. One main reason is to increase profits through the economies of large-scale enterprise. Combination brings purchasing advantages, manufacturing economies, easier and more adequate financing, selling advantages, and administrative efficiency and economies. Technology and research often lead to combinations to exploit the results. The desire to control raw materials and semimanufactured products going into a finished article may lead to combinations of plants for that purpose. The desire to eliminate competition is another cause. Idle plants and resources often induce a firm to enter different industrial fields. A company is often forced into the manufacture of many different products by the need for a full line, by changes in demand, by new methods of marketing, by consumer financing conditions, by requests of large buyers. Waste materials and salvage may result in a new plant. And so on; the reasons are practically endless. Each combination must be examined by itself in order to understand the reasons and conditions that influenced its formation. Certain basic patterns of integration appear, such as those found in horizontal, vertical, complementary, and other combinations involving functional organization. Others are dictated by some strong influencing factor connected with the organization or operations of an industrial enterprise. Still others occur by chance and have no rational basis for their appearance. Diversity should be approached with great caution and decided upon only after careful study because the enterprise as a whole may suffer from uneconomic operation or from organizational weaknesses.

SUMMARY

Basic industrial structures manifest themselves along two main channels: types of ownership and types of operation, as in the following outline:

Types of Ownership

Private:
  Individual proprietorship.
  Partnerships.
    General.
    Limited.
  Cooperative and mutual profit-sharing associations.
    Consumers.
    Producers.
  Corporations.
    Simple (single) unit.
    Complex (multiple) units and combinations.
Public (governmental: national, state, local):
  Departmental and special agency enterprises (nonincorporated).
  Public corporations.
Mixed:
  Partly public (governmental) and partly private.

Types of Operation

Independent single operating unit.
Central-office (multiple plant) operating units:
  Horizontal combinations.
  Vertical combinations.
  Combinations based on divergent functions.
  Combinations based on convergent functions.
  Combinations based on unrelated functions.

The whole development in the field of industrial organization and operational structures is in process of change. For more than two centuries, innovation in this field of economy was narrowly confined and slow to make its way. Changing forms of ownership and operation came about chiefly along four lines: (1) to overcome legal, social, financial, and customary limitations on industrial enterprise, (2) to reintegrate and coordinate enterprises, processes, and products as expanding specialization broke up production into minute operations and lengthened the span between raw material and finished product, (3) to respond to scientific and technological developments, and (4) to give organizational structure to the greater productivity which we popularly call "mass production." One or more of these factors shaped industrial structures from sole proprietorship to corporate combination. The dominating theme behind their formation (as it was the chief driving force of the economic system as a whole) was the hope of private profit. Conditions have changed sharply in the last two decades and once again business organization seems to be on the point of further advances. What these may be is perhaps best indicated by noting some of the problem areas that contemporary conditions seem to define.

CASE PROBLEMS

In the development of industrial structures to modern times, certain features call for constructive examination with an eye to the future. Some of these have already become basic issues confronting the managers of private enterprise. Chief among them are:

1. Can new private business structures be developed to meet new industrial conditions? With the corporate combination, reached at the turn of the present century, innovation and progress in the form of private business organizations seem to have bogged down. Subsequent years saw only the refinement of the holding company, already well known by 1900. In the past, new structural forms had come into being only where the element of profit to individual enterprisers was obvious.

But industry today is confronted with entirely new problems, many of which result in profit to the individual company only after the industry as a whole (involving many different companies) takes constructive action. The need for standardization of parts, processes, and products, for quality control, for patent sharing, for the handling of industrial health and accident problems, for concerted action in overcoming business crises and unemployment, for protection against abuses perpetrated by unscrupulous enterprises, and for bringing about labor participation with management in industrial operations are but a few of these new problems.

Conditions since 1900 have called for interindustry forms of organization, for regional corporations coordinating mining, agriculture, manufacture, and other processes, and for many kinds of new corporate types fostering different kinds of group action in various sectors of the private economy. Many corporations did develop interindustry organizations (corporate combinations) and regional holding companies, but they were conceived wholly in terms of individual companies seeking profits for their private corporate owners. Trade associations were formed to advance the common interests of particular industries. "Better business bureaus" fought unscrupulous enterprisers and did valiant work. Councils and committees were formed to bring about group action. Arbitration panels were set up to dispose of industrial controversies quickly and economically. But these were not new forms of organizational structures and they did not begin to reach the real problems that cried out for attention. Can the inventiveness and imagination of management extend the process of business organization to cover the new needs in industrial operation where individual companies are helpless to act alone?

2. Can management develop new private business structures to meet

the public responsibilities of industry? Although slight, there is a distinction between the problems in this group and those in group 1. In group 1 the problems mainly concern the management of particular business organizations and group action within industries—something like technical problems of industrial management. In group 2 the problems are not only interindustry problems, but they reach out to involve the public interest to such an extent that governments have already taken action on them.

When problems arose involving the public responsibility of private enterprisers, and private enterprisers did not attend those responsibilities or did so inadequately, governments rushed into the vacuum thus left open, taking action, as we have seen, along two lines: government regulations and controls, and expanding public enterprise. In some cases governments compelled private enterprise to do what it might have done for itself by imaginative thought and concerted action.

The problem confronting industrial management (and all private enterprise) is whether it is possible to create new private organizations to do for themselves and for the public those things which government has done and will do if private enterprise fails to act. Let us take some examples. Is it inconceivable that interindustry action might have set up its own workmen's compensation—a super, national insurance corporation to cover industrial health and accidents? By new nonprofit combinations of real estate, construction, industrial, financial, and raw material producing associations might private enterprise undertake huge slum-clearing projects? Might many other "public works" projects be undertaken by private enterprise in a similar manner? Would it be possible for a large interindustry combine—made up of banks, the large prosperous industries, insurance companies with excess funds, and with labor and public representatives on its governing board—to create and administer a pool of liquid funds for the financing of small enterprise, home owning, and other activities that are in need of credit? Why could not the private banking system set up a deposit insurance corporation of its own?

In other words, where concerted action is necessary to meet the public responsibilities of private enterprise, how can private interindustry groups develop new organizations and methods that will be capable of meeting the problems that arise? Is government action the only way to handle such problems? Does the fact that private enterprise does not possess many powers exercised by government constitute a barrier to action by private enterprise? Do antitrust laws stand in the way? Might new legislation be secured which would make concerted action by private industry possible?

3. Draw up as large a list as you can of the things which government regulations now compel private industry to do or which government enterprises do, that might be done by private interindustry action? What new organizations and methods can you suggest to private enterprise for the accomplishment of the things on your list?

Organization of the Industrial Enterprise

CHAPTER IV

INDUSTRIAL RISK AND FORECASTING

One of the great advantages of the free enterprise system is the ease with which anyone may start a new enterprise or introduce a new product. No restrictions of law or in economic life are so stringent that they prohibit the introduction of new enterprises and new products. Before any business venture may be launched, of course, some laws and regulations must be complied with. Every enterprise, and even a single product, must meet certain standards concerning the health, safety, and morals of the people. And the whole body of commercial law sets up a framework of conditions to which business enterprises must conform. Requirements will vary according to the nature and operations of the proposed enterprise. In the case of public utilities and other enterprises in which the public has a special interest, the preliminary requirements may be so complicated and severe that opportunities for starting new concerns are narrowly limited. But aside from special cases and from relatively simple legal preliminaries, the way is open generally for the promotion of new business concerns and products. This is certainly true in regard to the production and distribution of goods, *i.e.*, in the fields of manufacturing and marketing with which we are primarily concerned. This freedom, runs the common argument of those who oppose state-planned enterprise, prevents stagnation and insures a healthy, active, and progressive economy.

But freedom to enter business and to launch new products is a very small part of the conditions involved in an economic undertaking. It gives the individual merely a right to try his hand at a business venture. Like the hunting license, it permits a man to enter the field but it does not promise big game or even insure a successful venture. The disadvantage in free enterprise is that it opens the door to irresponsible persons, to half-baked projects poorly organized, to enterprises inadequately financed, to commercial fraud and piracy. Free enterprise beats a path of progress, but it also leaves the debris of business failures, economic waste, tragic disappointments, and losses along the trail. From a record taken in July, 1929, a year of active and prosperous business, the total number of business organizations of all kinds reached 2,213,000. In that year 453,000 new enterprises were started, but 483,000 discontinued. In the depth of the depression in 1932 there were 2,077,000 listed concerns, with 338,000 new enterprises and 454,000 discontinuances. With 2,102,000 listed concerns in 1938, there were 388,000 new enterprises while 365,000 closed their doors. In 1948 the number of listed concerns totaled 2,550,-000, including 651,000 new listings and 492,000 names deleted.[1] There is a close parallel between the birth rate and death rate in business history.

Not all the discontinuances represent failures or result in losses to creditors. Many disappearances are due to changes in ownership and mergers; other enterprises close voluntarily in solvent condition. True commercial failures are much smaller in number, but they represent a serious problem. At the depth of the depression (1932) 31,822 business failures were listed with liabilities close to a billion dollars. In 1938, 12,836 concerns failed with liabilities of $246,505,000 and of these 2,428 were manufacturing concerns with liabilities of $98,251,000. During the war, business failures dropped off to less than 1,000 but rose steadily again in the postwar years. In 1948 there were 5,252 business failures with $310,-566,000 in liabilities. Of this number, 1,481 were manufacturing concerns with $130,292,000 liabilities.[2] What business failure means over the long run may be seen from an analysis of the 18-year period, 1920–1937.[3] In that time a total of 858,858 enterprises went through bankruptcy liquidations. Their total liabilities were $16,510,103,000, and this was offset by only $1,372,943,000 realized upon their assets. The expenses of liquidation amounted to $299,145,000, and the creditors finally received a total of only $1,039,066,000. The large total of 521,235 concerns had no assets at all.

Distressing as it is, the loss in dollars and cents from business failures is probably the least of the harm done. In earlier business history the individual proprietor put up his own cash and property and, if he failed, the loss was a personal one. When creditors were involved they were few and the amounts lost were small. Enterprises were considerably inde-

[1] In July of each year, the "Dun & Bradstreet Reference Book" lists the concerns in the United States business population. See also, its "Vital Statistics of Industry and Trade."

[2] Ibid. See also Dun's Review, February, 1939: Analyzing the Record of Industrial and Commercial Failures.

[3] Louis P. Starkweather and Edward H. Bishara, reported by U.S. Department of Commerce, Division of Business Review, October, 1938.

pendent of each other and small in size, so that failure was confined to narrow compass. Today, the size of enterprises is much larger. Through specialization each enterprise is part of a large circle of interdependent firms. With the corporate form predominating as in manufacturing, the savings not of a few persons, but of hundreds of individuals, are staked in the business. Instead of a handful of workmen each trained in a well-rounded craft capable of sustaining them independently when the shops of an earlier day closed, today's factories employ hundreds and thousands of workers who cannot fall back on self-employment when the plant shuts down. Specialization has fitted them only for a minute operation in a long chain of integrated industries, and they do not have the rounded skill in a self-contained craft that will yield them an independent livelihood. In many cases today entire communities—retail stores, gas and electric systems, transportation, professional people, real-estate values, schools, and churches—are dependent upon one or a very few factories. In these conditions, the failure of an industrial enterprise is a serious and tragic event. A wide circle of persons, other firms, and entire communities may be affected. The situation is like the 15 balls tightly racked in a triangle on the pool table—hit the single lead ball hard and squarely, and all 15 are sent flying in all directions. Economic enterprises are likewise closely tied to one another: if failure strikes any one of them, the impact is felt by all.

When few were harmed by business failures, there were few who cared enough about the problem to demand action. But today, when the effects of business failures are serious and widespread, there are many who clamor for redress and preventive action. The many can speak only through political channels, and thus we have government interference in private enterprise on an increasing scale. In these circumstances, if enterprise is to remain free from political plan and authoritative control, leaders of private business will have to accept greater responsibility for industrial promotion and operation.

One field where the need for greater care is very obvious is that which is concerned with industrial risk. Business failures—whether they come from the hazards in launching new enterprises or concern merely the exploitation of a single new product—must be minimized. Not only is this necessary to avoid government intervention and consequent loss of freedom, but it is sound business economics to prevent losses if the enterprise is to be successful. Profit margins are slender in modern economy, and it does not take many losses to cut them to the point where the existence of the enterprise is threatened. Not that all losses can be avoided. The industrial machine cannot be so perfect that there will be no frictional loss. Constructive activities almost always result in some waste. To make an omelet, some eggs must be broken, and occasionally a bad one turns up. Many things have to be first torn down before we can build up again. And the best plans miscarry because no human vision can penetrate the blind spots, uncertainties, and mysteries of the future. The knowledge that some economic loss is inescapable should prove a powerful incentive to reduce those losses which are preventable. We should not wish by our own mistakes to add to the burdens that in any event are unavoidable.

The causes of business failures are numerous. It would take many pages merely to list them, which is one way of presenting them. But such a listing would be stiff and uninteresting and perhaps hamper rather than contribute to our understanding of them. Most business failures center around the product and the organization set up to exploit it. If we examine the major risks and problems concerning the product and the enterprise, we shall make an oblique but probably more understanding approach to the conditions necessary for a successful business venture. The product and the enterprise, of course, are interdependent and, although we may separate them for convenience of discussion, their essential interrelationship must be constantly borne in mind.

Risks and Problems concerning the Product.—Although there are many important functions of an economic system, its prime object is to provide goods and services. This means that the *product* is the all-important center of an industrial enterprise. It is for the sake of the product that the whole organization of management, plant, equipment, materials, and workmen exists. The product gives meaning to production. It is the source of profits, one of the chief incentives for which men labor. More product and better quality of product are the chief ends for all we do in the name of efficiency. In its widest sense product is the physical embodiment and essence of wealth.

Filling such an important part in the industrial scheme, it would seem that product should receive prime consideration from those engaged in industrial enterprise. That it does receive a great deal of attention is obvious. Years of research and constant study in production at great expense are lavished on the development of new products or upon the improvement of existing products. Hundreds of millions of dollars and every means that human ingenuity can conjure are used in advertising and marketing the product. Yet it remains all too true that failure of product in innumerable ways lies at the bottom of many business failures. By "failure of product" we take the larger, rounded view of the problem —failure in the relation of the product to the enterprise producing it, in marketing the product, and in calculating the place that the product fills in the scale of human needs. Contrary to the narrower technical view, individual business forecasting takes in all three of these aspects and attempts to correlate them with the product considered as the unifying element.

Forecasting for Industrial Enterprise.—Forecasting then, in the broadest sense, begins with a study of the product—its physical nature and its commercial possibilities. After the company determines from this that it has a well-conceived product for which there is a reasonably satisfactory demand, a further study of the product in its relation to other features of the company should be undertaken. The purpose of such an inquiry is to make certain that the venture will not fail for want of proper organization, financing, and other factors affecting the company or its plans to manufacture and sell the product. If these preliminary studies give promise of success and the company decides to go ahead with the venture, an intensive market study should be made as the basis for production schedules, cost, and price calculations, and for the actual sales and advertising campaigns. Many companies wind up their studies at this stage and proceed to put their plans into execution. Others take one further step—that of preparing a general business forecast so as to gage the future prospects of the venture under changing business conditions, although this step may be undertaken at any time, even after the product is well launched.

The whole process, in short, comes down to this: know the product; be sure there is a satisfactory demand for it; prepare the company for the undertaking; make an intensive market study as a basis for production schedules and for the sales campaigns; and cover the future by a general business forecast.[4] Wherever risks and problems crop up in this process, take the proper precautions to meet them.

Analyzing the Product Marketwise.—A thorough analysis of the nature of the product and of its commercial possibilities is one of the first essentials of forecasting for the individual enterprise. By the general term "product" we mean either the single article (a specialty) or a line of articles produced by a manufacturing concern. Product analyses may be made for many different purposes but, when used in connection with forecasting, the object of such studies is to make reasonably certain that all risks to the company from the possibility of product failure are minimized or eliminated. Many business failures are laid to inadequate financing, to adverse conditions of business cycles, and to other factors when the real cause is that the product is not well conceived as to struc-

[4] How this process is worked out in minute detail may be seen from an excellent study, "Forecasting Sales," Policyholders Service Bureau, Metropolitan Life Insurance Company, New York. The study outlines the general forecasting problem of manufacturing concerns.

ture, quality, and usefulness. A study of product, therefore, in relation to its commercial possibilities is of the utmost importance.

Is the Product Well Conceived and Useful?—In answering this question a detailed description of the product is the starting point. In other words, what have you got to sell? This involves a careful consideration of such factors as physical appearance, structure, functional style and design, component materials, and the detailed uses for which the product is intended (see Chaps. VII and VIII). Such a study will indicate what will have to be done in developing the product if it is decided to produce and sell it. From the same data it will be possible to identify the product in its industrial group and commercial class, and thus to determine its fitness to fill a need as compared to competing products. Is it a product to be used up directly by people in the process of living (a consumer good); or is it intended to be used by other manufacturers in further production (a producer good)? Is it a durable good (of long life when used), nondurable (consumed immediately or in a very short time), or semidurable? In which one of the 20 major groups and of the several hundred subordinate industry groups is the product to be classified? If the product is to be used in further production, what subsequent classification will it have? In making this part of the product analysis, reference to the "United States Census of Manufactures" and to the literature put out by trade associations will be very helpful.

When the product has been described and identified in its field, product analysis will go deeper. Do patents and trade-marks adequately protect the product? Here, one recalls the several companies that started in the manufacture of electric razors under the cloud of infringement on Schick patents. Each year hundreds of similar cases occur, and many company failures can be directly chargeable to unprotected products. If the patents of others are to be used, are the use and royalty agreements drawn carefully so that no subsequent barriers arise to the exploitation of the product? Have the effects of these agreements on production costs and marketing factors been carefully calculated and weighed so that competitive and profit margins will not be too narrow? Have government and trade regulations affecting the production and use of the product been checked so as to avoid interference with the business from these sources? Has a tax analysis of the product been made and due allowance made for the tax position of the product? An enterprise, sound in other respects, may be weakened by difficulties in any of these matters.

In connection with the use of the product, the problem of *service factors* should be carefully examined. Is the nature of the product such that the manufacturer's responsibility carries through to quality, form, and performance in the use of the product by others, to servicing, to replacements? What guarantees are to be made? What services are to be rendered along the line from manufacturer, wholesaler, jobber, industrial user, consumer? How are the responsibility and cost of servicing to be borne and by whom? Will service parts constitute a secondary line of products on which profits can be made? Many companies that are hopefully launched and many products that are in themselves well conceived often come to grief because of the neglect of the service factors.

Is There a Demand for the Product?—After it is certain that the product is well conceived (although it may not yet be completely perfected) and that no obstacles stemming from the product itself will hamper its production and sale, the next step is to find out if there is a satisfactory demand for it. This calls for a market study, which is best done in two stages: (1) the preliminary *survey* to determine potential demand and (2) the intensive market *study* which is to be used as a basis for the final production plans and for the sales campaigns. Where a company is reasonably certain that there is a demand for the product and wishes to measure and chart the demand only for production and sales purposes, these two stages may be merged into one. But for several reasons, the two-stage study is the best course. Enthusiasm for the product may lead executives to take for granted that a demand exists, only to find after they have rushed ahead with heavy expense that the market is insufficient. A preliminary survey brings out the real facts early in the game. It shows the probable nature and extent of the market. By sampling and other tests it probes the depth of the market in any section or typical market area. The preliminary survey thus provides an estimate of potential demand with the least expense of time and effort. If the market does not look promising, the heavy expenses incident upon production and sales plans need not be undertaken. The cost of an exhaustive market study is saved. The venture can be trimmed to a more modest scale. On the other hand, the preliminary survey may show that original plans have been too modest, that they are not scaled to take full advantage of the demand that really exists. Revisions can then be made at this stage at least cost. Moreover, the preliminary survey may bring out defects in the product, indicate desirable changes, and result in other suggestions that it would be wise to attend to before marketing the product on a wide scale. For all these reasons, a market study in two stages rather than in one appears to be the most desirable. The trouble and expense of the preliminary survey are not wasted because the facts it uncovers are equally necessary in the later, intensive market study.

Procedure in the preliminary market survey is very similar to that undertaken in the more exhaustive study. The difference is a matter of coverage and degree, and each is governed by the objects sought. In the preliminary survey the object is to reach an estimate of *potential* demand. What is the nature of the demand and how big is it likely to be? The intensive market study starts with these facts and then probes deeper. Its object is to get the data for actual production schedules and for the sales campaign. How much of the potential demand can be turned into *actual* demand at the outset? How must the sales campaign be organized?

It is a matter of judgment as to how much of the data sought by the intensive market study (page 65) should be uncovered in the preliminary survey. A working minimum is not difficult to outline. From product analysis the product is identified as a producer item or a consumer item, durable, semidurable, or for quick consumption. This will set the outer limits of the preliminary market survey. More detailed study will then be needed to determine the geographical extent and specific locations of the market. Certain facts about prospective buyers will have to be gathered and studied to determine classes of buyers, need for the product, quantities likely to be taken, and conditions of sale. Sampling or other tests of buyer receptivity might be made. The type and extent of competition should be charted.

Certain conclusions should be sought from this preliminary survey. What is the nature of the market and how dependable is it as the basis for a manufacturing venture? What is the possible volume of sales that may be expected over various periods of time and perhaps at various prices of the product? Insofar as tests or sampling of the market indicate, what is the probable cost per unit of selling the product? Are any changes in the product needed before proceeding with regular manufacture and sale? Does the marketing of the product, as revealed by the preliminary survey, require any changes and preparations in the enterprise itself—its organization, production plans, financing, and other operations?

Although the object of product analysis is to determine the commercial position of the product and to make reasonably certain that all business risks growing out of the product as such are safeguarded against, the study will also be useful to the company in other respects. The product almost always influences the company in general, but very often the nature and commercial position of the product have a special bearing upon the organization, financing, and operations of the company. It is to this relation of product to enterprise that we must now turn in our survey of business risks and forecasting.

Relating the Product to the Enterprise.—Important decisions will hinge upon whether the product is to be launched along with a *new* enterprise, or whether it is a new product of an *established* company. Of like importance is the question whether the company is to be based upon the single product, a line of related products, or several diversified products. In other words, the place that the product is to occupy in the company and the purpose for which the company conceives the product are of considerable importance in forecasting and calculating the risks.

Production factors are of first consideration in relating the product to the enterprise. Are the proposed or existing plant and equipment adequate for efficient production, for contemplated quality and volume? What raw materials are required; what substitutes can be used; how adequate is the supply, and how dependable is the source of materials? Is there anything in the processing, cost conditions, and transportation of the materials to be used from the crude state to the point where needed that will create risks for production and marketing plans? Is the labor supply appropriate and dependable for the manufacture of the particular product? Are proper provisions being made for product development and improvement; for product form, design, packaging, and shipment? Has an analysis of government laws and regulations, trade customs and requirements, labor laws and union agreements affecting plant, equipment, and production been made? Has a graph of projected production been made, taking into account seasonal factors, production for stock, market, and order; allowing for necessary idle time, use of machinery and equipment for other products; and covering similar factors affecting production? Where possible, from a pilot plant, from test runs, and from engineering estimates, has a careful cost analysis been made? Many chapters of this book are devoted to answering these questions. The object of inquiring about them here is to make certain that all risks concerning the manufacture of the product are disclosed and measures taken to safeguard against them.

In like manner the product should be considered in conjunction with other departments of the enterprise. Is the sales organization properly formed for the marketing of the product as a specialty or line of products? Has a careful promotion, advertising, and sales campaign been formulated?

Has a careful financing forecast been made? What demands will the manufacture of the particular product make upon financial arrangements? Almost every study of business risk and business failure repeats the story of "inadequate capital." A study of 270 establishments that had failed in three Minnesota communities showed that lack of capital was of prime importance in 116 cases. Financial inadequacy was obvious by the fact that 51 per cent of the manufacturers had a net worth of less than $2,000 or an uncertain amount of investment.[5] Lack of capital was the cause assigned to an average of 31 per cent of the failures reported by Bradstreet over the period 1890 to 1931.[6] Analyzing bankruptcies in Boston and surrounding territory, the U.S. Department of Commerce reported that approximately 48 per cent of the bankrupts laid their failures to insufficient capital and that 33 per cent of their creditors agreed with that conclusion.[7] An analysis of the reasons given by banks for refusal to make loans to small manufacturers shows that 36.8 per cent of the refusals were based on "inadequate working capital." This means that when the banks examined the condition of the proposed borrower they found too low a ratio between current assets and current liabilities. In 40 per cent of the cases the refusal was based on "inadequate net worth" which measures the long-run ability to pay by means of the relation between total assets and total obligations.[8] In other words, behind each glittering success story of the "shoestring-to-industrial-empire" variety lies the tragic drama of hundreds of enterprises whose "shoestring," in the form of insufficient capital, is the prime cause of failure.

These sober facts bear out the importance of a proper financial survey as a means of guarding against future risks to the success of the enterprise. Reference to Chap. V on Financing will show the many factors that have to be considered if a new enterprise has to be financed from scratch. If the financing problem is to be examined not for the requirements of a new enterprise but for the introduction of a new product or group of products, equal care must be exercised that there will be sufficient financing for the new product without endangering the existing established business. Many details will have to be examined in a thorough financial survey, but the main questions are two: (1) Is there sufficient money available to put the product into production and to launch it on a scale adequate for the market for which it is intended? (2) If the product gains a foothold, will the probable long-term capital supply be sufficient to supplement the current financing generated by the sales of the product itself? Affirmative answers based on careful studies of all factors involved will not eliminate all the risks, but the chances for failure will be greatly minimized.

[5] Senate Temporary National Economic Committee, *Monograph* 17, Problems of Small Business, p. 88.

[6] *Ibid.*, citing Paul H. Nystrom, Opportunities for the Improvement of Retail Management, *Journal of Marketing*, April, 1936.

[7] *Ibid.*, p. 89, citing U.S. Department of Commerce, Bureau of Foreign and Domestic Commerce, Domestic Commerce Series 69, "Causes of Commercial Bankruptcies, 1932."

[8] *Ibid.*, p. 224.

Tentative Price and Production Schedules.—A thorough knowledge of the product and the demands which its production will make upon the enterprise as a whole will be very helpful in forming tentative price policies and a production schedule. Later on, this tentative price and production schedule will have to be refined by a specific study of market conditions. Tentative unit price can be set on unit cost at graduated production volumes, plus the desired markup, and qualified by prospective terms of sale. A scale of allowances and discounts should be set up in connection with the proposed marketing channels. The point of application of the net price (f.o.b. factory, warehouse, delivered, etc.) should be covered in the price policy. Likewise, the policy on returns, order cancellations, damaged merchandise, etc., should be determined. Finally, an important phase in the calculation of price is the credit and collection policy that will be followed. From all these facts a tentative profit-graph can be projected for each graduated volume of production (or for varying percentages of capacity of plant operation) showing the relation between fixed costs, variable costs, and expected net income. The break-even point will serve as a careful reminder of the risks involved before a profit can be earned.[9]

The Intensive Market Study.—After the company is satisfied from its preliminary studies that its product is sound and marketable and that the company organization and operations are adequate to handle the product, a specific market survey should be made. The preliminary survey having yielded an estimate of the possible demand, an intensive study must now be made of all the factors that will operate in converting *potential* users into *actual* customers. Many new products and enterprises fail because they are launched on an estimate of the potential market which is never realized. The cost in time and money of a careful market study is relatively cheap insurance for the larger failures it helps to avoid.

In many instances it may be desirable to have an outside agency do the work. Many professional organizations—marketing specialists, advertising agencies, business engineering firms—perform this service. Newspapers, magazines, radio chains, and other advertising media make surveys of the markets tapped by their circulation coverage, and these surveys may be of very great help if adapted to the needs of the manu-

[9] Helpful discussions of the profit-graph may be found in T. B. Fordham and E. H. Tingley, "Organization and Budgetary Control in Manufacturing"; and articles in *Mechanical Engineering*, Vol. 54, No. 11, and Vol. 55, No. 8. *Fortune Magazine*, February, 1949, p. 82, contains an excellent brief description of a chart on How to Tell Where You Break Even. See also Chap. XXVIII, section on Cost Control.

facturer.   Or the company may wish to make its own survey.   In that case it may be done by the sales department, a special research department, or by one or more management executives delegated to do the work.   In any case, there are certain fundamental guides to be followed in gathering and interpreting the facts.   The immediate object of the study is to arrive at a *sales estimate* on which to base actual production schedules, materials commitments, price and sales terms, and financial requirements.   Likewise, it will form the basis for the scope of advertising and the nature of the sales campaign.   The long-run purpose is to forecast the probable success of the enterprise or product.

The data provided by the preliminary market survey identify the potential market.   This is the starting point for the intensive market study.   From there on, the object is to widen and deepen the study of the market, to develop the minute detail that will be required to turn potential buyers into actual customers.   Every effort should be made to identify the prospective buyers, to learn their circumstances and characteristics, to chart the conditions under which they are likely to buy, to determine the type of effort necessary to sell to them, to discover if and how they are being serviced by competing firms or with comparable products, and what obstacles your firm will encounter in any attempt to distribute the product in the market outlined.   No "assumptions" or guesswork in an inquiry of this kind can substitute for the patient collection and study of the most detailed information that can be found.   Markets, after all, are people (even when a product is to be sold to other producers) ; and it is the intimate details about people that will reveal the ways in which they can be turned into customers.

Consumer Market Surveys.—If a consumer market is to be exploited, the survey will begin with the population and its distribution in the market area.   The climate, seasonal problems, transportation facilities, business conditions, and other aspects of the natural and cultural environment will be noted.   The market will be further refined by studies of the age, sex, family status, occupations, property holdings, income, buying habits, tastes and likes, and other personal characteristics of the people expected to buy your product.   What factors of quality, style, and service will influence the introduction of the product to this market?   What standing does your enterprise have relative to the market?   A very careful study of the channels through which the buyer may be reached should be made.   Here, you will be dealing with others—wholesalers, jobbers, retailers, and other actual selling media—whose activities may greatly influence your venture.   A slip here may spell failure although you have taken every precaution in your own power to insure success.   What sales appeals will have to be made in matters of arousing interest, of price, and of terms of sale? For durable goods, how are consumer sales to be financed? Some conclusions should be formed on the magnitude of the sales effort required and upon the unit cost of sales. The competitive situation should be fully investigated and carefully charted. The relation of your firm and of your product to each of these factors should be especially noted. On entering the market what advantages and disadvantages will you have? What will be necessary to make the most of your advantages and to offset or overcome your disadvantages?

The material for a consumer market survey must be drawn from many quarters and by various means. If the company is an established one, with long experience in selling consumer products, the sales department should have built up a sizable body of knowledge. Road salesmen, if properly trained to record consumer market conditions throughout their territory, may become valuable sources of information. Materials dealers and salesmen calling upon your own purchasing agent may also yield considerable information. But much data will have to come from outside sources. Publications of the U.S. Bureau of the Census, the U.S. Department of Commerce, and other Federal agencies are indispensable to a complete understanding of market areas and their characteristics.[10] Many states and an increasing number of cities now publish considerable data useful in market research. Surveys made by newspapers, magazines, radio networks, advertising agencies, chambers of commerce, and like associations will also be of great help. University and privately endowed research organizations frequently make and publish detailed studies of business conditions and consumer markets.[11] Invaluable, too, as a source of data is the growing literature dealing with community life in the United States, urban and rural.[12]

Producer Market Surveys.—If the enterprise or the product is to serve the producer market, procedure will be similar, but many details will be different. Here, the market consists, not of ultimate consumers in homes and communities, but of other producers who will use your

---

[10] Government agencies and departments are listed periodically in the "United States Government Manual," Superintendent of Documents, Washington, D.C. An excellent aid in this connection is "Government Publications and Their Use," 2d rev. ed., by Lawrence F. Schmeckebier, Brookings Institution, Washington, D.C., 1939.

[11] Columbia University and the University of Chicago are especially active in publishing studies of this kind. The National Industrial Conference Board, Twentieth Century Fund, Consumers League (National), American Home Economics Association, and even the Metropolitan Life Insurance Company are random examples of the many private organizations publishing studies of this kind.

[12] Notably the two studies of "Middletown" by Robert S. Lynd and Helen Lynd, and the work of Howard Odum and his associates at the University of North Carolina.

product in further production of their own. They may be producing for still another producer who, in turn, will use the product in further manufacture. Sometimes the chain is very long before a raw material becomes a finished consumer product. The character and length of this chain will determine how to approach market research of this kind. Just as intensively as the researcher studies *people* in the consumer market, so does he study the *business population* (the firms) in the producer market. The survey will cover the nature and characteristics of the industry producing the product and of industries using the product, the firms actually falling in market areas, the buying habits and customs of the market, the nature of competition, channels of distribution, price policies, and selling methods, and the trend of business conditions in the trade. Details and conclusions of this external market will be related to the specific enterprise, with the object of discovering its status in the field, advantages and disadvantages, and what adjustments and adaptations must be made in the organization for an efficient exploitation of the market.[13]

Varied Usefulness of Market Studies.—From studies of consumer and producer markets a rough estimate of current possibilities should be made. This should be referred back to the preliminary internal study previously made of the product and the enterprise. Alterations may be necessary in matters of engineering, materials, design, quality, packaging, and other features of the product. Revised production schedules may be necessary. Costs and price policies should be rechecked. Financing may have to be reconsidered. Organization of the sales department and of other departments may have to be adapted to market factors. Results of the survey may indicate that a test or sampling trial of the product should be made before the full risk of launching the enterprise or product is undertaken. In the case of the introduction of a new product in an established business considerable help in this connection may be obtained through the questionnaire method for appraising consumer reaction. Many other methods are available and yield information for the same purpose.[14] A careful consideration of all the factors in the particular industry or concerning the particular product will indicate the best approach. Each enterpriser will have to determine these factors for himself.

When all the information in the various surveys has been carefully

[13] Very helpful guides in making production and marketing studies may be obtained in the form of charts prepared by O. C. Holleran, Marketing Research and Service Division, Bureau of Foreign and Domestic Commerce of the U.S. Department of Commerce, Washington, D.C.

[14] WHITE, PERCIVAL, "Marketing Research Technique," New York: Harper & Brothers, 1931.

weighed, and the product, enterprise, and market adjusted to each other, the way is clear to arrive at a working sales forecast. This may then be used as the basis for actual materials commitments, production program, and sales campaign. Expressed in dollar terms and related to the financial status of the business, these items can be set up in the form of an estimated profit or loss statement and in an estimated balance sheet which will show the probable effect of the venture on the enterprise as a whole over a given time period. Some firms will be satisfied if the calculations made in this way point to a favorable result; others may wish to consider the particular industry or product appraisal in the light of a general business forecast.

The General Business Forecast.—Business forecasting today is roughly comparable to the state of medical science and the healing art a couple of centuries ago. On a slender foundation of genuine technical progress and achievement there rests a colossal structure of conjecture and doubt adorned with rococo by the hands of charlatans. Fortunately for the businessman who limits his fortune gathering to the successful operation of his own enterprise, most of the quackery in business forecasting plays upon operators in the securities markets. In the general field of forecasting there is a growing body of competent and earnest men and women, working individually and in public and private groups, with the laudable objectives of studying, charting, understanding, interpreting, and possibly of controlling business conditions in the interest of progress and for the welfare of the country. But sincerity and competence do not of themselves supply data buried in the past and now impossible to retrieve. They cannot guarantee the collection of current information necessary to sound forecasting. Nor do they preclude wide differences of opinion among the experts on the causes of economic disturbances and on methods of analyzing and interpreting the facts.[15] Like any other science, forecasting has to make its way in time by persistent study and patient experiment. Much hope for progress exists, even though the absolute unpredictability of many events will prevent the science of forecasting from reaching perfection.

But to point out that a science or process falls short of perfection and that experts disagree is not to conclude that what is being done in business forecasting is useless to the businessman. The exact contrary is true. In the attempt to understand and to forecast economic fluctuations, the experts have achieved many things of great value in business. They have been responsible for the collection of great amounts of data, past and present, which are indispensable for the understanding of economic condi-

[15] For an excellent survey of the whole subject of forecasting, see Elmer C. Bratt, "Business Cycles and Forecasting."

tions. They have arranged, grouped, and correlated these data in an infinite number of ways useful to the businessman. And although they have produced no infallible methods for reading the future, they do offer many helpful guides to reduce the guesswork about the future. This much may be shown in a few observations on the nature of forecasting.

Forces Involved in Economic Forecasting.—The economic present and future are conditioned by three sets of forces or influences, each of which is made up of many different elements. These are the seasonal influences, the long-time trends, and the business cycle. All three are at work, effecting economic change, concurrently. Stated another way, seasonal influences and business cycles are of relatively short duration and occur, so to speak, within the longer time framework of the long-time trends which are also working economic changes. Economic forecasting studies each of these three sets of influences, seeks to discover the way they work and the effects they produce separately and in combination, and then tries to interpret them in terms of future probability as a basis for practical economic action.

Seasonal Variations.—Seasonal variations stem from the yearly cycle of weather and from the social seasons set up by custom and tradition. Each of the natural seasons is responsible for many economic changes, some of them very great as at harvest time. In like manner, each social season—such as Christmas, Easter, and the summer vacation period—influences the economy in many ways. Businessmen need no reminder of seasonal influences on their affairs; they know the minor and sometimes major business tragedies caused by seasonal fluctuations. But seasonal variations occur within a year and their tendency to repeat from year to year is fairly reliable. Moreover, the nature of many of the elements that make for seasonal fluctuations are well known to businessmen. They know substantially what to expect in spring, summer, fall, and winter. They know how to translate Christmas, Easter, vacation time, and other social seasons into economic terms. This has taken much of the mystery out of seasonal economic disturbances.

Businessmen prepare in many ways to cope with these easily predictable changes. They manufacture for inventory in off seasons, diversify the line of products so as to stabilize production and labor, offset weather by artificial devices, offer special sales inducements to off-season buying as in furs, adjust price schedules to take up part of the risk of seasonal business, anticipate the season as when women's spring hats are introduced in January, develop off-season uses for seasonal products, exploit complementary markets when the season in one closes while the season in the other opens, stagger vacations and residential moving days—the list of offsetting techniques is endless. Careful study of each individual enterprise is necessary, and plenty of imagination and ingenuity is required. Great progress has been made. Yet, despite all that is done about them, seasonal variations in total economic activity continue to work havoc in the economy. Where this is due to change and sudden variations, like cyclonic storms and hurricanes, probably little can be done about it except to meet the risk by insurance and similar compensations. But for the regular variations, forecasting offers much promise and has already developed a body of data of considerable value to industry, as we shall see below.

Long-time Trends.—Long-time trends indicate structural changes in economy occurring in a slow, cumulative way. They come about through changes in productive ability, social institutions, and individual habits and usually manifest themselves in industrial growth or decadence. Obviously, this involves many elements such as population trends, technological developments, condition and use of natural resources, long-time stages or types of economic growth, changes in social institutions and customs and in individual habits. The study of these trends requires data extended over long periods of time, and past data of a useful kind are extremely meager. Moreover, whereas some of these data are measurable in exact terms, like population, a large part of it can be appraised only by qualitative, logical reasoning which itself opens the door to great variation.

Forecasters study these long-time trends. They measure where they can and seek to classify the unmeasurable into various patterns such as time periods, eras, ages, epochs, stages, or resource-use. Where possible, an attempt is made to project these trends into the future and to interpret their significance in economic affairs. From this it is hoped to bring about more desirable regulation of fixed-capital investment, proper planning of public works, stabilization of employment, geographical location of plants and economic activities, desirable changes in regional and international trade, and better balance in economic life. The broader data and conclusions thus reached may be applied in part to industrial groups and even individual industries.

Even particular enterprises may make use of such data at least as a guide to action in many phases of the enterprise. Assume, for example, that forecasters of population trends are correct in that the population growth is leveling off—specifically that births are declining, that family units are growing smaller, and that the average age of the population will be older. This is a long-time trend of the kind we are here considering. Its influence on the economy will be slow, not spectacular; but over a period of twenty or thirty years (the life of many capital goods) it may work far-reaching effects in the whole economy. Industries manufacturing children's wear, toys, school equipment, various kinds of foods, and other products for babies and young people may have to make careful adjustments to the changing demand; while those producing for an adult population will experience different effects.   Real-estate developments will be affected.   Public works in the form of schools, community centers, parks and other recreation areas, and public services will take on a different significance.   So profound is population change that its effects can be traced through every phase of economic life—capital investment, production, employment, trade and exchange, and distribution of wealth and income. Many enterprises ignore such trends at their peril; and some learn by bitter experience, as did the railroads when they neglected to utilize the technological change that resulted in the automobile.   Anticipated changes in the quality or use of a product, for example, may prevent the growth of a competitive industry that might spell ruin for existing industries.

The individual enterprise can obtain or make up from available studies a list of these long-time trends, arranging them according to the degrees of positive and negative effects they may have on the enterprise.   It may then interpret them in terms of adjustments to be made in planning the future of the enterprise, in arranging its capital investment, in determining the type, volume, and nature of its production, in formulating labor and other policies and similar detailed applications.   Care will have to be taken that long-time trends serve only as a broad guide which must be brought into relation with seasonal and business-cycle changes.   The effort to do this will be valuable even though the reliability of long-time forecasting remains in considerable doubt.

The Business Cycle.—In duration, the business cycle covers a time period longer than seasonal fluctuations and much shorter than long-time trends.   Stated differently, many seasonal fluctuations take place within a business cycle, and many business cycles occur in the progress of a long-time trend.   The business cycle is made up of recurrent fluctuations revolving around a state of balance.   These fluctuations make up a pattern according to which business activity experiences an *upswing*, carrying it far above balance to what may be termed "overproduction," and then enters upon a *down swing* extending far below balance to a point we may call "underproduction."   These two extremes are popularly called "prosperity" and "depression."   A complete cycle is described when business activity moves, let us say, from the peak of prosperity through the down swing to depression and back up again to prosperity; or in similar manner from depression to depression.   The length of the cycle varies from 2 to 12 years, but most business cycles cover time periods ranging from 3 to 4 years.   Although the cycle is recurrent, *i.e.*, occurs again and again, it does not do so in clear, stated periods; and it does not swing from one extreme to the opposite extreme in any consistent pattern. The reason for this appears to lie in the two sets of factors seemingly responsible for the cycle.

One set of influences has been called "originating causes" which prevent production from taking place at balanced levels.[16] They may drive it upward, downward, or from one extreme in the direction of balance. A long list of these causes may be made up, but a few examples will indicate their nature. Weather and solar variations may have an influencing effect of this kind on business activity. So does war or threat of war. The commercial use of inventions and discoveries may operate in the same way. Any significant changes in the legal rules of doing business may have a similar effect. Government spending may also exert such an influence. These originating influences do not produce the business cycle. They introduce a disturbing element, an upsetting circumstance; and it is the reaction of other business forces to this disturbance that determines the course of the business cycle. A disturbance of this kind may be likened to a pistol shot fired close to a horse; it may cause him to rear up and thrash around, to bolt and dash away in any direction, to stop if he has been moving, or merely to stand quietly without reaction. The shot will cause the reaction, but the nature of the reaction depends upon other causes.

In the case of the business cycle these other causes are a series of *limiting forces* and *reinforcing forces* which are more or less self-generating in two respects. They gain their power from conditions within the business cycle, and they are parts in a chain of interacting influences. The course that the cycle will take depends upon the relative strength of the two sets of forces. The reinforcing influences accelerate the business movement in the direction in which it is moving. The limiting forces retard that movement and sometimes reverse the movement altogether. Production, employment, and purchasing power, interacting, are reinforcing influences working in the direction of an upswing. Credit expansion is another. Price rises, stimulating inventory accumulation, securities and land speculation are others. They are accompanied by an optimistic emotional reaction in which business confidence blossoms. Investment, expansion, and increasing business activity heighten. Many of these forces have a spiraling effect in that the influences set in motion by one force react to intensify that force. All are interacting and must be considered as a combination. They form a wide variety of patterns in different business cycles. They translate themselves into operating activities in all phases of the economy and may be readily

[16] BRATT, *op. cit.*, p. 184. In this description of the nature of business cycles much reliance has been placed on Dr. Bratt's study.

identified in whole industries and even in the individual enterprise. If strong enough, these forces eventually pull or push business activity up to prosperity levels.

Soon after the prosperity level is reached, business activity tends to run along a plateau for a time. Limiting forces are at work and probably are accumulating power. These forces grow out of the very elements that contribute to the boom and prosperity. During the boom period, for example, inventories are expanded; but a point is reached when storage facilities are used to the limit, when costs of carrying inventory rise, when the movement from inventory to market becomes progressively slower. These considerations lead producers to slow up on inventory accumulation, which means to reduce the pace of production. This condition and the decision to slow down production are limiting forces. Other limiting forces work similarly. As expansion during the boom takes place, interest rates on working capital and even on long-term loans rise. This curbs lending for production and thus acts as a brake on production. Expanding production during the boom also leads to higher variable and overhead costs. For a time, the state of prosperity will take these higher costs in the form of higher prices, but soon sales resistance sets in, and the higher costs can no longer be covered. When this point is reached, production is slowed down. In every prosperity period, too, efficiency gains at first, but later begins to fall off as production is speeded up. The less efficient firms find themselves at a disadvantage which increases progressively, and they are compelled to taper off production. All these signs of slackening are in fact limiting forces at work on the conditions of production. A general feeling of strain seems to pervade the business scene. Elements of unbalance between various industries and in many activities appear. Adjustments become more difficult to make. The boom is drawing to its end.

If the accumulated difficulties are large enough, they may precipitate a downward tendency in business activity. Or, while business conditions are thus strained and vulnerable, some originating cause may become the deciding factor and a down swing gets under way. Now, reinforcing influences analogous to those which accelerated the upswing hasten the down swing, as they function in reverse. Prices fall, profits disappear, production decreases, unemployment rises, purchasing power falls off, credit contracts, failures increase, and gloom colors the business outlook. The combination feeds on itself to accelerate and deepen the down swing. At some point the limiting forces, also in reverse from what they had been at the top of the upswing, reappear to check the fall. A period of stabilization sets in—"scraping along the bottom"—while forces, once more making for another upswing, gather. These up-and-down swings do not always go to extremes of the balance around which they revolve. There is constant oscillation, and there may be several minor rises and falls, as the longer cycle from prosperity to depression and back again to prosperity follows its course.

The Great Depression that began in 1929 was a vivid and unforgettable experience of the havoc worked in every phase of life by cycles of extreme severity. Major depressions of comparable severity occurred in 1815–1821, 1837–1843, and 1873–1878, although the relative degree of severity cannot be satisfactorily established. Between 1878 and 1933, some 15 cycles are traced, 7 considered major and 8 minor, according to the extent of deviation from normal.[17] Each cycle is unique in that different factors and different combinations of factors distinguish it from others. Confusion is further increased by seasonal cycles and long-time trends. The forces and fluctuations of the three different cycles, seasonal, long-time trends, and business cycles, meet in an endless variety of combinations in the changing economic scene. In an effort to understand business cycles, forecasters screen out the effects of seasonal and long-time trends, but the infinite variety of combinations possible with 40 or 50 different forces makes this extremely difficult, to put it mildly. Anyone familiar with the chances of hitting the right combination in the numbers game, of drawing a straight flush in poker, or 13 cards of the same suit in bridge will understand what forecasters are up against. And, to make things even more difficult for the practical businessman, it is believed that, in addition to these cycles affecting total economic activity, there is also a *specific* cycle for an individual industry or process.[18]

Yet business management must and does function in this environment of confusion and fluctuation. Plans are made; enterprises and products are launched; operations proceed; and individual managers make the best adjustment they can to these forces which seem beyond their control. That progress is made in the face of such difficulties shows that the situation is not so discouraging as it seems. It shows also that management and economic enterprise are extremely flexible. The cycles do not produce such ceaseless unsettlement, and their effects are not so destructive as to make working adjustments by management impossible. This means that there is much intelligent action that management can take to meet and possibly offset these economic fluctuations.

Industrial management executives cannot be business-cycle experts unless they are willing to devote all or the major part of their time to the subject. The most they can hope to accomplish is to assimilate the

[17] BRATT, *op. cit.*, table on p. 403, and Chaps. XI and XII on business-cycle history.

[18] MITCHELL and BURNS, The National Bureau's Measures of Cyclical Behavior, National Bureau of Economic Research *Bulletin* 57, July 1, 1935.

best thought of experts in the field. From the growing body of knowledge about economic cycles, businessmen can become familiar with the form and behavior of cyclic conditions. They can understand the general methods that the experts use to study and measure economic conditions. And they can learn how to use the forecasts worked out by the experts. An individual enterprise cannot hope to isolate itself from the business cycle, but, by judicious adjustment in accordance with the business "barometers" used by experts to study business cycles, management may go far to protect itself against the worst effects of cyclic changes.

Business Barometers.—Since business cycles affect every phase of economic life, forecasters have made minute studies of economic operations and conditions in an effort to find either the causes or the indicators of cyclic behavior. They have studied stock-market activity, industrial production, employment, prices, construction contracts, electric-power output, bank debits, income, inventories, trade, and similar features of economic activity. They have divided many of these larger activities into subclassifications for more intensive study, as for example, stock prices, world prices, commodity prices, retail prices, agricultural prices, industrial prices, and such aggregate price behavior as the general price level. By careful search of past conditions, they have succeeded in projecting many of these economic activities over fairly long periods of time to gain the perspective that business-cycle study requires. For example, Barron's Publishing Company has compiled a series to show physical volume of production and trade from 1875 to date; and the Standard Statistics Company, Inc., has compiled a number of industrial production series going back to 1884.

Aside from their use in studying economic cycles, these compilations of data may be used by the practical business executive as guides in operating the specific enterprise. As projected in time, the data on any given item, such as industrial production, bank debits, retail prices, or department-store sales, are termed a *series*. Wherever possible the data are converted into *index numbers* which are statistical devices used for convenience in measuring and comparing data. A single series may be used for many purposes; or many series may be combined in one general index (as they usually are) for the purpose of bringing related data together. In order to measure *general business activity,* for example, a compiler will select and combine several different series which he believes are keys or indicators to the course of general business conditions. *The New York Times* thus compiles a weekly index of business activity consisting of a combined index and six series currently listed as follows: miscellaneous carloadings, other carloadings, steel production, electric-power production, paperboard production, and lumber production. The Babson

Statistical Organization, publishing *Babson's Reports*, combines 54 series into a composite index of business activity. The more than half a hundred series are subclassifications under the following heads: manufactures, minerals, agricultural marketings, building and construction, railway freight, electric power, and foreign trade. Since the number of separate series is unusually large, the business executive will find a valuable aid in Donald H. Davenport and Frances V. Scott, "An Index to Business Indices," [19] which gives detailed information about the principal indexes and their compilation. Of equal value, especially in keeping up with current data, is the U.S. Department of Commerce *Survey of Current Business*, a monthly magazine with annual and biennial supplements, which carries about 700 series.[20]

Using Business Indexes in the Industrial Enterprise.—The best procedure, perhaps, is for the officials of each enterprise to examine and select a group of business indicators that measure and compare data having some direct bearing on the particular enterprise. They may select several separate series or various combinations, or use a set made up of selections from each type. In some cases, single series may be considered together as a tailor-made group. Much will depend on the use that is to be made of them. In any event, great care should be taken of the qualifications and limitations that the compiler places upon his work. Top executives will want indexes of general business activity; and for this purpose they may select a composite index like the "New York Federal Reserve Bank Index of Production and Trade," or the "Bureau of Foreign and Domestic Commerce Index of Total Income Payments," or any one of the other mentioned general business indexes. In some cases, a single series such as the "Federal Reserve Board Index of Industrial Production" or an index of general prices may serve this purpose. Whatever indexes are chosen, they will, of course, have to be interpreted for their bearing upon the specific enterprise and, in any case, used only as guides to action to be checked by other data.[21]

[19] Business Publications, Inc., Chicago, 1937.

[20] The Joint Congressional Committee on the President's Economic Report, in discharge of its functions under the Employment Act of 1946, now issues a publication *Economic Indicators* available to the public at a nominal charge through the Superintendent of Documents, Washington, D.C.

[21] The business executive may supplement the technical indexes with trade association publications and reports and with current, more general interpretations of business conditions such as may be found in commercial newsletters like the *Kiplinger Service;* or with the periodical magazines such as *Commercial and Financial Chronicle, Nation's Business,* and even popular magazines like *Newsweek.* Those mentioned are merely typical of the supplementary aids available which, along with the technical data, may be used in the formation of independent judgment in specific cases.

The sales department will also want to use both the broad guides to general business conditions and other, more pointed indexes. Some among the many indexes available and useful to the sales manager are measures of regional business conditions; indexes of producer and consumer goods; of production, shipments, and inventories; several of the indexes dealing with price behavior in many fields; of trade conditions, wholesale and retail; of national income, wage payments, credit conditions, and other monetary measures; of population changes; and of commercial failures and the state of business confidence. Bearing in mind the nature of his sales distribution and related problems, the sales manager may want to use many other indexes.

The purchasing agent will want to know the trend of purchases, production, inventories, general prices, commodity prices, and the prices of goods in various stages of fabrication. He will also be interested directly in money and credit conditions, the state of business confidence, and commercial failures. The production manager may want to follow the relations between durable and nondurable goods, production, inventories, unfilled orders, labor turnover and industrial disputes, wage rates, prices, changes in productivity, unemployment, and the various indexes dealing with goods in process and market conditions. The personnel manager will find much of interest in the selection of many indexes bearing upon employment, wages, and other labor conditions. The treasurer, controller, and budget officer will be interested not only in general business conditions but in such indexes as wage rates, interest rates, stock prices, general prices, national income, net profits; wage, interest, and dividend payments; tax payments, savings, and idle capital; bank loans, debits, and turnover of deposits; security flotations; and in commercial and bank failures.

In other words, from the top management down through all the departmental executives of any enterprise, there will be need for guides of trends and business conditions bearing upon departmental functions, upon the enterprise as a business unit, upon the industrial field in which the enterprise operates, upon related groups of industries, and upon the state of the economy as a whole, domestic and foreign. And thanks to the great and painstaking work of many individuals, private institutions, and government agencies, guiding indexes in almost all these matters are available. Where several executives in different departments of a single firm use different indexes for guides, care should be taken that there is fundamental consistency and harmony between the various indexes used. Many firms use a forecasting committee composed of executives from various departments in order to insure correlation of their findings.

Knowing the nature and scope of the indexes he has selected and the use he intends to make of them, the executive can devise his own charts of interpretations and adopt methods of relating the business indicators to the needs of the specific enterprise. Few general directions can be given here for these purposes. The available indexes are so many, and each enterprise is so highly individualized, that the job of selecting and interpreting the indexes falls upon each executive seeking guidance. A study of the business barometers, methods of interpreting them, and devices for correlating them with the enterprise will prove a profitable investment for every executive. He will learn the coverage of the various series, those which lead and those which lag, how to handle the timing of various relationships, and what opinions to form on the amplitude of recorded fluctuations. From practice, he will be able to build interpretative check lists increasing his knowledge of the behavior of economic conditions and of how they affect his own operations.[22]

Specific Risks in Industrial Operations.—So long as the future remains uncertain, economic activities will involve risk—the chance of loss or injury. We have seen with what great care an enterprise or a product must be launched in order to guard against the general business risks involved in such undertakings. Once in operation the enterprise will be subject to many other risks. They spring from many physical and natural causes, from uncertainties arising out of insufficient knowledge about many phases of economic behavior, from the unpredictable character of human conduct, from changes wrought by time, from chance happenings of events, from unexpected government action. The saving feature about most risks of this type is that they are more or less specific. Even though their occurrence is unpredictable, most of them are well known. Consequently businessmen have worked out many methods and techniques for dealing with them. In short, if management takes the matter firmly in hand, subjects every part of the enterprise to a searching study for the probability of specific risks, and adopts such measures as plain common sense often dictates, the danger of loss from risks of this kind may be greatly reduced.

The proper procedure is for the management to institute a thorough risk survey of its own enterprise.[23] A committee for this purpose may be formed of certain executive officers and department heads. With the help of selected employees, the committee may study and evaluate the

[22] Considerable assistance may be had from the following: L. H. Haney, "Business Forecasting"; D. F. Gordon, "Practical Business Forecasting"; J. L. Snider, "Business Statistics"; and William Wallace, "Business Forecasting and Its Practical Application." The article Forecasting Business in *Fortune Magazine*, Vol. 18, October, 1938, will also be very helpful.

[23] If it is desired, the original survey may be made by an outside firm of industrial engineers.

risks in each department or activity of the company. If the committee is made permanent and its work encouraged by proper publicity and incentives, a continuing vigilance may be kept over the major risks most likely to cause serious losses.

It is not the intention here to set up a complete classification of specific risks, but rather to point out the most common ones and to indicate some of the general methods of dealing with them. Specific risks will differ according to the nature of the enterprise, the location of its plant, the type of machinery and equipment, and the scope of the firm's operations. For this reason an individual risk survey is recommended. The greater part of these specific risks (other than market risk treated in connection with forecasting) center about (1) the enterprise as a whole and (2) its production activities. If the company is large enough to warrant a more detailed outline, risks can be catalogued by departments, by processes, by equipment, and the like; or a check list of risks may be worked out and used as a rating sheet for every phase of the enterprise.

Specific Risks Bearing upon the Enterprise as a Whole. *Risks Centering around the Physical Property of the Enterprise.*—Many risks center about the enterprise as a whole. A survey would define the nature of these risks in detail and indicate methods for eliminating or offsetting them. Attacking risks at the point of prevention rather than at the point of loss is good business all around. Title to the company's real estate, if defective, may cause great inconvenience and perhaps serious loss if not discovered and cleared as early as possible. This is work for the company attorney who may either institute proceedings to clear title or advise title insurance. A proper survey of boundaries will insure the proper location of buildings and of roadways affording ingress and egress to the plant, thus saving costly removals and relocations and avoiding damage suits for encroachment. Care in the examination of easements and riparian rights along waterways may insure uninterrupted and untroubled power sources.

The plant engineering department may be charged with the task of guarding against many hazards to the physical property of the company and to the safety and health of workers and all others attending to business on company property. Included here are risks from fire, earthquake, tornado, hail, windstorm, and flood; building collapse from overloading, from weak construction, or from deterioration of supports; dangers involved in improper location, weak anchoring, and unsafe operation of machinery, of power transmission, and of conveyor systems; hazards involved in defective electric wiring; explosions of steam boilers and from other causes; hazards involved in the use of dangerous substances and materials; dangers in hanging signs, in unsafe passageways, and in defective stairways. Engineers, maintenance men, and the working force, if given to understand that the company is in earnest in adopting a policy of preventive action, will uncover many risks such as these and will take the simple precautions against them. If new buildings are to be built, fireproof construction meets the fire hazard at the point of prevention. Sprinkler systems, properly placed sand buckets, water pails, and chemical fire extinguishers are always good investments. Fire escapes and periodic fire drills save human life and are the best insurance against personal damage suits and criminal actions against the company officers. Moreover, a company that is known to look after the health and safety of its workers will also find that the workers are interested in the welfare of the company. Fire and building inspection by city authorities and fire insurance underwriters should be welcomed and encouraged rather than regarded as a nuisance. Where else can a firm get such an inexpensive survey of its fire hazards? Other physical deficiencies, dangers, and hazards of all kinds should likewise be attacked from the side of prevention rather than viewed from the doubtful angle of compensation after loss. After the utmost has been done to make the physical property of the company safe from uncertain risks, the element of risk will still remain in part and in many forms. Where possible, insurance may be procured against loss as outlined below.

Risks Centering around Administration.—Building a proper administrative staff whose members can carry on satisfactorily if ill health, accident, or death removes key individuals is a better policy than taking out life insurance on selected executives. A good policy to follow here is the one that holds that no man is indispensable to the organization. Building the loyalty, honesty, and trustworthiness of officials who handle large sums of the firm's money is also better than relying upon fidelity insurance against innocent loss or embezzlement. Credit losses are best prevented by more careful extension of credit in the first instance—an account recklessly handled involves the double risk of the loss of your money and your customer too. Many financial losses are avoidable by proper accounting methods and budgetary controls. Balance sheets and profit and loss statements reveal financial weaknesses and profit leaks. A system of simple accounting ratios, adjusted to the particular enterprise, is a necessary element in forecasting risks. Moreover, ratios are what the bankers examine first when loans are sought. Advance budgets which achieve sound proportion in the allocation of funds to the various departments of the enterprise and which indicate financial needs ahead of time are far better than the "happy-go-unlucky" policy of waiting for something to "turn up" when financial problems are acute. A reserve for contingencies serves a double purpose; it is an insurance against loss and an investment. Pending the contingency, a reserve is an element of soundness that your bankers and business associates will respect. If the contingency occurs, reserves cushion the blow; and if the contingency never materializes, reserves are handy windfalls. Where possible, diversify the source of income, iron out seasonal variations, produce on order or with a backlog of orders, and avoid carrying the enterprise or its executive personnel in a state of frozen assets. The term "frozen assets" is a paradox; most of the assets disappear with the thawing. In short, in the handling of administrative risks as with all others, preventive action is preferable to trying to offset losses after they occur.

Production Risks. *Risks in Connection with the Laboring Force.*— Besides risks involving the enterprise as a whole, a second sector where many and large risks are likely to occur is that of the plant in production. The health and safety of the labor force are direct responsibilities of the enterprise. Many firms insist upon medical examinations for prospective workers and pay the cost. They encourage group health, hospitalization, accident and life insurance. An emergency sickroom with an industrial nurse in charge often catches injuries before they become heavy liabilities. Even if workmen's compensation insurance meets part of the problem of industrial accidents, it is better to go to the sources of trouble. Plant engineers and maintenance men should be responsible for safety devices on machinery in operation, for the proper use of dangerous materials, for sanitation, and for the elimination of all other hazards of the workplace and equipment in operation. The personnel department can do much in the way of worker training programs and safety campaigns to build safe work habits. Rest periods and restrooms, more comfortable work positions, fresh drinking water, and better lighting are not falderal coddling the worker, but essential elements in efficiency and for avoiding industrial accidents.

Treating the workers as human beings entitled to every consideration commensurate with efficient production is also good insurance against absenteeism and labor turnover, against damage to materials and equipment through carelessness and indifference, and against strikes. The losses here are not so spectacular as those which come through fire and floods, and for that reason are often regarded indifferently by management. But these are the slow, steady leaks that sap efficiency and drain away profits. Collective wage contracts often avoid wage bickering and inconvenient strike losses, but if poorly drawn or permitted to terminate at improper times, may themselves be a source of loss. Although of more direct benefit to the economy as a whole, unemployment, group health, and social security insurance results in better employer-employee relations even in the single enterprise. In short, an adequate personnel administration can go a long way toward preventing risks centering around the worker and his operations.

Risks in Connection with Materials.—Many risks arise in connection with materials. Proper forecasts of commodity prices will contribute toward the elimination of price surprises. Where a forecast is doubtful, forward buying or hedging to cover standard needs or contract requirements may be advisable. Supply deficiencies may be met by changes in inventory policy, by contracting out, by acquisition of the supply sources themselves, or by a careful survey of alternative sources and substitute materials. Simplification of product and standardization of parts often result in considerable materials savings where the risk of high-cost materials cannot be reduced. Careful attention to proper storage techniques will cut down losses from deterioration. Proper precautions and health and safety devices should be used in the handling of dangerous and other deleterious materials. Losses on materials is another one of those small, but often steady, leaks that drain away the profits of an enterprise.

Risks of Technological Change.—Many risks arise from changing technology. Firms that have developed a good product and have enjoyed a steady sale of it for years are likely to grow complacent as newer products are developed by competitors. Once the swing to a competitive product has begun, it is difficult for the original producer to hold his market. The changes he may then make in the product disturb the public familiarity with it and often hasten the turn to other products. Technological changes also take place in machinery, equipment, materials, and methods of production. These involve the risks of changing costs of production, which along with market prices lie at the heart of the profit equation. In other words, profits may come from larger returns through market price and volume; or price and volume may remain constant while costs of production are brought down. In either case the spread between cost and selling price—the profit margin—is widened and larger profits result. Risks relating to product change and development, and those springing from changes in equipment and production processes, are best met by a policy of constant research. No matter how small, a research department should be part of every enterprise. Even where the cost seems unwarranted, such a department will be found to pay many dividends which in the long run will exceed its cost.

This brief survey of specific risks centering around the enterprise as a whole, its administrative and production activities, merely indicates the type and range of risks likely to be encountered in the average industrial enterprise. A company survey will bring out the specialized and detailed risks that each individual enterprise will have to meet. Other chapters of this book develop many of these risks in detail and discuss the different methods of handling them. With the aid of this material a company committee may explore the nature of risk in its own plant. Knowledge of the risk is the first essential toward eliminating or reducing it. After the facts are thoroughly developed, methods to handle the risk may be put into operation. A residue of risk is likely to remain about which nothing, apparently, can be done. Here, a rough estimate of the probability of the event or happening must be weighed against the cost of compensating for losses, probably through insurance. If the chance of loss or injury is reasonably probable, and the approximate amount of loss is likely to be large, insurance should be sought as an offset.

Insurance.—Insurance should be the last resort, not the first, in meeting business risk. Insurance increases the current cost of doing business and thus narrows the profit margin and makes the product more vulnerable to competition. Insurance does not eliminate the risk. It never fairly compensates for all the loss. At first glance, it appears that insurance shifts the risk to others, but this means simply that others are also shifting part of their risks to you. Each enterprise does not escape its share of the total loss to the economy as a whole. If this merely shared the losses equally among all firms, only the economy as a whole would be likely to suffer. But all enterprises do not have the same cost of production. Some operate with very wide profit margins and can easily bear their share of total economic loss. Others are high-cost firms, operating with a very narrow margin between cost and selling price in what may be a highly competitive field. If total economic losses become large enough so that insurance premiums run high, the marginal firm is likely to find itself vulnerable to business failure and bankruptcy. The best policy for all firms is not to shift the risk, if it can be eliminated altogether, and to reduce all risks wherever possible. It is a better policy, for example, to use safety devices to decrease accidents than to rely upon workmen's compensation insurance to pay for injuries.

Where a residue of risk remains without possibility of elimination, insurance is perhaps the best method to cushion the loss if it should occur. The range of insurance has steadily widened over the years and now includes coverage for almost all calculable risks. There is the usual insurance against fire, earthquake, tornado, windstorm, hailstorm, flood, explosion, burglary and theft, riots, and public disturbances. Various grades and types of insurance cover rolling stock, delivery equipment, and other transportation risks. Personal liability insurance and property damage are available to cover almost every injury to persons and property. Surety and fidelity insurance cover cases such as defalcation and embezzlement. Where necessary, the lives of key executives can be insured to protect the firm against losses growing out of heavy dependence upon one man or a group of men. Insurance may be had against credit losses and to cover fixed charges and overhead during the incapacitation of the plant.

An increasing array of insurance services (even where the service is government supported or partly subsidized and not strictly on the insurance principle) covers contingencies affecting the labor force. Workmen's compensation insurance is firmly established; and group health, hospitalization, and life insurance is already widely acceptable. Unemployment insurance and the diverse coverage in the social security system are still in the formative stage, but there is every indication that such services will be enlarged and perfected as time passes. Extension of these so-called "social services" in the economy undoubtedly will work temporary hardships on many individual firms, but adjustment will come in the long run. Painful as the present adjustments are, they are deemed more desirable than to let the social risks of accidents, ill health, hospitalization costs, unemployment, and old-age dependency continue and accumulate until they burst forth in the often uncontrollable upheavals of revolution and reform. Even in normal conditions, much of what is called government "interference" in business may be traced back to the unwillingness or inability of the private economy to recognize and safeguard against the risks that affect large groups of people.

SUMMARY

Although most sections of this diverse chapter carry their own summaries, there remains the necessity of gaining an over-all view of what has been attempted. If a conscientious application of the principles and procedures herein outlined has been made, the student and management executive will have a series of surveys pertaining to almost every phase of risk involved in launching an enterprise or product and of risks encountered in the operation of a going business. There will be an analysis of the product marketwise, so to speak; an analysis relating the product to the enterprise; a specific market survey for the purpose of reaching price and production schedules and for formulating the sales organization and campaign; a general business forecast covering seasonal variations, longtime trends, and business-cycle behavior; and finally a survey of specific risks involved in industrial operations. Each of these analyses and surveys will have many uses in separate departments of the enterprise and for varied purposes. The problem remains of how they may be correlated so as to produce a general guide for the management.

Although statistical averages cannot be made for such diverse data, it is possible that a comprehensive chart can be constructed which will relate selected business indicators to each other centering around the product, a line of products, or the enterprise as a business unit. Point values may be given to quantitative data. Where the data are qualitative, the logical inferences may be set up in a list of favorable and unfavorable factors relating to the product or enterprise. Various degrees of favorability and unfavorability may be determined upon and represented by symbols. Interpretative conclusions can be worked out for each point value and symbol and for various groupings of indicators. A system of periodic ratings of business factors will be necessary because the business picture is constantly changing. For the individual enterprise, these evaluations should always be in terms of that enterprise. In other words, what may be an unfavorable condition in the business cycle as regards the total economy may be a favorable one in terms of the individual enterprise.

When the chart and the evaluation bases are carefully worked out, the points and symbols may be grouped into various patterns indicating different effects on the enterprise and pointing toward several possibilities for corrective action. Patterns may be related to certain key policies, operations, and decisions. Thus, definite patterns may be developed for guidance on over-all expansion or retrenchment, investment in plant and equipment, short- and long-term financing; on price and credit policies; on production schedules, inventory policies, labor force and wage rates; on sales campaigns and on budget construction. It is this end product of such a chart—these patterns high-lighting conditions and indicating actions and decisions required on key policies—that will be of most service to the general management. Much experiment, testing, and many mistakes will have to be made before a working tool of this kind can be constructed, but it is not beyond the range of possibility. Even if there should be complete failure in the attempt to make a reliable forecast of all business risks, the experience will yield many by-products in the direction of more efficient conduct of the business for those who make the try.

CHAPTER V
FINANCING THE INDUSTRIAL ENTERPRISE

Few influences play a stronger part in American industrial life than does the people's simple belief in material progress. And their faith in this regard has become all the firmer because it has been sustained by tangible works. The balance sheet of each generation from earliest colonial times to the present has recorded increasing material gains. The scarcities and hardships of pioneer life steadily gave way to increasing plenty and comfort. Each passing year showed improvement in equipment and processes. New tools and new products poured forth from the growing factories. Primitive one-man enterprises and family-sized workshops grew to be giant industrial corporations employing thousands. Although it constantly fluctuated, the physical volume of production continually increased on the average, each decade surpassing the previous one with few exceptions. The idea. of progress took the form of expansion and became the dominating force, if not the law, of industrial growth and economic life.

This faith in progress was so strong that it generated traditional attitudes which held particular implications in the matter of business finance. There was the belief, for example, that if a man made a better mousetrap, the world (including the bankers) would beat a pathway to his door. Every man sought to go into business for himself in the firm belief that, once the step was made, he was on something like a moving belt from poverty to riches. And akin to that was the idea that business is started on a shoestring and proceeds uninterruptedly to industrial empire. The effect of these and similar attitudes was to obscure the necessity and importance of a thorough study of industrial financing. It was taken too much for granted that, if a business enterprise held forth great prospects, the problem of financing would take care of itself.

Some justification for these views existed in the conditions of industry in its early stages. Shops were small. Tools, equipment, and other aspects of industrial technology were quite simple. Production was carried on without extended specialization and mainly for local markets. Only a limited use was being made of credit. Total investment was relatively modest, and industrial financing was largely a matter between individuals. Financing was always a problem, to be sure, but in these conditions it was largely a secondary problem rather than a prime one. But time worked radical changes. Factories became increasingly larger, requiring extensive administrative staffs to take care of thousands of specialized workers in the single and related plants. Plant, equipment, tools, and materials demanded a heavy investment. Production came to serve national and world-wide markets. Credit was used extensively all along the line from raw materials to finished product and followed through to consumer financing. Intense competition demanded financial soundness for survival. The corporate form of business unit turned the problem of industrial financing from a matter between individuals and small groups to one involving the savings of thousands of people. As these changes came about, industrial financing became a matter of major importance. It has remained so to the present day.

If the new enterprise is to be solidly launched and if the existing enterprise is to continue to survive, constant attention must be paid to the problem of financing. The capital structure of the new enterprise cannot be left to chance; it must be planned. The current need for working capital must be carefully gaged, and methods should be worked out to assure its availability. All enterprises will be greatly improved if a system of budgeting is followed. The industrial promoter and business administrator should be as familiar as is the banker with the sources of capital and with the methods of raising it. It is the aim of this chapter to outline the information dealing with these phases of industrial financing.

Kinds of Capital.—In common usage the word "capital" is the single term used to cover the land, buildings, machinery, tools, and materials of a productive enterprise. Technically, whereas land is capital, it is distinguished from the other means of production because they are reproducible and land is not. Rarely does the businessman make this distinction. In the word capital, he lumps together all the elements he will need to start an enterprise, including the land required. He also takes another step in his thinking which results in a different use of the word capital. He thinks of capital most often in money terms. Promoting a new enterprise is very largely a financial operation. Since money and credit are the chief means for acquiring the instruments of production, the word capital has this financial aspect. And this is the way we shall use it here. Applied to industrial financing, capital means the cash money and credit needed to start and to operate an enterprise.[1]

[1] The many technical meanings of the word "capital" are best understood when studied in the context in which they are used. In its broadest meaning capital is synonymous with wealth, all useful articles owned by man. Land and its resources are often called *natural capital* to distinguish them from produced or *artificial capital*

Fixed and Working Capital.—Financial specialization recognizes different classifications of capital depending on such features as the use that is to be made of it, the time element involved, and the sources and methods of raising it. These forms of capital are best understood when we examine the capital requirements of an ordinary industrial enterprise. In this way, too, the connection will be clear between money capital and productive capital, the tangible instruments of production. If an industrial enterprise is to be started from the ground up, so to speak, it will need land and buildings, machinery, tools, and equipment. Assets of this kind, intended to be used over and over again in production for a long period of time, are commonly called *fixed capital;* and the money and credit required to pay for such assets take the same name. An enterprise also requires funds to cover its operations—to maintain the plant, to purchase materials and supplies, to pay salaries and wages, to cover storage, transportation and shipping services, for advertising, and to tide over the enterprise during the time lag between the sale of its products and payment for them. These are current operations and the funds to cover them are commonly called "working capital."

Short-term, Intermediate-term, and Long-term Capital.—Capital funds, especially in the form of bank credit, are often classified according to the time period for which loans are made. Where money is needed to pay for materials, labor, transportation, and other items required in the quick production of goods for market, the funds are called *short-term capital.* The familiar 30-, 60-, and 90-day loans are of this type. The time element usually does not extend beyond one year. If machinery, tools, supplies, and other equipment having a life of several years are to be bought, funds advanced for that purpose are referred to as *intermediate capital.* The time period covered is usually two or three years and rarely exceeds five years. General or heavy financing needed by an enterprise for a long period of time and for major purposes—for the purchase of land, erection of buildings, and for heavy machinery having a long life—is described as *long-term capital.* Funds for this purpose are usually invested for periods of 10, 20, and 30 years or more. The classifications are not hard and fast, and there is much overlapping. Intermediate capital, for example, may become long-term capital through successive renewals of a loan before final repayment. And the borrower of long-term capital may gain some of the advantages of intermediate

---

such as buildings, machinery, tools, materials. In corporate finance, *paid-in capital* means the amount paid for that percentage of the stock which has been sold. In accounting, *capital net value* is the total assets of an enterprise less the debts owed to others. In other words, the meaning of the word capital depends on its technical usage and upon the context.

capital (such as a saving on interest) if he has the privilege of paying off the loan before maturity. But in the main the three classes represent different types of capital funds. The distinction between them is important not only because they show the different financial needs of an enterprise but also because they bear a close connection to the different sources and methods of financing.

SOURCES OF CAPITAL FUNDS

Where does the money capital to finance industrial enterprises come from? The simplest way for a new enterprise to get its needed funds is for one or more individuals who are interested in the project to contribute the money directly. Or, in lieu of money contributions, individuals may transfer to the enterprise the actual land, buildings, machinery, and materials needed to make up the productive capital of the firm. Here, the source of the capital is the savings and property of wealthy individuals. If the new enterprise gets its capital in this way, it does not have to enter what we shall call the regular commercial money market for its funds—the market made up of professionals whose business it is to accumulate money and credit for the purpose of financing industrial enterprise without themselves becoming actual participants in business ventures. Launching a new enterprise through cash and property contributions of individuals personally interested in the venture is one of the oldest forms of business promotion, and it continues to be an important method of financing even today.

When we turn to the existing enterprise in need of money and resources for current operations or expansion, we find that it, too, is often financed by the direct investment of individuals who are personally interested in the enterprise. Going concerns also finance themselves through undistributed profits, depreciation, and depletion; i.e., they build up reserves through these means to cover their capital needs. This is, in effect, a form of financing through the price mechanism. The consumers of the product of the enterprise provide the capital by being compelled to pay a price for the product high enough to include a capital charge. In addition, as we shall see later when we consider the problem of raising capital, the going concern may finance expansion in many other ways without entering the commercial money market for funds. But regardless of what independent sources they may tap, almost every industrial enterprise does enter the money market for funds for some purposes and at some times. The financial requirements of modern industrial enterprise are so great that a large network is needed to mobilize the money and credit resources needed. The money market does this and is therefore one of the chief sources of capital.

The Money Market.—What is meant by the commercial money market? Definitions are always stiff and rarely adequate. If one were attempted here it might read something like this: In its broadest sense, the money market is the total of individuals, firms, institutions, and the process by which money and credit are collected, accumulated, and administered for the financing of economic activities. Even if correct, such a definition as this is academic and practically meaningless; the process has to be explained to be understood.

The Role of Savings in the Capital-generating Process.—To finance modern industry, large-scale savings are necessary. By large-scale savings we commonly mean money savings arising in a variety of ways throughout the economy. Individuals, rich and poor, save. The rich save directly, largely because their income exceeds even the large spending they do for themselves and their families. They also save indirectly as when they pay life insurance premiums, purchase annuities, establish funds, etc. From the wealthy to the lower income groups—to the range between $1,500 to $2,500—there are gradations in amount of direct savings like savings bank accounts, building and loan shares, postal savings accounts; and much of the steady saving is done through such indirect means as life insurance. The very poor cannot save for themselves at all; their income is all used up in living expenses. But the spendings of all individuals from the very poor to the wealthiest contribute indirectly to the stream of savings through the prices paid for goods that work back through the entire economic process, providing business profits and reserves that are invested. It is through this element that a second large group of savings—business savings—take place. In a survey of business plans for 1950, the McGraw-Hill Publishing Company found that profits and reserves were expected to provide 92 per cent of the 1950 investment funds of manufacturing companies. Some two-fifths of the country's gross savings come from the retained earnings of business enterprises plus the reserves they set up for depreciation and depletion. Governments make up the third large group of savers. There are about 180,000 government units in the United States—Federal, state, and local. When any one of these units collects more in taxes than is used for operating expenses and uses the balance for public works, the part so used represents government savings.[2] The savings take the form of public works such as highways, river and harbor construction, sewage disposal and water systems, transportation facilities, and public buildings. So far as the stream of savings and

---

[2] Although government savings result from excess tax collections devoted to public works, public works built with money currently borrowed by government are not government saving.

investments is concerned, government savings perform very much the same function as do business savings. Each takes money from the people's incomes—the one in the form of prices and the other in taxes—and spends part of it for capital goods.[3]

Main Channels for the Transfer of Savings into Capital Investment.— All these savings—of individuals, business enterprises, governments, and others—flow into the capital markets directly and indirectly through many channels. (The flow of funds in the national economy is illustrated by the chart in Fig. 2.) These channels and the process by which they transfer savings into capital funds make up the money market. The market is not a single place, or channel, or institution, but a network of many markets distinguished by the different areas they cover, by different types of loans they make, and by the variety of borrowers they serve. Life insurance companies collect millions of dollars annually in the form of premiums from rich and poor, accumulating a pool of funds on which they draw when making investments. They may invest funds directly as in a large housing project, or indirectly by buying industrial stocks or bonds of public-utility companies which use the money for plant and equipment. The banking system—mutual savings banks, other savings deposit banks, commercial banks—collects the savings of individuals and handles the funds in each community, and thus administers a large reservoir of funds which may be drawn upon for industrial financing. In addition, commercial banks have the power to create deposit accounts, which they do in financing enterprise. The postal savings system, building and loan associations, and investment trusts likewise accumulate funds and direct them into channels of investment. Colleges, universities, religious organizations, and various philanthropic foundations have large accumulations of funds which are invested directly or indirectly in all sorts of undertakings. Corporate and individual trustees place the funds in their control at the disposal of the capital market. Investment bankers, financial brokerage houses, real-estate brokers, commercial credit houses, finance companies, and other lending channels place their own and the funds of others in the capital markets.

---

[3] Many distinctions in other respects are drawn between government and business savings. The chief one, perhaps, is that business savings are said to be "productive" in the sense that money is spent for goods to be used in further production like factory buildings, machines, and tools; government spendings are declared to be "unproductive" because they go into school buildings, roads, bridges, and other public works, which yield no direct increase in material goods. Although this distinction has been shown repeatedly to be invalid, it still persists in common opinions debating the merits of private enterprise vs. government undertakings. The word "savings" is used here in the economic technical sense and differs somewhat from the lay idea of money deposited by an individual in a bank savings account.

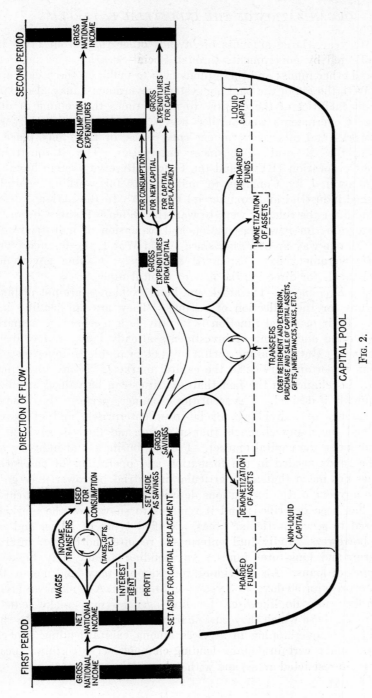

DIRECTION OF FLOW →

FIRST PERIOD

GROSS NATIONAL INCOME

NET NATIONAL INCOME

WAGES

INCOME TRANSFERS (TAXES, GIFTS, ETC.)

INTEREST

RENT

PROFIT

USED FOR CONSUMPTION

SET ASIDE AS SAVINGS

SET ASIDE FOR CAPITAL REPLACEMENT

GROSS SAVINGS

SECOND PERIOD

GROSS NATIONAL INCOME

CONSUMPTION EXPENDITURES

GROSS EXPENDITURES FOR CAPITAL

FOR CONSUMPTION

FOR NEW CAPITAL

FOR CAPITAL REPLACEMENT

GROSS EXPENDITURES FROM CAPITAL

MONETIZATION OF ASSETS

DISHOARDED FUNDS

LIQUID CAPITAL

TRANSFERS (DEBT RETIREMENT AND EXTENSION, PURCHASE AND SALE OF CAPITAL ASSETS, GIFTS, INHERITANCES, TAXES, ETC.)

DEMONETIZATION OF ASSETS

HOARDED FUNDS

NON-LIQUID CAPITAL

CAPITAL POOL

Fig. 2.

Of late years, large amounts of savings other than from taxes have been collected by governments through Social Security, pension, retirement, and other funds; and these funds help to make up the great capital pool. With the aid of the banking system, governments may also expand the credit facilities of the country to many times the volume of direct savings. Governments may either invest such funds directly, as in public works and other government enterprises, or they may place the funds at the disposal of business enterprises. The Reconstruction Finance Corporation (RFC) and the Federal Reserve System have each been empowered by Congress to make loans for working capital to established industrial and commercial business. In the national defense crisis and after the country went to war, the Defense Plants Corporation lent huge sums for new construction and expansion of industrial enterprises. In one way and another since World War I, the financial activities of government have expanded enormously, making governments prime channels for directing the flow of capital funds.[4]

Security Exchanges.—The stock and bond exchanges are not primarily institutions for the collection of savings. They are not lending institutions. Their principal function is to provide a mechanism, a market, for the buying and selling of investments already made and evidenced by securities. But in making such a market available to investors, they render an important service to the capital markets. Many investments are made in reliance on the fact that securities can be valued and liquidated quickly if desired. The securities exchanges perform this function.

The savings of individuals, of business enterprises, and of governments, and the many channels that mobilize and deal in savings and credit comprise the capital market. From it business and industry may draw the funds needed in the formation and operations of enterprises. This does not mean that any particular industrial borrower may go for funds to any one of the institutions described. Only the general capital market has been described; and it remains to show how the market is specialized to serve particular areas, specified types of loans, and particular borrowers. Individual enterprises require short-term, intermediate-term, and long-term funds. Any lending agency may make all three types of loans. An individual, for example, may lend money to a local enterprise for 90 days, or 3 years, or 10 years. A bank or an investment broker may do likewise. Lending agencies may make loans in areas outside those which they customarily serve. In other words, there is considerable overlapping in services among capital-lending agencies. But in the main, certain definite lending channels serve certain types of borrowers, in restricted areas, and with only certain types of loans.

[4] See Chap. II.

Sources of Long-term Capital.—For long-term capital, industrial borrowers may tap several channels. Large investment banking houses serve large industrial enterprises by undertaking to underwrite and to market stock and bond issues. Insurance companies have lately become an important source for long-term capital funds by taking the security issues of industrial enterprises (particularly utilities) by direct, private placement. Institutional and endowment trust funds may also supply capital by direct placement, but usually they do their investing by purchasing securities distributed by other agencies. In the past, commercial banks dealt mainly in short-term loans, but financial changes in the last twenty years have induced them to seek outlets for their funds in fixed-term investments for as long as 10 to 15 years' maturity. Rarely do wealthy individuals make independent capital loans in competition with these agencies. The sums wanted by the borrowers are too large for any but institutions of great resources and wide connections. But the wealthy do participate in the process indirectly by purchasing stocks and bonds distributed by the large financing agencies.

Intermediate and Short-term Loans.—Whereas intermediate and short-term loans represent different types of financing, both are virtually serviced by the same types of lending agencies. This is the field occupied by the regular commercial banks which in local communities throughout the nation have traditionally served the current credit needs of business enterprises. But in recent years, economic conditions and particularly banking problems have been working to cut down the activity of commercial banks in this field. For one thing, the very large industrial companies increasingly tend to finance themselves in matters of intermediate and short-term credit. On the other hand, the need for liquidity, the high lending standards, and the riskiness of small business tend to make commercial banks reluctant to serve the credit needs of small enterprises. In consequence the role of the commercial bank appears to be changing. It has become a heavy investor in government bonds. More and more it tends toward becoming a service agency in the community, merely handling the flow of funds. Where it does lend, it turns more frequently to fixed-term loans of from 5 to 15 years for the sound medium-sized business concerns, leaving large and small enterprises to seek other sources. To fill the gap left open by the commercial banks in loans to small enterprise, various lending agencies have become active. These include mortgage companies, miscellaneous finance and investment companies, commercial factors, and outright "loan sharks."

The mortgage, finance, and investment companies operate very much as do the orthodox commercial banks, except that they are less institutional and less stable. The rates they charge are likely to be higher, the conditions put upon the borrower more burdensome, and the resultant total cost of the loan much higher than regular bank credit. Originally the commercial factor performed merchandising functions for the manufacturer, and in the process realized financial credits which were made available to producers. In time, the factor came to deal extensively in the financing operations through the purchase of accounts receivable, promissory notes, and other commercial paper. Commercial factoring firms of this kind now operate widely throughout the small industrial loan field.

The Small-loan Field.—Equally active, particularly in lending to small firms, is a group of miscellaneous personal-loan companies, personal-loan departments of banks, private lenders, and the like. They usually require a high ratio of security and usually sweep up all forms of collateral the borrower has, including his personal insurance policies. Where these financing agencies are legitimate, they are usually high cost and otherwise troublesome to producers. Not being institutionalized, there is an element of uncertainty about them which often makes them unreliable as a steady credit source or embarrasses the small enterpriser in his relations with them.

The Loan Shark.—The instability of the small-loan field, together with the lure of high interest rates, also makes it fertile ground for the loan shark. Although following the letter of the law, these lenders employ every subterfuge to exact the maximum return with the minimum risk on the loans they make. In most cases they deal with borrowers who are in desperate straits and who are virtually compelled to put their business and personal affairs completely within the power of the unscrupulous lender. Government authorities and legitimate lenders in the small-loan field are active in seeking to expose the loan sharks in the interests of sound finance and public policy. But loan sharks, like those in the world's oldest profession, cannot be stamped out by exposure and prosecution alone. The time always comes when vigilance is relaxed and the unscrupulous lenders reappear to ply their trade. A more positive, constructive approach is needed on a bold scale. New institutions and new methods for making money available to small enterprisers at reasonable rates and conditions should be explored by legitimate financial interests with a view toward meeting the need within the framework of the private economy. Otherwise, the pressure for government intervention will become irresistible. And experience shows that when government acts to curb abuses perpetrated by even a small minority, it usually places burdensome restrictions on the innocent majority as well.

Trade Credits.—Not mentioned as yet, because it is not exactly a lending agency, is the trade credit. This is the mainstay of intermediate and short-term financing particularly for the small enterprise. It covers not only commodities and supplies, but also machinery, fixtures, equipment, and other items of longer term financing. The small manufacturer simply finds himself partly financed, at least for materials and small equipment, through his regular purchases on credit. In boom times and even in times of normal economic activity, trade credits play an important part in short-term financing, but in times of business recession the method tends to fail. At all times, other disadvantages operate to limit its effectiveness as a desirable source of financing.

Credit Instruments.—Credit instruments are the legal forms through which loans are made. They differ with the type of loan, the length of time it is to run, the use to which the funds are to be put, and the type of borrower. They differ also by the way in which they affect third parties. Only the more general types of credit instruments can be touched upon here because each case is more or less individual and must be studied specifically.

Long-term credit, if required for equity or fixed capital, usually takes the form of securities—*stocks* or *bonds* of the borrowing company which ultimately come to be held by individuals, banks, investment trusts, and other investors. Commercial credit for other than fixed capital of permanent nature is usually represented by *promissory notes,* backed by collateral of various kinds, and almost always negotiable. In some cases the collateral takes the form of mortgages against the firm's real estate, machinery, equipment, and other chattels. In other cases the collateral may be securities owned by the firm. Loans may be made, of course, on straight promissory notes, without collateral, but in that case the lender often requires two or more comakers or guarantors.

Short-term credits or commercial loans intended to finance single transactions or a group of transactions that are to be completed in short time are ordinarily evidenced by *promissory notes, drafts, bills of exchange,* or *trade acceptances.* These may or may not be supported by *bills of lading, warehouse receipts,* or *chattel mortgage contracts* as against materials involved in transactions, and other claims upon property. When *accounts receivable* are accepted as collateral to a loan, or taken over outright by a lending agency, the usual form is to *assign* such accounts to the lender. If the firm markets its products direct to the consumer and takes *installment notes* or *conditional sale contracts,* these may be grouped in series and assigned either outright or as collateral for a circulating capital loan from many lending agencies.

PLANNING THE FINANCIAL STRUCTURE OF THE INDUSTRIAL ENTERPRISE

Few people will deny that enterprises may still be started on a shoestring and may be developed into large-scale companies. This is less possible in the old-line industries where established firms offer strong competition than it is in the newer industrial fields where demand and supply forces are not fully established. In the last two decades the automotive industry is an example of the established field, while the radio, refrigerator, plastics, light metals, electronics, and airplane industries are examples of newer fields. On the other hand, there are the cases of the piano and phonograph-recording industries which suffered a devastating decline in the early 1920's only to stage remarkable comebacks almost as new industries in more recent years. In any case, the problem of starting a new enterprise is always much more difficult than that of expansion for existing firms. But whether the problem is one of financing a new venture or the expansion of an existing enterprise, modern conditions make financial planning a necessity.

The Capital Structure of the New Enterprise.—The new enterprise will require land, buildings, machinery, tools, and equipment. This is the fixed capital that is to be invested in the firm for a long period of time. The enterprise will also require working capital funds to finance a continuing series of transactions or, in other words, circulating capital. In addition it may require commercial loans from time to time to finance single, self-liquidating transactions which are to be completed within a very short period. What does the planning of these types of financing involve for the new enterprise?

Noncorporate Capitalization.—If the enterprise is to be a nonincorporated enterprise, such as a business owned by a single individual or by a partnership, the problem of capitalization is a simple one. In the case of the individual proprietor, a simple decision as to what part of his wealth shall be devoted to the business is all that is necessary. So far as the public and creditors are concerned, the single proprietor is personally liable for the debts of the business to the full extent of all his wealth. Capitalization is equally simple for the partnership. In the partnership agreement there will be outlined the value of the property each has contributed toward the enterprise and what respective shares in the business each partner shall have. For all practical purposes, this is all that is involved in the matter of capitalization.

Corporate Capitalization.—It is the corporate enterprise that is most concerned with problems of capitalization. Fixed or equity capital must be secured either in direct form, as contributions of land, buildings, and machinery by the organizers of the enterprise, or indirectly through the sale of securities. In either case, the problem arises as to how to arrive at the total amount at which the enterprise should be capitalized and what forms the capital structure should take. In Chap. IV there was outlined a procedure for analyzing the product, relating it to the enterprise, conducting a market survey, and making a general business forecast of the prospects of the enterprise. From a consideration of the factors involved in those studies it should be possible to arrive at an estimate of the total amount of fixed capital required in the undertaking. If real estate, buildings, or other tangible property is contributed by the organizers, the cost or value of such assets will naturally be part of the total capitalization. To this sum there will have to be added an amount sufficient to cover necessary promotion, engineering, and developmental expenses. Where the probable earnings of the enterprise can be fairly definitely estimated, such an estimate may be formed and used as a guide in arriving at the final total of the initial capitalization. In some few cases, the capitalization may take account of good will, patents, secret processes, trade-marks, and other intangible items, but in the untried enterprise there is scarcely any real basis for anything other than nominal values on these items. Their value in most instances can be established only in operational experience over a period of time. In forming a judgment on the total capitalization of the enterprise, some consideration should also be given to other factors. Current legal requirements—state and Federal—will have to be weighed because they affect franchise fees, taxation, and other affairs of the enterprise. If the enterprise has great promise, initial capitalization should be planned with an eye toward future expansion and toward the problem of future marketing of the corporate securities.

Under- and Overcapitalization.—Care should be exercised against under- and overcapitalization. A corporation that issues its total capital stock at a nominal or par value that is below the fair value of the assets and low compared to the earning power of the business is undercapitalized. If the business thereafter is successful, the earnings will appear unduly large, which may cause considerable public disapproval, labor troubles, loss of trade, and increased competition. These will more than outweigh the advantage of financial strength which undercapitalization brings out. Overcapitalization is the reverse condition in which the total outstanding capital stock is greater than the fair value of the net assets or more than is justified by the probable earning power of the business. This may result in excessive incorporation fees and large annual franchise and capital stock taxes. It may give rise to charges of fraud in the sale of securities. Subsequent dividends may have to be very low, and the credit standing of the company is likely to be impaired. These and other disadvantages more than outweigh advantages expected from putting on a big front.

Authorized Capital Stock.—From the studies involved in the formation of the enterprise; from estimates of the value of assets acquired or to be immediately acquired, and of the probable earning power of the business; and from a consideration of all other factors affecting the problem of capitalization, it should be possible to reach a grand figure for the total capitalization of the enterprise. This is the figure that will be used in the application for the corporate charter and, when divided into various classifications of stock, it will indicate the authorized capital stock of the enterprise.

Classification of Stock.—Before the basic financial structure of the enterprise is complete, the total authorized capital stock will have to be classified. Stock classifications determine the relations of stockholders to the enterprise. That is, they set forth the rights and limitations of those who have an ownership interest in the business. They also influence the relations between the corporation and the public, with creditors, and with the capital market from which the corporation hopes to draw its funds. Classifications of stock are made with these factors in mind.

Common Stock.—All the authorized capital stock of a company may be issued in a single classification, *common stock*. No special rights or privileges are attached to common stock. It bears the full risk of the enterprise, its successes and failures. Common stockholders are in law the real owners of the enterprise, and they are entitled to the net assets of the business. They usually exercise control over the business through the voting power of their stock. All the income remaining after prior claims of creditors are satisfied belongs to the common stockholders; and in the going business they collect this income in the form of dividends. In the early days of corporate organization, many corporations were based solely upon common stock; but as corporate finance developed it became more specialized to gain advantages not only in corporate organization, but also in the securities markets. The result has been a variety of stock classifications.

Preferred Stock.—Preferred stock is the second of the fundamental classes into which authorized capital stock may be divided. This class of stock carries with it a qualified ownership in the enterprise. It enjoys certain preferences and is subject to certain limitations. It may be preferred as to dividends, or as to assets on dissolution of the company. It may be convertible into common stock at the option of the holder. It may or may not have voting power. A sinking fund may be set up to retire preferred stock, thus assuring the holder of the return of his investment. It may be limited as to the extent of its participation in the earnings of the business. These are but a few samples of the types of preferences and limitations that may be attached to preferred stock.

In each case of preference or limitation, some object is sought to be attained. By giving a stock preference as to dividends, it is made attractive to those investors who seek only a fair, assured return on their money and who do not wish to incur the risks of great loss in the hope of large gains. But if they are given this advantage, they may be denied the voting privilege on the ground that if they do not wish to share in the ultimate success or failure of the enterprise, they are not entitled to a voice in its management. Each preference and each limitation has to be considered on its merits and with reference to the ends sought to be achieved.

No arbitrary rules can be set for the division between common and preferred stock, or for attaching various qualifications to the preferred issue. Decisions of this kind are a matter of judgment in each case of corporate financing and many different factors have to be weighed in reaching them. A list of the objects sought to be achieved by the classifications, together with lists of advantages and disadvantages involved, is perhaps the best way to approach the problem of classifying capital stock. How and by whom is the enterprise to be controlled? Which is more desirable from all points of view—risk capital (common stock) or investors' capital (preferred stock) on which a specified income return must be guaranteed? To what extent is it wise to burden the company with a preferred dividend overhead? What are the legal and tax advantages and disadvantages attached to each type of stock and how will they affect the company and the various parties in interest? How will the sale of securities be affected by the different classes of stock? What is the most desirable basis for the division of earnings, and of assets of the company on dissolution? These are a few samples of the many questions that should be considered in setting up the common and preferred stock, and in qualifying the preferred stock as to rights and limitations.

After the basic decision is made for classifying the stock into common and preferred, similar calculations will have to be made to set up classes of preferred stock if that is desirable. The common stock itself may be partly qualified by setting up special classes such as A and B common. Preferred may be *first preferred* and *second preferred*, and each further classified ad infinitum according to rights, privileges, and limitations surrounding each subclass.

Par and No-par Value Stock.—Both stocks, common and preferred, may have a *par value*, or face value, stated in the stock certificate. What this shall be is dependent upon the number of shares or units into which the total class is to be divided; and the decision will be influenced by many of the same factors that bear upon the class as a whole. A stock with a low par value may be attractive, for example, to many small investors; and it may be considered desirable to have a wide distribution of the company's stock. If $100 is written on the face of a stock certificate, it often has great psychological value to investors and to the company. Theoretically it fixes the amount of the original investment represented by the certificate. In fact, however, the value of a stock is not set by the amount appearing on its face, but by the assets and earning power of the company. It is partly for this reason, and partly on account of corporate interests and the sale of its securities, that no-par stock came to be issued. In this class of stock no value whatever is stated in the certificate; merely the number of shares of the total authorized capital stock of the class. This leaves the price of shares to be fixed arbitrarily by the company or according to the true relationship between the stock and the assets and earning power of the enterprise.

The fixing of the total authorized capital stock and its division into classes completes the basic financial structure of the enterprise. After the company is chartered, part of the stock is issued to pay for property transferred to the company and in pursuance of cash sales. The balance of the stock constitutes *unissued stock* to be used in subsequent financing. This is not to be confused with *treasury stock*, which is stock lawfully issued by the company and reacquired by it. Supplemental financing, largely for capital purposes, may be arranged through corporate borrowing. This is usually done through bond issues and other types of financing that are not considered part of the basic financial structure of the enterprise. Moreover, bond issues are rarely floated in the case of a new enterprise, if for no other reason than that such issues require tangible assets to secure the loan, and new companies have not had time to build up sufficient security of this kind.

Capital for Expansion. *From Current Operations.*—Ordinarily the established enterprise will accumulate capital for expansion through operational techniques. Where the competitive price structure allows, the unit price of products may contain a fractional sum to be set aside in the form of reserves for expansion of the business. Many of the public utilities and larger industrial firms have been following this practice for years. The sum so accumulated is over and above, and added to, normal earnings and is applied toward the development of the business. The practice raises some interesting economic questions that cannot be explored here, but the main point may be mentioned in passing. If through the price mechanism, for example, industrial financing can make itself independent of the capital markets, what is to become of the whole institution of savings and investment which, until recent years, has been the mainstay of economic progress?

Closely analogous to financing through the price mechanism, but not quite the same in all effects, is financing expansion through "plowing back the earnings" and through depreciation and depletion reserves. The funds for these purposes also come through the price mechanism; and they also have a tendency to make the company independent of the capital markets. The difference is that here all enterprises engage in these practices as a matter of course, while only the largest companies, capable of administering a set price schedule, can use that schedule as a specific instrument to build up expansion capital in excess of normal earnings, depreciation, and depletion. But whatever the economic or social effects may be, all four methods arising in the course of current operations are used to accumulate expansion capital independent of the regular capital market. To exploit these methods to the best advantage, it is practically essential to install a budget system.

Raising Equity Capital for Expansion.—Where reserves built up through earnings, depreciation, and depletion are insufficient to finance expansion, other methods may be resorted to. The firm may seek equity capital through the sale of unissued stock. If the firm has no such securities in reserve, having previously distributed its entire authorized capital stock, proceedings may be started for an enlargement of the authorized capital. This will require consent of the existing stockholders and an amendment of the corporation charter. When such stock is made available, it may be marketed in various ways. *Existing stockholders* must first be given the opportunity to buy the new shares. In most states this is a rule of law. The method is to issue *stock rights* to existing shareholders, giving them the right to purchase new shares at a stated price and in proportion to their holdings of the old shares. Equity shares may also be sold to the *employees;* and if the company is a large one a sizable issue may be disposed of in this manner. Not only does it provide a source of capital, inexpensively raised, but it is held to have the further advantage of improving the company's relations with its employees. A move in the same direction, but very infrequently used, is the sale of stock to the company's *customers.* In the case of small companies, well known in their own localities, shares may be sold directly to business and professional men by personal solicitation of the officers of the company. On rare occasions, and usually for reasons closely connected with their own interests, *creditors* may be persuaded to take equity stock. The final method is to market the company's stocks through the regular capital market, which in the case of equity capital means investment bankers, commercial banks, investment brokers, and other agencies dealing in long-term financing.

Borrowing on Long-term Securities.—Where the earnings record is good as to steadiness and rate and if the prospects of expansion are definitely favorable, the best method of raising the needed capital is to borrow it. On this point several factors have to be considered. In most cases the company will have to be well established in order to gain a hearing for a bond issue. The assets pledged to support repayment of the loan will have to be acceptable in banking circles. Bankers will be very exhaustive in seeking an answer to the question, "If we have to liquidate this loan by selling the property, what are the chances of getting our money back?" The state of the company and the industry, as well as the position of the country in the business cycle, will have to be studied. The purpose of the expansion should be carefully considered, as well as the length of time it will take to realize earnings on the new overhead and to liquidate the loan. The company president's enthusiasm over what he can do with the new setup and the sales manager's dream of an avalanche of orders will have to be tied down to the solid earth of realities. There should be a good working margin between the interest rate on the borrowed capital and the expected level of earnings. A decision should be reached on the type of borrowing, short- or long-term. Conditions may make it advisable to carry out the immediate financing on a short-term basis, refunding the loan at a more favorable time by a long-term bond issue. Whereas borrowing for industrial expansion has many advantages, it also carries with it the possibility of great risk of loss. Even a temporary failure to pay the interest charges may throw the company into a receivership. Money raised through the sale of capital stock is free from this risk.

Bond Issues.—If capital for a major expansion is to be borrowed, the usual way is by bond issue. In essence, bond issues are company promises to repay the loan and are backed by a mortgage on part or all of the company's property. In most cases, the total amount of the issue is divided into denominations of $100, $500, or $1,000 which constitute the *bonds, debentures, certificates,* or *notes* of the issue. The mortgage takes the form of a *trust agreement* or *indenture* which contains all the rights and obligations between the company-borrower and the lender-bondholders. The instrument designates a *trustee* who represents the bondholders and it defines his powers and obligations. The bond issue may mature as a whole or serially; and there is usually a provision in the trust agreement for a *sinking fund* arranged to cover the retirement of the issue. In the event of default in payment of interest or principal, the trustee named in the trust agreement has the power to take various actions to protect the bondholders. In many instances, long before such a critical stage is reached, bondholders or their representatives may bring influences to bear upon management to correct dangerous tendencies in the condition of the firm. The essential relation between the company and the bondholders is that of debtor-creditor. While this means that the bondholders have no ownership interest in the company, it also implies that their rights are paramount to those of the stockholders who are the company owners.

The size of the bond issue will depend upon the character of the enterprise, the length of time the company has been in business, its general financial condition, and the ratio between the amount of the loan and the value of the property that is to secure it. A speculative enterprise in which earnings fluctuate or are uncertain will have difficulty in floating a bond issue. One which deals in necessities or which has stability of earnings for other reasons (as, for example, public utilities) is more likely to succeed. If an organization has been in business for a considerable length of time, building up sound assets and income stability, the chances of placing a successful bond issue are very favorable. Usually, the amount of the loan is 50 per cent of the value of the property pledged to secure it, but there is no set rule on this point. It varies considerably with different enterprises, depending upon a consideration of the same factors examined in deciding to borrow on a bond issue in the first place. If the general financial condition of the company indicates an additional margin of safety over and above the value of pledged property, a higher ratio is quite possible. From the company's point of view, the loan represents an opportunity to improve the enterprise and to increase its earning power; but it also carries the great risk that it may be the means of disrupting the business (through receivership on default) or of ending the enterprise altogether (as in liquidation under court proceedings). Additional funds may be as harmful to a business as a lack of funds may be, if the business itself is not soundly conceived and efficiently administered.

A company contemplating a bond issue should make a careful study of the many different kinds of bond issues. They differ according to the purpose of the issue, the nature of the security, terms of payment, and miscellaneous conditions affecting the interests of the various parties. For example, there are construction bonds, improvement bonds, equipment bonds, reorganization bonds, general bonds, etc., indicating the purpose. Some of these, and others also, show the nature of the security. Still others, like income bonds, profit-sharing bonds, general mortgage bonds, and first- and second-mortgage bonds show the nature of the lien. Term bonds, callable bonds, serial bonds, sinking-fund bonds, and convertible bonds indicate the time period of the issue and method of payment. At one time, bonds also indicated the medium of payment, such as gold bonds, but these have been abolished by Congressional legislation (Joint Resolution of June 6, 1933, Gold Reserve Act of 1934, etc.), which was validated by the Supreme Court in the "gold cases" decided in February, 1935.

In arranging the type and conditions of the bond issue, four parties in interest are involved: the company, the bankers who are to market the issue, the prospective bondholders (represented by the trustee), and the general public (represented by government agencies). In principle, the interests of these four parties need not conflict. In practice they often do. Perceiving a possible future conflict, the principal parties often approach the initial arrangements in this way: the company and the bankers reach a compromise on their respective interests because one wishes to borrow and the other is willing to arrange the loan. Compromise is necessary to bring them together. Each seeks to protect its future interests through the trustee and the trust agreement. Both are reluctant to recognize the fact that the trustee should be independent and above the parties in interest, acting for the good of them all when contingencies arise. Both too often ignore the public interest except as law compels them to conform to certain regulations when floating the bond issue. This note of caution is inserted here because abuses in this field of finance in the recent past have led directly to Congressional investigations and to regulatory legislation which has been denounced as "interference with business." [5] In this, as in so many similar situations, the sins of minorities are often visited upon the innocent majority. By far the bulk of industrial bond issues are sound and fairly administered.

[5] Investigations which have disclosed flagrant abuses in capital financing are: Hearings on stock exchange practices, pursuant to S. Res. 84, 72d Cong., 1932; Report of Committee on Banking and Currency on stock exchange practices, pursuant to S. Res. 84, 72d Cong., and S. Res. 56 and 97, 73d Cong., Rept. 1455, 73d Cong., 2d Sess., 1934.

Hearings on utility corporations, pursuant to S. Res. 83, 70th Cong., 1st Sess., 1927.

Hearings on the sale of foreign bonds or securities in the United States, pursuant to S. Res. 19, 72d Cong., 1st Sess., 1932.

Investigation of railroads, holding companies, and affiliated companies, pursuant to S. Res. 71, 74th Cong., 1st Sess., 1935.

Reports on protective and reorganization committees, by the Securities and Exchange Commission, under Sec. 211 of the Securities Exchange Act of 1934.

Reports on investment trusts and investment companies, by the Securities and Exchange Commission, under Sec. 30 of the Public Utility Holding Company Act of 1935.

See also BRANDEIS, LOUIS D., "Other People's Money and How the Bankers Use It," National Home Library Foundation, Washington, D.C., 1933.

But abuses in a minority of cases arouse the people and move government to pass laws severely regulating the entire process of financing through bond issues. And often, the requirements prove unduly expensive and burdensome on the sounder issues without providing much protection to the investor against the bad practices. In its own interest, the company should take an active part in securing a fair balance in the rights and obligations of these parties; and when that balance is written into the transaction, it ought to be lived up to, instead of circumvented.

Expansion through Combination.—One of the chief methods of expansion, not heretofore mentioned except in passing, is through the combination of two or more enterprises.[6] The method has been used extensively in the last half century, giving rise to a vast literature dealing with the many phases of the problem under such heads as business combinations, concentration, and monopoly. Business combinations in general give rise to great economic and social problems, with which we are not here concerned. Regardless of the questions surrounding business combinations in general, the combination of two or more specific enterprises is a common method of contriving expansion. The combinations are effected in various ways: through merger, consolidation, and holding companies. The result may be a general expansion of the company surviving or controlling the combination; or special purposes may be effected such as the strengthening of all capital assets, acquisition of raw-material supplies, enlargement of the line of products, control of patents, elimination of competition, and the acquisition of established markets. So far as financing is concerned, the combination is a method of raising equity or fixed capital, and often of strengthening the working-capital position of the surviving enterprise.

Expansion by combination should not be attempted lightly. Many complex questions have to be studied thoroughly. A careful analysis of each of the concerns to be combined should be made. Are the plant and physical property adequate for the enterprise and in good condition? How long has each concern been in business? What advantages and disadvantages are derived from its position in the industry and trade? A study of the financial history and of its record of earnings should be made. Will the combination gain the services of the competent men in charge of the separate concerns and be able to eliminate the incompetents?

After a thorough analysis of each concern has been made, it will be necessary to consider the effect of the combination. Do the earnings of the combination promise to exceed those of the separate concerns? Will they justify the full costs of acquisition? In order to bring about the combination, it is often deemed necessary to pay in stock to the old

[6] See Chap. III, Corporate Combinations, pp. 39–42.

owners a value in excess of that warranted by the earnings of the new company, with the result that the new concern is overcapitalized with what has been called "watered" stock. This may be fatal to the new concern in the long run. How will the price schedules of the new concern compare with those of the old? Will combination give them an advantage in the competitive market? Does the new concern promise definite efficiencies and other advantages in management? What hostile elements—in the industry, in labor, in finance, among competitors, and in public circles—will be created by the combination; and are they likely to hinder success of the enterprise? What legal barriers may be thrown up against the combination?

A financial plan for the proposed combination will have to be drawn as carefully as should be done in the case of every new enterprise. Its various classes of securities and the plan of their distribution to the owners of the old companies and to the new investing public will have to reconcile the many interests involved, as well as safeguard the financial structure of the combination. Will the financial structure of the new company offer a sound basis for subsequent financing of the combination? Does financial control of the combination rest with those who have a sincere and definite interest in the concern as an industrial enterprise? If formation of the combination and subsequent control over it rests only in the hands of promoters who see profits in the manipulation of companies rather than in running a sound industrial enterprise, the combination is likely to be a spurious one, as were so many combinations formed during the 1920's.

Whereas combination is a common method of expanding an enterprise, great care should be taken that the weight of advantages lies with the new concern over the former separate concerns. It is questionable whether a successful, going concern should combine with an unsuccessful, dormant one. If the successful company wishes to expand, it may be better for it to float a bond issue on its own merits and acquire outright the facilities it needs for expansion. The lure and dazzle of greater profits through expansion should not be permitted to obscure the cold realities and risks that often result when a new concern is fashioned out of the patchwork of older companies.

Working Capital.—In the new enterprise, working capital must come largely through the initial financing. After the firm is in operation, other sources will be open to it. Chief of these sources, of course, is the current operations of the enterprise. These operations should be sufficient to produce all the financing required to meet the routine, current needs of the enterprise. They may, in addition, yield sufficient in excess earnings to provide for working capital and other permanent investments.

A well-planned enterprise follows a plan to set aside regular sums in surplus and reserves for the small but steady enlargement of the business. These are usually expended periodically over the years, with the result that business growth and vitality are steadily maintained.

In common usage, *working capital* is the total of current assets consisting of merchandise and materials, cash, accounts receivable, and other liquid assets, less current liabilities. Proper ratios should be sought between current assets and current liabilities and between current assets and capital assets. What these ratios should be depends upon the type of enterprise and other factors; no fixed rule can be applied to all concerns. In general, working capital should be sufficient to meet current liabilities and to enable the company to take immediate advantage of opportunities that present themselves from time to time. These opportunities may take the form of an advantageous purchase of special machinery, a chance to acquire a needed piece of real property, the acquisition of a patent right, the chance to make a particularly advantageous purchase of raw materials, or an opportunity to make considerable profits by a temporary expansion of production. Without adequate working capital or quick access to capital-lending sources, a company may have to stand by and see such opportunities lost to it.

A budget plan is the best device to develop and control the flow of working capital. It sizes up the prospects of the business in advance, proportions the various parts of the enterprise in proper relation, sets the timing of income in relation to expenditures, prepares for contingencies, and keeps a reserve in readiness for unexpected opportunities.[7]

Where a firm is chronically short of working capital, and for many other firms on occasion, it is necessary to resort to short-term financing. In the case of the well-established firm in sound financial condition otherwise, but in need of a considerable sum of money for a special purpose, the financing may take the form of short-term notes, secured or unsecured. This is in effect a short- or intermediate-term bond issue, with many although not all the features of the regular, long-term bond issues. The company usually reserves the right to take up the notes before maturity. Where the company follows the practice of resorting to such financing regularly, it may be under the disadvantage of high-cost financing, particularly when depression or other conditions tighten the money market. And unless the firm carefully budgets its current operations, it may find itself embarrassed in having to meet a short-term loan at an inopportune time.

Other sources of short-term financing, as previously mentioned, include the commercial banks, miscellaneous finance and investment com-

[7] See Chap. XXIX.

panies, trade credits, personal loan companies, and private lenders. Except for the commercial banks and similar orthodox lending agencies, short-term financial sources are likely to be unreliable in the sense that funds cannot always be had when wanted, and the rates charged are usually high. This introduces an element of dangerous uncertainty into the affairs of companies compelled to resort to such sources; and the high rates may increase the company's cost of doing business beyond what it can recapture in the prices received for its products in a competitive field.

Reserves.—So far as current operations are concerned, most of the soundly managed companies set up a series of reserves for various purposes. Such reserves may be to maintain working capital, to provide for expansion, to cover improvements, to extinguish debts, to build up sinking fund requirements, and to cover such contingencies as fire, theft, flood or storm damage, and accident liabilities. Other reserves will be set up to cover depreciation, depletion, and obsolescence. Reserves for bad debts will be set up against uncollectible accounts receivable. In some cases, a reserve will be used to offset price fluctuations on inventories. Reserve funds are not necessarily cash or property set aside for the purpose of meeting future contingencies, although some funds exist in that form. But they are reflected in the financial operations of the company and are carried on its balance sheet. They constitute that part of profits withheld from surplus (and thus not available for dividends) for the express purpose of covering the losses and contingencies incident to the conduct of the enterprise.

Laws Affecting Financing through Securities. *State Laws.*—An extensive body of law has been developed to regulate the issuance of securities and to protect the interests of investors and of the general public. It is impossible within the scope of a small section to set forth all these laws in detail; nor is this necessary, because in almost every security issue there will be an attorney or some other competent person charged with supervising the legal aspects of the financing. In general, however, almost every state prescribes conditions that must be complied with by companies incorporated within the state and disposing of their securities there. Another set of regulations governs corporations formed in other states and intending to sell securities or do business within the regulating state. Aside from the general requirements concerning incorporation, these laws usually relate to the size of initial financing, the type of securities intended to be offered, the relation of the securities to the real assets of the company, the methods and agencies through which securities are marketed to the public, and to the protection of the public from speculative issues and from fraud. Most of these laws require the filing of statements qualifying the company or its fiscal agents to sell the securities proposed; and, if the statement gains the approval of the state commission or other agency having jurisdiction over the matter, a certificate or permit is issued authorizing the company to proceed. Some states provide for recovery of losses suffered by those who have been sold securities in violation of law.

Federal Laws.—As industrial enterprise spread out from local operations to interstate and national activities, industrial financing likewise overflowed state boundaries. State commissions found it increasingly difficult to protect the public from abuses and outright fraud that accompanied the widespread sale of securities in the boom period preceding 1929. The subsequent loss in the depression of millions of dollars through worthless stocks and bonds and the inadequacy of the remedies owing to the interstate character of business financing led to the demand for Federal protection of investors and the public. Congress responded with a series of laws designed to regulate the issuance and sale of securities in interstate commerce. Chief among these measures is the Securities Act of 1933, the Securities Exchange Act of 1934, the Public Utility Holding Company Act of 1935, and the Investment Company Act of 1939.

Designed to prevent misrepresentation and frauds in the sale of securities, the 1933 act required a full public disclosure of the essential facts involved in the flotation of every security issue of more than nine months' maturity which is publicly offered in interstate commerce. It required the filing of an elaborate registration statement with the Securities and Exchange Commission, the delivery of an informative prospectus to security buyers, and provided for a waiting period for a check on the facts before the issue could be floated. The Commission was invested with effective controlling powers to compel observance of the law, and certain civil and criminal penalties were attached to violations of the law. The Securities Exchange Act of 1934 set up machinery for the systematic supervision of stock exchanges and security-market activities. The Holding Company Act gave the Commission power to protect the public in the matter of public-utility financing. It also sought to put an end (through the "death sentence" provision) to uneconomic combinations and pyramids of superholding companies. The 1939 act regulated investment companies and investment advisers. In addition, the bankruptcy laws dealing with the reorganization of corporations were revised with a view toward protecting investors. Other legislation, such as banking and monetary laws, widened the power of the Federal government to regulate and control securities operations.

ADMINISTRATION OF EXTERNAL FINANCES

Financing of all kinds from outside sources and the handling of company investments may be treated as the *external finance* of an enterprise to distinguish those operations from financial operations connected with the internal functioning of the company. Where the enterprise is a sole proprietorship, the individual owner administers the funds. In the partnership, one of the partners may be designated by agreement to perform these functions. In the corporation, it is usually the treasurer who does this work, while the controller attends to the internal financing operations of the company. There is no hard and fast rule in this respect however. Whereas the administration of external finance usually devolves upon the treasurer, other officers of the corporation may be selected to handle specific financing problems like the floating of a bond issue, the negotiation of short-term notes, or the investment of company surplus. And no matter what officer is designated for these functions, it is usual to provide him with an advisory committee made up of several of the top-ranking management officers. In corporations large enough to employ a separate budget officer, the practice is to have him work in close cooperation with the treasurer in all matters of external finance.

With or without the assistance of a budget officer, it is the treasurer's duty to keep account of the receipts and disbursements of the company. In companies where both a treasurer and a controller are employed, the controller may take charge of the operational receipts and disbursements. As a general rule, the principal item in receipts will be on account of goods sold and services rendered, evidenced by cash, and accounts and notes receivable. These items may be supplemented by income from company investments. The treasurer plans the use of these, together with other company assets, to cover the firm's liabilities. The object of good financial management is to plan to have current receipts realized so as to meet current liabilities; and further to build up capital assets to meet such long-term liabilities as shall mature from time to time.

Where the normal operations of the company call for current borrowing, and where expansion policies require long-term financing, the treasurer (usually assisted by other officers of the firm) determines the forms that the loans shall take, explores the sources from which funds may be secured, and ordinarily conducts the negotiations involved. For current needs, he may select any of the several forms and channels through which short-term and intermediate-term loans are obtained. For long-term capital needs, he may market some of the firm's own securities or attend to the arrangements of a company bond issue.

As chief financial officer of the company, the treasurer also attends to the investment of surplus funds. His object is to make these funds as productive as possible, but at the same time to keep them in such form as will be most appropriate for the company's affairs. At times this may counsel temporary investments that may be readily liquidated; at others, the funds may be placed in long-term investments. Subject to the general policies of the company and to any specific instructions of the board of directors, the management of invested funds is left to the discretion of the treasurer.

SUMMARY

Where industrial enterprises cannot finance themselves through operations, *i.e.*, through the pricing mechanism, profits, depreciation, and depletion, the alternative is to seek capital in the commercial money market. This market may be thought of as something of a great money concentration process and a dispatching agency. Individual savings, business and government savings flow into a great capital pool. The commercial banks are part of this pool, and the funds in their hands enable them to create additional deposit credit which supplements the volume of actual savings. A great variety of financial agencies act as dispatchers and channels, sending funds from the capital pool in the form of loans to business enterprises. Industrial enterprises need long-term, intermediate-term, and short-term financing or, in other words, money for fixed capital and credit for current operations. They may satisfy their need for fixed capital either through the sale of their own equity securities—company stock of various kinds—or through borrowing on bond issues. Their need for short-term funds is met by the manipulation of commercial paper of various kinds and by trade credits. For each type of financing, the industrial enterprise has access to many financial channels specialized for the making of different kinds of loans: investment bankers, commercial banks, mortgage and finance companies, commercial factors, and personal loan companies. The well-managed industrial enterprise carefully plans its permanent capital structure and budgets its current operations to anticipate its financial needs. In this manner, funds to finance enterprise follow a circular flow—from those who save into a great capital pool; from there through many financial agencies and channels to business enterprises in the form of investments and short-term loans; and finally the greater part of the funds so placed come again into the hands of savers who replenish the capital pool.

THE SPECIAL PROBLEM OF FINANCING SMALL ENTERPRISE

It should be obvious from a study of this financing process that, although all kinds and sizes of enterprises will have their peculiar financial problems, small enterprise faces the most serious predicament of all. Small enterprise is beset with more intense competition than affects medium-sized and large enterprises. It cannot, therefore, utilize the price mechanism for a financing device as they can do. Its normal earnings are minute when proportioned to its need for long-term capital and, consequently, it is limited in its capacity to build depreciation and other capital-accumulating reserves. The limited capital and scope of small business prohibit it from employing the specialized management that it needs for the efficient conduct of the enterprise. It has no company staff of lawyers, accountants, financial specialists, and public relations counselors to draw its financial plans and set them in the right light in the eyes of investors.

Equity Financing.—Limited in its opportunities to finance itself internally through current operations, small business must place heavy reliance for its financing on the money market. All the sources of long-term capital—investment bankers, commercial banks (which now tend toward fixed-term loans), insurance companies, institutional and endowment trusts, and other security buyers—are theoretically open to the smaller companies. But the true state of affairs is otherwise, as small business managers sadly testify. In many respects small enterprises are at a disadvantage in these long-term capital markets. The sums they need are too small to make their stock and bond issues attractive to large investors. The condition of most small companies is not up to the high standards set by these lenders. The element of risk is believed to be too great in the case of small enterprise for the assured safety of investors' capital, although this is an assumption not always warranted by experience. Big business has become so impressive in the eyes of long-term capital investors as to create the feeling that small enterprise does not have a chance for industrial success. The result of such an attitude is that financing agencies are not receptive to the needs of small enterprise. Where small companies do get capital, it is often at excessive cost. Examining a group of 217 issues registered in 1937, the Securities and Exchange Commission found that the expense of a common stock issue of less than $250,000 is 22 per cent compared to 16 per cent in expense for issues of more than $1,000,000. For preferred stock issues the expense is respectively 17 per cent to 9 per cent. And in the case of bond issues the comparison is 9.2 per cent to 4.8 per cent.[8] Moreover, while most of the large issues sell 100 per cent of the registered amounts offered, the small issues are not always entirely sold.[9]

[8] NICHOLSON, J. L., The Fallacy of Easy Money for the Small Business, *Harvard Business Review*, Autumn, 1938, p. 33.

[9] "Selected Statistics on Securities and on Exchange Markets," Securities and Exchange Commission, August, 1939, p. 35.

Short-term Financing.—For the reasons mentioned and for other causes in the same vein, the small enterprise is at a great disadvantage in the long-term capital market. Where small companies cannot find wealthy individuals in their own localities to provide them with long-term capital, they are compelled to seek accommodation in the short-term money market. In the past this was not such a hardship. With a modest investment of their own, they could rely on the short-term loans of commercial banks. The rates were reasonable, and the conditions of the loan were not overburdensome. Often renewed from time to time, this short-term credit operated something like a long-term capital investment. But for reasons of liquidity, high standards, fear of the risk of small enterprises, and increasing legal limitations on their activities, the commercial bank is steadily limiting this type of short-term financing.

The upshot is that small enterprises are more and more compelled to seek funds from a growing group of miscellaneous financing agencies—commercial factors, mortgage and finance companies, personal loan agencies, and in some cases, the outright loan shark. These agencies borrow money wholesale from banks and investment houses and retail it to small business. By painful experience, small business concerns have become aware of the disadvantages of this type of financing. The source cannot always be counted upon. Where it is the policy of the lender to direct funds into the most profitable loans (as is usually the case with most of these types of lending agencies), a new borrower will sometimes get the funds that might have been available to older borrowers. In any event, renewals are uncertain. Loans may be called at embarrassing times for the borrower. Even where legitimate, the cost may be excessive. Many such loans contain hidden charges and holdbacks for "services," "business advice," and other dodges, in addition to interest, regular service charges, and other fees. In other ways, these types of loans are embarrassing and burdensome to the borrower. Heavy collateral in the way of mortgages, liens, reserve deposits, and assignments of receivables greatly in excess of the loan on them are required. Many finance companies retain collections on excess receivables for considerable periods of time on one pretext or another "for the account of the client," although these funds belong to the borrower-client and should be turned over to him. In addition to sweeping up all the collateral the traffic will bear, many finance companies insist upon various measures of control over the borrower's business.

Management of Small Enterprise.—But before financial sources of this type are too forthrightly criticized for their tactics, the problem they have to contend with should be brought into view. Small enterprises are often very badly managed. Accounting practices are loose and confusing. Small enterprises are often too liberal in granting credits to others, making for a high ratio of uncollectibles. Small enterprisers are too willing to borrow their way out of situations that should be solved by better management. They withdraw too much money for salaries and personal use. They are too eager to expand, taking on broader activities and obligations than a careful survey of probabilities would warrant. Economic conditions tend to make small concerns unstable. The over-all result is that a high risk element colors small enterprise. Those who lend to them often have to share in that risk and, therefore, seek their compensation in high rates and protective devices. Although there is no excuse for the loan shark who takes full advantage of the borrower's desperate plight, a fair case can be made out for the legitimate lending agencies even though the loans they make are costly and burdensome to the borrower.

Trade Credits.—Trade credit is the mainstay of small enterprise. It covers materials purchased for further manufacture and resale. It also covers machinery, tools, fixtures, and other equipment purchased on long-term account. Thus trade credit is both short- and long-term, current operational credit, and capital investment credit. Why is not this sufficient to cover the financial needs of small enterprise? There are several reasons. Trade credit covers only the tangibles needed in current operations—materials, equipment, etc.—but the small enterprise requires liquid funds for many other purposes which it cannot get through trade credit. Trade credit compels the small enterpriser to deal with certain firms, preventing him from shopping around for price advantages. Discounts are lost and, if bargains in materials present themselves, the opportunity cannot be seized. If the small enterprise gets too deeply in debt to its suppliers, it is often subject to their dictation in the conduct of the enterprise. And finally, economic fluctuations greatly affect the trade credit, often cutting it off entirely and forcing the small enterprise into liquidation.

Economic Status of Small Enterprise.—Examined from many angles, the problem of small enterprise is thus a grievous one. Small business is by no means an unimportant part of the economy. Numerically, it is the largest sector of the economy.

Although the line between small- and large-scale enterprise cannot be arbitrarily fixed, latest reports show that of the total number of 240,881 manufacturing establishments in the United States, employing 14,294,304 persons and adding by manufacture $74,425,825,000 to the value of their products, plants with less than 100 employees numbered 216,339 establishments, employed 3,578,448 persons, and the value added to their products by manufacture was $17,597,114,000. In other words, the ratio between plants of this small size and total manufacturing in the United States is that these small manufacturers make up 89.81 per cent of the total number of establishments, employ 25.03 per cent of manufacturing personnel, and add 23.64 per cent to the value of their products through manufacture.[10]

Small enterprise complements big business by carrying on the specialized production and services which standardized big business does not perform. A survey of every large-scale enterprise would reveal its reliance upon dozens, perhaps hundreds, of small enterprises for materials, accessories, parts, and services.[11] Nor should it be overlooked that small enterprise is an important market for the products of big business. Much of the independence, self-reliance, and experimentation in business ventures which we associate with the free enterprise system is fostered through small enterprise. And by providing a wide field for the gainful employment of the population, small enterprise performs an essential social and economic function for the nation. For these reasons, its problems command attention.

Suggested Solutions.—Whatever solutions are attempted, it seems clear that they will have to be part of a rounded program for providing equity capital, term credits, and management assistance to small enterprisers. How shall this be done? The following suggestions are interesting but by no means exhaustive of the possibilities.

Equity Capital.—In the case of *going* concerns in need of equity capital, encourage investment bankers and investment trusts to occupy the field as they do that of big business. And since commercial banks show a tendency to develop along the lines of the fixed-term loan, encourage them to make capital loans of this type. A third suggestion points to the establishment of regional or national industrial financing corporations, either privately owned, government owned, or in some mixed form, to perform this function. Parallel to this, several legislative proposals have been made to establish a system of industrial banks covering the nation in a way similar to the Federal Reserve System. Many other proposals would support these lending agencies by agencies which would guarantee or insure the loan or compensate for losses somewhat

[10] U. S. Department of Commerce, Bureau of Census, release of Aug. 1, 1949, Series MC100–6. These are preliminary figures on the latest census of manufactures. Although they are not strictly comparable, similar data for the last complete census before the war may be found in the 1939 Census of Manufactures.

[11] As a prime contractor for more than 2,000 items for the armed forces at a rate of more than $10,000,000 per day, General Motors Corporation reported its reliance on 18,735 subcontractors and suppliers of which 74 per cent employed fewer than 500 persons, and 43 per cent employed fewer than 100 persons. *The New York Times,* July 6, 1943.

along the lines that Title I of the Federal Housing Act supports bank loans for the modernization of dwellings, or the way in which the Federal Deposit Insurance Corporation covers bank deposits.

New enterprises may or may not be financed by these agencies. Whereas the risk element is present in the case of both new and established enterprises, the going concern offers a better opportunity to appraise the risk. It has assets, a functioning organization, a market record, the equity of its owners as a margin of safety, and other features by which its condition and prospects can be judged. A new venture relies heavily upon estimates and probabilities that may or may not be realized. Yet the new venture in prospect may be sounder than the older enterprise in operation. No general rule covers all cases, but when all things are taken into consideration, it would seem that where the case is purely one of venture financing, unconnected with any existing concern, the enterprise should be left to find its capital where it can, as such enterprises do now.

Short- and Intermediate-term Credits.—Any tendency the commercial banks may have to decrease their activities in the field of short-term loans to industrial enterprises, it seems, should be reversed. This is traditionally their field and fits in well with their functions of providing banking services to the community. If they suffer from any disadvantages in the making of short-term loans, it would be better to remove the drawbacks rather than permit them to withdraw from short-term lending. If necessary, the Federal Reserve Banks, the RFC and other government agencies might devise measures to safeguard their liquidity and guarantee them against losses. Where they are not functionally organized or equipped to service the short-term loans of small enterprise, they might establish departments for that purpose.

Another suggestion holds that since commercial factors, finance companies, personal loan agencies, and other retailers of credit have grown so rapidly and have developed special techniques for handling short- and intermediate-term credits of small companies, they should be encouraged to increase and stabilize themselves in that field. By coordination of their activities and aided by proper legislation, it is possible that they can reduce costs and make the conditions of loans less burdensome. Since the great risks involved are given as a reason for high charges and stringent terms, some form of guarantee against losses may enable these finance agencies to lend on more reasonable terms. Where no insurance device can be set up by the private economy, the government might provide it.

Other suggestions propose industrial loan corporations, specialized banks in addition to the existing banking system, certain forms of subsidies to small enterprises, tax relief to small concerns, and certain forms of collective action like large credit pools. From another point of view further consolidations of small enterprises have been suggested. From the broader aspect, greater consumer purchasing power is considered a remedy.

Management Assistance.—Not all people recognize that the problems of small enterprise go deeper than finance. Small concerns lack skilled management, research facilities, and modern technical equipment. The ease with which anyone may start a business tends to overcrowd the field. Large companies often control basic materials, patents, and machinery which they either withhold from small concerns or for which they demand a price that greatly increases the costs of the small user. Any solution of the small-enterprise problem will have to reach these and other difficulties, and not alone the financing problem.

Conclusion.—Indeed, certain broader problems may be closer to the root of the predicament of small enterprise than are either finance or management difficulties. How necessary is small enterprise to economic vitality in the nation? Does the trend to larger business units mark a desirable economic development which the attempt to uphold small enterprise simply retards? Where the economic fabric of the country is so closely knit that failure of its weak parts endangers the whole economy, is it wise to permit anyone who pleases to start a business on the mere chance that it will succeed? On the other hand, where an economic society is continually growing, is not waste in the form of small-business failures a necessary element? Moreover, where the plight of small enterprise arises out of maladjustments and failures in other sectors of the economy, should not these be remedied before small enterprise is sacrificed? In any event, the deterioration in the position of small enterprise seems to mark a crisis in the nation's economic system which has been years in the making and which may take many more years to resolve.

CASE PROBLEMS

I. On the Problem of Financing Small Enterprise

1. Make a comparative study of the economic position of small-scale and large-scale manufacturing in the United States in 1870 and 1950. Discuss your findings in terms of production, employment, markets, and finance.

2. Construct a case for or against the following proposition: Investment credit should be controlled by the Federal government.

3. What plans can you suggest for the financing of small enterprise by private sources independent of government aid?

II. On the General Problem of Industrial Financing

Case A [12]

An established Seattle businessman, who had specialized for some years in the salvaging of waste and the recovery of commercial products from waste, often using original methods and apparatus of his own invention, decided to establish a plant at Ketchikan, Alaska, for deriving meal and oil from the fish waste of the salmon canneries. Many tons of such waste were dumped daily into Ketchikan harbor with the loss of iodine and vitamin-rich materials valuable for stock feed, as well as creating a health and navigation problem. Initial capital of $25,000 for the venture was obtained by the pledge of business assets in Seattle and Portland and through small personal loans. Of this, $12,000 was expended upon initial construction and lost when the Forest Service canceled a permit previously granted. The project was saved through the granting of a personal loan of $4,000 by the head of a small bank in Ketchikan, a $4,000 mortgage on the proprietor's home, and a $6,000 loan against machinery. A new site, including an excellent small harbor, was purchased. A plant was constructed and operations were begun on a small scale in 1935. These proved profitable, but a second difficulty arose when the town of Ketchikan passed legislation forbidding the canneries to dump further salmon waste into the harbor. This amounted to a compulsion upon the new plant to handle all the waste of the 13 near-by canneries, which it was not equipped to do, and the need for expansion to meet the new demands placed upon it has embarrassed the enterprise ever since.

In the first five years of its operation, the plant's entire production was profitably sold and all its profits were plowed back into the business, not a cent having been withdrawn by the proprietor. At the time of the study, the situation was such that all the fish-waste of Ketchikan harbor could be handled; a single good year would retire the bulk of the debt; and a demand by a single major creditor would go far toward bankrupting the enterprise. The need was for the consolidation and amortization of a $25,000 indebtedness on a three-year basis. No Alaska bank could undertake this refinancing; the Seattle banks regarded the enterprise as outside their territory and in addition were not making capital loans. The RFC had declined to refinance a debt incurred through past expansion. Credits from different non-bank sources—food and other supply houses, machinery concerns, an oil broker, and the Seattle enterprises owned by the proprietor, although not large, were a source of constant embarrassment. This original-minded enterpriser had no desire to sell an equity in a business which, once launched, might conceivably spread to other Alaskan canning centers and grow to large proportions. Tests had shown that an added investment of a few thousand dollars in refining equipment would develop a medical product which the United States today imports largely from abroad. But capital could not be obtained.

[12] Temporary National Economic Committee, *Monograph* 17, Problems of Small Business, pp. 337–338.

Preparatory Questions

1. Take the position of a banker and discuss the reasons why you would be reluctant to undertake the financing of this company.

2. Criticize this enterprise from the following viewpoints: (*a*) business organization, (*b*) business forecasting, (*c*) financial planning.

3. Draw up a financial plan that you believe would solve the problem of this enterprise and detail the steps you would take to put the plan into execution.

Case B [13]

The manager of a well-established typewriter and office machine sales and service business had invented and patented a paper-grip feed roll, applicable to any typewriter. In 1935, one large typewriter parts concern purchased 2,670 of these devices; in 1936, 7,010; 1937, 27,050; 1938, 27,960; January to May 3, 1939, 8,000. The inventor attempted to obtain a loan of $2,500 for machinery, $1,000 for sales promotion and $1,000 for raw materials. Despite the existence of a market for his product, he had been unable to do so.

Preparatory Questions

1. From a banker's viewpoint, what are the weak points in this financing problem?

2. Describe the data you would want and the studies you would make preliminary to drawing a financial plan for this enterprise.

3. Plan a financial structure to meet the needs of this concern and indicate the sources from which financing funds may be drawn.

Case C [13]

A skilled mechanical engineer, formerly retained by the General Electric Company for experimental work on small Diesel engines, became chief mechanical engineer at the Bremerton Navy Yard and continued his experiments, developing a small marine engine suitable for use by the fishing fleet. Later, he succeeded in organizing a company for the development of this engine. Over a period of years $77,000 was earned and was largely plowed back into the business. In 1937, additional capital was added through the entry of a partner. At the time of the study, many local fishing boats were using this engine and a fisheries-supply concern had offered to contract for 20 engines a year. The company's assets included machinery, $17,000; patterns, $12,000; jigs and dies, $8,000; stock parts and receivables, $3,000, or a total of $40,000. The liabilities included amounts payable of $2,000 and a balance due on a mortgage loan obtained from a local bank amounting to $1,650, reduced from $3,000. The needs of this company were $30,000 for increased production facilities and $15,000 to $20,000 for long-term working capital. But here, again, the commercial bank can be of no assistance.

[13] *Ibid.,* p. 339.

Preparatory Questions

1. Give at least three reasons why you think the investigator of this case concluded that the "commercial bank can be of no assistance."

2. Prepare a prospectus to be used in soliciting capital for this enterprise.   Indicate the sources you would seek to tap, and explain fully why you have selected them.

Case D

Figure the ratios explained below on the accounting data of the two companies and tell which is more eligible for a bank loan and why.

Ratios

$$\text{Current ratio} = \frac{\text{total current assets}}{\text{total current liabilities}} = current \text{ credit strength}$$

A 2:1 ratio is generally considered satisfactory.   Each dollar of current liabilities is covered by two dollars of current assets.

$$\text{Liquidity ("acid-test") ratio} = \frac{\text{total current assets} - \text{inventory}}{\text{total current liabilities}}$$

These are the "quick" assets (dollar assets or assets readily convertible into dollars) divided by total current liabilities. The "acid-test" ratio is more stringent than the current ratio.   A 1:1 is acceptable; *i.e.*, for every dollar of current liabilities, there should be one dollar of current assets with inventory excluded.

Ratios indicating the earning power and financial efficiency of a company:

$$\text{Proprietary ratio} = \frac{\text{total capital}}{\text{total liabilities and capital}}$$

This ratio indicates the dependency of a company upon its creditors for working capital.   Considered together with the current ratio over an extended period of time, it provides a trend analysis and shows whether the degree of debt pressure is increasing or decreasing.

$$\text{Rate of earnings on total capital employed} = \frac{\text{net operating profit}}{\text{total liabilities and capital}}$$

This ratio gives the percentage return from business production for every dollar of liabilities and capital employed.

$$\text{Operating ratio} = \frac{\text{cost of goods sold and operating expense}}{\text{net sales}}$$

This shows the percentage of every dollar received from net sales which is needed to meet the cost of production and operation.

Ratios indicating the efficiency of management:

$$\text{Turnover of capital} = \frac{\text{net sales}}{\text{total liabilities and capital}}$$

This ratio undertakes to show what percentage is realized in net sales for every dollar available to management in total liabilities and capital (total assets). It indicates the efficiency of financial management.

$$\text{Number of days' sales in receivables} = \frac{\text{receivables}}{\text{net sales}} \times \begin{cases} \text{number of days} \\ \text{covered by profit} \\ \text{and loss statement} \end{cases}$$

This is the collection ratio. It shows the average length of time accounts are outstanding and is a measure of the efficiency of credit management.

$$\text{Merchandise turnover} = \frac{\text{net sales}}{\text{average inventory}}$$

This is the number of times that inventory is replaced during a given period of time and indicates the degree of efficiency in a company's merchandising.

Ratios important to management in the control of internal operations:

$$\text{Margin percentage} = \frac{\text{gross profit on sales}}{\text{net sales}}$$

For every dollar received from sales, a certain percentage is gross profit. This figure must be large enough to cover all other expenses (not operating expenses alone) if the company is to be profitable. If the quotient in this ratio is subtracted from 100, the percentage of net sales going to cost of goods sold is obtained.

$$\text{Net profit ratio} = \frac{\text{net income (before dividends)}}{\text{net sales}}$$

Shows percentage of net income for each dollar of net sales.

PROFIT AND LOSS STATEMENT
for the year ended December 31, 19—
(Thousands of dollars)

	Company A	Company B
Net Sales	$5,500	$3,170
Cost of Goods Sold	2,700	1,375
Gross Profit on Sales	$2,800	$1,795
Operating Expenses:		
Maintenance and Repairs	$ 150	$ 100
Depreciation	380	300
Bad-debt Expense	90	80
Selling Expense	925	800
Administrative and General	315	275
Total Operating Expense	$1,860	$1,555
Net Operating Profit	940	240
Other Income	75	40
Other Expense	425	200
Net Income	$ 590	$ 80

BALANCE SHEET

for the year ended December 31, 19—

(Thousands of dollars)

	Company A	*Company B*
Current Assets:		
Cash	$ 1,500	$ 750
Marketable securities	300	400
Accounts Receivable	475	635
Inventories	2,000	1,200
Total Current Assets	$ 4,275	$ 2,985
Fixed Assets:		
Investments	$ 800	$ 1,000
Land, Buildings, and Equipment (net)	8,650	6,280
Total Fixed Assets	$ 9,450	$ 7,280
Prepaid Expenses	260	75
Total Assets	$13,985	$10,340
Current Liabilities:		
Notes Payable	$ 175	$ 400
Accounts Payable	800	780
Other Current Liabilities	1,450	1,200
Total Current Liabilities	$ 2,425	$ 2,380
Fixed Liabilities:		
Mortgage Payable (due 10 years from date this statement)	2,790	4,500
Total Liabilities	$ 5,215	$ 6,880
Capital:		
Preferred Stock—6%, cumulative, nonparticipating	$ 2,100	$ 1,000
Common Stock	3,000	1,700
Total Capital Stock	$ 5,100	$ 2,700
Surplus:		
Appropriated Surplus	$ 1,200	$ 540
Unappropriated Surplus	2,470	220
Total Surplus	$ 3,670	$ 760
Total Capital	8,770	3,460
Total Liabilities and Capital	$13,985	$10,340

CHAPTER VI
BUILDING THE INTERNAL ORGANIZATION

In the days of the nineteenth century manufacturing plants were relatively small. Contact between the owner and the workmen was comparatively easy. Each workman was familiar with all parts of the product manufactured and was acquainted with its various uses and adaptations. He was skilled in all the work required in the manufacture of the product. The owner was frequently the manager or superintendent of the company. All men reported directly to him. He was the man who established policies, assigned the jobs to be done, and followed up on the jobs for the purpose of direction and coordination.

Many small industries of this type still exist, although for many years there has been a rapid trend toward consolidations and mergers into large organizations. In times of war or other periods of increased business activity many small industries suddenly grow large. At this point of transition, from small to large, we reach the critical point in organizational procedures. Too frequently the company attempts to struggle along under its former organization. The heads of the company, who may have grown up in the business, may know only one procedure and that is direct personal control of all activities. If such is the case, we soon find the business jammed with orders delayed beyond the promised date of delivery, grumbling and dissatisfaction on the part of the badly managed working personnel, and a nervous collapse on the part of the president, or a financial collapse on the part of the company.

Today we find companies, such as General Motors, General Electric, and many of the aircraft industries, divided into as many as 80 divisions scattered throughout the nation, some of which employ as many as eight or ten thousand men. Each division is, within itself, a huge industrial enterprise, yet all divisions must be brought into coordination and harmony, all working toward a common purpose and in conformity with established policies. This is the problem of *organization*. By organization a framework of authority and responsibility is established through which policies established by *management* are administered. Thus a distinction is made between the functions of *management* and the functions of *administration*.

It is the function of the board of managers, frequently referred to as management, to establish policies regarding the type of product to be manufactured, finance, channels of distribution, service, personnel, and other factors affecting the operations of the enterprise. Furthermore, it is the responsibility of management to outline an organizational structure for the carrying out of these policies.

Industrial Engineering.—As industry itself widened its horizons from rule-of-thumb and empirical methods to precision and scientific techniques, the character of industrial management also changed. Specialization carved out new occupations for the management personnel who directed the constantly enlarging subdivisions of an industrial enterprise. As in every evolving field, there is a tendency to define and crystallize functions and to find some distinctive name for them. This will be obvious from descriptions in this text of functions practiced in modern industrial organization and management. In this chapter, dealing with the internal organization of the whole enterprise, we shall mention a term commonly applied to one whose functions have come to touch upon many phases of an enterprise—the industrial engineer.

Not so many years ago the term "industrial engineer" had a precise meaning. Reflecting the words "industry" and "engineer" the term was used to mean a production engineer who specialized in such things as factory layout, time and motion study, materials handling, production operations, and control. He usually was a qualified engineer by education, training, and experience. His aims were so to organize production equipment and operations as to produce efficiently at constantly lower costs in time, effort, and money. In the course of these technical functions the industrial engineer found himself drawn into other phases of industrial management. For example, in studying factory layout, the industrial engineer was drawn into inventory control, safety engineering, cost systems and controls, and other functions associated with policies and general management; time studies led to merit rating, supervisory training, selection, placement, welfare programs, and other phases of industrial relations; machinery and product design led to excursions into advertising and marketing.

Much of the success and growing acceptance of the industrial engineer is rooted in the management system of Frederick W. Taylor, the father of scientific management.[1] Taylor is so known because of his systematic development of management techniques starting at the Midvale Steel Company in Philadelphia around 1880. His work began with an effort

---

[1] Taylor himself called his system "task management" until the last five years of his life. It was given the more popular misnomer by attorney Louis Brandeis (later a justice of the Supreme Court) in 1910 at hearings on railroad-rate increases. In the United States the term "scientific management" still refers to "Taylor system." In England and much of the rest of the world "scientific management" is used to mean merely "modern management."

to develop a piecework system, but he soon found all management actions closely interrelated.   Taylor spent the next 30 years perfecting his system in wood-pulp mills, machinery plants, building-construction projects, the Bethlehem Steel Company, etc.   When installed at the Link Belt Engineering Company in 1905, the system included cost accounting, unit time study, inventory control, production control, planning, output scheduling, functional operation, standardized procedures, a mnemonic system of classification, and means for maintaining quality production.   All these were developed by the application of inductive research to industrial operations.   Management continues to perfect these and gain new techniques by the application of Taylor's four principles of management—*research, standardization, control,* and *cooperation*—to present-day problems under the new title of industrial engineering.

Pioneers of Scientific Management.—Associating with Taylor in these early years were important pioneers of scientific management to whom Taylor gave much of the credit for perfecting the system.   Carl G. Barth was one of the earliest.   At first as a draftsman at Midvale and later as Taylor's assistant at Bethlehem, Barth merged research mathematics, a capacity for details (which Taylor hated), and machine-tool knowledge to develop a number of shop slide rules.   These brought Taylor's recommendations within the reach of many shop supervisors.   Henry L. Gantt, Taylor's first helper at Bethlehem, contributed much of the recognition of worker psychology and a bonus plan with a guarantee to replace Taylor's differential premium plan.   Gantt also developed the charts widely used in production control and scheduling.   One of Taylor's closest associates was Sanford E. Thompson, who helped him invent the decimal-dial stop watch and perfect cost-accounting methods for the building trades.   H. King Hathaway worked out one of the earlier plant installations.   Following closely on the pioneer trail were such men as Harrington Emerson (the first to use standard costs and the "popularizer" of efficiency), the Gilbreths, Professors Harlow S. Person and Morris L. Cooke, Wallace Clark who dispensed American know-how in Europe, and manufacturers Henry S. Dennison and Henry P. Kendall. It was the advisory work of men such as these that gave rise to the new field of management counseling, for many of them organized consulting firms.[2]

These firms specialized in applying the methods of research and scientific discipline to industrial organization, planning, methods, coordination, and control.   For a fee they offered to business enterprises the services of a group of consultants capable of dealing with organization,

[2] The Association of Consulting Management Engineers, New York City, lists 33 member firms in its 1949 directory.

financing, production, budgeting and accounting, personnel relations, and marketing. Some of these practitioners were engineers in the technical meaning of the word (mechanical, electrical, civil, etc.), but more often than not they formed something of a new profession based upon a working knowledge of engineering principles, scientific research, and modern principles of commercial and industrial management. In common application in the United States the term "engineer" took on a broader meaning, as one who puts through an idea, superintends a plan, manages an enterprise in which engineering technology is only a small part. In many quarters the term was broadened still further to the meaning of "manage" in general, as to "manage" a business deal. Engineering thus came to be closely associated with the general management of an enterprise. While the number of titles for practitioners of this kind are numerous, recent usage tends to name the field of their operations "industrial engineering." [3]

While the movement in this direction seems apparent, it is still in process of development. The field of industrial engineering as yet has no fixed boundaries, no exact content, and no universally recognized professional status. At most, it consists of a conglomeration of highly valuable although only slightly related management functions.[4] In essence, an industrial engineer is a functional staff management member or an independent practitioner or firm who offers an integrated viewpoint to management based upon the application of scientific research methods to business problems or industrial enterprise. He is the modern practitioner of scientific management in the great tradition of Whitney, Taylor, and the Gilbreths. Although there are many charlatans in the field, taking advantage of the current emphasis on science, technology, and modernization to sell glib advice, tricky systems, and technical hocus-pocus to industry at lucrative fees, the legitimate industrial engineer (in the broad sense) may well come to occupy an important place as something of a new profession in industrial enterprise. Although there are only about 10,000 industrial engineers in this country, they occupy an increasingly important place in business and industry.[5]

Where the industrial engineer functions in the broad sense, he works directly in association with top management, reporting to the president or board of directors, depending upon the nature and scope of his work.

[3] See *Proceedings* of the Fall Meeting (Middle Atlantic Section) of the Society for the Promotion of Engineering Education, New York, Dec. 2, 1944, pp. 14 *ff*.

[4] A survey reported in March, 1949, *The Management Review,* listed over 50 separate industrial-engineering functions ranging from "wage standards and incentives" to "marketing, trade customs, and standards."

[5] Estimate of the "Occupational Outlook Handbook," *Bulletin* 940, p. 72, U.S. Department of Labor, Bureau of Labor Statistics, Washington, D.C.

Where he functions in the older, technical sense, he reports to the vice-president, general manager, plant engineer, or other officer in charge of engineering (see Fig. 5, Organization Chart of a Large Corporation). What each one does for the economic success of the enterprise can best be understood by the careful study of all the principles, parts, and functions comprising industrial organization and management, as presented step by step in this book.[6]

THE ANATOMY OF THE MODERN COMPANY

A company is usually divided into divisions or departments. Division in some instances is made according to product. By this method a hardware industry might have one division for the manufacture of locks, another for the manufacture of cutlery, etc. Or a company may be divided by processes or operations in order to permit greater specialization in the division of labor. In this case, patternmaking would be assigned to one division, molding to another, plating to another, and so on through the various operations common to the products manufactured.

Administration is concerned with converting policy into practice. At the head of each division is a person responsible for the division and in possession of authority for supervision and control. Each division may be organized into a framework of *departments* with an operating head of each department.

All orders authorizing work in accordance with prearranged schedules must pass through the administrative organization of a company to the man at the workplace. In the same way, responsibility for material, equipment, and personnel must travel through designated channels. In order to facilitate the work of administration, routines are established into a *system*. Administrative officers, through the adoption of systematic standard procedures for the handling of orders, records, reports, and complaints, are able to free themselves of miscellaneous day-by-day tasks and direct their attention toward more constructive work. System, therefore, becomes a tool of administration. Unfortunately, in many instances, administrators become slaves to their systems. It should be recognized that a system cannot be made infallible nor can it be constructed in a way that will properly serve all needs that may arise. An administrator should realize that all rules and regulations comprising a system must be interpreted in consideration of the circumstances of a particular case. Exceptions may be expected to arise. They should be looked for rather than shunned. In fact, systems are estab-

[6] For a more comprehensive treatment of the functions of the industrial engineer (in the technical sense of the term) see Chap. XVII.

lished in order that the administrator may have time to deal with exceptions.   This is frequently referred to as the *exception principle*.

Principles of Organization.—The primary purpose of organization, as previously stated, is for coordination and control over the activities of the company.   There are many factors to be considered in building the organizational structure of a given company.   No two companies are identical.   Each company must be studied in terms of its purposes, its size, and the nature of the product manufactured.   There are, however, a few basic principles that can be used for guidance in considering the organizational needs of any company:

1. Definite lines of responsibility and authority must be established.
2. Provision must be made for the grouping of specialized work and the appropriate division of labor in terms of the manufacturing requirements of the product.
3. Consideration must be given to the abilities and specialized skills of existing and available personnel in order that they may be used to the maximum.
4. Unauthoritative lines of coordination and facilitation must be developed for the promotion of harmony and understanding.

Lines of Responsibility and Authority.—It is easily recognized that in any sizable organization there must be delegation of responsibility. In the first place, it is a physical impossibility for any one man to control effectively all the work of a large organization through personal contact with it.   He must rely on other individuals to be responsible for designated phases of the work.   Secondly, no one man possesses the skills essential to guide personally the highly specialized activities in a modern industry.   Instead, he procures an expert on finance to assume responsibility for the financial activities of the enterprise.   He obtains an industrial engineer to study the manufacturing processes of the company and develop the most efficient methods for manufacturing a product of maximum quality at minimum cost.   And so, throughout the organization, he must segregate these highly specialized activities and obtain individuals with the necessary knowledge and skill to be responsible for them.

This principle of delegation of authority extends all the way through the company from the president and general manager to the heads of divisions, the supervisors, the straw bosses, and the workers at the bench. Lines of responsibility must be fixed.   Each man in a company should know to whom he is responsible.   Lines of responsibility that are "fringy" or indistinct lead to grumbling and misunderstanding throughout the personnel of the organization.   One supervisor will order the work performed in one way and another will order the worker to stop operations and proceed in a different way. The result is dissatisfaction on the part of workers and supervisors and loss in the efficiency of operations.

Consider also the position of the supervisor who cannot be sure of the bounds of his responsibility. He lives in fear of the possibility that he is either "meddling with someone else's business" or that he is neglecting a responsibility of which he is unaware. Lines of responsibility work two ways: from the executive to the personnel and to the work that comes under his jurisdiction and, conversely, from the worker to those who are in authority over him. These lines must be kept clear at all times in order to facilitate the ready flow of communication and control.

The Meaning of Responsibility and Authority.—A famous professor of administration is credited with a definition of "hell" as *responsibility without authority*. Many people, by their actions, seem constantly to seek authority but evade responsibility. The latter we refer to as "buck passing." Yet, both authority and responsibility must go together. We are much more willing to agree to the necessity of authority in doing a job than to accept the resulting responsibilities once we are aware of the full implications of these responsibilities.

If you as an individual were given the complete authority for the selection of production processes and equipment, would you also be willing to assume the complete responsibility? These elements not only require extensive research but also in the end require selective experience for the exercise of judgment in making final choices. These are elements which play an important role in determining the relative competitive position of the manufacturer. Industry must continually exploit all its resources for the improvement of processes and equipment lest it be knocked out of the market by a more efficient competitor. Would you be willing to assume this responsibility alone? [7]

If you were given authority to act in disciplinary cases including suspension or discharge, would you be willing to assume complete responsibility for the avoidance of strikes and consequent shutdowns that might result from an unintentional error in your actions?

If your answer to these questions is in the affirmative, your employer should very quickly put you in isolated quarters where you can cause no serious destruction to life or property. No one is infallible. We are all capable of errors. You as an individual might be willing to risk the possibility of such errors, but the stockholders, the board of directors, the president, your management superiors, and the employees cannot afford to place that much confidence in you.

---

[7] If you question the relative importance given to the selection of processes and equipment, glance at Chap. X.

These reasons are the source of the principle which says that *authority can never be completely delegated—it can only be shared.* The president is still held responsible for quality of product and for the causes of strikes. Then why does he delegate any of the authority and responsibility? He does so because he knows he must *share* if he expects to obtain the necessary counsel of specialists in production, cost, labor relations, and the many other varied activities of the company. Such counsel, given by persons who do not share in the responsibility, would be of questionable value.

Yet even with the aid of responsible specialists there is always the element of risk in decisions. The true scientist will be the first to admit the possibility of error in his findings and recommendations. Who is to assume this risk? Who is to make the decision? Probably the best answer is that decisions should result from *the pooling of judgment* of those who share in the responsibility and authority in the situation in question.

In the selection of processes and equipment, basic policies governing the procedures to be used in the selection are established and approved by top management. However, even these policies are the outgrowth of recommendations coming from specialized staff personnel and approved by the production foremen, the production-control manager, the cost-control manager, the superintendent, the maintenance superintendent, the union representative, and any others who may be directly affected by the policies.

Characteristics of the Pooled-judgment Process.—Ellis C. Maxcy, assistant vice-president of the Southern New England Telephone Company, lists six characteristics of the pooled-judgment process: [8]

1. A common body of information for discussion. All parties to the process should have full access to the same information.

2. A common understanding and use of words or terms important to the subject being discussed. The semantics of human relations is an area of increasing importance because words not only suggest ideas but attitudes as well. In forming a judgment it is not only important that we say or write what we wish to convey but that we avoid using words or terms which convey other than intended meanings.

3. An agreement regarding the facts and the issues involved in the decision. Agreement becomes easier as meanings are clarified.

4. A cross stimulation of ideas through discussion. This can incorporate points of view developed at different organization levels by persons of differing status, which when reconciled, improve over-all organization communication.

[8] MAXCY, ELLIS C., Pooled Judgment Process in Human Relations, *Personnel,* March, 1947, p. 362.

5. A development of common conclusions. The general support of conclusions is a by-product of participation. It is not to be assumed, however, that conclusions need be unanimous to be an effective product of the process.

6. A check of the conclusions by application to a sample group or test situation.

Policies growing out of this pooling of judgment and approved by top management should include statements of principles governing the procedures to be followed and the group to be consulted when the situation warrants. This does not mean that every time a piece of equipment is bought a committee must be called together for approval of the purchase. Instead, the individuals directly charged with the responsibility are given prescribed areas of responsibility in which to act. In the purchase of miscellaneous supplies, a department may requisition through purchasing within the limits of its budget without further authorization. Selection of minor replacements might fall in the same area of responsibility. However, major replacements or additions might be placed by policy in another category requiring consultation with a larger number of affected parties. The extent of agreement or disagreement within a group also may determine how many people in the ladder of responsibility and authority must be included.[9]

There may be instances when the president or chief executive officer is in disagreement with the majority judgment of the group. In such case he has two alternatives:

1. He may exercise his right of final authority and reverse the majority recommendation. In such case he assumes the burden of responsibility and is by his action releasing those in opposition to his decision from responsibility for the possible error of the decision.

2. He may carry the issue to the board of directors for recommendation.

Utilization of these alternatives should be necessary only on rare occasion. Frequent use will lead to a "one-man company." If such reversals prove to be necessary on frequent occasions, the company is not receiving the quality of specialized counsel which it is seeking and deserves. Therefore, ultimately, the company should call for changes in personnel.

Division of Labor.—In contrast to the days when a machinist would perform all operations on a given part or product, the various manufacturing operations of today may be performed by as many different machines as there are operations. The operations are scheduled in their logical sequence so that the product, in the process of manufacture, travels through the plant from machine to machine, each operation adding

[9] See Fig. 118 for an illustration of prescribed responsibility and authority.

one more step in its progress toward completion. This means that machines and the personnel that operate them must be grouped according to the dictates of the operation sequences. These required groupings must necessarily be given due consideration in forming the organizational structure of the company. This influence on organization will be discussed more fully in a separate section.

Available Personnel.—The organization of a company is dependent not only upon the type and arrangement of work in the company but also upon the special abilities and skills of personnel to perform the work. This is especially true in the establishment of leaders, supervisors, and foremen. Two factors are here especially significant: (1) the need for close supervision as judged by the skill of the workmen and the difficulty of the operations, and (2) the availability of experienced and trustworthy personnel capable of acting in supervisory capacities. Operations of a routine, unskilled nature might require little supervision. In this case a large number of operators could be grouped together under one supervisor or foreman. On the other hand, during a period of rapid expansion when large numbers of new personnel are being brought into the plant, it is usually advisable to decrease the number of operators per supervisor in order that each worker may receive more attention and help in becoming familiar with the work.

The case of Cutler-Hammer, Inc., illustrates the change that is necessary in the supervisory organization during a period of rapid expansion. Cutler-Hammer, prior to World War II, normally billed eleven to twelve million dollars' worth of business a year. In 1942, because of war business, billings had suddenly risen to fifty millions a year. Instead of a personnel of 3,000, they then employed 7,000. Thus 4,000 new employees had been added to the organization within a period of a little over a year. Most of the new group were inexperienced in industrial work and totally unfamiliar with the work of this particular company. Realizing early the need for an immediate change in the supervisory organization, the company set about to find experienced employees from within their former personnel who possessed the qualities necessary for positions of leadership. Heads of the manufacturing divisions were asked to select young engineering assistants and put them in charge of subdivisions. Capable and experienced men of the operating force were designated as supervisors within the subdivisions. They in turn selected outstanding workmen of their respective groups and appointed them straw bosses, thus making it possible to establish groups of four and five employees working under the direct leadership of a workman of long experience in the company. Straw bosses continued on an hourly basis in their regular operating function. Thus, the valuable skill of these men was not sacrificed but, instead, was multiplied several times by the men working beside them and under their skillful guidance.[10]

There are occasions, however, when a company suddenly finds itself without personnel available for supervisory work. Perhaps the company has been able to maintain a very even volume of production year after year and has not felt the necessity for preparing employees to assume responsibilities of leadership. A nucleus of old-time supervisory personnel has been maintained under a good salary scale. While men at the workplaces could be bought for a "dime a dozen" during the period when labor was plentiful, why should the company be concerned if there was a rapid turnover in the personnel of this classification? Then suddenly an upturn in business requires the doubling of personnel. Trained personnel are not available because now there is a scarcity of labor. Young inexperienced help are brought in. The foremen tear their hair and the workers tear up the machines. The waste pile mounts. Idle time of puzzled workmen is added to the costs of production because of the inability of the supervisors to give proper attention to the greatly enlarged group. Labor disputes arise, and the company concludes that there must be a change in the supervisory organization. But the company has neglected to establish a reserve of young men to be used in anticipation of such a need as this. It then faces a problem of organization that cannot be dealt with in terms of the ideal. It must reorganize around the leadership that is available and gradually move toward a more ideal structure as additional leadership becomes available. This may involve the complete rearrangement of operation sequences with a regrouping of machinery and workplaces in order to utilize the peculiar skills of members of the supervisory staff. The more experienced employees may be grouped together where they can work with little or no supervision and assistance, thus relieving supervisors who may devote their attention to other departments. Frequently, it is necessary or advisable to analyze the abilities of a single man and organize the work of a department around his abilities. This is one reason why we find such wide variation in the scope of work in given departments of different companies.

Lines of Coordination and Facilitation.—Many executives object to the charting of lines of authority and responsibility for, they say, an organization does not work that way. Here a distinction can be made between authority and facilitation or persuasion. By authority men in parallel positions are responsible not to one another but to superior executives. Actually, however, the majority of problems affecting these

[10] For a complete discussion of this case, see *Fortune Magazine*, August, 1942, p. 97.

two men may have been solved by mutual agreement before ever reaching the superior officers. This is merely a recognition of the fact that courteous, informal discussion by individuals nearest a problem may simplify the solution and avoid extraneous influences such as misunderstanding and distrust.

Of course, free interplay of discussion between individuals of different departments can develop into a serious weakness in organization. First, it can result in a needless waste of time if a supervisor can call an employment interviewer and discuss in detail the routine requirements of a job to be filled or if he can call a follow-up clerk in the purchasing department and ask for special consideration on an order of material. Such abuse would also serve to destroy lines of coordination and control. Executives who are supposed to be in positions where they can view problems in better perspective and with recognition for the welfare of the department or the enterprise are "by-passed" and made ineffective.

For these reasons lines of facilitation are recognized for their value but are carefully confined to points where they are actually needed as illustrated in Fig. 7.

Types of Organizations.—It has been stated that details of organizational structure may differ in terms of the peculiar needs of a given industrial enterprise. There are, however, five principal organization types with varying degrees of complexity appropriate to the enterprise in terms of its size and type of product. These types are (1) line or military, (2) line and staff, (3) functional (pure), (4) line and functional staff, and (5) line, functional staff, and committees.

Line Organization.—Line organization is the simplest form of structure. It is the framework on which a more complex organization may be built as needs arise. It assumes a direct straight-line responsibility and control from the general manager to the superintendent, to foremen, and to the workmen.

Line organization has frequently been referred to as military organization. It acquired this name through the fact that there are direct single lines of authority and responsibility between an officer and his subordinates. However, any similarity that might have existed previously between this form of organization and the organization of the military services is now outmoded. Branches of the military service now have special divisions with horizontal as well as vertical lines of authority and responsibility.

Line and Staff Organization.—Industrial leaders have recognized, as their companies grew from simple to complex organizations, that a small number of executives could not personally assume direct responsibility for all functions such as research, planning, distribution, public relations, industrial relations, and the many other varied activities. Therefore, one of the first moves toward reorganization as a company grew in size and complexity was to appoint assistants to executives. Specific advisory responsibilities were delegated to these assistants. Executives and

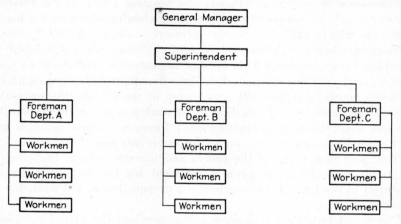

Fig. 3.—Line organization.

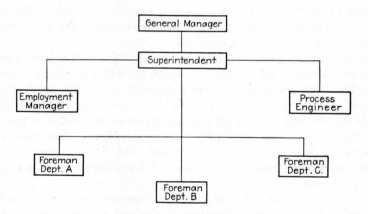

Fig. 4.—Simple line and staff organization.

general foremen retained supervisory authority and control over the activities of the personnel of their particular departments. They were the coordinating force that worked toward the preservation of harmony and good personnel relations between the workmen and the special executive assistants. These assistants frequently carried the title of process engineer, design engineer, industrial engineer, or budget officer, as shown in Fig. 4. As the activities of these assistants increased, other personnel were added to assist in the activities. Eventually, the work centering around a special assistant was organized into a department which was known as a *staff* department, supplementing the *line* organization of the enterprise.

Functional Organization (*Pure*).—As business grows and a company enters the field of competition with mass production, the need for leaders with specialized skills is greatly increased. Frederick W. Taylor, a pioneer in what was known as Scientific Management, developed the *functional* organization. This type of organization undertook to break the job of the old line foreman down into four parts: (1) the preparation of work for the machine, (2) supervision of machining, (3) inspection, and (4) maintenance. Each division of work was under the responsibility and supervision of a functionalized foreman. These foremen were called *gang boss, speed boss, inspector* and *repair boss*.[11]

The gang boss received the orders and directions from the planning department of the company and arranged for the tools and fixtures essential to the job. He supervised the preparation of the work for the machines.

The speed boss then took over and supervised the actual machining operations. It was considered essential that he should be a skilled operator of the machines in order that, if necessary, he might demonstrate and teach the most efficient operating procedures. He was supervisor and teacher of machining operations.

The inspector was responsible for the quality of the work produced. He inspected operations while in process, especially during the first runs on a given job, and also made final inspections on the finished part or product.

The repair boss supervised the maintenance of machines and workplaces. It was his responsibility to see that all machines were kept in proper condition, oiled and cleaned, and that the operators were good housekeepers in maintaining the floor and workbenches in a clean and orderly manner.

The advantages of the functionalized foreman organization was that it permitted greater specialization in the skills and abilities of those responsible for the supervision of work. Each foreman was an expert in the work under his supervision. This naturally gave him prestige which was an asset to him in gaining the cooperation of the workmen and in the establishment of proper working procedures. However, the principal objection to the plan was the fact that the workmen must serve four masters. The clear-cut lines of responsibility and authority of the

[11] TAYLOR, FREDERICK W., "Shop Management," Harper & Brothers, New York, 1911.

line organization were totally lost. This had a tendency to cause friction and dissatisfaction between the workmen and the foremen.

Line and Functional Staff Organization.—The functionalized organization of foremen as advocated by Taylor led to the establishment of functional staff departments whereby many of the advantages of both the line and staff organization and the functional type of organization could be retained. This has come to be known as line and functional staff organization. Through this type of organization, functional staff departments were given responsibility and authority, within company policy established in consultation with the line organization, over specialized activities such as inspection, time study, employment, purchasing, internal transportation, and shipping. Note that these are service functions performed by specialized personnel apart from the line operators who are responsible to their line supervisors.

Line, Functional Staff, and Committee Organization.—In order to facilitate a cooperative relationship within a large industrial enterprise, many companies now add a network of committees to the line and staff organization. Committees are formed for the performance of special duties. These committees may be either "permanent," sometimes referred to as standing committees, or they may be organized to serve a temporary function only.

The Need for Committees.—The test of an administrator is his ability to get others to work with him toward a common goal. Following the exception principle previously referred to, he should be free to devote attention to special problems as they arise and to new developments for the general improvement of operations. However, if he attempts to dictate quickly the solution to a problem or the structure of a new project, he finds that he alone must follow it through to completion. His subordinates and colleagues are far behind him in their thinking. They have no enthusiasm for the plan. Probably the most common faults of the administrator are his impatience and his failure to take time to share the process of planning with those who must work with him in developing and operating the project—those who must translate plans into action.

The importance of enthusiastic, cooperative effort can best be explained through studying the probabilities of a given situation. For example, let us consider the organization of a training program. The director of industrial relations, of the dictatorial variety, would probably call the foremen together and announce that the company is to have a training program. He would set forth the details of the program as he had planned them. He would make it perfectly clear that the plans were to be followed and were not to be questioned. Under these circumstances the foremen and all executives through the company would have a natural tendency to resist the development of the program (1) because of their dislike for the methods of the director and (2) because some of their own pet ideas have not been included. The result of such a situation would undoubtedly be an accumulation of hindrances to the program such as enforced overtime for trainees, unwillingness to transfer trainees from one department to another, and unwillingness on the part of supervisors to take an active part in training on the job.

Neither can the administrator be one who sits idly by and expects others to provide all the ideas and the work required for their development. An idea must be nurtured. It must be given support through the personal assistance of the administrator and other personnel of the organization who can contribute to its development. A suggestion should seldom be quickly answered "yes" or "no." If the answer is "yes" and the individual is told to go ahead, there will almost inevitably be floundering, disagreement, and delay. Usually the idea is only in an embryo stage. It lacks clarity of definition. Its full pattern has not been thought through. If the answer is quickly "no," the one making the suggestion feels that he has not been given adequate consideration and is discouraged from making other suggestions in the future. Instead, he should patiently be assisted in arriving at his own decision that the suggestion lacks sufficient merit to receive adoption. Frequently this can be attained only through permitting the individual to attempt an elaboration of plans with the help and criticism of his associates.

A committee is a tool for the development of ideas and recommendations of policy and procedure. It is a means whereby ideas can be pooled and offered for criticism. It is the strong right arm of a tactful administrator who realizes the importance of getting his people to work together in the solution of their own problems.

Basic Principles of Committee Organization.—Committees, like other phases of organization, should be varied in terms of the needs of a given enterprise. However, there are at least four basic principles to be considered:

1. The organization of a committee should grow out of a need that is recognized by representatives of the departments and the personnel affected.

2. The personnel of a committee should be representative of the function and the personnel concerned and should represent variations in opinion among personnel.

3. Duties, authority, and responsibility must be clearly defined even if, owing to circumstances, they must be subject to change.

4. The organization and operation of a committee should be a cooperative development.

The application of these principles can best be explained through referring again to the problem of organizing a training program. The director of industrial relations, in order to receive counsel and support, would first talk informally with individual representatives of his own department regarding the need for training. He would also consult individual representatives of other departments. He would carefully choose the occasions for these individual consultations, watching for opportunities when the need for training was especially apparent within the individual's own department. He would attempt in every way possible to draw the suggestion from the individual as his own. This may require time and patience but is usually well worth the effort in the long run.

By the very process of the first step the director automatically chooses the personnel of his training committee. However, he will make a mistake if he selects only those who have offered enthusiastic support to the idea. Quite to the contrary, a good committee should include the dissenters if they, by their position, should be represented on the committee. Full recognition must be given to the opinions of all concerned. It may develop that, through the collective thinking and planning by the representatives on the committee, the dissenting minority opinion may lead to the abandonment of the idea. On the other hand, it is more probable that, if the need actually exists, the dissenters on the committee will alter their attitudes and offer at least mild endorsement of a plan in which they have had a part. At least the director can feel that the plan evolved is the result of representative planning and has a reasonable chance of success.

The first meeting of the committee should include a thorough discussion of the responsibility and authority which it is to assume. In all probability the committee will be advisory in nature. It will be expected to make recommendations to the training staff responsible for actual operations. There should also be an understanding regarding the relationship between the director of industrial relations, the director of training if one has been appointed, and the training committee.[12]

[12] The point in the development at which a director of training will be appointed will vary. If there is a person already employed in the company who is thoroughly qualified for the position, it would be well to appoint him as chairman of the committee immediately following the first step. He would then take over the leadership, and the director of industrial relations would gradually fade into the background. If a new man must be brought into the organization, it may be advisable to organize a temporary committee to serve through the beginning stages wherein it is to be decided whether there shall be a training program. A director of training would then be appointed. He, in turn, would form a new and more permanent committee to advise on the actual developments of the program.

Weaknesses of Committees.—The principal criticism of committee operation is that it is slow. But this is a criticism of the democratic process in general. When two or more persons of different backgrounds and ideals are brought together for the consideration of a problem, disagreement will occur. It may be that they merely lack understanding, that they misinterpret each other's statements, or that they lack mutual confidence. Continued relationship under expert leadership should aid in clearing these differences. This is one of the objectives of committee organization. On the other hand, in a committee composed of capable individuals, it is to be expected that real differences will occur that will alter and improve any original suggestion or plan proposed to the committee. It has been said that two heads are better than one, but only if they disagree. A good committee should provide a check on proposals and recommendations coming from executives or from workers, but it should also provide constructive suggestions for improvement of the proposal.

A second criticism of committees is that they are a needless waste of the time of individuals who are neither skilled nor interested in much of the work of the committee. One critic has defined a committee as a group of individuals who meet to *discuss* what they should be *doing.* Others contend that *lines of facilitation* between individuals are more effective and less time-consuming.

Proposed as a third criticism, many companies seem to find it difficult to dissolve committees once they have served their purposes or to confine them to their advisory capacities. This weakness may result from negligence on the part of an executive in the statement of purpose in the original organization of a committee or it may be that the executive is either "weak-kneed" or "committee-mad." In any event, inactive committees or committees continued as operational units are to be recognized in the long run as a weakness and a hindrance to the total organizational structure. If the executive disagrees with the majority recommendation of his advisory committee, he should feel bound by courtesy and by modesty to seek the recommendations of his superiors, perhaps the executive committee of the enterprise or the board of directors.

Recognizing that action by committees is slow, there are times when emergencies call for executive action. The wise executive does not fear or shirk these emergency decisions; at the same time he recognizes them as temporary expedients.

Principal Subdivisions. *The Management Section.*—In a large corporation the stockholders, through their board of directors, select a president who is placed in charge of the formation and supervision of the policies of the corporation. He in turn delegates to the treasurer responsibility for carrying out the financial policies, and to the secretary responsibility for corporate records. He may also appoint assistants to aid him in specific fields of corporate policy. It is common practice for him to appoint a legal counsel and a public relations counsel, depending somewhat on the scope of this work in his particular company. There are occasions when it may be necessary to establish a whole department to serve one of these specialized functions. In such a case the department frequently is organized as a *staff* department reporting directly to the president.

In a small company the president may also serve as general manager, and the secretary and treasurer may assume responsibility for the supervision of actual operations within the company. The treasurer would supervise the accounting and general offices, and the secretary might be assigned to any one of the other divisions depending upon his background of training and experience.

The Operating Section.—Factors causing variations in organizational structure have been discussed in earlier sections. It should be remembered that the central function of organization is coordination and control. It is important, therefore, that the lines of responsibility do not require that too many men report directly to one man. This is accomplished by dividing the company into divisions, frequently five in number: (1) internal finance and office services, (2) sales, (3) industrial relations, (4) manufacturing, and (5) product development. The head of each of these divisions reports to an executive vice-president or general manager as shown in Fig. 5. Each of the separate divisions may be organized into departments according to functions, with their designated heads. Each of these main divisions will be discussed briefly in separate sections.

Internal Finance and Office Services.—The general and personal qualifications of available leaders will have much to do with the organization of this division. If internal finance and office services can be centralized under one division head, usually known as the "controller," better coordination and general efficiency can be attained. However, it may be that the best man available to serve as the head of internal finance is not qualified to serve as an executive over general office functions. On the other hand, a good supervisor of the general office may be very limited in his background of training and experience in finance. In such a case there are two possible alternatives: (1) a third man can be appointed controller if one is available either within the present personnel or outside the company or (2) the general office can be broken down into several departments, each reporting directly to the general manager.

Considering the preferable organization, wherein these two related functions are organized into one division, a still finer segregation of functions may be established.[13]   The function of the general offices includes all general services such as stenographic, duplication, filing, mailing, telephone, and messenger.   The accounting department assumes responsibility for the general and control accounts of the company.   The cost department serves a very specialized function that becomes more important, as a separate unit, as the company increases in size and in the number of variations in the product manufactured.   The work of this department includes the recording and analysis of all costs pertaining to the operation of the company.   The credit department, as its name implies, takes care of credit ratings for customers and the collection of outstanding customers' accounts.   Accounts payable and receivable represent specialized divisions of accounting.   The work of the payroll and tax departments has become especially significant because of the many Federal taxes and deductions that affect employee payroll and company earnings.

The Sales Division.—The sales division is usually divided into at least two departments, such as sales and promotion.   A third department, service, should be added in case the company manufactures a product for which service by the company is required.   For example, a machinery manufacturer would need a service department while a manufacturer of paper boxes would not.

Promotion is considered a specialized function requiring personnel qualified for the handling of all types of advertising and customer relations.   There is, of course, a considerable amount of effective promotion work performed by the salesmen in the field.   The promotion function, therefore, cannot be segregated entirely from the selling function.   This will be discussed more fully in a later section.

Industrial Relations.—The industrial-relations function has had especially significant growth during recent years, both in scope and recognition.   The American labor movement and a growing social consciousness have been strong contributing factors.

The industrial-relations division of a large organization may be divided into five or more departments: (1) employment, (2) labor relations, (3) training, (4) health and safety, and (5) supplementary employee services.   The training function was given special emphasis with the coming of World War II.   It has been found that a good training program not only increases the quantity and quality of production but that it also has many by-products that are substantial aids toward the improvement of general personnel relations.

[13] Note the organization and functions of this division in Figs. 5 and 6.

The labor-relations department has charge of union-contract relations, labor grievances, and relations with Federal labor boards and committees. Although a separate department is established to handle this function, it is exceedingly important that top management keep closely informed of and actively participate in the work of the department.

The health and safety department is responsible for preventive and emergency services to the employed personnel. This involves the maintenance of a clinic and medical staff and also a program of education for the dissemination of information regarding the rules of health and safety. Supplementary employee services include various miscellaneous items that are promoted and maintained by the industrial-relations department as special aids to personnel.

The Manufacturing Division.—The vice-president or works manager in charge of manufacturing is in charge of all departments directly relating to the manufacture of the product. Reporting to him are the heads of various staff departments. This organization will vary greatly among companies owing to abilities of the personnel in charge of the production and staff departments and the "family problems" which may have arisen from the peculiarities of personalities. For example, it might appear logical for the purchasing division to report to the works manager. Yet, in practice, this is probably one of the most frequent points of friction and disagreement. For this reason it is advisable in many cases for the purchasing division to be directly responsible to the executive vice-president. As a general rule, the scope and size of a staff department in a given company will also be significant factors in deciding whether it should come directly under the executive vice-president or the works manager. Detailed discussion of the function and organization of each department of the manufacturing division including production planning, standards, and methods, and plant engineering will be reserved for later chapters.[14]

Product Development.—The place of research and engineering in the organizational structure of a company is determined to a great extent by the nature of the product. For example, in the automobile industry, research and design hold a significant place in the work of the company. The automobile industry is highly competitive. Also, by the very nature of the product, extensive research and experimentation are essential before changes in design can be accepted for production. Compare this to the manufacture of cutlery. In the latter, research is essential but because the product does not have moving parts and mechanical gadgets,

[14] See Figs. 5 and 6 for study of the organization of this division.

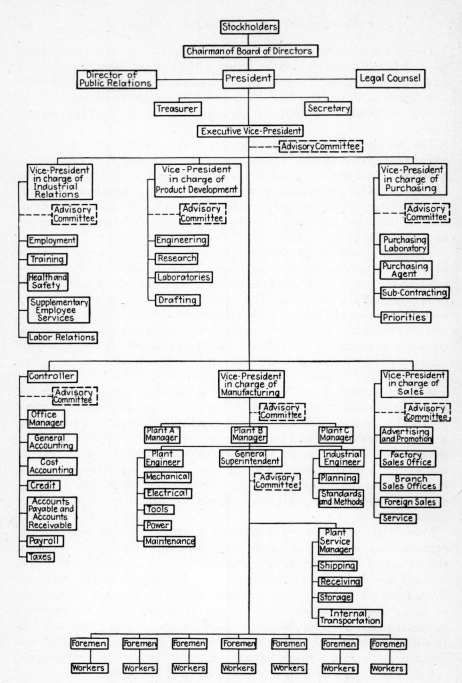

Fig. 5.—Organization chart of a large corporation.

146

the problems of design are more limited and more simple. In this case the function might be assigned to a staff department reporting to the works manager.

In the case of a product requiring a large amount of research and engineering it is advisable that a separate division be established reporting directly to the executive vice-president. The division may be subdivided into departments to fit the needs of the company such as engineering, research, laboratories, and drafting. Each department would serve a designated function, and all would be coordinated in their activities under a vice-president as head of the division.

Manufacturing Organization of a Company of Medium Size.—The manufacturing organization illustrated in Fig. 6 is of a Connecticut company employing a personnel of 1,700. It may be observed that many more functions are placed under the works manager than in the larger company illustrated in Fig. 5. For example, in the smaller company, staff functions such as industrial relations, product development, and purchasing are placed under the works manager while in Fig. 5 they are under the executive vice-president. This is possible without loss in efficiency because of the limitations in scope and volume of each of the functions. In Fig. 5 the works manager has control over three plants, while in Fig. 6 there is only one plant. Actually the positions of works manager and executive vice-president are combined in Fig. 6.

Note that the position of superintendent has been eliminated in the smaller company. In this case each general foreman is responsible for a department of approximately 200 workers. He in turn has foremen under him responsible for smaller groups.

The chart in Fig. 6 incorporates an interesting and useful feature in its listing of the functions within each department. This feature is a valuable aid in bringing about an understanding among the personnel regarding responsibility and authority throughout the plant. The broken lines represent lines of coordination and facilitation as referred to previously in this chapter.

The General Electric Company.—The organization of the General Electric Company is an example of one of America's large industrial enterprises. It also represents a type of organizational division by product which is common among larger industrial enterprises. This company, as it exists today, represents the merger of a number of related organizations over the past sixty years. It would be expected that each company joining the General Electric would bring with it certain interests, patents, and skills for the manufacture of one or more products. Over a period of years these interests and abilities have been interchanged and knit together so that the total enterprise holds four major divisions of interest: [15]

1. *The Apparatus and Supplies Business.*—This is essentially the business of producing and marketing goods that will be used by customers to make money in their own business enterprises. Broadly classified, this division may be termed the company's producer-goods business.

2. *The Merchandise and Appliance Business.*—This is the business of producing and marketing goods to be used by ultimate consumers. Again using a broad classification, this is the consumer-goods business.

3. *The Lamp Business.*—Incandescent lamps, and more recently sodium, mercury-vapor, and fluorescent lamps, are used by all who require artificial light whether it be in industry, service trades, on the highways, or in homes.

4. *The Electronics Business.*—The manufacture and sale of radio transmitters and receivers, television transmitters and receivers, and electronic devices for both radio and other uses are the responsibility of the electronics department.

In addition there are a number of separately incorporated affiliated companies which have been created to accomplish specific tasks that can be performed better with the freedom of action that comes from autonomy than if they were handled as a department of the parent company.

Included in the list are manufacturing companies selling their products largely to the General Electric Company, manufacturing companies with their own sales organizations, selling companies, and special-purpose companies.

Corporate Organization.—As the chart of the corporate organization of the General Electric Company indicates, the company is owned by its stockholders. The common stock is the only corporate security now outstanding. At their annual meeting held at Schenectady the third Tuesday in April, the stockholders elect the Board of Directors.

The *board of directors* exercises the powers conferred upon it by the act incorporating the company. It elects all the executive officers and directs the management of the company's estate.

The chart shown in Fig. 7 indicates all the executive officers and the general responsibility assigned to them by the board of directors.

The *advisory committee* functions in an advisory capacity to the executive committee and the board of directors as a whole. It passes upon questions of internal policy and management. The committee is composed of the chairman of the board, the president as chairman, the executive officers shown in the chart, the president of the International

[15] The following material is adapted by special permission from the General Electric Lecture Series, summer-fall, 1942.

General Electric Company, four honorary vice-presidents, and the secretary of the company as secretary of the committee.

The *general operations committee* is a smaller committee composed of the president and ten vice-presidents, which meets weekly to review the operations of the four departments of the company and to assist the officers in charge of these departments in making decisions pertaining to operations and in making recommendations to be reviewed later by the advisory committee and acted upon by the board of directors.

The *general functions division* has been established for the purpose of providing special services of a company-wide nature and the coordination and promotion of services decentralized into departments within each of the other four main divisions. Note, for example, that each product division has its own distribution and publicity departments. On the other hand, the patent department and the law department of the general functions division are set up to provide specialized services to all divisions.

SUMMARY

When an enterprise grows in size to a point where one man can no longer exercise direct and personalized control over all its activities, he is compelled to delegate authority and responsibility to others. He then assumes a new responsibility for himself, *i.e.*, the management of an organization. His job becomes one of coordination. He must learn that, to obtain the most in the way of initiative and thoroughness from his subordinates, he must be willing to delegate authority. This authority and corresponding responsibility must be specifically outlined. He must learn to exercise patience, realizing that group action is necessarily slower than the independent action of any one man. He must be willing to accept at times what he may consider imperfections in the plans and actions of others.

To facilitate the operations of this organization, consideration must be given to the appropriate grouping of work, both in terms of manufacturing operations and of the abilities and specialized skills of available personnel. The organizational structure will necessarily vary, therefore, in terms of the requirements of each company.

In spite of the many weaknesses inherent in a large organization, there are strengths that are seldom present in the owner-manager type of small enterprise. The large enterprise demands group action if, for no other reason, coordination is to be attained. Personal interests, although always present, are placed more in the background, and factual information becomes the basis of action. Neither the strengths nor the weaknesses of any one man can hold absolute and personal control over the destinies of the large organization. The president of one of America's largest enterprises frequently says to a department head, "I am only the president of this company. As such I am an adviser. If I cannot convince you of the merits of my ideas, don't buy them. And furthermore, if you don't agree with my suggestions and decide to pursue a contrary course of your own, you will be judged only in terms of the resulting efficiency of your department." Industry, large and small, would do well to look carefully at the managerial philosophy of this company president.

CASE PROBLEMS

The K Manufacturing Co.[16]

The K Manufacturing Co., a concern established over thirty years ago, produces a line of precision machine tools and equipment. Up until 1939, the factory manager was in charge of both the factory and pro-

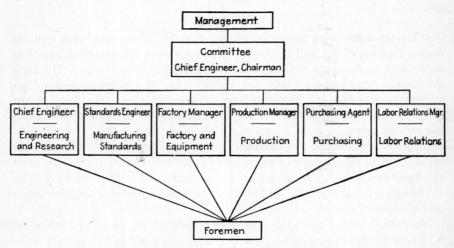

Fig. 8.—Organization chart of the K Manufacturing Company.

duction personnel. Having no assistants, he dealt with all production and factory problems himself by persistent and frequent personal contacts with the foremen under him.

In 1939, when incoming orders began to increase and production schedules were raised, it became rather apparent to the management of the company that the factory manager's organization resulted in over-centralization of effort. As a result, the factory manager was asked to:

[16] Fictitious name.

1. Provide for a more adequate factory organization by setting up a purchasing department, a production control department, and a manufacturing standards department.

2. Increase the production at a certain rate that was specified by the management.

In collaboration with one of the officers of the company, the factory manager proposed an organization somewhat on the functional type. A new man was hired to take over the duties of purchasing agent and to form the purchasing department. The production control function was assigned by the factory manager to a new man who was to be the production manager. Furthermore, the factory manager proposed and received authority to expand the manufacturing facilities so as to increase the production as requested.

After some 6 months of operation under this organization plan, the management became dissatisfied with the progress of the reorganization and the rate of production expansion. The main reasons advanced for the failure were:

1. Because of his previously centralized, one-man control of all factory operations with well-established short cuts and personal contacts, the factory manager found it difficult to adjust himself to the new organization, to delegate the proper authority to his assistants, and to send problems through the proper channels.

2. As a result of an increase in union activity, a factor that had not been present to any great degree previously, the factory manager became greatly burdened with labor problems, and the time that he was forced to devote to these problems seriously distracted his attention from other urgent factory problems.

Therefore, at the end of the 6-month period, the management decided to make another revision in the factory organization in an attempt to improve its functioning. After this second revision, the factory top organization consisted of six department heads who were required to act together as a committee in making all decisions on factory policy. The departments and their heads were as follows:

Engineering and research	Chief engineer
Factory and equipment	Factory manager
Manufacturing standards	Standards engineer
Production	Production manager
Purchasing	Purchasing agent
Labor relations	Labor-relations manager (a new man who was hired for this job)

This organization was of a pure-function and committee type, each department head having authority over all the factory foremen in matters with which his department was concerned. When problems arose which were a matter of policy and which affected more than one department, a committee meeting was held with all members concerned. Each had equal authority and the members assembled made the decisions. The chief engineer, an officer in the company, presided at the meetings, and when the members could not agree, he acted as arbitrator. As soon as one department head overstepped his authority, the matter was brought to the attention of his colleagues as it became the subject of a committee meeting. Once decisions were made, however, it then became the duty of each department head to carry out those phases which affected his branch of the organization.

Preparatory Question

List the strengths and the weaknesses of the reorganization of the K Manufacturing Co.

THE NATIONAL CHEMICAL CORPORATION [17]

The National Chemical Corporation is a large chemical-manufacturing company with ten divisions located in various parts of the United States. Each division has its own distinct line of products.

The main office of the company is in New York City. The principal executive officers are located in the main office. The main office also maintains staff departments in design and development, materials procurement and control, production control, sales, quality control, methods, finance, cost control, and personnel. One or more representatives of each of the staff departments is located in each of the divisions of the company and is responsible directly to the home office. Market surveys, product designs, specifications, schedules, etc., are submitted by the home-office staff departments to the executive committee for approval. These form the bases for the orders which are issued to the division managers.

If a division manager disagrees with policy, specification, or schedule, he may discuss his disagreement with the appropriate staff representative assigned to his plant and then, if he desires, may carry his complaint to the vice-president of manufacturing, to whom he reports. Since the division managers are not members of the executive committee, their first official notification of plans comes with the production orders. However, new developments are discussed in general with division managers at periodic meetings with the vice-president. Staff representatives

[17] Fictitious name.

may also seek any assistance from within the division plants that may be helpful to developments.

Friction has developed between the staff representatives of the home office and the people of the division plants. The staff representatives are not placed in the category of "one of the boys." Plant personnel feel that these home-office "fair-haired representatives" are merely theorists who have no knowledge and appreciation of the know-how of the plant. Furthermore, plant personnel is not inclined to share this know-how with the representatives.

The home-office methods department, after what was considered to be a thorough analysis, recommended a methods change in one of the divisions that would result in considerable savings in production hours. The recommendation was approved by the executive committee, piece rates on the job were reset, and orders issued. No disagreements were received from the division manager, although none were solicited.

After two months of operation under the new method, it was discovered that workers on the job were earning 90 per cent more than under the old method. The methods department had anticipated the reduction in rate for the new method would result in earnings to the worker equal to earnings under the old method.

Upon discovering this error in calculations, the methods department recommended a further reduction in rate that would bring worker earnings back to the original level. The workers, however, had grown accustomed to this increase in earnings and wished to retain it, claiming that the increased earnings were due to their own efforts over and above the expectations of management at the time of the methods change. The grievance was carried to the union committee and ultimately resulted in a strike.

Preparatory Questions

1. Who was responsible for the error and the resulting strike?
2. What changes in organization and in responsibility and authority would you recommend for the future avoidance of similar situations?

CHAPTER VII

DEVELOPING THE PRODUCT—
RESEARCH AND ENGINEERING

Production has been defined in an earlier chapter as the transformation of raw materials by factory methods into things wanted by society. This definition implies that an industrial enterprise engaged in production supplies society with a service through the manufacture and distribution of its products. For that matter, one of the justifications for the existence of an industrial enterprise under our competitive economic system lies in the ability of that enterprise to make and sell form utility, *i.e.*, a product or range of products, and to do so at a profit. It follows, therefore, that one of the prime considerations in the organization and continuous operation of an industrial enterprise is the development of products that can be made and sold at a profit.

An enterprise has the alternative of supplying society with an entirely new service by pioneering a new and original product, or of attempting to compete with another enterprise in supplying society with an existing type of service in the form of a competing product. Where products are competing, they may be similar in design or manufacture providing patent regulations permit, or one product may depart radically in design and manufacture from the other and merely compete with it in service rendered. Perhaps this can be better explained by an example. Some time ago Polaroid, the first really practical material for polarizing light to be produced commercially, was developed primarily to eliminate the glare from oncoming automobile headlamps without appreciably reducing night vision. As such it attempted to provide an entirely new service. Before long, however, it was found that Polaroid could be used in sun glasses and, when thus used, it went into direct competition with sun glasses fashioned from smoked or colored glass. Thus Polaroid began to render a competing service in the form of a product that was similar in design and manufacture. A third use to which Polaroid was subsequently put was in the field of photoelasticity in instruments for determining stresses and strains. When a piece of transparent plastic is bent or strained and examined under polarized light, bright bands of color appear where stresses are present. The location and number of these color bands give an accurate picture of internal stresses. By this method the design of highly stressed parts such as automotive brake pedals and front-spring control arms can be tested by viewing plastic replicas under polarized light. Where Polaroid is thus used, it competes in service with other stress- and strain-measuring mechanisms, but the application is entirely different as regards design and manufacture.

Naturally when an enterprise attempts the manufacture and sale of a competing product, the service supplied in terms of quality, price, and availability must be comparable or superior to that supplied by a competing enterprise. Otherwise the concern will find little demand for its product. If your mousetrap is not equal to or better than those currently in service, the world is not interested in beating a path to your door.

Once a successful product or range of products is established, the enterprise must then endeavor to keep itself abreast or ahead of the field by the constant improvement of its products. In this rapidly changing world, the demand for products is constantly changing with it. Unlike individuals who inevitably become old and die, industrial enterprises may through the continual development of new products find a sort of "fountain of youth" by which they can retain their youthful vigor and vitality. Many of the "ghost" plants and towns that were to be seen in some sections of the United States in the late twenties and thirties were silent monuments to a type of management that was not awake to the necessity for the continual development of new products.

Until shortly after the turn of the century, little thought was given by industry to organized product development. Most new products resulted from the activities of free-lance inventors like Edison, Bell, and Wright. These inventors worked alone or in small independent groups, relied financially upon their own capital or that of friends interested in their projects, and employed cut-and-try methods in their laboratories, which more often than not were located in their kitchens or in near-by barns. Relatively few ever achieved prominence; in fact, many of them were quacks or were ill-advised individuals who squandered their time and money in the search for impossible devices such as the traditional perpetual-motion machine. Very few of those who did contribute worth-while discoveries ever realized any wealth from them. Free-lance inventors did not concern themselves with yearly and seasonal style changes of products, and in general the progress of products remained static until the same or another free-lance inventor hit upon a new and better basic idea.

In the early 1900's, however, the increasing complexity of manufactured products and processes together with the speeding up of the American way of life through faster transportation and communication facilities left the free-lance inventor unable to cope with the more advanced state of the technical arts. Whereas, previously, new materials, products, and processes had sprung primarily from practical men and from curious amateurs of an inventive turn of mind working in their own shops, new developments began to come mainly from the organized efforts of trained scientists and engineers engaged cooperatively in specific fields of investigation. Although it is true that lone inventors are still with us, and we hope they always will be, nevertheless their basic inventions usually require the organized effort of a well-equipped research laboratory to test, modify, and extend their ideas before products supplying society with useful services and capable of being manufactured may result. In the past 40-odd years, organized industrial research through the coordination and specialization as well as the intensification of inventive effort has brought about a rate of industrial development previously unequaled. Today organized industrial research stands unchallenged as our greatest medium for achieving better living through new methods and new products.

CONSIDERATIONS IN PRODUCT DEVELOPMENT

Before discussing the matter of industrial research, however, we should understand certain basic considerations that are influential in an appraisal as to whether or not a specific project in the field of product development is worth while. These considerations usually include [1]

A. The possibility of consumer acceptance.

B. The relationship between costs of development and manufacture and the returns to be derived therefrom.

C. The utilization of existing manufacturing and distributing facilities.

D. The effect of the product upon other products in the line offered by the enterprise.

E. The possibility of patent control as a protection against competition.

F. The utilization of by-products or waste.

Consumer Acceptance.—It should be readily apparent that the possibility of selling a product can result only from an acceptance of the product by consumers. What, then, does the consumer look for in accepting or rejecting a product? Usually the consumer's decision depends upon the factors of

1. Appearance: Is it pleasing or attractive to the eye?
2. Convenience: Can it be used readily?
3. Usefulness: Does it meet a need?

[1] Additional considerations for analyzing the product marketwise and relating the product to the enterprise have been advanced in Chap. IV from the standpoint of industrial forecasting and the calculation of business risks.

4. Durability: Will it stand up under use?

5. Cost of operation: Is it inexpensive to use and keep in good order?

6. Purchase price: How does it compare competitively and in terms of needs met?

7. Diversity of types and sizes from which to choose: Does the variety meet a specific preference?

Frequently consumers base their decision to buy more on appearance than on the other considerations, and producers endeavoring to cater to that desire stress it in their product designs to the detriment of the other factors. Industrial designers have long been wrestling with the problem of *form design* vs. *functional design,* of appearance vs. utility, for the best design from the standpoint of appearance is not always the best as regards performance. Perhaps it is a valid complaint against the automotive industry that it has catered to form design in the development of the automobile to the detriment of functional design. The excessive over-all length of the modern car, the minimum clearance between road and running gear, the excessive use of sheet metal making maintenance difficult, the glittering dashboards with illegible instruments—all of these are indicative of the sacrifices that designers have made in convenience, usefulness, and cost of operation simply for the sake of appearance.

In general, the producer must weigh carefully the relative importance of each of the above consumer-acceptance factors as they bear on the particular product under consideration. Only by achieving a proper relationship or balance between these factors can an intelligent decision be made.

Costs of Development and Manufacture.—Usually before undertaking to develop a particular product, the management of the enterprise must be able to envisage a return on the product that is commensurate with the cost of development. It goes without saying that this requires not only a forecast of the market for the product but also some knowledge of the time, effort, and equipment required in its development. Also important is the estimated cost of manufacturing the product. A product that is developed merely to the point of performing a service is of little practical use unless it can be reproduced commercially. Hence the product design must be carried to a stage where it can be labeled "production design," *i.e.,* a design that can be manufactured in the quantity desired and at a cost in line with the price obtainable for the product.

Utilization of Existing Manufacturing and Distributing Facilities. A live management is always on the alert for new products that will round out the line of goods sold, articles that may be produced or sold during the dull seasons or that will utilize existing equipment not being used to capacity.   Products falling into any of the foregoing categories are known as "complementary" products.   Products may be complementary as regards their production or distribution, or both.   The Gillette Safety Razor Company added the manufacture of shaving cream to its line of razors and razor blades because the cream could be distributed through the same sales organization and to the same distribution outlets, even though the cream required different techniques and equipment in its manufacture.   One of the quick-freezing processes now widely used in preserving foods was originally developed as a better method of freezing fish.   However, it was soon discovered that the same preparation and freezing equipment could be used during the off seasons for the freezing of fruits, vegetables, and meats, and what is more, these products could be marketed through the same distribution channels and in the same storage equipment used for fish.

Any analysis of the effect of a new product on the utilization of manufacturing facilities must consider, first of all, the question of the plant buildings and manufacturing equipment.   Are these adequate or can they be adapted to the manufacture of the proposed product?   Secondly, man power possessing the required skills or attributes for learning those skills must be available.   Finally, the supply of materials of the kind necessary to manufacture the proposed product must be adequate.   In the field of distribution, analyses should be made to discover whether or not the proper marketing organization, the necessary outlets, and the required sales, promotion, and advertising personnel are available.

Effect on Other Products in the Line.—The management of an enterprise usually has to consider the effect of proposed products on its established products.   Sometimes the addition of a new article tends to fill out the line of products; othertimes the new product competes directly with another product.

As the recession of 1949 made itself felt in the form of a buyers' strike against high prices, manufacturers of household appliances (particularly washing machines and vacuum cleaners), automobiles, and other durable goods introduced lower priced "competitive" models devoid of some of the frills and gadgets found on their more expensive deluxe editions. In most cases, the cheaper model further dehydrated the already dry market for its costlier counterpart.   But in each case the action was certainly taken with full realization of the consequences and recognized as the only way to bolster over-all sales volume.   Thus, the question as to whether the addition of a new product is beneficial or detrimental to the established line of products is one that must be answered on the merits of each specific case.

Patent Control.—Before a decision is made to embark upon an expensive development program, the degree of protection obtainable from patents should be thoroughly explored. A company that is unable thus to protect itself against competition may find that it has lost in part, at least, the value of its pioneering efforts. Under the present-day American patent system,[2] patents are issued on basic processes, parts of processes, new products and materials, equipment, techniques, catalysts, and improvements on any of the foregoing. The duration of a patent is 17 years from the date of its grant, after which time the invention passes into the public domain. In actual practice, however, the patent grant has been used — or misused—by a few corporations and corporate combines to perpetuate their control over basic inventions as well as to further monopolies, dictate prices, and regulate production.

Under existing patent regulations, this perpetuation of control may be accomplished in any of four possible ways. First, there is the simple and usually very reputable practice of obtaining successive improvement patents on a basic invention. Such improvement patents, however, sometimes lose their respectability when they are obtained for the obvious purpose of keeping a basic article on which the patent is about to expire from being thrown on the open market.

The second practice, the so-called "fencing-off device," is that by which the holder of a basic patent surrounds his grant with patents on every conceivable combination of elements, processes, machines, and products, thus heading off competing products developed by different means.

The third use sometimes made of patents is the "fencing-in device." This is just the reverse of the second practice in that a powerful enterprise sometimes is able to secure patents on every possible combination of elements surrounding a basic patent secured by another inventor or company. Thus is the competitor's invention blocked off from further development.

Finally, there is the infringement suit. Nominally, this is purely a legal device for preventing someone from stealing a patented invention. However, it can be used as a controlling device as well. For instance, a competitor desiring to delay or prevent the use of a new discovery may challenge it with or without a clear basis for an infringement suit. So costly and long drawn out is such litigation that a financially strong con-

[2] The U.S. Constitution gave Congress the "power to promote the progress of science and useful arts." Revised Statute 4886 provides that a patent may be obtained by "any person who has invented or discovered any new and useful art, machine, manufacture, or composition of matter, or any new and useful improvements thereof."

cern may use it as a threat to force into submission a legally right but financially weak competitor.

It is important that the above ramifications of the patent system and their relation to the development program under consideration be carefully studied. Of course, it is sometimes possible for progressive organizations unable to gain patent protection to keep one or more jumps ahead of their competition by improving their products constantly or by introducing new products at frequent intervals. Furthermore, an efficient monopolistic enterprise can often effectively discourage competition simply by manufacturing and marketing its products very cheaply.

By-products or Waste.—A product-development program designed to find ways and means of utilizing by-products or waste frequently is very worth while. Consider, for example, the leather belting company which found that it could utilize waste leather pieces by developing, as by-products, shoe soles, dog collars, skate straps, and leather washers. Or consider the manufacturer of materials-handling equipment who utilizes his short odds and ends of stock and small scrap pieces of steel plate in the manufacture of small hand trucks, dollies, and carboy tippers. Both these concerns have found that money consumed in the development of such by-products is well spent.

PRODUCT DEVELOPMENT THROUGH ORGANIZED RESEARCH

Research, broadly defined, is the systematic search for new knowledge. More specifically, research may refer to investigation for its own sake— *pure research,* or it may refer to investigation for a definite industrial purpose—*applied research.* Pure research, sometimes called "fundamental research," is the type that deals in the basic sciences. General Motors Research Laboratories for years have been endeavoring to find out why the grass is green. As Charles F. Kettering, head of the laboratories has said, "If plants did not know how to catch sunlight and preserve it for us, we would be in a devil of a hole so far as food, clothing, and fuel are concerned. If we could find out how they do it, it would help us to keep healthier and live longer." [3] Fundamental investigations are made principally for the sake of knowledge itself. The directions in which such investigations are to be pursued frequently are not prescribed in advance, for the avenues of study are determined as the investigations proceed and as promising leads are uncovered.

Applied research, on the other hand, is usually directed principally at some specific industrial problem. It specializes in adapting the basic sciences to industrial materials, products, and processes. Under this category are included research studies directed toward the improvement

[3] *The New York Times,* Aug. 29, 1943, magazine section, p. 12.

of existing industrial techniques. True it is that applied research frequently is a direct result of pure research. Subsidiaries of the Union Carbide and Carbon Corporation have made mass-production industries out of the gases, carbides, batteries, and plastics that are the applied results of some of their pure research discoveries in carbon and oxygen. The DuPont Laboratory's fundamental experiments with coal, air, and water led to the development of a plastic now known the world over as Nylon. Then by an applied study of the substance, DuPont developed applications and uses for it and, what is more important, manufacturing processes whereby it could be made commercially into rope, brush bristles, stockings, and numerous other items.

The primary objective of any industrial-research program is naturally enough the search for new knowledge. New ideas, new materials, parts, and products, improvements in present products, better methods of production, new uses for new and old products alike—these all result from the acquisition of new knowledge.

Fields for Investigation.—Applied research, the type with which we shall be primarily concerned from this point forward, may be directed toward any of the following fields: (1) marketing, (2) materials, (3) products, (4) processes.

1. *Marketing.*—Marketing research, or market forecasting as it is sometimes called, was discussed in detail in Chap. IV; hence we shall consider it rather briefly at this point, primarily for the purpose of ascertaining how it fits into an industrial-research program.

The testing or, more exactly, the pretesting of consumer acceptance, which is a major function of marketing research, has become a vital part of industrial research primarily because of the size of modern industrial enterprises. In years long past, when practically all goods were produced in one-man shops, the heads of such enterprises through intimate contact with the customer were able to understand his wants, desires, and tastes. However, in the larger modern institutions with their specialized internal departments and external selling organizations, the producer is widely separated from the consumer, and it becomes difficult for him to keep himself abreast of customer requirements. The situation has been likened to a broken circular chain in which marketing research supplies the missing link (see Fig. 9).

Marketing research is vital to an industrial-research program not only through its pretesting of the consumer acceptance of a proposed product but also because it is a source of new ideas for development. The observations of the sales organization, executives, and plant employees often serve as an informal medium for gathering data on consumer needs that may be worth investigating. However, marketing research of the type carried on for years by the General Motors Customer Research Staff is a much more thorough and systematized method of search for new ideas. This technique makes use of repeated consumer surveys, usually in the form of mail questionnaires designed to sample consumer needs

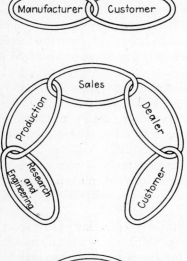

Relationship which existed between manufacturer and customer under conditions of the one-man shop.

In the large modern business institutions, the producer has become separated from the customer, and the intimate relationship no longer exists.

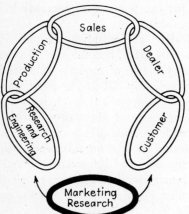

Marketing research supplies the missing link to the broken chain and thus rejoins the producer and customer.

FIG. 9.—The broken chain of modern industry.

and desires to the end that the manufacturer may direct his development program toward meeting these needs (see Fig. 10).

2. *Materials.*—The search for materials is linked with the development of products as the discovery of new materials frequently leads to new

product applications. For example, the sintered metallic substances formed by the process of powder metallurgy have in recent years found ever-increasing application in industrial products. This process is essentially one that with the aid of pressure and heat converts metallic powders into finished physical shapes without melting, forging, rolling, extrud-

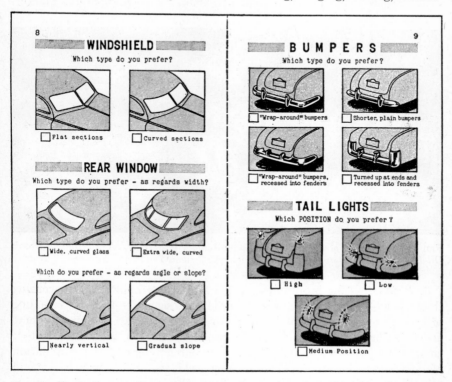

Fig. 10.—Typical pages of a marketing-research questionnaire as issued by the General Motors Customer Research Staff to gather new ideas for development and improvement. (*From "Your Car as You Would Build It," Customer Research Staff, General Motors Corporation, Detroit, Mich.*)

ing, or machining. By this means, hard metals and alloys, such as those of tungsten, that cannot be worked into usable forms by any other method can be put to worth-while industrial usage as in cemented-carbide cutting tools and in the wearing surfaces of inspection gages. Also by this process of powder metallurgy, the softer metals can be worked quickly and economically into small machine parts. Self-lubricating sleeve bearings and ball-bearing retainers, long-wearing oil-pump gears for automobile engines, oil-injector nozzles for Diesel engines, fine wire-mesh filter screens, friction faces for brakes and clutches, self-oiling automobile door striker plates—these are but a few of the many applications toward which metal-powder materials have been directed. This type of research and development has played a big part in recent years as plastics, aluminum and magnesium alloys, synthetic-rubber substances, and other new materials became available in quantity and were adapted to existing products as well as to new products then coming on the market.

Fig. 11.—A camera study in powder metallurgy. (*Courtesy of the Bound Brook Oil-Less Bearing Company, Bound Brook, N. J., and Industrial Equipment News.*)

3. *Product.*—The importance of the search for knowledge concerning the product—otherwise known as "product research"—to the continuing prosperity of the enterprise has already been stressed. In general, there are two classifications into which product research may be divided: *creation* and *improvement.* Creative research refers to the stimulation of new ideas, the development of new products, and new and original uses for existing products. It includes the adaptations of extensive research principles to intensive product applications. Improvement research, on the other hand, refers mainly to the betterment of existing products, a furtherance of their convenience and utility, and an enhancement of their appearance, packaging, and general sales appeal. Allied with these activities are studies to open up new possibilities of by-product utilization. A well-rounded research program includes activities for both creation and improvement.

4. *Processes.*—Research pertaining to industrial processes is usually directed toward the development of methods of manufacture, tools, and equipment, as well as handling devices that tend to increase productivity. The replacement of human skill and heavy labor by mechanical devices to better the operating efficiency, and the development of methods and

mechanisms for increasing the safety of processes are both fertile fields for study.

The decision as to alternative processes is one that is usually vested with the research staff in cooperation with representatives from the industrial- and plant-engineering,[4] production, and cost departments. The part played by the research department in this regard is usually to experiment with available processes, techniques, and equipment and to suggest and try out new ideas. A careful analysis of the relative merits of each process would be made by the research department in cooperation with the other departments concerned to determine which is the best for the product under consideration. Once the basic process has been named, the exact operations and details of the process may be determined by the same cooperative groups.

Important to the manufacture of a product is the development of processes that are adequate to produce it in the quantity and quality desired. Frequently a product can be made on a minute scale in a research laboratory, whereas the manufacture of that product on a large scale, utilizing the laboratory process, may be quite impracticable. It is then the function of process research to develop methods of manufacturing it on the scale desired. Similarly, certain standards of quality may be set up for the product which may not be easily adhered to in large-scale production. Here again, research study is required to develop methods of maintaining quality in production manufacture.

The responsibility for *pilot plants* is frequently vested in the research staff as an adjunct to the process-research program. A pilot plant is essentially a miniature manufacturing plant used to carry the manufacture of the product from the test-tube stage to the small-lot stage and designed to iron out the manufacturing problems before manufacture of the product is attempted on a large scale. The research staff prescribes the process to be attempted in the pilot plant as well as the equipment required. Once the pilot plant is in operation, this staff diagnoses and attempts to rectify any manufacturing difficulties that develop. When the process is perfected, it is ready for production on a large scale and is then turned over to the plant engineers and production men. The pilot-plant technique is commonly used in the chemical industries and is a relatively simple and inexpensive medium for perfecting any process.

Types of External Research Organizations.—Industrial research is performed by a number of external agencies as well as by internal organizations set up within the industrial enterprise. *Government agencies*

---

[4] The work of the industrial- and plant-engineering departments is discussed in Chaps. XVII and XVIII, respectively.

perform extensive work of a research nature covering today all kinds of research (fundamental, applied, commercial, statistical) in many fields. While almost every department and agency of the Federal government is engaged in some research, the range may be indicated by a few examples. The Agricultural Research Administration engages in extensive research in the whole field of foods and food materials, agricultural and industrial chemistry, home economics, and agricultural engineering. The National Advisory Committee for Aeronautics for many years has engaged in fundamental research in the aeronautical sciences. The National Research Council together with its parent organization, the National Academy of Sciences, for a long time has conducted scientific research on specific subjects at the request of the various government departments. The Research and Development Board established under the National Security Act of 1947 is engaged in development work for national security. The Atomic Energy Commission has set up divisions for exploring raw materials and medicine in the atomic field. The Bureau of Mines engages in research, investigation, and development of mining and mineral products. Of course, with the exception of certain projects over which military secrecy prevails, the results of government research studies are available to all industries and enterprises.

Trade associations are frequently instrumental in carrying on research projects that do not affect the relative competitive position of the member companies. An association may act simply as a clearinghouse for the exchange of technical information, as has the Manufacturers Aircraft Association acting in its capacity of licensing agent, royalty collector, and arbitrator for all new patentable developments of member companies. Or the association may go further and set up committees for carrying on market research or product research of a nature that will benefit the industry. *Special industrial groups* within an industry frequently gather to further the development of projects of mutual interest. For example, some years ago, five major airlines collaborated in drawing up specifications for a new and what was then a huge transport plane. The specifications were then turned over to the Douglas Aircraft Company which designed and constructed the plane, the cost of the entire project being financed by the airlines as a group. The advantage of such an arrangement is that much duplication of effort and development expense is eliminated. Or again, different enterprises within the metals industry have cooperated in studies of corrosion, each enterprise adapting the findings to its particular product or application. Still other groups gather to make use of certain technical facilities which may be owned collectively or individually by one or more of the cooperating companies.

Commercial laboratories specializing in industrial-research projects are frequently employed by manufacturing enterprises for problems requiring certain equipment, technical knowledge, or ability not possessed by the particular enterprise, where the project is in a field in which the company has had no previous experience, where it wishes to take advantage of the "state of the arts," or where time is of the essence and the results are required so promptly as not to permit the enterprise to conduct its own investigation. The firm of A. D. Little, Inc., of Cambridge, Mass., is one of the best known of the commercial laboratories. This firm, which once made a "silk" purse out of a sow's ear just to prove that it could be done, has in recent years engaged in such widely diversified activities as the development of a synthetic shellac that in several respects is better than the original, the synthesizing of spices from chemical substances, and "chemical" analyses of smells according to their basic components.

Educational institutions in recent years have entered the commercial research field, and it is now considered ethical for an educational institution to do secret research for a specific concern providing that research is of a sporadic nature, cannot be performed by private laboratories, and makes use of unique facilities not available elsewhere. Such institutions should not attempt to compete with commercial laboratories and should limit the scope of their projects primarily to adaptations of extensive or pure research. The wind tunnel at the Massachusetts Institute of Technology for studying the behavior of new aerodynamic designs and the differential analyzer at the same institution for the solution of complicated calculus equations are random examples of the type of unique facilities which educational institutions frequently make available to industrial concerns. So also has the University of Michigan's School of Engineering maintained an open door to the Detroit automotive industry in the solution of its technical problems.

Administration of Industrial Research within the Enterprise.— Research conducted within the enterprise may be of two types: (1) that which originates with the suggestions and ideas of employees or with the unsolicited inventions of itinerant inventors and (2) that which is undertaken entirely within the functionalized research department. Both avenues of research are vital to the progress of the enterprise. The company that refuses to set up a formal research department and instead relies solely on the decentralized development of ideas is almost sure to find that its research has degenerated into a hit-or-miss procedure. Similarly, the enterprise that closes its eyes to the suggestions of its employees just does not see the woods for the trees.

The ideas of employees and others may be fostered through the use of a "suggestion box"[5] or through the establishment of a standard procedure for carefully considering each idea or invention offered. Also an arrangement should be made for the further development, remuneration, and possible patenting and licensing of acceptable discoveries. The Thompson Products Company, for example, has employed a "director of screwballs" to interview inventors, pass on ideas that may benefit the business, aid the inventor in gaining a patent, and arrange the royalty contract between the inventor and the company. A number of companies have employees' patent remuneration plans designed to assist employees with their patentable ideas. Under such plans the patent department aids the employee-inventor in making models and drawings, applies for the patent in his name with the company as assignee, negotiates licensing, and collects any royalty derived therefrom. Furthermore, employees are then given an equitable share in the income derived from their inventions. Such programs as these effectively encourage employees to bring forth suggestions of value to the concern.

The fact that there is also a centralized research department within the enterprise does not remove from the foremen and line executives the entire burden of development activities. It is still the duty of the supervisory force to search for and promote improvements within the area of its jurisdiction. Also, it is good practice for the research department to cooperate with the foremen by seeking their advice, if possible, and by showing them research projects already under investigation together with the benefits to be derived therefrom. This is a simple device for eliminating what may be a natural suspicion on the part of the foreman of that seemingly mysterious and unworldly creation known as the "research department."

The position of the research department in the organizational structure of a company has been discussed in Chap. VI. The administration of the research department may be carried on by a director of research or by a research policy committee. In the former case, the director originates all policies for the research department, subject, of course, to the approval of his immediate superior. In the latter case, the research policy committee, composed usually of representatives from the research, production, sales, and finance departments, meets to determine research policy and to pass on suggested activities. The director of research then carries out the decisions thus made. For example, in a well-known paper-products company, a "research activities committee" groups together representatives from the sales, development, and production departments under the direction of the chairman, who is vice-president in charge of research. The committee meets monthly to re-

[5] See Chap. XVII, p. 420.

view the progress of new developments and to approve budgetary allotments for future work.

The actual research investigations are the province of the research department, but even these activities would be subject to the advice and cooperation of the engineering, production, cost, and sales departments. Where the project concerns a new product, that product must be more than merely designed—it must be manufactured and sold with the entire transaction consummated at a profit to the enterprise. Hence the need for intelligent coordination of these departments in truly effective research.

Internal Organization of the Research Department.—In a small enterprise or where the research department itself is not large, the internal organization of the department is simply a matter of selecting a director of research to head up the group of laboratory technicians and assistants. Where the department is large, however, it becomes necessary to organize the research personnel into effective working units. The three common ways of subdividing the research department are: (1) by manufacturing departments or plant units, (2) in terms of specific purposes, and (3) in terms of research techniques.

1. Where research effort is segregated by departments or plants, each manufacturing unit has its own research laboratory and personnel whose activities are directly or indirectly under the control of some central research executive. Each research unit is concerned with problems and projects pertaining to the particular manufacturing unit with which it is affiliated. The disadvantages of this type of segregation are that (*a*) it tends to break down collaboration between the research units, (*b*) the men keep their ideas and problems wholly within their branch of the department, and (*c*) there is considerable duplication of men, equipment, and effort with a resulting waste of money when projects are conducted along parallel lines.

2. Research divided in terms of specific purposes refers to the segregation of effort in terms of products, specific problems, or processes. Regardless of the exact nature of this subdivision, much of the duplication of effort described above is eliminated, since one branch of the research department works for the common good of all manufacturing divisions. For example, one research unit may be concerned with the development and control of raw materials, another with new products, while a third branch of the department might be engaged in an investigation to locate the source of trouble connected with a particular manufacturing operation. A group of men assigned to solve a certain problem usually disseminate the knowledge thus gained to all manufacturing divisions concerned with the problem. However, the danger of this method

is that men tend to become too closely restricted to the assigned problem. Frequently they fail to follow leads developed as by-products of their assigned investigations simply because such leads happen not to be a part of their assignment.

3. The third possibility, of subdividing research into the techniques involved, is perhaps the most natural and wisest segregation. It is based on a specialization of skills. A problem of how to reclaim the minute metallic particles from grinding sludge might be a problem of physics, one of metallurgy, or one of chemistry. Hence it might be turned over successively or simultaneously to the physicists, metallurgists, and chemists, each a specialist group within the research department and each trying to arrive at the best possible solution within its technical field or in collaboration with other fields. As may be expected, close collaboration of the groups is very necessary for complete harmony and effectiveness of the department.

In large companies, a combination of all these groupings is employed. For example, General Motors has divided its research according to its manufacturing divisions, each unit having its own research organization for its specific product and manufacturing problems; at the same time, the parent corporation maintains the General Motors Research Laboratories, a separate division which has devoted its attention to specific investigations such as antiknock fuels, vibration, and springing. The results of such investigations as these are made available by the laboratories to the respective manufacturing divisions concerned. Or again, a large shoe-machinery factory directs its research effort primarily according to purpose, but when the regular research men encounter a phase of their study that employs a specialized technique, as, for example, a stress-analysis problem in the design of a machine, this study is turned over to a specialist who is trained in that particular field of work. This procedure saves the general-purpose research men from a great deal of work poring over textbooks to brush up on a specialized field with which they may not be too familiar.

Biography of a Research Project.—The basic idea for a research project may originate in the sales department, the production or manufacturing departments, or in the research department, depending upon whether the idea pertains to a product or to manufacturing processes, or is the result or by-product of some previous research investigation. Of course, any individual in the company may suggest some avenue of study. For example, the president of one of the large food organizations once asked his research director to try to find him "something a dog likes as well as a cat likes catnip." But it is usually the duty of the research department to maintain a close relationship with the problems

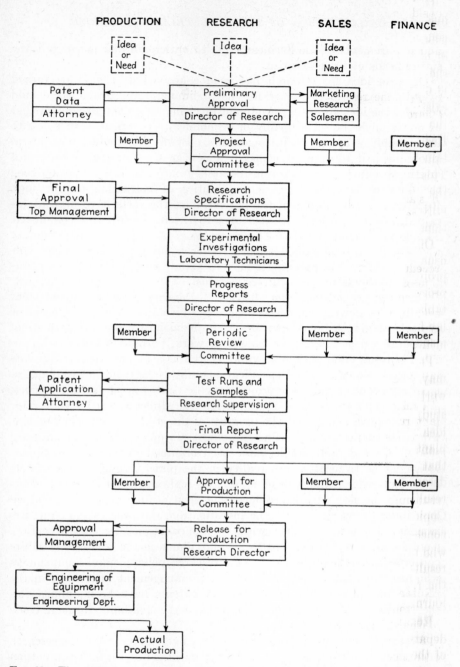

PRODUCTION　　　RESEARCH　　　SALES　　　FINANCE

Idea or Need — Idea — Idea or Need

Patent Data / Attorney ← Preliminary Approval / Director of Research → Marketing Research / Salesmen

Member → Project Approval / Committee ← Member　　Member

Final Approval / Top Management ← Research Specifications / Director of Research

Experimental Investigations / Laboratory Technicians

Progress Reports / Director of Research

Member → Periodic Review / Committee ← Member　　Member

Patent Application / Attorney ← Test Runs and Samples / Research Supervision

Final Report / Director of Research

Member → Approval for Production / Committee ← Member　　Member

Approval / Management → Release for Production / Research Director

Engineering of Equipment / Engineering Dept.

Actual Production

Fig. 12.—The path of a typical research project from its inception to its incorporation into production.

and requirements of the business so as to anticipate and investigate the future needs of the enterprise.

Once an idea for research has been conceived, it should be turned over to the research director for his preliminary approval. He should consider the idea from the standpoint of company policy, decide whether or not it might be scientifically or economically practical, and look into the possibility of patent infringements. Before his tentative approval is obtained, if the project concerns a new product or a revision of an existing product, the marketing-research group should then be assigned the duty of investigating the possibilities of marketing the product. Regardless of the nature of the project, once the facts have been ascertained, it should then be turned over to the research-policy committee. This group should consider the project from all points of view, balance the benefits to be obtained against the costs involved, and, if the committee grants final approval, it may formulate certain general specifications as to the nature of the investigations.

Once the project has been authorized, the director of the department usually lays down precise specifications which include the scope of the project, its aim, a breakdown of the problem into its parts, methods of procedure, an assignment of phases of work, perhaps a tentative timetable of results and periodic review, as well as a budget of financial outlay for the project. These specifications may be then subject to management review after which the project may be started in its proper sequence.

Periodically during the investigation the director or the committee may be required to review the progress of the study, decide whether it is worth continuing, and redefine the objectives or direction for continued study. Once definite results have been obtained in the laboratory, the idea may be translated into reality in the plant through test or pilot-plant runs which finally lead up to full-scale operations. Refinements that may be needed are provided and then a final report is prepared describing the work done in the investigation, the progress and findings resulting from it, together with recommendations for future action. Copies of this report are sent to all individuals in the company who are concerned with the project and to the research-policy committee members who may then meet to recommend to top management the release of the results for production purposes. After patents have been applied for, the results of the investigation may be made available through trade journals, technical papers, etc.

Research Operating Procedures.—The over-all budget of the research department may be based on a given percentage of sales, a summation of the project cost estimates, a lump sum subject to periodic review, or on the probable financial returns. Where the appropriations are based on sales, research must then become lean in depression years—a time when the need for research is actually most acute. Where the project costs are totaled, the tendency is to hold down the research department to that amount so that it is unable to take advantage of new ideas as they develop. The lump-sum method does not take into consideration any allocation to projects and gives the research director excessive control and responsibility over expenditures. Estimates of financial returns from a specific project are difficult to forecast accurately, and the organization that follows this procedure is apt to leave stones unturned in its search for knowledge. Perhaps the best procedure for budgeting the research department is to utilize the summation of the approved-project cost estimates for the period as a base and to superimpose upon this base a lump-sum allowance for possible additional worth-while projects that may be forthcoming during the period. This practice tends to insure that, for the prescribed sum of money to be spent, a certain minimum amount of progress will be made.

It is natural to expect that not all research projects will turn out profitably. Some encounter insurmountable difficulties and have to be abandoned. Others prove to be economically unsound. Still others may be shown to have no direct present or future application to the business in which the enterprise may be engaged. Obviously it is desirable for unsuccessful projects to be weeded out as early as possible so that additional funds will not be wasted on such projects. One common method for locating "bad" projects is to make only partial appropriations for each project when it is authorized so that it must come up for subsequent review and reconsideration when the original allotment has become exhausted. These reviews, which should be made at set intervals or progress points such as every week, month, or quarter, together with the necessity for granting additional appropriations tend to keep the projects crystallized in the minds of the research chiefs.

Progress reports not only are an aid in reviewing projects but they prevent research employees from falling into the dangerous habit of keeping in their heads all information pertaining to their work and findings. Daily records and progress reports enable another man to carry on should the original investigator be taken ill or leave the employ of the company. Furthermore, such records may subsequently be invaluable should patent litigation develop.

It is generally good practice to assign one man the authority and responsibility for the result of each investigation started, even though he may delegate much of the actual work to others. Where one man has charge of expediting a project through to its conclusion, it tends to eliminate any "buck passing" from one person to another and results in a more comprehensive reporting of progress and a quicker completion of the work.

Selection and Control of Research Personnel.—The industrial research director may be a major executive of the enterprise and devote all or part of his time to the research department, he may be a subexecutive who carries out a policy determined by higher authority, or he may be a college faculty member or a professional research engineer on the staff of some commercial laboratory. In either of these latter cases he probably devotes only part of his time to the research work of the enterprise. He should possess personal research ability, have an orderly mind, and think clearly and instinctively. He should possess one research field in which his talents are recognized, for a director who has won his spurs in research commands the respect of his subordinates.

The research worker, on the other hand, should be a man with a specific area of curiosity together with a facility in that area. His talents should be of the type that combines imagination with sound engineering—the coined word "imagineering" has sometimes been used to describe this trait. Facility in any research area is usually best gained by fundamental scientific training of the type offered by the major scientific schools. However, as is the case in any other field of endeavor, some good research workers still gain their facility in the school of experience.

It is of course desirable to stimulate the interest and output of research personnel without demanding predetermined results. Direct wage incentives are therefore not usually applied to research workers, but indirect incentives in the form of a bonus for good work on a specific project or annually at Christmas time for outstanding work throughout the year furnish financial stimuli to research employees.

Frequently, however, nonfinancial rewards mean more to a research worker. Professional or public recognition through publication of his achievements, recognition by colleagues, naming of products after the research man responsible for them, the issuance of patents in the name of the discoverer rather than in the name of the head of the department— all these are prime incentives to the research worker.

Engineering the Product.—Another phase of product development, and one that is closely allied with that performed by the research department, is the *product-engineering* function. While this department may be a part of the research organization, it generally is a separate division under the direction of a chief-product engineer. The duties of the product-engineering department include the preparation of engineering data, drawings, models, and patterns; the control over product simplification; and the setting of industrial standards, particularly those bearing on the product or its design.

The engineering data commonly developed by the product-engineering function include stress calculations for highly stressed parts together with the redesigning of such parts as may be necessary to achieve the strength characteristics required. Calculations pertaining to performance of the product, its operating speeds, permissible loads, and life characteristics are prerogatives of the product-engineering group, as are the preparation of data and specifications for lubrication, servicing, and replacement of parts.

The engineering department also is responsible for the preparation of engineering drawings. These are usually transparent tracings from which blueprints or whiteprints can be made. Drawings are usually prepared for each part, subassembly, or assembly and serve as the foundation of all instructions issued to the manufacturing units. They show front, side, and "plan" views of the object to be manufactured together with all necessary dimensions, tolerances, clearances, and specifications. Frequently the establishing of these engineering details, since they vitally affect the manufacturing of the product, is the subject of consultations between the product engineers and the industrial and plant engineers, the latter two groups being concerned with the technical problems arising out of manufacture.

The fields of product simplification and industrial standardization are today so important to product development that Chap. VIII will be devoted entirely to a treatment of these subjects.

CHAPTER VIII

DEVELOPING THE PRODUCT— SIMPLIFICATION, DIVERSIFICATION, AND STANDARDIZATION

Important to any product-development program are three principles that have a direct bearing on the consumer acceptance of the product as well as on the ease with which it can be manufactured. These principles are known popularly as simplification, diversification, and standardization.

Definitions.—*Industrial simplification* means essentially the elimination of extraneous or marginal lines of products. It concerns itself with a reduction of the range of products, their types, and sizes. Simplification also includes the elimination of extraneous basic materials used in the manufacture of these products and likewise tends to reduce the complexity of the methods of manufacturing procedure.[1]

Diversification, on the other hand, is the direct opposite of simplification. It involves the addition of lines of products, types, and sizes, for the primary purpose of achieving variety. It likewise affects basic materials and methods of manufacturing procedure but in the sense that it tends to increase their complexity.

Factors Affecting Simplification and Diversification within a Given Enterprise.—Simplification and diversification within a given enterprise are dependent upon several factors, the first of which may be listed as the nature and use of the product. If the product is classed as a producer or capital good, fewer types and sizes are necessary than would be the case if the product were in the consumer-good classification. The general public, influenced by promotional advertising, is usually more interested in appearance, in a choice of styles and colors, and in ornamentation than it is in performance. Producer goods, however, are usually purchased first on performance and economy of operation and purchase. Hence an enterprise manufacturing consumer goods tends more toward diversification than does the enterprise making producer goods.

Secondly, the matter of competition within the industry has an effect on simplification and diversification. Where an industry is highly com-

---

[1] *Product simplification* should not be confused with *work simplification,* which is discussed in Chap. XVII.

petitive, each enterprise usually endeavors to outdo its competitors in offering a more varied line of products. Frequently where competitive products are involved, sales appeal and diversification go hand in hand. However, where the enterprise is somewhat monopolistic, it may find that a varied line of products adds little to its sales volume but greatly to its complexity of manufacture, under which conditions a program of simplification can achieve very beneficial results.

A third consideration is the effect of simplification or diversification on the price of the product and on its sales volume. A program of simplification, for example, might tend to reduce the sales appeal of the product; at the same time it might permit substantial manufacturing savings. If these savings were then responsible for substantially lower prices, in a flexible market the lower prices might more than offset any lowering of sales appeal with the result that the volume of sales would actually increase because of the simplification. Conversely, a program of diversification for another kind of product might increase the sales appeal to such an extent that any adverse effect on sales volume due to increased manufacturing costs and prices would be more than nullified, and the net result would be an increase in sales volume for this product through diversification.

Benefits Derived from Simplification Compared with Those Derived from Diversification.—The benefits to be derived from simplification are those resulting from the manufacture of fewer products, or from products that are less complex to manufacture. In either case, simplification means that fewer types and sizes of raw materials are purchased, smaller and less varied inventories are possible, and larger quantities of the remaining materials may be purchased with resultant quantity discounts. Simplification likewise reduces manufacturing costs by reducing the complexity of the manufacturing processes. It makes possible the utilization of special-purpose machines or machines tooled up to handle one type of product, as compared with general-purpose or utility machines which may sacrifice productivity for the flexibility that would otherwise be required to handle a variety of products. It eases the problems of supervision and of production planning. Simplification may also be extended to individual operations to the end that a greater degree of specialization of work tasks may result. This naturally leads to greater ease in training employees and a greater proficiency of work. Lower manufacturing costs, particularly lower labor costs and lower inventories, mean less money tied up in the enterprise.

The benefits to be derived from diversification are principally those resulting from a more balanced line of products. Where sales appeal is extremely important, a greater variety of products tends to meet more exactly each consumer's individual needs and desires. Goods that are seasonal, or those for which the demand is not stable, may be augmented in a diversified line by complementary products that can be produced and sold by the same manufacturing and distribution facilities during the slack periods. Diversification of products reduces the danger of a change in demand. If the demand for a particular product falls off, the enterprise that is making a variety of products is less seriously affected than is the enterprise which specializes in that product alone. Similarly the effect of business depressions is lessened where a variety of products are manufactured—a factor that frequently makes for a more steady employment of equipment and personnel.

However, diversification increases the manufacturing "headaches." Larger and more varied inventories are often required, a greater range of manufacturing equipment must frequently be utilized, more skills are required from employees, sometimes to the point where they are expected to be "Jacks-of-all-trades." Supervision under such operating conditions usually must be increased, and the difficulties of planning production of diversified manufacture are increased several fold.

In past years diversification has in many instances been carried to great extremes. Frequently such a practice was as unwise as it was uneconomic. Primarily to outdo competitors, manufacturers of consumer goods continued for years on end to add fancy, and in some cases useless, gadgets to an ever-widening range of products. Frequently the demand for this ever-increasing variety came not from the customer but from the salesman who clamored for additional selling points or features in his line of products.

A wise management before deciding to diversify its line of products asks itself the following questions about the proposed product:

1. Can use be made of present sales and distribution mechanisms?
2. Can present manufacturing facilities be utilized and are they available?
3. Can existing brains—technical, managerial, and supervisory—be used?
4. Will it level off production?

Only if the answer to all or a majority of these questions is in the affirmative, will a wise management favor a policy of diversification of its line of products.

Industrial Standardization.—A *standard* is essentially a criterion of measurement, quality, performance, or practice, established by custom, consent, or authority and used as a basis for comparison over a period of time. The setting of standards and the coordinating of the industrial factors to comply with these standards and to maintain them during the periods for which they are effective are known as "industrial standardization."

It is rather unfortunate that the terms "simplification" and "standardization" are sometimes loosely used interchangeably. However, it should be noted that simplification, as already defined, refers to lines of products and methods of manufacturing procedure, whereas standardization is concerned principally with a particular product or process. When a manufacturer of electric appliances reduces his line of electric irons from five models to two, he has *simplified* his line of products. When the same manufacturer establishes for each model iron a heating element of a certain wattage and design, a beveled sole plate with tapered toe and made from a casting, a finish of chrome plate of a specified thickness, and also when he stipulates that each iron will bear a 5-year guarantee, he is said to have established *standards* for the product and its manufacturing processes.

Industrial standards may be either *technical* or *operative*. A technical standard is one that involves technical or engineering elements and usually specifies *what* and *how*. An operative standard, on the other hand, deals with the human element and specifies *who, when,* and *why*. Some standards fall naturally into one or the other of these classifications, whereas other standards represent a combination of both types as they involve both technical and human elements. An engineering specification relating to the properties of steel billets, for example, is a technical standard, whereas a set of regulations governing employee-grievance procedure in an industrial plant is an operative standard. A fire-underwriter requirement that suitable exits shall be provided in a public building (technical element) and that these shall be inspected periodically to insure that they are unlocked and that no obstructions are present (operative element) combines both types of standards.

Range of Industrial Standards.—The range of industrial standards is wide indeed, for they may pertain to any of the operating activities of the enterprise. Nevertheless, the more common standards are those dealing with the product, engineering design, materials, quantity, and industrial processes.

Product standards are frequently established to regulate the form, size, quality, and performance of a particular product or range of products. For example, a number of years ago the National Bureau of Standards (see page 182) prepared specifications for dry cells and batteries which included standard cell sizes, arrangement of batteries, types of qualification tests, and required battery performance. Since that time, as new developments have been made in battery construction, the specifications have been revised to keep abreast of the changes. The Bureau of

Standards has checked periodically the products of those manufacturers who have been willing to cooperate, testing several thousand cells each year for compliance with the requirements of the standards. As a result of these coordinated activities, not only are dry cells and batteries manufactured in a few standard and interchangeable sizes but also the quality

Fig. 13.—A shoe-testing machine. This walking machine in a laboratory of the National Bureau of Standards is testing sample shoes. As the spokes of the wheel turn, a shoe presses and rubs against the moving belt. This wears and strains the upper leather, linings, stitches, and heels of the shoe just as if a person were wearing it. Within a short time, a shoe has walked many miles on this machine. The data gathered through such tests as this frequently form the basis for standards of product performance. (*Courtesy of National Bureau of Standards.*)

standards in terms of battery life have been extended three- to fourfold since the standards were originally made effective. In another phase of its work, the Bureau of Standards has conducted experiments for the purpose of determining the essential performance characteristics of women's leather shoes. A machine was developed for testing various types of shoes with respect to their ability to hold shape and resist breakdown. As a result of such tests, performance data for each type of shoe construction have been gathered to the end that performance standards may be established.

The foregoing are typical of the product standards existing today. Some are determined or regulated on a nation-wide basis by the industry concerned. Others are set up by an individual enterprise in the form of specifications regulating the quality of its parts or products as well as their over-all performance. (For a further discussion of standards of quality see Chap. XVI.)

In general it may be said that product standards amount essentially to a set of compromises between the desires of consumers and the restrictions of manufacture. Product standardization frequently protects and benefits the consumer by assuring him of articles that are interchangeable, uniform in quality and performance, and often lower in price.

Engineering design standards are concerned directly with the component parts that make up the product. A company making several similar products may standardize on certain sizes of bolts, screws, fittings, etc., which are to be used in the design of its products. Drawings and specifications for these parts are usually catalogued by number so that a designer or draftsman confronted with the need for some such part has only to look in the catalogue for the standardized part that best serves his purpose. Instead of sketching the part, he merely refers to it by number on his drawing. The burden of proof for a request to modify or add to the list of standardized parts rests with the designer.

Interchangeability is one of the principal benefits to be derived from the application of engineering-design standards. Screw threads,[2] wire sizes, structural-steel members, automobile-tire valves, and electrical sockets and plugs are among the many items that are interchangeable the world over by virtue of having been standardized.

Steel shelving for industrial storage bins and racks, as well as for lockers and cabinets, offers a fine example of what can be accomplished by the use of standardized parts. Almost any rack or bin that is special as regards length, height, or depth of the section, its shelf spacing, or its weight capacity can be constructed from standard back pieces, sides, shelves, spacing bars, angle pieces, etc., all with regularly spaced, punched holes for flexible rearrangement. It is through the usage of parts of standardized design that the cost of both design and manufacture as well as the length of time required for delivery may be considerably reduced.

Material standards are those which concern the composition, form, size, and finish as well as the types of materials used. Any material standard can be readily set forth in a set of specifications listing the required properties of the material desired. For example, a specification

[2] It was only in 1948 that British and American standards groups reconciled the differences which for years had existed between the screw threads used in the two countries and married them into one universal standard.

for Manila rope might include a notation as to the kind of fiber desired, the diameter, the weight per foot of length, the oil content, as well as the breaking strength. Raw materials are almost always purchased to specifications, but it is equally important that standard specifications also be established for supply items such as tool bits, drills, cutting and lubricating oils, grinding wheels, and belting, as well as for repair parts.

Standards connected with materials will be discussed further in Chap. XII in connection with purchasing specifications. However, for our purpose here, it suffices to say that material standards are prerequisites not only to the proper control of quality in the finished product but also to the control of the manufacturing processes and their quantity and process standards.

Quantity standards, which will be considered in later chapters dealing with the control of materials, production, and cost, relate to the quantity of the finished product to be completed within a given period, the amount of raw, in-process, and supply materials required, the production rate per man or per machine, the overhead cost per machine-hour, and any number of other similar standards that are in constant use in industry today in the operation of productive facilities.

Process standards include the standardization, first of all, of operating methods and, secondly, of operational performance or work effort, both of which subjects will be treated in Chap. XVII from the point of view of procedures. Considered here primarily from the standpoint of their function, both of these phases of process control are necessary to the efficient operation of the enterprise, the former dealing primarily with the efficiency of the equipment and plant operating practices, and the latter with the efficiency of the employees. In either case, the standards are established from scientific analysis, from past experience, or from both, to define what should reasonably be expected in the control of processes. Any deviations of the actual results as compared with the standards are carefully scrutinized for opportunities of correction and improvement.

Agencies for the Establishment of Standards.—Foremost among the agencies that establish industrial standards is the National Bureau of Standards, a government agency which, at the request of private industry or other government bureaus, will test and establish reference or working standards on anything from a baby carriage to a steel I beam. Also included in its activities are the custody and maintenance of the standards of weights and measure, publication of data on the units of measurement, formulation of standards of quality and performance, development of testing apparatus and methods of testing, and research on the properties of metals. It further acts as a clearinghouse through which the pro-

ducer, distributor, and consumer all can operate to eliminate needless variety of types and sizes—in other words, to simplify product lines. Commercial quality standards established through the National Bureau of Standards by business and consumer groups usually set up limits below which the grade or quality of a commodity cannot fall if it is to be acceptable under the industry's prevailing practice. These standards not only facilitate the production of the vendor by giving him a working quality range or tolerance but also assure the purchaser of a voluntary guarantee of quality.

Likewise engaged in important work in the field of standardization is the American Standards Association. This association is composed of a number of trade associations representing industry, the various engineering societies, and several government departments. The function of the American Standards Association is to coordinate the standardizing activities of committees of its member groups, to approve and publish engineering and industrial standards and safety codes, as well as to represent American industry in international standardization attempts.

The Army, Navy, and other Federal agencies charged with procurement have in recent years been rather active in establishing industrial standards. For example, standards were set for the implements of war to insure that they would function properly in the field. Also food purchased as a part of the Federal government's agricultural control programs has required standards, to make for uniformity of quality and to determine value received. State and local agencies likewise usually establish standards for purchases upon which they wish to entertain bids. Of course, prime contractors set standards for their subcontractors as do all enterprises in the purchase of their major raw materials.

Introduction of Standards.—The National Resources Committee in 1937 made a study of the sociological effects of new inventions and found that the period from the origin of a new invention to the time when its social effects become evident averages about thirty years. The first airplane was flown in 1903, but it was not until some three decades later that it had developed to the point where its sociological influence on the country's living habits was felt. A similar case can be made for the automobile, television, the sound movie, and a host of other inventions.

Invention is usually a slow process, starting with faint beginnings, proceeding gradually to development, diffusion, and finally to a state where its social influences are felt. The progress of any new invention can be shown to be a function of time and may be depicted graphically by what is known as a *progress-time curve* (see Fig. 14). The life of a new idea is marked by three successive stages: (1) the incipient period, (2) the development period, and (3) the saturation period.

The *incipient period* begins at point *a* in Fig. 14 with the conception of a basic idea, discovery, or invention.   Usually there are many technical and economical difficulties which, temporarily at least, hinder the development of the idea and render impossible any immediate practical application of it.   Thus during this first stage, the idea makes little progress with the interval of time, and the progress line is nearly horizontal. Some examples of ideas now in this incipient or latent stage are facsimile

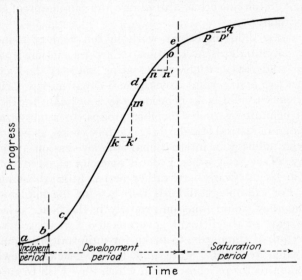

Fig. 14.—Progress-time curve.

or radio transmission of newspapers, plastic automobile bodies, electroplating of color on metal, extraction of gold from sea water, and three-dimensional movies.

The second or *development period* starts at point *b* where the slope of the curve begins to increase.   Perhaps some secondary invention or discovery has come to light which facilitates the development of the basic idea (as the discovery of the electron tube speeded the development of the radio), or perhaps economic or demand conditions stimulate its development (as World War II stimulated the development of synthetic rubber).   In any event, the practical application of the idea reaches reality, and a product is manufactured in small quantities and tried out commercially.   Gradually the problems and difficulties are ironed out, the manufacture leaves the small-lot stage and, by the time point *c* is reached, quantity manufacture has started.   Between points *c* and *d*, improvements in the product and in its manufacture take place very rapidly, and the progress curve reaches its greatest slope. The airplane, air-conditioning equipment, vacuum concrete, synthetic rubber, television, and prefabricated houses are some of the products in various stages of their development periods at this moment.

By the time point *e* is reached, most of the major improvements have been effected, and the third or *saturation period* begins. Since by this time any improvements are relatively minor, progress levels off. The automobile has been in this period for a number of years; the telephone, the incandescent lamp, and the typewriter are likewise in this stage. During the third period the manufacture of the product continues with little change, either until some other competitive product takes its place or until a new basic idea is introduced to change the "saturated product" so radically that a new progress curve is at once set up. For example, the incandescent lamp is now being gradually replaced by the fluorescent lamp, one of its competitors. Or the perfection of the facsimile newspaper may radically change the nature and methods of issuing newspapers, in which event the new product will introduce a new progress curve.

The establishment or introduction of standards at any point on the progress curve results in a temporary fixation of existing conditions. Thus, if standardization is introduced at point *k* on the curve, there is a tendency to stabilize conditions at that level (horizontal line *kk'*). By the time point *k'* is reached, progress has proceeded to point *m*. Thus the line *k'm* represents the magnitude of the "pull" of progress on the existing standardized level which tends to force an upward revision of that level of standards so as to incorporate the improvements made since the standards were established. It is apparent, however, that, as the progress curve levels off at point *e* and the improvements successively come less rapidly and are of a relatively minor nature, any level of standards established thereafter increasingly approximates the curve of progress. Thus there is less "pull" [= magnitude ($p'q$)] to change the standards during this third period. Hence standards set during this period are valid for a greater length of time.

From the progress-time curve explained above, three basic principles of industrial standardization can be evolved:

1. Standards cannot be effectively established before the third or saturation period in the development of a product. To do so at an earlier stage makes necessary almost continual revision of the standards to keep pace with progress.

2. Standardization "fights" progress by tending to stabilize conditions at an existing level. The upward "pull" of progress exerted on a standardized level at any point along the progress curve also creates an

equal and opposite downward "pull" operating against the path of progress with the net result that progress is retarded.

3. Since standards must frequently be revised to keep pace with progress, it is quite necessary that as few basic standards as possible be established so that the program for compliance with, and maintenance of, these standards will be as flexible as possible.

Let us examine how these principles work out in their practical application. We have seen that airplanes are still in their development stage, yet during World War II the armed services found it necessary to standardize on one or two models of each class of fighting airplane required and, regardless of company design or manufacture, all production was concentrated on these models. The Boeing Flying Fortress and the Consolidated Liberator, both planes of the heavy bomber classification, are perhaps the best remembered illustrations of this premature wartime standardization. As would be expected of products in the development period of the progress curve, these heavy bombers as standardized repeatedly felt the effect of the changes in war technology. To keep progress with the new uses of heavy bombers in warfare and new developments in airplane design, the standards were revised successively upward, each revision incorporating additional refinements and improvements in the original basic model, and each reflecting the pull of progress on a group of standards that of necessity were established prematurely.

Another example of premature standardization in recent years occurred in the case of television. During the middle 1940's, when this invention was entering its development period, the Federal Communications Commission standardized on 12 television channels and on "black-and-white" video in order that commercial television sets might be manufactured and sold in quantity. This standardization served only to retard subsequent progress in the science of television. Adoption of additional ultrahigh-frequency channels to reduce interference between stations and the introduction of "full-color" video, both fundamental improvements aimed at better television quality, were apparently delayed simply because the changes would make existing television equipment obsolete and discourage prospective purchasers.

However, some articles still in their development period escape the rigid standardization of their neighbors. The practice in the case of such articles is to standardize only the assembly dimensions or the dimensions for matching the article in question to its mating part or in some other manner keep the standards to a minimum. Some years ago in the case of aircraft-engine carburetors, standards were applied only to the carburetor mounting. Thus research men were not hindered in improving the internal design of the carburetor, and any better product could be assured of fitting existing equipment. Here then was a case of flexibility attained through the establishment of as few standards as possible. Or again, to meet the problem of transition as higher octane gasoline is introduced into the automotive field, some motor-car manufacturers have announced that their present engines can be adapted to the higher octane fuel simply by replacing the present cylinder head with a head which gives the higher compression ratio required. Thus flexibility is obtained by standardizing in the present engines the strength and other characteristics required to meet future developments in gasoline. The only design change necessary is then limited to a relatively minor item, the cylinder head.

SUMMARY

In Chaps. VII and VIII we have seen how industrial products can be developed through organized research. Likewise, we have been concerned with the principles of product engineering, simplification, and diversification, and finally with the field of industrial standardization.

Now, in summary, it is fitting that we examine briefly the place that these phases of industrial endeavor occupy at the high table of American industry. Certainly product development is today a major industrial activity, and no enterprise can better prepare for its future than by mending its research and engineering fences. Now the nation's productive capacity is much greater than ever before. Technological progress during the past ten years was so vast that its full potentialities and complete range of consumer applications cannot be realized for perhaps another decade. Thus any enterprise wishing to maintain or better its competitive position must place greater emphasis on its product-development program.

The simplification of consumer goods of all sorts and the standardization of materials, parts, industrial equipment, methods, and even terminology that took place during and after World War II have almost certainly effected a permanent change on the producing and buying habits of the nation. People to some extent have lost their inclination to see five models or designs differing only in appearance when perhaps one or two functionally designed articles would suffice. In addition, the public as a whole has become less brand-conscious and more standard-conscious. Industrial standards are of themselves undergoing drastic revisions upward as the tremendous progress made during recent years in connection with materials and their fabrication leads to improved consumer goods. Thus can industrial standardization point the way to a nation of the future that produces huge quantities of quality products with a maximum of efficiency—a nation in which more people enjoy better living.

CASE PROBLEMS

Product Development

THE VARIPRODUCTS CO.[3]

The research department of the Variproducts Co. has developed a rather novel electric paint remover designed to take the place of a blowtorch or chemicals in the removal of paint. The device, remotely resembling a household electric iron in size and construction, has a flat, rectangular heating surface and a handle at one end. Heat from the unit "ironed" against a painted surface causes the old paint to blister and soften so that it can be removed with a putty knife or wire brush. Over-all weight of the device is about 1 pound. It achieves maximum heat within 2 minutes. Its nichrome-wire heating element operates on 115-volt a-c circuits. The remover could be made to sell for slightly over $10.

Preparatory Questions

Before deciding whether or not to add this paint remover to their range of products, the executives of the Variproducts Co. ask you, a member of the research department, to

1. Draw up a list of possible applications or uses for the device.

2. Present a résumé of its advantages in the field of existing paint removers.

3. Develop a series of specific research tests to be conducted on the device to prove out the claims made for the device in (1) and (2) above.

Product Design

1. Assume that you are an automotive engineer in charge of the design of a new automobile body. List in detail the procedure you would follow to develop the new body from the time you receive the mechanical specifications of the engine and running gear until you are ready to turn the new body design over to the engineers who prepare the shop production drawings.

2. Assume that after your model has been in production for a short while, complaints are received that its dashboard lights are reflected in the windshield in front of the driver at night. Assume also that in your model, to achieve symmetry, provision was made for an ash tray on both sides of the dashboard, but in the interest of economy only the left-hand ash tray was installed, the other opening being covered with a plate. Suppose also that advices received from dealers indicate consumer prefer-

---

[3] Fictitious name of an actual company.

ence for the ash tray on the right rather than on the left-hand side. What action, if any, would you take to meet these objections and why?

Product Diversification and Simplification

Unexcelled Specialties Co.[4]

One of the largest of the present-day manufacturers of specialty paper products, Unexcelled Specialities Co., was organized to produce quite a different line of goods: jewelry boxes. In the early days of its existence, the company added jewelry tags to its products because, marketwise, they were allied with jewelry boxes. Such tags, however, required quite different manufacturing equipment and did not make full-time use of these facilities. So to increase its equipment utilization the company soon added shipping and marking tags to its line of paper products.

From a marketing standpoint, marking tags are closely associated with marking and pinning machines, and hence the company next turned its attention to the development and manufacture of such equipment.

Since tags and labels are first cousins from a selling standpoint, the company's entrance into the label business was practically inevitable. Printed labels soon followed, requiring the installation of printing equipment. Then, since this equipment was idle for a part of the time, the company added job printing to its endeavors. The company salesmen soon demanded further additions to their line of dealer items in the form of gummed labels (this leading to Christmas seals), paper reinforcements, and even poker chips.

The sales of gummed labels became so great that the company found itself unable to purchase sufficient gummed paper stock. The best solution appeared to be the manufacture of its own paper. However, the picture then changed from famine to feast, for the paper equipment installed could turn out more gummed paper than was required by the company for its own use. Thus the company next began to market its surplus to other label manufacturers including its competitors.

Crepe paper was the next step. This required not only crepe-paper making but decorative marking and printing equipment as well. Again the equipment was more than adequate to meet the demand, and gift wrapping paper and wallpaper were added to the line to minimize equipment "down time" from the lack of work.

Any manufacture of paper products involves some odds and ends and other waste. Consequently the production of gummed hearts, gold and silver stars, and similar items was undertaken to utilize waste gummed paper. Confetti was likewise added as a salvage proposition.

[4] Fictitious name of an actual company.

Preparatory Questions

1. What factors were influential in causing the Unexcelled Specialties Co. to diversify its line of products? Specify also any advantages or disadvantages derived therefrom.

2. Recommend to the management of the company a specific program of action for gradually simplifying its line of products, outlining the major considerations that you believe should influence a decision to drop any specific item.

Product Standardization and Diversification

THE PIN-TUMBLER CYLINDER LOCK

In 1861, a Philadelphia lockmaker named Linus Yale, Jr., filed a patent on a revolutionary type of lock: the pin-tumbler cylinder lock. Prior to that time, locks were complicated devices made individually by the skilled hands of locksmiths. All locks and keys were fitted manually, reproduction was extremely difficult, and standardization impossible. However, Linus Yale's lock, the essential principles of which are applied almost without change in our present-day cylinder lock, not only was a more tamperproof device but also its few standard parts were capable of being mass-produced on machines.[5]

The essential parts of a modern cylinder lock (see Fig. 15) are as follows:

1. The *cylinder,* or fixed portion of the lock, is the part that screws into the door and is essentially a hollow bronze cylinder with a hole bored through it eccentrically. Along the length of the cylinder is a rib in which are drilled several vertical holes.

2. The *plug,* or small bronze cylindrical section that is fitted into the bore of the larger fixed cylinder, likewise has several holes drilled into it mating those of the cylinder.

3. The *key* is a grooved bronze or brass blank with "saw teeth" on one edge. It is accommodated in the plug, which is slit lengthwise, the opening being known as the *keyway.*

4. The *pin tumblers* are thin bronze or brass bars each split into two separate sections. The upper section is known as the *driver;* the lower section engaging the key is called the *key pin.* These pins fit into the mated holes in the cylinder and plug and are constantly pressed downward by small helical *springs* placed uppermost in the holes.

[5] The simple key could be punched or stamped by dies. Pin tumblers were a machine product from the outset and eventually came to be made on automatic-screw machines in a single operation. Springs were formed mechanically, and the cylinder and plug could both be turned on a machine.

5. The *bit* is a "banjo-shaped" section of brass affixed to the end of the plug. It operates the bolt mechanism of the lock.

In its normal state the mechanism is locked. The springs press down on the pin tumblers so that the drivers prevent the plug from turning

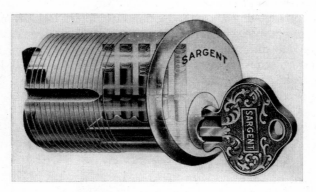

Fig. 15.—A modern pin-tumbler cylinder lock with key in place and tumblers of cylinder partly thrown. When the proper key is inserted, the pins part at the line of separation between the cylinder and the plug, thus permitting the latter to rotate. The bit is attached to the end of the plug and operates the bolt mechanism of the lock. The springs which press the pins down into their proper operative position are shown in the cylinder above the plug. (*Courtesy of Sargent and Company.*)

in the cylinder, just as nails running through two pieces of wood prevent the pieces from sliding one against the other.

However, when the proper key is inserted in the narrow slit in the plug, the saw teeth on the key raise all the pins to such a height that the junctions between their two sections are flush with the joint between the plug and the cylinder hole. This permits the plug to turn and the mechanism can be unlocked.

Each lock and key must be different from every other—a problem in diversification. At the same time, where the cylinder lock is used in large industrial or commercial installations, it is desirable that certain individuals be given access to a number of the locked-in areas with but a single key—a problem in standardization. For example, in a hotel each guest's key should unlock only his own room. However, the chambermaid's master key must unlock any of the rooms on her floor, and the manager's grand-master key must permit access to any room in the establishment. Thus through the use of master or grand-master keys, certain individuals can gain entrance to the desired number of areas without resorting to the unwieldy procedure of carrying a chainful of duplicate keys—one for each area.

Preparatory Questions

1. What determines or limits the number of key combinations possible in a pin-tumbler cylinder lock?

2. How can master and grand-master keys be applied to individually keyed cylinder locks?

3. In the present-day mass production of cylinder locks from standard parts, the assembly is performed by semiskilled employees. Applying your answers to questions 1 and 2, how would you provide assemblers with the information necessary to assemble each individual lock keyed to a master and grand-master system?

ORGANIZING THE PHYSICAL FACILITIES —PLANT LOCATION AND BUILDINGS

The physical facilities of an industrial enterprise consist of the manufacturing plant, its buildings and premises, as well as the machines and equipment necessary to make, in the quantities desired, a product or a range of products. The organization of these facilities usually includes the following main steps:

1. Selection of the plant location.
2. Selection and erection of the plant buildings.
3. Selection of the building installations.
4. Selection of the productive equipment.
5. Preparation of the plant layout.
6. Installation of the equipment.

SELECTION OF THE PLANT LOCATION

The decision as to the location of an industrial plant is frequently one that has a vital effect on the success or failure of the operation of that plant. Hence it should be based upon a careful consideration of all factors pertinent to the business of the particular enterprise. The nature and emphasis of the factors in plant location vary among industries and with changing technical and economic conditions. Some industries have tended to follow their markets in the location of their plants; others, such as the textile industry in Massachusetts, have located around the sources of power; still others, notably Pennsylvania's iron and steel industries, have tended to seek the source of their raw materials. From time to time new or special factors have arisen to outweigh the usual considerations involved in plant location. For example, in recent years an entirely new factor has come into the picture as the possibility of atom-bomb attacks on highly industrialized areas in a future war has been in part responsible for the decentralization of some war-vital plants into less highly concentrated regions.[1]

Determining the Region.—The first step, the selection of the general region or area in which the plant is to be located, usually requires con-

[1] For a report on Air Force policy regarding the "strategic situation" of aircraft manufacturers, see the article "Air Force Shifts B–47 Contract from 'Too Vulnerable' Seattle," *New York Herald Tribune*, Aug. 20, 1949, p. 1.

sideration of five prime factors, namely, (1) proximity to market; (2) proximity to necessary materials; (3) transportation facilities; (4) adequacy of public and private services, such as power, water, fuel, and gas; and (5) climatic conditions.

In this country in the past there has been a relationship between the centers of population and of manufacturing—a relationship indicating that industry in general tends to seek its market. As the center of population has moved westward, the center of manufacturing has followed it but always has lagged slightly behind. The pull on a plant to locate near its market is very strong where the product is perishable (bakeries, dairies), where the product is "service" (repair depots, laundries), and where professional skill is important (photographers, tailors, and others whose style or craftsmanship the customer wants to see before buying). Furthermore, the market factor is of consequence where processing adds weight. The preparation of bottled drinks, for example, involves perhaps 90 per cent water plus the weight of the bottle. Hence, that industry tends to keep its market areas small and to locate its plants near the center of each area.

The materials factor is most vital if the processing removes considerable weight. Ore smelting and refining must locate near the source of its principal materials (ore and coal), since the end product (metal) carries but a small fraction of the weight of the raw materials taken from the mines. If, on the other hand, the principal materials are universally available (as are air and in some regions water), if the material is readily mobile, or if the cost of moving it is small in relation to its value, then the source of materials is only a minor consideration. So also is it of little importance if the material cost is but a small part of the total cost of the end product, as is the case with the raw materials that eventually find their way into your television set.

It has been said that plant location was liberated by transportation. This is perhaps true insofar as the transporting of light products and materials is concerned. But when the material is heavy or bulky, the proximity of the plant to its market and raw materials is directly tied in with the optimum means of transportation for the material involved. Water transportation where available, although it is slow, is the most economical way to ship bulky freight, such as oil, iron ore, or coal. Rail freight is faster, somewhat higher in cost, and accommodates bulk and package carload items as well as less-than-carload shipments. Faster still are motor truck, railway express, and air express, the last two being limited principally to lightweight items and perishables because of the high cost involved. Thus, where heavy materials are involved, the

location of a plant is usually limited to areas proximate to both the source of materials and the market and served by the optimum method of transportation.[2]

Manufacturing thrives in an area where the supply of power and water is plentiful. The electrolytic reduction of aluminum, for example, requires the location of plants near ample power supplies, witness the Aluminum Company of America plant at Niagara Falls. Huge public water-power projects such as have been carried to completion in the Tennessee Valley and in several Western states are indicative of the importance of adequate power to a successful industrial economy. The necessity for dissipating great amounts of heat generated by some present-day manufacturing processes, together with the more frequent application of air conditioning to industrial buildings, calls for increasingly greater amounts of water for cooling purposes—hence the importance of sufficient water supplies in the location of plants today. One of the principal plants for processing atomic-bomb components was located at Hanford, Wash., because, in addition to the advantages of isolation and abundant power, the nearby Columbia River provided one of the best sources of pure, cold water in the United States—water required in tremendous volume for process cooling.

Climatic requirements vary with the type of industry, but in general cool but not cold winters and warm but not hot summers are desirable. Frequent changes in weather are also sometimes advantageous. Southern New England, the California coastal strip, and the southern part of the Great Lakes region are generally considered to be areas with good industrial climates.

[2] The whole matter of cost of transportation and proximity to materials and to market has been given changed emphasis in recent years by a decision of the Supreme Court holding that the so-called "basing-point system" of pricing goods, resulting as it did in identical delivered prices, indicated collusion and was therefore illegal. Prior to this decision, buyers of certain products — cement and steel among them — paid the cost of freight from an arbitrary "basing point" to the buyer's plant, regardless of whether the supplier was located a lesser or greater distance away from the buyer than the basing point. Thus, in effect, the more distant suppliers absorbed the freight differential to meet the prices of competitors located more strategically to the various customers, and nearby customers paid "phantom" or extra freight on their material. Following this decision, the steel industry among others adopted an *f.o.b.-mill system* of pricing whereby each customer paid the actual freight cost between the supplier's plant and his own. Although Congressional action is almost certain to rule out some of the principles laid down in this decision, nevertheless the long-term result may well be that plants using high-freight-cost items will be drawn more strongly toward their source of materials and companies supplying such items will be inclined to locate closer to their large customers.

Determining the Community.—Once the general area has been determined, the search for a plant site narrows to the selection of a particular community. Which of all the communities in the region chosen can best supply the needs of the individual enterprise? The answer generally is determined after consideration of the following factors: (1) labor supply, (2) wage scales, (3) other enterprises in the community, (4) industrial attitude of the community, (5) taxes and restricting laws, and (6) living conditions and standards.

An adequate supply of labor means one that is adequate not only in numbers but also in types of skills required. An energetic and capable type of personnel in the community is an asset to any enterprise. Communities vary in labor skills and interests. The very apparent trend toward the removal of skill from jobs both by application of the sub-division-of-effort doctrine and by design of machines with built-in skill is gradually decreasing the importance of this factor in choosing the community. Yet it is still an important consideration for some industries. Providence jewelry workers and Detroit toolmakers are two examples attesting to this fact. Labor interests may be relevant particularly if the work is undesirable. When jobs are easy to find, foundries, in spite of elevated wage scales, frequently are unable to attract employees needed, while other types of plants in the same communities are able to expand their personnel fairly readily. The reason is not hard to find. Foundry work is considered to be undesirable, and the available labor just is not interested in that type of work.

Wage-scale differentials are not permanent, and a plant should not be located in a particular community solely because for the moment it happens to pay lower wages. Nevertheless, where labor costs represent a large part of the sales dollar, any saving therein may more than offset the differential in all other factors combined. Regional wage differentials, *e.g.*, between the North and the South, were formerly of considerable importance to plant location. However, the present trend and aim of labor unions to level all wage rates have greatly reduced this differential and, of course, with it the over-all importance of this factor in determining plant location.

Sometimes competing, complementary, or supplementary enterprises in a community may influence the decision to locate or not to locate there. Competing companies may drain the supply of certain types of labor skills, with the result that both companies are at a disadvantage. Complementary companies, particularly where the finished product of one is the raw material for the other, are, respectively, near their market and source of materials. Such an arrangement can work to their mutual advantage. Seasonal enterprises usually must locate in large communities where enough other firms are located to supplement their personnel needs and to supply and reabsorb employees.

The attitude and cooperativeness of the community as a whole are of some importance. An anti-industry or anticompany attitude sometimes cannot be overcome by the best public-relations man. A community beset with labor-union strife, factions, and intra- and interunion squabbles or politics does not generate a healthy atmosphere in which new plants are encouraged to settle. The continuing supply of good managers and line supervision is likewise a vital consideration for almost any plant. A community which has not previously been industrialized cannot be counted on immediately to furnish good key personnel. In spite of some good training programs, the education of supervisors is an evolutionary process that takes time. Experience is to a foreman what aging is to a fine wine. An acceleration of it only sacrifices quality. State and local legislation are also important. Incorporation laws are more stringent in some states than in others, and some enterprises locate in a particular state almost for that reason alone. State wage and hour laws, tax laws, local restricting ordinances—these are typical of legislative factors that point to the state and community attitudes toward industry.

The living conditions and standards of each community are frequently important to plant location. Executives and key personnel as well as the rank-and-file employees often refuse to locate in certain towns or cities because they feel that the educational advantages, residential facilities, class of people, private clubs, or civic advantages are not equal to those of another town or city.

A consideration of the foregoing factors will probably narrow the search down to a few communities in the area. Final decision, however, occasionally reverts to one of the prime regional factors previously discussed. For example, a town without regular railroad service might be scratched on that score alone. Or electric-power rates might tip the scale in favor of a particular community, as might an unlimited supply of water, etc.

Choosing the Plant Site.—The final step is, of course, to select the exact plant site in the favored community or communities, the latter because there may not be an available or adequate plant site in the first community selected.

In the search for a site, the principal consideration is land. Is it ample in size, including room for expansion and for the parking of employees' cars? Is the topography right for the type of building desired, and are the soil content and drainage such as to provide the proper foundation?

The second factor in order of importance is very likely to be transportation. Is the potential site as readily accessible to rail, motor, water, or air transportation as may be required? Can employees with and without automobiles conveniently reach the plant?

Then come the miscellaneous factors pertaining to the site's surroundings. Will employees consider it a good place to work? Are there any building and zoning restrictions that would not permit the type of building planned? Is the community fire protection adequate and available to the site? Will the cost of bringing in power and other utilities as well as sewage disposal be prohibitive?

Plant location today is generally a matter of costs tempered by circumstance. Theoretically the most favorable location of a plant is that spot where, in consideration of the business as a whole, the total cost of producing and delivering goods to all the customers is the lowest. This total cost includes the cost of all the factors listed above which may be pertinent to the enterprise involved as well as any special considerations peculiar to that enterprise. Actually, however, the decision as to plant location is not always based on reason, for, more times than management is willing to admit, corporate or financial ties of the enterprise or personal whims of some top executive exercise the balance of power in this regard, and circumstance then takes precedence over cost.[3]

Present Trends in Plant Location.—Most industrial observers today recognize two rather definite trends in plant location. The first is the tendency to locate plants in the proximity of cities rather than in rural areas or directly in cities. The suburban areas today offer practically all the advantages, facilities, and services supplied by city areas and

---

[3] In 1949, the Federal Reserve Bank of Boston conducted a survey of 106 manufacturing establishments which had been set up in New England during the intervening period since World War II to determine why these plants had located in the New England region and also what factors had dominated their choice of community. These firms included new companies, branch plants of established enterprises, and also plants which had relocated in the area.

The FRB concluded: *"The regional decisions of new firms were based primarily on personal considerations* (as the president or partners desired to maintain established residences, or they were personally acquainted with a few workers who formed the nucleus of their employees, or they were personally acquainted with jobbers who furnished initial markets, etc.) ; *those for branch plants were heavily influenced by production relationships* (with other plants located in the area) ; *and those for relocation depended largely on market and personal considerations."* The FRB further concluded: *"A . . . result of this analysis has been to point out that personal considerations dominated not only the regional decisions but also the community decisions of new firms.* Insufficient attention to this aspect of their actions could result in misinterpretation of the location decisions of new firms." From *Monthly Review,* April, 1949, Federal Reserve Bank of Boston.

possess the added advantages of lower assessment values and of sufficient land space to spread out the plant, to allow for expansion, and to provide parking areas for the cars of the plant personnel.

The second trend in plant location is toward *decentralization*. Decentralization, the spreading out of plants of a particular enterprise into new locations, is a trend that began a number of years ago and still continues today but with significantly new motivations. Formerly, industry set up branch plants principally to garner new markets and to provide cheaper and more rapid service to customers.

In recent years, however, a new motive for decentralizing plants has resulted from a recognition of the clumsiness of the elephantine plants so characteristic of the mass-production industries. A large plant is not necessarily more efficient than a smaller plant. On the contrary a large plant frequently becomes unwieldy, difficult to manage, and a victim of inertia. The management of such a plant is usually so far removed from the operating functions that its decisions become quite impersonal and it tends to lose its perspective of the plant problems. Also the span of administrative control of any one top executive or group of executives is usually such that regardless of the assistance of subordinates, the top management of an extremely large plant is very often unable to comprehend clearly the vastness of the plant under its control. Other factors, such as the difficulty of providing the tremendous supply of personnel necessary, as well as the internal transportation, servicing, and maintenance problems of a large plant, are quite apparent. Consequently the mass-production industries, following a practice advocated by the late Henry Ford, have within recent years spread out their plants on the theory that N plants in different locations, each producing X units, are preferable to one plant producing NX units. Not only are several smaller and scattered plants frequently easier to manage than one extremely large plant, but also the production cannot be completely tied up by a strike or fire at any one point.

Basically, decentralization may be accomplished by one of two methods: (1) by the unit or *horizontal method* or (2) by the subsidiary or *vertical method*. Under horizontal decentralization, each branch plant is set up to manufacture a complete product or line of products. Each starts out with raw materials and ends up with the finished article, and the production at each plant is merely *supplementary* to that of the others. The National Biscuit Company buys flour, sugar, shortening, and eggs for its bakeries in various cities throughout the country, and in each one it ends up with bread, crackers, and pastry items to be distributed to its local selling outlets.

With the vertical type of decentralization, on the other hand, the basic idea is to remove the manufacture of parts and subassemblies from the main plant to one or more subsidiary plants. The subsidiary or *complementary* plants ship the parts and subassemblies to the main plant which then performs the assembly operations on the product. Many home-appliance manufacturers have set up a spider web of branch plants to make plastic cases, handles, etc., required on appliances, others to supply electrical parts, and still others to furnish electronic devices. All these items are then assembled into finished appliances at the central plant. A variation of this vertical decentralization is employed by many of the automotive companies, in that the main plant ships parts and subassemblies to its branches scattered about the country, where cars are finally assembled, generally within the market area served.

SELECTION AND ERECTION OF THE PLANT BUILDINGS

In the selection of the plant buildings, there are two basic building types, the relative merits of which should be weighed with respect to the requirements of the enterprise involved. The two types, the *single-story building* and the *multistory building,* each offer certain definite advantages. Those usually listed for the single-story building over the multistory structure are

1. Greater ease of expansion through extension to existing buildings.

2. Greater floor-bearing capacity and less vibration where heavy equipment and materials are employed.

3. Soil requirements for foundations less severe.

4. Better natural light and ventilation.

5. Greater flexibility for plant layout.

6. More usable floor space because no space is required for elevators and stairways.

7. More efficient routing possible, particularly for serialized manufacture.

8. Lower materials-handling costs.

9. Better supervision possible.

The advantages usually given for the multistory building over the single-story structure are

1. More efficient use of land space, particularly where that space is limited.

2. Lower cost of construction per square foot of floor space.

3. Cheaper to heat because of less roof area through which heat can escape.

4. More fire-resistant because reinforced-concrete construction is commonly used.

5. Better type of construction for sloping terrain.

6. Upper stories freer from street noises, odors, and dirt.

7. Use of gravity flow of materials permitted.

8. More compact layouts permitted by vertical arrangement of production areas.

Once the type of building is determined, its arrangement and positioning on the site should next be considered. This will in many cases depend upon the shape of the land available but, in general, buildings are constructed in rectangular sections located in an interconnecting fashion to minimize their mutual interference with light and ventilation. Common industrial building arrangements are in the form of a U, H, L, T, F, or E. Future expansion requirements should always be considered when the initial arrangement is planned, to the end that provision is made for the erection of future building extensions to the original arrangement.

The engineering profession recognizes three general classes of industrial-building construction: third-class, second-class, and first-class.

The *third-class building* is a frame structure wherein all structural parts and practically all the walls, flooring, and roofing consist of inflammable materials. Frame buildings are generally light-duty structures made of wood and not more than one or two stories in height. Such buildings can be erected quickly and cheaply, require considerable maintenance, will take only light floor loads, and possess the serious drawback of being readily combustible.

The *second-class building* is a heavier type of structure in which the external walls and main partitions, and usually the stair towers, elevator shafts, entrances, and exits as well, are of a fireproof construction. However, the structural supports for the floors and roofs and the remaining interior construction are composed of inflammable materials. The slow-burning, mill-construction (plank-on-timber building with brick siding) so common to the southern New England landscape is typical of this classification. The trim and finish, both inside and out, are generally inflammable. However, the heavy wood timbers and planking are fire-resistant to the extent that, in the event of fire, their exterior surfaces char readily only to a depth of perhaps $\frac{1}{2}$ inch. A sufficient cross section is left to support the building structure, thus providing a reasonable length of time for controlling the fire. Also, the fireproof partitions together with self-closing fire doors form closed fire units which tend to localize any fire that may start. Furthermore, with the installation of automatic sprinklers, the danger of a major fire in this type of construction becomes quite remote.

One of the advantages of this type of construction lies in its adaptability. Its interior may be readily revamped as layouts are revised, and openings are quickly made in the flooring to accommodate plumbing and electrical installations, vertical conveyors, and transmission belts. Where heavy floor loads are employed, a deviation from the standard mill construction in the form of laminated flooring may be employed to handle the greater loads. Also the demolition cost of this type of construction is low. Its drawbacks are to be found in its noise- and vibration-transmission characteristics, its fairly high maintenance costs, and its restricted light and ventilation due to the small window areas permitted by its load-bearing walls. In addition, its timber posts and fire walls frequently so cut up the usable floor space as to render the layout of such buildings difficult and at times rather inefficient.

Steel-frame construction, which likewise comes under this classification, is well adapted to single-story buildings requiring wide spans and few supporting columns, for steel trusses can be made to support large roof areas. Rigid steel-frame construction with non-load-bearing walls for both single- and multistory buildings has found widespread favor in a variety of industries.

The *first-class building* has all its main structural members and most of its exterior and interior partitions, flooring, and roof composed of non-inflammable materials. Generally the only inflammable materials permitted under this building classification are those in the interior trim, doors, and windows. The structural members are usually steel completely encased in concrete or masonry or are made of reinforced concrete. The reinforced-concrete building is in wide use today as the successor to the mill-construction building. Its erection time is rapid, its materials are readily available, wider and longer bays between columns are possible, vibration and noise are minimized, maintenance costs are lower, and it is virtually fireproof. Precast concrete blocks, slabs, or planks used for siding and in some cases roofs are coming into favor because of lower cost and greater construction speed. Disadvantages of most concrete buildings center about their high cost of alteration and demolition and the fact that concrete floors are "hard on employees' feet."

A few words about industrial building materials are perhaps in order. Wood, masonry, and steel are the three basic materials used, the application of each depending upon the characteristics desired. Wood in cents per pound is the most economical building material available but, unless specially treated, is quite inflammable. That it is still a useful material for industrial buildings was conclusively demonstrated during World War II when the scarcity of structural steel caused many a plant building to be erected with wood trusses, columns, roofs, and partitions. Unit masonry, such as brick, stone, or concrete, is fire-resistant and can support a greater load than can wood. Exposed structural steel and steel sheathing twist and buckle under the heat of a fire and thus are not fireproof.

Furthermore, the expansion and sagging of steel-truss members in a hot fire distort the exterior walls to the point of collapse. But when steel is encased in concrete, the combination is almost completely fireproof and quite exposure-resistant. Encased steel or concrete reinforced with steel rods has the unique characteristic of being a completely integral, monolithic unit, whereas other steel and wood structures usually rely on rivets, plates, caps, and similar ties to bind the members together. It is this integration of the concrete structure that provides its unusual load- and shock-bearing characteristics.

Present Trends in Building Construction.—Allied with the present trend toward the location of plants in suburban areas is a trend toward the erection of single-story buildings in preference to multistory buildings.

Fig. 16.—Modern food-processing plant of the Hill Brothers Coffee Company, Edgewater, N. J., is both attractive and functional. It was located on tidewater for low-cost distribution. This multistory plant was designed and built around the process to provide the facilities for maximum operating efficiency and high quality product. (*Design and construction by The Austin Company, Engineers and Builders.*)

Suburban locations frequently offer sufficient land area to accommodate a one-story structure of sufficient floor space. This fact together with the present emphasis on the flexibility of plant layouts, on serialized manufacture (see page 228), and on lower routing and materials-handling costs, presents a strong inducement to management to erect single-story structures. This is not to imply that the multistory building is no longer in demand. On the contrary, for light manufacturing and where the gravity-flow principle can be utilized, it still has a definite place in the list of industrial structures.

Typical of other recognized trends in building design and construction are those pertaining to the spacing of columns, the utilization of basements, and the construction of walls, roofs, and floors. The present thought on the spacing of *columns* is in the direction of wider and higher interiors. Undoubtedly this trend has been influenced by the increased need in recent years for flexibility to meet rapidly changing conditions in manufacture as well as by the more widespread use of assembly-line techniques, which require wider and longer bays. Today minimum di-

Fig. 17.—Single-story plant of a music publisher. Limestone entrance, set in long, low, light brick wall gives a modern functional appearance. With landscaping, this plant is an attractive addition to the community. [*From Factory, Vol. 107, No. 4, p.* B–80 (*April,* 1949).]

mensions for the bays between columns are 20 by 20 feet, and such bays are to be found principally in multistory buildings where heavy equipment is employed. At the other extreme are single-story aircraft plants, some 300 feet wide, constructed for the assembly of large airplanes, that are entirely free from columns their entire length and breadth. In passing, a word of caution should be said about "columnless" plants and plants with large bays. Whereas they are a necessary type of construction for large assembly operations, they are frequently a waste of money where used to house small machinery or to manufacture small products. Not only do they involve an expensive type of construction, what with the heavy girder work to bridge the large bays, but also, because of the type of the roof structure, they furnish considerable headroom, which for the manufacture of light products represents many idle cubic feet of air that must be heated throughout the winter.

Basements and *subbasements* of manufacturing plants are being used more and more for the storage of raw materials, for "dead storage," for service tunnels, and for employee-servicing facilities. One aircraft manufacturer in the design of a single-story building has incorporated a large basement space laid out somewhat in the form of a cross under the manufacturing floor. The basement contains corridors through which employees pass on their way to and from the work areas above. At convenient intervals along the corridors are stairways leading up to the main floor level. Along the corridors are locker rooms, washrooms, and an air-conditioned cafeteria. This arrangement smooths out the confusion and interference that occur during the change of work shifts.

FIG. 18.—Large plant of the Western Electric Company at Allentown, Pa. A feature of this building is its controlled atmosphere furnished by air-conditioning equipment to provide dust-free air of almost constant temperature and humidity. Also, thick insulated walls and roof provide considerable time lag in solar-heat transmission. Note, too, the 30-inch-high insulated window "vision strip" around the building and the effect gained by landscaping. (*The Austin Company, Builders and Engineers.*)

One of the great difficulties with concrete *walls* is their inflexibility. When changing conditions require the installation of pipes and blower outlets through a section or where a wall must be removed to permit a building addition, concrete makes such changes rather costly. Consequently brick or insulated metal-panel siding is frequently favored for walls. Likewise, cinder or gypsum block is finding wide use in partitions because alterations are easier to effect. Some new plants rely principally on natural daylight, and in these there is a distinct trend toward walls with more sash and less masonry, with continuous-type sash around the building growing in favor. In others, the preference is for artificial, "controlled" illumination, which permits solid masonry walls with perhaps only a glass "vision strip" to cater to the habitual human desire to "see out."

Monitor or saw-tooth *roofs*, while still popular for single-story buildings because of the improvement in natural lighting that they afford, have given way to flat roofs, in some cases because of lower initial and subsequent maintenance costs. Tar and gravel on planking, steel, or concrete provide a serviceable roof construction. A few plants in crowded locations have used their roofs for employee parking areas at a considerable saving in land space. Some others use roof ponds or spray systems for reflective and evaporative cooling. Plant areas under such roofs are reported to be as much as 10 degrees cooler in summer.

Present-day heavy-machinery installations require solid *flooring*. Concrete, poured or precast, or wood blocks on a concrete base are common types of flooring. White concrete is favored in some aircraft assembly plants because its light-reflecting qualities provide upwards of 60 per cent more light on the underside of wings and fuselages. Concrete has the property of chipping with heavy usage and tends to be dusty, thus requiring the frequent use of dustproofing compounds. Wood blocks on end, soaked with creosote, form a long-wearing, durable, if somewhat more expensive flooring that is easier than concrete on the feet of the employees and can be repaired simply by replacing the damaged blocks.

SELECTION OF THE BUILDING INSTALLATIONS

The building installations and facilities discussed in this section, although not all-inclusive, are those to which industry is today devoting major attention. They point up current trends in management's thinking as regards installations for better process control and manufacturing efficiency as well as for employees' increased comfort and safety. Lest these last named appear to be purely philanthropic benefits, it should be pointed out that they pay dividends in the form of greater productivity and lower accident-compensation costs.

Air Conditioning.—Practically all machine tools generate heat. Some are dust, fume, moisture, or smoke producers. Human occupancy of a plant results in lower oxygen content and higher carbon dioxide content. At the same time, human lungs and bodies give off heat and moisture. Odors and bacteria are introduced. Sunlight and artificial lights as well are responsible for an appreciable amount of heat. Winter weather in most sections of the country tends to cool plant interiors. Thus it can be appreciated that industrial air conditioning in its broadest sense requires control over (1) temperature, (2) humidity, (3) motion, (4) dust and other air-borne particles, (5) odors, and (6) purity.

1. *Temperature.*—Generally the control of temperature involves heating the air in winter and cooling it in summer. However, in some plants where operations generate considerable heat and are run practically continuously, the problem is one of cooling the air the year around.

Other plants have processes which require constant temperatures throughout the year.

Heat may be generated in a central heating plant, with the heating medium—usually hot water or steam—piped to the area. Heating of the area is then accomplished by conventional radiators, by radiant-heating pipes in the floor or ceiling, or by fan-type unit heaters which force air over heating coils. Where the building is small or remote from other structures, heating frequently is accomplished by "direct-fired" heaters containing a heating element through which air is forced.

Air cooling may be accomplished by passing air over cooling coils, with the heat removed through a refrigerating cycle. Large air-conditioning systems usually pipe the coolant from a centralized compressor plant to local areas where air is run through cooling coils. Otherwise, individual, self-contained cooling equipment is located in or near the area to be cooled. Oftentimes well water at 50 to 55° F. serves as an inexpensive cooling medium.

2. *Humidity.*—Control of moisture content is a very important factor in some industrial processes. In a rayon tire-cord plant, the process requires maintenance of 65 per cent constant humidity. In a precision steel-products company, corrosion is such an important factor that constant humidity of 40 per cent is vital. Apart from process requirements, humidity control is also a major factor in employee comfort.

Excess moisture in summer air is generally condensed by the "dew-point" method. Air is cooled until in a moisture-saturated condition it carries only the desired amount of moisture. Then when the air is heated to the ultimate temperature, the predetermined humidity percentage is attained. The low moisture content of winter air can be increased by heating the air and adding water.

3. *Motion.*—Air movement in a closed room is second only in importance to temperature, for without it the occupants will have a sensation of stuffiness and stagnancy. Frequently the natural movement of air in a room is augmented by placing the conditioned-air inlets at floor level and the exhaust outlets at ceiling or roof height. If this is not practicable, incoming air ducts may be located about the area to achieve the desired air motion.

4. *Dust.*—Certain forms of dust encountered in industry are injurious to employees' health and may bring on diseases such as silicosis. Other dusts are explosive if widely prevalent in a finely divided state. Many processes require dust-free air. For example, dust particles clinging to the inside of fluorescent lamp tubes during their manufacture produce irregularities in lamp performance. Thus, the removal of almost all air-borne particles in tube plants is a "must."

The easiest way to remove dust from air is to take it out at its source, particularly if the source is a machine, tumbling mill, sandblast equipment, crusher, or the like. Then a hood over the dust source, piping, and a blower to furnish suction carry the polluted air to collectors. Another and very efficient way of removing not only dust but oil mist and smoke from air is by electrostatic precipitation. Here dirt particles in the air are given a positive electrical charge, then the air is passed over negatively charged plates which attract the particles and from which the dirt is subsequently washed or cleaned. This electrostatic principle of "washing" air is applied both to the conditioning of large areas and to removing objectionable particles at individual machines.

5. *Odors.*—Odors and fumes likewise may be toxic or harmful to the respiratory system or may simply be disagreeable. In any event, their removal is accomplished by exhaust equipment similar to that for the removal of dust, with the possible addition of activated carbon units if necessary to remove certain common odors.

6. *Purity.*—Each person in a closed area requires a minimum of 10 cubic feet per minute of fresh air if its purity is to be maintained at a level satisfactory for breathing. Generally this requirement is designed into equipment for controlling air temperature, humidity, and motion. Ultraviolet lamps and other devices for destroying bacteria are becoming increasingly common and may soon be generally employed in plant and office areas to prevent epidemics of colds and other ailments among employees.

Before leaving the subject of air conditioning, a few words should be included as to its limitations. Complete air conditioning is costly to install and expensive to operate. In many types of work where the process does not demand exact temperature, humidity, and purity control, winter heating equipment plus simple and relatively inexpensive ventilators can heat the air and move it (in summer as well as in winter) sufficiently for the comfort of employees. More complete air-conditioning equipment should be installed only where the need justifies the expense (as in inspection areas, gage rooms, or areas involving critical processes) or where morale, public relations, or other more intangible factors dictate (as in sales rooms or office areas).

Plant Illumination.—Light and paint are the Siamese twins of illumination. Together they are a team which can banish darkness; one without the other will only half do the job. Good illumination in a plant soon pays for itself in greater productive efficiency, improved morale of employees, fewer accidents, and better housekeeping.

The rapid progress in artificial lighting is attested by the rapid rise in standards of plant illumination. Only a decade and a half ago the average industrial illumination achieved by artificial lighting was about 7 foot-candles. Today well-lighted work areas receive 20 to 50 foot-candles, and drafting rooms or other areas for very fine work up to 100 foot-candles.

Nevertheless, proper intensity for the type of work performed is only one part of good illumination. Even brightness throughout the area without dark shadows is very important, as is elimination of the tunnel or cave effect which was so characteristic of old localized lighting. Furthermore, glare from improperly shielded or poorly placed light sources and reflections from highly reflective walls or shiny surfaces should be minimized. Finally, the light should be "cool," or give off little heat.

Fluorescent lighting is the type of artificial lighting that is most widely used by industry today, having to a great extent replaced incandescent lamps. Used on alternating current, fluorescent lamps are usually mounted in pairs on a fixture and run out of phase to minimize the stroboscopic effect. The advantages of fluorescent lighting are high efficiency, low glare, large area of light source (fewer shadows), little heat, and its availability in colors (daylight, white, green, gold, blue, pink) for different effects and applications. Furthermore, it is more economical in

Fig. 19.—100-watt daylight fluorescent lamps in reflectors mounted 24 feet above the floor and with rows spaced 10 feet apart furnish 40 foot-candles of even, shadow-free, general illumination. (*Courtesy of the General Electric Company.*)

operation, 100 watts of fluorescent lighting being approximately equivalent in foot-candle illumination to 300 watts of incandescent lighting.

For the future, certain lighting trends are now discernible. Lights will become an integral part of many machines, since frequently that is the best method of directing light squarely on the work center. Already lights built into tool grinders and into magnifying glasses have proved their worth, and an expansion of this scheme is sure to follow. It is reasonable to expect that such lamps will be recessed into the machines and covered with dust- and oiltight lenses. Similarly, trends toward the illumination of control panels, dials, and pointers and toward lighted signal buttons are already evident. Miniature lamps, fluorescent circular tubes of varying diameter, plastic rods to bend light—these are only previews of things to come in the realm of illumination.

Color Conditioning.—The other phase of good plant illumination—interior painting—has assumed its present importance only within the past several years. During this period industry has learned how to apply the science of color—"three-dimensional seeing," it is sometimes called—to increase the "see-ability" in its plants. Even today the natural resistance to change has prevented some plant managers from finding out that it is possible to salvage many foot-candles out of a can of paint.

It is well known that white paint reflects from 75 to 90 per cent of the light hitting it whereas black paint bounces back only from 3 to 5 per cent. Usable light in a plant can be increased over 200 per cent by using white paint instead of black. Although from the standpoint of brightness alone white is the logical color for a plant, its high reflectivity causes glare and it is hard to keep clean. Furthermore, an all-white interior is most monotonous for employees.

The principal objective of industrial color conditioning is to achieve uniform brightness but with sufficient contrasts so that the job is more interesting to an employee's eyes than is the surrounding area. This means that walls and machine bases must provide uniform seeing conditions without eye-tiring light-dark contrasts. The contrasting colors are then saved for the operating area of the machine upon which the operator should focus his attention.

Color technology tells us that color possesses three general properties or qualities which stimulate the human eye: (1) *hue,* or the property by which red, yellow, etc., are distinguished from each other; (2) *value,* or the intensity whereby darker colors are distinguished from lighter shades; and (3) *chroma,* which refers to the purity, strength, and richness of color. The value and chroma of a color measure its ability to attract attention. Walls and ceilings, which should fade into the background, require low values and chromas but light, neutral hues to retain brightness of seeing. Work areas as well as protruding machine parts, low overhead obstructions, pits, and other hazards should be high in value and chroma to drown out the weaker background colors and to compel attention.

Reducing these color principles to actual shop practice, we find the following color code recommended by some authorities:

1. Ceilings—white, cream, or ivory.
2. Upper walls—buff, very light green, blue, peach.
3. Lower walls and machine bases—slightly darker color to harmonize with upper walls.
4. Working areas—buff, "eggshell," or very light gray.
5. Floors—as light a color as is consistent with serviceability.
6. Hazards:

> Obstacles—yellow or yellow and black stripes.
> Dangerous machine parts—orange.
> "Hands-off" objects—blue.
> Fire-fighting equipment—red.
> Stretchers and other first-aid equipment—green.
> Traffic lines on floor—white.

Noise Control.—During the past few years industry has displayed an increasing interest in the control of industrial noises. While a reduction or elimination of objectionable noises in a plant lessens the wear and tear on employees' nerves, reduces mental fatigue, and improves morale, such a program is far from philanthropic. An increase in the amount of work performed, improvement in its quality, as well as a reduction of costly accidents—these definitely result from the control of noise.

As far as industry is concerned, all noise can be defined as undesirable sound. Industrial noises may be steady (from machines, motors, blowers), intermittent (presses, pneumatic tools, forging machines), or random (people talking, handling of tools and material). The disagreeableness of noise is dependent on (1) sound intensity or degree of loudness as measured in *decibels*, (2) noise fluctuation or irregularity (a clap of thunder is more disturbing than a regularly recurring noise of the same or greater intensity), and (3) pitch or frequency (the higher pitched police whistle is more disturbing than a locomotive whistle of comparable intensity).

Noise and vibration are partners in crime, and in fact, noise transmitted to the air directly from the noise-producing equipment may be unimportant compared with that transmitted through vibration of the equipment base to the building structure. Hence the emphasis of much acoustical treatment is on vibration. Briefly, the most widely used methods for controlling industrial noises fall into four classes: (1) quiet the noise-producing element through the repair or redesign of the machine, bearings, gears, spindles, etc.; (2) isolate the noise source by damping or mounting machines and other equipment on rubber, springs, or felt; (3) enclose the noise source with sound-resistant partitions; and (4) treat ceilings, walls, and floors acoustically to absorb sound.

Power and Power Transmission.—*Electric power,* or the electric energy required in the operation of a plant and its equipment, may be purchased from a public-utility power station or be generated in the company's own power plant. Power is commonly generated by steam turbines; by gasoline, Diesel, or other engines; or in a hydroelectric plant.

Alternating-current power is usually brought into a plant at high voltage (usually 4,160 or 13,200 volts) to a set of transformers which reduces the voltage for in-plant distribution. For supplying power to machines, 460 volts is usually preferred to 208/120- or 230-volt distribution because smaller wire sizes can be used. However, lights and fractional-horsepower motors operate on 120 volts, and 208/120-volt circuits also are generally required.

Load-center distribution of in-plant power has gained wide favor. This system brings high-voltage power into the center of each load area where unit substation transformers reduce the voltage to that required in the area. Considerable copper is saved that would otherwise be required for low-voltage transmission to the load areas from a central substation. Particularly is this true of large plants and shipyards where the load centers are widely distributed.

Flexibility of internal transmission of power is the key word in most plants to meet the demand for flexible layouts and for rapid positioning of machines. Hence, an overhead *busway* with multiple outlets is commonly placed along the lines of machines to provide the flexibility desired. When machines are moved, they can be disconnected from the busway and plugged in at a new location (see Fig. 20) almost as simply as you plug in your household bridge lamps. Although it is true that a much neater power-duct arrangement can be achieved with underfloor busways, some sacrifice in flexibility and the danger of water seeping in or flooding the "subway" are introduced.

Efficiency in the power system depends to a great extent upon its *power factor.* This may be simply defined as the percentage of energy in a circuit that can be applied to useful work. Low power factor means overloaded lines, and conversely, high power factor permits saving in the size of power lines, transformers, and generating equipment. Furthermore, power companies generally penalize plant power systems with low power factor by charging higher rates. To achieve a power factor close to unity (= 100 per cent), plants usually take corrective measures such as selecting motors so as to run well loaded and introducing static condensers (called "capacitors") into circuits which have low power factor.

Once electric energy is transformed into *mechanical power*, there is still the problem of transmitting that energy to the productive equipment.

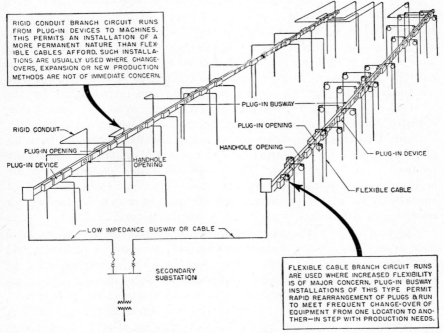

FIG. 20.—Two common methods of bringing power to machines are shown in the above diagram. One makes use of rigid conduit and the other, flexible cable. Both are fed by plug-in busways, which are, in effect, long switchboards with plug devices spaced usually at 2-foot intervals along their length. (*From booklet "Electric Power Distribution for Industrial Plants," p. 75, published by the American Institute of Electrical Engineers.*)

Generally this resolves itself into a question of *group drive* vs. *individual drive*. Group drive, as the name implies, involves the transmission of power to a group of machines from but a single motor or source of mechanical power. This transmission is commonly via line shaft and countershafts with pulleys driving flat leather belts. Sometimes, however, V belts are used either singly or in sets. Chain drives, combinations of gears, speed changers, clutches, and flexible couplings—any or a combination of these—may be used as the application requires.

Individual drive, on the other hand, requires the use of one or more motors mounted integral with or adjacent to each machine and used to drive the moving components of that machine. Here again, flat or V belts, chains, gears, speed changers, clutches, and flexible couplings may be used to transmit power from the motor to the working parts of the machine.

Group drives are more efficient where regular amounts of power over long periods of time are required by a series of machines in an area. Individual drives generally transmit power with less slippage under load and are far more efficient where machines are used at irregular intervals and under varying loads. They permit much greater flexibility of machine arrangement and do not cause ceilings to be cluttered up with shafting, nor do they interfere with lighting and housekeeping by the creation of a forest of belts in working areas. Wherever practicable, industry today is equipping its machine tools with individual drives.

Plant Utilities.—No treatment of plant installations would be complete unless mention were made of the various plant utilities commonly required in industry today. Three separate *water* systems often are necessary: (1) potable water, (2) water for fire-fighting equipment (usually under higher pressure), and (3) process water for cooling, air conditioning, and toilets (can be drawn from well, lake, or river). *Gas* is also piped through plants to provide process heating. *Steam,* as we have seen, is used in power-generating equipment, for process purposes, and sometimes for heating. *Oils,* where used in large quantities, may be stored in underground tanks and pumped to the point of use. This is an efficient way of distributing mixed oils such as machine cutting oils, slushing oils, and solvents, and furthermore it saves trucking, handling, and spillage that otherwise go with the distribution of oils. *Compressed air,* often required as a part of the process and for pneumatic equipment, is supplied by large compressors and piped to the point of use. *Liquid-waste disposal* systems are increasing in importance today as antipollution regulations are enacted affecting the effluent of plants into rivers and lakes.

Vital to effective plant operation is the multitude of plant-communication facilities in use today. These include an intraplant *dial-telephone system* with switchboard linking to outside telephone service, *bells* and *horns* to denote shift changes or fire calls, and *teletypes* and *telautographs,* the former for transmitting and receiving outside telegrams and both the former and the latter for dispatching orders and receiving production reports. Now firmly entrenched as one of the most useful of communication facilities is the *public-address system.* Installed with speakers throughout the plant, it is widely used for paging purposes, announcements, morale-building talks, music for reduction of fatigue, and notifying employees of important news bulletins.

Not to be forgotten also is that silent watchman, the *automatic sprinkler system*. The sprinkler heads let go and douse the fire before it can gain headway. Frequently an alarm is installed that sounds as soon as water starts to flow through the sprinkler pipes. Allied *fire-fighting equipment* includes portable fire extinguishers and fire engines which, depending upon the type of fire hazard involved, may be filled with a soda-acid solution, foam, powder gas, carbon tetrachloride, or carbon dioxide. Hydrants, hoses, fog nozzles, fire walls, and fire doors, likewise, should not be overlooked as a part of the plant fire protection.

Employee Facilities.—Included in the category of employee facilities are locker rooms, rest rooms, showers, water coolers, eating facilities, time clocks, plant hospital, and first-aid equipment. Criteria for the design of any of the above installations dictate that they be (1) adequate in capacity for the employee concentration required, (2) readily accessible to the bulk of employees with a minimum of lost production time, (3) easy to keep clean and sanitary, and (4) located and accessible for ease of maintenance. Some recently designed plants locate all employee facilities in the basement or on mezzanines in the center of the production area. Basements also provide the opportunity for subterranean aisles, entrance tunnels, and service passageways without interrupting production. Off-street parking for employees' cars is a requisite in today's plants. Also, as a morale booster and for its public-relations effect, more and more companies are landscaping that part of the grounds visible from streets or employee entrances.

CHAPTER X

ORGANIZING THE PHYSICAL FACILITIES—PLANT EQUIPMENT AND LAYOUT

SELECTION OF THE PRODUCTIVE EQUIPMENT

This section is concerned with the principles that underlie the engineering and selection of the productive equipment or that used directly in the production of goods in the plant.

Which Productive Process?—The first consideration in the selection of productive equipment is to establish the basic types of productive processes to be used. Product development and process engineering generally go hand in hand. Often the product is designed specifically for fabrication by a certain process, as, for example, an aircraft-engine cylinder head which is designed to be sand cast. Other times, where no sacrifices in the quality or usefulness of the product are concerned, the product may be designed to be made on existing equipment. But even here, efficiency usually requires some retooling or other adaptation of equipment to product.

Still other situations bring no limitations, and the plant engineers have free rein. Consider, for example, the production of steel rings such as might be used for ball-bearing raceways. Certainly they can be machined out of steel bars or tubes or forged out of slugs of steel. At least these are the first processes that would come to the mind of a plant engineer. But utilizing newer techniques, centrifugal castings, or even welding together the ends of strips of flat steel rolled into rings are not beyond the realm of possibility. All available processes must then be carefully considered for their relative merits.

What are the productive processes in use by industry today? Enumerated in succeeding paragraphs are some of the more common processes employed by the metalworking industries. Yet many of them are equally adaptable to the fabrication of nonmetallic materials. Plastic articles, for example, can be molded (cast), extruded, drawn or formed on a press, or machined from rods or tubes. Glassworking often makes use of forming, welding, and tempering techniques. Also to be noted is the fact that certain other materials such as textiles, liquids, and chemicals require specialized types of processes, the categorization of which is difficult if not impossible.

Sand casting requires an exact pattern of the article to be produced. This pattern is set in sand, and the metal (iron, steel, bronze, brass, or aluminum) is poured into the resulting impression. Sand-cast articles may be of irregular shape and range in size from small belt buckles to mammoth machine bases, with tolerances of medium-sized items on the order of magnitude of $\pm \frac{1}{32}$ inch. Of course, further accuracy can be achieved by machining. The pattern is the principal item of tooling, but because of the manual work involved in the actual casting, it is a relatively slow process more adaptable to job-lot than to continuous manufacture.

Under the general heading "metal-mold casting" are three specific casting techniques. The so-called *permanent-mold casting* method is similar to sand casting but makes use of metal or refractory-lined molds and is warranted for volume production at greater precision than is permitted by sand casting. It is used principally for irregularly shaped articles of moderate size such as automotive engine blocks. *Centrifugal casting* likewise requires a metal mold, but as the metal is poured, the mold is rotated. The result is a casting which has a dense, clean structure near its outer surface. While centrifugal castings may be of irregular shape, generally they are cylindrical items such as wheels or cylinder barrels. *Die casting,* which at present is limited to the lower melting alloys of zinc, copper, aluminum, or magnesium, has been defined as "the art of producing accurately dimensioned parts by forcing molten metal under pressure into a steel die." Dimensional tolerances are in the neighborhood of 0.001 inch, very little surface finishing is necessary, and complex and intricate articles ranging in size from the zipper fastener on a lady's handbag to the "massive" radiator grille on her automobile can be produced by this method. Plastic molding is essentially a die-casting technique employing compression and heat on plastic powders. While the cost of the die and the casting machine used for metal items both are high, the process is incredibly rapid. Consequently die casting is essentially a volume-production process.

Investment (or "lost wax") *casting* requires first of all a mold of any suitable substance for casting wax replicas of the article. Each wax replica is then "invested" into or surrounded by a ceramic material which upon hardening is fired. During the latter operation, the wax melts away, leaving a ceramic mold into which the metal is cast, generally under pressure or by the centrifugal method. As in die casting, dimensional accuracy is in the neighborhood of 0.001 inch. Noteworthy is the fact that carbides and certain alloy steels that are difficult to machine or otherwise form can be cast to the shape desired by this method.

Also on the family tree of casting methods is the technique of *powder metallurgy.* Metallic powders poured into dies and compressed can then be sintered in a furnace to produce parts of varied strength and porosity to meet specific needs. Small gears, "oilless" bearings, model-train parts, and numerous other items can be produced rapidly and to considerable accuracy (measured in a few thousandths of an inch).

Forming methods include various forging and extrusion processes. "Impact-die" or *drop forging* as well as *hot-pressed forging* are performed

FIG. 21—An automobile crankshaft is forged under the impact of a steam drop hammer. The crank starts out as a white-hot steel slug, and during a series of passes under the hammer, it takes on the form of the dies, as shown above. (*Courtesy of Chambersburg Engineering Company.*)

on heavy forging machines with dies. The metal usually is heated and then pressed or hammered to shape, although smaller articles such as bolts, rivets, and small balls are "cold-headed" at room temperature. Forging dies are fairly costly, making the process one for quantity manufacture. Accuracy in terms of hundredths of an inch is not uncommon, particularly if the item is coined subsequent to the initial forging treatment. Strength of the metal is improved by the forging process. Larger items which cannot be machine forged can be *hand forged* on an anvil under a steam-driven hammer. This process is essentially a craft operation limited to simple, plain shapes (large crankshafts, steel plates, steel rings) in small quantity (see Fig. 21).

In the process of *extrusion*, ductile material or material made ductile by heating is caused to flow into the desired shape in dies by the action of a press plunger against the material. In this fashion are produced metal bars and tubes of uniform cross section as well as plastic and rubber-base articles. Closely allied with this process is that of *cold drawing* by which to produce the desired cross section (hex, channel, elliptical, etc.). Another similar process is *impact extrusion* in which the blow of a punch press forms and extrudes ductile metal in a die. Tooth-paste tubes are produced by this method.

Machining is a term used to embrace the reduction of material to specified shape and dimensions by the action of cutting tools mounted on machinery. Round articles or articles with circular sections, round holes, threads, knurling, etc., can be machined to an accuracy of a few thousandths of an inch on an engine lathe, turret lathe, automatic lathe, hand screw machine, or automatic screw machine depending upon the complexity of the section and the quantity needed. Where only holes or tapped internal surfaces are required, a single- or multiple-spindle drill press may be used. Flat surfaces can be machined on any of the diversity of milling machines, shapers, or planers to similar tolerances. In each of the above cases, "stock," or material, is removed by movement of the part and cutting tools (hardened alloy steel or cemented carbide) against each other. Machining techniques are used on a host of materials other than metals, including various plastics, rubber, and wood.

Should further accuracy down to a fraction of 0.001 inch, as well as a smoother surface finish, be required, the part can be fed against a *revolving grinding wheel* of suitable abrasive. Cylindrical surfaces are produced on universal grinders, holes on internal grinders, flat areas on surface grinders. In addition there are centerless, cutter, and thread grinders, and honing, superfinishing, and polishing machines for special grinding and finishing applications. Further descriptions and data as to the characteristics and potential of each type of machine mentioned above can be found in any standard shop-machinist manual.

Stamping consists of pressing or drawing sheet metal (copper, aluminum, steel, or their alloys) into dies on a foot-operated, hydraulic, or power press. Intricate shapes, cutout sections, and deep drawings are all possible to tolerances of about 0.001 inch by this method. While it is essentially a process for quantity manufacture, small quantities which do not warrant the high die cost can usually be turned out in an inexpensive "soft" die or by use of a hand-operated shear, bender, and brake. A press-forming method employing heated dies is used to mold slabs of rubber and to bond rubber-to-metal items into various shapes.

Cutting may be accomplished in a reciprocating, rotating, or band saw or by means of an abrasive cutoff machine using a cardboard-thin abrasive wheel. Still another process is flame cutting, employing an oxy-acetylene torch directed by hand or pantograph.

Heat-treating embraces several processes for changing the physical properties of metals by means of heat. *Hardening*, which is usually applied to steel, consists of heating the metal above its critical temperature and quenching suddenly in water, oil, or air blast. *Tempering*, or draw-

Fig. 22.—A roller-hearth conveyor-type bright-annealing furnace which anneals parts under a controlled atmosphere so as not to discolor them in the process. (*Courtesy of the General Electric Company.*)

ing to give desired "toughness," is accomplished by a subsequent heat soaking to relieve hardening stresses. *Annealing* is a heating process to soften parts hardened by heat or cold working (see Fig. 22). The foregoing heat-treatment processes may require heating the entire part in a gas, oil, or electric *furnace*. Or if localized heating is prescribed, it may be done by an *induction heater* wherein heat is generated in any conducting substance by means of a high-frequency magnetic field. Or localized heating can be accomplished by an *acetylene flame* moving along the exterior surface of the part. Both of these processes for local heat-treatment are commonly used for casehardening (as gear teeth), for annealing, and for brazing. *Infrared heating* is an efficient means of preheating, dehydrating, paint drying, or shrink-fitting some articles. Since it utilizes radiated heat of lamps which at the source are between 3000 to 4000°F., the resultant heating is very rapid. Nonmetallic articles may be heated by *radio-frequency power*. It is also useful in pressure-bonding laminated wood, in plywood manufacture, for "compreg" woods, and in the molding of plastics. *Mild heating*, as for process baths or washing equipment, may be achieved by steam or gas-fired units or again by electricity.

Surface treating includes a variety of processes for chemically or mechanically altering the surface characteristics of any article. *Plating* is an electrolytic process for adding beauty, providing an anticorrosion finish, or enlarging dimensions (of worn or undersized parts) by the addition of chromium, nickel, cadmium, or copper to the surface. *Galvanizing*, a hot-dip process, provides an antirust zinc coating. *Porcelain enameling* gives a hard if somewhat brittle, baked-on, highly protective finish commonly used on kitchenware and on some household appliances. *Metal-blackening*, e.g., gunmetal, embraces electrochemical processes for improving appearance and adding slight antirust protection without increasing the dimensions of the article. *Painting* for appearance and as a preservative makes possible the use of colors or can be "wrinkled" for added attractiveness. *Plastic coatings* are, however, encroaching into the domain of paints because of their better and more durable finishes. Other surface treatments include surface abrasion by either *tumbling* or *shot-blasting* for purposes of cleaning and brightening and *shot-peening*, a means of achieving surface hardness and resistance to fatigue through compressive surface stresses. A youngster in the family of surface treating is the technique of *metal spraying*, in which molten metal is sprayed on parts to build up or alter surfaces.

Assembly methods are legion. *Soldering* and *brazing* join two metals by fusion with a lower melting and softer metal. *Welding*, which has enjoyed phenomenal growth in application in recent years, can produce a joint stronger than the surrounding metal. Depending upon the metal, the type of joint, and the speed required, electric-arc, oxyacetylene, resistance, helium-arc, atomic-hydrogen, thermit, or automatic welding may be used. However, all welding relies on heat to soften the edges to be joined. Contrary to the impression conveyed by some Sunday supplements, welding is not the only assembly technique employed today. *Mechanical connectors*—bolts, screws, rivets, bent metal lugs, and even "old man" friction—are still enjoying wide usage.

Selecting the Exact Type of Productive Equipment.—Once the basic manufacturing processes have been determined, the next step is to select each item of productive equipment along with its tooling, jigs, fixtures, etc.

Usually this entails first of all a decision as to the flexibility or adaptability desired in the equipment to be selected. While product designs are seldom "frozen," some items are subject only to infrequent design changes; others are more unstable, depending upon their relative position on the progress-time curve (see page 183). The more likely that

Fig. 23.—Industrial welding. (*Courtesy of Linde Air Products.*)

frequent changes in design will occur, the more necessary it becomes to build flexibility into the productive equipment.

Machine tools can be classed as either *general purpose* or *single purpose.* General-purpose machines are the more flexible and constitute the bulk of machine tools in use today. Included in this category are many of the equipment items mentioned in the foregoing section: engine and turret lathes, screw machines, universal grinders, welding machines, and induction heaters. Each of these types of machines is designed to perform one or more operations on a variety of sizes or items. A change in product design simply means changing a tool, a head, or a fixture, and the same piece of equipment is again ready to start production.

By contrast, special-purpose machines are designed to do one job and that job alone. Such machines generally possess the advantage of performing specific operations more rapidly than do general-purpose machines—an important factor in volume manufacture. However, they are likely to be inflexible, and a change in product design may require scrapping or a complete conversion. Usually the choice between general- and single-purpose equipment is a matter of economics: (1) initial cost which must be charged off during the anticipated useful life of the equipment, (2) direct labor cost, and (3) preparation cost including tooling and setup.

Machine tooling refers to the selection and design of cutting tools, jigs, fixtures, and dies required to perform a specific operation. This field, which is generally called *tool engineering,* has much to do with the operating efficiency of machines. Decision as to whether an air chuck or a mechanical chuck should be used; whether a cemented carbide tool or one made from high-speed steel will perform better; what speeds and feeds produce the most satisfactory results; whether water, oil, or air will serve best as a coolant—these are typical of the problems encountered by the tool engineers.

A decision as to the machine *actuation, i.e.,* the means of achieving motion, must likewise be made. Common actuating methods are electric, hydraulic, pneumatic (compressed air or steam), and mechanical (train of gears, cams, or levers). Each of these actuating means has its advantages for achieving certain motions, but this factor being equal between two such means, the limitations of space, over-all cost, and ease of change or maintenance govern the exact choice.

In the design or selection of any machine, there are two cardinal principles which should be taken into consideration: (1) The machine should be easy to set up, operate, service, and repair, and (2) it should be provided with safety devices to prevent costly breakdown from improper operation. Examples of the latter are electrical heating coils which cut off the power when the equipment has been overloaded and photoelectric-interlock devices on furnaces which shut off fuel flow in the event of interruption of the flame. Adequate safety guards should be provided to prevent the operator from being caught in protruding moving parts. Start-stop controls should be placed so that quick stopping is possible. Levers and control movements should be so rigged that their direction coincides with that of the machine part being regulated—otherwise even the best of operators is apt to make a wrong move in an emergency. If possible, the machine should be so designed that the operator may sit comfortably at the machine.

Finally in making the choice of equipment, there is the question whether to build or buy. Many factors bear on such a decision. Where the machine is designed by and purchased from an outside firm, the purchasing company may find itself in the unenviable position of having at least partially financed the development of that equipment and provided the vendor with experience which he can then make available to the company's competitors. Also, an in-plant-designed and -built item of equipment sometimes more nearly fits that plant's needs than does a similar item of general-purpose design purchased from a machine-tool manufacturer. Other times, the ability of the plant to make the equipment, the availability of replacement parts, the knowledge required in that field of design—any of these may govern the decision. And apart from the foregoing considerations there is always the important matter of relative costs.

Determination of Productive Capacity.—The most accurate and in fact the only scientific method for fixing the number of machines of each type required makes use of production data.

The first datum or information utilized is a forecast of the production required. This forecast usually is based on a breakdown of the sales forecast, and although it may at best be something of a guess on the part of the sales department, nevertheless it is information that is essential to an intelligent appraisal of the production equipment required.

Next a work-shift policy must be formulated so that the number of hours that the equipment is to operate per week can be calculated. The question of the length of the working day together with that of single- or multishift operation is an integral part of the calculation of the available hours of operation. In general, it may be stated that, where floor space and other conditions warrant, single-shift operation for hand jobs and assembly work is preferable because it eliminates the bonus commonly paid to night-shift employees for working less desirable hours. A single-shift schedule is also desirable where the equipment cost is low and hence where the machine-rate charge against the operation performed is correspondingly low. Multishift operation frequently is favored where costly equipment is involved and where 16- or 24-hour-per-day utilization produces a more favorable machine-rate charge against that equipment. Furthermore, in continuous-process industries (as chemical production, papermaking, steel rolling, or brass casting), the 24-hour day is a virtual economic necessity because of their high "warm-up" costs.

Standard production-rate data in the form of minutes per piece or pieces per hour for each product or part to be processed on the equipment involved, together with proper allowances for setup time, maintenance, and repairs, must likewise be considered. These may be obtained from time studies [1] of the equipment and operations performed. If past production records over a period of time are available for that or similar equipment, they may be used as a check against the synthetic data evolved by time

[1] See discussion of time study, Chap. XVII.

studies. Of course, idle-machine allowances or "down time" for setup, maintenance, and repairs will vary considerably among types of machines, nature and precision of the work required, length of the runs permitted, and a host of other conditions. Nevertheless, most enterprises figure that their equipment should be operating between 75 and 80 per cent of the theoretical or available hours of operation possible under the work schedule in effect. Failure to measure up to that percentage is usually prima-facie evidence that some control is breaking down.

Once the data as enumerated above have been assembled, a large sheet is frequently prepared, listing vertically along the left-hand side the parts and operations together with the quantities to be manufactured. Across the top are enumerated the various machines and equipment required. Sometimes a separate card with spaces for the foregoing data may be made up for each type of machine. In any event, the standard production times plus the idle-machine allowances are listed in the appropriate columns. These, when multiplied by the quantities to be manufactured per week and totaled, give a result equal to the total operating hours per week required for each type of machine. This figure divided by the number of hours available per machine per week furnishes the number of machines required.

The primary objective in selecting the number of machines required is, of course, the elimination or prevention of bottleneck operations. Each type of machine must be capable of absorbing work received from prior operations and of supplying subsequent machines with sufficient material to utilize them to the desired capacity.

Trends in Design of Productive Equipment.—Of particular note in current design trends is the increasing use of electronics as a part of the process (as for rapid and precise heating), for automatic inspection (particularly for automatic dimensional control at the machine), as well as in timing devices (for processes controlled by time), electric-eye overload protective devices (comparable to the safety valves on steam boilers), dynetric balancing (of motor shafts and other rotating parts), cathode-ray oscilloscopes, speed indicators and regulators, voltage regulators, etc.

Electronics are also responsible for an important development in machine design. Infinitely variable speeds and feed rates have long been recognized as the secret to a machine's optimum rate of production and to maximum tool or grinding-wheel life. Or it may be desirable to synchronize the speed of several machine components or several interdependent operations. Yet with a-c electric power, which is practically universal for transmission reasons, only "step" changes in speed frequently are possible—not the 1, 3 per cent, etc., variations in speed so often desired.[2]   However, d-c motors make possible infinitely variable speeds without gearing or speed changers.   In the past for certain applications, a-c to d-c motor-generator converters have been used to permit installation of d-c motors, but this practice has not met with wide favor. However, it is now possible to achieve infinitely variable speeds and feeds with a-c power converted to d-c electronically (usually with a thyratron tube) right at the machine.

Finally, a trend has been noted toward the design of machines with "built-in skill and intelligence."   In this category fall not only the various types of machines classed as automatic (such as those which make incandescent light bulbs), but also such machines as tracer-controlled millers, profilers, and others which take most or all of the guesswork and judgment out of their operation.   These machines relieve operators from the tedious mental and physical work that otherwise is a part of highly repetitive production.[3]   Furthermore, the human mind and faculties can operate only just so rapidly.   Automatic mechanisms, on the other hand, can function with incredible speed.   Hence, machines thus equipped are capable of much higher rates of production than are those which must rely solely on human activation.

PREPARATION OF THE PLANT LAYOUT

Principles of Plant Layout.—In any plant, the ideal procedure is to build the layout around the product and then design the building around the layout, thus achieving a plant that is completely *functional*.   How-

---

[2] Step changes are usually accomplished by gearing or by one of the types of speed changers available.   It should be mentioned, however, that some speed changers do provide for infinite speed change.   One of the more common types makes use of a pair of "split-V" pulleys, one the driver and the other the driven, connected by a special belt.   The effective pitch diameter of one pulley is decreased by spreading the V in that pulley as the pitch diameter of the other is increased by narrowing its V. Nevertheless, such speed changers do not lend themselves to high-speed ranges and are costly to maintain.   Hence their application is limited.

[3] Ford Motor Company's Mound Road Plant, Detroit, Mich., has almost entirely accomplished the ideal of removing the burden of physical effort from men and placing it on machines.   Ford terms this *automation* and defines it as the "loading, processing in machine, unloading and transfer to the next operation without resorting to manual handling."   Automation requires that the machines, tooling, and mechanical handling devices between machines all be so integrated as to become, in effect, one continuous machine.   In this plant, steel tubing is processed into rear-axle housings for Ford cars.   From the time the tubes enter the plant until they emerge as finished axle halves, after many operations have been performed on them, they are handled manually only three times!   The story of automation at Ford may be found in *Production Engineering and Management*, August, 1949, p. 51.

ever, this ideal method cannot always be followed. In the case of a going enterprise, some if not all buildings may be in existence. Or perhaps the plant site has been selected, in which case its terrain, size, and shape may not permit the construction of a building to house the layout desired. Plant layout, therefore, is usually a compromise between the ideal or functional layout and the limitations of buildings and plant site.

Plant layout is influenced by the type of productive process involved. A *synthetic* process is one that involves the assembly of the component parts of the product. For example, the manufacture of Portland cement is a synthetic process involving the mixing of limestone and clay. Automobile assembly lines likewise are typical synthetic processes. An *analytic* process is one that resolves the raw material into its various elements or constituent parts. Such industrial processes as meat packing, which develops a multitude of by-products, and petroleum refining, which converts crude petroleum into naphtha, gasoline, paraffin, tar, kerosene, etc., are typical analytical processes. A *conditioning* process involves a change in form or physical properties. Most metalworking industries, foundries, and leather-tanning shops condition their raw materials to achieve the product. The fourth type of process is *extractive*. It is essentially a process of separation, such as the obtaining of magnesium and bromine from sea water, or metal ore from the earth. Usually, however, manufacturing involves not one but a combination of these productive processes. For example, the manufacture of machine tools involves conditioning processes in the fabrication of the various machine parts, and synthetic processes as far as their assembly into finished products is concerned.

It is imperative that any layout be based on the types of processes involved. For example, a synthetic process will usually be laid out to resemble a river. Just as a river's tributaries merge together as the river continues downstream, so also do the various materials and parts of a synthetic process merge into the completed assembly as one follows the layout path through the plant. An analytic-process layout, on the other hand, takes the form of a tree as it starts out with a single material or substance (the trunk) and spreads out into a variety of resultant materials (the branches, leaves, and fruit). A conditioning process often calls for a layout to accommodate "batch" or "lot" manufacture. In such a layout, the material undergoes no merger or separation but is simply subjected to physical conditioning as it flows in separate lots through the variety of operations and processes. However, regardless of the type of process, plant layout is not an end in itself but is concerned only with achieving the best means to an end, the end in this case being a smooth flow of materials through the required productive processes.

Also of importance among the principles of plant layout is the question of whether it should be engineered for serialized manufacture, for job-lot manufacture, or for semiserialized manufacture. Each of these types of manufacture will be considered in Chap. XI in its relation to production planning. However, we are here concerned with the effect of each on the layout of the plant.

Layout for Serialized Manufacture.—Serialized manufacture or the production-line type of manufacture, as it is sometimes called, involves continuous flow of materials from one operation to the next and is used in the quantity production of a standardized product. The simplest application of the production-line technique is the *line within a machine.* A multiple-spindle automatic-screw machine successively indexes the work from one machining position to another so that several operations are performed in what amounts to a continuous flow of material within the machine. An industrial washing machine for cleaning metal parts may, by means of a conveyor belt within the machine, carry the work through successive washing, drying, and oiling operations. A second application is the *sporadic production line* involving a battery of machines or several continuous or closely allied processes (see semiserialized manufacture, page 230). *Lot fabrication with line assembly* and *line fabrication with line assembly* are the two remaining applications of the production-line technique. The former is the accepted type of manufacture in airplane plants where parts and subassemblies are made in batches and assembled into the finished product on an assembly line. The automotive industry, of course, employs both line fabrication and assembly.

In production lines other than those involving only a single machine, the machines and equipment are laid out according to the sequence of operations required for that product and are usually grouped around the conveying mechanism which is the heart of serialized production flow. This arrangement of equipment speeds up the manufacturing cycle by reducing the inventory and congestion of goods in process as well as the time required for their handling, makes production easier to control, and eliminates backtracking of materials. It greatly simplifies the problems of supervision, since the foreman is generally concerned with just one part or product per production line. Also the line usually sets and regulates the pace of the operators. It likewise exercises a certain amount of "holding power" to keep operators at their workplaces. The responsibility for the quality and output of the part or product is vested in one foreman which greatly simplifies administration and eliminates interdepartmental bickering and complaints.

The disadvantages of any production line are that it makes for an inflexible layout not adaptable to the manufacture of any other type of product, and that a tie-up or machine breakdown at any one point along the line will stop the entire line of machines and personnel. Production lines are practical only where the rate of flow is such that all machines and operators can be kept busy virtually 100 per cent of the time. Even if the line is theoretically designed for the complete utilization of all equipment and personnel, variations in the rate of output of certain operators, absentee problems, and other human factors invariably affect the rate of flow of work so as to reduce the utilization of other machines and operators in the line. Also the volume and length of the production run must be such as to make the high installation costs of the line economically practical. However, in spite of the fact that many companies still think of minimum production-line runs in terms of several months or even a year, there is at least one organization on record that has found that it pays to set up a completely new line for a 2-weeks' run, after which the line is torn down and another one installed for a different product.

Wherever serialized manufacture is contemplated, much planning must go into the line itself. The machines, tooling, and auxiliary equipment must all be carefully selected both as to type and capacity to handle the rate of flow desired. This, together with the determination of the number of operators required and the positioning of those operators so as to provide near 100 per cent utilization of their time, is known as *balancing out* the production line. Finally, as a part of the planning of the line, the *float* or bank of material required between each operation must be ascertained and provision made for the storage of that float as an integral part of the line installation. After the line is installed, the continuing availability of materials and man power must be assured if the ultimate efficiency of the line is to be realized.

Layout for Job-lot Manufacture.—Job-lot manufacture, on the other hand, involves an intermittent flow of materials. For that reason machines are grouped according to the type of operation they perform. For example, under this so-called "layout by process," all lathe turning might be done in one production center or department, grinding in another, plating in a third, assembly in still another, etc. Where a variety of products are produced at irregular intervals, job-lot manufacture is obviously the only type possible. It has the advantage of offering maximum flexibility as far as machine usage and capacity are concerned, provides a better opportunity for less duplication and greater control of tools, jigs, and fixtures, and makes for lower setup and repair costs.

Furthermore, when one machine or group of machines becomes loaded with work or where a machine breakdown is involved, it is possible to shift work readily to other machines so as to balance the load and avoid or minimize delay.

Of course, in a plant laid out for job-lot manufacture, backtracking is the rule rather than the exception, and more material is tied up in inventories. Material must be moved in and out of storerooms, production centers, and inspection stations in lots. Delays occur between operations, since any particular batch of work is not as a rule moved to the next station until the entire lot has been completed at the previous operation or inspection center. Routing, scheduling, dispatching, and follow-up of the material in process involve a great variety of paper work and leg work by the inevitable "expediters." Handling of material between operations is slow and costly, for work is usually moved by hand or power-driven trucks, and the distance between operations is frequently great. Where the product is heavy or bulky, this handling problem may be a serious drawback to this type of layout, whereas for smaller products the handicap is not so important. As an example of the latter, in the manufacture of drill chucks process layouts have proved to be quite advantageous, for the parts and finished product itself are small, and handling is not a serious or costly problem.

Layout for Semiserialized Manufacture.—A compromise can sometimes be achieved in certain plants between the two foregoing types of manufacture. This compromise can be labeled *semiserialized manufacture.* Companies that have perfected this type of flow have found that a very advantageous arrangement can be devised by performing several operations on a single product within a department. Such an arrangement groups together into a battery the machines used in successive operations, possibly connecting them with conveyors. Or, the manufacture may be serialized as far as possible except for a few operations requiring fixed, extremely heavy, or very objectionable equipment (such as that used in heat-treating, plating, forging, or large sheet-metal work), which is then located centrally. However, the aim of any layout for semiserialized manufacture is to decrease handling costs and lower the in-process material without seriously detracting from the flexibility of the machines—thus retaining the principal advantages of both serialized and job-lot manufacture.

Size of the Production Center.—The size of the production center or department is also an important consideration in the making of the layout. Its size is usually dependent more upon the span of administrative control than upon any physical factors involved. A department should not be so large that it is difficult for one man to control. Of course, wherever possible, natural subdivisions should be utilized, as for example, grouping together men with the same or allied skills, interdependent or related machines, parts subassemblies, or products.

Service areas should be a part of each production center, or if community service areas are found to be practical, they should be located conveniently to the production men and equipment that they serve. In general, it has been found that *one-third of any plant or department area should be devoted to servicing facilities.* These include the storage of materials, clerical and supervisory offices, tool and gage cribs, and lavatory, washing, and locker facilities. Thus, in laying out any manufacturing area, it is usually advisable to rule off immediately one-third of the space as that which must be devoted to servicing.

Provision should be made in the initial layout for future expansion or a possible rearrangement of machines in the event that the design of the products, methods of manufacture, or production requirements are changed at some subsequent date. To do so may save much grief and costly rearranging of machines should some such changes later take place. Aisles should be adequate not only for the internal transportation of production material and the passage of employees to and from their machines but also for the passage of any of the machines should one or more of them have to be removed from the production center for overhaul or for major repairs.

However, since floor space in an industrial plant represents money, it is desirable to utilize it to the utmost. Among plants making similar products, the degree of utilization is known as the *relative production density.* A high production density makes for a compact plant, one that is an integrated unit. Furthermore, the plant that can raise its production density to a high level thereby prevents the over-expansion of its facilities.

Tools of Plant Layout.—There are certain tools of plant layout in common use today which are a distinct aid in making or improving the layout of any plant. The first of these is the *process-flow chart,* a graphic map that follows material through its manufacturing cycle and records the sequence of the elements of that cycle as they occur (see Figs. **24** and **25**). In analyzing a process, five major elements are sufficient for most purposes:

- ◯ Operation.
- ○ Transportation.
- ▽ Temporary storage (less than **24** hours).
- ▽ Permanent storage (greater than **24** hours).
- ☐ Inspection.

PROCESS FLOW CHART

Job No. *Sub contract 5624*   Part No. *FL5*   Date *1/27/44*
Part *Forged link*   Chart No. _____77_____
Division *Link*   Chart By: *K.H.R.*

Old Method

Distance (feet)	Means of transport	Dept.	Symbol	Process description
15	HT		◯	Receive steel bars
		A	▽	In racks in raw-material storage
30	HT		◯	To forge room
		H	①	Hot forge
30	HT		◯	To tumbling barrels
		I	②	Tumble to remove flash
80	HT & E		◯	To chucking machines
		J	▽	"Float" ahead of chucking
		J	③	Form-turn
55	HT		◯	To machining inspection
		K	④	Inspect for size, magnaflux, and visual inspection
25	HT & E		◯	To tumbling barrels
		I	▽	"Float" ahead of tumbling
		I	⑤	Tumble to remove burrs
75	HT		◯	To plating barrels
		L	▽	"Float" ahead of plating
		L	⑥	Cadmium plate
95	HT & E		◯	To plate inspection
		K	⑦	Inspect % for plate appearance and plate thickness
20	HT		◯	To drill presses
		J	⑧	Drill and tap hole
25	HT		◯	To thread inspection
		K	⑨	Inspect for thread depth and fit, visual inspection, and pack
40	HT		◯	To finished goods storage
		B	▽	In racks awaiting shipment
50	HT & E		◯	Ship to prime contractor
540 ft.	Total			

KEY:
- ① = Operation
- ④ = Inspection
- ◯ = Transportation
- ▽ = Permanent storage
- ▽ = Temporary storage

- HT = Hand truck
- E = Elevator
- C = Conveyor
- GC = Gravity chute

FIG. 24.—Typical process-flow chart—old method. Note that each element in the process is systematically listed to reveal a great deal of hand trucking over considerable distances. Note also that the intermittent flow of material between departments and operations requires a temporary storage or "float" of material at several points in the process. (See also process flow diagram, Fig. 26.)

232

PROCESS FLOW CHART

Job No. *Sub contract 5624*   Part No. *FL5*   Date *2/23/44*
Part *Forged link*   Chart No. *78*
Division *Link*   Chart By: *K.H.R.*

New Method

Distance (feet)	Means of transport	Dept.	Symbol	Process description
15	HT	A	O	Receive steel bars
		A	▽P	In racks in raw-material storage
30	HT		O	To forge room
		H	(1)	Hot forge
95	HT, E & C		O	To tumbling barrels
		J	(2)	Tumble to remove flash
25	C		O	To chucking machines
		J	(3)	Form-turn
15	C		O	To machining inspection
		K	[4]	Inspect for size, magnaflux, and visual inspection
15	C		O	To tumbling barrels
		J	(5)	Tumble to remove burrs
15	C		O	To plating barrels
		J	(6)	Cadmium plate
15	C		O	To plate inspection
		K	[7]	Inspect % for plate appearance and plate thickness
20	C		O	To drill presses
		J	(8)	Drill and tap hole
15	C.		O	To thread inspection
		K	[9]	Inspect for thread depth and fit, visual inspection, and pack
12	GC		O	To finished goods storage
		B	▽P	In racks awaiting shipment
25	HT		O	Ship to prime contractor
297 ft.	Total			

KEY:

(1) = Operation		HT = Hand truck	
[4] = Inspection		E = Elevator	
O = Transportation		C = Conveyor	
▽P = Permanent storage		GC = Gravity chute	
▽ = Temporary storage			

FIG. 25.—Typical process-flow chart—new method. Rearrangement of layout now permits the use of conveyors and a gravity chute eliminating much hand trucking and use of the elevator. New layout also consolidates departments and provides continuous flow of material between most operations to eliminate need for "floats." Total distance traveled by material is reduced from 540 feet to 297 feet. (See also process-flow diagram, Fig. 27.)

The process-flow chart permits a process to be visualized in such a compact form that possible improvements are usually readily discerned. Repeated static elements of storage, for example, indicate delays in production and perhaps unnecessary transportation of material. The inefficiencies disclosed by such a chart may require the rearranging of

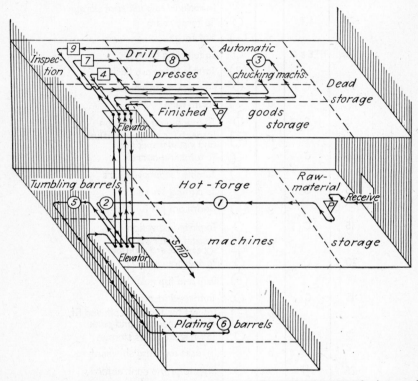

Fig. 26.—Typical process-flow diagram—old method. Such diagrams depict graphically the flow of work, emphasizing the existence of backtracking and long hauls of material. (For description of operations, see process-flow chart, Fig. 24.)

work stations or may point the need for better transportation facilities. Analysis may disclose that some operations that add little or nothing to the final value of the product can be eliminated by minor changes in the product design, or that certain tasks previously split into two operations may be combined into a single operation. Similarly, an opportunity may be disclosed by which the sequence of the various elements in the process can be rearranged to eliminate backtracking and unnecessary handling. Once the process has been analyzed through the use of the process-flow chart, any improvements effected can be incorporated into the layout as it is made.

Another similar layout tool that is sometimes used in place of, and at other times in addition to, the process-flow chart is the *process-flow diagram*. This will take the form of a floor-plan sketch of the building or in

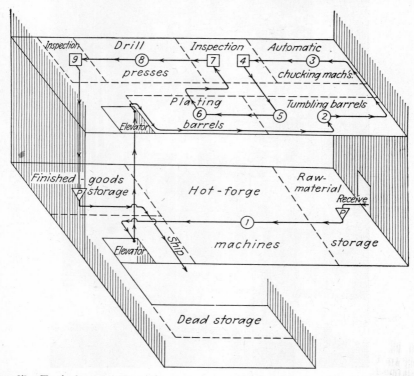

Fig. 27.—Typical process-flow diagram—new method. Note how the rearrangement of the plant serves to minimize the distance material must travel and permits the use of conveyors between operations. A gravity chute carries material from the second floor down to the finished-goods storage on the first floor. Such a process-flow diagram as this depicting the new method not only shows improvements already effected but also may point the way to further economies. (For description of operations, see process-flow chart, Fig. 25.)

the case of a multistory plant, a perspective diagram of the building plan upon which the flow of materials through the various operations is depicted. The process-flow diagram is a fine method of showing up long material hauls and the backtracking of present layouts, thereby indicating how the layout may be improved; or it may be used to check a proposed layout against similar pitfalls.

The next layout tool is the familiar *template layout*. It is prepared by cutting out scale templates to denote machines, racks, and other equipment and laying them on a plan drawing that shows elevators, stairs, columns, and other limitations of the buildings that might affect the

Fig. 28.—Light-colored templates cut to scale for each machine, bench, conveyor line, etc., are used against a dark background in making the layout at North American Aviation, Inc. Note that where space is required for large subassemblies and assemblies (in this case, airframes), templates are made for these also. Large layouts may take the form of wall charts, as shown here, or can be made in sections for ease of preparation and handling. (*Photograph from Modern Industry, February,* 1944.)

layout. A scale of ¼ inch to the foot is perhaps the most satisfactory. Where the equipment and plant are large, ⅛ inch to the foot may be more desirable. The templates may be moved around on the drawing at will until the optimum layout has been achieved. Approval of all interested parties is then obtained after which the layout is transferred to blueprints or photostats for installation and recording purposes.

Another aid is the *scale-model layout* consisting of scaled reproductions of all pieces of equipment laid out on a floor plan of the plant area. Resembling a child's doll house, the scale model aids in determining the amount of space and headroom required by each equipment item. Sometimes substituted for the template layout, it likewise enables the layout men to visualize the flow of work through a plant.

In "selling" a revised layout plan to the top management of the enterprise, a *cost and savings estimate* is frequently prepared. This is simply a report of the estimated cost of making the moves proposed, as balanced or overbalanced by the annual savings to be derived therefrom. For example, direct savings of labor through the elimination of handling and trucking as well as indirect savings such as less clerical work, fewer inspection operations, and better supervision should be included in the dollar-and-cents column if possible or, if that is not possible, certainly under a list of intangible savings.

INSTALLATION OF THE EQUIPMENT

Once the layout has been approved and reproduced, copies are usually distributed not only to the manufacturing supervision involved but also to the construction engineers, plumbers, millwrights, and electricians so that necessary preliminary work may be completed by the time the installation of equipment is desired.

It frequently is possible to build flexibility and lower maintenance costs into the layout when such work is performed. Examples of such features that can be incorporated into the layout and installation of the equipment are floor trenches adequate for all utility lines to the equipment and with sufficient space for servicing them, T joints in pipes at regular intervals for additional outlets without cutting the pipe, cleanout traps in drain lines, coolant tanks placed for ready accessibility for cleaning, "plug-in" type electrical connections, catwalks where needed for servicing overhead equipment, conveyors with removable sections, movable office and crib partitions, and automatic or single-application oiling systems. These not only make for ease of subsequent alteration and maintenance but also increase the safety of the machine operation and minimize any lost production which might be caused by machines "on repair."

The actual moving of machines is done by millwrights who are skilled in the art of moving heavy equipment. Frequently for large installations, firms of industrial movers are called in with their heavy tractors, winches, and cranes to perform the job. Where production must continue during a change in plant layout, considerable coordination among the engineers and various trades specialists is required to minimize the lost production time while equipment is moved. Sometimes it is possible

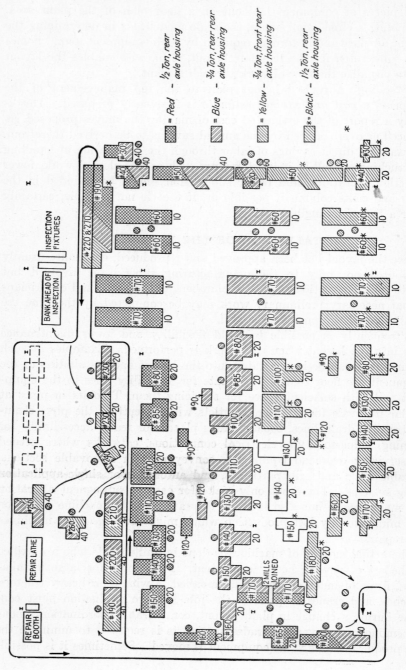

Fig. 29.—For descriptive legend see opposite page.

to make the moves on nights, week ends, or holidays, when there is no interference with production.

Who Selects the Physical Facilities?—In these last two chapters we have been concerned with organizing the physical facilities of the enterprise—the plant location, buildings, installations, equipment, and layout. Before leaving this subject, mention should be made that these activities are usually the function of the *plant-engineering department*. Other functions of this department will be considered in some detail in Chap. XVIII. However, we should note here that in making its choice of facilities this department is guided variously by the counsel of the research and product-engineering, industrial-engineering,[4] cost, personnel, purchasing, and production-control departments. Similarly the maintenance department usually will figure in decisions pertaining to plant and equipment. Of course, the physical facilities invariably involve a rather substantial outlay of the funds of the enterprise, and the ideas and recommendations of all these departments are presented to top management for final disposition.

SUMMARY

A few general observations on the subjects discussed in the past two chapters stand out as worthy of reconsideration. Industrial facilities

[4] Frequently the industrial engineers because of their closer contact with plant methods, work simplification, and time standards (see Chap. XVII) prepare plant layouts and turn them over to the plant-engineering department for installation and procurement of materials handling and any other necessary servicing equipment.

FIG. 29.—A template layout of the axle housing department at the Highland Park plant of the Chrysler Corporation, showing how color may be used in laying out an area for the production of several items. In this case the items are four sizes of axle housings, each of which is assigned a different color. These colors used on the machine templates indicate which housing size or sizes are routed to a particular machine. For example, the initial operation (20) for the red, blue, and yellow housings is performed on a single machine, the template space for which is tricolored accordingly.

The path of each housing during fabrication can be readily traced by following the corresponding color and operation sequence. Thus the red housings travel right to left from operation 20 to 180 inclusive, then are hung on an overhead, continuous-loop-chain conveyor (solid line), which carries them through the washing machine (operation 190) and finally to inspection. The number under each machine indicates the hourly rate of production for that machine. Colored circles denote the positions of the machine operators and the housing sizes upon which they work.

In addition to showing where to locate machines common to more than one housing, the Chrysler layout attempts to obtain the maximum utilization of machine equipment and manpower, keep material handling to a minimum, use overhead monorail-and-hoist conveyors (not shown in this reproduction) and gravity-flow racks (likewise not shown) to accommodate the desired banks of material between operations.

All these considerations can be quickly visualized through the use of color. The result: an effective semiserialized layout. (*Chart and accompanying description from Factory, March, 1944, p. 113.*)

should be thought of simply as tools in the hands of the plant engineers. The effectiveness with which these tools are applied and the ends that they are made to serve depend upon the vision, foresight, and imagination of the men to whom they are intrusted. It is important to note that there may be no "one best way" of using these tools. The sole test is empirical: Does it work? One group of men in selecting a plant site might choose a crowded city area whereas another group would elect instead a spacious suburban site. One group might decide on a compact multistory unit; another, on an expanded single-story structure. Some might mold together the plant facilities for job-lot manufacture; others would work toward a completely serialized plant. Some might install elaborate facilities for servicing the personnel, whereas others would decide that the money could be better spent in providing better handling equipment and working conditions at the machines. What works under one set of conditions and with one group of people may be far from the answer with other conditions and people. Thus are experience and a separate consideration of each case the best and perhaps the only guides in matters pertaining to plant facilities.

If current trends in plant facilities were to be summed up in one word, that word would most certainly be *flexibility*. Until fairly recently, it was the accepted procedure to move all materials to the men and machines. Today, however, plant engineers realize that it may be more efficient in many cases to move men and machines to the materials. Flexibility is the offspring of mobility. It is gained through motorized machines with their own unit coolant systems, blowers, and accessories. It results from the use of standard sections of conveyor, shelving, and other servicing equipment. It likewise demands more adaptable buildings which permit of easy alterations and in which the necessary utility lines are laid so as to provide ready service for each equipment unit wherever it may be positioned. Of course, large heat-treating equipment, steam hammers, presses, and other big machines are generally quite immobile. But with most of today's equipment of the mobile type, it may truly be said that progressive plants are "on the move."

CASE PROBLEMS

Selecting the Plant Location

THE MAP METHOD

One objective approach to the problem of selecting a plant location is known as the map method. The practice is first to draw on a map an outline of the market area to be served by the plant. In the case of a bakery, for example, the area might be on the order of magnitude of a 20-mile radius; for a manufacturer of electrical appliances, it might be nearer 200 miles, etc. Next the sources of materials, including parts and major supplies, should be indicated on the map as should the transportation facilities available in the area.

Such a map fairly well defines the region in which the plant should be located and can indicate the communities in which the search should be conducted. This map technique has applicability not only for plants looking for new sites but also for existing plants to check their present location and to ascertain if a move is warranted.

Preparatory Question

Select a manufacturing plant in your locality which serves a regional or local market and check the suitability of its present location by the map method. Use a road or atlas map and plot the pertinent factors, employing the following key:

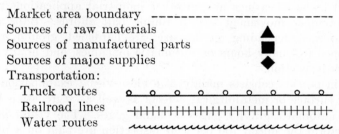

Indicate whether or not the plant you have selected is strategically located and why.

Selecting the Building Installations

SPORTING GOODS, INC.

Sporting Goods, Inc., is a firm located in a small community and employing about 500 people in the manufacture of tennis, squash, and badminton rackets and wood golf-club heads. Its processes require a steam kiln for drying lumber directly as it is taken from boxcars, a series of woodworking operations, a lacquering section, and areas for assembly, storage, and shipping of completed rackets.

The management of the company has decided to build a new plant to consolidate and streamline its manufacturing operations and to enlarge its warehouse space to take care of peak seasonal inventories so characteristic of the sporting-goods industry. The building is to be a moderate-cost, one-story steel-frame manufacturing building with brick and steel-sash walls, concrete floor, and steel-deck flat roof.   An attached two-story office building is to be of similar construction.   The total floor space will approximate 250,000 square feet.

Preparatory Question

You, as plant engineer of Sporting Goods, Inc., are asked to provide your top management with a list of specific building installations you feel should be provided in this new plant for efficiency, safety, low-cost maintenance, and good employee and public relations.   (*Example:* A central steam plant to furnish process steam for the drying kiln.)

Process-flow Charts and Diagrams in Plant Layout

THE COOLIDGE BALL CO.[5]

The Coolidge Ball Co. manufactures high-grade hardened steel balls ranging in size from $\frac{1}{16}$ to $4\frac{1}{2}$ inches in steps of $\frac{1}{32}$ inch.   These balls are used in ball bearings and in other industrial applications requiring the freedom of movement that a rolling ball affords.   Balls are hot- or cold-forged depending on the size, are hardened, ground, reground, and lapped for many hours on automatic machines, and finally given a thorough inspection.

This inspection consists mainly of a close visual examination of each ball for surface or metallurgical defects as well as segregation by exact size on automatic gravity gages or hand gages.   The visual inspectors who perform the initial 100 per cent inspection are paid on a piecework basis.   Then reinspectors, who are paid by day rates, inspect 30 per cent of the work of each first inspector to make sure that the pieceworkers have not permitted some defective balls to slip through.   The entire inspection procedure is responsible for a high percentage of the total cost of manufacturing balls.   Hence, a few years ago the management of the company, upon analyzing the cost of inspection, decided to examine the layout of the inspection department to determine whether or not any improvements could be effected to lower the inspection cost.

Figure 30 shows the original layout.   Tote pans of balls were delivered from the final-process department and placed on the floor in the center of the room.   A few balls in each pan were first taken to the master size- and surface-check benches for a spot check of the size and surface finish of that lot of balls.

The first visual inspection was performed by girls at the benches along the north and west walls of the department.   Assigned to a pan of balls of a particular size, each first inspector stooped to the floor, secured

[5] Adapted from *Factory*, Vol. 100, No. 11.   Company name fictitious.

a quantity for convenient handling from the pan, and carried this quantity to the weigh-and-cleaning bench. When this operation was completed, she took the balls to her individual inspection station along the benches. Frequently two girls went to the center of the room to help

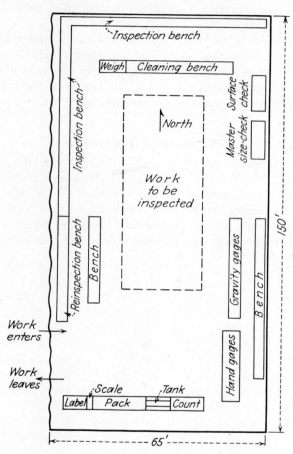

Fig. 30.—Original layout.

one another lift an entire pan, instead of one girl making two or more trips in order to handle all the balls in the pan.

At the inspection bench, each first inspector scooped balls onto a ground-glass plate immediately in front of her. Under this plate was a wooden box into which the inspected balls fell. After this inspection she then carried the box of balls to the reinspectors' bench, and returned to the center of the room to repeat the cycle of stooping, lifting, and walking. The reinspectors handled the balls at their bench in the same fashion as the first inspectors, except that they inspected only 30 per cent of each lot. The reinspectors carried the balls from their positions to a bench placed behind the gravity- and hand-sizing gages. After sizing, the last inspection operation, balls were counted, oiled, packed, and taken to the shipping room.

The management of the Coolidge Co. was fairly well convinced that the nature of the inspection operations and their general sequence could not be readily altered without detracting from the control of quality. However, it did appear that changes in the layout of the room could be effected to reduce the amount of handling and improve the flow of material.

Preparatory Questions

1. Make a process-flow chart and a process-flow diagram of the original layout. On the chart, estimate the distances traveled.

2. Advise the management of the Coolidge Co. of the steps they might take to improve the layout. Substantiate your suggestions with a process-flow chart and a process-flow diagram, incorporating your improvements and noting any cost savings effected and any materials-handling aids used.

Operation of the Industrial Enterprise

A. Manufacturing the Product
B. Administration of Industrial Relations
C. Selling the Product
D. Managing the General Offices

A. Manufacturing the Product

CHAPTER XI

PLANNING FOR PRODUCTION

Modern manufacturing, sometimes defined as the creation of material goods by hand or machinery, is based on an accumulation of knowledge which has become codified and systematized over a period of time. Thus, manufacturing is an *art,* for its foundation is systematized knowledge, its principles have been proved in actual usage, and it has been made more efficient through the acquisition of experience. Modern manufacturing may be shown to consist of three main phases: the *planning* of production, the *supplying* of materials, and the *controlling* of production, quality, and processes. Each of these phases, as will be subsequently developed, is interrelated with every other and is necessary to the efficient and effective brand of manufacturing for which the United States has long been famous.

These phases of the art of manufacturing are analogous to the three phases of military science: strategy, logistics, and tactics. *Strategy* may be defined as the science of projecting or directing military troops or ships to advantage over the enemy. As such it involves the planning of warfare. The military decisions of World War II as to those battlefronts on which the enemy could be most advantageously engaged, the relative priority of activities in each theater of operation, and the degree of concentration of air warfare over Europe, were all a part of the strategy of the United Nations in that conflict. *Logistics* is the science of moving and supplying combat forces in military operations. It involves supplying the right thing in the right amount, in the right place, and at the right time. In World War II the responsibility for this phase of military warfare for the United States was vested in the Army Service Forces. Included in the activities of the ASF were not only the movement and control of the implements of war but also the procurement of these items from the various war plants and arsenals. Finally, *tactics* is the art of using troops, munitions, or equipment in battle or in the presence of the enemy. It is thus the execution of military plans. The battle of Midway, the siege of Stalingrad, and the atom-bomb attacks were all a part of tactics in World War II.

From the foregoing, it can readily be seen that for the effective prosecution of any war, strategy, logistics, and tactics are all mutually interdependent. For example, while strategy determines tactics, at the same time good tactics can advance and strengthen strategy, whereas poor tactics can undermine it. While strategy certainly dictates logistics, nevertheless logistics limits strategy, for without the necessary materials supplied by logistics, strategy and the resultant tactics are both doomed to failure.

Now to complete our analogy. Strategy (the planning of warfare) is directly comparable to production planning. Logistics (the moving and supplying of combat forces) is analogous to the procuring and controlling of industrial materials. And tactics (the execution of military plans) is comparable to the controlling of production, quality, and manufacturing methods. The mutual interdependence of these phases of manufacturing to the same degree that the military phases are interdependent should at once be apparent. Thus, planning determines the degree of control attainable in production, quality, and manufacturing methods. For example, well-planned production can be executed with a minimum of control, whereas poor planning may make unworkable even the most excellent control of production. Conversely, the success or failure of current controls has a bearing on future planning. Also, the supplying of materials is formulated on the production plan, but limitations to the materials supply frequently limit the scope of that plan.

It is the purpose of this and the remaining chapters in this section dealing with the manufacture of the product to develop further these three phases of manufacturing with due consideration not only to their functions and interdependency but also to the principles and techniques employed by industry in their application.

Purpose of Production Planning.—The question: *For whom and for what are we planning?* is one that should be kept in mind continually by those responsible for planning the operations of any industrial enterprise. Why is planning necessary? What purpose does it serve?

To answer these questions we should first define what we mean by planning. *Production planning* is that management function which systematizes in advance the factors of men, materials, machines, and money to achieve an output which is predetermined in relation to: (1) profit desired, (2) market demand, (3) plant capacity, (4) jobs created, and (5) plant facilities utilized.

These then are the reasons for production planning. In our competitive-enterprise system, the *profit motive* is still predominant, for upon it may rest the justification for, and in fact the very survival of, the enterprise. Planning provides the necessary information upon which are based decisions that enable that profit to be realized. For, as someone has said, "Information is knowledge, knowledge is protection, and protection is profit."

Any enterprise to realize a profit must sell its products. Thus its planning agency must take into consideration the *market demand* for the products it is capable of manufacturing. This, of course, involves the translation of the sales forecast, program, or orders into production or manufacturing requirements. The amount of material planned to be manufactured will differ from the forecast sales only by that amount of increase or decrease in the inventory of finished goods desired for the period under consideration. For example, if in anticipation of rising prices or of future increased sales or to stabilize year-round employment, it is desired to increase the inventory of finished goods, the quantity planned to be manufactured will exceed that forecasted by the number of units that the inventory is increased. Of course, in the case of many products manufactured in a diversified line of styles, models, sizes, or colors, the over-all quantity of goods planned must be broken down into quotas for each variation offered.

One ideal aim, if not always attainable, of any plant management is to operate its facilities at their most efficient level of production. This level is seldom the plant's peak capacity, for peak production in any plant involves certain inefficiencies in the usage of men, equipment, or space, whichever is the limiting factor. At some point below the peak level, then, there is an *optimum plant capacity*. This may be defined as that rate of production which makes the best utilization of men, equipment, and space combined and which results in the lowest unit cost with respect to all the cost factors involved. In practice, however, the optimum level of production is seldom strictly attainable. It is always interrelated with the other four considerations of production planning herein discussed. It may be subject to certain predetermined decisions such as the number of hours per week the employees wish to work, the number of work shifts the management wishes to employ, or the desires of the owners to expand or contract the plant facilities. At any rate, effective planning procedure takes all such factors into consideration, together with those which determine the operating efficiency, to the end that a rate of production may be achieved with respect to the sales forecast, stock program, or orders that most nearly approximates the optimum plant capacity.

Frequently, as in lines of endeavor in which business is temporarily or perhaps permanently slack, planning resolves itself into a question of the *utilization of plant facilities* and the *creation of jobs*. The narrowing margin between cost and selling price in recent years has raised the "break-even point" (see Chap. XXVI) to the stage where a high percentage of the plant's optimum capacity must be utilized if a profit is to be realized. Idle equipment involves many dollars of fixed charges just to pay for its "board and keep," yet it brings in not one cent of revenue. Only when the equipment is producing can it pay its way. Likewise, fixed charges and maintenance costs on the plant building as well as the wages of the key executive, engineering, and plant supervisory personnel exist whether the plant is operating with full or only partial throttle. Thus production planning of the enterprise is of necessity charged with keeping its plant busy.

As for the creation of jobs, where in a short period of time a plant successively hires, lays off, rehires, etc., any fair percentage of its personnel, there is prima-facie evidence of poor planning. Pressure of government, unions, and public opinion in recent years has made managements more conscious of their responsibility for keeping people employed. In some states, unemployment-compensation regulations penalize companies with large layoff lists by upping their rates paid for such compensation. This adds a financial stick ready to strike management's posterior if the moral carrot dangling in front of management's nose is not an adequate incentive. Furthermore, seniority-layoff rules in union contracts frequently make layoff and rehiring procedures complicated and costly to the enterprise. Finally, communities do not look favorably upon companies in their midst wherein there is instability either of work force or of number of hours worked. Thus has production planning assumed a role of increased importance in stabilizing the use of plant facilities, the number of jobs, and the working hours.

This stabilization is achieved by leveling off, as far as is practicable, the normal cyclical and seasonal peaks and valleys in production to the end that equipment and men may be kept busy in all seasons and regardless of the trend of the business cycle. Various means are used, such as manufacturing to stock during slack periods in anticipation of future sales, requiring vacations to be taken during such periods, or using idle manufacturing employees for long-term maintenance work. Sometimes, particularly where the slack period is prolonged, certain complementary products can be added to the line of goods made and so selected as to be active during periods when the manufacture of other products would normally be slack.[1] Finally, failing otherwise to keep its employees continually busy, a company can sometimes arrange with other enterprises or agricultural groups to absorb its people temporarily.

In summary, then, to the question "For whom and for what are we planning?" it can be said that we are planning for the owners of the enterprise when we plan to achieve a profit, to operate at the optimum plant capacity, and to utilize the available facilities. We are planning for the employees when we plan to create or maintain jobs. We are planning for the consumers when we plan to meet the market demand. Furthermore, since owners and employees are all consumers, their interests and hence these seemingly divergent objectives of planning are all interrelated. Thus, in effect, are we planning for the productive enterprise in its social setting.

Scope of Production Planning.—Planning as here defined is considered to mean "preplanning" or the systematizing in advance of the various industrial factors vital to production. Planning thus includes any and all activities that determine in advance the manufacturing techniques to be used. It decides what has to be done and where, when, and how it is to be done. One phase of planning is the analyzing of products and parts, as well as the required manufacturing operations, to foresee the sequence of steps necessary to the completion of each article and to set up routines that will cause each step to be performed in a stipulated manner and at a designated time. As such, planning is a major activity of the production department[2] in its control of production. But the function of planning embraces more than just production control, for it is a coordinating function—one that is designed to effect a concerted effort from a series of disassociated departments. The quantitative planning of purchased materials and supplies as a cooperative venture of the materials control, production, and purchasing departments constitutes a vital part of production planning. The activities of the plant- and industrial-

---

[1] The subject of complementary products is discussed in greater detail in Chap. VIII.

[2] Terminology relating to this department as used in industry today varies from one enterprise to the next. What is the *production department* to one company is the *production-planning department* to another and simply the *planning department* to a third. As used hereinafter, these terms will be considered to be interchangeable.

engineering departments in planning the procedures to maintain the quality standards established, the development of methods and work-simplification techniques as applied to the contemplated manufacturing processes, and the planning of the required tools, jigs, and fixtures not only as to type but also as to quantity necessary to accomplish the desired production—all these are an integral part of the planning activities necessary to achieve a smoothly operating industrial enterprise.

Thus in summation, it can be said that production planning is a series of related activities performed by not one but a number of different departments, each activity being designed to systematize in advance and to coordinate the manufacturing efforts of the entire enterprise.

Prerequisites to Production Planning.—The planning of production is founded upon certain prerequisites or tools which must be utilized in achieving the results described above. The first of these is a *going enterprise*. As was developed in Chap. V, the going enterprise must have a financially sound capital structure with adequate working capital to carry on the production activities planned. Next, there must be an *internal organization* (see Chap. VI), which must be a dynamic structure alive to changing conditions and with coordinated lines of delegated responsibility and authority. It must be filled with men possessing the necessary "know how" to perform the various technical phases required in the operation of the enterprise. Then there must be a *product* (see Chaps. VII and VIII) capable of being manufactured and for which there is a market (Chap. IV). And finally, there must be the necessary *physical facilities* (see Chaps. IX and X), the land space, buildings, and equipment required to make the product in the amount desired.

Check List to Good Planning.—The best evidence of effective planning procedure is the elimination of the wasteful conditions noted in the following check list: (1) idle men, (2) idle machines, (3) idle materials, (4) idle money, (5) idle delivery promises, (6) idleness of the product.

The plant that repeatedly sends its employees home in the middle of the day because a particular department or battery of machines has run out of work reveals prima-facie evidence of poor planning, as does also the plant in which the production operators spend a large portion of their time waiting for machine setups, repairs, materials, and supplies. Machines which are idle one week and loaded beyond capacity the next or which are poorly designed and tooled for the duties required of them are likewise indicative of poor planning. The enterprise that has large stocks of slowly moving raw materials or a low turnover of material in process reveals similar planning inefficiencies. Money invested in idle stores of raw, in-process, or finished material brings no interest, and money invested in equipment not utilized may well have been invested unwisely. Idle delivery promises that are made only to be broken are as provocative of the loss of good will and the alienation of affections as is any other type of broken promises. Finally, the product that is manufactured and not sold not only involves a freezing of the funds invested therein, but also is subject to the risk of obsolescence as well as perhaps to a material storage problem.

Thus good planning procedure aims to eliminate the idleness that may evolve from the foregoing factors. Men and machines which are busy and which have a moderate bank of work ahead of them at all times, materials progressing through the plant from one operation to the next in what approximates a thin, smoothly flowing stream of work, money turning over at a rate commensurate with the length of the manufacturing cycle, delivery promises that are based on fact rather than on fancy, and a product that is invoiced rather than inventoried—these are the dynamic factors that are indicative of effective planning.

Organization for Planning.—In virtually every enterprise, the production-planning function, because of its close association with manufacturing, is located in the organization structure as a part of the manufacturing division. At this point, however, unanimity of practice ceases as regards organization for planning. Nevertheless, from the many and varied types of planning organizations to be found in industry, three general classes can be established differing from one another primarily in the degree of centralization each affords.

The simplest type of planning structure, and one that, if employed at all today, is found only in the smaller enterprises, makes use of the *line organization*. With this structure, all planning, if it can be called that, is vested in the manufacturing division heads and their subordinates, the foremen. These manufacturing line executives make all decisions pertaining to the product, quantities, processes, methods, etc., and transmit them to the foremen for compliance. Frequently, because of the pressure of routine duties, these executives tend to let much of the preplanning slide—particularly if conditions seem to be running smoothly—and all control is by exception, *i.e.*, as troubles occur. Thus the planning is "after the fact" as the foremen suddenly report to their superior that they are out of a certain material or supply, or that no steps have been taken to tool up a particular machine to perform the job required of it, or that a machine is down and no action has been taken to stock in advance the necessary replacement parts, or that a bottleneck has developed because there is an insufficient number of a certain type of machine to handle the existing volume of orders.

A second and somewhat more formalized type of planning organization is the *routine production department*. This department usually acts simply in an advisory capacity to the manufacturing units. It translates the market or customer demands into manufacturing requirements, plans the quantities and time data necessary to meet these demands, and then turns over the information to the foremen. From this point on, all responsibility is assumed by the foremen. They must check all equipment and tools, plan their own methods, perhaps even requisition the purchase of their own materials and supplies. The only control that the production department then exercises on the manufacturing departments is through the medium of periodic reports which reveal those areas that are not producing satisfactorily. A stock-chaser type of control is then invoked to ascertain the difficulties and to see that they are rectified. Here again control is primarily by exception—after the delay has occurred.

The third type of organization for planning, and one that is still more formalized, is what may be called the true *production-planning department*. It is a functionalized-staff department about which center all the production-planning activities of the enterprise. In this type of organization, preplanning is the order of things. No work is done by this department that would not otherwise be done by some other group in the enterprise. The main difference lies in the fact that the responsibility and authority for all planning are centralized in the hands of specialists—not decentralized in the hands of a host of foremen, supervisors, and other line executives. Furthermore, by a fixation of the responsibility and authority, it becomes a certainty that all planning activities will be performed in their proper sequence and to the greatest benefit of the enterprise as a whole. Uniformity of procedure, thoroughness of action, and a close regard for the time element almost invariably result from centralized planning.

Although it is true that actually the production-planning department under the direction of the planning head may perform only certain phases of planning (usually the production-control functions of routing, scheduling, dispatching, and follow-up), nevertheless, the responsibility and authority of that department are usually broadened so that it also coordinates and checks the progress of those phases of planning which are delegated to other departments. For example, sales orders upon being translated into production orders usually are cleared first through the planning department and then are referred to the product engineering department for drawings, bills of materials, specifications, etc. In the event that this information is not supplied completely or on time, the planning department becomes responsible for following through to see that the necessary information is obtained. Or, again, production orders awaiting the delivery of purchased materials or of tools and other equipment from the plant's toolmakers become the concern of the planning department to the extent that its representatives would follow closely the delivery of the missing articles to the end that production schedules might not be delayed.

Edmund Mottershead [3] notes that some of the more detailed functions of the typical production-planning department include:

. . . advice as to the design of the product, perhaps even determining that design; providing necessary patterns and manufacturing tooling, such as jigs and fixtures, dies and other tools; determining and specifying the kinds and amounts of raw materials, half-finished materials, finished materials, machines and equipment to be purchased; selecting and discovering methods for doing the work as it goes through the shop; setting standards of quality and quantity. It should employ whatever cost accounting or time study engineering or other skills that expedite the work and turn out the finished goods on schedule or ahead of schedule, up to standards for quality or better, at the predetermined costs or less. Stock room control, supervising the maintenance of equipment, keeping and interpreting production control records of all kinds, outlining labor requirements, selecting methods of transportation, developing the safety program which will aid the production effort and keep the plant layout in tune with production requirements, are other functions of such a department.

It can readily be appreciated that many of these duties are rather highly technical and require the attention of engineering specialists. These specialists, the plant and industrial engineers, are responsible for seeing that goods are produced as required with a minimum expenditure of the plant's resources. More specifically, they concern themselves with the technical functions of production planning already listed, as well as with the production-control systems described in Chaps. XIV and XV.[4]

Of course, there are dangers resulting from overcentralizing the planning function in the hands of a production-planning department. For example, the central planners may fail to take into consideration the equipment characteristics or human variations that often play a large part in the effective planning of production orders. Again, if a change in routing is contemplated by the planning department without the advice or approval of the engineering, methods, and cost groups, the repercussions from the change may be anything but pleasant. Or where the planning department excludes the foreman from the planning activities, his "nose tends to go out of joint" or at the very least, his whole-

[3] MOTTERSHEAD, EDMUND, Productive Planning, *Machine Tool Bluebook,* March, 1943, pp. 133 *ff.*

[4] The activities of the industrial engineer are discussed in Chaps. VI and XVII and those of the plant engineer in Chap. XVIII.

hearted enthusiasm and cooperation may be lacking—factors which in themselves can cause the plans to fail. Thus it becomes quite important that the advice and assistance of the other departments and the foremen concerned be sought by the planning group, even though the responsibility for planning remains with the planning department.

Planning Adapted to Different Types of Manufacture.—Production planning is merely a means to an end and not an end in itself. Therefore, planning should be adapted to the type of manufacture involved; rarely should the type of manufacture be varied to conform to the planning procedure. To do so is akin to burning down the barn to get roast pig. Furthermore, whenever a change in the product or demand necessitates a change in the type of manufacture, the planning techniques should likewise be altered if maximum manufacturing efficiency is to be obtained.

Actually there are almost as many variations of production planning as there are types of manufacture. The latter can be grouped into eight basic classes as follows:

1. Few pieces never reproduced.
2. Many pieces never reproduced.
3. Repeat orders at irregular intervals (few pieces).
4. Repeat orders at irregular intervals (few to many pieces).
5. Repeat orders at irregular intervals (many pieces).
6. Repeat orders at regular intervals (few pieces).
7. Repeat orders at regular intervals (few to many pieces).
8. Repeat orders at regular intervals (many pieces).

At one extreme then, we have the manufacture of a few pieces which will never be reproduced as would be the case in the manufacture of large telescopes, great passenger liners, etc. Obviously such products call for manufacture to specific customer or job order and an arrangement of machines presumably grouped functionally according to the nature of the process performed (see discussion of job-lot manufacture, Chap. X). At the opposite extreme is the production of large quantities repeated at predictable intervals, such as the manufacture of automotive products and a host of other so-called "mass-production" articles. Efficiency demands the manufacture of such products to a master schedule based on depletion of stock inventories, and with machines arranged on a production-line basis (see serialized manufacture, Chap. X). Between these two extremes we have all possible permutations and combinations of types of manufacture and machine arrangement, most of which fall into the category of semiserialized manufacture (again, see Chap. X, semiserialized manufacture).

To generalize on the planning techniques required to meet these variations in manufacture, it can be said that, for serialized manufacture, most of the planning effort goes into the design of the production line, a study of the best methods, and a careful selection of equipment, especially conveyors, to the end that a *balanced production line* may be achieved. Once the line is established with its failings and "bugs" ironed out, planning becomes somewhat routine. It is primarily a matter of planning for the control of materials and the control of quality so that the line may continue in operation without the traditional bottlenecks creeping into the picture.

Planning for semiserialized manufacture is similarly first a problem of setting up all possible production lines and batteries of related machines and, where this is not practical, grouping machines by process. Secondly, it is a problem of planning the control of materials and quality. However, semiserialized manufacture, by virtue of the fact that it is not entirely continuous, must facilitate its flow of materials through the use of *balanced schedules*. For this reason subsequent planning is of a more complicated nature than where a fully serialized production line can be employed. Those production lines that can be devised must be sufficiently flexible to manufacture a variety of products or a variety of types and sizes of the same basic product. Hence, to employ all equipment to its optimum capacity, a balanced schedule or relationship usually must be maintained between the sizes and quantities that can be manufactured at any one time on those lines or within the machine groupings. Of course, as we shall discover in Chap. XIV, the problem of planning a balanced schedule of production can be eased through the use of matching centers but, nevertheless, the planning of semiserialized manufacture is considerably more complicated than planning where manufacture is serialized.

When we come to the planning of job-lot manufacture, the problems are still more complicated. With the machines grouped by process, the main consideration becomes that of *balanced machine loads*. Scheduling, then, involves careful planning of the work for each machine or battery of machines to insure that the material in process is spread out evenly among the available equipment and is produced in the desired sequence. Also, since separate production orders are required for each article fabricated, more paper work is involved, materials handling and control of quality may become infinitely more difficult, and the reporting and tracing of the progress of material through the plant are invariably more intricate. Here then, we have some of the prime arguments for the adoption of serialized or at least semiserialized manufacture methods wherever the volume of production permits, for it can readily be seen that the difficulties and expense of planning may be sharply reduced if such methods can be introduced.

Estimating as a Phase of Planning.—Of considerable importance to some plants, particularly those engaged in the job-lot manufacture of products that seldom if ever are reproduced, is the function of *estimating*. As we shall see in Chap. XII, when we consider the problem of bids and proposals through the eyes of the purchasing agent, a customer who wishes to buy a particular product for the first time generally entertains bids from the vendors of such a product before he actually places his order. The bid must contain among other information the selling price of the article (which requires an estimate of the manufacturing cost) and an estimate of the time required for delivery. These in turn can best be determined through an analysis of the manufacturing techniques required. Thus the estimating of bids is frequently a cooperative function of the production-planning, industrial- and plant-engineering, and cost departments.

The sales department, upon receipt of a request for a proposal, refers it to the planning department which, in the case of new products, variations on standard products, or significant changes in quantity to be manufactured, solicits the aid of the engineering and cost groups. This last-named department makes a cost analysis of the item and prepares a cost estimate, upon the accuracy of which depend not only the opportunity the enterprise has for meeting competition but also the certainty that the expected profit will be realized from the sale.[5]

In the case of products made from standard parts, a price list of such articles or parts can be prepared for use by salesmen in the field. For example, sales engineers for industrial conveyor equipment are supplied with price lists for standard conveyor parts from which the price of most individual installations can be calculated. Also, knock-down wire-grill partitioning used in industrial plants is quoted by sales representatives on a rule-of-thumb price per lineal foot.

Of course, products frequently reproduced require virtually no estimating by the planning department, for past records furnish actual cost data from which the new bid can be prepared. Also, in some cases when a new product is requested, it may be possible to compare it with some similar product previously manufactured, and the new estimate can be readily projected without a complete analysis.

SUMMARY

We have seen that production planning in its broadest sense embraces many activities. It may be said to start with the production plans of the board of directors and to permeate down through the plant organiza-

---

[5] For a further discussion of cost analysis and the problems of pricing, see Chap. XXVIII.

tion to the lowest supervisory level. The functions of production planning may be decentralized in the hands of the line organization or may be partly or completely centralized under the production-planning department and the industrial and plant engineers. This latter practice is perhaps to be preferred in most industrial enterprises for it results in uniformity, in better coordination, and in a fixation of responsibility that minimizes "buck passing."

The prime requisite of all individuals who carry on production planning is that they have vision—vision to preplan, to anticipate requirements of all sorts, and to analyze objectively the production problems that may be encountered. Regardless of how carefully they are laid, production plans "gang aft agley," and the production planners must be equal to such situations as require the application of control techniques. Finally, all production planning must be *productive* planning, for nonproductive effort has no place in effectively planned manufacture.

CONTROLLING MATERIALS—PURCHASING, SHIPPING, TRAFFIC, AND RECEIVING

Materials control pertains to the kind, amount, location, and movement of the various materials used in an industrial enterprise. Time is likewise "of the essence" in this control, for the materials must be available *when* required for use. We have seen in Chap. XI that materials control is akin to the military science of logistics and that it is inevitably linked with the planning and control of production as well as with the control of quality and manufacturing methods.

Materials, one of the five "M's" of an industrial enterprise (Management, Money, Machines, Materials, Man power), have occupied a rather large share of management's attention during recent years. Successively during and since World War II, industry has been faced with government-controlled materials, problems arising out of substitute materials, black markets, decontrolled materials in scarce supply, rapidly rising prices, gradual or, in the case of some items, sudden transition from scarce to ample supply, and then falling markets requiring liquidation of inventories and dictating hand-to-mouth buying. Furthermore, since materials now represent such a large part of the sales dollar of many items, the control of material costs is under management's scrutiny as never before. Price has once more become perhaps the foremost factor in the buying of materials, and this, in turn, has led to more careful control of the size of inventories so that advantage may be taken of price changes. Also, more efficient methods of storing and handling material are under constant study in most enterprises. For the foreseeable future, as more and more manufacturing processes reach the point where further improvements become mere refinements, the potential savings resulting from better over-all control of materials will come into ever greater importance.

Consequently, the challenge before Chaps. XII and XIII is to present what seems, in the light of present emphases, to be contemporary thought as to the basic principles underlying the control of materials. Likewise to be considered are the more important techniques and procedures that are the tools by which this control is effected.

Nature of the Control of Materials.—Any effective procedure for the control of materials must involve four phases, which in a sense define the nature of materials control as well as set forth its scope. These may be listed as follows:

1. Procurement—purchasing.
2. External transportation—shipping, traffic, and receiving.
3. Materials storage—inventory control.
4. Internal transportation—materials handling.

No one of these phases adds form utility to the materials involved, for materials subjected to any or all of these stages of control undergo no change in their physical characteristics. However, materials control does increase place utility, and to a limited degree time utility, since the materials controlled can thus be made available at the right time and place as required for use.

Materials control is one of the necessary expenses or overhead costs of doing business. In fact, any management that refuses to spend the required money to carry on this type of control probably will not be doing business long. Since one of the purposes of materials control is to reduce the cost of supplying materials used in the operation of the business, the saving in this connection should always be considered in the light of the expenditure necessary to achieve that saving. Usually the cost elements of materials control are hidden and difficult to identify. Most of them are quite indirect and are not immediately chargeable to any one department, process, or product. For this reason, these costs are all too often neglected by management, and no measure of efficiency is even attempted. If, however, the materials-control activities are clearly defined and if an accounting procedure is established for allocating indirect costs (see Chap. XXVIII), it is then possible to compute the efficiency with which these activities are conducted.

Organization for Materials Control.—Distinct as are the scope and duties of the four phases of materials control, nevertheless, they all serve as links in the chain of action by which that control is achieved. If one link is weak or is improperly coupled to the next, the entire chain may fail. Thus must the phases be closely coordinated if they are to operate successfully.

Perhaps this coordination can best be achieved by placing all four phases of materials control under the direct authority of a single individual. However, in actual practice it is quite common to find the various phases under separate authorities in the organization structure. Where the purchased materials represent a considerable portion of the sales dollar—as would be the case in the manufacture of tin cans, a fully automatic process in which relatively little labor on the product is required —the work of the purchasing agent is of such extreme importance to the profitable operation of the enterprise that he may be made one of the major executives of the enterprise, often with the title of vice-president. In perhaps a majority of companies, however, the purchasing department is a responsibility of the works or plant manager, since most of the purchases are made for the manufacturing divisions. Yet it is not uncommon to find the purchasing department working under the direction of the treasurer, apparently because of the purchasing agent's close relationship with the company's purse strings.

The external transportation, storage, and internal transportation activities are sometimes consolidated under a "plant service manager" who is then responsible to the works or plant manager. Where these activities are left in separate departments, the traffic manager generally reports directly to the works manager or perhaps to the purchasing agent. Shipping and receiving, allied activities in which the work is comparable, are often combined under one head who operates under the direction of the purchasing agent, the traffic manager, or the works manager. The same lines of authority might prevail even if the two functions were separate entities. Whereas storage and internal transportation usually function under the works or plant manager, in some cases because of the close alliance of these functions with the control of production, they are made the responsibility of the production manager. Thus it can be appreciated that the workable organization structures for controlling materials in an industrial plant are many and varied, and the one that is "correct" for any particular enterprise depends upon the circumstances and individuals involved. The sole test in each case is empirical: Does it work?

Regardless of its position in the organization structure, each of the four phases of materials control should be organized as a staff function with functional jurisdiction over all matters within its defined operating area. Thus all buying activities should be cleared through the purchasing department, all incoming and outgoing shipments handled by the receiving and shipping departments, respectively, all external transportation problems referred to the traffic manager, and the handling and storage of all materials within the plant considered the duty of the internal transportation department. Coordination between the phases can be achieved not only through the organization structure but through operating procedures as well. Duplicate records are generally quite effective in this regard. For example, copies of the purchase orders supplied to the receiving department and copies of the notices of receipt of material furnished the purchasing department work to their mutual advantage.

Let us now analyze the function, scope, and techniques of each of the four phases of materials control, remembering that, in spite of the fact that the phases are hereinafter considered separately, they are naturally interrelated one with the other and in practice must be closely coordinated for maximum effectiveness.

PURCHASING

The purchasing function deals with outside vendors on all matters pertaining to the procurement of materials, parts, supplies, equipment, and tooling. The importance of the function to the successful operation of the enterprise ranges from minor, where purchased items represent a low percentage of the value of goods sold, to major, where purchases comprise a high percentage of the sales dollar.

Scope of the Purchasing Department.—In general, the purchasing agent is made responsible for maintaining the four major procurement factors of *quality, quantity, time,* and *price.* *Quality,* of course, refers to the kind of goods desired as established by the specifications emanating usually from the engineering department. The *quantity* of the purchase will generally be determined directly or indirectly from the production and material requirements set forth by the routing division of the production department, and the *time* allowed for delivery is linked with the production schedules of the scheduling division. Thus these three factors—quality, quantity, and time—are generally established *for* the purchasing department, and its responsibility in this connection then becomes principally a matter of securing vendors who will maintain the factors established. The fourth factor of *price,* however, is essentially the responsibility of the purchasing department, for that department with its contacts with outside markets is in the best position to determine what is a fair price. Nevertheless, just as any business activity is most effectively carried on through the cooperation of all interested departments, so can the best results be secured where prices—and for that matter, all the procurement factors—are discussed among and approved by the various departments concerned.

More specifically as to the activities of the purchasing agent and his staff, they are expected to:

1. Know and maintain records showing possible materials and substitutes, sources of supply, prices, and quantities available.

2. Review specifications for possible simplification and standardization of materials or for unreasonable requirements.

3. Negotiate with vendors.

4. Accumulate and analyze quotations.

5. Place purchase orders with vendors.

6. Follow up purchase orders for delivery as specified.

7. Audit invoices to check compliance with agreed terms.

8. Maintain records of all purchases.

9. Coordinate with other departments on all matters pertaining to procurement.

Likewise a major duty of many purchasing departments is the handling of subcontracts. Practically all enterprises at one time or another "farm out" the manufacture of some parts or production items. Usually these represent but a small portion of the total purchases of a manufacturing organization. However, during periods of high business activity, subcontracting is frequently the solution as overburdened plants seek to increase their production. Also, it is common practice to farm out dangerous, obnoxious, or expensive operations to other concerns whose know-how and equipment permit them to perform the work better, safer, or cheaper. Other instances involve companies desirous of providing competition in costs for their own departments or of escaping royalty payments or burdensome labor agreements. Since the appraisal of a potential subcontractor's productive facilities and questions of product quality are often beyond the scope of the purchasing function, the technical phases of subcontracting are usually turned over to the engineering, production, and inspection groups, while the purchasing agent acts primarily as a liaison or contact man between the two or more firms involved.

There is a blurred line between the responsibility of the purchasing department for materials-quality standards and that of the engineering department concerned. Both may exercise some jurisdiction, but usually the duty of the purchasing agent is only to see that materials bought meet requirements established by specification or, in the case of items not regularly purchased, entered on the purchase requisition—in either case, the responsibility resting on the engineering department. But where materials are requisitioned without special quality standards, the purchasing agent assumes the responsibility for quality, as is natural for any purchaser.

Last but far from the least of the purchasing agent's duties is that of acting as the eyes and ears of the enterprise in finding new and useful materials or effective substitutes. Large companies may even create a section in the purchasing department to perform this service.[1] In small companies, the purchasing agent and his assistants generally read periodicals dealing with new equipment and materials and interview

---

[1] The General Electric Company has set up a "Value Analysis Division" of the purchasing function to work with vendors as well as with G.E.'s own manufacturing and engineering personnel in the study of existing and new products. Ways are sought to lower costs through the elimination, alteration, or simplification of purchased parts or material items.

vendors to find out "what's new." If the proper individuals concerned are thus kept informed, some of these new developments may be applied with attendant monetary savings to the enterprise.

Purchasing Procedures. 1. *Specifications.*—A prerequisite to any purchasing contract is a meeting of minds as to the exact nature of the materials that are to be the subject of that contract. Material standards (see Chap. VIII), which are established by an enterprise to define its major material requirements, are commonly termed "specifications." They define the form, shape, composition, performance, etc., of the material involved and are established in writing by the product-engineering department, generally with the help and cooperation of both the production and purchasing departments. These specifications are furnished to the vendors, and purchased materials thus covered are assumed to be as per specification unless all parties concerned are previously advised otherwise.

Many materials, however, are purchased by catalogue number and description or by brand name. This practice makes for simplicity, but in the case of major procurement items is not always the wisest purchasing procedure since specifications of branded and catalogue items are often subject to change.

2. *Purchase Requisitions.*—Every purchase should originate in writing on a standard purchase requisition form (see Fig. 31). This form, which essentially authorizes the purchasing department to make the purchase, specifies *what* kind of material is desired (*i.e.*, by description or specification, brand name, or catalogue number), *how much* is desired, *when* it is required, and *where* it should ultimately be delivered in the plant. Each requisition should be signed by the foreman or individual requesting the material and then O.K.'d by his superior or by some other individual who has this delegated authority and through whom all requisitions must clear on their way to the purchasing department. Many companies require three copies of the purchasing requisition, the first of which goes to the purchasing department as its authorization to make the purchase. The second likewise is sent to the purchasing department but is subsequently returned to the individual requesting the material with the price and/or delivery information marked on it. The third copy stays with the originating individual for his follow-up purposes. It is good practice for the requisition forms to be serially numbered so that they may be keyed with the purchase orders as an aid in filing and for ready reference.

3. *Proposals.*—Once authorized to make the purchase, the purchasing department looks over its sources of supply and by letter, telephone, or telegram, depending upon the proximity of the vendors and the urgency

PURCHASE REQUISITION

To Purchasing Agent:
Please order the following:
 Ship to........................
....
  Via............   F.O.B.............
Date Material Wanted...............

Dept..............................
Requisition No.....................
Date..............................
Requested by.......................
Approved by.......................
Checked by........................
      Terms..........

Quantity	Description	Material on Hand	Average Consumption	Price

Special Instructions

Ordered from......................
Date Ordered......................
Purpose...........................
Charge to.........................

Purchase Order No..................
Approved by.......................
Checked by........................
....

Fig. 31.—A composite purchase requisition form prepared by the National Association of Purchasing Agents and based on an analysis of the requisition forms of some 120 companies of all sizes and in all industries. (*From "Purchase Requisition Forms," National Association of Purchasing Agents, Inc.*)

of the requisition, asks for quotations as to price, delivery, and the amount and exact description of the material that each vendor is in a position to furnish. This last is necessary where each vendor's product differs in some respect but may be equally satisfactory for the purpose intended, in which case specifications may not be established. For example, many branded products, such as solvents, oils, and slaked lime, are each prepared to their own company brand standard.

Once the proposals are received, the purchasing agent with the cooperation of the individuals requesting the material analyzes them and makes the selection as to which vendor's goods shall be purchased. Where the goods vary as to description, price, or delivery, this selection may be automatically determined for the purchasing agent. Again, laboratory analysis or trial under actual manufacturing conditions may show which vendor's product is preferable. However, where all factors are virtually equal, it is then generally the purchasing agent's prerogative to select the vendor.

Materials bought under continuing contract or those purchased repetitively do not require proposals from the vendors since all necessary information would then be available to both parties. In the case of repeat orders, the purchase order might include the phrase, " . . . as previously furnished on our Purchase Order No. ———." In actual practice, many of the major material items are purchased repeatedly, and it is thus imperative that the purchasing agent develop adequate and dependable sources, preferably two or more, from which to obtain such items, rather than shop around at each repeat order. Of course, the purchasing agent may check the quality, price, and delivery of the usual sources by asking for occasional proposals from other vendors.

4. *Purchase Orders.*—When the vendor has been selected, the purchasing department then prepares the purchase order. This form (see Fig. 32) contains the information as to what and how much material is desired and when delivery is requested (taken from the purchase requisition) together with a stipulation as to how shipment is to be made (express, freight, cheapest way, etc.). The unit price and discount expected will likewise be shown as will the purchase-order number and that of the originating requisition.

At least three copies of the purchase order are customarily employed. The first copy goes to the vendor while the second is generally issued to the receiving department so that material received may be identified and checked as to description and quantity against that which was ordered. The third and perhaps the fourth copy, if there is one, are retained by the purchasing department for its records and follow-up.

5. *Follow-up of Purchase Orders.*—Generally the vendor acknowledges receipt of all purchase orders and supplies the customer with a tentative or actual date upon which shipment will be made. It is customary for a separate division of the purchasing department to be assigned the duty of following outstanding purchase orders to insure that delivery is made as specified or as promised. Thus the purchasing agent's time can be devoted to his proper function: the making of purchases. A common exception to this procedure is in the case of major procurement items, the importance of which warrants the purchasing agent's personal attention.

Follow-up procedure varies among industrial plants and, for that matter, among materials. Supplies and minor equipment items are generally followed up by filing one copy of the purchase order in a tickler file according to date due. Another procedure sometimes employed is to file the purchase order by vendor name and to use various colored tabs attached to the order in such a fashion as to indicate the due date for that particular material. Major production items which are scheduled for a series of successive shipments may be followed up by a form of the Gantt chart (see Chap. XIV) on which the schedule is laid out by days,

DOE SAWS

DOE MANUFACTURING COMPANY
10 IVANHOE ROAD
CLEVELAND, OHIO

PURCHASE ORDER No.

REQUISITION No.

IMPORTANT
Both above numbers must appear on all correspondence, invoices, shipping papers and packages.

To..

DATE

Account No.

Class No.

SHIP TO   VIA

                                     DELIVERY WANTED

F.O.B.   TERMS

Please enter our order for the following material subject to all the instructions and conditions contained on the face hereof.

SPECIAL NOTICE TO SELLER

INSTRUCTIONS
Invoice in Duplicate and mail with Bill of Lading or Express Receipt to 10 Ivanhoe Rd., Cleveland, Ohio, the day EACH shipment is made. Terms as previously arranged or specified on this order.
CONDITIONS
1. **Acceptance.**—Acknowledgment of this order must be made in writing by return mail. Acceptance of this order constitutes acceptance of all conditions herein stated.
2. **Prices:**—This order must not be filled at higher prices than last quoted without authority of the buyer.
3. **Packing and Cartage Charges.**—No charge allowed for packing or cartage unless designated on this order.
4. **Quality and Inspection:**—All material furnished must be as specified and will be subject to inspection and approval of buyer after delivery. The right is reserved to reject and return at the risk and expense of the supplier such portion of any shipment which may be defective or fail to comply with specifications without invalidating the remainder of the order. If rejected it will be held for disposition at expense and risk of the seller.
5. **Quantity.**—The specific quantity ordered must not be changed without buyer's permission in writing.
6. **Non-Performance.**—Buyer reserves the right to cancel this order or any portion of same if delivery is not made when and as specified, time being of the essence of this order and charge seller for any loss entailed.

7. **Patents:**—The seller hereby guarantees the buyer against all losses of profits, damages, or both, resulting from any patent infringement by reason of purchasing goods covered by this contract. This guarantee also includes the reimbursement to the buyer of all litigation costs which he may suffer as a result of any patent suit, in addition to the recoveries which may be secured against him of profits and/or damages.

DOE MANUFACTURING CO.

By..
                              Director of Purchases.

Fig. 32.—Typical purchase order form. This form was suggested as to general content and arrangement by the National Association of Purchasing Agents after a survey of some 237 forms from companies of all sizes and in all industries. The principal advantage of a standard industry-wide form is, of course, uniformity leading to faster processing of the orders and fewer misunderstandings and clerical errors. (*From "Purchase Order Forms," National Association of Purchasing Agents, Inc.*)

weeks, or months, and the receipts are shown by projecting a horizontal line indicating progress against that schedule. Where a number of different items are purchased from one vendor, it is often desirable to employ a separate sheet for each vendor. Then when discussions are carried on with a particular vendor, it is possible for the purchasing agent to have before him a concise picture of the orders placed with that vendor, his promises, together with shipments made against them. From this picture, the overdue items can be readily discerned and used as a basis for the discussion.

Routine follow-up of vendors is conducted through the use of follow-up form letters or cards on which the order number and other necessary information can be filled in and which request the desired delivery information. More urgent items demand telephone calls or telegrams to ascertain the current status of the material on order.

Organization for Effective Purchasing.—The industrial procurement function can best be made effective if all purchasing is channelized and centralized through one agency—the purchasing department—and under one head—the purchasing agent. All vendor inquiries and contacts as well as purchasing commitments should then be arranged through the purchasing department. This centralization of purchasing almost invariably makes for more efficient ordering of materials, eliminates much duplication of effort, and simplifies purchasing procedure and the payment of invoices.

However, there are circumstances which, for reasons of efficiency, dictate a decentralization of the purchasing function. Occasionally plants or points of material usage are so widely scattered as to make centralized procurement a hindrance rather than a help. Particularly is this true for high-quality or technical items wherein control over purchases made from a remote point may be difficult to achieve. Also where the materials involved are heavy and bulky commercial items (such as oil products, fuels, sawdust, and paint), transportation costs and speed of delivery may dictate the purchase of these items by each plant from its own local vendors. Nevertheless, small items of fairly high value, such as tool bits, micrometers, and grinding wheels, as well as those for which quantity lots bring discounts, may best be bought by a central purchasing department. Since the transportation costs on such items would be relatively insignificant, such an arrangement might thereby be more economical than would be the case were each plant to make its purchases separately. Furthermore, centralized purchasing may in many cases specify branch-plant delivery and still gain quantity discounts. However, centralized purchasing for scattered plants requires systematized control in each plant over quantity and quality supplied. Otherwise, full value for the company's monetary expenditure may not be realized.

Whereas an incompetent or not too energetic purchasing agent may waste many of the company's dollars, so on the other hand will a competent buyer repay his salary many times over. The purchasing agent should be able to deal with vendors on technical details, use, and cost of the materials he is required to buy, and he should be familiar with the markets that supply those materials. An individual with an analytical mind and perhaps with an engineering background frequently makes a good purchasing agent. He should be willing to lean over backward to be helpful to the rest of the plant organization. In fact, "service" is the middle name of any good purchasing agent.

In most concerns where the purchasing agent is considered to be one of the major executives of the firm, he has the power to execute purchasing contracts for the company. Where such power is not granted, generally some other executive such as the treasurer or controller reviews all purchase orders before they are sent out.

Where the purchasing department is large and several purchasing agents are required, it is common practice to divide the duties among the personnel according to the type of purchases made. One buyer may be assigned to purchase the major raw material; another, the supplies; another, plant equipment; etc. This functional division of effort makes for increased specialization and permits each purchasing representative through close association with a particular trade to gain a better "feel" of the market to which he is assigned.

Constructive Purchasing Policies.—The reputation of many an industrial organization rises and falls on the policies of its purchasing department. An enterprise wherein the purchasing department is noted for its *fair dealings* with vendors is very likely to gain for itself the respect and confidence of the trade. *Sharp practice,* on the other hand, will breed only sharp practice in return. It is poor policy for a purchasing agent, instead of negotiating and bargaining for a fair price, to use means fair or foul to browbeat the vendor down to an absurdly low price. The man who takes unfair advantage of the vendor in one transaction is likely to find that the difference is recouped in a subsequent deal. Furthermore, a price that is too low may force a supplier out of business and thus be a factor in destroying a sound source of supply for the purchaser.

It is, however, the duty of the purchasing agent to see that a vendor does not take advantage of him in the matter of price. The wise purchasing agent, therefore, makes it his business to know what he can of the vendor's manufacturing processes. By piecing this information together and upon consideration of the vendor's proposals, he generally can determine whether or not the price is fair.

In a sense, the purchasing agent should maintain a *judicial attitude* on the disposition of all matters between his enterprise and its vendors to see that both parties are dealt with fairly. He should practice at all times the golden rule—not the David Harum version: "Do unto others as they would do unto you, only do it first."

Everyday *social and business courtesies* apply in the relationships with vendors and their representatives. For example, the practice of either interviewing salesmen promptly or advising them immediately when an interview must be delayed is a small but important consideration in good purchasing relationships. Yet altogether too many purchasing agents are careless in this respect and frequently keep their vendors' salesmen waiting for considerable periods in the reception room.

The *acceptance of personal gifts and favors* from vendors, particularly Christmas gifts, world series or prize-fight tickets, and free dinners and entertainment, is a rather controversial issue. Some purchasing agents are not opposed to accepting personal gifts and maintain that in their subsequent relationships with vendors they do not let the gifts influence their decisions. However, other purchasing agents state that ultimately in one form or another their company always pays for the cost of vendors' gifts. Hence they refuse to accept all gifts which are for their own personal use or which cannot be construed as institutional advertising.

Broken delivery promises and the vendor's inability to make delivery on the date specified are continual causes of friction between vendor and customer. The reasons for this lack of performance may be many. The customer may not forecast his requirements sufficiently far in advance to allow the vendor adequate time to make delivery. Or the customer may arbitrarily engage in the inefficient practice of specifying "Rush" or "Wanted at Once" on all his orders. Should this happen, the vendor either endeavors to accommodate the customer and make quick delivery—which invariably runs up the prices asked of that customer—or the vendor gets the impression that the customer is "crying wolf" on every order and hence pays no attention whatsoever to any of his urgent delivery requests. Still another cause of broken delivery promises is that which results from the vendor's insufficient knowledge or control of the backlog of orders in his plant. As a result he promises delivery of goods beyond his capacity to produce.

Cancellations of purchase orders violate the purchase contract and are often destructive to good business relationships between vendor and customer. However, cancellations frequently are necessary and may result from design or model changes, improvements in manufacturing methods, or conditions beyond the customer's control. Thus it is customary to permit concerns to make cancellations on purchases, provided that the material has not been placed in process and that no binding commitments (such as for new machines or equipment) have been made from which relief cannot be gained. If, however, the material is in process or such commitments have been made and a cancellation becomes necessary, the purchaser may agree to pay the costs incurred up to that point rather than have the material carried through to completion.

Another and rather interesting purchasing policy is that which determines whether the department is to be permitted to engage in *speculation*. Speculation may be defined as the purchase of materials in excess of normal requirements and in anticipation of a price rise or a market shortage.

Pure speculation occurs when the materials are purchased primarily for subsequent resale at a higher price and hence for a profit. Since manufacturing enterprises are not generally incorporated to engage in such transactions for profit, pure speculation should be discouraged. If, however, it is permitted, the profit or loss resulting therefrom should be segregated from the normal operating profits of the enterprise; otherwise a true picture of the operating efficiency is not obtainable.

Operational speculation is simply advance buying for manufacturing purposes in an attempt to cover the operating needs for some future period. Although it is more readily condoned and more commonly engaged in by industry as a whole, even so, this practice can be somewhat dangerous as it tends to decrease the liquidity of the enterprise by tying up money in more materials than should normally be carried, involves greater storage and carrying costs (space charges, insurance, taxes), and increases the business risk of obsolescence.

Of course, in the purchase of certain commodities, there is the perfectly legitimate practice of *hedging* or the use of the "futures contract" to protect against a price rise. By contracting both to buy and to sell at some future date, the purchasing agent in a sense operates on both sides of the fence and is assured of at least breaking even in the event of a change in price in either direction.

Reciprocity is simply that purchasing policy whereby the enterprise makes a practice of buying from its customers. Some purchasing agents feel that it is not fair to let the prospects of future sales to a customer influence their purchasing decision or to force them into buying from that customer an inferior article or one at a higher price. Others feel that a valued customer is entitled to a fair share of their business and tend to favor their customers if at all possible. The prevailing opinion on this matter seems to be that reciprocity in moderation builds up customer good will. Thus when a customer's product can be used, it is generally believed that he should be given the same opportunity to bid for the business as is given all other vendors. The factors of quality, quantity, time, and price being relatively equal, the enterprise may then justifiably buy from its customer if it so desires.

SHIPPING, TRAFFIC, AND RECEIVING

Shipping refers to the preparation of goods for outgoing shipments, traffic to the external transportation of goods and materials both outgoing and incoming, and receiving to the acceptance of incoming items.

Packing for Shipment.—Virtually all outgoing material is packed, marked, and weighed preparatory to shipment. Packing containers in general are subject to three cardinal rules:

1. They should be designed to minimize breakage in transit.
2. They should make for ease of handling.
3. They should conform to the commodity classification regulations contained in the "Consolidated Freight Classification," the "Official Express Classification," or the "Postal Laws and Regulations" which provide the necessary data for economical shipping by the standards of the type of carrier to be selected. Copies of these publications should be available in every shipping department and consulted whenever there is any doubt as to classification.

Efficiency dictates certain additional rules that apply to packing. Container and package sizes and styles should be standardized as far as is possible. Interior closures and dividers can often be utilized for odd-sized items rather than adding to the variety of containers used. Paper waste, particularly old newspaper, can often be used as fill-in material. Multiple wrappings and containers should be avoided through the design of a single container and adequate protective provisions. Cartons, wooden boxes, and other containers can often be reused and should be handled and opened with this thought in mind. Wherever possible, packing should be made an integral part of the manufacturing process to avoid rehandling.

Among the more common types of containers are the corrugated cardboard box and the wire-bound or strap-bound wood shook. *Unit load* packages have enjoyed ever-increasing popularity in recent years. These are constructed by bundling one or more parts on a standard low-cost wood pallet which is used as the base of the package. For example, a unit package can be made to ship automobile radiators by properly wrapping and protecting 32 of them, building them up in layers on the egg-crate principle, and strapping them to a pallet. Material shipped in this fashion can be readily handled by fork-truck (see Chap.

XIII) which makes for low-cost handling and simplifies the storage problem at both originating point and destination. Furthermore, packaging costs are comparable with other means, and the pallet base permits a nesting of the material so as to reduce the possibility of damage in transit.

However, the advantages of pallets are somewhat offset by the initial cost of the pallet itself, by its adding shipping weight to the package, and by the cost of returning it to the shipper. Many concerns have found that these added costs more than offset the reductions in handling and storage costs. Also, it has not been found practical to standardize on pallet construction and size throughout industry so as to permit interchangeability and reuse. Nevertheless, the introduction of lightweight, low-cost, "expendable," wood and pasteboard pallets for one-way usage only has tended to minimize the aforementioned disadvantages at least for small, fairly light loads.

Modes of Transportation.—There may be several alternate modes of transportation available for the shipment of goods. Where *boat* transportation is available, it provides a slow but inexpensive means of shipping large quantities of bulk material. *Railway freight* is perhaps the best means of hauling heavy or bulky goods long distances, particularly in carload lots, where waterway transportation is not available. *Railway express* and *parcel post* are fast and handy methods of shipment for small articles but involve considerably greater cost. *Motor truck* is an excellent way of shipping over short hauls, particularly where full carload shipments are not possible and where door-to-door delivery with but one handling is desirable. *Air express* is perhaps the fastest means of transporting goods but, because of its relatively high cost, it is generally limited to light articles.

The method of shipment and the routing over which the material travels may be specified in the purchase contract, but if not they are the prerogative of the shipper. Selection of the mode of transportation frequently involves a knowledge on the part of the traffic manager of the classifications into which all commodities are grouped by the carriers and from which the tariffs are determined.

A number of companies that regularly make shipments to customers over a limited area find it more economical to maintain their own fleet of trucks rather than use the common carriers. These concerns argue that they thereby can give their customers faster and more dependable service and can likewise simplify their packing and shipping procedures.

Loading and Stowing.—An important phase of shipping is the supervision of loading and stowing of articles into the truck or railroad car. Even the most firmly packed article may be damaged if improperly loaded. Generally, railroad boxcars are loaded from end to center; trucks from front to rear. Good practice dictates the grouping and loading of boxes of the same type and size together. Loading should also be carried out in the proper geographical sequence; *i.e.*, those articles to be unloaded last should be stowed first. Proper identification

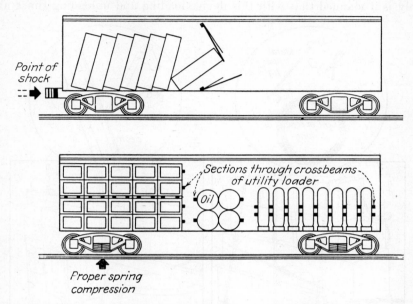

Fig. 33.—Division of load into small units which may be locked securely in place to prevent shifting. (*From The New York Times, Feb.* 14, 1943.)

in easy-to-read printing together with any "Handle with care" or "Fragile" warning should be made plainly visible during both the loading and unloading.

Goods placed in freight cars must be secured so as to stand the cumulative effects of sudden starts and stops (particularly those resulting from the common practice of switching railroad cars by "humping"), sidesway, and vertical vibrations—all of which can combine to cause no end of damage to poorly fastened articles. To prevent articles from shifting around in a car, it is common practice to resort to the use of "dunnage"—lumber, strap iron, and nails. These are constructed into bulkheads and supports and are nailed to the car. Or the strap iron may be used alone, passed around the goods, and fastened in place. One development, which may do away with the dunnage method of securing articles for shipment in freight cars and trucks, is the much publicized Evans "utility loader." Making use of permanently fixed vertical braces in the cargo area, detachable notched rails and adjustable crossbeams, this loader is designed to divide the load into small units each of which is locked securely in place so as to give it no opportunity to shift (see Fig. 33). It will hold all sorts of articles from bags of flour to storage batteries and from cartons of lamp bulbs to stoves. Not only is it claimed that with this device loading and unloading times are

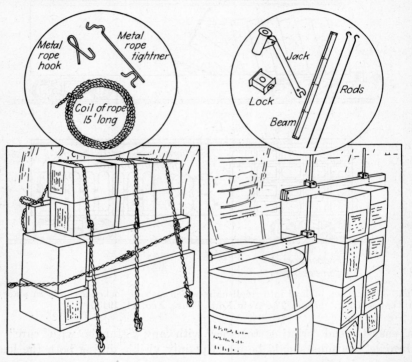

Fig. 34.—Loaders used in cargo airplanes. (*From The New York Times, Aug. 29, 1943.*)

reduced, but shipping space is saved through the elimination of dunnage, and the possibility of damage to articles thus loaded is considerably lessened. Similar loaders are also available for use in cargo airplanes (see Fig. 34).

As each shipment is made, certain paper work is necessary to record the transfer of goods to and from the carrier and to notify the customer that the goods are in transit. Where the goods are shipped by common carrier, this record usually takes the form of a *bill of lading* which not only serves as a promise from the carrier to deliver goods to the customer (consignee) but is also the means by which the carrier acknowledges receipt of the goods from the shipper (consignor). Where large or important shipments are involved, the vendor generally sends the customer shipping papers or a notice stating when and how the shipment has been made. If rail transportation is used, this notice will list the car number and routing so that the car may be traced if necessary. Where the shipment is by motor truck, the name of the truck company involved is usually furnished. While the freight car is at its point of origin or destination, records are generally kept showing where the car has been "spotted" on the sidings and to record the sealing or unsealing of the car, as the case may be.

Tracing and Expediting Shipments.—In the game of chess by which cars are moved about the country, there are a thousand and one possible combinations that may serve to delay the progress of a particular car. These may range from chance mechanical failure in the form of a hotbox to bad weather conditions and even to overburdened switching yards and terminals. It then becomes the duty of the traffic manager to trace and expedite cars en route, both inbound and outbound. The railroads check the progress of all cars at certain key points along all freight routes and will telephone or telegraph this information to consignor or consignee upon request. Thus, once the number and route of a particular car are known, its progress may be ascertained fairly readily.

Damage Claims.—Generally speaking, common carriers guarantee the safe delivery of all goods they accept. Hence they are responsible for all damaged goods and losses except those which are caused by acts of God, war, riots, strikes, negligence on the part of the consignor, and those which are inherent in the goods themselves (such as shrinkage in gasoline due to evaporation, etc.). Where goods arrive in a damaged condition, it is considered prima-facie evidence of the carrier's liability. However, the carrier relieves himself of the burden of proof by asking the consignee to sign a receipt for the goods. Thus it is very important that the receiving department of the consignee inspect the goods for possible damage before accepting them.

When goods are received in a damaged condition, it is the duty of the traffic manager to file a claim and to make negotiations toward collecting for the damage done. However, a wise traffic manager whose own goods frequently arrive at their destination in a damaged condition asks for the return of the damaged containers to ascertain, if he can, whether the carrier was entirely to blame or whether the design of the container, its packing and sealing, or the loading procedure were in part responsible and should be changed.

Demurrage.—Demurrage has been defined as the higher mathematics railroad men use to penalize shippers for delays in handling cars. Shippers are granted 48 hours' free time to load and receivers the same amount of time to unload each car. Demurrage is charged thereafter at rates of \$2 and up per day depending on the kind of car being held. Through intelligent planning, demurrage can be virtually eliminated. By scheduling cars to arrive only as fast as they can be loaded or unloaded, by educating suppliers to send shipping notices in advance of receipt of the material, and by holding department heads strictly responsible for the loading or unloading cars within the free period, this charge can be minimized.

At times some companies have loaded boxcars with goods and had the cars shipped to distant rail terminals consigned to themselves. The cars were then held at those points as floating warehouses from which quick delivery could be made when customers in those areas ordered the goods. When a few simple calculations of demurrage costs are made, however, it can readily be shown that the practice is economically unsound.

Receiving.—The receiving department is responsible for making and checking all receipts both for condition and count, for seeing that the material is delivered to its desired location, and for reporting the receipt

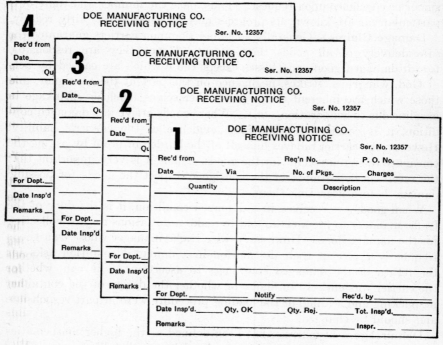

Fig. 35.—Typical receiving notice form.

to the proper individuals.   As discussed above, the receiving department is charged with the nonacceptance of all articles that are visibly damaged. It is also required to report promptly all articles found to be damaged when the container is opened together with any shortages discovered in the shipment.

The purchasing department usually supplies the receiving department with a copy of each purchase order from which the latter department may ascertain the quantity and description of the material on order as well as other pertinent information as to its point of use, vendor, method of shipment, etc.   The incoming material may then be checked for completeness against this purchase-order copy.

The receiving department may notify the purchasing department that the material has been received by returning its copy of the purchase order properly marked.   Or it may use the invoice memorandum or bill of goods supplied by the vendor to serve the same purpose.   Better still, the receiving department may use a *receiving notice,* or "inbound notice" as it is sometimes called.   This form (see Fig. 35) generally is serially numbered for easy posting and reference.   In general, the receiving-notice form is preferable to the other notification methods mentioned, for several copies can be supplied, and it simplifies the procedure where partial shipments are received.   Copies of this notice are sent usually to the purchasing department and to the department or person where the requisition originated.   A copy is also included with the material for identification purposes, and a file copy remains with the receiving department.

Where material is sent first of all to a receiving-inspection department for a thorough quality check, the receiving notice may be used also to record the inspection results, or a separate inspection form can be used for those data.   The receiving-inspection department is generally a part of the plant's inspection function as it checks the quality of raw materials received and therefore is closely linked with over-all quality control.   When substandard material is discovered, it is reported usually to the purchasing agent who arranges with the vendor for its disposition.

CONTROLLING MATERIALS—INVEN-
TORIES AND MATERIALS HANDLING

INVENTORY CONTROL

Effective inventory control insures that an adequate but not excessive bank of materials is on hand at all times to meet operating requirements. Under Utopian plant operation, materials would move through the plant in a thin smoothly flowing stream, and no storage of material would be required at any point. However, seldom if ever is this entirely practical, for segregation and storage of material are necessary to permit flexibility of production schedules, to facilitate manufacture in economic-lot quantities, to take advantage of quantity purchases, and to prevent possible pilferage or the "selection" of work by the production operators.

The size of the inventory carried is based principally on the relative costs involved. Dormant materials represent a considerable cash investment, and their storage incurs certain carrying costs. However, the costs of not maintaining an adequate inventory are likewise great for, as production delays develop, other and often more serious cost factors are introduced. Hence, it is the function of effective inventory control to maintain an inventory of such size that the costs of carrying too large an inventory are balanced against those resulting from an inadequate bank of materials.

In addition to regulating the bank of materials stored, inventory control is concerned with the systematic location, storage, and recording of materials in a manner that supplies the desired degree of service to the operating departments and minimizes the cost of that service.

The following financial and operating economies were shown in a survey of industrial organizations made by the Policyholders Service Bureau of the Metropolitan Life Insurance Company to result from the systematic controlling of inventories: [1]

1. It facilitates purchasing economies through the measurement of requirements on the basis of recorded experience.
2. It eliminates duplication in ordering or in replenishing stocks by centralizing the source from which purchase requisitions emanate.

[1] "Inventory Control Methods," Policyholders Service Bureau, Metropolitan Life Insurance Company, New York.

3. It permits a better utilization of available stock by facilitating inter-department transfers within a company.

4. It expedites the work of the planning department in developing production programs and in scheduling operations.

5. It provides a check against the loss of materials through carelessness or dishonesty.

6. It facilitates cost accounting activities by providing a means for allocating material costs to products, departments, or other operating accounts.

7. It enables management to make cost and consumption comparisons between operations and periods.

8. It serves as a means for the location and disposition of inactive and obsolete materials.

9. Perpetual-inventory values provide a consistent and reliable basis for preparing financial statements.

That the stocks of materials required by any industrial enterprise represent a large financial outlay and investment is a fact occasionally overlooked by the plant personnel and supervisory force. The story is told of an operating executive who at one of his periodic foremen's meetings with apparent carelessness dropped some coins from his pocket to the floor. The foremen promptly rushed to gather up the coins for him—for which efforts the executive duly gave his thanks together with the subtle reminder that materials in the plant represented a considerably greater investment than that represented by the company's cash. He then proceeded to contrast their interest in retrieving cash from the floor with the way in which they willingly permitted materials to be left on the floor and around machines and benches where these materials frequently became damaged, lost, or stolen.

Types of Inventories

Generally speaking, there are five main types of inventory items necessary in the operation of any industrial enterprise:

1. Raw Materials.—Included in this category are all materials used directly in the product which have undergone no major change since their receipt by the company. What is a finished product for one manufacturing enterprise may then become the raw material for another. For example, the steel producers turn out steel bars, rods, tubes, billets, and flat stock as their finished products. These are then used by a host of metalworking industries as their raw materials. Similarly, castings, forgings, leather hides, cloth, and commercial chemicals are all finished products that may in turn become raw materials subject to further processing.

2. Materials in Process.—These materials are likewise used directly in the product and are those upon which work has been performed to change their form, shape, and physical or chemical characteristics. Value in the sense of processing time and labor has been added to such materials. Examples of materials in process include a bar that has been turned in an automatic screw machine into a machine-tap blank, a leather hide cut into an upper for a shoe, a casting that has been sandblasted and painted.

3. Finished Products.—As the title implies, a finished product is one that is in a condition such that it can be shipped to a customer.

4. Supplies.—Supplies are materials which aid in production but which do not become a constituent part of the product itself, such as files, emery wheels, taps, drills, belting, sandpaper, oils, sawdust, plating supplies, lumber, shooks, stationery, and pencils.

5. Equipment Items.—These include "expendable" parts of machines and other equipment in the nature of jigs, fixtures, fittings, gages, minor machine parts—all repair or replacement items not exactly in the category of materials but subject to the same controls, techniques, and procedures.

Elements of Systematic Materials Control

Any materials-control system must provide certain elements or "tools" that can be used in achieving the degree of control desired. These tools can generally be classified under the following headings: (1) an effective stockroom location and layout, (2) adequate storage facilities, (3) a system of material symbolization and identification, (4) an accurate inventory-recording procedure, (5) a sound method of pricing materials, (6) intelligent stockroom operation.

Stockroom Location and Layout.—One of the prime considerations in the location of a stockroom relates to whether it should be centralized or decentralized. The centralization of all storage into one area affords a better opportunity for stores control, is easier to supervise, and usually involves a lower operating cost. Furthermore, a well-coordinated central stockroom can often provide faster and better service to the operating personnel. Centralization of the stores is usually desirable in small plants and in single-story plant structures where the storeroom can be located centrally for all work areas served. However, for large plants and for multistory plants, the time lost by personnel walking to and from centrally located stockrooms makes them all but prohibitive. In such organizations and where the points of use for the material are scattered, storerooms are usually decentralized throughout the plant so as to be near the points of use. Bulky items by their very nature lend themselves to such an arrangement, for although the costs of operating a series of small stockrooms may be higher than where only one large one is involved, nevertheless this cost may be more than offset by lower materials-handling and transportation costs.

The type of material to be stored exercises a great influence on the location of the stockroom. Heavy and bulky materials are frequently stored on the first or ground floor either near the point of receipt or the point of use and preferably near both. Steel billets, bars, and sheets, castings, bulk oil storage, and similar materials are likewise generally best stored on the ground floor. Light materials, particularly those which lend themselves to gravity flow through the plant, can often be located on the top floor. Liquids may even be pumped to the desired location and piped by gravity to the points of use. Valuable articles require a secure location. For example, industrial diamonds are often stored in a safe. Other portable and marketable items must of necessity be kept under lock and key to prevent pilferage. Inflammable materials should be stored in fireproof areas but, if this should not be possible, adequate first-aid fire-fighting equipment must be provided.

A location in which the light is good and the ventilation plentiful is usually desirable. Temperature and humidity are likewise factors that should be given consideration. Many materials may be preserved in storage for a greater length of time if the air is relatively dry and the temperature even throughout the year. Moisture in particular is important, for it will readily attack ferrous materials to form rust and will decompose or otherwise damage perishables and semiperishables. Paper articles, for example, must be kept in a very dry area. A location that, by virtue of its proximity to dusty or dirty manufacturing processes, introduces dirt into the storage area should be avoided or by all means partitioned off.

The stockroom, like the home kitchen, should be neither too large nor too small. An area that is too large for the material contained therein is not only wasteful of space but is likewise wasteful of the stock clerks' time and shoe leather. However, at the other extreme, an area that cramps the storage makes for inefficient operation as the clerks get in each other's way and are handicapped for space to store incoming material. Flexibility in the size of the area to allow for changing conditions, new and different materials, and a variation in the type and size of containers for bulk materials should invariably be provided. No business is static, and the stockroom for which no expansion or alteration space is provided will sooner or later cause trouble. During World War II, the shortage of standard 55-gallon steel oil drums led some oil producers to develop and use a smaller and nonreturnable fiber drum.

Those companies which previously had arranged their oil-storage facilities to accommodate the standard steel drums then had to revamp their stores areas and facilities to handle the substitute drums.

A well-laid-out stockroom provides space for the receipt and inspection of incoming materials and for making disbursements as well. Materials brought or conveyed into the area may have to be checked, sorted, or inspected, and even stored temporarily before they are placed in the storage racks. Where no provision is made for this temporary storage, the tendency is to use the aisles as receiving areas, which makes for a dangerous and inefficient condition. Main aisles should usually be between 4 and 8 feet wide, depending upon the type of material involved and the amount of traffic to be accommodated. The subaisles between racks and bins may in some cases be a minimum of 30 inches wide.

Where the order-filling requires the selection of a few pieces, each of a wide variety of items, it may be desirable to split the stockroom into a main or bulk stores area and a "substockroom," the latter containing a small quantity of the variety of items ordinarily required a few at a time. Since, in the main stores area, the storage of large quantities requires much space, the order-filling of a variety of items normally makes for considerable leg work on the part of the stores clerk. In the substockroom, however, the many items can be stored in a small area, and order-filling of small lots from this area is relatively rapid. Substockroom stocks can, of course, be replenished as necessary from the main room, which may be used both for this purpose and for filling bulk-lot orders.

If portable and salable items are to be stored therein, the entire area should be enclosed with wire-mesh partitioning or with a solid-frame structure. An information or service window can be provided as a part of the enclosure, and material requisitions and small items may then be passed through this window. Thus, shop and operating personnel can be kept out of the stores area, a condition absolutely necessary for effective control.

Storage Facilities.—The major precepts upon which the selection and installation of storage facilities are generally based may be stated as follows:

1. Allow for easy, quick, and sure receipt, storage, and disbursement of material.

2. Provide space and storage equipment adequate both as to size and load-bearing capacity for the material to be stored.

3. Protect against damage and deterioration.

4. Provide means for identifying and readily locating contents.

5. Provide for the selection of the oldest material first.

Many items in a range of sizes can best be stored in racks or bins (see Figs. 36 and 37). These can be either steel or wood, but preferably the former, since they are more flexible, durable, and economical and are also fireproof. Steel racks are assembled from standard shelves, uprights, and backs and are so designed that the shelf openings are ad-

Fig. 36.—Efficient use of steel-shelving bins for the storage of large castings. (*Courtesy of Lyon Metal Products, Inc.*)

justable. Such racks or bins are usually procured in standard heights but may be designed in some cases to extend virtually to the ceiling. This naturally reduces waste air space in the stockroom. After all, the effective capacity of the stockroom is dependent upon its usable cubical space, which in turn is dependent upon the height to which material is stored. Accessibility to the top spaces in such racks may be gained either by the use of ladders or by attaching protruding "counter" racks to the lower part of the high rack. The counter can be used not only for clerical and stock-filling activities but also as a built-in ladder.

There is a wide variety of commercial storage equipment available for the storage of common materials that cannot be put in conventional shelving. Typical of these are tiering racks for the storage of steel oil drums in as many rows high as may be desired; large tanks up to many thousands of gallons capacity which can be sunk in the ground and used for the storage of all sorts of liquids; various arm, U-shaped, and pipe-frame racks for storing metal bars and tubes; mixers and batchers for the storage and preparation of various granular materials; silos for the accommodation of sawdust and other pulverized material; and

Fig. 37.—Interesting application of steel shelving and wire partitioning to make for the neat and orderly storage of tools and supplies in the toolroom at the R. K. LeBlond Machine Tool Company, Cincinnati, Ohio. (*Courtesy of Lyon Metal Products, Inc.*)

skids and platforms as well as pallets that can be employed in conjunction with lift trucks and fork trucks in the vertical storage of bulky material.[2]

The "tote box" (see Fig. 38) and other types of shop containers have wide usage in the handling, storage, and segregation of small parts. The size and design of the container depend largely upon the material for which it is to be used but, by all means, when full the box should not be too heavy to be lifted by the handling method provided. Where lifting of boxes is done manually, the rule of thumb generally em-

[2] For a further description of materials-handling and storage equipment, see pp. 300–315.

ployed for a man of average strength is that he should not be required to lift alone boxes weighing more than 65 pounds, especially if he must carry them for some distance. An interesting and useful type of tote box is the stacking box which nests, one on top of the other, without need for shelving. Obviously where any number of boxes are stored,

Fig. 38.—Use of straight-side and open-front tote boxes together with steel shelving in the storage of small parts at the Nineteen Hundred Corporation, St. Joseph, Mich. (*Courtesy of Lyon Metal Products, Inc.*)

this type of box saves floor space. Some types of stacking boxes have open bin fronts for easy order-filling and ready access of parts for assembly.

Materials in the storage area should be placed in such a manner that they may be identified quickly both as to contents and to length of time in storage. Frequently it is desirable to use the oldest material first in order that stocks can perpetually be kept fresh. Thus it may be practical to divide the racks into two sections, one for current stock and the other for the storage of new stock as it is received. Some bins are designed so that incoming material stored in bulk may be put in at the top of the bin and disbursements made from the bottom. Oil drums stored in tiering racks may frequently be received at one side of the rack and issued from the other, again insuring that the oldest material is drawn first.

Material Symbolization and Identification.—It is standard industrial practice to classify, through the use of symbols, all materials, parts, and finished products, as well as operations, departments, machines, factory accounts (for cost-accounting purposes), and occupations or jobs (as a part of job-evaluation analysis, for consideration of which see Chap. XXV). Symbolization of such industrial items is necessary to identify them with the greatest possible ease and simplicity, to save time in writing or referring to them (in the same manner that abbreviations and nicknames are timesavers), and to aid in sorting or segregating them according to their respective classifications or group headings.

In general, symbolization may be either *numerical* or *mnemonic*. Numerical symbolization, which is perhaps the simpler to set up but not always the easier to operate, assigns numbers to each item to be classified. One familiar numerical system is the Dewey decimal system widely used in libraries to classify and identify books by subject matter. However, any numerical system makes use of the decimal positions, *i.e.*, units, 10's, 100's, 1,000's, etc., to identify the various class groupings. Thus machine No. 6503 may indicate that it is located in department 6, is type 5 (an automatic-screw machine), and is machine 03 in a battery of several machines. Factory account No. 728 for costing purposes might refer to the supplies account No. 28 in department 7. Among products classified numerically are ball bearings. For example, one bearing manufacturer, The New Departure Division of General Motors Corporation, classifies its single-row radial bearings as type 3000, and the various bearing sizes in that classification are listed as ranging from 3200 to 3222; the double-row bearings as type 5000 with sizes again similarly arranged from 5200 to 5222; shielded bearings as type 7000, etc. Such product designations not only aid in controlling production of material in process but serve as well to classify the part or product in the company's catalogue.

The second system of symbolization and that which enjoys perhaps the wider industrial application is the mnemonic system. The word "mnemonic" is defined as that which assists or aids in developing the memory. The system of identification bearing that name makes use of a combination of letters and numbers which identify each item and which are readily memorized. Frequently the letters used suggest the name of the class or part. Thus the New Departure clutch-throwout bearings are given the prefix CT, as CT27. The Mathews Conveyer Company makes use of a form of the mnemonic system to identify its various types of conveyers. For example, 2CO33-2¼-14-6-S-G1 refers to a 2-rail gravity-roll conveyer with type C rails on which the legs are turned out(O), No. 33 bearings, rolls 2¼ inches in diameter and 14 inches long, are spaced 6 inches on centers. Strap couplings (S) between rail sections are called for and the guard-rail clearance is equivalent to the roll length plus 1 inch (G1).

Material in storage may be located either by *symbol* or by *index*. Where the former is used, one row of bins may take only parts carrying, for example, numbers in the 1000 series, the next row of bins, series 2000, etc. Each item in a grouping is permanently assigned to a bin section. Obviously such a system of storage is apt to waste space in one section and make for an overcrowded condition in the next, since the stocks of each item are seldom constant over a period of time. Thus it is common practice under such a material-locating system to provide a bin for each item that is adequate in size to store an average supply of that item and to allow additional space or bins in the same general area for surplus stock when, as, and if required.

A system of indexing, on the other hand, permits material to be stored in any bin that happens to be free at the moment, but of course requires that a record be made of the location or locations in which each item is stored. Under any index system, each bin section is classified in a fashion similar to the designation of houses in a city area. Thus each main aisle (avenue), subaisle (side street), and bin (house) is appropriately labeled with numbers or letters for ready identification. Very large warehouse areas frequently require use of charts or maps of the storeroom layout in order that all items may be located quickly. Storage of material by index makes the most effective use of the storage space available but does entail accurate records and postings of receipts and disbursements if material is to be located.

Other systems of storeroom identification make use of paint, tags, or distinctive marks to segregate material. For example, the ends of rods, bars, and tubes, or the edges of metal sheets are often painted with identifying colors to aid in segregating them by size, alloy, date of shipment, or vending company. Buckets or wagons used to collect turnings and scrap pieces of various alloy metals are frequently painted distinctive colors as are the machines on which the respective alloys are used, thus aiding in keeping alloy turnings and scrap segregated for resale and remelting.

Most job-order companies have the problem of identifying specific materials for specific production orders. Frequently similar or identical material may be in process concurrently, and the problem then becomes one of identifying and segregating each batch of material through the various operations. This problem has been solved in various ways, depending upon the nature of the material involved. Sometimes paint is used, the color identifying the lot. Tags can be employed either attached to the material itself or, in the case of small parts, to the container in which they are stored. For machinery parts, the machine or order number may be imprinted or stamped on the part itself. Finally, materials that do not lend themselves to one of the foregoing procedures often can be kept separate by segregation alone as in separate bins, on separate pallets or skids, or on individual materials-handling trucks.

Inventory-recording Procedures.—The quantitative control of materials is based on the "three R's" of stockkeeping: *records, requisitions,* and *reports.* Most stockrooms regardless of size employ records of the perpetual-inventory type. These usually show the movement of material in and out of stock as well as the current balance of each article carried. Practically all such records are prepared in terms of unit quantities such as number of pieces, pounds, gallons, etc. Many likewise include evaluation data so that the value of the stock carried can be ascertained for factory accounting purposes. Perpetual-inventory records not only provide the information necessary for effective monetary and quantitative control of materials but are vitally necessary to the scheduling of production as well. Where the backlog of production orders is great, as it was during the recent war years, this backlog must be translated into material requirements which are to be ordered and made available as necessary to meet this backlog. Thus, where this apportionment of material is large in relation to the amount of material carried in stock, it is common practice to provide scheduling information by recording the material "apportioned" with respect to that "available."

There are many types of perpetual-inventory records in use by industry today, and each is individually tailored to meet the needs of the enterprise and the nature of the materials control involved. Typical perpetual-inventory records are shown in Figs. 39 and 40. For further description of a specific inventory-record system, see A Typical Record Adaptation, Chap. XXX.

Clarification of the following terms commonly used in perpetual-inventory records may be required:

1. *Ordered* or *On Order:* Quantity of material on order with the plant through a manufacturing order or on order with the purchasing department through a purchase requisition.

2. *Received* or *In:* Quantity of material supplied to the storeroom in response to a manufacturing order or purchase requisition.

3. *Issued, Delivered,* or *Out:* Quantity of material issued to the plant, sent to a customer, etc., in accordance with a material requisition or customer order.

4. *Balance* or *Stock on Hand:* Quantity and/or value of material physically on hand as of the date indicated.

5. *Applied* or *Allocated:* Quantity of material apportioned or ear-

RECORD OF INDIVIDUAL M. O.'S.						ALLOCATION RECORD			
M O NO		ARTICLE	M O. NO		ARTICLE	ALLOCATED		AVAILABLE	
DATE	DELIVERED	BALANCE	DATE	DELIVERED	BALANCE	M O NO	QUANTITY	ADD-P. O. NO. DED.-M.O.NO.	QUANTITY
M O NO.		ARTICLE	M. O. NO		ARTICLE				
DATE	DELIVERED	BALANCE	DATE	DELIVERED	BALANCE				
M O NO		ARTICLE	M. O. NO.		ARTICLE				
DATE	DELIVERED	BALANCE	DATE	DELIVERED	BALANCE				

a.

INVENTORY CONTROL RECORD										
VENDORS:- 1 2			3 4			LBS.	QUANTITY UNIT FT.	PCS.		
ON ORDER:- PURCHASE RECORD						STOCK ON HAND RECORD				
DATE	V	ORDERED P. O. NO.	QUANTITY	RECEIVED P. O. NO.	DATE	RECEIVED P.O. NO.	UNIT PRICE	QUANTITY	DELIVERED M. O. NO.	DEP'T.	UNIT PRICE

DESCRIPTION OF MATERIAL

b.

Fig. 39.—Perpetual-inventory control cards designed for a visible index file.

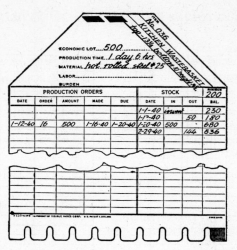

PRODUCTION ORDERS					STOCK			
DATE	ORDER	AMOUNT	MADE	DUE	DATE	IN	OUT	BAL.
					1-1-40 *invun.*			230
					1-17-40		50	180
1-12-40	16	500	1-16-40	1-20-40	1-20-40	500		680
					2-29-40		144	536

Fig. 40.—Simple perpetual-inventory-record card used to control the inventory of finished goods at an enterprise making cans and containers. This form of card is used with a bin type of file in which the cards are shingled horizontally to serve as a visible index. Note that on 1–12–40 as the balance on hand went below the established minimum of 200, a production order was placed with the plant to replenish the stock.

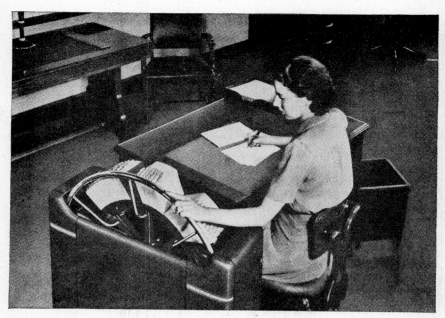

Fig. 41.—Typical application of a rotary file. Wheel may be rotated in either direction. Cards can be quickly picked from the wheel, the information obtained or posted, and then cards are readily snapped back in place. Postings may be made without removing cards from the file. Speed, visibility, and convenience are the principal advantages of this type of file. (*Courtesy of Diebold, Inc.*)

marked for future orders already planned but not necessarily issued to the plant or to a customer.

6. *Available:* Quantity of material available for the plant or customer in the sense that it is either actually on hand or on order but not already earmarked.

Descriptive and identifying information such as the name and part number of the material, location in the stockroom, and annual consump-

Fig. 42.—A recent development in the field of visible-index files is this mechanized unit which holds flat, shingle-type, slide-trays of record cards. Advantages claimed for this unit are that it saves space and operates swiftly to position slides at proper level for flipping up cards and making entries. Colored tabs are used for signaling records. (*Courtesy Remington Rand, Inc.*)

tion is entered either at the top or bottom of the record card depending upon the type of file in which the card is placed. In a vertical bin type of file (or "drawer file," as it is sometimes called) this information will be at the top of the card for easy reference. The same is true where rotary files are used (see Fig. 41). Where the file is of the flat-drawer, visible-index type (see Fig. 42), the cards or sheets are filed in these drawers in a horizontal position and are "shingled" so that the bottom of each card is visible when the drawer is pulled out. Thus the identifying information would be placed at the bottom of the card for such purposes. Various colored signal clips and tabs are often attached to the visible portion of the record card (see Figs. 42 and 78) to indicate the time to reorder, to note important follow-up dates for material on order, to denote obsolescence, and for other similar purposes.

The minimum or *min* usually refers to the ordering point or flag point at which a new order should be placed to replenish used stock. At this point, sufficient material is generally ordered to bring the stock up to a maximum or *max*. The max and min are usually stated in terms of number of units, as a min of 100 pieces and a max of 700 pieces. Occasionally, it may be preferable to translate these into time units, as a min of 3 weeks' supply and a max of 10 weeks' supply. Some companies add an *absolute min* below the regular ordering min. This is the danger point below which the on-hand stock balance should never go. However, if the absolute min should ever be reached, it indicates that the on-hand stock is dangerously low and that the material on the replacement order should be expedited for immediate delivery lest the stockroom run out of that material.

Another and perhaps the simplest type of perpetual inventory record is the *bin tag*. This is a tag that is kept with the material in stock at all times and contains running balances of receipts, issues, and balance on hand. A bin-tag system is used primarily where the type of inventory control is elementary and where no centralized perpetual records are maintained. However, it makes for easy checking of the physical inventory with the record kept—a feature wherein the other forms of perpetual-inventory records are especially weak. The main hazards connected with the use of bin tags are that they frequently become lost or placed with the wrong box or bin of material and the fact that clerks in their haste to make receipts or disbursements from that material fail to make the necessary postings.

Materials are issued from the storeroom only upon receipt of a formal requisition properly signed by an authorized individual. The form shown (see Fig. 43a) has spaces for the date, the department to which the material is to be delivered, the account or production-order number, the amount and description of the material, the unit price, and the total cost. Requisitions are analogous to bank withdrawal slips or checks, and they are, of course, presented for "payment" in materials at the stockroom. Frequently these forms are numbered serially so that all slips may be checked and accounted for. Returns of unused or overdrawn goods call for the use of *stores credit slips* which are materials requisitions in reverse and are quite similar in form and information included (see Fig. 43b).

Physical inventory involving an actual count of materials on hand is

From stores	Date delivered	MATERIAL REQUISITION	Order No.	To dept.
	Delivered by	Charge to	Authorized by	
Quantity	Description		Unit price	Total cost

1. Salmon: To stores control.   2. Manila: to department with material.

Fig. 43a.—Typical material-requisition form prepared in duplicate.   No material may be drawn from the storeroom without a written requisition.

From dept.	Date returned	RETURNED MATERIAL	Order No.	To stores
	Returned by	Credit	Authorized by	
Quantity	Description		Unit price	Total cost

1. Yellow: To stores control.   2. Blue: To stores with material.

Fig. 43b.—Returned-materials slip to accompany overdrawn material that is returned to the storeroom.

taken periodically so that adjustments may be made to correct cumulative errors in receipts and disbursements, incorrect postings or extensions, and possible omissions. Count of large items is taken mentally or by weight; small items are usually weigh-counted on counting scales (see Fig. 44). Three methods of taking the physical inventory are in wide

FIG. 44.—Counting scales used by an electrical manufacturer. The scales are so designed that by counting a few pieces in the small scoops, the virtually exact count of several hundred pieces can be quickly determined. (*Courtesy the Toledo Scale Company.*)

use, the application of each depending upon specific conditions involved in each case. These methods are:

1. Inventory at a stated time annually (as on New Year's Day), covering all items at that time. Generally, inventory is taken either at the end of the fiscal year for the enterprise or during a period when the stocks of the inventories as a whole are low. When the inventory is taken by this method, all production generally must stop and a special crew is organized for the job.

2. Periodic physical inventory of all items during the course of the year so that each item is inventoried at least once during the year. This

method does not disrupt operations in the plant and places a steady load on the personnel taking the inventory.

3. Inventory of each item whenever the stock on that item reaches its lowest point. Under this system, items are inventoried irregularly, but the time for the actual inventory is reduced to a minimum because of the small quantities involved.

A form of physical control of inventories takes place where the minimum or stand-by quantity is bonded in stock by tying together the required number of boxes or units, binding them with scotch tape, etc. When the bond on such material must be broken to meet requirements, it becomes a signal to the stores clerk that stocks should be replenished by sending through a new order. This form of control can be used either to supplement and furnish a double check on the perpetual-inventory records or, in cases where only a very elementary form of control is necessary, it can be used in place of perpetual records.

Ordering Quantities.—A detailed study of ordering amounts and ordering points, their formulas and methods of calculating is perhaps beyond the scope of this treatise. The subject is one that is quite involved because of the many variables that must be taken into consideration. Thus the reader is referred to some of the books now available and devoted extensively to a presentation of this subject.[3]

However, it is important here to understand the principles upon which any calculation of *economic-lot quantities* is based, for a knowledge of these is essential to any intelligent ordering procedure. These principles may be grouped as follows:

1. Material is generally reordered for stock when the balance on hand has reached the prescribed minimum or ordering point (see page 292). Minimums are set so that, when fresh stock arrives, a small reserve of material is still on the shelves. This dormant reserve stock prevents the stockroom from being entirely out of that material should some slight delay in getting the fresh stock develop, but of course this reserve increases the *average inventory* carried.

2. Material in stock incurs certain *carrying charges* which make it desirable to carry a low average inventory:

a. Material in stock represents an outlay of the company's cash funds. Money invested in any enterprise is subject to certain interest charges that are based on the business risk factors for the enterprise involved. Unless the money so invested brings a return to its investors, that money will be withdrawn and invested elsewhere. Money spent

[3] Suggested references for a treatment of economic-lot sizes are F. E. Raymond, "Quantity and Economy in Manufacture" and F. L. Eidmann, "Economic Control of Engineering and Manufacturing."

in idle or dormant stocks of material is not bringing any return on its investment.

b. Stocked material occupies space that must bear its proportionate cost of heat, light, taxes, repairs, and depreciation on the building.

c. Insurance is generally carried on all material in stock, thus introducing another cost factor.

d. Material in stock is always subject to possible deterioration or damage. Also there is the risk of obsolescence as technical advances or changes in methods and materials render the stocked material valueless for the purpose for which it was originally intended.

3. Each time material is ordered, certain *preparation costs* are incurred which make it more desirable to order large quantities infrequently than to order small quantities frequently:

a. In the case of purchased material, expense is incurred in the preparation and placing of the purchase order, the receiving, handling, and voucher paying.

b. In the case of manufactured material, there is the cost of production planning of the order, clerical costs, costs connected with the issuance of tools, gages, tickets, work orders, and blueprints. Also a part of this cost is the foreman's time spent on the order in question as well as that of setting up the machines to run the material.

From the foregoing it can readily be seen that the carrying charges and preparation costs operate at cross purposes with each other. Low carrying charges require a low average inventory and hence small ordering quantities. Low preparation costs are gained only through large ordering quantities with a resultant high average inventory. However, in general, it may be stated that the most economical quantity to order (economic-lot quantity) is that for which the preparation costs equal the carrying charges and hence for which the total variable costs are at a minimum (see Fig. 45).

The importance of the principles of economic-lot quantities varies with the type of manufacture. At one extreme is the A. O. Smith Corporation's automatic automobile-frame machine. This machine occupies two city blocks, handles steel direct from the railroad siding, inspects it, punches the rivet holes, forms it into the desired shapes, trims and assembles the component parts of the X assembly, and finally rivets the parts together. Performing 552 automatic operations, it is designed to turn out 10,000 completed frames per day. Yet this machine requires the services of some 200 men for 8 hours to make the change-over and setup from one size to another. At the other extreme is an operation that involves drilling a hole in a small automotive casting. The setup of the hand-operated drill press used in this operation consists simply of inserting the proper sized drill and locating the stops against which the castings are held in place.

Contrast the importance of determining the proper lot quantities in the manufacture of automotive frames with that of establishing the proper lot quantities for the drilled casting. The quantity of frames

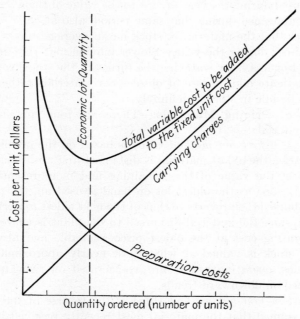

Fig. 45.—How the quantity ordered affects the carrying and preparation costs. Where these two lines cross, the total variable cost (= carrying charges + preparation costs) is a minimum.

manufactured in any one run has an important bearing on the total cost of the article. As for the casting, provided the carrying costs are likewise low, the quantity manufactured has little influence on the cost of the article and thus is relatively unimportant.

Furthermore, economic-lot quantities as determined empirically or by formula must be tempered by other factors. Quantity discounts that vary with the quantity purchased often outweigh the carrying and preparation costs. Transportation costs, particularly where carload lots are involved, frequently have an important bearing on the size of the lot purchased. Or again, a rising or falling market may be a major factor. From the standpoint of competition and customer good will, it may be desirable to store larger quantities of finished goods than the formulas dictate simply so that sizable orders may be filled promptly from stock.   Thus the theoretical lot size must often be modified in accordance with the other considerations involved.

Allied with the question of quantities to order is that of the *turnover* of material in stock.   Turnover is the rate at which material moves in and out of stock and may be defined technically as the ratio of the value of material used during the year at cost to the value of the average annual inventory maintained during that same period, also at cost.   A turnover of 4 indicates that the material in stock on an average moves in and out of stock 4 times during the year.   Slower moving materials may have a turnover of 1 or less.   By watching the turnover, the stockkeeper may be able to investigate and dispose of obsolescent materials rather than permit them to lie idle in stock indefinitely.

Methods of Pricing Materials.—There are four common methods of pricing materials:

1. The *first-in-first-out method* (fifo) is based on the premise that, almost invariably, the oldest material is disbursed first and should not continue to affect the value of the remaining and more recently received material.   As soon as the oldest lot on hand is used up, the price of the material disbursed then reverts to that of the next oldest material.   Under this method, since the material disbursed to the plant is charged into the current operating cost at the oldest price available and also since the material in stock is valued at what most nearly approximates current market values, operating profits are exaggerated on rising prices [4] and are minimized on downward trends.

2. The *last-in-first-out method* (lifo) is the reverse of the one above, since it is assumed that the material most recently received is disbursed first, and hence the material is charged out accordingly.   The underlying theory in this case is that in stocking materials for normal manufacturing operations, a reserve bank of materials must be maintained which in a sense represents a fixed asset that is seldom if ever taken out of stock. Therefore, the theory continues, this reserve should be valued at a more or less constant figure and any fluctuations in the prices of new materials received should be absorbed currently in the cost of operations.   This method has been said to reduce profits on the upswing of prices and to accentuate them on declining price trends.

3. Under the *cumulative-average method* all materials of like specifications are valued and charged out at the same unit-cost figure.   This figure is obtained by dividing the total value of the material on hand at any one time by the number of units of that material.   As can be readily appreciated, each time a new purchase of material is received,

[4] Many of the high industrial profits recorded for the years 1947–1948 can be attributed to this fact alone.

the average must be recalculated. Thus this system involves considerable clerical work, may admit of clerical errors, and is considered by some accountants to be a costly and complicated pricing method.

4. Under the *standard-cost method* [5] a standard cost is established for each material. This standard may be simply a cost estimate or may represent an average of the cost of that material as taken from past purchases. All disbursements are charged out as an operating cost at the standard value, regardless of the price actually paid for the material disbursed. As the price of receipts of new material varies from lot to lot, this overage or underage is debited or credited to an inventory-variation account which is finally cleared at the end of the year into the profit-and-loss account. Only as a seemingly permanent change in the price of that material appears to have been made is the standard-cost figure revised more nearly to approximate the new price.

Which of the above methods is applicable in any specific situation depends upon the type of material, its price-fluctuation pattern, and the manner in which it conforms to the over-all accounting procedure followed by the enterprise in question. No one method is the best for all situations. However, in all cases the method followed should be consistent from year to year and should be acceptable to the Collector of Internal Revenue if it is to be used in the computation of Federal taxes.

Stockroom Operation.—A major premise of stockroom operation is the fixation of responsibility for the operation and control of that stockroom in the hands of one individual. Only this man and his subordinates should be allowed access to the stores area; all others should be permanently locked out. Unless this is done, it is hopeless to expect that the records and stocks will be kept in good order. The storeskeeper and his subordinates should be carefully selected and trained to be exacting, meticulously neat, and production-minded.

As pointed out above, the heart of the quantitative control of materials lies in the use of perpetual-inventory records. Hence, it is important that orders, receipts, and disbursements are posted to the records promptly and that a close check is constantly made on the stock balances to ascertain when the minimum is reached. Also when the stock becomes dangerously low, this fact should likewise be made known so that overdue orders may be given special attention. If a constant watch is maintained for those items the consumption of which is unusually high, an investigation may be made to reveal the breakdown of some type of control in the plant. Where slow-moving items are involved, it may be possible to see that these are used up before any new or better substitutes are permitted to be withdrawn.

[5] For further information on standard costs, see Chap. XXVIII.

Prima-facie evidence of an efficiently operated stockroom is a well-organized and speedy stores service which prevents as far as is possible idle time on the part of operating personnel waiting for material. Frequently, good arrangement and housekeeping in the storage area will prevent the accumulation of hidden stocks and will greatly reduce the toll of damaged articles. A good stockkeeper is ever on the watch for possible ways in which materials can be simplified and standardized. He likewise carefully watches for potential savings resulting from the purchase of bulk material in place of packaged material and for possible changes in the package size or in the quantity ordered that may enable him to take advantage of a lower price. Packaged material, provided it does not have to be opened for inspection, should ordinarily be stored and disbursed in package-lot quantities to save handling and counting. Regardless of the accounting procedure followed, the oldest material should be used first, and the incoming material should be so segregated that this is possible.

Finally, since standard items often invite theft and are possible of resale, the stock system should be such that petty thievery of this type is soon discovered. Just as a daily balance system relieves bank clerks of any temptation they may have to steal the money they handle, so also are stock clerks and others who handle industrial materials relieved of temptation through the knowledge that pilferage will be promptly discovered. The importance of this problem and the limits to which some thieves will go cannot be overestimated. There is on record the case of a plant employee who tripped and fell on his way home from work and then was unable to rise even with the assistance of two other men. An investigation showed that he was carrying on his person 200 pounds of bar solder in a specially built belt! Furthermore, it has been found that unless cigarette lighters are installed on automobile dashboards as one of the last operations in the assembly line, they are often stolen. Thus where the possibility of pilferage is present, the removal of temptation is one of the requirements of effective materials control.

MATERIALS HANDLING

It has been said that today the greatest opportunities for the reduction of industrial costs and for increased manufacturing efficiency lie in the more economical handling and transporting of materials rather than in the more economical manufacturing and processing of materials. Strikingly enough, the development of machines that move materials is not new. In fact, prehistoric man's earliest mechanical implements were those which enabled him to move rocks and other heavy articles. But rather the application of such machines for industrial use has tended in the past to lag behind the introduction of machines that produce goods. The automotive industry was perhaps the first to realize that the extensive use of materials-handling equipment should be an integral part of manufacturing. World War I led to some notable advances in the application of such equipment, but it remained for World War II to demonstrate to industry once and for all that a production machine is only as efficient as is the machine supplying it.

Production men in general have now finally realized that materials-handling equipment is not merely a substitute for a man with a strong back and a weak mind, but instead is a vital element in the continuous flow of goods through a plant. True it is that production machines make the goods, but it is equally true that, were it not for their servants, the materials-handling devices which wait on them hand and foot, congestion of materials in the work areas and delays in the supplying of materials would be such that their full productive capacity could not possibly be realized.

There is now available such a wide range of mechanized handling and transporting devices that most industrial materials and products can be moved mechanically about a plant. The advantages of completely mechanized handling over that whereby materials are moved primarily by man power with perhaps the occasional assistance of a floor truck or overhead device may be summed up as follows:

1. The nonproductive time of the production process is lessened through the more rapid handling and movement of material. Carl F. Dietz, president of the Lamson Corporation, manufacturers of mechanical conveyors, has stated, "materials-handling operations consume at least 30 per cent of the total time required to produce manufactured articles." [6] Mechanical equipment tends to reduce this time for moving materials between operations, and if Mr. Dietz's statement is to be considered for industry as a whole, it points the need for the greatly increased application of mechanical-handling devices in industry today.

2. Human fatigue in lifting and handling by hand is reduced and even entirely eliminated. Thus much of the backbreaking labor that was once a part of many industrial processes is no longer required.

3. Idle machine time and idle operator time can be brought to a minimum. Much of the waiting for work that occurs where intermittent and nonmechanical delivery of materials is involved can be eliminated by equipment that insures a steady, constant flow of materials.

4. The productivity of production operators is increased by a reduction of the time they would otherwise spend in handling materials.

5. Increased safety of handling results where materials are not "man-

[6] *Mill and Factory*, May, 1943, p. 61, advertisement of Lamson Corporation.

handled." Mechanical equipment never suffers back injuries, hernias, or toe accidents.

6. Storage space is conserved, particularly where the mechanical equipment piles materials vertically. Where only man power is available, heavy materials seldom can be piled more than 4 feet from the floor.

7. Nonproductive labor is released for more productive endeavors. This particular advantage was a major factor in the greatly increased use of mechanical-handling equipment during World War II. Acute man-power shortages then prevailing in many areas placed a premium on materials-handling men, stockkeepers, and other servicing personnel, with the result that industrialists became intensely interested in mechanical-handling devices.

8. Mechanized equipment can be used to set the pace of production. This pace-setting feature is the very backbone of serialized manufacture, for all machines and work stations are built around the handling device in such numbers and in such a fashion that each operation can be performed at a rate that is predetermined in the handling equipment.

Mechanical-handling equipment may be used by industry for the warehousing and storage of materials, or it may serve as a production tool. Equipment as used in the first-named application may provide for the moving of raw materials into storage, in-process materials about the plant between operations, or finished products through to the point of shipping. Where the equipment serves as a tool of production, on the other hand, it might, for example, move materials through one or more continuous processes, such as heat-treating, painting, plating, baking, and drying. Or it might be used as an integral part of the assembly process to move materials from one assembly station to the next. The traditional example commonly associated with such an application is, of course, the automobile assembly line.

The best answer to any problem concerned with the handling of materials is: *Don't!*—if it can possibly be avoided. There are always three elements involved in such a problem: men, materials, and machines. Any one of these may be stationary, but the other two must then be moved. Traditionally, it has been considered most economical to move materials and men to the machines, which are kept stationary. However, many industrialists now realize that with today's flexible, unit-powered equipment, machines and men can be moved to the materials for the best all-round results. Such an arrangement really amounts to a serialized-production line (for a discussion of which, see Chap. X).

If, on the other hand, it is found necessary to move the materials, the nature of the equipment to be used must then be considered. The effectiveness of any materials-handling equipment item can generally be determined from the answer to the following question: Does the equipment pick up the load and transport it to its destination without any intermediate hand labor or rehandling by nonmechanical means? Unless the answer to this question is "Yes," the equipment is doing only half the job. Some types of equipment, as for example, chain conveyors and traveling cranes, are capable of both picking up and transporting. Others, notably most gravity conveyors, simply transport and, where heavy materials are involved, auxiliary hoists or other pick-up devices must be provided.

Types of Mechanical-handling Equipment

Functionally, there are two general classes of handling equipment: the *floor type* and the *overhead type*. Under the first classification there are:

1. *Hand Trucks.*—These include the 4-wheel hand-lift truck used for transporting skids and platforms; the 4-wheel wood-stake truck used for all-purpose carrying; the stock-handling cart or "tea wagon" type of truck for handling small, light items of all sorts; and the general-purpose 4-wheel truck. In addition there are special-purpose hand trucks designed to accommodate beer kegs, barrels, paper cement bags, carboys, etc.

FIG. 46.—Hand-lift truck used to carry a skid bin full of parts on the way to assembly. (*Courtesy of The Yale & Towne Manufacturing Company.*)

Fig. 47.—A battery-powered hand-lift truck. Such trucks are widely used because they provide fast, low-cost, maneuverable transportation. (*Courtesy Automatic Transportation Company.*)

Fig. 48.—The low-lift electric platform truck is shown here transporting skids of aircraft-engine cylinder-barrel blanks into the machine area. (*Courtesy of The Yale & Towne Manufacturing Company.*)

2. *Truck Tractors.*—These are generally small but powerful gas-powered tractors used with trailers. Frequently they are of the single-wheel-in-front, short-wheel-base variety to provide a small turning radius and all-round maneuverability. Although they are generally employed in out-of-door applications, with suitable exhaust equipment they may be

Fig. 49.—One of the many uses of a very versatile piece of mechanized handling equipment. The high-lift fork truck is transporting a large roll of jute weighing more than a ton. No skid or pallet is required. The tapered fork slides under the roll, the lift mechanism and load are tilted back, and the truck is on its way. (*Courtesy of The Yale & Towne Manufacturing Company.*)

used to advantage inside as well. Their high-draw capacity makes them a useful tool for moving machines and other equipment as well as heavy production materials.

3. *Power Lift Trucks.*—A very useful type of equipment in any plant, these trucks are generally powered electrically and are provided with either an elevating platform, a set of tiering forks, a ram, or a crane, depending upon the application for which they are intended. They may be either low-lift for simply transporting and low-stacking materials, or they may be of the telescoping high-lift type to permit stacking clear to the storehouse roof.   Tiering forks are used in conjunction with wood pallets which are inexpensive and may be carried and stacked in much the same manner as the conventional skid on the platform truck.   The ram is used with special classes of materials, such as coils of strip steel and wire which may be handled by their hollow interior.   For small

Fig. 50.—A high-lift truck stacking all-metal skid bins into a stack-rack. This combination makes for efficient handling and storage of heavy parts both indoors and out. (*Courtesy of Towmotor Corporation.*)

loads, generally under 1 ton, a powered hand-lift truck (see Fig. 47) likewise made with either a platform or a fork, low- or high-lift as the occasion demands, is an economical vehicle for transporting and stacking.

4. *Stackers.*—Being only moderately mobile, this type of equipment is used primarily for the vertical stacking of heavy or bulky articles. One common type is the barrel stacker for handling standard oil drums and other barrel products to and from a barrel stack rack wherein they may be stored vertically as high as is desired.

5. *Gravity-roll Conveyors.*—Constituting perhaps the most widely used conveying means employed in industry today, gravity-roll conveyors

are used to convey materials on ball-bearing rollers down a gentle grade by utilizing the natural force of gravity. The articles moved on roll conveyors may range in size from a few ounces to 20 tons or more. For example, department-store roll conveyors take packages of hosiery weighing only a few ounces. In steel mills, roll conveyors are used to handle

Fɪɢ. 51.—Electric-crane trucks have great load-lifting and load-carrying capacity. The truck shown here is storing seamless steel tubes. (*Courtesy of The Yale & Towne Manufacturing Company.*)

many tons of sheet and bar steel. Between these two extremes, almost all kinds of commodities in a wide variety of containers are conveyed on the various types and sizes of roll conveyors now available. The length of such conveyors may vary from a few feet between machines or operations to several hundred feet between departments. Conveyor manufacturers stand ready to provide a variety of standard curves (to permit material to turn corners or go around objects) and roller spirals (to accomplish a considerable vertical drop in a short distance). They

Fig. 52.—Air-brake reservoirs are handled on heavy-duty roller conveyors through Ingersoll machines for milling and then proceed to further machining areas. The castings shown have been discharged from the trolley conveyor at the right and are fed into the machines one at a time by means of combination stops and roll-over devices. Pneumatic tongs facilitate handling of castings from conveyors into machines. (*Courtesy of Mathews Conveyer Company.*)

Fig. 53.—Flat-belt conveyors are furnished with a belt supported on ball-bearing rolls of the regular gravity type or on wood or steel slider bed. This belt conveyor handles airplane parts through manufacturing operations. Conveyor is slider-bed type with work boards on both sides. (*Courtesy of Logan Company.*)

will also provide storage decks of conveyors (to facilitate storing a "float" of material between operations), gate-hinge mechanisms (to permit the lateral passage of employees), and power boosters (to provide increased elevation).

6. *Power Conveyors.*—Power conveyors are frequently used in applications where gravity-roll conveyors are not practicable as would be the

Fig. 54.—Pipes are frequently used to convey chemicals. Shown above is the main tower group of an alkylation unit used in the production of 100-octane aviation gasoline. (*Courtesy of Pan American Petroleum and Transport Company.*)

case where small individual parts are conveyed separately or where vertical or sloping changes in elevation as from one floor to the next are required. The exact type of conveyor will depend upon the application. Belt conveyors are in common usage and generally consist of powered endless belts traveling over rollers. Slat conveyors, apron conveyors, and push-bar lifts are simply adaptations of the belt type. Vertical-lift conveyors of the finger type and of the "dumb-waiter-elevator" type have wide application. Hoppers and chutes, frequently provided with electric vibrators, are used for handling coal, ores, and other bulk materials. Grain, pulverized coal, and chemicals are a type of materials that are sometimes lifted pneumatically through pipes to the top of storage silos or "elevators."

The most widely used varieties of overhead-handling equipment include:

1. *Chain Conveyors.*—These are of a number of types but usually employ an overhead monorail on which run trolleys attached at regular

FIG. 55.—Pneumatic conveyors used at the Seattle, Washington, glue plant of the Monsanto Chemical Company. Soybean meal is fed from above to the five hammer mills shown, where it is ground and then fan-blown up 40 feet of piping to a collector. (*From Factory, August,* 1949, *p.* 92.)

intervals to an endless chain. Under each trolley is placed a hook or other carrying device. The principal advantages connected with these conveyors are that they are located overhead and out of the way, that they thereby do not take up valuable floor space, and that they can be used to pre-position the material at the level and at the point in the plant where it is desired for use. Many continuous-process conveyors are of the chain type. Some, instead of being located overhead, are placed under the floor (see Fig. 59).

2. *Cranes.*—There are so many varied types of cranes, that any generalization as to their characteristics is somewhat difficult. How-

FIG. 56.—This full-length view of a foundry core room shows a trolley conveyor with trays loaded and handling cores past work stations. Transverse bends lower the trays to working height and the trolley maintains a constant flow of material through working area. This method of handling cores is extremely effective because of the smoothness with which the trolley moves the load through the room. There is no jolting and consequently breakage is kept at a very minimum. Note clear aisleways made possible by overhead equipment. (*Courtesy of Mathews Conveyer Company.*)

ever, all of them, whether they be classed as traveling, locomotive, tractor, jib, or gantry, both pick up and transport the material. Their application is generally for extremely heavy materials sporadically handled.

3. *Tram-rail and Monorail Hoists.*—These are simply standard chain, electric, or pneumatic hoists mounted to a single rail by means of a trolley. Horizontal movement may be controlled electrically or by hand. Such an arrangement adds mobility to what would otherwise be a stationary hoist.

Fig. 57.—An effective materials-handling system involving a combination of traveling cranes and roller conveyor. Note also the well-planned warehouse with high ceiling, few obstructing columns, and ample loading-dock facilities which permit rapid and low-cost storage and shipping of crated electric ranges. (*Courtesy of The Cleveland Crane and Engineering Company.*)

Fig. 58.—A motor-operated single-leg gantry crane in a large motor manufacturing plant. It is used for placing heavy motor armatures in position for assembly. This equipment is completely push-button controlled. (*Courtesy of The Cleveland Crane and Engineering Company.*)

Fig. 59.—A large airplane plant showing the first automobile-type continuous assembly-line conveyors ever installed in the airplane industry. Note that the chain is located in floor recess. (*Courtesy of Mechanical Handling System, Inc.*)

Selecting the Equipment

There is no rule-of-thumb basis applicable to the selection of materials-handling equipment, for materials handling is still classed in most quarters as an art, not as a science. Just as the selection of an automatic-screw machine as against a hand-operated turret lathe is dictated by the conditions involved in the specific case, so also is the choice, for example, of a gravity-roll conveyor vs. a belt conveyor vs. an overhead chain conveyor affected by the exact nature of the individual problem. However, if sales engineers from reputable manufacturers of materials-handling equipment are consulted about the handling problem, they are

Fig. 60.—Electric hoists are widely used in the vertical movement of materials. The one shown above picks up motor blocks and moves them along an I beam to assembly. (*Courtesy of The Yale & Towne Manufacturing Company.*)

often in a position to recommend the equipment best suited for the job and will prepare an engineering layout together with an estimate of the cost of the proposed installation.

Mechanized handling equipment to be worth while should pay for itself in a reasonable length of time. Some companies figure that the cost of such equipment must be returned in the form of savings from its use inside of one year. Others believe that equipment that pays for itself inside of three years is worth installing. At any rate, estimates of the cost vs. savings are frequently a major factor in selling management on the need for such equipment. These estimates should include all the tangible cost and savings elements involved. When these are totaled and compared with each other, the length of time required for the equipment to pay for itself can readily be calculated. In addition, any intangible savings, such as increased customer good will because of a reduction of the in-process time cycle, fewer handling accidents, less fatigue, better working conditions, and more regular production flow, should be enumerated in presenting to management the arguments in favor of the installation.

Occasionally, management becomes oversold on the idea of some type of mechanical-handling equipment and, based on a hunch alone or on the thought that by its installation the concern will evidence its progressiveness, an installation is made without consideration of all factors involved. There is a case on record of one manufacturer who installed an expensive conveyor that required the full-time attention of two men. It replaced a single husky individual who previously had done the job handily with the help of a very inexpensive wheelbarrow. But the management decided that the conveyor was modern, whereas the wheelbarrow looked like a carry-over from the stone age and, without consideration of the cost factors involved, the change was made.

Or consider another example. A number of the large aircraft companies have devised complicated power-driven conveyors as an integral part of their assembly lines. Douglas Aircraft Company, on the other hand, at their Santa Monica, Calif., plant designed to produce attack bombers during World War II hit upon an extremely simple and relatively inexpensive solution to this same problem. They employed a gravity-feed assembly floor. The concrete floor sloped 6 inches in 200 feet so that carriages on which planes were placed during assembly traveled of their own weight along a guide channel set in the floor. With this arrangement, no power was required to move planes from one assembly station to the next.[7] Thus does the old adage "Look before you leap" apply to the installation of any mechanized handling equipment.

In addition to selling top management, it is often necessary that the foreman who will have to make use of the equipment be sold on its advisability. Unless the foreman is convinced of the need for the equipment and is acquainted with its possibilities, the full advantage of the conveyor may be realized very slowly if ever. A vindictive foreman may even take pains to prove that it does not work. If, however, the foreman is consulted on the details of the equipment and if his advice is sought in planning the installation, he generally becomes personally interested in the project and will endeavor to make it work properly.

SUMMARY OF CHAPTERS XII AND XIII

In Chaps. XII and XIII we have been concerned with the principles and techniques by which materials are controlled in industry today. We have seen that there are four main phases of this control: procure-

[7] For an interesting discussion of this see *Steel,* Aug. 9, 1943, p. 72.

ment (purchasing), external transportation (shipping, traffic, and receiving), material storage (inventory control), and internal transportation (materials handling).

If a full measure of control is to be achieved, each of these phases must inevitably intermesh with the other three. This requires close coordination which may be achieved through the organization structure, through the operating procedures, and especially through the system of operating records. Like the other forms of control (those of production, quality, and processes), materials control is an indirect or overhead cost of doing business. In a sense it is a necessary evil. It is a means to an end: that whereby materials are made available in the desired amount and at the right time and place.

Of these four phases, perhaps the one that foretells the greatest opportunity for future development and improvement is internal transportation—materials handling. The techniques of procurement, external transportation, and materials storage have been fairly well established and are generally practiced in industry today. This does not, however, hold true for the art of materials handling. In that field, probably a majority of companies have barely scratched the surface. However, the need for scientific materials handling is rapidly becoming apparent. A wide variety of handling equipment has been made available. Only a widespread knowledge of the art, the techniques, and the applications seems to be lacking. But if recent trends are any indication, industry is rapidly striving to make up these deficiencies.

Some wide-awake managements are now discovering the real meaning of materials handling. They are finding that its effects pervade the activities of their plants. Machine design, plant layout, and in some cases even the plant buildings to be completely effective are best molded around the materials-handling equipment. The rate of production is often governed by it. The entire production-control system is inevitably linked with it. Truly the field of materials handling offers immense possibilities for furthering the operating control of an enterprise.

CASE PROBLEMS

Purchasing

1. The K Co. is improving its employee dressing-room facilities and is planning the purchase of 100 steel lockers. Each locker is to be 15 inches wide, 15 inches deep, and 72 inches high. Write a complete set of specifications establishing all the essential features that the vendor must provide in these lockers.

2. The machining division of the L Co. has placed a requisition with

the company's purchasing department for 400 small mechanical counters. These devices, used by the L Co. to count the daily production of machine operators, will gradually be installed on machines as the counters currently in service wear out or become broken. The purchasing department has asked for quotations on this item and has received the following bids:

Vendor A: $7.00 ea. list price, less discount of 20%.
Vendor B: $7.00 ea. list price, less 15% and 5%.
Vendor C: $7.25 ea. list price.
        Discount:
                10 or more 5%
                20 or more 10%
                50 or more 15%
                100 or more 20%
                500 or more 25%
        Terms: 2%—10; net—30. (= 2% if paid in 10 days; net if paid in 30 days)

What decision should the purchasing department make in placing its order and why?

3. The M Co. uses large quantities of grinding wheels made to their specifications as to grit size, bond or "adhesive" material, and degree of hardness (rapidity with which the bond breaks down to expose new grit cutting edges). The M Co. maintains two or more suppliers for each type of grinding wheel used. However, the manufacturing supervisor whose department uses these wheels specifies on his purchase requisitions which vendor to buy from. He argues that he is in a position to know which supplier's wheels give the best service, and he feels the company's interests are best served by buying the preferred wheels. The purchasing department, on the other hand, claims it should have the say as to which vendors get the orders. On what basis would you settle this dispute?

4. The N Co. uses commercial-grade hydrochloric acid (HCl) in the cleaning operations that are a part of its plating process. Carboys [8] of this acid are stocked by the plant's central supply room and withdrawn as needed by the plating department. On July 26, 1944, the supply room ran out of stock of this acid, thereby completely tying up the production of plated parts. The purchasing agent immediately made arrangements for an emergency shipment. Then the works manager summoned both the purchasing agent and the stockkeeper in charge of the supply room to ask for an explanation. The stockkeeper produced records to show that on July 5, three weeks prior to the 26th, he had

[8] Large glass bottles enclosed in wood and generally used in the handling of acids.

requisitioned from the purchasing department a shipment of the acid, scheduling it for the 19th. This shipment had not been received as of the 26th, by which time the supply room's reserve stock had been reduced to zero. The purchasing agent countered with the statement that deliveries of acid were running late, and he further blamed the stock-keeper for not having notified him a day or so in advance of the time he expected to go out of stock. If this had been done, he argued, emergency arrangements might have been made. If you were works manager of the N Co., what suggestions would you make to the purchasing agent and to the stockkeeper?

5. The purchasing agent of the O Co. receives the following Christmas presents from vendors: 1 quart of whisky, 1 necktie, 10 calendars, 2 daily memo pads—desk type, 1 paperweight, 1 box of candied fruits, and 1 dozen golf balls.

Which of these should he accept and why?

Packaging

THE ACE RADIO CO.

A few years ago the Ace Radio Co. was faced with the problem of developing containers for shipping its newly designed radio chassis and dynamic speaker, items that were sent to cabinetmakers, dealers, and even to customers for installation in radio cabinets. The chassis, typical of that in any home cabinet-type radio receiving set, consisted of a metal base serving as anchorage for the wiring, many condensers, resistors, etc. Mounted on this base were the several radio tubes, transformer, and tuning and control mechanisms. The dynamic speaker, which was shipped in a separate container, consisted of the magnet portion—a dead weight of solid metal—and suspended from it the fiber speaker cone with its delicate sound-reproducing center section.

Preparatory Questions

1. What characteristics were desired of the containers to be used by the Ace Radio Co. for shipping its radio chassis and speaker unit?

2. Suggest composition and design for a container that would have met the conditions listed in question 1. How would you secure each article in its container?

Three Inventory Control Systems [9]

ALPHA CO.

A machinery builder carries in its materials inventory large quantities and varieties of bolts, nuts, and other low-priced items that are subject to frequent

[9] Reproduced from "Inventory Control Methods," *op. cit.,* pp. 30, 35.

issue in small quantities. The issues are all made on stores slips that are priced in the cost department. The minimum quantity to be carried is made up into a separate package at the time a replenishment is received. A tag is attached to the package showing the date and quantity last received. The package is placed in the bin or on the shelf, adjacent to the loose material of the same type from which issues are made.

When the loose material is used up, the package is opened and the tag is sent to the office. The tag is automatically a notice to purchase or manufacture additional parts. The replenishment quantity is established from the rate of usage computed from the tag data.

BETA CO.

A duplicate bin system is used for controlling branch warehouse stocks of service parts by a maker of business machines. All of the models in current use have an aggregate of about 80,000 parts, most of which are made of stamped sheet metal and have a low unit value. A three months' supply is kept in branch warehouses. They are housed in steel cabinets which are arranged in rows with a walking space between rows and with drawer openings facing both ways. The cabinets have many drawers of varying width and depth. Each drawer is divided into compartments with one part number allocated to each. Stock numbers are inserted on compartments by use of gummed paper labels.

The drawers in one aisle of the stockroom contain the stock currently being used. The drawer immediately across the aisle in the same position contains the minimum quantity of the same stock number. The branch warehouse clerks withdraw stock from the active section until it is consumed. They then transfer some or all of the stock from the reserve bin across the aisle to the active section and make a decision as to the amount to reorder.

The reserve bin holding the minimum quantity contains a loose paper tag showing the date of the last replenishment and the quantity received at that time. This quantity incidentally is equal to the amount held in reserve because the minimum quantity is one-half the maximum. At the time the active stock is exhausted, the entire minimum is moved to the active section, provided the rate of usage, as shown by the elapsed time on the tag, justifies this move. If the maximum has been properly set, there would be a reorder every six weeks. If, however, the item is slowing down in usage, the stock clerk inserts another date on the tag (crossing out the old date) and he enters the quantity transferred to active stock (crossing out the old quantity). The amount that he transfers under these conditions would depend on his judgment regarding the actual rate of usage. The information entered on the tag, together with the earlier information which has been crossed out, provides a basis for recalculating usage when this becomes necessary.

In cases where the stock clerk transfers the entire reserve supply to the active bin and makes a complete reorder, he inserts the amount of his order on the bin tag, erasing previous figures. He also inserts the date of the reorder. When the replenishment arrives, he changes this date to the date of receipt.

Gamma Co.

A lithograph house having annual sales of over $1,000,000 has three principal kinds of materials, (*a*) paper, (*b*) ink, and (*c*) maintenance materials and shop supplies. Each is carried in a separate general-ledger account, office supplies being charged to expense when purchased. The procedure described here is restricted to the third classification, as the control of paper and ink, the principal direct materials, is effected through unit inventory records.

Shop supplies and repair parts, constituting about 1,200 items, are kept in a locked enclosure which is provided with adequate metal shelving. Access to the stockroom is available only to one stockkeeper, who is responsible for receipts, issues, and physical custody. No detailed stock records are kept. The stockkeeper's duties include reordering each supply as it gets low. To assist him, each bin or shelf space has a label showing the name of the item, and maximum and minimum quantity limits. The risk of serious embarrassment through stock shortage is slight, because most of the items could be secured in an emergency from local sources.

The company's only control over the accumulation of excess or obsolete inventories is an annual audit of the physical inventory. This is done primarily by the chief accountant and the factory superintendent. The accountant lists questionable items, especially those having a substantial value, and investigates these personally. The superintendent sees this list, and he also scrutinizes the entire inventory list. This is the basis for finding additional uses for such items, changing the maximum and minimum quantities to be carried, and selling them to outside sources if they are entirely obsolete.

Preparatory Questions

1. Criticize the effectiveness of the inventory-control systems of the Alpha, Beta, and Gamma companies.

2. Describe the operating conditions under which physical inventory control is to be preferred over perpetual inventory records and vice versa.

Ordering Quantities

The Webster Co.

The Webster Co.'s yearly consumption Y of a certain size of grinding wheel is 1,000. The unit cost C of these wheels is $1. The yearly carrying rate I on the average stock carried is 12 per cent (based on 6 per cent interest, insurance, and taxes; 4.5 per cent depreciation and obsolescence; and 1.5 per cent storage). The average preparation cost P, which equals the cost of placing one additional order to replenish stock, is $0.80.

Preparatory Questions

1. Calculate the economic-lot quantity Q, *i.e.*, the most economical quantity to order.

NOTE: The stock on hand varies from R to $(Q + R)$ where R equals the reserve quantity in stock when the new lot Q is received. Thus the average stock carried is

$$\frac{R + (Q + R)}{2}$$

However, for the purpose of this problem, assume $R = 0$ and the average stock carried is

$$\frac{Q}{2}$$

2. Under what conditions may it be assumed that $R = 0$ without seriously affecting the economic-lot quantity Q?
3. Still assuming that $R = 0$,
> *a.* What is the total variable cost for the year if quantity Q obtained above is ordered each time?
> *b.* If 20 orders for 50 wheels each are placed during the year, what is the total variable cost for the year?
> *c.* If 2 orders for 500 wheels each are placed, what is the total variable cost for the year?

Materials-handling Problems

In each of the situations determine what kind of materials-handling equipment can be used to best advantage.

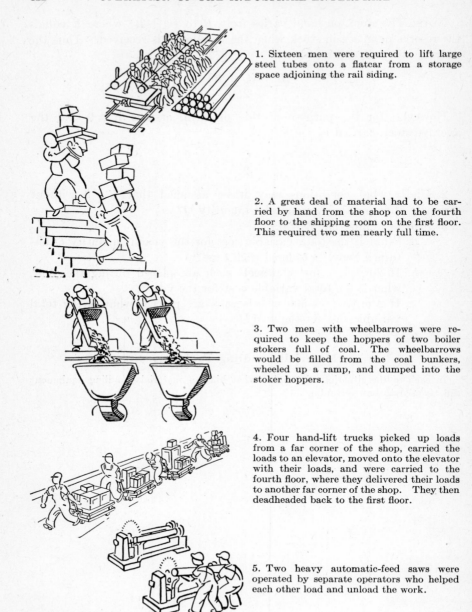

1. Sixteen men were required to lift large steel tubes onto a flatcar from a storage space adjoining the rail siding.

2. A great deal of material had to be carried by hand from the shop on the fourth floor to the shipping room on the first floor. This required two men nearly full time.

3. Two men with wheelbarrows were required to keep the hoppers of two boiler stokers full of coal. The wheelbarrows would be filled from the coal bunkers, wheeled up a ramp, and dumped into the stoker hoppers.

4. Four hand-lift trucks picked up loads from a far corner of the shop, carried the loads to an elevator, moved onto the elevator with their loads, and were carried to the fourth floor, where they delivered their loads to another far corner of the shop. They then deadheaded back to the first floor.

5. Two heavy automatic-feed saws were operated by separate operators who helped each other load and unload the work.

FIG. 61.—Figures and descriptive material adapted from industrial applications of materials-handling equipment as described in *Mill and Factory*, Vol. 33, No. 5, *Nov.*, 1943.

6. Two men using cable slings together with a crane and operator were required to unload bundles of sheet steel from freight cars.

7. Metal drums were placed on their ends directly on the warehouse floor. As the quantity of drums in storage increased, they soon began to take up too much floor space and required two men with hand trucks to handle them.

8. The haphazard temporary storage of parts being manufactured covered too much floor space and required three men to keep parts moving in and out in an orderly fashion.

9. Each time a freight car had to be moved into a loading or unloading position along a railroad siding, and a switching engine was not available, it was necessary to call out a crew of men to move it with a pinch bar and brute strength.

10. Two men were required to load and unload open coils of wire on platform trucks and haul them to shipping platforms.

Fig. 61.—(*Continued.*)

CONTROLLING PRODUCTION—ROUTING AND SCHEDULING

Production control is essentially the control of quantity in manufacture. By definition, the word "control" means to restrain, curb, regulate, or check. Yet, production control not only exercises the check rein but also applies the whip. That is to say, it not only regulates production but stimulates it as well. It is concerned with the motion or tempo by which an industrial plant operates. Rhythm is as important to the flow of material from an industrial plant as it is to the flow of music from a jazz band. As one production expert once said, "I am more interested in the hum than in the horsepower."

Indirectly, production control also controls costs for it is concerned with eliminating or reducing to a minimum the inefficiencies in manufacturing. Such inefficiencies may result from the performance of operations on incorrect equipment or under improper conditions. Or operations may be unbalanced; time and effort may be wasted on nonproductive work; and duplications or omissions in planning or executing work may make for confusion and delay. Thus do losses and waste run rampant where control is lacking. To put it another way, efficiency is born of and fostered by control.

Production control regulates the orderly flow of materials within the plant from the raw state to the finished product. It takes the influx of sales orders, boils them down into production orders, and feeds them to the plant at a rate and in a sequence that enable the plant to digest them most readily and with a minimum of internal disorder. It aims to produce the right product, in the right quantity, of the right quality, at the right time, and by the best and least costly methods. Good production-control procedure means less work in process, decreased stock inventories, and more rapid turnover which in turn results in less capital tied up in idle material and greater earnings on money thus invested. As such, production control, like materials control, is a facilitating activity which, with the possible exception of additional time and place utility, adds nothing directly to the value of the product (in the sense that work on the product increases its value). Production control involves both planning and control: the advance planning necessary to achieve an orderly flow of materials, and the execution of that plan to insure that the desired control is maintained.

Since production control occupies such an important place in all industrial operations, we shall explore at some length in Chaps. XIV and XV not only the functions and underlying principles upon which the control of production is based but also some of the control practices, procedures, and systems that are typical of those in use in industry today. In considering production control, as, for that matter, every other industrial control, we must remember that, although the fundamentals apply for plants small as well as large, the former do not need nor do they have the detailed systems found in their larger counterparts. For example, in a plant of 100 or so employees it is not at all uncommon to find a one-man production-control system. During the course of the day this person does all the things—probably in a more simplified manner—that are performed by the variety of specialists required in a large plant.

Administration of Production Control.—The diagnosis of the proper system of production control to fit an individual enterprise and the subsequent administration of that system is entrusted in most large industrial plants to a *production manager* or in small plants to the superintendent. The production manager usually reports to the top manufacturing executive, the works manager, and his department has functionalized staff authority over the various manufacturing departments in all matters pertaining to the control of production.

Briefly, the scope of activity of the production manager and his department includes the development of production-control procedures, forms, and techniques. He is also concerned with breakdowns in control as they occur. Furthermore, he coordinates the production activities of the various manufacturing divisions and other staff functions concerned with the production flow, *e.g.*, materials control, quality control. Thus the duties of a production manager may range from the installation of a $10,000 production-control system to the investigation of a falling-off of production in department *B*, an investigation revealing that the cause is simply poor performance on the part of Joe, the new dispatch clerk who suffers almost daily from alcoholic hangovers.

Sequence of Production-control Procedure (see Fig. 62).—Any production-control procedure must of necessity start with certain information supplied by other branches of the organization of the enterprise. This prerequisite information includes, first of all, an authorization for the production department to arrange for the manufacture of a particular product in a specified quantity and within a desired length of time. The authorization may be in the form of a production *stock-order* if the

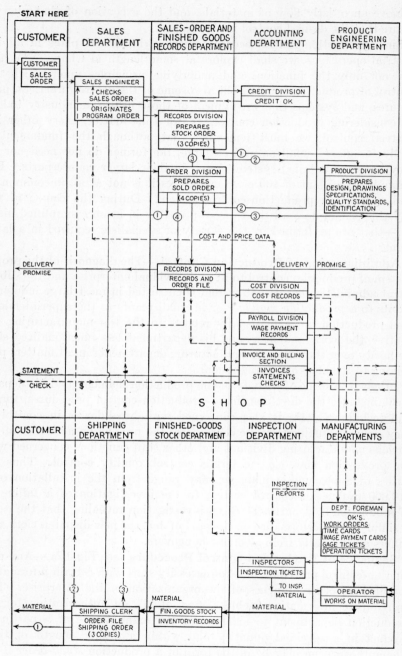

FIG. 62.

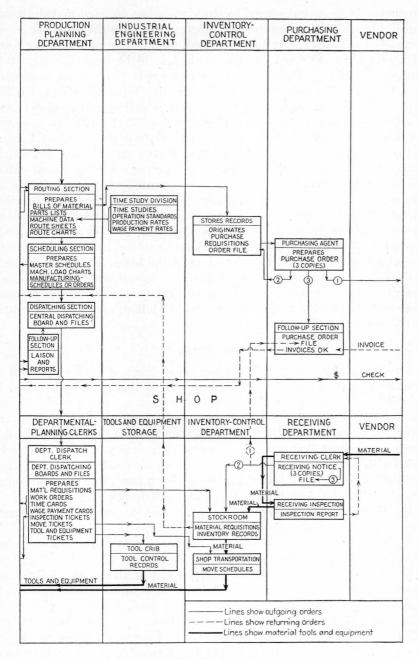

Fig. 62.—(*Continued.*)

product is to be manufactured to stock replacing depleted inventories of finished goods or to an established program based on the sales budget of forecasted sales for the period. Or the authorization may take the form of a production *sold-order* if the product is to be made directly to a customer's order. Secondly, before actual production-control procedure can be started, *product information* in the form of design details, drawings, specifications, quality standards, identification symbols, etc., must be furnished by the engineering department. Finally, the required *machine data* pertaining to the product involved are supplied by the industrial engineers in the form of time studies or estimates, operation standards, machine-production rates, and perhaps wage-payment rates. Whereas this prerequisite information is essentially the responsibility of the department in which it originates, at the same time best practice dictates that its preparation should be a cooperative venture. Decisions as to quantities to manufacture, specifications, and quality standards frequently require the consultation and advice of the various departments concerned and should not be left entirely in the hands of one department.

Once the production department has been armed with the credentials described above, it may then proceed with the four main steps of production-control procedure: (1) routing, (2) scheduling, (3) dispatching, and (4) follow-up.

ROUTING

Fundamentally, routing determines what work shall be done on a product or part as well as where and how it shall be done. Thus it establishes the operations, their path and sequence, as well as the proper class of machines and personnel to be utilized in performing these operations. Routing is an adjunct to the field of product development in designing a product that can be readily manufactured. Also it is closely allied with industrial engineering in setting up the most efficient operating methods and with plant layout in establishing a flow of materials through the plant that involves the least handling and backtracking.

Routing Procedure.—The routing procedure for a new product or part usually consists of six principal steps:

1. *An Analysis of the Article and Its Component Parts to Determine What to Make and What to Buy.*—The decision as to whether to fabricate a part or to purchase it will be based first of all on the relative cost involved and secondly on the availability of equipment and personnel. Cost is always a prime consideration in industrial decisions. Normally, quality and time for delivery being equal, the cheaper of the two methods will be selected. However, in slack periods, there is a tendency to make as much of the product within the plant as is possible simply to keep men

and machines busy. Also, in periods of great industrial activity the pendulum swings in the other direction, and plants tend to purchase much of their products simply because their facilities may not otherwise be adequate to handle the volume required. Thus, in such "abnormal" periods, the availability of equipment and personnel may take precedence over costs, whereas in more normal times costs exercise the balance of power in the decision as to whether to make or buy.

2. *An Analysis of the Article to Determine the Materials Needed, as to Both Kind and Amount.*—Blueprints of drawings, engineering illustrations, specifications, standards of quality, identification symbols, etc., as

Date 3/27/44	PARTS LIST			Sheet 1 of 2
Article	100-Q-VARIAC (135 V.)			
ITEM	NAME OF PART	DWG.	PART NO.	NO. REQ.
1	Spring Washer	4	100-90	5
2	Coil Insulator	6	100-771	6
3	Spacer (⅞" long)	–	222-99	3
4	Terminal	–	139-285	1
5	Washer B.D.	4	100-72A	1
6	Hex. Nut (std. ½"-20) Steel–			
	Cad. Plate	–	139-549	3
7	Hex. Nut (⅜"-24) Steel–			
	Cad. Plate	–	139-401A	3
8	Steel Lockwasher ⅜"			
	Cad. Plate	–		3
9	1⅛" Bd. Hd. BMS *6-32	–	–	3
10	½" R. Hd. BMS *10-32	–	–	4

Fig. 63.—Typical parts list.

prepared by the product-engineering department are usually condensed by the routing division into a *parts list* (see Fig. 63) showing the name, identification number, and quantity of the parts required, together with the drawing number, pattern number if any, and application in the product. Sometimes combined with the parts list, but more often a separate form, is the *bill of materials* (see Fig. 64), which lists the kind

CMP-2
11-14-42

Form Approved
Budget Bureau No. 12-R468-42

PROCUREMENT ITEM (Gun)................................   REPORTING CONSUMER (Victory Corp.)
Type (3 inch)................................   ADDRESS Detroit, Mich.
MODEL (M6)................................
Material for (100) procurement items

Line	Drawing or Part No.	Part Name	Material Name	Material Code No.	Specification or Chem. Anal. of Material	Size of Material	Weight (lbs.)		No. of Parts	Total Weight (lbs.)	
							Net	Gross		Net	Gross
1	D1700	Tube.........	Alloy Steel centrifugal casting.	....	3 % Chromium, 0.15 % molybdenum, 1.5 % manganese, Remainder C. P. S. & Fe.	....	825.0	2500.00	100	82,500	250,000
2	D1792	Breech block..	Alloy Steel, bar, hot rolled......	....	SAE 3000........	6″ x 6½″....	125.00	150.00	100	12,500	15,000
3 etc.	C3765	Fixed ring.....	Bronze casting............	....	QQ-B-700 (Fed. Spec.)......	....	48	60	100	4,800	6,000
Spares											
1	D1700	Tube.........	Alloy Steel, etc. (see above).	....	3 % Chromium, etc. (see above)..	6″ x 6½″...	825.0	2500.00	10	8,250	25,000
2	D1792	Breech block..	Alloy Steel, bar, hot rolled.....	....	SAE 3000........	6″ x 6½″...	125.00	150.00	10	1,250	1,500
3	C3765	Fixed ring.....	Bronze casting............	....	QQ-B-700 (Fed. Spec.)......	....	48	60	20	960	1,200

Signature of authorized official (John Doe) Date (11/9/42)   Sheet No. (1) of (4) Sheets

FIG. 64.—Typical bill of materials. (This form was originally suggested by the War Production Board for use by industry during World War II in complying with the requirements of the Controlled Materials Plan.)

and specifications of the materials required for each part, as well as the amount of material used per piece or per 100 pieces. From this last information, the individuals charged with supplying the necessary raw materials can determine the adequacy of the materials on hand or on order to meet the requirements of the article to be manufactured, and they can then requisition the purchase of any additional material needed.

Another tool of routing used frequently in connection with job-order products involving the assembly of many component parts (as for example, an engine lathe or a milling machine) is the *parts short list*. This form is very similar to the parts list except that it omits those parts which are available either as stock parts already on the shelf or as purchased parts on order and contains a listing of only those parts which are "short" and hence must be manufactured in the plant.

3. *A Determination of the Operations Required Together with the Sequence in Which They Should Be Performed.*—Next the routing division analyzes the operation standards or estimates and the production-rate data supplied by the industrial-engineering department together with data as to machine capacities and characteristics—information usually on file with the routing division. From these data it establishes the operations necessary to manufacture the article or part and lists them in their proper sequence on a *route sheet* or an *operations sheet*.

A route sheet of the type used by Thompson Aircraft Products Company is shown in Fig. 65. It is called the "production routing sheet" (1) and contains the part name and number, customer's name, materials required, operations listed in their proper sequence, and production rates for each operation in hours per 100 pieces. The data for the master production routing sheet for each job are first typed on a die-impressed stencil and 50 copies are run off on a stencil duplicating machine using the prepared form (1). Next the data for the last three columns are blocked out and four copies of the cost record are run off on another prepared form (2). Finally all but the first four columns are blocked out and the number of production routing cards (3) that may be required are run off. After being used, stencils for repeat products are placed in a file of master routings.

Copies of the Thompson Products production routing sheet are sent to all manufacturing departments concerned and to the production-scheduling and control divisions. They serve as maps to guide the material through the plant. However, as is the case with the routing sheets in most plants, these forms do not constitute an authorization to manufacture material. Instead, the plant must await release of a written order from the scheduling unit before work is started. The Thompson Products cost record sheet is used by the factory cost department in the preparation of cost estimates. The production routing cards are sent to the department originating the material. From this point they are subsequently released with the first trays of work. In the preparation of these

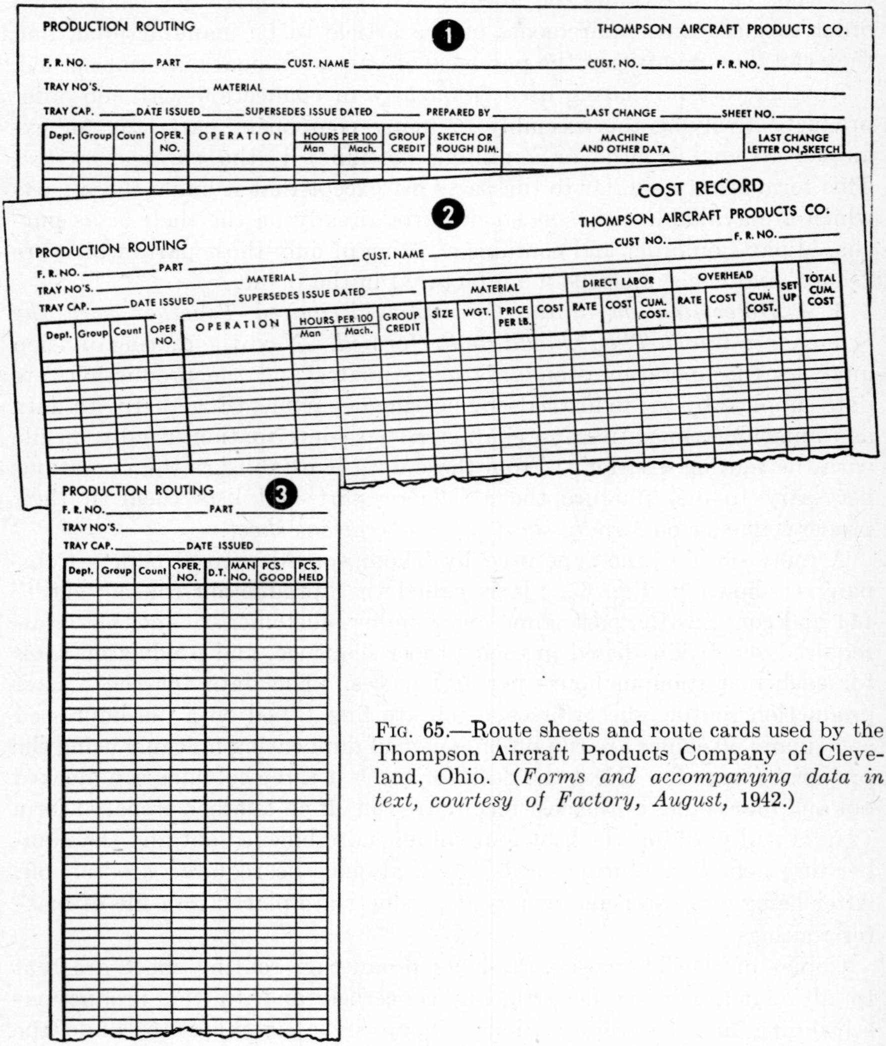

FIG. 65.—Route sheets and route cards used by the Thompson Aircraft Products Company of Cleveland, Ohio. (*Forms and accompanying data in text, courtesy of Factory, August, 1942.*)

cards a hard-set ink is used that will resist the abrasion, water, grease, oils, and solvents that the routing cards encounter in the course of operations.

Also frequently used as an aid in laying out the routing of material is the *route chart*. In their more detailed form, route charts are essentially process-flow charts (see Figs. 24 and 25), but simplified in that they show only the sequence of operations as in Fig. 66. Route charts are an aid in visualizing operations that may be eliminated, combined, or simplified, or the sequence of which may be changed to make for a smoother flow of materials.

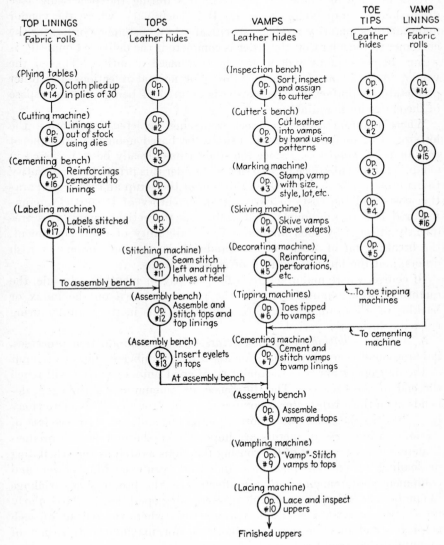

FIG. 66.—Route chart. (*From Bethel, Tann, Atwater, and Rung, "Production Control," New York: McGraw-Hill Book Company, Inc., 1948.*)

4. *A Determination of Lot Sizes.*—The number of units to be manufactured in any one lot or order as established by the routing division depends primarily upon the type of manufacture involved. If the product is to be manufactured strictly to a sold-order, the quantity to be made will usually equal that required for the customer's order plus a certain overage or allowance for rejections during the processing (see discussion of scrap factors below). It is customary, where the vendor manufactures quantity products specifically to a customer's order, for the customer to consider that the order is complete if the delivered quantity is within 10 per cent over or under the purchased quantity. Thus if the vendor in his planned quantity allows for normal rejections and other predictable manufacturing losses, he is assured of being able to dispose of the entire lot manufactured.

Where manufacture is to stock replacing depleted inventories, the lot size to be manufactured will usually be based upon the principle of *economic-lot quantities.* Since the subject has already been discussed in Chap. XIII, it will suffice here to say that under this principle the quantity to manufacture is that for which the sum of the setup and other preparation costs and the costs of carrying an inventory of the article manufactured is at a minimum. Naturally this theoretical quantity is frequently affected by such factors as the availability of plant equipment, the breaking off of stock runs to sandwich in customer orders or rush orders, and the unpredictability of seasonal items.

Of course, where manufacture is to a weekly or monthly schedule, the quantity to be manufactured for the period is based on the influx or backlog of sales orders subject to any limitations in the manufacturing capacity during the period.

5. *A Determination of Scrap Factors.*—In most production processes, it is reasonable to expect that, for any given number of pieces of input at the first operation, a lesser quantity of good units of output will reach the end of the process. The difference, or amount of "shrinkage," depends upon the *scrap factor* encountered in the process. This factor may be defined as the anticipated normal scrap encountered in the course of manufacturing. Scrap factors are important in the planning of production quantities as a part of the routing functions as well as the scheduling or loading of various machines and work centers. Man-power and equipment requirements both are affected by the progressive shrinkage in number of good pieces available at succeeding operations. Particularly is this true in serialized or line manufacture, where the output of each employee and machine must be balanced for maximum utilization of manufacturing facilities.

It is important to know where scrap is most likely to occur—whether it occurs progressively during the parts fabrication and assembly or all at once after a certain operation or after completion of the assembly. If scrap occurs at but one point in the process, a *single* scrap factor to take care of the anticipated scrap at that point is generally satisfactory. If,

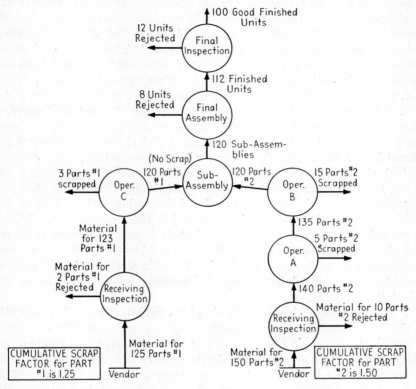

Fig. 67.—Illustration of an over-all manufacturing process wherein 20 per cent of the material used for Part 1 and 33⅓ per cent of that used for Part 2 is lost in rejections somewhere between receipt of the material and shipment of the finished product. The cumulative scrap factors are as noted above. Thus is shown the nature of typical cumulative scrap factors or the changing quantity requirements at various points in the line to produce a specified number of finished units.

on the other hand, scrap is progressive, *cumulative* scrap factors more accurately determine the expected load at each stage in the process (see Fig. 67). Note that it is necessary to start with the desired result (finished units) and work backward (toward the raw material).

Best practice dictates the establishment of *standard* scrap factors (either single or cumulative) for use in routing and scheduling. These are based on experience—on records giving scrap history—and, if cumulative, are set for each control point [1] in the process. Actual scrap in each lot or schedule is then recorded at the various control points. From these records, adjustments are made to schedules and to man-power and equipment requirements to compensate for differences between scrap anticipated and that experienced. Furthermore, if actual scrap is excessive, it may be necessary to initiate replacement lots. Actual-scrap records also serve to localize the responsibility for such scrap and point to areas or operations which should be investigated for cause of trouble. Similarly, such records encourage accurate reporting of scrap figures and localize any investigation of unreported or "covered-up" scrap.

6. *The Organization of Forms and Procedures to Furnish the Plant with the Necessary Information to Carry Out the Routing as Planned.*— Here again the type of manufacture exercises considerable influence upon the forms required by the plant departments. In job-order manufacture, almost invariably among these forms will be a production order—"manufacturing" or "factory order" it is sometimes called [2]—containing the name, number, description, and quantity of the part to be manufactured together with a serial number or other information to key it in to the routing sheets. Also prepared are such job tickets, inspection tickets, move orders, and tool and equipment tickets as may subsequently be required for that particular order. When released to the plant, the production order constitutes an authorization to begin work on the material in accordance with the date-and-hour information supplied thereon by the scheduling division.

Where the product is relatively simple to manufacture, it is frequently desirable to combine as many plant forms as practicable into one sheet. For example, The Steel Company of Canada, Ltd., employs a combination routing sheet, bill of materials, specification sheet, part drawing, and production order all tailored into one factory order (see Fig. 68). This order, prepared from master stencils, shows the size and description of the material required, machine number and class, dimensions, and tolerances, together with a sketch of the article and the shop routing, and contains a place for the schedule information. When this sheet is duplicated, it serves a multitude of purposes and thereby eliminates considerable paper work that would otherwise be required if a series of forms were employed. In this connection it should be remembered that production-control forms are a necessary evil and should be reduced to a minimum consistent with achieving the degree of control desired.

[1] A control point, as the name implies, is a stage in the process at which production quantities and schedules are recorded. Usual control points: dispatch stations, prior to or following major operations and assemblies, or between departments.

[2] For the use of the manufacturing order, see p. 343.

Or again, if the manufacture is on a schedule basis, the preparation of the plant forms may be somewhat simplified because of the repetitive nature of products usually manufactured to a schedule. Frequently

DESCRIPTION			NO.	
OVAL HEAD MACHINE SCREW			11 – 4688	
PART NO.	MATERIAL		SCHEDULE NO.	
	Steel			
SIZE	QUANTITY			
1¼ × 10/24	1500 C			
CUSTOMER				
A. & B. Mfg. Co.				

DEPT. & MACH. NO.	LBS. TO MAKE		BL. WT. PER C. FIN	
	1450		.926	
N. SLOT	O. SLOT	SHAVE	BEND	R. T. AUTO	R. T. HAND
	X			X	
CUT THRD.	NUT	SORT	PLATE		

SPECIAL INSTRUCTIONS

SPECIFICATION DESCRIPTION		NO.	
Oval Hd. Mach. Screw		O-M 10/24	
MATERIAL	WIRE DIAMETER	BLANK DIAMETER	
Chain St. S.D.	.158 – .157	.162 – .160	
	MACH.	STYLE	DIE
	1W 2W 11W	3/16N –	.159

	THREAD D DIA.	A WIDTH	H HEIGHT	F HEIGHT OVAL	J SLOT WIDE	T SLOT DEEP	R RADIUS	X	Y
MAX.	.190	.380	.116	.061	.055	.103			
MIN.	.183	.367	.098	.050	.041	.084			

Fig. 68.—Factory order for an oval-head machine screw as used by The Steel Company of Canada, Ltd. (*From Factory, August, 1942.*)

all that is necessary is a weekly or other periodic release from the scheduling division showing the quantity to be manufactured for the ensuing period.[3]

Use of Master Routing Sheets and Cards.—Some of the foregoing steps in the routing of a new product can be eliminated in the case of repeat products through the use of master routing sheets and cards. Once the initial routing procedure is completed, it can be transferred to appropriate cards and filed away for use when the same product is repeated. Where a variety of products all take the same basic routing—

[3] See manufacturing schedule, p. 342.

as would be the case where a certain style of product is manufactured in a variety of sizes—master route sheets may be made up, assigned a routing number or symbol, and supplied to the individuals concerned. Thereafter, the routing need not be written out for each order but may simply be referred to by number or symbol on the order, thus saving much listing of operation sequences. At other times, master stencils for each routing are made out and filed, and copies are subsequently run off as required.

Considerations Affecting Routing Procedures.—1. Routing, as we have already seen, is affected primarily by the *type of manufacture employed*. Where serialized manufacture is used, the path and sequence of operations usually are incorporated into the production-line layout. Then routing becomes quite automatic except when changes are made in the product or processes, necessitating a change in the production line. The automotive industry has for many years incorporated its routing into its fabrication and assembly lines and then has left them basically unchanged until a subsequent model is introduced. Much the same thing is true of "batch" manufacture as developed particularly in the chemical industry. In the case of practically all items processed by some of the large chemical concerns, production is accomplished in a few operations on an interrelated equipment group, and routing consists simply of assigning production to the correct equipment. Once assigned, the flow of material is virtually automatic.

2. Routing is affected by the *individual characteristics of the physical equipment in the plant*. Of course, the rule-of-thumb procedure in all routing where two or more machines can be used to achieve the same end result in the product is to select the cheapest method. Usually the cheapest method is that which utilizes the fastest machine. However, in some cases a slower machine may prove to be cheaper than the faster one, for the latter may entail higher setup and overhead costs which, particularly in the case of short-run jobs, could more than offset any direct operating savings. Then again, the operation may be performed on two or more machines of different size and capacity but with the same rate of production. Here, even if there were no differential in the operating costs in favor of the smallest machine, as there usually is, common sense would dictate the use of the smallest machine that will conveniently do the job simply because a larger machine generally possesses greater flexibility through its greater capacity range. Hence by employing the small machine, the greater utility of the large machine is preserved for other jobs.

Where routing is concerned with the selection of one machine out of a battery of basically similar ones, special individual traits inherent in that machine may have to be considered. Standard-purpose machines frequently are equipped with different gearing, spindles, type and capacity of coolant solution, as well as a variety of jigs, fixtures, and other tooling —all of which must be taken into consideration in any decision as to which machine can best handle the job in question. Where standard-purpose machines are thus equipped with a variety of accessories, it is common practice for the routing division to prepare and place on file a *machine-data card* for each machine, listing its individual characteristics and job range.

Not only should consideration be given to the machine characteristics, but also to that of the conveyors, cranes, hoists, skids, pallets, tote boxes, and other handling equipment that may be available in one section of the plant but not in another. Here again a record of such equipment data prepared in card form is useful to the routing division.

3. Routing is affected by the *availability of physical plant equipment*. Quite frequently because of machine-load conditions, breakdowns, and absentee operators, the cheapest machine or method cannot be utilized. In such cases it is desirable that the routing division have ready alternative routings to substitute for the standard route. These alternative routings may be in the form of detours around the bottleneck machine or operation or may simply involve a change in the sequence of operations, particularly if the tie-up should be of a temporary nature.

4. Attention should be given to the *human elements* involved. Particularly where the routing requires a selection of specific machines upon which work is to be performed, the experience of the operator should be considered. High-precision work is normally given to the more experienced operators; easy work generally is routed to trainees. Also, many employee grievances originate with the type of work routed to an individual. One typical objection concerns the size of runs assigned to incentive operators since those employees who receive the short runs feel that their earning capacity is impaired. Furthermore, the size of work assigned is frequently a grievance factor. Heavy work necessitating a greater physical demand and very small work requiring greater visual acuity are generally considered more disagreeable than moderate-sized work.

SCHEDULING

Scheduling is that phase of production control which rates the work in the order of its priority and then provides for its release to the plant at the proper time and in the correct sequence. Thus scheduling is concerned with *when* work shall be performed on a product or part.

The function of industrial scheduling closely resembles that branch of modern railroading which schedules the usage of railroad-track facilities. Similar to the route or path over which materials must flow in an industrial enterprise is the railroad bed with its main lines, detours, sidings, junctions, and switch terminals. Under usual railroad procedure, timetables are established for all passenger trains indicating the precise moment of their arrival and departure from each station and terminal. But trains run at different speeds—some through trains operate on fast schedules; commuter and local trains operate at slower rates. Furthermore, certain feeder trains are geared to the arrival and departure of other through runs, as their passengers, express, and mail loads are transferred either to or from the through trains. And finally, not operating on fixed timetables are the freights, both fast and slow, that must be sandwiched in between fixed-schedule trains over the same roadbed.

The aim in railroad scheduling is to run as much traffic over the same tracks as is safely possible without interference or collisions. Similarly the aim in industrial scheduling, within the limits of the customer orders available, is to schedule as great a volume of work as the plant equipment can conveniently handle without similar interference or "collisions" resulting in material stoppages along the route. Naturally, the work of devising railroad timetable schedules is closely allied with that of the dispatchers along the right of way who guide the trains in and out of sidings and spur tracks to permit the passage of faster trains or of trains running in the opposite direction. So also are the fields of industrial scheduling and dispatching closely related, and in many smaller companies both functions are performed by the same individual or group. This fact should be kept in mind as these subjects are herein developed separately.

A production schedule that establishes the starting and finishing dates of all material in process is subject to the limitations of the availability of (1) physical-plant facilities of the type required to process the material being scheduled, (2) personnel who possess the desired skill and experience to operate the equipment and perform the type of work involved, and (3) necessary materials and purchased parts. Failing the adequacy of any one of these three factors, or at least failing the knowledge as to when the missing factors will be made available, no intelligent production schedule can be developed.

Sequence of Scheduling Procedure.—Scheduling usually starts with the *master schedule,* a typical example of which is shown in Fig. 69. This schedule is simply a weekly or monthly breakdown of the production requirements for each product for a definite period of time (as a quarter, six months, or a year). As new orders or requirements are received, they are scheduled on the master schedule with due regard for the available plant capacity. Where the requirements noted on the schedule indicate that the plant capacity for a particular week (or month) is absorbed, it is obvious that the new requirements must be carried over to a subsequent period, or the present schedule for the capacity period must be rearranged to accommodate the additional orders.

The type of master schedule shown in Fig. 69 permits the addition of new requirements as they are received and at any time a total can be

MASTER SCHEDULE   NAME OF PART *Spark Plug*   PART NO. *J-5*

MAX. RUN PER WEEK *10,000* MIN. RUN PER WEEK *5,000*

Date	Assign. No.	JANUARY Week of 1/2	Week of 1/9	Week of 1/16	Week of 1/23	Week of 1/30	Cum. to	FEBRUARY Week of 2/6	Week of 2/13	Week of 2/20	Week of 2/27	Week of	Cum. to	MARCH Week of 3/6	Week of 3/13	Week of 3/20	Week of 3/27	Week of	Cum. to
For'd		7,968	5,742	3,041	2,221	1,689	12/15	3,520	1,089	786	556		12/15	0	0	332	56		12/15
12/16	33	700	700	700	700	700													
12/18	43							1,100	1,100	550	550			550					
12/19	51	45	68	68	45	45											2,500		
12/21	59	1,000	2,000	2,000	2,000	2,000													
		9,713	8,510	5,809	4,966	4,434	12/21												
12/23	76		1,300	2,600	2,600	2,600		2,600	2,600	2,600	2,600			2,600	2,600	1,300			
12/26	81		15	23	68	31													
12/29	87							1,000	1,000	2,000	2,000								
		9,713	9,825	8,432	7,634	7,065	12/31	8,220	5,789	5,936	5,706		12/31	3,150	2,600	1,632	2,556		12/31

Fig. 69.—Master schedule.

drawn off in red (as underscored here) showing what is scheduled in advance for each week. In this way it is possible to ascertain when the maximum plant capacity for the article in question has been reached.

The master schedule not only provides a convenient means of keeping a running total of the production requirements but also enables the production manager to plan in advance for any shifting emphasis from one product to another or for a possible over-all increase or decrease in production requirements. In addition, the master schedule furnishes the necessary data for calculating the backlog of work or the load ahead of each major machine. Furthermore, once a new order has been entered on the master schedule, it is then possible to furnish the customer with a provisional or perhaps even a definite shipping date for the material on his order. In summary, then, the master schedule provides the information that becomes the basis for all subsequent scheduling activities.

Next, depending upon the type of manufacture involved, a manufacturing schedule or manufacturing order is prepared. The *manufacturing schedule,* or "shop schedule," as it is sometimes labeled (see Fig. 70), is used primarily in serialized or semiserialized manufacture where a single product or a relatively few products are manufactured continuously or are repeated at regular intervals. It serves the purpose of authorizing

SHOP SCHEDULE		Part No. *J-5*
Name of Part	*Spark Plug*	
Book No. *5*	Date *6/3/44*	Dept. No. *22A*
Shop Schedule for Week of		*6/5/44*
Amount of Schedule This Week		*9825*
Behind Schedule Last Week		*651*
Over Schedule Last Week		
TOTAL SCHEDULE THIS WEEK		*10,476*

PRODUCTION

Day	Amount	Cum. This Week
Monday		
Tuesday		
Wednesday		
Thursday		
Friday		
Saturday	*11*	*11*
Total Production This Week		
Behind Schedule This Week		
Over Schedule This Week		
Remarks:		

Fig. 70.—Typical shop or manufacturing schedule.

the plant departments concerned to manufacture the stipulated quantity of parts or products designated within the period for which the schedule applies. In serialized or semiserialized manufacture, such items as shop instructions, routing information, blueprints, and specifications ordinarily are readily available in the departments requiring them. Furthermore, since the proper tooling is provided when the production line is erected and since the product is manufactured repeatedly, all tooling equipment would normally be subject to a standard control system which provides automatically for periodic replacement. Thus, with all the physical equipment available without advance notification, the only information necessary on the manufacturing schedule is the name and number of the part or product plus the quantity to be manufactured each day, week, or other time period, in the department concerned. However, if the product is made in a variety of sizes, weights, colors, types, or styles, the manufacturing schedule will show the quantity of each required and the sequence in which each is desired. The length of the period covered by the manufacturing schedule may be a week, month, or quarter, depending primarily upon the length of the manufacturing cycle of the product involved.

The *manufacturing order,* on the other hand (see Fig. 71), is generally used for job-lot manufacture or where a variety of products, if repeated at all, are made at infrequent or irregular intervals. Since the manufacturing order invariably contains information required by the plant to make the part or product named thereon—the quantity to

DELIVER TO:	Dept. 1	Dept. 3 ✓	Dept. 5	Dept. 10-11	Dept. 18	Dept. 27	Dept. *Insp.*	Dept.
Finish Date:	1/23	1/26	2/7	2/10	2/15	2/19	2/20	
MANUFACTURING ORDER								

Date Issued	*1/15/44*	
Order No.	*D 6728*	
Article	*WORM GEAR*	
Art. No.	*912*	
Quantity	*200*	
Delivery	*2/22/43*	

B. P. No. *A 5654*
Spec. No. *E 5*
Routing Seq. *R.O. SHEET D*
Instructions: *NONE*

Issued By: *M.J.R.*   *17*

Equipment Ordered

O.K.

Form P10   OK'd By: *RAM*   Date *1/15/44*

Fig. 71.—Typical shop or manufacturing order. Check mark with "Dept. 3" indicates copy to be furnished that department.

be made, specifications, blueprint numbers, routing sequence, any necessary shop instructions, and equipment required—it is generally prepared by the routing division and turned over to the scheduling division for a starting or finishing date. When the manufacturing order is finally released to the plant, it constitutes an authorization to each department concerned to start work on the article at the time scheduled.

Scheduling Adapted to Different Types of Manufacture.—Just as a chain is only as strong as its weakest link, so the capacity of a serialized production line is limited to that of the slowest operation along that line. Scheduling of serialized manufacture, then, becomes primarily a matter of translating the sales or program requirements into a schedule of the amount of material that can be manufactured on the production line in any given period. The length of time required for the production cycle of a serialized production line is usually established when the line is set up, and material entering that line usually finishes the cycle without change of sequence. Thus, once the starting date of a particular lot of material is determined, the completion date is automatically established, and no intermediate scheduling of operations along the production line is required. The same is true of "batch" manufacture of the type that is so common to the chemical industries. Usually when a batch of material is released for production, it follows through its complete and predetermined cycle, and rarely is its cycle interrupted to permit another batch to pass by.

Semiserialized manufacture, on the other hand, usually does permit some storage and reshuffling of the orders along its production lines,

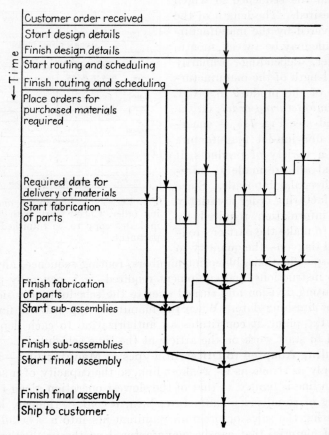

FIG. 72.—Diagrammatic sketch depicting the scheduling of a job-order product involving both fabrication and assembly.

particularly if a range of products or parts with varying process times is fabricated on a single production line. Where several mating parts are involved, it is common practice to interject "matching centers." These are simply storage areas between certain key manufacturing operations designed to take up the slack and to smooth out interruptions and delays caused by parts or materials not being at the right place at the right time. (For further discussion of matching centers see the Westinghouse case at the end of Chap. XV.) These matching centers serve also as key points for the intermediate rescheduling of material in process.

The scheduling of job-order manufacture, particularly where a range of parts is required for one assembly project, becomes infinitely more difficult, for the fabrication of each part and the assembly of each group of parts must be scheduled with due regard for the availability of equipment, personnel, and materials. Figure 72, a diagrammatic sketch, depicts the factors involved in scheduling a job-order-assembly project. It should be noted that the starting and finishing dates for each part and subassembly are related to the length of their manufacturing cycles. The scheduling of intermediate operations is fully as important as the scheduling of the initial operation. Since little or no progressive flow of material is attempted in job-order manufacture, material not so scheduled soon becomes overlooked or otherwise hopelessly delayed in process. Frequently in job-order plants where the material must be routed through several departments and where the operations in a particular department are not extremely intricate, the scheduling of each operation may be omitted. In such cases the relatively more simple procedure of scheduling the date for the completion of the material in each department may serve to furnish the degree of control desired.

In the scheduling of several component parts of a job-order assembly, each with a different process time, theoretically each part is scheduled so that it will be completed immediately prior to its being required for assembly. In practice, owing to the limitations of equipment, personnel, and materials as described above, it is seldom possible to complete all parts exactly at the time required. Breakdowns, excessive rejections, and inaccuracy of estimates creep in. Also certain standardized parts are made more economically if manufactured not in small lots to a particular order but rather in large lots manufactured in advance to stock. Thus storage facilities must be provided immediately prior to assembly for parts that are being held pending the arrival of those not yet completed. Warner & Swasey accomplishes this by what is known as "the loose-assembly department." Here each turret lathe in the process of manufacture is represented by a series of portable bins. As the various gears, shafts, collars, stop bars, and spindles are completed in the shop, they are sent to be stored in their respective bins until all parts of the lathe are accounted for. Not until then are the parts hauled to the assembly line and the project scheduled for completion.[4]

It is important to remember that schedules are made only to be revised! After all, a schedule is based on the priority or relative urgency

[4] *Fortune Magazine*, October, 1942, p. 172.

of the work involved, and as conditions and customer requirements change, so also does the relative urgency change. A "rush" order may be sandwiched in ahead of a regular or customer order, and even the rush order may be later moved aside to make way for an order in response to a customer's breakdown. Thus must a schedule be flexible to meet changing conditions.

The question as to whether scheduling should precede routing or vice versa is like the perennial question: Which came first, the chicken or the egg? The answer is that routing comes first in practically all types of manufacture except job shops or where extremely crowded conditions are present. In such cases manufacturing requirements necessitate first of all that the important jobs be scheduled on the key machines or equipment and then routed in a manner that will enable them to meet that schedule as nearly as possible. However, in most other cases, best practice dictates that the routing (path) be established first, followed by a formulation of the schedule (timetable) as to when the work will traverse that path.

Control Charts.—Charts are widely used in industry today for control purposes, particularly in the field of production scheduling where they often constitute the foundation upon which all scheduling activities are

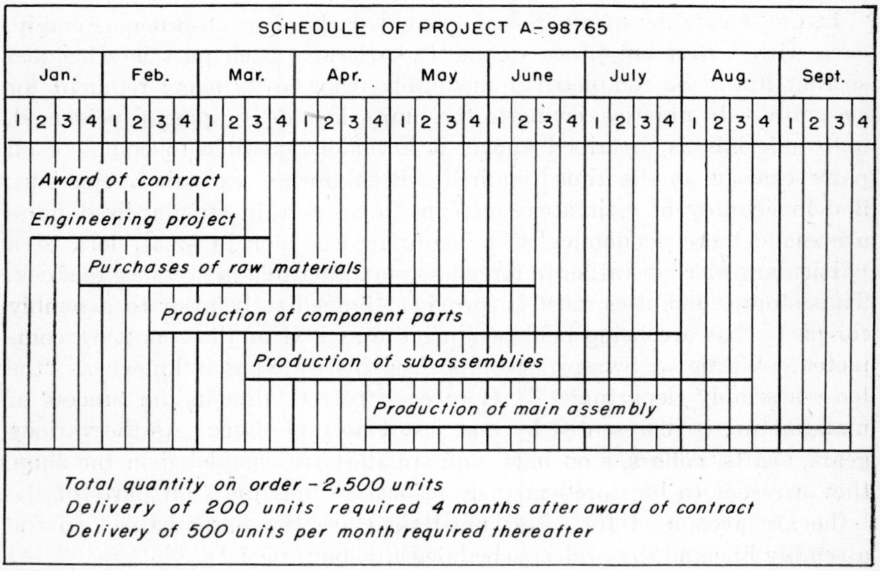

Fig. 73.—A project-layout chart showing when the contract was awarded, delivery promises, and key dates that must be kept. (*Chart from Plant Efficiency, U.S. Government Printing Office,* 1942.)

based. Control charts have the advantage of supplying a quick, compact, and visual means of recording information, both that which sets forth a plan and that which records what has been done in the line of accomplishment against that plan. Charts are useful in establishing "control by exception," for the exception in the form of poor accomplishment in relation to the original plan readily stands out when charted and thereby points the need for investigation and possible correction. Control charts are usually dynamic. That is to say, as conditions change, the charts are successively revised so as to furnish a moving force for current as well as for future action.

Among the more common classes of control charts used in industry are:

1. The *man-machine chart*, which depicts graphically both the potential and the actual performance of the operator in relation to his machine and hence shows up the idle time of each. This type of chart is primarily a tool of the industrial engineer rather than that of the production specialist and will be discussed more in detail in Chap. XVII.

2. The *project-layout chart*, which schedules in advance the work ahead of either men or equipment, or both, and determines the relative importance and hence sequence in which that work should be performed. Figure 73 is a compact chart which sets forth the plan for a project.

Figure 74a illustrates a project-layout chart for the order under observation. This chart provides a complete picture of the entire project. It shows what parts are needed, where they originate, where they are to be processed, where assembled and what quantities are required. It serves to point out weak spots in deliveries of materials.

Information that is added as the order progresses is shown in Fig. 74b. Receipt of all materials is recorded, with notches in the horizontal line representing specific deliveries.

The control chart as shown here represents conditions existing at the end of the fourth period in June. For that date the original schedule called for 1,250 completed units. The heavy bar of actual production indicates 1,300. Apparently there is no difficulty in meeting the schedule for completed units. The first subassembly is progressing smoothly. Component parts are drawn from raw-material stores. Deliveries are excellent. The wide spacing of notches in the horizontal lines indicates that requisitions for substantial quantities are filled without difficulty.

The trouble is readily visible with the second subassembly. It is already 150 behind, having finished only 1,900 of the 2,050 units scheduled for completion on that date. Close analysis shows ample supplies of all parts except P–72412. Irregular and closely-spaced notches point to delivery problems. The weak spot is flagged with a thumbtack so that

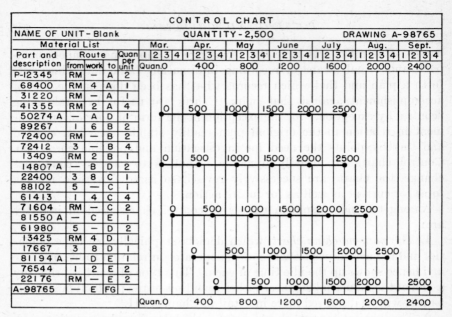

Fig. 74a.—The control chart is based on master schedules. *RM* signifies raw material stores; *FG* finished goods stores; odd numbers in routing column, the departments from which materials are to be drawn; even numbers, the machining or finishing departments; letters, assembly departments.

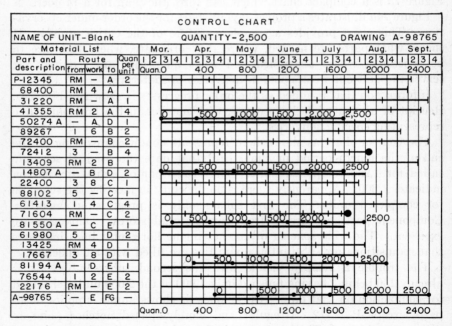

Fig. 74b.—The control chart here represents the condition of the order at end of June. Although deliveries of completed assemblies are ahead of schedule, the chart warns of weaknesses.

corrective action can be taken before the final-assembly schedule is disturbed.

At the third subassembly, part P–71604 is holding up production. As it is drawn from raw-material stores, the difficulty apparently arises from poor deliveries by the supplier. Here again a visible danger signal is attached to the chart.

At the fourth subassembly there is a slightly favorable margin, with 80 assemblies ahead of schedule. But one of the parts required in this assembly is the second subassembly which is running behind schedule. According to the final schedule dates, there should be a four-week interval between the second and fourth subassemblies, but the current interval is only three weeks. Unless the danger point is corrected at the second, there will soon be trouble at the fourth.[5]

3. The *load chart*, which represents as a function of hours, days, or number of jobs the amount of work ahead of a particular machine, battery of machines, department, division, or plant. (See Fig. 76 for a typical load chart.)

4. The *progress chart*, which indicates by means of comparison the progress or accomplishment made against a prescribed plan, pointing out readily where failure is occurring and enabling appropriate investigation and action to be taken. (See Figs. 74 and 77 for typical progress charts.)

Charts also differ according to construction, among the most common structural types being:

1. The *curve chart* is simply a graph with the ordinate or vertical axis scaled to one function and the abscissa or horizontal axis to another. Points are plotted in accordance with the relationship between the two functions and lines drawn connecting the points to show peaks and valleys as well as trends. As an example of such a chart, Fig. 75 depicts the backlog of production scheduled for the various fabricating departments of a shipbuilding company, the figures being drawn up weekly, and plotted, with connecting lines drawn to show the trend in each department.

2. The *bar chart* is used primarily to show accumulations or "running totals" of one function against another. For example, the bar chart reproduced in Fig. 76 depicts the accumulated load or amount of work ahead of each machine in a machine shop with respect to time. In general, it may be stated that both the curve and bar charts are primarily historical in that they show what has already occurred and are not too readily adaptable to current or future action. They are used primarily because

[5] Above charts and descriptive material for Figs. 74*a* and 74*b* taken from Plant Efficiency, U.S. Government Printing Office, 1942.

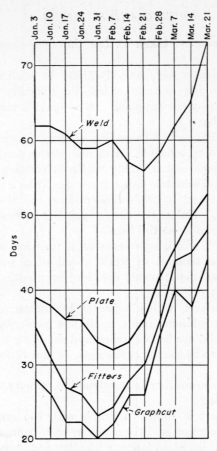

FIG. 75.—Curve chart or graph showing the number of days' work scheduled ahead of each department of the Manitowoc Ship Building Company, Manitowoc, Wis. (*Courtesy of Factory, July, 1942, p. 75.*)

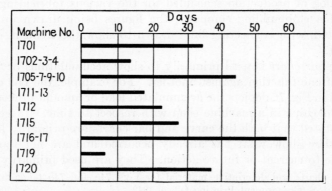

FIG. 76.—Bar chart showing the load in terms of number of days of work ahead of machines in a machine shop.

they are easier to read and to analyze than are the interrelated data from which they are derived.

3. Much has been written and said about the *Gantt chart,* which takes its name from the individual who developed its format and industrial application, one of the pioneers in the field of Scientific Management, Henry L. Gantt. Perhaps in some quarters this chart has been over-rated, but nevertheless it, together with its various modifications and adaptations, has certain advantages that make it a rather useful tool of the production specialist. Fundamentally, the Gantt chart is an oper-

Month estimated sales							Material supplier					Weight cost	Max. Min.		
ORDERS BOOKED				SCHEDULED DELIVERIES								IN STOCK			
Date	Order No.	Quantity	Total on order	Date	Scheduled Daily	Scheduled Total	Date	Delivered Daily	Delivered Total	Date	Order No.	Rec'd.	Issued	Balance on hand	
4-6		1,000	1,000	5-1	10	10	5-2	50	50						
				2	10	20									
Part No.	Description			Day deliveries completed											

1 | 2 | 3 | 4 | 5 | 6 | 7 | 8 | 9 | 10 | 11 | 12 | 13 | 14 | 15 | 16 | 17 | 18 | 19 | 20 | 21 | 22 | 23 | 24 | 25 | 26 | 27 | 28 | 29 | 30 | 31

Fig. 78.—One widely used modification of the Gantt chart is the visible index record shown here in simple form. The body of the card carries the production order or orders scheduled against a particular product or part. The lower margin of the card (which, being hinged to the upper margin and "shingled," is the only part of the card that shows in the visible-record type of file, Fig. 42) bears the part number and is also divided into days or other convenient time units. A given quantity, as 10, being scheduled for daily delivery, a flag or marker on the lower edge of the card is advanced a corresponding number of days' production as deliveries are made. Thus if 50 parts were delivered on the second day of the month, deliveries of 10 per day being scheduled to commence on the first, the card would show the orders 3 days ahead of schedule on that day. The comparison line, the current day of the month, moves one space to the right every day. Four days later, if there had been no subsequent deliveries, the order, instead of being 3 days ahead of schedule, would be a day behind. The follow-up clerk can tell by a glance at this card which orders are in need of attention. (*Adapted from H. P. Dutton, Factory Management and Maintenance Plant Operation Library Pamphlet: Production Control.*)

ating chart in that it furnishes information for action. It may depict plans for the future, progress on present operations, and may at the same time serve to record past achievements for possible future reference.

An understanding of the Gantt chart rests upon the knowledge of a few of its simple principles.[6] Each subdivision of space on the chart along the horizontal represents at once three factors:

a. Passage of a set increment of time (as an hour, 8-hour shift, day, etc.).

[6] Adapted from Wallace Clark, "The Gantt Chart," New York: Pitman Publishing Corp.

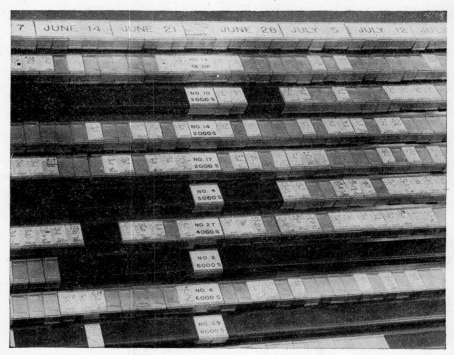

Fig. 79.—Schedule board used by the Steel Improvement and Forge Co., Cleveland. It makes use of metal clips, each representing one day's production on a piece of equipment. A scheduling card for each order is entered in its proper position by date and machine. Blank clips to the right of an order indicate additional days required for completion. If necessary, schedules can be completely revised in a matter of minutes simply by reshuffling the cards on the board. (*From Factory, August*, 1949, *p*. 106.)

b. Amount of work scheduled to be done in that increment of time.

c. Amount of work actually done in that increment of time.

Light lines indicate the amount of work scheduled (or actually done) during the increment of time represented by that space. Heavy lines indicate the cumulative amount of work scheduled (or actually done) up to any given date or hour.

Typical of the many Gantt chart applications is the Gantt load and progress chart shown in Fig. 77 which depicts the amount of work scheduled daily and even hourly for each machine shown, together with the cumulative actual production in relation to that scheduled. This chart serves to keep the scheduling man posted as to when each machine will be available for additional orders.

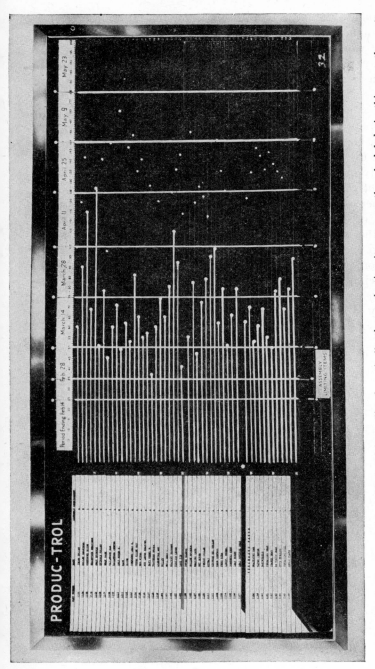

Fig. 80.—Production-control board on which are listed vertically the production items currently scheduled—in this case, the parts to an assembly. Each item with its history is listed on a sheet or strip attached to the left of the board. Running horizontally to the right are two lines of peg holes for each item. The upper line is used for any itemization or comparison desired and the lower is used for the spring tape or progress line.

The background of the visualization board is black, the tapes and tape pegs are white, and the comparative information pegs are in bright colors. Vertical cords stretched from top to bottom of the chart can be used for scheduling the production to be accomplished for each day or other work period. The progress of the horizontal tapes reveals at a glance the accomplishment against the preplanned schedule. Items for which accomplishment is lagging are evident at once and may then be investigated. (*Courtesy of the Wassell Organization, Westport, Connecticut.*)

The limitations to the use of Gantt charts for scheduling-control purposes may be summed up as follows:

a. Necessary calculations and the actual plotting to keep the chart up to date may require more time than would be involved were the scheduling man to ascertain the same information from a table, record, or report.

b. Errors in calculations and posting are hard to detect and are apt to be cumulative.

Nevertheless, Gantt charts have a definite place in scheduling, particularly where the information presented would in any other tabular or report form defy quick visual and mental analysis.

4. *Mechanical charts,* in which are grouped the various wall boards, charts, and other mechanical devices that are available from the leading manufacturers of production-control equipment and also those that are made by the enterprise for its own use. Usually such charts are simply enlarged adaptations of one of the three foregoing types of charts with the addition of mechanical clips, pegs, or other devices to enable the production specialist to visualize and focus on the basic facts requiring action. Not in any sense all-inclusive, but typical of the mechanical charts currently in use in industry are those shown in Figs. 79 and 80.

CHAPTER XV

CONTROLLING PRODUCTION— DISPATCHING AND FOLLOW–UP

Production control has been said to involve two fundamental steps:

First plan your work;
Then work your plan.

Up to this point in our discussion of production control, we have been concerned primarily with the planning of work, or more specifically, with routing and scheduling. Now we are ready to work the plan by dispatching the production orders and then following up these orders to insure that the routings and schedules are maintained.

DISPATCHING

Dispatching, the initial action element of production control, consists essentially of the issuance of orders in terms of their priority as determined by scheduling. It includes the assignment of work to the operators at their machines or workplaces. Thus, dispatching in effect determines *by whom* work shall be done.

We have seen in Chap. XIV that there is a close analogy between the scheduling of production orders and the scheduling of railroad trains over a roadbed. So also is there a similarity between the dispatching of production orders and the dispatching of trains over a busy track section. Just as the railroad dispatcher must know every foot of the railroad and the speed of each locomotive, so must the production dispatcher know exactly his routing for each product and the productive capacity of each piece of manufacturing equipment to which he dispatches the work. He must know at all times the position or progress of all orders (trains) under his control. He would prefer to have all items run on a prescribed schedule, but he too is confronted with orders of different degrees of priority ranging from those which suddenly become classed as "rush," to those on a prescribed manufacturing schedule, and finally down to those which have a lower urgency standing, such as stock orders. Production orders (like trains) move at different speeds as dictated by the dispatcher. If his judgment is faulty, the efficiency or capacity of the plant (railroad) is impaired; if his errors are serious, a production bottleneck (wreck) almost invariably results.

From the foregoing, some of the activities frequently delegated to the dispatcher are apparent. In summary they may be listed as follows:

1. The assignment of work to the machines or workplaces.

2. The authority to prepare, assemble, and issue to their point of use the necessary materials, tools, fixtures, and gages.

3. The issuance of the orders and production forms necessary to the performance of work and to the reporting of production, payroll, and cost data.

4. The responsibility for controlling the progress of material at each operation; for making the necessary adjustments to schedules and work assignments as conditions change or as unpredictable emergencies occur.

5. The authority to move work from one operation to the next.

6. The liaison function linking the plans of the routing and scheduling office with the performance of the manufacturing divisions.

The complexity of the activities of the dispatcher varies with the type of manufacture. The dispatching of repetitive orders, particularly where the manufacture is serialized, is infinitely more simple than is the dispatching of work, materials, tools, and other equipment for a job-order project that is seldom if ever repeated. In the case of the former, the equipment necessary to line production will either be incorporated into that line or will be readily available. It is then simply necessary to dispatch the raw materials and supplies required to manufacture the product. However, for the job-order manufacture of a product infrequently repeated, new tooling is often necessary, equipment must be checked, and the missing elements supplied. Gages usually are set up for each job as it is run. "Bugs" often develop and must be ironed out. One machine may be used for a variety of operations. Some machines and operators become overloaded with work; other machines run out of work. Emergency or rush orders must frequently be dispatched to the detriment of orders previously dispatched. Seldom can a progressive flow of materials be completely achieved in job-order manufacture, and consequently the movement of material between operations must be controlled closely by the dispatcher. Otherwise material is very apt to become delayed or lost in transport, and banks of material are soon stored ahead of some operations with a subsequent dearth of material ahead of others. Hence, the degree of responsibility vested with the dispatcher of job-order manufacture to maintain a smooth flow of materials is much greater than is that required of the dispatcher of serialized manufacture.

Sequence of Dispatching Procedure.—In Chap. XIV, we noted that for serialized and semiserialized manufacture the scheduling division prepares a manufacturing schedule for each production item showing the quantity to be produced at each successive operation during the period for which the schedule is effective. These schedules are then turned over to the dispatching division for temporary filing. They are subsequently issued to the departments or machines concerned just prior to the start of the period. We also saw that in the case of job-order manufacture, an individual work or manufacturing order is used for each production item in place of the manufacturing schedule. The scheduling division usually enters on that order the "date required" as determined by the relative priority or urgency of the order in question. The dispatching division may then file the work order for issuance either to the originating department in the sequence determined by its relative priority or to a particular machine, depending upon whether the dispatching is decentralized or centralized.

Decentralized dispatching consists of issuing manufacturing schedules or work orders in blanket fashion to the foreman or "dispatch clerk" within each department who must then determine the relative sequence in which those orders will be started within that department. It is likewise the duty of the foreman or clerk to dispatch the orders and material to each machine and operator. The only restriction placed on the departmental dispatcher is that the material be completed in the department on or before a prescribed date. Good practice dictates that the foreman be required to acknowledge in writing acceptance of the schedule or order upon its receipt, by which act he subsequently accepts responsibility for completion of the material within the time allowed him. Or, by the same token, he may take exception to the time allotment when the order is issued to him. However, should breakdowns or other unforeseen events subsequently occur to delay completion of the work, he should then be required to notify the central-dispatching division of the production department that a revision of the "finish date" has become necessary.

Centralized dispatching, on the other hand, involves the dispatching of orders from the central-dispatching division directly to the machine or work station. Under this procedure, the capacity and characteristics of each machine as well as the backlog of work ahead of it are known and recorded in the central-dispatching station, and all dispatching is controlled from that point. The foreman merely takes the orders assigned to his machines and runs them as assigned. However, in most cases the foreman has the privilege of objecting to orders dispatched to his machines if he can show cause why it would be difficult or impossible to carry through with the assignment. For example, the operator of the machine in question might not have the necessary experience to perform the operation required, or perhaps the mechanical condition of the machine will not permit the degree of precision required.

The effect achieved by decentralized dispatching is to minimize much of the red tape, the duplication of postings, the elaborate reporting, and the "absentee control" that are usually present in most centralized dispatching systems. Hence it is an inexpensive system from the clerical standpoint. Nevertheless it entails more leg work on the part of the dispatcher for he must visit the various departments regularly to retain his control and to keep in touch with their difficulties. As for centralized dispatching, it can achieve a greater degree of control—control that is typical of all centralized effort. Also it is more flexible, particularly in peak periods when the plant is running near or at capacity. As changes occur in the relative urgency of orders, they can readily be effected at the central-dispatching station without greatly upsetting the plans and schedules of the individual foremen. As all reporting of production clears through this central station, the progress of all material can readily be ascertained at any time. This makes for less telephoning and running back and forth between the central production office and plant departments.

Regardless of whether dispatching is centralized or decentralized, it is customary for the department foremen or their clerks to keep themselves informed of the starting date and progress of each order by means of a wall chart, visible-index file, or one of the several types of department dispatching boards. A common type of departmental dispatch board is shown in Fig. 81. A three-pocket unit is provided for each machine or work station in the department. Work orders, job tickets, or prewritten time tickets for each operation scheduled can be filed on such a board against the machine on which they will be run, as follows:

1. In the back pocket, jobs for which material and equipment are not yet available, arranged either in the sequence in which they are to be run or in the sequence of order numbers.

2. In the front pocket, jobs for which material is available, arranged in the sequence in which they are to be performed.

3. Under the spring clip, the job currently on the machine or in operation.

The status of each machine is readily visible, orders are easily arranged and rearranged, and machines for which no future orders are available readily show up as the pockets become empty. Posting of production daily or by shifts to the orders under the spring clips enables the foreman to ascertain at any time the progress of each order.

To systematize the issuance of authorizations and instructions to the various shop units, virtually all plants employ tickets, cards, and orders which are printed forms filled in usually by the routing and scheduling divisions with the appropriate information and sent out to the respective plant department or individual with each batch of material dispatched to the plant. These forms either authorize the department or individual to originate some action or furnish a means for reporting such pertinent information concerning that material as may subsequently be required.

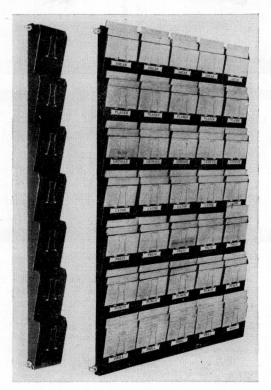

FIG. 81.—Departmental dispatch board. Each three-pocket unit controls the backlog of orders ahead of a particular machine. (*Courtesy of McCaskey Register Company.*)

Among the more common forms dispatched are:

1. *Work orders* and *operation tickets* (see Fig. 82), which authorize a department or employee to start work on a certain lot of material and which also serve as a means of recording the production performed on that material.

2. *Time cards* and other *wage-payment cards*, which are used to report the time utilized in the performance of work on a lot of material by each operator and to supply other vital information used in the preparation of the payroll. For a typical wage payment card, see Fig. 83.

3. *Inspection tickets*, which are employed to report the quantity of

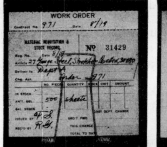

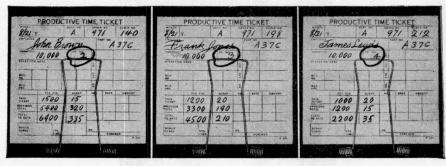

FIG. 82.—Typical record of the progress of an order through successive operations. The work order is shown under one spring clip with the material requisition covering withdrawal from stock of the required material filed on top of it. Production time tickets (operation tickets) are here shown for successive operations 1 to 4. These are placed under the spring clips at the end of each operation and the total production of each operation is recorded on the last ticket as it is posted by simply carrying forward the total from the previous ticket and adding the current quantity. Such a record system makes use of a dispatch board with spring clips as shown above. Note that with this system the progress of all material between operations (or between departments, if departmental control only is desired) can be quickly ascertained. (*Courtesy of McCaskey Register Company.*)

FIG. 83.—Type of wage-payment card used in reporting employee's production where incentive wage payment is involved.

360

work passed and quantity rejected at each inspection operation (see Fig. 84).

4. *Move tickets,* which authorize the movement of material between operations (see Fig. 85).

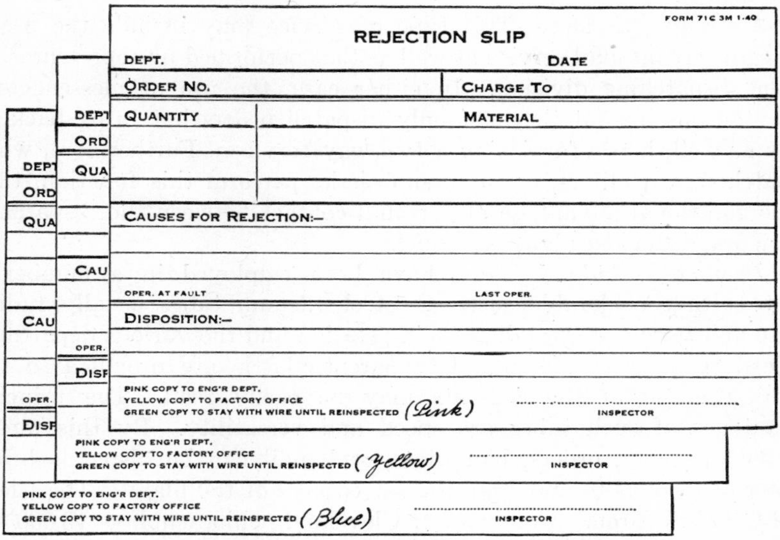
FORM 71C 3M 1-40

REJECTION SLIP

DEPT. DATE

ORDER NO. CHARGE TO

QUANTITY MATERIAL

CAUSES FOR REJECTION:—

OPER. AT FAULT LAST OPER.

DISPOSITION:—

PINK COPY TO ENG'R DEPT.
YELLOW COPY TO FACTORY OFFICE
GREEN COPY TO STAY WITH WIRE UNTIL REINSPECTED (Pink) INSPECTOR

PINK COPY TO ENG'R DEPT.
YELLOW COPY TO FACTORY OFFICE
GREEN COPY TO STAY WITH WIRE UNTIL REINSPECTED (Yellow) INSPECTOR

PINK COPY TO ENG'R DEPT.
YELLOW COPY TO FACTORY OFFICE
GREEN COPY TO STAY WITH WIRE UNTIL REINSPECTED (Blue) INSPECTOR

FIG. 84.—Inspection ticket. Note use of the three copies.

MOVE TICKET		
Date	Office order No.	Charge to
From dept.		To dept.
Quantity delivered		Quantity accepted
Foreman		Foreman
Moved by		
Remarks		

FIG. 85.—Typical move order or ticket required in the movement of material between operations or departments.

5. *Tool, gage,* and *equipment tickets,* which must be furnished to the tool crib or gage room before such equipment can be supplied.

Dispatch-communication Facilities.—Some of the more common methods employed in the dispatching of orders and the reporting of work performed are:

1. *Messenger Service.*—This type of service may include the use of the regular plant mail service as well as that performed by representatives of the dispatching division. In either case, the use of messengers is advantageous in that they not only dispatch orders but bring back reports as well, hence furnishing a two-way service. Furthermore, where dispatchers, expediters, or follow-up clerks perform this function, there is the additional advantage of personal contact between the dispatching division and the key plant personnel.

2. *Pneumatic Tubes.*—These have been employed in a number of plants with considerable success. Steel vacuum tubes usually radiate out to and from a central dispatching station and the various department centers. Carriers made of a transparent plastic are provided so that the destination of the contents may be easily read. The principal advantages of such tubes are speed and versatility. By this means, written messages, orders, blueprints, and mail can be dispatched in a matter of seconds to and from the far corners of the plant. The Cleveland Graphite Bronze Company of Cleveland, Ohio, employs 13,000 feet of steel tubing along 22 routes to dispatch some 1,200 to 1,500 messages per day. The far end of the plant is 1,200 feet from the dispatching station and requires 8 minutes of walking time between the two points. Dispatching by pneumatic tube over the distance takes about 40 seconds.

3. *The Telautograph.*—This is a commercial installation used to transmit sketches and written orders instantaneously to the department or individual concerned. The sender holds a pencil-like stylus with which he writes on a plate. The sending stylus is mechanically connected to a pair of rheostats set at right angles to each other which serve to vary the voltage at the receiver and thus to translate the impulses into pen motions on recording paper at that end. A permanent record of all messages can be thus obtained at each end. No attendance at the receiving end is required, periodic attention being all that is necessary to read the messages as time permits. Perhaps its principal advantage lies in the fact that it is the only shop dispatching method by which sketches, dimensions, and other symbols can be transmitted instantaneously over long distances.

4. *The Temperator.*—Another commercial device, it makes use of a dial similar to that on a dial telephone to send coded messages. Its most successful application probably is in the various manufacturing and in-

spection departments where employees dial in to a central control station their starting and completion of production orders along with other pertinent information. The message appears on a panel in front of both sender and receiver so that the former can easily detect any mistakes in dialing and the latter can transcribe the information before releasing the station for the next message.

5. *The Teletypewriter.*—This is the standard teletype machine similar to that used by the telegraph companies and newspapers. If machines are spotted at key work centers throughout the shop or in each of several widely separated departments, the system can then be used to transmit dispatching information and to report production information in return. Wallace Barnes Company Division, Associated Spring Corporation, of Bristol, Conn., has used this method with considerable success to replace the longhand reporting of the status of production orders. Each work center is equipped with a teletype machine over which once an hour a report is made of the production performed during the previous hour. The information, reported in code, is received at the central-control station on gummed telegraph tape which is then moistened and pasted on the reverse of the office copies of the production orders involved. By this means, Wallace Barnes is able to know within an hour the exact status of some 8,000 production orders running at any one time in the plant. Perhaps the principal disadvantage of this type of dispatching facility is its rather high equipment cost.

6. *The Telephone.*—The telephone has in many plants been overlooked as a dispatching and reporting device primarily because it is considered to be an inaccurate method for transmitting letters and figures. However, this is not altogether true. A telephone properly employed by trained operators can be a very swift and accurate facility. If proof is required, the Southern New England Telephone Company has long dispatched its installation and repair men by telephone, transmitting the job number and all other pertinent information via the phone. Its principal advantages are its speed and the fact that the communication is on a personal basis; its disadvantage lies in the fact that no permanent record is available for messages thus dispatched.

7. *Interstation Loudspeaker Devices.*—These are essentially multiple-station amplifying units over which conversations can be carried. Each station consists of a small cabinet containing a microphone and speaker. At each station, communication is afforded by simply throwing the switch for one or more other stations with which contact is desired and talking in a normal voice. The advantages and disadvantages of this method are essentially the same as for the telephone. However, this type of device is normally faster and more convenient to use.

FOLLOW-UP

Follow-up or "expediting" is that branch of production-control procedure which regulates the progress of materials and parts through the production process. Although it is the agency charged with the responsibility for the production orders after they are dispatched, it, nevertheless, is closely interrelated with dispatching. Follow-up serves as a catalytic agent to fuse the various separate and unrelated production activities into the unified whole that means progress. It concerns itself with the reporting of production data and the investigating of variances from the predetermined time schedules. As such, follow-up endeavors to see that the promise is backed up by performance.

Types of Follow-up. 1. *Materials.*—The follow-up of purchased materials is, as was noted in the section on Purchasing (page 265), primarily the responsibility of the purchasing department. The original requisition upon which the purchase of materials is based usually specifies the date on or before which the material is required, and it then becomes the duty of the purchasing department to insure that the material is received so as to be available by that date. However, certain orders for material or for subcontracted items may be extremely vital to the maintenance of delivery promises to the customer, whereas other orders may simply be required to maintain a normal bank of raw material or parts in anticipation of future customer orders. Or changed conditions may require that the delivery date of certain material be advanced.

Thus it is frequently advisable for the follow-up division of the production-control department to follow outstanding material requisitions placed with the purchasing department which are deemed vital to the maintenance of preplanned schedules. This follow-up may be accomplished most simply by filing one copy of the requisition in a daily follow-up file or in a tickler file according to the date the material is due to be received. Delivery information as obtained from the purchasing department through this type of follow-up can be transferred to the stock records to supply a ready cross reference for the source of the information.

2. *Work in Process.*—The follow-up of work in process in serialized manufacture consists primarily of checking the materials required for that process and recording the production accomplished by the production line for comparison purposes with the preplanned schedules. Once material enters the production line, it cannot easily become sidetracked or dormant. Thus, when the material is put into process in the desired sequence, follow-up of that material is a relatively simple matter. In fact, follow-up of serialized manufacture can rely on a daily production

record (see Fig. 86) or make use of a control chart (see pp. 346–354) to reveal any delays in production items along the line. Thus by the use of the principle of exception, late items can be given special attention.

However, the same cannot always be said for the follow-up of work in job-order manufacture. Where products are diversified and where a

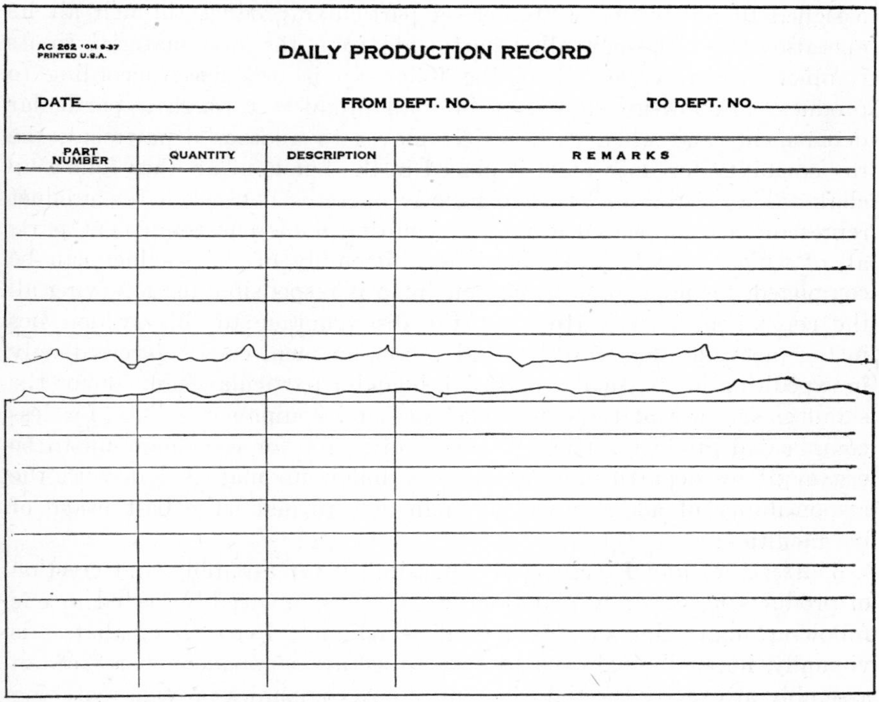

PART NUMBER	QUANTITY	DESCRIPTION	REMARKS

DAILY PRODUCTION RECORD

AC 262 '0M 9-37
PRINTED U.S.A.

DATE_____ FROM DEPT. NO._____ TO DEPT. NO._____

Fig. 86.—Daily production-record form which can be used both for the daily reporting of a department's production against a manufacturing schedule and as an aid in follow-up. If the department fails to meet its assigned schedule, the foreman must note under "remarks" the reasons for poor performance.

number of orders are running currently in the shop departments, it is possible for the sequence in which work on these orders is performed to be changed as conditions may dictate. Hence it is the duty of the follow-up men or expediters to advise the foremen as to the best sequence in which orders can be run so that the necessary parts will be fabricated and brought together at the right time and place for completion of the finished product.

As a part of the follow-up activities of job-order manufacture, a time record is usually made of the start and completion of each job or operation, together with the number of pieces made and those which are defective or spoiled. Allied with such records are those showing the idle time of men and of machines which thus reveal lost-time conditions requiring investigation.

Follow-up of job-order manufacture may be organized either by product or by department. Under the first system, a follow-up clerk is assigned to follow up or "father" a particular product through all its operations and through all departments from the raw material to its completion. However, where the follow-up is organized according to product, a follow-up clerk expedites all products through a particular department, and when each article moves to another department, the responsibility for its control is placed in the hands of another follow-up clerk. The "fathering" system usually operates best when the product represents a complicated assembly requiring numerous component parts all of which must be available before assembly of the product can be completed, for under this system one man is responsible for following all the component parts. However, the disadvantage to this system lies in the fact that frequently several follow-up men, each interested only in expediting his particular material, hound a particular foreman for the simultaneous use of the same machines and equipment. Thus for less complicated products, it is frequently advisable for the follow-up to be organized by departments so that one follow-up man is left with the responsibility of advising the foreman how to make the best usage of his facilities.

3. *Assembly and Erection.*—Responsibility for assembly and erection of products in assembly manufacture is almost invariably vested in one follow-up man using the "fathering" technique. Recognizing that it is virtually impossible always to bring together component parts of an assembly at exactly the right instant, many companies provide matching centers (see reference to Warner & Swasey's "loose assembly department," in Chap. XIV) for temporary storage of the component parts awaiting assembly. When all parts are available, the follow-up man permits assembly or erection of the product to start.

In the case of large and complicated products, the assembly and erection as well as the subsequent servicing of the product may of necessity take place at the purchaser's plant. This type of erection frequently is required for machinery and for other highly technical articles where the follow-up man must be thoroughly acquainted with the engineering details of the product, with the applications in the field, as well as with the trouble shooting and servicing of the product after it goes into service.

Preventing Production Delays.—As can be seen from the foregoing, the follow-up man or expediter is concerned with the delays that creep

---

PRODUCTION DELAY REPORT

PROGRESS ON..OPERATION IN MY DEPARTMENT
WAS HELD UP BECAUSE OF THE ENCIRCLED CAUSES.

PREMISES: Physical conditions, Floors, Stairs, Working Areas.

MATERIAL: Insufficient, Wrong, Spoiled, Inaccessible, Not designated, Unclear specifications.

EQUIPMENT: Inadequate capacity, Breakdown, In use, Being repaired, Unsafe, Shortage of parts, Lack of needed equipment.

METHODS: Unsuitable, Unsafe, Being revised, Misinterpreted, Unclear or Not specific.

MEN: Inadequate, Inexperienced, Incapable, Unsafe practices, Disobedience of rules.

OTHERS: ....

EMPLOYEES INVOLVED: ....

....

DESCRIBE INTERRUPTION COMPLETELY: ....

....

....

....

....

....

DAMAGE OR INJURY: ....

NORMAL OPERATIONS WILL BE RESUMED: ....

....

PREVENTIVE MEASURES TAKEN: ....

....

....

Supervisor	Production Clerk	Superintendent	Safety Man	Manager

Fig. 87.—The production delay report of the type shown can be used when the foreman is required to report delays in the production in his department as they occur. This report can then be forwarded to the proper individual for appropriate investigation and action.

into industrial production.   He gains his information concerning present and past delays from production records, from delay reports of the type pictured in Fig. 87, and, most important of all, from personal observation.   It is his duty not only to take corrective action after delays have developed, but to anticipate and prevent delays that would otherwise occur.   An ounce of prevention is far more valuable than a pound of cure where industrial production is concerned.

The following check list of the causes of production delays is applicable to both serialized and job-order manufacture, and it further suggests some of the preventive measures that may be required of the industrial expediter:

1. *Errors in Routing, Scheduling, and Dispatching.*—These are essentially errors of management whereby equipment is scheduled with work beyond its capacity to produce, or too many setups are introduced through the scheduling of uneconomically small lots and through not grouping similar production items.   The follow-up man by his close association with plant conditions can often discover and rectify such errors before they cause trouble.

2. *Lack of Materials.*—Because of the extreme importance of this phase of follow-up and also because of the special techniques required, a separate section has already been devoted to the follow-up of materials (see page 265).

3. *Labor Difficulties.*—Strikes, walkouts, slowdowns, and sitdowns, of course, delay production.   However, the solution of problems in personnel relations is far beyond the scope of the follow-up man and is logically the province of the personnel division (see chapters on Industrial Relations).

4. *Breakdowns of Equipment.*—These may involve electrical or transmission difficulties, those in bearings or spindles, or inaccuracies caused by general wear and tear on the equipment.   Of course, preventive maintenance and duplication of vital pieces of equipment help to minimize delays due to breakdowns.   Nevertheless, the follow-up man must see that alternative equipment including all necessary tooling is kept available in the event that breakdowns do occur.

5. *Lack of Proper Tools, Jigs, and Fixtures.*—The expediter can see that tool lists are sent to the tool-room well in advance of the need for such tools.   Furthermore, the chasing of undelivered tools is a logical counterpart of his other duties.

6. *Inadequate Material in Process.*—Where the "float" between operations becomes so low that slight spurts or lags in production at any of the operations cause operators to run out of work, the follow-up man

must then take steps to build up this float so as to reduce idle-man-and-machine time attributable to this cause.

7. *Excessive Rejections.*—Materials scrapped at any point in the production process in excess of the permissible rate of rejections subsequently show up as shortages in the finished article. Thus it behooves the expediter to investigate every case where rejections seem excessive. He must then set in motion the machinery to have the defective material replaced and, what is more important, to have the cause of the spoilage eliminated for subsequent material.

SUMMARY OF CHAPTERS XIV AND XV

Chapters XIV and XV have dealt with the principles and techniques of production control, which as we have seen is a quadripartite function composed of:

1. Routing—determination of the path.
2. Scheduling—establishment of the time sequence.
3. Dispatching—issuance of the orders and work.
4. Follow-up—expediting the flow of work.

Current trends in production control indicate for the future increasing emphasis on the word "control." Tighter control is a natural by-product of intense competition. It can be made possible by the increased centralization of mechanical or electrical dispatch and reporting devices as well as by greater knowledge and mastery of equipment characteristics. It is facilitated by the growing application of the principles of serialized and semiserialized manufacture. Mechanized handling equipment of the fixed-conveyor type likewise provides the means for closer control over production.

Whereas in many companies today manufacturing schedules, reports of production, and movement of materials are considered to be adequate if handled on a day-to-day basis, the production managers of the future will find use for both clock and calendar in their control techniques. This forthcoming emphasis on control, virtually minute by minute, is a counterpart of the general quickening of the industrial tempo made possible by our rapid communication and transportation facilities. It is likewise a part of the over-all attempt to produce more and better goods faster and at a lower cost.

It is important to note that the heart of the material developed above rests in the basic philosophies underlying production control, not in the exact techniques, procedures, forms, records, and reports presented. The latter have been included simply as illustrations and guides to effective practices—practices which in each case must be adapted to the individual circumstances and conditions involved.

CASE PROBLEMS

Control of Production

THE WESTINGHOUSE ELECTRIC AND MANUFACTURING COMPANY [1]

The Cleveland, Ohio, Lighting Division plant of the Westinghouse Electric and Manufacturing Company specializes in the manufacture of industrial and commercial lighting fixtures, marine and aviation lighting equipment, and the well-known Precipitron electrostatic air cleaner. Although nearly all designs are standard, customers very frequently specify some individual feature (such as special finishes or parts) to accommodate an architectural requirement, and local building codes often necessitate some departure from the standard designs.

Material is received either by truck or by rail in the receiving department. Every piece of material is checked, then sent to the raw-material storeroom, production dispatch station, or finished-parts storeroom, depending upon the type of material and where it enters into process.

We can now follow a hypothetical product through a typical manufacturing cycle, assuming that it originates as raw material in the raw-material storeroom. The correct quantity and size of material are sent by the storeroom to the production dispatch station. The storeroom cuts, shears, weighs out, or otherwise supplies the correct amount for a given order. The material is then sent by conveyor or caster truck to the dispatcher.

When all the material required for the first operation is on hand, the dispatcher routes the order to the manufacturing department, usually with drawings and tools necessary to perform the specified operations. If the material can be accommodated in tote boxes, it is sent over by conveyor, automatically controlled from the dispatch station. If the material is too large for tote boxes, it is delivered on caster trucks by a "move" man. By this means, the dispatcher can control production very readily. The shop can work on the various orders in the proper sequence since only such work is dispatched as may be required and all other material is held in the dispatch station. This then becomes the first "matching center" in the layout.

After the specified operations are completed on the first assignments, the material is returned to the dispatch station for reassignment until all so-called "feeder operations" are completed. These may be any or all of the following processes: metal stamping, machining, spinning,

[1] Condensed from C. H. Smith and R. W. Mallick, Plant Layout Facilitates Defense Lighting Production, *Machine Tool Bluebook,* January, 1942, p. 181.

welding, subassembly, cleaning, plating, painting, or polishing. The dispatcher has full control of work assignment and in this way can route jobs to the best advantage and stabilize the work in the shop as well as give preference to specific orders.

Should any one department be low on work, he may start out jobs that may not be required immediately, then hold the parts in the dispatch station before routing for succeeding operations. Or, he may hold up less important orders to give way to urgent work.

When all the "feeder operations" have been completed, the material is sent to the finished-parts storeroom or dispatch station 2, depending upon its classification. Material that is made for stock and carried on ledgers is held in the finished-parts storeroom until requisitioned. If it should apply on a customer's order, it is sent to the dispatch station for matching with other parts applying on the order and is held there until it can be released for assembly and shipment. This now becomes a second "matching center."

When an order is ready to assemble, the dispatcher collects all of the special material required for the order, and requisitions the stock parts from the finished-parts storeroom which is located adjacent to the dispatch station. When all is in readiness, he sends the order by caster skid to the head assembly lines.

With exceptions, such as apparatus that cannot be moved on conveyors owing to physical dimensions or design, all assembly is done on gravity-roll conveyors. Each unit is assembled progressively and, after the final operation, is inspected and ready for packing. Assembly conveyors extend to the packing floor, and this operation is also done on conveyors or special benches designed to keep all material within the effective working radius of the operator.

After the material has been packed, it is turned over to the shipping department, located on the same floor, for shipment or warehousing. If it is for warehouse stock, it is transferred by caster truckload on an elevator to the upper floors that are used for that purpose. If it goes into direct shipment, it is moved to the loading platform.

Preparatory Questions

Appraise the Westinghouse treatment of the following basic issues raised by this case study:

1. Routing procedure and type of manufacture used in the fabrication and assembly of essentially standardized articles requiring some special features and nonstandard parts.

2. Use of matching centers.

3. Centralized and decentralized dispatching.

Control of Production

The Cheshire Company

The Cheshire Company is essentially a service mill which takes hot-rolled steel of any desired analysis, cold-rolls it to specified size and finish, and heat-treats it to the desired temper. Rush work and frequent specification changes are a regular part of the service offered, and the company frequently juggles its production plans to take care of the emergencies of its customers.

The plant, employing some 300 people, is a modern structure with modern equipment. However, the production-control system in use at the plant has not kept pace with the physical progress of the company, a fact that can perhaps be appreciated from the following outline of the system:

A sales order, upon receipt, is sent from the sales department to the works manager, thence to the credit department, and finally to the production office. From the production office a notice of acceptance is sent to the purchaser with a delivery promise or verification of the promise that previously may have been made by the salesman.

Next, a production order is made out in quadruplicate. Two copies are retained by the production office, one filed by production-order number and one by customer name. The third goes to the sales office, and the fourth to the shipping room. Also, a shop order is made out in triplicate. Two copies go to the shop office, one for use by the dispatcher and the other for the timekeeper. The third (on cardboard backing) is sent to the pickle-room foreman to be kept with the material and to show the operations required as it moves through the mill.

The pickle-room foreman has charge of the raw-material stock, the scale-breaking operation, and the pickling—initial steps for all orders. He looks over the new orders daily and decides how much of what material to start. He tries to lay out enough work so that no one will run out of material. If in doubt, he confers with the dispatcher, shop superintendent, production office, or even the works manager.

Once past the initial operations, the material moves to the next department provided (1) the pickle-room foreman hails a passing electric truck and tells the driver to move it, or (2) the foreman of the next department comes to the pickle room looking for his next job, or (3) the dispatcher from personal observation or upon being notified by either of the foremen learns that the job is ready and orders it moved. Information on the progress of each job is recorded by the dispatcher on his copy of the shop order only.

Thus does work proceed through the various operations required until the material reaches the shipping room. Here a notice of partial or total completion is made out in several copies, one each going to the shop office, production office, billing department, and the shipping room.

Any variation on the material in an order, such as change in quantity or delivery date requested by the customer, is recorded by the production office on a change notice form from which the information is transferred to all copies of the production order and shop order that have been filed throughout the plant. Upon receipt of a change notice, the dispatcher then endeavors to meet the new requirements of the customer concerned— a phase of his work that often means shuffling a number of other orders.

If, as frequently happens, a customer inquires about his order, one of the production-office clerks checks its status by going through the following procedure:

Steps	Comments
1. Ascertain customer order number and item desired.	1. Be diplomatic.
2. Obtain production-order number from file according to customer.	2. If not there, try unfiled orders awaiting action by the sales department, works manager, credit department, or production office. If this search is successful, skip to No. 6 below.
3. Check production-order copy in sales binder for any shipments.	3. Record balance open. If all shipped, skip to No. 7 below.
4. Check production office for any completion notices or shipping slips not yet posted.	4. Find these on production clerks' desks.
5. Check dispatcher's mill binder for schedule.	5. If schedule not listed or delayed, get in touch with dispatcher.
6. Estimate best delivery.	6. Be conservative, allow a factor of safety.
7. Advise customer.	7. Be sympathetic to his needs.
8. Follow up material.	8. Send out rush slips with dispatcher and check item periodically.

Preparatory Question

Refer back to Fig. 62 (chart showing "Sequence of Production-control Procedure"), and draw up a similar chart for the control system of The Cheshire Company. From a comparison of this chart with Fig. 62 and from the descriptive case study, outline why The Cheshire Company's control system is outmoded. Suggest corrective measures for each weakness you find.

Control of Production

THE REX MACHINE COMPANY [2]

The Rex Machine Company manufactures lathes in a variety of sizes. The heart of the production-control system in use at Rex is its master schedule sheet retained in the production-control office upon which are listed the serial number and size of each lathe ordered. The "legs" of this system are the stock chasers who operate in the plant departments to maintain a constant checkup on parts in process, keep replenished the supplies of parts in assembly and subassembly departments, expedite special jobs, and regularly follow one or more types of material or parts from receiving to shipping.

Stock chasers report to a centrally located desk between the machining and assembly departments. All work passes this desk from the machining department on its way to inspection, which is located at the stock storage room. Depending on the rate at which parts are being used, some material delivered to inspection may be forwarded immediately to the assembly or subassembly departments, eliminating double handling of material. The balance is put in stock storage, and from there stock chasers requisition it out to replenish individual stock supplies. Supplies of parts in the stock storage room are replenished at regular intervals under the direction of the stock chasers who are in a position to know when it is time to start orders for more parts through the necessary machining and finishing operations.

One stock chaser stays at the central desk at all times to act as a dispatcher for the material flowing uninterruptedly past this point. Two stock chasers circulate all the time through the assembly and subassembly departments. The rest of the chasers follow definite assignments throughout the plant, always with a view to keeping production going at top speed.

These assignments are made so that each chaser follows certain kinds of parts. One man makes it his primary responsibility to see that the right lathe beds get on the right planers and grinders at the right time. Another stock chaser follows up small screw-machine parts. A third keeps track of quick-change gearboxes and aprons. Still another looks after certain sizes of forgings, and so on. In this way every item in process is closely expedited through the entire plant.

Preparatory Question

Comment on The Rex Company's production-control system, making note of its sound features as well as of possible weaknesses.

---

[2] This case has been adapted from the study of an actual machine tool company as reported in *Factory*, Vol. 100, No. 5, p. 85.

Production-control System for Minimizing Inventories

In periods of rapidly expanding business activity, many normally successful production-control systems break down from a depletion of available materials that are required to maintain production. What formerly was a month's supply of some items then, because of the increased rate of consumption, may be reduced to perhaps a week's or even a few days' supply. Thus, as its production rapidly gathers momentum, an enterprise often runs itself right out of materials and parts.

Conversely, during a hasty contraction of business activity, many production-control systems wind up with excessive stocks of inventory items. For, as the plant's production slackens, what was a few days' or weeks' supply of materials stretches out into a stock that will last for a period of months.

During World War II, the U.S. War Department, Office of the Chief of Ordnance, issued a pamphlet [3] suggesting a control system by which companies holding war contracts could minimize commitments, work in progress, and inventories in anticipation of the eventual cancellation of these contracts. The principles of this system likewise have general application in meeting the expansion and contraction problems outlined above. Its essential features can be shown in the following abbreviated explanation [4] of the forms shown in Fig. 88:

The upper or general data card containing information on customer orders for part W55 shows orders still not completely filled. Delivery rates of each customer are resolved into percentages of total deliveries. The optimum amount of work in process is calculated at the bottom of this card as days of working bank ahead of operations multiplied by the daily schedule.

The bottom or control card keeps a progressive Balance on Order representing the gross amount of parts still due all customers. This amount is progressively reduced by Shipments made and increased by new orders received.

The addition of Work in Process and Finished Inventory gives the Total Available parts for subsequent delivery which, when divided by the daily delivery schedule, results in Days Supply ahead of orders or the number of days for which material has been cut up and put into process. For quick visual reference, the visible marker at the bottom of this card is continually set at the current number of days ahead of orders.

[3] "Control System for Minimizing Commitments, Work in Progress, and Inventories," U.S. War Department, Office of the Chief of Ordnance, Washington, D.C., 1943.

[4] Adapted from pamphlet, *op. cit.,* p. 13.

Part No. _W 55_   Part Name; _Adjusting Screw_ _____   Daily   P.C.
                                                            Del'y   of
Customer; _X Co._   Sched   Total

| Order No. | C-17445 | C-19007 | C-20888 | C-23113 | | | | |
| Quantity | 1,000,000 | 800,000 | 700,000 | 600,000 | | | 50,000 | 66.7 |

Customer; _Y Corp._

| Order No. | 42-21761 | 42-25601 | 43-16476 | 43-18009 | | | | |
| Quantity | 900,000 | 1,000,000 | 850,000 | 900,000 | | | 15,000 | 20. |

Customer; _Z Co._

| Order No. | 20-717 | 36-411 | 44-916 | | | | | |
| Quantity | 75,000 | 1,000,000 | 800,000 | | | | 10,000 | 13.3 |

Customer;
Order No.
Quantity

Maximum Daily Capacity; _80,000_   (_16_ hrs/day)   TOTAL ; _75,000_   100%

MATERIAL: _Steel Rod .069" dia. x 12'. CD or CG X-1335_   (_80_ lbs. per 1000)

Work in Process:- (Operation No.; Days Working Bank) (#6 ; 1) (# 11 ; 1/2)
  (#12 ; 1/2) (;   ) (;   )   (;   ) (;   )
  (;   ) (;   ) (;   )   (;   ) (;   )

Total Days of Work in Process; _2_ _____   Total Pieces in Process; _150,000_

Fig. 88a.—A control form.

	ORDERS		MATERIAL AND EQUIV. PARTS			W. I. P. AND PARTS AHEAD OF ORDERS			
Date	Balance on Order	Shipments	In Stock	Equivalent Parts	Days Supply	Work in Process	Finished Inventory	Total Available	Days Supply
6-8	2,075,000	60,000	1487#	1,860,000	24.8	170,000	125,000	295,000	4.
6-9	1,993,000	82,000	1487#	"	24.8	"	115,000	285,000	3.8
	a (a-b)	b	c	d c/1.80 x 1000	e d/75,000	f	g	h (f+g)	i h/75,000
				Visible marker set at 3.8 days					
							(Limits; 2 to 10 days)		
Part No. W 55		Days Ahead of Orders;		0 10 20 30 40 50 60					

Fig. 88b.—A control form.

Of course, these forms of necessity are supplemented by detailed purchase, in-process, and finished inventory records showing individual transactions.

Preparatory Questions

1. Record the effect of the following transactions on the forms in Fig. 88, entering the new figures and totals on the control card, columns (*a*) to (*i*) inclusive:

Date: 6–10.
Received from the Z Co. Order 45-722 for 1,000,000 pieces to be delivered at the rate of 10,000 per day starting with completion of Order 44-916.
Shipped total of 70,000 pieces.
Received 1,000 pounds of raw material.
Put into process 100,000 pieces.
Delivered into finished inventory 76,000 pieces.

2. What are the advantages of this control system?
3. Suggest general classes of materials, parts, and products for which this system is especially applicable.

Production-control Forms

THE R Co.

See Fig. 89.

Preparatory Question

Comment on the format, arrangement, method of preparation, and use of The R Co.'s production-control forms. Would you eliminate or improve any of the forms?

CHAPTER XVI
QUALITY CONTROL

Quality control in its broadest sense refers to the systematic control of those variables encountered in a manufacturing process which affect the excellence of the end product. Such variables result from the application of materials, men, machines, and manufacturing conditions. All materials are derived either directly or indirectly from the land, sea, or air and, being thus subject to the caprices of nature, differ greatly as to composition and physical characteristics. Men vary in their degree of skill, proficiency, and application to their work. Machines are built by men using the materials of nature, and the interaction of their variables on the machines thus made introduces an entirely new set of variables. Furthermore, machines, machine equipment, and measuring instruments are subject to wear and tend to go out of adjustment with use. Manufacturing conditions—temperature, humidity, building vibration, composition of coolants, dust and dirt in the air—are likewise factors that of themselves admit certain variations. Only when these variables are regulated to the extent that they do not detract unnecessarily from the excellence of the manufacturing process as reflected in the quality of the finished product can the control of quality be said to exist.

Quality control is never absolute—it is always relative to certain other considerations. For one thing, the word "quality" is meaningless unless the *end use of the product* is also stipulated. The term "good quality" means that the article is good for the purpose for which it was intended. For example, a high-quality automobile tire jack might pass every test for quality required of tire jacks but, if it were subjected to tests given jackscrews designed to raise buildings, it would fail miserably. Its quality is adequate only for its intended end use, that of supporting 2 tons—not 20. Also, quality is an abstract word unless related to *definable and measurable characteristics of the product* involved. Thus the quality of a piece of metal should be stated in terms of its chemical and physical properties; a paint in terms of its viscosity, color, drying time, resistance to foreign substances, etc. Quality is likewise related to the *economics of manufacturing*. The degree of quality that can be maintained under a designated manufacturing process, the percentage of imperfect goods, if any, that are acceptable to the producer and/or to the consumer—these are typical of the economic considerations linked with quality control. Furthermore, quality has a bearing on *manufacturing costs* and on *selling price*. High quality generally results in high cost of manufacture, whereas a relaxation of quality standards often permits costs and hence prices to be lowered. Finally, quality bears a relationship to *quantity*. The higher the degree of quality demanded, the tighter become the controls imposed on the manufacturing process and the more difficult it is to achieve quantity output.

In the past decade industry has seen a tremendous advance in the preciseness of its quality standards. Quality has changed from a generic art to a specific science complete with definite standards and devices for measuring product characteristics against those standards. Instruments now available and in use measure in millionths of an inch. The degree of accuracy involved can be appreciated when it is recalled that one-millionth of an inch is the equivalent of splitting the human hair 2,500 times! Other characteristics such as color, hardness, surface finishes, and noise, to mention only a few, have in recent years become measurable to great exactness on specially designed instruments. Thus has industry been required to adapt itself to rapidly developing quality standards, measuring equipment, and control techniques. Furthermore, its manufacturing technology has time and again been taxed to keep pace with the ever higher degree of precision demanded by advances in the science of quality.

Scope of Quality Control.—A program for controlling quality has in its toolbox certain essential tools of the trade. These, when arranged as below, serve to define the scope of quality-control activities:

1. *Standards and specifications* that determine the quality objectives to be measured or evaluated.
2. *Inspection methods* for selecting good quality from bad in accordance with the established standards.
3. *Statistical techniques*, including sampling and the collecting, sorting, and analyzing of data to indicate whether or not quality is under control.
4. *Inspection records* and charting techniques for recording inspection data so as to single out indications of lack of control.
5. *Salvage methods* by which defective goods are effectively disposed of.
6. *Inspection devices* which embrace all items of equipment used for objective and measurable comparisons of actual quality against established standards.

It should be noted in passing that in actual shop parlance the terms "quality control" and "inspection" are often used interchangeably. This, no doubt, is the result of the historical concept of inspection as the principal tool of quality control. Important though inspection is, we must remember that, whereas a program of quality control by bringing variables under control enlarges the production pile, inspection, by its separation of the good from the bad, merely enlarges the scrap pile.

STANDARDS AND SPECIFICATIONS

The subject of manufacturing standards was discussed at some length in Chap. VIII. However, it is important here to consider how the establishment of standards relating to quality affects the maintenance of a program of quality control.

There is a well-known axiom in industrial circles to the effect that *perfection in manufacture is impossible to attain and costly to approach.* We have seen that imperfections are caused by the variables in a manufacturing process and that, through control, the effect of these variables can be minimized to reduce the imperfections. However, the economic law of diminishing returns applies to quality control as it does to everything else: as perfection is approached, costs rise disproportionately.

Tolerances.—To be salable, a product must be acceptable to customers as regards both quality and cost. Somewhere along the scales of quality and cost there is a point of compromise at which the quality meets the customer's minimum requirements and the cost fits his pocketbook. At this point, then, is established what might be termed the "basic standard" of quality. In practice, however, there is no such thing as an exact standard, for such a thing is as difficult to attain as is perfection itself. So, recognizing that while it is impossible to avoid variations from any basic criterion it is possible to restrict such variations, industry usually states each standard in terms of a *tolerance* or permissible deviation from the basic criterion. This tolerance defines by means of limits the *zone of acceptability*—a zone of variation that may be permitted without altering the functional fitness of the article involved.

In order that we may better understand the principles underlying the establishment of standards of quality, we must explore further the nature of the manufacturing variables that make tolerances necessary. Basically, manufacturing variables can be grouped into two classes:

1. *Chance Variables.*—These include all variables which are inherent in the manufacturing process and which, even if located, cannot be corrected except by a significant change in the manufacturing process itself. They are "chance" in the sense that they are sporadic and may have no regular or predictable effect on the product. Such variables include materials that are not entirely homogeneous, imperfections inherent in the design of the machines employed, natural inaccuracies of inspection instruments, the "feel," eyesight, or judgment of the production operators — all variables that cannot be removed without a major change in materials, equipment, or methods.

2. *Assignable Variables.*—These are the variables not inherent in the manufacturing process. Generally they result from such extraneous causes as improper operation of a machine, incorrect sequence of manufacturing operations, machines or inspection instruments worn and in need of repair, room temperatures that vary during the day or in different parts of the same room, vibration of the plant building affecting the performance of the machines—all variables that can be assigned and controlled without altering the manufacturing process.

From the foregoing, it can be seen that, in general, the tolerance limits or zone of acceptability should be set sufficiently wide to include within those limits at least all the variations singly or compounded, that are caused by the chance variables in the manufacturing process. If this is not done, an inspection operation must be introduced to segregate defects resulting from chance causes, and part of any lot of goods will always be rejected as not falling within that acceptable zone for reasons impossible to control under the existing manufacturing process. However, where tolerances are sufficiently broad to include all chance variables, any variations in the quality of the goods beyond those limits can be assumed to be due to assignable variables which, when once located, can be readily corrected. Thus a lathe designed to machine parts to within 0.001 inch requires a tolerance of at least 0.001 inch for such parts. Otherwise some parts will be rejected for reasons that are beyond the powers of the machine or operator to control.

The width of the tolerance that is permissible often depends upon whether interchangeable manufacture or selective assembly is involved. *Interchangeable manufacture* may be defined as "The procedure which requires all mating parts to assemble without selection or fitting, the final assembled product conforming to specified dimensions within limits of variation establishing the closest and loosest fits permissible." [1]

Selective assembly, on the other hand, may be defined as "The procedure by which mating parts are accurately gaged and sorted into classes according to tolerance. Units of each class are assembled with companion parts of its corresponding class." [1]

Interchangeable manufacture requires close tolerances in order that all parts falling within those tolerances will mate properly without selecting or fitting. Thus it calls for precision manufacture in order that the chance variables may not cause the rejection of a considerable portion of the material produced. Its advantages are, of course, cheaper and faster assembly and the interchangeability of replacement parts, the last named being an important factor from the standpoint of field

[1] Definition from "Dimensional Control," prepared and distributed by The Sheffield Corportion, Dayton, Ohio.

servicing. Interchangeable manufacture is the *sine qua non* of mass production. However, only in recent years has it been found possible to apply interchangeable manufacture to high-precision products. That such products can be produced interchangeably was demonstrated conclusively by the Ford Motor Company shortly after it went into the production of the Pratt & Whitney aircraft engine during World War II. An engine made by Ford was shipped to the Pratt & Whitney plant and together with a Pratt & Whitney engine was torn down, part by part. The parts were next scrambled and the two engines reassembled from parts selected at random, each then working perfectly.

Selective assembly permits looser tolerances and hence requires less exacting manufacturing methods. This reduces the cost of fabrication but may well result in higher assembly costs as each part must be selected and mated with a part in its corresponding size bracket. Also servicing of the article is complicated, for parts are not interchangeable, a factor which in some lines of products may be a definite disadvantage. Thus any comparison of interchangeable manufacture with selective assembly for a particular application rests upon the relative ease of fabrication and assembly, the comparative costs, and a consideration of the replacement parts and servicing problems.

Setting of Standards.—In general, standards establishing the quality of products determine standards of engineering design, process, and material. Quality standards should be reasonable, measurable, available, and understandable. Best practice dictates that they be reduced to writing and that copies be given to all individuals concerned with their maintenance. Furthermore, like all other types of standards, they are subject to the progress-time-curve theory and the principles of industrial standardization developed in Chap. VIII. Within a particular enterprise, quality standards are generally set by the company's product-engineering department in cooperation with the sales, production, cost, and inspection departments. Under no circumstances should standards be established by the inspection department alone, for then that department becomes a bureaucratic agency serving as lawmaker, prosecutor, and judge all rolled into one.

Of course, in the last analysis, the customers set standards of product quality by their decision to buy or not to buy. Yet this customer control over quality is completely effective only in the case of industrial purchasers who buy on technical specifications. The average private consumer is confronted with complicated or technical goods he does not understand, with a wide range of choices that generally cater to eye appeal, with conflicting and confusing advertising claims—all of which prevent him from thinking through on quality. Consider, for example, the plight of Mr. Johnnie Q. Public peering intently into the cabinet of a television set with its many tubes, wires, gadgets, and gimmicks, and trying to appraise its "works." Or again, what can Mrs. Housewife know of the quality of a particular can of fruit, of the expected life of a lamp bulb, of the validity of advertising claims for a certain brand of toothpaste?

Because of this helplessness on the part of the average consumer in judging quality, he has been compelled to take certain steps in his own defense. Since the turn of the century, consumer leagues and testing organizations have sprung up. Books, magazines, and newspapers have exposed sales frauds and entered the field of consumer education. Colleges and universities have inaugurated courses in the domestic sciences. Legislation has been passed regulating the quality of foods and drugs, setting forth uniform standards of size, proper labels, outlawing unfair practices. Government bureaus have disseminated consumer bulletins telling how to judge, buy, and conserve many products. One of these agencies, the National Bureau of Standards (see Chap. VIII), has for many years been influential in setting standards of product quality. Thus have consumers collectively and with the help of semipublic and governmental agencies taken an ever stronger hand in defending themselves from predatory producers.

Certainly this trend will continue until industry in general and individual companies in particular assume a greater responsibility for setting standards of quality. In all fairness it should be noted that many companies have already assumed this responsibility by guaranteeing satisfaction or money back, by granting time and service guarantees, by truthful advertising and honest prices. But as in any other field of endeavor, a few culprits must be controlled if the great majority are to be free of indictment.

INSPECTION METHODS

Inspection serves two main purposes in any quality-control program, namely,

1. *To segregate defective goods and thus insure that the customers receive only goods of adequate quality.* This type of control is of paramount importance, for upon its success rests the good will and satisfaction of the users of those goods. The principal objective of all "final" inspection (the inspection of finished products) as well as much of the inspection of raw and in-process material is to insure that no, or at least very few, defective goods leave the plant.

2. *To locate flaws in the raw material or in the processing of that material which will cause trouble at subsequent operations.* This phase of

quality control is purely a tool of manufacturing in that it is designed to anticipate and prevent manufacturing difficulties that might otherwise occur. For example, by such inspection, oversize or undersize parts of an assembly are located and segregated before the assembly operation, at which stage such defective parts would cause trouble.

Organization for Inspection.—The successful control of quality in an industrial enterprise is to a great extent dependent upon the operating efficiency of the inspection organization charged with the maintenance of that control. Trying to control quality with a poorly organized and inadequately staffed inspection crew is akin to trying to sandbag a flooded river: you plug it in one spot and it leaks in another.

The inspection department is naturally enough a part of the operating branch of the enterprise and as such should be made a responsibility of one of the operating executives. In the case of precision products, the importance of quality in the manufacturing processes warrants placing the inspection department directly under the plant or works manager. In manufacture in which precision is not a major factor, the lesser importance of quality permits subordinating the inspection department to the division or plant superintendent. Although inspection has been known to operate effectively under the wing of an operating foreman or other supervisor charged with the maintenance of production schedules, this practice definitely is risky. For when rush orders arise or when the pressure is on quantity, an operating foreman has a tendency to sacrifice quality for quantity. Best practice dictates setting the men responsible for quantity and for quality on a par with each other and under an impartial authority.

In spite of the use of measuring instruments and control devices, infallibility of inspection almost invariably depends on competent inspectors; hence, the importance that is attached to their selection and training. An inspector should be conscientious, thorough, exacting about details, and not afraid of routine. Important too is his ability to carry out orders and instructions faithfully. Keen eyesight as well as the manual dexterity required to handle small gages and parts in inspection and to ascertain the correct feel are often important requirements. Women readily become good inspectors for they seem to be particularly adaptable to light, repetitive work and excel where nimble fingers are required.

One important point sometimes overlooked in the training of inspectors is that they should be instructed not only in the techniques of their own particular inspection operation but also in its relation to the end product. That such training is not always given is shown by the true story of a new inspector in a large plant who after a month's service was questioned as to the sort of work he did. To this question he replied, "Oh hell, there's nothing to it. All I do is put a little metal thing into a gadget and watch a pointer. If the pointer stops in one place, I put the thing in one box. If it stops in another place, I put the thing in another box. Why, it's easy." Obviously what he was inspecting, the reason for the inspection, and why the material was segregated had never been explained to this individual. Such an explanation takes but little time and may seem unimportant, yet it often spells the difference between a conscientious and a disinterested inspector.

Just as a chain is only as strong as its weakest link, so also is the chain of quality in a product only as strong as the poorest inspector—hence the stress that is usually placed on the maintenance of a high morale and degree of exactness among the inspection personnel. Adequate pay, light, airy, and clean inspection areas, inspection equipment always in good repair, intelligent supervision ready to back up the inspectors when they are right and to guide them properly when they are wrong—these are typical of the factors that maintain inspection morale.

The ability to cooperate and deal with the personnel of the manufacturing departments is an important attribute of inspection supervisors and inspectors alike. Generally, inspectors deal with people fully as much if not more of the time than they deal with inanimate equipment and material. All too often manufacturing personnel gain the impression that the primary aim of inspectors is to prevent production. A cooperative inspection organization often can do much toward promoting the main objective of quality control: that of preventing *defective* production before it occurs.

Who is responsible for quality—the operating foreman or inspectors assigned to his department? In other words, should production foremen and their subordinates be responsible for checking the quality of work coming off their machines or should inspectors representing the inspection division and assigned to floor inspection in that area properly be given the responsibility? These are questions that are in the forefront of management's thinking on the subject of quality control today. One school of thought maintains that the function of foremen is to supervise their personnel, to take the proper care of their equipment, and to achieve the quantity of output assigned to them. It is too much, this school of thought maintains, to expect foremen to spend their time gaging work. Their duty in the field of quality, once defective work is discovered by the inspectors, is simply to see that causes of error are promptly corrected. Another school of thought argues that the foremen are as responsible for quality as for quantity and that, if necessary, they should have sufficient subordinates to check regularly and at frequent intervals the quality of work right at the machines in their departments. Under such a system, the argument continues, independent inspectors should perform no floor inspection but simply check completed work as may be required for control purposes. Responsibility for defective work then rests squarely on the shoulders of the foremen involved. Actually industry seems to be about evenly divided on this question of the responsibility for quality, and no definite trends are discernible in favor of one system over the other.

The duties generally delegated to an inspection department include:

1. Authority to pass or reject all raw material, in-process material, and finished products.

2. Inspection of supplies and tools, both purchased and company-made, which in any way affect the quality of the finished product.

3. Issuance, control, and inspection of all gages, instruments, and other measuring devices for use by both inspection and production operators.

4. Supervision of work allied with or incidental to inspection, such as final cleaning or buffing operations, oiling and greasing, wrapping or packing.

5. Joint or even complete supervision of salvage of rejected work and the disposition of scrap to insure that no defective material is returned to the productive flow.

Inspection Practices and Procedures.—The following inspection practices and procedures are generally recognized as being the principal steps by which quality can be controlled through inspection:

1. *Control Raw Materials.*—The quality of raw materials is usually established through definite standards and specifications, put in writing and furnished each vendor concerned. Then as the materials are purchased, they are ordered according to specification.

However, this procedure often must be supplemented with personal contacts and consultations between purchaser and vendor as questions arise as to interpretations of a specification, or as substitutes are offered. Particularly is this close liaison between purchaser and vendor important where subcontracted parts and assemblies are involved. In such cases, it may be desirable for the purchaser to keep a resident inspector in the vendor's plant to handle such problems and to inspect the material prior to its shipment.

As material is received in the plant, all possible steps should be taken to identify each lot so that the name of the vendor, the order number, and/or date received may be known. And as far as is practicable, this identification should be retained during the production processes, particularly if a defect in the material might be revealed during such processes. Many companies wherein metal products are involved use paint of various colors for this purpose; others etch or inscribe the material with symbols; and still others key the information as to the source of the raw material into their identification cards and tickets which accompany the material through the operations. This practice of identifying raw material aids in assigning and correcting the causes of defects in that material. It makes assignable and hence controllable variables out of what otherwise would probably pass for chance variables. Furthermore, it forms a concrete basis for discussions with vendors regarding the quality of their material, particularly that which turns out not to be serviceable.

2. *Make Inspection and Production Operations as Foolproof as Possible.*—This generally means a thorough investigation into operating methods to see that the most efficient practices are instituted and followed. It involves the elimination of all assignable variables and, through the changing of methods where economically feasible, the elimination of many of the chance variables.

More specifically, such steps frequently include the elimination of eyesight and feel methods of inspecting, both by production operators checking their own work and by the regular inspectors. Inspection involving judgment on the part of any of the human senses is far from reliable. Human senses may vary with the weather, the reaction of a person's digestive system on his breakfast, his mental attitude, his like or dislike for his work, and other fully as nebulous chance variables. Tests have revealed that human inspections are on an average only 98 per cent reliable where the inspections involve large quantities checked over long periods. Thus, wherever the nature of the inspection operation permits, it is frequently desirable to substitute comparator-type instruments or other mechanical devices for the human element.

It is likewise important that operators be provided with all necessary inspection instruments at the machine or workplace. These generally should be of the same type as used in the subsequent inspection operation so that the results obtained therefrom will be comparable. It is also important in the setting of the production standard for each manufacturing operation that time be allowed for the use of such inspection instruments and, once allowed as a part of the operation, that operators be required to use these instruments regularly.

The principles of motion economy (see Chap. XVII) apply to the methods employed by inspectors as well as to those of production operators. Wherever possible, automatic gaging equipment, drop-delivery chutes, mechanical materials-handling equipment, semicircular workplaces, and the other motion-saving devices should be used.

3. *Gain Control of Quality through Strategic Location of Inspection Points.*—Much control of quality is lost or gained by the location of inspection stations in relation to the points at which defects occur.

In general, important raw materials purchased in large quantities and involving high transportation costs are most economically inspected at the vendor's plant. Wood, steel, coal, and similar materials are often inspected in this manner. Depending upon the amount of material to be shipped and the nature of the inspection, the purchaser might station a resident inspector at the vendor's plant, send out one of his inspectors when each shipment is ready, or hire some organization or individual to perform the inspection. For other less vital raw materials, of course, the most economical point of inspection is immediately after receipt in the plant of the purchaser.

The military services have followed a policy of resident inspection at the plants of their major vendors. They also make regular calls at the plants of smaller producers of military goods. The assignments of such inspectors include the inspection of raw materials and in-process work, as well as of finished products, for their adherence to the specifications established by contract.

Material in process may be inspected at each major machine or work station as a floor inspection, or it may be checked at centralized inspection stations located strategically throughout the plant, or both. *Floor inspections* by virtue of their location at the machine or in the production line minimize the material handling and are, in fact, an integral part of serialized manufacture. *Centralized inspection stations,* although frequently requiring the handling of materials over longer distances from the individual machines to the area of the nearest inspection station, do improve inspection supervision and make for better control of the output of inspectors. Regardless of which of the two methods is employed, the main objectives are to prevent a defect from being concealed (as might be the case where the next operation involves assembly or painting), to prevent the defect from affecting a subsequent operation (for example, a crack in a forging which might break tools and ruin the setup of a subsequent machining operation), and to prevent additional work from being performed on "rejectable" material.

Most finished products are inspected immediately before they are packed. As we have seen above, one of the primary purposes of inspection is to insure that the customer receives only good material, and this often can best be accomplished by a "final" inspection. As soon as the finished goods are passed as O.K., they should be at once protected against possible damage or alteration. Generally this can be accomplished by the prompt packing or boxing of the articles either for temporary storage or for immediate shipment.

Tools and gages should be inspected in the tool or gage crib immediately prior to issuance and also directly after use, the latter inspection being designed to discover any damage at once, fix the responsibility for that damage, and segregate the article for repair or discard.

4. *Establish the Minimum Amount of Inspection Consistent with the Degree of Quality Desired.*—Inspection is one of the indirect costs of doing business. It is nonproductive in the sense that it adds nothing directly to the value of the product. Wherever an inspection operation can be eliminated or the amount of inspection reduced without interfering with the control of quality, the cost of manufacturing the article in question is reduced just as surely as if an improvement in the manufacturing methods were consummated. Thus in answer to the question of how much to inspect, we can phrase the reply: The least amount to furnish the control required.

For some control requirements, 100 per cent inspection furnishes the best if not the only means of achieving that control. In many plants, 100 per cent inspection of finished goods is customary for this very reason. Also in visual inspections for finish, appearance, condition, or other surface defects, those to control dimensions and to check performance (where the test is nondestructive as in the testing of electric motors and of the calibration of thermostats)—in such cases as these 100 per cent inspection is often inevitable.

However, for other types of control, "sampling" or percentage inspection may be desirable and, in the case of destructive tests, the only procedure possible. Typical of such tests are those for longevity (electric lamps), for performance (electric fuses, ammunition), and for ultimate physical properties (tensile strength of metals, ductility of plastics, strength of welded joints, and flash points of oil products). Thus it can be seen that the nature of the inspection has a bearing on the amount of inspection required.

Furthermore, in determining how much to inspect, the nature of the product and of the particular processes involved must also be taken into consideration. An inexpensive product designed to retail say through a "five-and-dime" store will bear far less inspection expense than will a high-priced article from which the customer expects guaranteed quality. Also an enterprise making a product such as a radio tube that is "inspected" for performance by the retail sales clerk at the time of sale can be relieved of some inspection expense since the 100 per cent inspection at that point eliminates the possibility of the customer's getting a defective article.

It is well to note that articles processed on automatic machines or equipment are less susceptible to chance variables and hence require less inspection. Contrast, for example, the amount of inspection required of a part machined on a hand-operated turret lathe and that required of a similar part produced on an automatic-screw machine. In the case of the former, the chance variables introduced by the human element might make a 100 per cent inspection necessary in order that quality could be controlled. On the automatic-screw machine, many of these chance variables are removed, and a percentage inspection of the parts machined will usually show whether or not the entire lot is acceptable. Percentage or sampling inspection today leans heavily on statistical techniques and will be considered further in the section of this chapter devoted to that subject.

5. *Set Up Inspection Control by Which Defects Are Located Promptly.* Usually this can be accomplished by prompt inspection immediately following points at which variations are apt to occur. Prompt inspection aids in fixing the responsibility for the defect. It prevents the covering up of mistakes by making it impossible for an operator to spoil work without the knowledge of his superior.

Many companies prefer that their inspectors occasionally be kept waiting for work rather than permit the work to bank up ahead of inspection. Where a "float" of material is permitted to wait for inspection, it is claimed that some degree of control is lost. Operators may not be apprised of their mistakes for some time, nor may improperly operating machines be corrected, and additional defective material may be produced in the meantime. However, in this connection a word of caution might be added. It is possible to go too far in the direction of prompt inspection, for if the intervals during which inspectors wait for work become too frequent or too prolonged, there is a tendency for some of them to become lazy and to "stretch out" what work they do have.

Prompt inspection can aid in controlling quantity as well as quality. Where the articles involved are small, production operators sometimes take parts home on their person. In the case of marketable articles, resale to a "fence" may be the object. Or where the operator has scrapped some material and wishes to hide the fact from his superior, he may deposit the scrap pieces in his lunch box or other personal belongings. In fact, the pilferage problem in some industries has been so marked that at the height of one of the "scrap drives" of World War II, a pseudo-serious suggestion was advanced in one city that a pond located amidst several large metalworking plants be drained. Workers passing that pond on their way home were known to have used it as a depository for their rejected work to such an extent that, the suggestion continued, its aggregate scrap-metal content would make the draining worth while. Weigh counting or manual counting of work at key points throughout the manufacturing process as a part of the inspection routine can do much to control quantity. Furthermore, when this quantity inspection is tied in with the production-control system for the issuance of all material to the workplaces, it becomes quite difficult for material to be stolen or scrapped without the fact being made known.

6. *Control Inspection Output.*—In general there are three means by which inspection output may be controlled. The first and perhaps the most common method is that whereby a standard rate of inspection is established for each inspection element or operation. For example, it may be found that a visual examination of a particular part should be made at the rate of 700 pieces per hour, a micrometer inspection at 500 pieces per hour, etc. These standards should be definitely stated, be reasonable, and should not tend to encourage inspectors into slipshod work. The actual performance of each inspector can then be recorded over a period of time and compared with the predetermined standard. In a sense this procedure reveals an inspector's efficiency and, when this efficiency is used over a period of time as a basis for wage increases, the system is essentially one of measured daywork (see Chap. XXIV).

Occasionally one of the direct forms of wage incentives (again see Chap. XXIV) is used as a stimulus for inspection output, but unless carefully controlled, it may be a risky practice, for inspectors become so conscious of their output that quality is bound to suffer. Some concerns, rather than pay inspectors directly for quantity, have devised bonus schemes based on the percentage of defects located. Even so, any inspection on incentive wage payment requires the use of checkers or superinspectors who reinspect a percentage of the work passed by the regular inspectors just to insure that their work is satisfactory. One electric-clock company has found it practical to pay a bonus to its packers for every clock discovered in packing with a visual defect that has escaped its regular line of inspectors.

The third method of controlling inspection output—one which has gained wide favor in serialized manufacture—is that whereby the inspection operation is geared directly into the production line. By setting a standard rate of output for that inspection and balancing out the inspection station against the desired output for the line, as are all other operations in the line (see Chap. X), inspection output is thus automatically regulated.

7. *Set Up a Standard Procedure for Judging Slightly Off-color Material.*—The disposition of borderline material or that where the product quality is just outside the tolerance is often a debatable issue. Should the article be automatically relegated to the scrap heap or can it be passed if the defect is deemed to be so slightly beyond the tolerance as not to be serious? Some quality-control men contend that if inspectors

are permitted to use judgment and to pass some slightly off-color material, the standards and specifications that have been set up for that material are of no avail. If slightly off-color material is satisfactory, it is argued, why not broaden the tolerances and then adhere to them?

The practice of exceeding tolerances can become dangerous unless skillfully handled, for otherwise inspectors tend to disregard them entirely. Consequently many companies require as standard inspection practice that regular inspectors set aside all off-color material, thus insuring that they pass only material definitely within tolerances. The material set aside is then subsequently reinspected by a special inspector qualified by his knowledge of the article and its application to pass or reject it depending upon the importance of the defect to the ultimate service and to the fabrication and assembly of the article. Regular inspectors, if they are permitted to know of the subsequent passing of some of the material they have rejected, should be made to understand the nature of the reinspection and the fact that their judgment is not thereby being questioned. Unless this is done, the morale of the inspection force—an important factor in the maintenance of quality—is bound to be undermined. Also, before any slightly off-color material is sent to a customer, it may be desirable to advise the customer of the nature of the minor defect and to ask his consent to ship the material.

STATISTICAL TECHNIQUES

When at the mid-century mark we contemplate the advances in management technology made since the turn of the century, we are impressed by the fact that the application of statistical techniques to the field of quality control has been one of the leading advances of this period. While many statisticians and quality-control engineers have contributed to this advance, it was fathered in 1924 by Dr. Walter A. Shewhart of the Bell Telephone Laboratories. A few years later through a cooperative program between the Bell Laboratories and the Western Electric Company, practical shop techniques were perfected. Thus much of the work on statistical quality control was performed over 25 years ago, yet not until the 1940's did industry in general start using the techniques. Perhaps this lag in application can be traced in part to lack of knowledge on the part of management as to what statistics could do in this field. Also, industry lacked personnel versed in basic statistics, and without such specialists, no application of the techniques was then possible. However, in the 1940's when workable shop tables eliminating most of the statistical calculations were published and when at the same time certain charting devices were popularized, statistical techniques really "caught on" in industry. They brought startling reductions in inspection costs and permitted more fundamental control of quality than had previously been possible. For the future, as the techniques are improved and additional applications developed, statistics promises even further to liberate quality control from the bonds of empiricism.

How Statistical Techniques Are Used.—The applications of statistical techniques are many, and only a few will be discussed here to illustrate their possibilities. For example, in measuring a quality characteristic of a particular item, a company usually wishes to know whether or not the present level of the quality is satisfactory. If not, and if some specific action on the process is taken to change the quality, the question then arises whether the change is the result of the action or comes out of the chance variables inherent in the process. In other words, is the change significant? The *frequency distribution curve* (see Fig. 90) based on the *laws of probability* [2] is used to shed some light on these problems by indicating present level of quality, the stability of the process, and whether or not it is capable of producing to the tolerances set, *i.e.*, whether or not the chance variables are too great. Then as action is taken to change the quality, a statistical technique termed *analysis of variance* can be applied to test for the significance of such changes. The effect of assignable variables on the quality is thus indicated. It should be pointed out here that such statistical tests merely suggest significance—they do not offer conclusive proof. They must always be used along with other evidence in judging quality results.

In the field of sampling or percentage inspection, the size of the sample, the probability that the sample will reveal the true condition of the entire lot (known technically as the population), the risks assumed by a consumer or producer that a lot of merchandise will or will not be acceptable or that not more than a specified portion of the lots supplied by the producer will be unacceptable to the consumer, based on the sampling system—these are typical of the answers that can be supplied by statistics.[3] The tools used in constructing these answers are available in published form,[4] and once the terminology and basic principles are mastered, they can be easily applied by mathematically minded shop personnel.

It is important to remember that, where sampling is involved, some

---

[2] For further amplification of laws of probability, see SKF case problem, p. 410, or any standard text on basic statistics.

[3] For an actual industrial application of sampling techniques, see SKF case problem, p. 410.

[4] One source: Dodge, and Romig, "Sampling Inspection Tables," New York: John Wiley & Sons, Inc., 1944.

defects invariably are passed. Only 100 per cent inspection can even attempt to catch all the bad pieces, and even here, because of the reliance on the human element, some defects will be passed. Also in any percentage inspection, for proper control the sample must be selected at random. Liquids are seldom homogeneous throughout. Tools machining metal parts

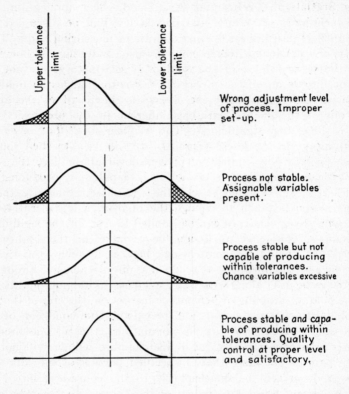

Fig. 90.—Application of frequency-distribution curves to indicate whether quality is under control.

are gradually subject to wear; grinding wheels that finish precision parts continually break down. Thus samples taken only from one part of the entire lot are not always representative of that lot. A representative sample from a tote pan of parts is one that contains pieces selected at random from the top, middle, and bottom of that pan. Similarly, good metallurgical practice calls for the testing of a steel billet by the selection of samples from the top, middle, and bottom of that billet. Also, tests on coal for heat-unit properties usually require repeated quartering processes to insure that a representative sample is obtained.

Randomization is likewise subject to the honesty of production operators. In more than one instance on record, a not-too-honest operator observing that inspectors were checking only material on top of each box, has succeeded in getting defective material past those inspectors by simply placing the rejects at the bottom of the box.

Advantages of Statistics.—From the foregoing, certain advantages of using statistical techniques for controlling quality are now discernible. A reduction of inspection costs is realized through sampling, through elimination of needless inspections, and through knowledge that quality is under control. Proper tolerances for the process and, conversely, whether the process is proper for the tolerances both can be indicated. Definite assurance of incoming or outgoing quality is obtainable. Last but certainly not least, when statistics are teamed up with control charts (see below) to furnish a running record of quality, rejections and scrap are reduced, impending process trouble can be avoided, and needless interruptions in production (*e.g.*, machine adjustments when the work is well within control) are automatically eliminated.

INSPECTION RECORDS

Standard inspection records start with inspection cards or tickets showing the quantity inspected and the number rejected, together with the individual reasons therefor. These cards or tickets are customarily made out in multiple, and copies may be supplied to the foreman or superintendent concerned, to the production operator responsible for the work, to the production department for posting to production records, to the accounting department for payroll purposes, and to the inspection division as a basis for its records. When these cards are summarized and analyzed over a period of time, they indicate points in the manufacturing process at which control has been breaking down. Assignable causes of past defects can be located by this analysis, responsibility for them fixed, and their recurrence prevented. Furthermore, points in the process at which there has been a dearth or an excess of inspection are indicated. Finally, this analysis can prove or disprove the manufacturing practicability of the product design, reveal quality standards which have been set too high, and show up processes that are set to a point of excellence where they are uneconomical to the manufacturer. This sort of investigation, which makes use of past records for future control, frequently employing the statistical techniques described above, can be labeled *quality research*.

Where large, highly complicated, or technical products are involved, it is frequently advisable to retain all inspection records, keyed to the individual product by serial number, for a definite period so as to fix responsibility and to locate sources of trouble that may subsequently develop in the field.

Control Charts.—These charts rode into popularity in the 1940's along with statistical techniques. They are a form of inspection record that advises of the need for investigating conditions, processes, or workers for causes of defective work beyond that caused by chance variables. Stated another way, these charts keep a running record right at the machine or on the job to indicate when production is driving down the

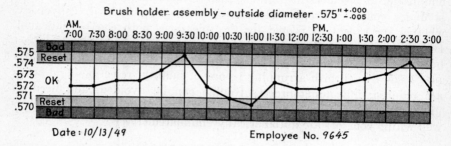

FIG. 91.—One type of control chart used at the machine to keep the process under control by showing when to reset the machine. Note that machine was reset following the readings taken at 9:30, 11:00, and 2:30.

paved road of good quality, when it is wandering off onto the dangerous soft shoulders of borderline quality, and when it definitely is in the ditch and out of control. Control charts are used on the spot for testing tight tolerances, selecting preferred vendors, clarifying disputes between vendor and customer, and improving process quality (by the prompt location of assignable variables). Applied to a specific machine, they show the effects of tool wear, point to changes in methods or equipment, and indicate when to adjust or reset the machine. One type of control chart is shown in Fig. 91.

SALVAGE METHODS

Up to this point we have been concerned with *prevention:* preventing defective goods from reaching the customer, preventing manufacturing trouble caused by defects, and preventing the defects themselves through better control. Salvage, however, deals with the *rehabilitation* of defective goods after they have been located and segregated. Through a careful study of the possibilities of salvage, much rejected material that would otherwise be relegated to the scrap heap can be put to useful purpose. Furthermore, the salvage of rejected production materials is a major economic problem, and the savings resulting from a thorough salvaging program are often of considerable significance to the cost of manufacturing.

In general, there are three possible approaches to the salvage of material which has been rejected:

a. The defect may be corrected or the material itself reworked to conform with the tolerances established. Such material after a careful inspection to insure that the defect has been eliminated may then be returned to the production flow or shipped as grade *A* material, as the case may be. For example, oversized metal parts can usually be reworked down to size, parts not properly painted can be given another coat of paint, small blow-holes in castings can often be filled by welding, etc.

b. Material that cannot readily be corrected and sold as first-grade merchandise can sometimes be disposed of at slightly lower price as "seconds." Thus are second-grade shoes and clothing as well as numerous other articles marketed through "bargain basements," and some second-quality automotive parts distributed by repair and service dealers for replacement parts.

c. Material that cannot be salvaged by either of the foregoing methods usually can be sold for scrap value of the basic raw material from which it is made. Frequently finished goods that are scrapped as defective and sold for scrap value to a scrap broker find their way back into the market and are offered at cut-rate prices in competition with first-class material. In such cases, it is quite important that the article, before being sold for scrap, be defaced or in some other fashion destroyed. For example, metal products are frequently crushed or burned, cloth products torn or cut into small pieces, etc.

The subject of industrial salvage is covered further in Chap. XVIII.

INSPECTION DEVICES

Glaucon, replying to Socrates in Plato's "Republic," is reported to have said, "Yes, the tools which would teach men their own use would be beyond price." Today this baffling reply is practically translated into reality by modern precision gages and measuring devices, for through the use of such instruments, any operator, however inexperienced, can be taught the most delicate and precise inspection operations. If we had to depend entirely upon human feel and eyesight, precision inspection would be a myth. Even inspections of only moderate exactness might take inspectors months and perhaps years to acquire the proper degree of accuracy. In fact, our high-volume precision manufacture is possible today largely as the result of the great strides that have been made in recent years on the instruments for inspection.

Types of Inspection Devices. 1. *Inspection Gages for Dimensional Control.*—Particularly has this progress been noteworthy in the field of inspection gages.   A *gage* may be defined as a device for investigating the dimensional fitness of a mechanical element in relation to its predeter-

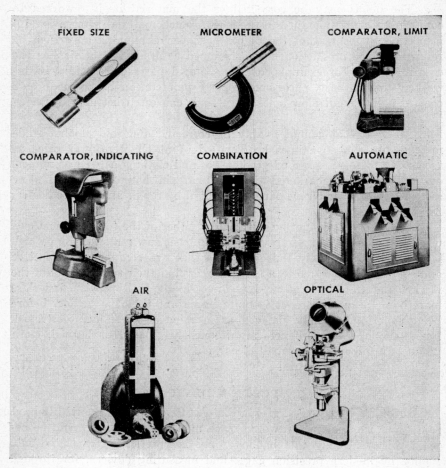

FIXED SIZE   MICROMETER   COMPARATOR, LIMIT

COMPARATOR, INDICATING   COMBINATION   AUTOMATIC

AIR   OPTICAL

Fig. 92.—Types of gages. (*Courtesy of Sheffield Corporation.*)

mined dimensional standards.   Figure 92 shows several of the more common types of gages.

Typical of the *fixed-size gages* are the plug gage (shown in Fig. 92) for investigating bores or internal holes, and the ring gage, which as its name implies is simply a ring of known size for checking external diameters of round articles.   Any fixed-size gage is in a sense a single-purpose gage. It can be used to check only one dimension, internal or external, and is declared obsolete when a change is made in that dimension. Its surfaces are subject to wear each time the gage is used, and its dimensions are not always capable of being corrected. Furthermore, such a gage does not always tell the whole story. For example, a plug gage usually will not show whether the hole is bell-mouthed, out of round, or has an irregular diameter. Fixed gages require of the inspector a sense of feel and tend to jam where tolerances are narrow. Since fixed-size gages never reveal exact dimensions, they are generally paired as "go" and "no-go" gages made to the upper and lower limits and are designed to show whether a part is within those limits.

The *micrometer* gage (see Fig. 92), in which category are included outside, inside, and depth micrometers, was the first of our modern, adjustable precision gages. Invented in 1848 by a Frenchman named Jean Palmer and first made in this country in 1877 by J. R. Brown and L. Sharpe,[5] the micrometer rapidly gained favor as the best instrument of precision inspection then available, and its use became practically universal. It relies on the screw principle for magnification, one revolution of the thimble advancing the spindle 0.025 inch. Graduations on the thimble and barrel enable readings to be taken to the nearest 0.001 inch, and on some micrometers a vernier permits readings approximately to the nearest 0.0001 inch. Although the micrometer has today been largely outmoded as a tool of quantity inspection, it is still widely used at machines and for precision toolroom work. The micrometer possesses flexibility in that it can be used to check a range of sizes and is useful for inspecting a variety of dimensions where the volume of production does not warrant setting up special-purpose gages. Furthermore, compensating adjustments can be made quickly as wear develops.

Comparator-type gages are available in a variety of types. Some show only whether or not the article falls within the established limits; others indicate exact dimensions. Still others can be arranged in multiple to check a combination of dimensions at one reading, or they can be made the brains of devices that automatically inspect and segregate parts according to size. All comparator gages make use of some sort of magnification device, the more common types of which are shown in Fig. 93.

Among the comparator gages finding wide application is the precision dial indicator which, operating on the principle of a rack and pinion together with levers, can be obtained to read accurately to a fraction of 0.0001 inch. Sheffield gages employing the reed mechanism (see the comparator-limit and comparator-indicating gages, Fig. 92) are comparatively new and are remarkably fast and accurate. Gagings have

[5] "Shop Theory," Henry Ford Trade School, 1942, Section on Micrometers, p. 37.

been made with such instruments to the nearest half of 0.0001 inch at the rate of 3,000 per hour. Furthermore, the reed mechanism does away with the need for gears, knife-edges, and levers which admit errors through backlash and wear. In fact, with such an instrument, 130,000,000 gagings

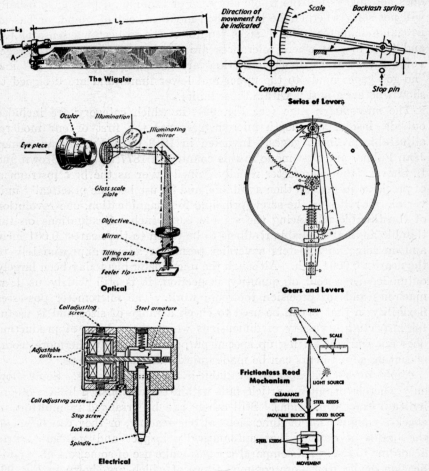

Fig. 93.—Magnification devices. Device in lower right-hand corner is the Sheffield reed mechanism. A movable block is joined to a fixed block by horizontal alloy-steel reeds. Two vertical reeds, one from each block, are joined together and extended to a pointer. Vertical movement of the movable block in the gaging operation tends to cause the two vertical reeds to slip past each other. However, being joined at the end, the reeds instead of slipping cause the pointer extension to swing in an arc. This motion of the pointer is further magnified by a light beam operating through a series of lenses that project the motion on a scale in the form of a shadow. Such a "shadow gage" is the comparator-indicating gage shown in Fig. 97. (*Courtesy of Sheffield Corporation.*)

have been made without perceptible wear. Gages employing the reed principle can be used for internal as well as external readings and for the electric control of sizing instruments or machines (see Fig. 92).

Comparator gages can also be used in combination for multiple readings. For example, a *combination gage* to check aircraft-engine pistons has been developed which inspects 11 dimensions simultaneously. A mas-

FIG. 94.—Automatic machine control. The gaging head is often mounted on a machine, in this case a grinder, and arranged to stop the machine when the work has been brought to size. It may be used to control either external or internal diameters. (*Courtesy of Sheffield Corporation.*)

ter amber light indicates that all dimensions are within tolerance. Pistons over size or under size in one or more dimensions flash a green or red master light, respectively, and individual lights reveal which dimension is beyond the tolerance permitted. Interchangeable heads can be inserted on such gages for flexibility in checking different-sized parts.

Automatic gages are frequently practical for special high-production applications. For example, a gage developed during World War II for inspecting 50-millimeter shells checked automatically the chamber depth, diameter of ejector, depth of primer, head diameter, over-all length, and the head thickness. The instrument was hopper-fed, and each dimension was checked in sequence. Rejects were ejected at the proper stations, thus automatically sorting out the defective material. Furthermore, as a part of the inspection, the good pieces were then weighed and those under weight likewise ejected. This entire process took place at the rate of 3,500 pieces per hour per gage. Yet such gages as this undoubtedly furnish us with a mere preview of things to come in the line of automatic gaging equipment.

Any comparator-type gage, as its name implies, must be compared or calibrated against some fixed standard. *Gage blocks* are commonly

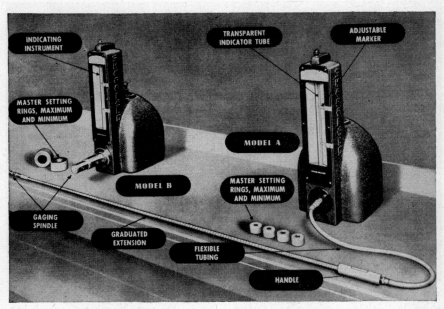

Fig. 95.—The "Precisionaire." An air gage of the flow type for checking internal diameters, taper, and out-of-round conditions in long or small bores (such as rifle barrels) or relatively inaccessible holes in assemblies which cannot be brought to the gage. (*Courtesy of Sheffield Corporation.*)

used for this purpose. These blocks are rectangular pieces of alloy steel, hardened, ground, seasoned, and accurately finished. The well-known Johansson gage blocks are produced accurate to 0.000002 inch. A full set consists of 81 blocks which can be used in combination with each other to produce some 120,000 different-sized gages from 0.2000 to approximately 12 inches in gradations of 0.0001 inch.

One extremely interesting gage development for dimensional control is the *air gage* (see Fig. 95). It operates on the principle that the volume of air flowing through an aperture under constant pressure varies directly with the size of that aperture. In the air gage, the aperture is represented by the clearance between the inside wall of the hole being gaged and the spindle of the instrument which contains an air outlet. The greater the clearance between the fixed-size spindle and the hole gaged, the greater the volume of air that escapes. The air gage is simple in construction, is surprisingly accurate, and there is virtually nothing to wear out. It can be used to check both internal and external dimensions.

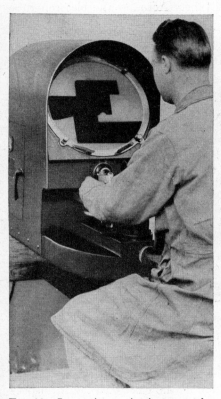

Fig. 96.—Inspecting an intricate part by comparison at 62½ magnification on a bench-type optical comparator. (*Courtesy of Jones & Lamson Machine Company.*)

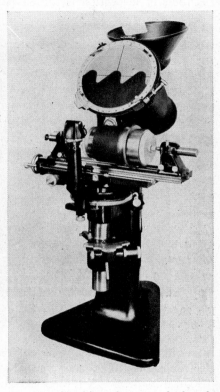

Fig. 97.—Checking the ground threads at the base of an air-cooled airplane-engine cylinder barrel on a pedestal-type optical comparator. (*Courtesy of Jones & Lamson Machine Company.*)

Another valuable comparator instrument for dimensional control is the *optical comparator* of the type made by the Jones & Lamson Company (see Fig. 96). A flexible and accurate instrument, it is widely used for checking the profiles of exterior shapes and forms, for measuring the dimensions of contours, and for other similar applications.

Not only has progress been made in the line of dimensional-control instruments but the materials from which such gages are made also have undergone marked improvements. Various sintered-carbide plug gages, gage points, and gaging surfaces have been developed and are popular because they are extremely long wearing. Chrome-plated gage surfaces are now likewise in favor for their wear-resistant qualities.

2. *Electronic Inspection Devices.*—One of the newest and most promising tools of inspection is the electron tube. Actually the electron tube

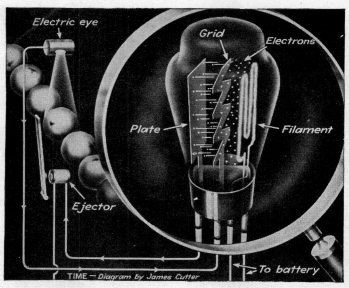

FIG. 98.—How fruit can be inspected and sorted electronically. *(From Time, Feb. 8, 1943, p. 48.)*

is as old as radio itself,[6] but only in very recent years has the field of electronics been broadened and adapted to industrial inspection.

Figure 98 depicts a typical application of the electron tube in inspection: to check the quality of citrus fruits. Electrons from the filament to the plate in the electron tube are stimulated by faint electrical impulses traveling to the grid from the electric eye. The electric eye in this case is made immune to the correct color of healthy oranges. When it "sees" a defective orange, it sends a slight current to the grid. This impulse steps up the current from the filament to the plate and causes a magnet to operate an ejector device that instantly sends that orange out of the packing line.[7]

Leading fruit packers now use such electronic methods for protecting

---

[6] In fact, the electron tube is often erroneously referred to as the radio tube.

[7] Adapted from *Time*, Feb. 8, 1943, p. 48.

not only the public but also their own investment as well. Fifty per cent of the fruit mistakenly discarded by California packers with other inspection methods has been found to be in A–1 condition by such devices, resulting in a saving to these packers alone of several millions of dollars each year.

Similar electronic devices are used to test milk for pasteurization, gage the thickness of paint, match colors and finishes, and to measure, control, or record pressure, temperature, humidity, smoke, and acidity. Automatic electronic sorters reject defective oversize, undersize, and off-color articles. Furthermore, the electron tube can be used to inspect the inside of articles which the eye cannot possibly see. Still other electronic devices convert the noise made in rotating devices (motors, bearings, etc.) into graphic displays of frequency and amplitude of the causal vibrations and inspect the lips of bottles and jars faster and better than the human inspectors formerly employed.

Electronics is playing an important part in another field as well—that of *industrial radiography* or the process by which the interiors of metals, welds, castings, armor plate, and molds are photographed by the radiation of rays of short wave length. Actually this process involves an adaptation of the surgical X-ray instrument to locate metal defects instead of human ailments. However, vastly more powerful equipment is required. Present 1,000,000-volt X-ray units are capable of penetrating and revealing cracks, holes, or other metallurgical defects through 8 inches of steel. The University of Chicago's new 100,000,000-electron-volt betatron makes it possible to photograph through foot-thick slabs of steel. A competitor of electronics in the field of radiography is radium and its gamma rays. These can penetrate steel to similar depths and possess the added advantage of radiating equally in all directions. Thus it is possible to photograph large sections as well as a number of pieces of work at a time if they are located in a circle about the radium. Furthermore, radium photography equipment is readily portable and can be brought to the work. Although radium has been used for this purpose only a few years, this field is now second only to that of cancer treatment as a market for radium.

3. *Other Types of Inspection Instruments.*—Actually the range of inspection devices is limited only by man's imagination. The instruments discussed below, far from all-inclusive, are simply representative of those now in use. Several *special-purpose gages* are shown in Fig. **99**. Figure **100** pictures a special-purpose gage for sighting rifles by optical methods. The final inspection of fluorescent lamps is likewise performed on a special-purpose instrument (see Fig. 101).

A widely accepted inspection technique for disclosing hidden flaws in ferrous metals is the *Magnaflux device*. This is a commercial process by which finely divided iron filings are distributed over a part that has been magnetized electrically. The iron particles arrange themselves in a symmetrical pattern on a surface thus magnetized. Wherever a flaw

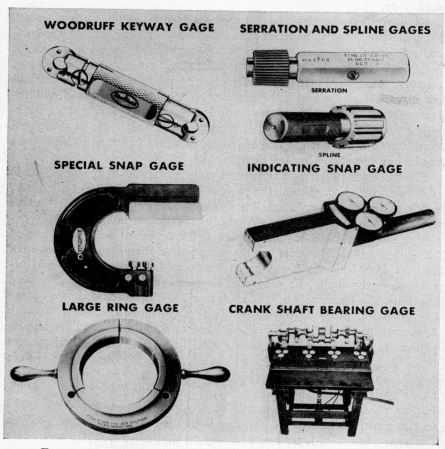

FIG. 99.—Special-purpose gages. (*Courtesy of Sheffield Corporation.*)

occurs in the steel, be it an inclusion, carbide, or crack, a break occurs in the lines of magnetic flux which in turn interrupts the pattern of the filings. Thus the flaw is readily disclosed. A similar process using a fluorescent penetrant and developing powder has been perfected for inspecting nonmagnetic materials under "black light." *Magnetic testing devices* have been developed to inspect the hardness of steel parts and to show up cracked articles. The testing of stressed parts is now accom-

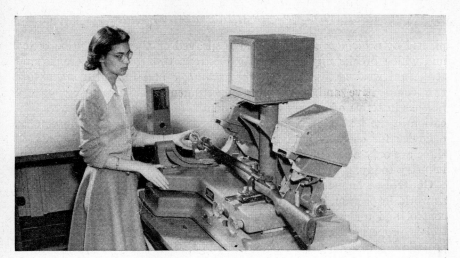

Fig. 100.—The General Electric optical rifle-sighting gage. Saving 13 rounds of ammunition formerly used in sighting each gun and permitting a girl to do a job in 2 minutes that formerly took two men 4 minutes, this optical gage "fires" light rays at a mirrored target. The rays, magnified 25 times, are mirrored to a ground-glass screen in front of the operator. The rear gun sight, similarly magnified, is adjusted until the gun is properly sighted. (*Courtesy of General Electric Photo News Service, No. 297, May 15, 1943.*)

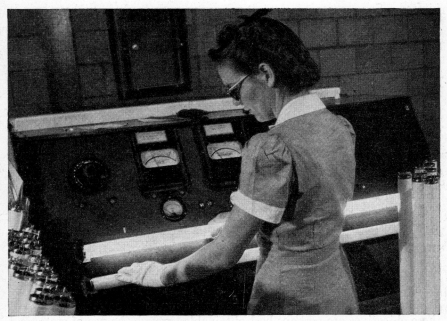

Fig. 101.—Another typical special-purpose inspection instrument. For testing the electrical characteristics of fluorescent lamps at the Fairmont Works of the Westinghouse Electric and Manufacturing Company.

plished by a *lacquer coating* which is sprayed on the article to be tested and which breaks up under localized stress, thus revealing cracks and structural weaknesses. The *surface analyzer* and the *profilometer* are two competitive and widely used instruments for measuring surface finishes in terms of microinches (millionths of an inch). Finding application in the textile, dye, and paint industries is the *spectrophotometer,* a device for checking and matching colors. Yet, such instruments as these are only a few of the many types of inspection instruments used in industry today.

Control of Inspection Devices.—All inspection devices whether used as work, inspection, or master gages must be under systematic inventory control and undergo periodic inspection. As already noted, such control is properly the function of the inspection department. The usual procedure is to issue gages from enclosed gage cribs only to operators and inspectors presenting gage tickets or job cards properly authenticated. Each gage may then be charged out to the employee, either through the use of a ticket-record system or by means of a metal tool check.

Good practice dictates that gages be checked at least once each shift— and in the case of some gages even more frequently. The "bunking" of gages by employees in drawers or at machines should be rigidly prohibited. Some companies catalogue every gage to find out how long it takes to wear off-limits. On gages subject to progressive wear, if the exact dimensions of each are recorded at every check-in, as wear approaches the fixed limit, the tool-stores department can be advised so that it can plan for repair or replacement.

SUMMARY

The foregoing material has been concerned with the principles and techniques by which the variables in a manufacturing process are controlled to achieve the degree of quality desired. Involved are not only the setting of the necessary standards of product quality but also the establishing of an organization and the procedures for sufficient inspection and control to maintain those standards effectively.

Several particulars stand out as worthy of emphasis in this brief review. Inspection, a necessary yet costly evil, should be reduced to a minimum consistent with a realization of the quality required. Competitive conditions today demand that an enterprise *know* when its products are of a satisfactory quality level—not too good, not below par. Also an enterprise wants to keep its scrap pile as low as possible. Production interruptions because of quality failure must be minimized. All these objectives are perhaps best obtainable through the use of statistical techniques and control charts. Backed up by the great interest and rapid rate of adoption of these tools today, we can fairly state that they are the most useful implements currently available for getting quality really under control.

There is a gradual but definite metamorphosis from manual to mechanized inspection. Greater speed, reliability, and accuracy are almost invariably obtained where mechanical methods can be substituted for the human element. Particularly is this true where specialized, automatic inspection devices are applicable. The field of electronics alone has tremendous possibilities and of itself may radically change inspection methods. For even though electronics applied to industrial inspection is still in its infancy, already its uses are legion. Furthermore, it is quite conceivable that in the future, automatic inspection devices may customarily be installed as an integral part of many production machines. Thus parts emerging from such machines will be automatically inspected and segregated. Truly it may be said that in the development of inspection equipment, industry has to date only scratched the surface.

CASE PROBLEMS

Establishing Inspection Procedures

A Co.

The A Co., a well-known coffee-processing firm, makes use of a weekly management inspection to check the quality of its coffee as passed by the regular inspectors. A laboratory representative collects cases of coffee at random in the company's shipping department and tests them in the laboratory. The report is sent directly to top management.

B Co.

The following printed statement is enclosed with each new deck of plastic playing cards manufactured by the B Co.:

I personally have inspected this deck of cards and found them to pass our rigid standards. In the event of any claim, I would very much appreciate your following the instructions on the guarantee card and sending your letter marked to my attention. Thank you.

Hazel (Signed)

C Co.

In the machining operations at the C Co. use is made of a system of double tolerances. The tolerance permitted machine operators is shown on the blueprint with which they work. Inspection or "secondary" tolerances which permit an additional leeway are shown on the working blueprint with a code letter.   Operators work on piecework and are paid only for pieces they produce which are within their work tolerances. However, if owing to the carelessness of the operator a part is machined slightly off size but falls within the secondary tolerance, the inspectors have the right to pass the part instead of scrapping it.   The theory behind this procedure is that parts passed under the secondary tolerance may give trouble and have to be scrapped at a subsequent machining or assembly operation.   In effect, the company is gambling that such off-size parts will turn out to be acceptable.

Preparatory Question

In each of the foregoing three cases, comment on the inspection practices followed.   Indicate whether or not they are effective, and suggest any difficulties that might arise from them.

Statistical Methods in the Control of Quality

SKF Industries, Inc.[8]

SKF Industries with its four plants in the Philadelphia area produce ball and roller bearings ranging in size from those 4 feet in diameter, weighing 3,800 pounds, and anchoring the central shaft of an armor-plate mill, to those ½ inch in diameter, weighing 0.05 ounce, and acting as pivots for a microscope lens.   Regardless of size, antifriction bearings must support the shaft or other moving part to give it the desired freedom of rotation without wobble or other eccentricities.   Thus, their manufacture requires much high-precision work supported by a close control of quality.   The importance of this last-named factor is shown by the fact that quality control at SKF is responsible for 40 per cent of its total man-hours.

SKF places considerable reliance on statistics in the control of quality. The system in use in its plants consists of two parts: (1) the Shewhart "average" and "dispersion" charts and (2) the Universal Double Sampling Plan, statistical tables that show a short cut to sampling, developed by Shewhart's Bell Laboratories colleagues, Harold F. Dodge and Harry G. Romig.   The Dodge-Romig tables derive from the capricious laws of probability, first discovered in games of chance and later endowed with respectability by a long line of mathematicians.

The "expectancy" calculations, as worked out in abstruse equations by Messrs. Dodge and Romig, yield the same result as if they had actually taken, say, 970

[8] The following material has been reprinted by special permission of the editors of *Fortune Magazine*, from the October, 1943, SKF Case History.

white balls and 30 black balls, mixed them in a bowl, and drawn out any number more than 30, counting the number of each color. This procedure, when repeated, say, 100 times, would show the black balls recurring nearly 3 per cent of the time; the more tests that are made, the nearer the average will come to the exact percentage of black balls. However, in any single draw all 30 black balls may appear, or none at all; in terms of quality control this would be the same as 30 defects or none.

By the same token, quality cannot be assessed from a single sample; in short, when a customer inspects a lot of goods (white and black balls) he cannot be sure that the lot is acceptable merely because a sample he chooses at random is without defects (as if it consisted only of white balls). In its disproportionate lack of defects, this sample reflects a probability error. But the frequency with which such errors occur can be determined by the mathematics of probability.

The risk of error for the customer will vary according to the proportion of defects (black balls) to the whole (black and white balls together). The producer is up against a similar problem since a lot is accepted upon the basis of a sample that is expected to have no more than a certain percentage of defects. But it might happen that a single sample from a particular lot would contain a preponderance of defects (much more than the 3 per cent of black balls). The lot would therefore be rejected—even though the over-all production it represented were running at a satisfactory quality level. However, over the long pull, the effect of this caprice is corrected. While the customer will get more defects in some lots, he will get less in others; so that his total purchase will not contain more than the guaranteed limit of defects. The producer, on the other hand, can always reinspect his rejected lots 100 per cent, sorting good from bad, to rectify the disproportion of defects, or black balls to white.

The Dodge-Romig tables, as used at SKF and elsewhere, guide the process inspector in choosing a sample size that will (1) provide a stipulated degree of protection, such as not permitting more than 2 per cent of defectives in the outgoing quality, and (2) do this with the smallest possible personnel.

The tables have been worked out for the inspectors so that they do not have to concern themselves with the necessary mathematical calculations.

A process inspector at SKF checking steel balls of a certain size finds himself, for example, with a lot of 1,400 after the lapping operation, before discharging them from his section.

He knows that the cost, engineering, and quality-control departments have guaranteed to the customer that the average quantity will contain no more than 0.1 per cent defects; this is called the Average Outgoing Quality Limit (AOQL). From his daily experience he sees that the process average, or average of defects, has been running at 0.03 per cent. He refers to his Dodge-Romig tables, which under these conditions, prescribe a total sample of 670 balls to be divided into two groups, the first of 430 and the second of 240. If no defects are found when he goes over the 430 group, the entire lot of 1,400 is acceptable. But if one ball out of the 430 has one defect, he has to inspect the second group of 240. If out of the total sample of 670 only one defect is discovered, he can let the lot go; but if he finds two, it is unacceptable. He reports this to the production foreman, and search for the root of the trouble, whether in the steel, or machine, or the operator, is promptly begun. (The tighter the AOQL, the larger the sample size must be. If, in the above case, the AOQL had been 2 per cent instead of 0.1 per cent, a sampling of only 70 balls, 33 in the first group and 37 in the second, would have been indicated.)

WESTINGHOUSE ELECTRIC AND MANUFACTURING COMPANY [9]

During World War II, the East Springfield, Mass., division of the Westinghouse Electric and Manufacturing Company pioneered the manufacture of a fuse used in aerial bombs consisting largely of screw-machine parts of steel, aluminum, and brass, two small gears, a pinion, and a few punch-press parts.

. . . Statistical methods (were employed) . . . in the control (of) parts . . . (inspections) to avoid 100 per cent inspection operations . . . (for most pieces). With this method . . . (it was found possible to) predict whether any pieces of a given lot (would) fall outside the preestablished limits and if so, what percentage. Whether any pieces outside the specified limits were permissible depend(ed) on circumstances surrounding a particular case. Each piece . . . (was) studied from the point of view to establish . . . (its relative importance). . . . (It was found that the parts to an assembly, or individual dimensions on the parts), divide themselves naturally into four broad classifications as follows:

1. Important parts or dimensions, for which no subsequent check is available. Whenever a dimension or part is vital to the proper functioning of the completed device and subsequent quality checks will not determine the correctness of the piece, every effort must be made to detect defective pieces at the source and prevent their use. In these cases, 100 per cent inspection is required, and it should preferably be of such a type as to minimize the possibility of human element error.

2. Important dimensions or parts, errors in which will not be detected by subsequent operations here but which will definitely be detected by later operations prior to use. In cases of this sort, the shipment of incorrect parts involves inconvenience and expense but does not involve inoperative equipment in the field. Defective pieces used must be held to a minimum, but the importance is clearly not so great as in the first case. A limiting percentage of defects has been tentatively set as 1 per cent, and the actual percentage is materially less than this.

3. Important dimensions, errors which will be detected during assembly operations or later quality checks. Here the disadvantage of sending to the assembly

[9] Adapted from Quality Control in Bomb Fuze Manufacture, article by A. L. Atherton, Manager Quality Control, Westinghouse Electric and Manufacturing Company, East Springfield, Mass., in *Steel*, Jan. 19, 1942.

section parts that fall outside the acceptable tolerance limits is purely economic. The defective pieces will not find their way into the completed product. In these cases, the percentage of defects which is tolerable is determined by economic calculation for each piece and, generally speaking, it falls into the vicinity of 2 to 3 per cent. Holding the percentage lower increases the cost of inspection in the machining division more than is justified by the saving in the assembly operation.

4. Unimportant dimensions. When a surface "fits air," no real harm results from failure to meet the specified dimensions. Here, the percentage of parts that can properly be used, even though outside of the drawing tolerance, is merely a matter of what we mean by the "standards of good workmanship." Here a total of 5 per cent defects, if they are not extreme, is not unreasonable.

Preparatory Question

What specific advantages and disadvantages do you see in the statistical methods used by SKF Industries, Inc.? By Westinghouse Electric and Manufacturing Company?

CHAPTER XVII

METHODS ANALYSIS AND CONTROL

Why Consider Methods Improvement?—Whenever an industrial enterprise ceases to move forward, it does not stand still but slips rapidly into a decline, losing ground not only in comparison with all its competitors but also in contrast to its own peak of attainment. The Industrial Revolution which started in 1769–1770 is not yet over!

Modern industry constantly studies its methods to reduce costs to a minimum, to improve the product where possible, to simplify work, and to standardize production methods for uniformity of output, accuracy of fit, balance of related activities, and ease in interchanging operators.[1] We are separating motion study from time study, which is treated in Chap. XXIV, because methods analysis can be used to advantage in companies that do not employ time studies either for wage payment or for cost and production estimating. Any operation or product of industry can be studied for improvement, but the operations on which a piece-rate price is to be set must be improved and standardized before the price is set.

Origin of Methods Analysis.—The modern search for better methods originated as part of the scientific-management movement described in Chap. VI. There were many facets to the integrated application of the experimental method to business management by such men as Taylor, Gantt, and Thompson, but we are concerned here with only the methods side. Taylor, whose name is used as a synonym for Scientific Management, was an assistant foreman in a steel-plant machine shop who tried to decide on a fair day's work for his men. He found that all of them worked differently and that the methods used by some were more effective than those used by others. He gradually developed by research, standardization, control, and cooperation what seemed to be the best method and taught it to his men. The results were so spectacular that Taylor rose to chief engineer of his plant in a period of only six years. He then became a consultant and trained a whole generation of other scientific managers, who in turn originated industrial engineering as we know it today.[2] One of his 20-year-long experiments enabled him to develop the

---

[1] These efforts are called *methods analysis, motion study,* and *work simplification* almost interchangeably.

[2] For more details on these early developments see the following biographies: Frank B. Copley, "F. W. Taylor," New York: Harper & Brothers, 1923; L. P. Alford,

first high-speed tool steel (Taylor-White) at Bethlehem Steel Company.

To Frank B. Gilbreth and Lillian M. Gilbreth goes the credit for the origin of *motion study* through emphasis upon the nature of movements.

Ask yourself:

"If this were my business, what could I do to...

ELIMINATE waste?

COMBINE forms, routines, or functions?

COORDINATE operations?

REDESIGN machines or equipment?

PREVENT accidents or spoilage?

SAVE time or materials?

IMPROVE processes or appearances?

HELP increase personal efficiency?"

Make a suggestion every week!

Fig. 102.—Showing poster used by General Mills Company to encourage employee participation in a suggestion system, as part of a work-simplification program.

The Gilbreths also sought the "one best way." Their chief contributions were the use of micromotion study in preparing process charts and the identification of *17 basic elements* of motion. These 17 elements they dubbed *therbligs*.[3] Micromotion study uses slow-motion cameras [4] and

"H. Gantt," New York: Harper & Brothers, 1934; and Edna Yost, "Partners for Life" (Gilbreths), New Brunswick, N. J.: Rutgers University Press, 1949.

[3] Therblig is Gilbreth rearranged. In "Cheaper by the Dozen," New York: The Thomas Y. Crowell Company, 1948, a popular biography, two of the twelve Gilbreth children report the origin of the term.

[4] The Western Electric Company's Bell Laboratories have developed the Fastax high-speed motion-picture camera, used largely for analysis of machinery motion patterns, with operating speeds from 150 to 4,000 exposures per second on 16-millimeter film and 300 to 8,000 exposures per second on 8-millimeter film.

extremely accurate time recording. The Gilbreths counted time in *winks:* 1/2,000 minute. Present-day motion analysts use a decimal time compilation for ease of addition and computation. Time as used in motion study is essential for durational knowledge but is not necessarily preliminary to establishing *work task* as it is in time study.

Group 1: Useful elements which usually accomplish work, although not always in the most effective way.	*Group* 2: Elements which retard work usually by slowing down group 1 elements.	*Group* 3: Nonaccomplishment elements in which operator adds nothing to complete task.
Reach Move Grasp Position Disengage Release Examine Do	Change direction Pre-position Search Select Balancing delay Plan	Hold Unavoidable delay Avoidable delay Rest to overcome fatigue
Action: Study to uncover possible improvements in performance using the laws of motion economy and corollaries.	*Action:* Eliminate first five by better workplace layout. Reduce Plan by supervisory preplanning, go-no-go gages, and workplace layout.	*Action:* Substitute mechanical holding devices for human action, rearrange motion sequence, and improve workplace layout to eliminate first two. Reduce last two by improved supervision, adequate incentives, and removing causes of fatigue.

FIG. 103.—The three groups of basic motion elements of which every human performance is composed. These are grouped according to the productivity of the action comprising the element. Recommended steps for increasing accomplishment are given. (*Based on ideas from "Methods-time Measurement" by Maynard, Stegemerten, and Schwab. The nonstop-watch time-study aspect of MTM is discussed in Chap. XXIV.*)

There have been several additions and variations developed in the original Gilbreth basic elements. As presented by the Methods Engineering Council the basic elements are broken into three groups (see Fig. 103). Each basic element is further broken down into subclassifications, and considerable attention is given to the exact starting and stopping point for each element. As an example of breakdown, under the basic element *grasp* the following classifications are identified: [5]

Case G1a: Pickup grasp—small, medium, or large object by itself, easily grasped.
Case G1b: Pickup grasp—very small ($\frac{1}{8}$ by $\frac{1}{8}$) object or flat tool handle lying close against a flat surface or cloth or paper in layers.

[5] MAYNARD, STEGEMERTEN, and SCHWAB, "Methods-time Measurement," New York: McGraw-Hill Book Company, Inc., 1948.

Case G1c: Pickup grasp—interference with grasp on bottom and one side of object as when cylindrical parts in a box touch one another.

Case G2: Regrasp, where fingers "juggle" the part within the grasp, as a pencil is turned and positioned in writing.

Case G3: Transfer grasp as when a part is passed from one hand to the other.

Case G4: Grasp when object is jumbled with other objects so that *search* and *select* occur.

Case G5: Contact, sliding, or hook grasp as when a coin is slid along a surface or a hinged lid is pushed closed.

Methods analysis has been applied to many other fields as well as to manufacturing. In homemaking it gave rise to home dishwashing machines, a new type of collapsible bath tub for babies, and the "Heart Kitchen" designed to limit movement by cardiacs. In agriculture it led to improved farm layout, crop-handling and storage equipment, and a redesign of the barn-workshop. Combined with systems work, motion analysis in finance and office developed tub files, money counters, and microfilming of records. In transportation both routing and loading-unloading have benefited on land, sea, and air. A quick look around will show you many other things in your daily life and work developed by methods analysis and control.

Methods-Analysis Economics.—Motion study believes in improvements to increase productivity. Years ago it anticipated the "Work or Want" element of the British austerity period, and its American counterpart of "production to beat inflation." *Overproduction* is not considered as a possible problem. Employment for all willing to work and effective distribution for consumption are accepted as natural results of more efficient output. Monopolistic restriction of output—scarcity prosperity—is condemned. The ultimate good of the entire social fabric—workers, owners, and public—is thought to be best served by conditions that result in the maximum production of goods and services with the minimum expenditure of human time and effort. Waste is to be eliminated. Work is to be simplified. The man power saved is to be employed in efficient production to turn out more goods for more people in more places. This must be understood to grasp the almost crusading zeal for better methods that governs many industrial engineers.

Organized labor with its often unconscious "lump-of-labor" theory [6] has a history of opposing scientific management on the grounds that it caused workmen to work themselves out of a job and imposed intolerable burdens upon health and the technological unemployed. Most workers

---

[6] The "lump-of-labor" theory holds that there is only a certain amount of work to be done and that, therefore, it is to labor's interest to do it as slowly as possible. An example is the painters' union restriction on the width of paint brushes and total barring of spray painting, in order to make more hours of work for hand painters.

without specific instruction and careful supervision do restrict their output, even when paid piecework.[7]

Thoughtful labor leaders are beginning to realize that, when more is produced, there will be more to divide.   As early as 1925 the A.F. of L.

WMC-T-4

HOW TO IMPROVE

JOB METHODS

A practical plan to help you produce GREATER QUANTITIES of QUALITY PRODUCTS in LESS TIME, by making the best use of the Manpower, Machines and Materials, now available.

STEP I—BREAK DOWN the job.

1. List all details of the job exactly as done by the **Present Method.**
2. Be sure details **include all:—**
   - Material Handling.
   - Machine Work.
   - Hand Work.

STEP II—QUESTION every detail.

1. Use these types of questions:

   WHY is it necessary?
   WHAT is its purpose?
   WHERE should it be done?
   WHEN should it be done?
   WHO is best qualified to do it?
   HOW is the "best way" to do it?

2. Also question the:
   Materials, Machines, Equipment, Tools, Product Design, Layout, Work-place, Safety, Housekeeping.

16—31488-2

STEP III—DEVELOP the new method.

1. **ELIMINATE unnecessary** details.
2. **COMBINE** details when practical.
3. **REARRANGE** for better sequence.
4. **SIMPLIFY all necessary** details:

   To make the work **easier and safer**
   - **Pre-position** materials, tools and equipment at the best places in the **proper work area.**
   - Use gravity-feed hoppers and drop-delivery chutes.
   - Let both hands do useful work.
   - Use jigs and fixtures instead of hands, for holding work.

5. **Work out your idea with others.**
6. Write up your proposed **new method.**

STEP IV—APPLY the new method.

1. Sell your proposal to your "**boss.**"
2. Sell the new method to the **operators.**
3. Get final approval of all concerned on Safety, Quality, Quantity, Cost.
4. Put the new method to work.   Use it until a **better way** is developed.
5. Give **credit** where credit is due.

———

JOB METHODS TRAINING PROGRAM
TRAINING WITHIN INDUSTRY SERVICE
BUREAU OF TRAINING
WAR MANPOWER COMMISSION

GPO   16—31488-3

a   *b*

FIG. 104.

adopted the productivity theory of wages with these words in its annual convention report:

We hold that the best interests of wage earners, as well as the whole social group, are served by increasing production in quality as well as in quantity and by high wage standards which assure sustained purchasing power to the workers and, therefore, higher national standards for the environment in which they live and the means to enjoy cultural opportunities.

[7] This is again reported by Collins, Dalton, and Roy, Restriction of Output and Social Cleavage in Industry, *Applied Anthropology,* Summer, 1946.   This field report of personal experience reiterates the restriction of factory output known to all factory supervision—at least at the lower levels.   Such restriction exists whether or not the workers are unionized.   See also "Trade Union Regulation and Restriction of Output," 11th Special Report of the U.S. Commissioner of Labor, 1904, and Stanley D. Mathewson in "Restriction of Output among Unorganized Workers," New York: The Viking Press, Inc., 1931.

This faith in production continues to be held by important labor leaders. A joint study by a famous industrial engineer and the president of the C.I.O. endorsed it.[8] The A.F. of L. *Monthly Survey* for May-June, 1949, advises local negotiators to consider improving their employer's competitive position. Union cooperation is suggested to prevent waste, save expenses, cut costs, improve production. The belief is not universal, however, and some leaders favor work restriction.[9]

Methods Analysis in Action.—Many products of industry have features which are not advantageous to the user and which retard economical production. Improvements in manufacturing methods are often forthcoming from *eliminating, combining, changing the sequence of, or simplifying* certain steps in the process. Methods as well as quality can be "out of control." Market research (Chap. IV) and manufacturing research (Chap. VII) often indicate ways to improve the product. These answer the questions: Does it need to be made this way? With these features? In this variety? Methods analysis answers the questions: Does it need to be made by this process? By these manufacturing steps? In this order? Indeed, since the methods department may devise industrial processes as well as improve and standardize them, methods analysis may answer the question: Can it be made? *i.e.*, Can the industrial establishment obtain material and equipment capable of economical production of the product as designed? Simplification of design or the creation of the "production model" (see Chap. VIII) may thus be methods analysis.

The standardization of the material to be used, or steps in that direction, taken at this stage of process control, may result in the development of entirely new materials. These new materials in turn may make new products possible or themselves become products. Many of the special alloys of steel with their multiform uses were developed through the efforts made to standardize steel as a material. ˙

All large-scale unit manufacturing is a succession of combining individual operations into parts, parts into components, components into subassemblies, subassemblies into unit components, unit components into major assemblies,[10] and these major assemblies into the final product, such as automobile, locomotive, or prefabricated house. This is the secret of the assembly line, as interchangeability of parts is the secret of mass-

[8] COOKE and MURRAY, "Organized Labor and Production."

[9] This is well reviewed by G. J. Anyon, Trade Unionists and Scientific Management, *Advanced Management,* Vol. 12, No. 2, pp. 65–73, with the conclusion that there is no permanent incompatibility between scientific management and trade unions.

[10] It is not intended that these specific combinations of lower-order parts into higher-order wholes *must* follow this sequence.

production industry.   The opportunities for methods analysis in selecting and recombining the subassemblies are endless.   Savings in both time and money of *unit assembly* over *progressive assembly* [11] are illustrated by shipyard experience in prefabricating multiple-ton unit assemblies, then using giant construction cranes to assemble these major unit assemblies into ships in one fortieth of the usual shipbuilding time.

Suggestion Plans.—A successful system for harvesting employee ideas is an important part of methods analysis and control.   Not only must employees be conditioned to expect changes to be made in the job, but morale improves when employees' suggestions are accepted, and the suggestions made are often extremely worth while.

Industrial-relations departments promote suggestion plans to improve employee morale.   Employee cooperative spirit may be estimated from the attitude shown in the suggestions made.   Suggestion systems have operated continuously since the closing years of the nineteenth century in such companies as Yale and Towne, National Cash Register, Eastman Kodak, and Bausch and Lomb.   The labor-management committee (LMC), a type of suggestion system operated with employee participation, developed as a part of the World War II drive to increase production.   Most such committees were discontinued in 1945, but a nucleus of the most successful carry on, largely because of the methods improvements and savings they contribute (see *A.M.A. Report* 14, 1949).   Company-tailored systems complete with blanks for recording ideas (numbered stubs for anonymity), display boards with monthly posters, and plant mailboxes (see Fig. 137) can be purchased from several sources.   The more important part of the installation must originate within the adopt-

[11] Unit assembly takes parts and subassemblies and brings these to relative completion before joining them into the final product; progressive assembly takes one piece or part at a time and joins it to the growing whole.

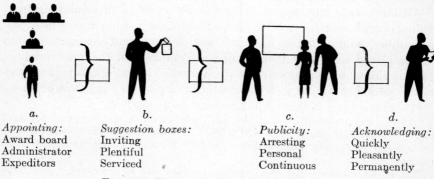

a.	b.	c.	d.
Appointing:	*Suggestion boxes:*	*Publicity:*	*Acknowledging:*
Award board	Inviting	Arresting	Quickly
Administrator	Plentiful	Personal	Pleasantly
Expeditors	Serviced	Continuous	Permanently

Fig. 105.—These seven steps will make your suggestion system

ing company. This consists of demonstrating to employees that their ideas are given full consideration, of actually making changes suggested promptly, and of rewarding contributors. Installing a plan is not easy, and nine out of ten attempts fail. Only 1 out of about 14 employees has a chance at making suggestions under a formal plan. Figure 105 is a flow chart adapted from Socony-Vacuum showing the steps in installing a successful suggestion system. Under a suggestion system about 30 suggestions will be received each year for each hundred employees eligible to participate. About one-quarter of these suggestions will be usable.

Since the most common reward is 10 per cent of the expected savings during the first year, an idea of savings made can be obtained from the awards paid. A giant company like General Motors will pay out millions and has—4 million in the first 6 years of its plan. The Illinois Central Railroad paid out half a million over the first 10 years. Smaller enterprises have made proportionate savings. Altogether the total is over 2 million a year—and could be 30 million if all plants had suggestion plans (reported A.M.A., Production Series 165).

Patent protection is usually given to employees whose ideas are good. Often the methods-engineering laboratory staff helps the employee with the perfection of a half-formulated idea. It is important in all cases that the employee, the foreman, and others who made a contribution be given full credit, even though the engineers perfected the improvement.

The methods engineer and the employee thinking up an idea for improving production on his job may both use the same tools of methods analysis. The engineer may introduce refinements such as scale models and three-dimensional templates or resort to photographic micromotion study, but the search for a better way is the same. Process-flow diagrams and work-flow charts described in Chap. X are tools of methods analysis.

Subsequent sections of this chapter will discuss right-and-left-hand charts, man-and-machine charts, and motion analysis through the use of therbligs.

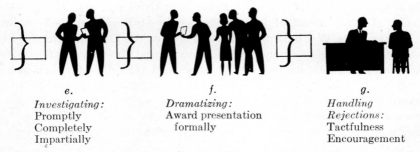

e.	*f.*	*g.*
Investigating:	*Dramatizing:*	*Handling*
Promptly	Award presentation	*Rejections:*
Completely	formally	Tactfulness
Impartially		Encouragement

successful. (*Illustrations, courtesy Socony Vacuum Oil Co., Inc.*)

Employee Training in Work Simplification.[12]—When methods-analysis techniques are taught to the employee by management, the term "work simplification" is often used to designate the cooperative project. Employee acceptance of methods-study activities and control is essential to any program. If in addition their enthusiastic participation can be

FIG. 105a. This shows how pre-positioning tools and the location of material within the normal work-area improves the operation.

obtained, results and savings skyrocket. In addition to training in methods analysis the program often includes a suggestion system such as was described earlier. Although work simplification is sometimes wrongly restricted in management thinking to improvements in small, light benchwork usually of an assembly nature, it can really cover all phases of the industrial enterprise, including office and sales as well as factory production and maintenance. The employee, being closer to his job, can often suggest improvements in it that would elude even a trained methods man. The more people in the organization who are thinking about improved methods the better. Employees, supervisors, top management, all might learn methods analysis and suggest improvements. Usually a central department exercises control over the function.

Where Does Work Simplification Fit into the Organization?—Because of the training of employees involved and the suggestion system, the work-simplification program is sometimes placed in the industrial-relations department. Since methods engineering is an important function of the industrial-engineering or standards department, this is sometimes confusing organizationally. It need not be so. The Glenn L. Martin Company in Baltimore and the American Rolling Mill Company

[12] This is the term used by Alan H. Mogenson for methods analysis and control.

both report the training department well able to handle work simplification. In the Murray Corporation of America at Detroit, the time-study department handles the assignment. Experience proves that either setup will work satisfactorily. Indeed there is no reason why both the industrial-relations department and the industrial-engineering department should not deal in work simplification simultaneously. Certainly both have logical functions in the field and both will benefit from closer interrelationships.

Industrial engineering might contribute skill for major changes, an experienced sounding board for radically different ideas, and mechanical assistance in developing hazy ideas. Industrial relations should provide the training, operate the suggestion system, and add sympathetic guidance of employee development. Both need the strong interest of top management. In either case attention should not be restricted to simple jobs only. That is not the meaning of "simplification." Motion study has been successfully applied to complex procedures including surgical operations and air-transport flying. At the Marchant Calculating Machine Co., in California, these methods have been applied to subassemblies requiring 2 hours each to assemble from a myriad of parts.

Control in Methods Study.—The methods-study program must include at least the following four important features: (1) *Uniform application.* A new and improved method developed and installed in one department may well be applicable in other departments of the same company. Those other departments must be checked, and the supervisors there persuaded to adopt the new method or perhaps even improve it. Too often the quality of methods used in different departments reflects directly the enthusiasm of the departmental foremen for methods improvement. An alert methods-control follow-up not only raises the foreman's enthusiasm but spreads the effect of improved methods plantwide. (2) *Established standard practice.* A new method must not be forgotten between orders as it sometimes is in job-lot manufacturing. Standard-practice instructions developed for each process make control of manufacturing processes possible, but unless a check is made regularly, standard practices may not be followed. Enough detail should be recorded to make possible the exact duplication of the original best method even though several years may elapse between runs. (3) *Continuous review.* An old operating procedure may not be the best procedure, even though it represented the best that methods study could do at the time of its adoption. There is always a better way, and if it is found, that, too, is only a pause on the march to a still better way (see Fig. 106). Control implies, therefore, that old set-ups are regularly reviewed, that especially long-running jobs are given extra attention, and that the

FIG. 106.—This shows how the "better method" of loading rings on a peg, instead of packing them one at a time, was further improved. The improvement was developed by R. R. Nicodemus at the Lake Placid Training Course of Alan H. Mogenson. (*From a booklet prepared by Johns-Manville, Inc.*)

methods department is never satisfied. (4) *Credit distribution.* The enthusiastic cooperation of every member of the organization is needed for successful methods study. To gain that cooperation a careful control of credit given for new ideas is essential. The employee-suggestion system described in a previous section helps give recognition to employees, but supervisors, toolmakers, draftsmen, and others who may have contributed to the new method must be recognized. A good methods department rarely takes credit for an original idea. Its glory lies not in thinking up new ways (we all do that in daydreams) but in getting new ways adopted—promptly, universally, continuously, and cooperatively.

Charts as Tools of Motion Study.—Three main kinds of charts are used in motion study. Whether investigation is made by personal observation or by analysis of motion pictures (particularly valuable for close study since a "loop" of film will repeat an operation endlessly), the written records are similar. First is the *general process chart,* of use in studying the flow of work, discussed in Chap. X. Second is the *man-machine chart* giving in detail actions, simultaneous or in tandem, of both members of the productive team. A circular form of the man and machine chart is shown in Fig. 107. This tool is especially useful in eliminating idle time of either the man or the machine through advance planning. For instance, a study of the man-machine chart shown in Fig. 107 might suggest that the provision of an extra lathe dog might enable the operator to prepare in advance for subsequent processing during time now wasted.

The third graphic tool is the *right-and-left-hand chart* illustrated in Fig. 108. When this chart is carried further and all parts of the body are charted in greater detail, it is called the "simo-motion" chart. Used in micromotion study, perhaps with wire patterns of the motions involved,[13] such charts become exceedingly complex. In function the right-and-left-hand operation chart makes it easy to spot idle time on the part of either hand. Once the waste is discovered, its prevention is often simple. Davis [14] has suggested a standardization in the "right-and-left-hand chart" including (1) always charting the same motion elements so that time-study and motion-study results are interchangeable, (2) using only five identifiable elements and symbolizing these by letters instead of geometrical shapes (suggested are G—get, P—place, O—process, I—idle, H—hold), (3) including the distance each hand (or body part)

---

[13] Called "motion models." The pattern for such models is obtained by attaching lights to the hands of the operator and photographing the motion path against a three-dimensional background.

[14] Davis, Louis E., Introducing the Operator Chart, *Modern Management,* Vol. 9, No. 6, pp. 8–10, August, 1949.

travels in the element, (4) summarizing each chart for workplace layout, elements, distances, etc.

After a methods engineer has considerable experience with process and operation charts, he does not have to resort to detailed studies to suggest many improvements. Bad practice stands out. The charts are useful, however, in training new motion analysts or in selling a new process. In

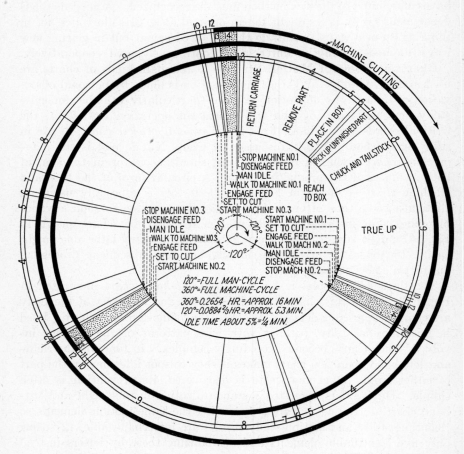

Fig. 107.—Man-machine chart of one man running three lathes.

It is different from the conventional chart. The time-honored method is to draw a man-machine chart as a set of parallel, theoretically endless lines. Each line represents a machine and is marked at appropriate intervals. Thus time marches on, down the long chart, and sooner or later everything comes out even.

Only one cycle is shown on the circular chart. It is a simple matter for the reader to begin at the top of the circle with the operation, "disengage feed," and follow the operator through the various steps required in running the three lathes. (*From Factory, September,* 1943, *p.* 93.)

Job No. 844	Part No. 1974-16	Dept 89		Date 3-6-44

Part Name *Forming Pin Bar*   Chart by *H. Stackman*

Operation *Closing Two Rivets in Opposite Side of Flat bar*   Chart No. *107*

Chart Type *Left - Right Hand*   Method *Present*   Time Unit *2000* of *Min.(winks)*

—Summary—					
	Man—	—Machine—		Summary *Single cycle*	
Use				Simultaneous Motion Chart	
Idle			Best Cycle		
Total			Ideal Cycle		
% Efficiency					

LEFT HAND —MAN—	Therblig	CLOCK OR METER READING	Therblig	RIGHT HAND —MACHINE—
Reaches for rivets	Transp. empty	4 — 8	Transp. empty	Reaches for flat bar
Selects and grasps two rivets	Selects grasp	10 — 4	Select grasp.	Selects and grasps one bar
Carries rivets to bar	Transport loaded	12 — 10	Transp. port loaded	Carries bar to modified arbor press
Positions two rivets in prepared holes	Assembl	5 — 5	Hold	Holds bar in place
Assists right hand in placing piece in fixture	Transp. loaded	8 — 12	Transp. loaded	Carries piece to fixture in modified arbor press
Moves hand to clamp and grasps clamp handle	T.E grasp	6 —		
Clamps piece	Use	6 — 12	Position release load	Inserts piece in fixture and releases it
Holds clamp in place	Hold	12 — 4	Transp. empty	Reaches for and grasps lever
Opens clamp, releases clamp handle	T.E release	6 — 10	Use	Closes first rivet
Moves hand to fixture	T.E	6 — 6	Release	Releases lever
		8	Unavoid able delay	Waits for left hand
Grasps bar, turns it around and releases	Grasp position release	16 — 8	Transp. empty	Reaches hand to fixture
Moves hand to clamp and grasps clamp handle	T.E grasp	6 —		
Clamps piece	Use	6 — 16	Position	Assists left hand in reversing bar in jig
Holds clamp in place	Hold	16 — 4	T.E. grasp.	Reaches for and grasps lever
		10	Use	Closes second rivet
Opens clamp, releases clamp handle	Release	4 — 6	Transp. empty	Releases lever (drop delivery)

FIG. 108.—Right-and-left-hand chart.

NOTE: Therbligs only approximate. Chart form may be used as either right-left-hand or man-machine chart.

addition, the final improvements are often found only after a complete chart work-up. Where it is desired to record exactly how a job is performed, charts are indispensable.

Sound Motion Practice.—The Gilbreths originally formulated a group of laws of motion which have been modified in wording, but not in concept, by each group of succeeding engineers. As formulated by Lowry, Maynard, and Stegemerten [15] these are:

[15] LOWRY, MAYNARD, and STEGEMERTEN, "Time and Motion Study," New York: McGraw-Hill Book Company, Inc., 1940.

1. When both hands begin and complete their motions simultaneously and are not idle except during rest periods, maximum performance is approached.

2. When motions of the arms are made simultaneously in opposite directions over symmetrical paths, rhythm and automaticity develop almost naturally.

3. The motion sequence which employs the fewest basic divisions of accomplishment is the best for performing a given task.

4. When motions are confined to the lowest practical classifications, maximum performance and minimum fatigue are approached.

5. When conditions are the same, the time required to perform all basic divisions of accomplishment is constant for any given degree of skill and effort.

To this basic list of laws these authors have added the following "corollaries to laws of motion economy."

1. Hesitation, or the temporary and often minute cessation from motion should be analyzed, studied, and its cause accounted for and, if possible, eliminated. When various parts of the body do not begin or complete their motions simultaneously, the resulting balancing delay should be recognized and recorded as being necessary.

2. The shortest time taken for each motion during the course of the study made on an expert operator should be considered the desired standard; all variations of time from this standard should be analyzed for each motion and the causes determined and recorded.

3. The best sequence of motions for any one class of work is useful for suggesting the best sequence for other kinds of work.

4. Where delay occurs, consideration should be given to the advisability of providing additional work which will permit utilizing the time of delay, if study indicates that the delay is unnecessary for overcoming fatigue.

5. All materials and tools should be located within, or as near as possible to, the normal grasp area.

6. Tools and materials should be located so as to permit the following of the proper sequence of motions. The part required at the beginning of the cycle should be next to the point of release of the finished piece of the preceding cycle.

7. Tools and materials should be pre-positioned in order to eliminate the search and select basic operations.

8. Hands should be relieved of all work that can be done with the feet or other parts of the body, provided there is other work which the hands can do at the same time.

That no set of motion rules is complete may be demonstrated by comparing this listing with that of other authors in this field. A further group of check rules which will be useful in evaluating motion practice has been added to these by Chane.[16] A warning should be sounded

[16] CHANE, GEORGE W., "Motion and Time Study," New York: Harper & Brothers, 1942.

against attempting to follow any of these suggestions too literally. First, find out what the originator meant.

1. Gravity feed containers should be used to deliver the material as close to the point of use as possible. The delivery point should be near the height at which it is assembled in order to eliminate any lifting or direction change in carrying the parts to the assembly.

2. Containers should be designed to facilitate the grasping of parts and materials.

3. The location of materials and tools should be slightly above the point of use.

4. Ejectors should be used whenever possible to discharge finished pieces.

5. Workplaces should be designed with proper regard for lighting and ventilation. Arm rests should be used when practicable.

6. Barriers in the motion path should be eliminated.

7. Finished pieces should be placed by drop delivery.

8. Chairs and workplaces should be designed to fit the operation and must be of the type and height to permit good posture.

Office Motion Study.—As applied to the office operations of the enterprise this subject has two aspects: (1) actual motion study of body movements and tools used in the clerical functions and, (2) the organization and methods survey. Office motion study is much the same as in the shop. The same methods of analysis, charts, and techniques are used. Wherever physical motion is involved, the same laws of motion economy apply. Where mental and sensory functioning enters, further information may be sought in psychology and physiology. In office studies even more than in shop studies, a thorough investigation needs to be made of the ways in which other offices have solved the same problem or do the same work. This may be applied both to the large and the small office.

Hints such as the use of eradicable typewriter ribbons, round disks to mark refiling of cards removed from drawers, foot-powered staplers, are common; basic improvements require study. Of especial importance is new office machinery. It would be impossible for any motion analyst to eliminate the waste motion in shifting a typewriter as effectively as the push button on the electric model does. Several of the office-equipment manufacturers have used methods analysis to develop machinery better fitted for the job. Not all latest machinery is necessarily better, but much of it is faster, more positive in action, and simpler to operate. The publications and meetings of the National Office Management Association present useful reports on modern office methods.[17]

[17] Notable is the program for standardizing office furniture, machines, paper, forms, and supplies, with the American Standards Association and 38 other national organizations, sponsored by N.O.M.A.

Office employees take particularly well to instructions in work simplification. The General Foods Sales Co. has each employee make a job breakdown for training purposes asking questions about each step: "Is it necessary? Is it in proper sequence? Is it simplified?" Paper tools such as charts and diagrams fit into office workers' experience. They will use them if given a chance. The suggestion system in the office can be particularly useful, although suggestions made are most often for improving systems rather than motions. Office employees accept themselves as "experts" in their own line and can work well on labor-management committees.

The organization and methods survey [18] is relatively new in office management, and methods engineers often find themselves drafted to do such work. Some companies have tried to make separate surveys of organization and of office procedures, but the two are so interrelated that both had best be done at once. An organization and methods survey is interested in standardizing, simplifying, and modernizing existing organizational structure and methods. Too many managers tend to consider organization only at the executive-officer level (where it is not too important to daily operation) and forget it among cost accountants, file clerks, and stenographers. Elimination of unnecessary reports, copies, and records is a great field for office economies. The tools used in an organization and methods survey will be office modifications of the regular analysis charts. The flow of forms and papers throughout the office can be shown on *procedure charts*. Regular process charts and operator charts show what is done. Sometimes new chart symbols for operations not found in the shop are needed. *Work-distribution charts* show who spends how much time, where, doing what, to produce certain office records. It may be decided, when the cost of an activity is known, that it is not necessary. A *forms analysis* may show that dozens of items of information used on several different forms can be dropped and the forms all combined. Rarely will the methods engineer find that any office procedure is as efficient as it should be. Even the "best methods" he develops will be outdated by the invention of new equipment and by realignments within the organization. Then the organization and methods survey starts all over again.

Value and Limitations of Motion Study.—Work simplification for its own sake is desirable. In a profit-driven business, however, certain limitations must be kept in mind. It does little good to study in detail, with camera, charts, and "brain-sweat," a process of short duration. Savings

[18] A series of articles by W. A. Gill outlines the procedure in *Modern Management*, Vol. 8, No. 8; Vol. 9, Nos. 1, 2, 3, 4, 5, 6.

realized on small orders take a long time to add up. The motion engineer must, therefore, decide whether or not the probable savings will pay for the cost of the investigation proposed. Short-running jobs should receive cursory examination. Long-running and bottleneck operations should be "given the works." Among the considerations that should appear on the balance sheet of a proposed motion study project are:

1. The capital required to produce: buildings, machines, equipment.

2. The working force required and labor relations: wages, working conditions, training required, union restrictions, ratio of labor costs.

3. The duration of the job: Will the company continue to make this part? Is it a high-demand, good-profit item or a marginal product? How many pieces like this were made last year? How many months has it been running?

Motion study can pay for itself. Indeed, it can show a bigger "profit" than any other single staff department. Because of natural human resistance to change, it is often necessary to draw up a brief balance sheet proving without doubt that the innovations suggested are savings. Labor alertness to possible worker displacements require that these proposed changes be considered from the employee's viewpoint as well as from a pure "costs-and-savings" angle.

Work Simplification Pays Its Way.—RCA developed a revolutionary method of packing radio receiving tubes as part of its work-simplification program. Among other savings are 30 per cent in material, 20 per cent in labor needed for testing, branding, handling, and warehousing. Annual money savings over $24,000 are being realized from this change. In another company a change in design of a shaft so that the necessity of cutting a tapered thread was eliminated, saved 25 per cent of the production time. Time and expense needed to make the necessary changes are rarely great. At the Murray Corporation in Detroit a worker's idea to use back-up boards to replace girls who held wooden blocks behind sheet-metal surfaces for drillers required 3 hours and $40 to install. It saved 31,500 man-hours in one year by halving the working force needed. Sometimes no new equipment but simply a better use of old equipment is required. At the Saginaw Steering Gear Division (G. M.), two operators were required on the ball stud to tie rod assembly. One made the initial assembly on an air press, and the other subsequently hammered it secure on a riveting machine. The operations were combined. The press operator now places the assembly in a riveting machine for automatic hammering while he presses a ball stud into the next tie rod. Output has been increased 94 per cent.[19]

[19] See *Factory,* July, 1949.

SUMMARY

Any industrial operation can be improved.   It is human nature to resist change.   We are often too busy to find ways to be less busy.

The field of management designated as "methods" has more to contribute to the greatest good of society as a whole than any other.   The envied position of American industry in the world picture is a direct result of American industrial methods.   Mass production, standardization, specialization of function, work simplification, all are American bench marks.   The chief difference in American industrial thinking is not only the constant search for new and better ways of doing the job, but the American willingness to junk old ways of doing the job when superior methods are discovered.

Wider instruction of all of the working force in tools such as flow charts, man-and-machine charts, right-and-left-hand charts, workplace diagrams, etc., characterizes the future in this field.   There is little danger that there will ever be an excess of attention devoted to methods improvement.   The repercussions of technological change on the industrial community, especially the introduction of laborsaving devices, have profound effects.   Industry must avoid idle man power and other social consequences of its methods changes.   Business existence requires the extension of the analytical approach to developing new methods by eliminating, combining, rearranging, and simplifying present activities in the production field to other parts of the business.   The office and distributive functions seem particularly ripe for thorough-going methods analysis.

CASE PROBLEMS

Man and Machine

1. It is desired to toast three slices of bread in a standard toaster, such as that shown in Fig. 109.   This machine toasts one side of each of two pieces at the same time.   Time to toast a side is exactly 0.50 minute. One side of each of two pieces can thus be done in 0.50 minute.   Time to turn over is 0.02 minute (two can be turned at a time using two hands). Time to remove toasted slice is 0.05 minute and to put another slice in is also 0.05 minute.   It takes two hands to do this, as shown in the figure. Only one slice can be changed at a time.

What is the minimum total time to toast three slices on both sides, starting with bread on plate, and returning toast to plate?   Assume that the toaster is warmed and ready to go.   Chart your analysis on a man-and-machine chart such as is illustrated in Fig. 108.

2. Obtain in your library several industrial magazines.   Go through the advertising sections and draw off a list of the mechanical improve-

ments and new machines offered. Pay particular attention to the copy writer's use of the terms "new," "revolutionary," "leader in its field," etc.

3. Select some simple operation you perform daily, such as shaving, putting on your shoes, or preparing a cup of tea. (An actual industrial example is better if you can recall one.) Study the operation from all angles, applying each of the laws of motion and their corollaries in turn. Write out a list of the improvements you can suggest.

The Lynal Co.[20]

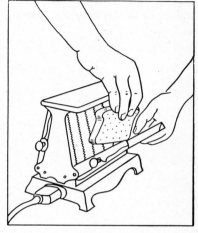

Fig. 109.

The Lynal Greeting Card Co., in common with all other card manufacturers, used steel dies and linseed-oil ink in its card printing. Demands for dramatic effects required deeper cuts in the dies. When cards were printed in this way, the ink, instead of being thinly spread, was massed on the card in thick ridges. The oxidation from the air, necessary to dry linseed-oil ink, penetrated these thick ridges slowly and unevenly. A skin was created by the drying of the outer surface under which the ink remained fluid for some time. To speed up the drying, mechanical engineers devised various schemes utilizing heat and draft. Each color still required several days to dry, and a multicolored card took weeks to manufacture. Considerable careful handling was required to transport the wet cards from press to drying room and back to press. The spread-out cards occupied badly needed space and the drying ovens added materially to costs.

Preparatory Question

Suggest ways in which the Lynal Co. can solve its production problem, utilizing the principles of methods engineering discussed in this chapter.

Everyman, Inc.[21]

In the home office of Everyman, Inc., a great many mimeographed instruction sheets and reports are prepared for the field sales organization. These range from 3 to 35 pages and require collating and stapling. Since a deadline must be met, there is always a rush for completion and

---

[20 and 21] Fictitious name.

often overtime expense. The usual collating method is to place each page in order around a table. The collating girls then walk around the table, each picking up one page from each pile, stapling on a large-size stapling machine (able to penetrate 35 pages) at the end of the walk, and depositing the completed reports in a final pile. Can you suggest improvements in this procedure which may save time and cost?

CHAPTER XVIII

PLANT ENGINEERING

Scope and Place of Plant Engineering in the Organization.—In earlier chapters on organizing the physical facilities, we saw that the engineering and selection of plant buildings, installations, productive equipment, and tooling normally are functions assigned to the plant-engineering department (see Chap. X). Now we are to consider further the work of the plant engineers as it pertains to the operation of the enterprise. In many enterprises this work embraces (1) plant and equipment maintenance, (2) replacement of equipment, (3) plant safety, and (4) waste control.

The position of the plant-engineering department in a large organization usually is that of a functionalized staff department reporting to the plant manager and serving all manufacturing departments in the plant (see organization chart, page 140). The section heads, usually a maintenance supervisor and a mechanical supervisor, each have line responsibility to the chief plant engineer (see Fig. 110). In a small plant, the plant super-intendent may personally perform many of the plant-engineering functions assisted by an all-round handy man to do the actual maintenance and machine-repair work.

PLANT AND EQUIPMENT MAINTENANCE

In Oliver Wendell Holmes' narrative of an earlier century, "The One-Hoss Shay," we find a twofold lesson for modern industry. First, nothing is "so built it couldn't break daown," and, second, unless a constant watch is kept for the evidences of "a general flavor of mild decay," disaster inevitably befalls. Applied to industry, these two principles lead to but one conclusion: Effective maintenance of a plant and its equipment is prerequisite to efficient plant operation and uninterrupted production.

Plant buildings deteriorate because of (1) the effects of the weather—sun, rain, cold, heat, wind—and (2) wear and tear resulting from general usage, vibration, fumes, etc. While deterioration cannot be stopped, it can be greatly retarded by maintenance.

Machines and equipment likewise are subject to wear and tear from use. Furthermore, machines gradually tend to go out of adjustment not only as the result of use but also because of temperature changes, vibration, "seasoning" of machine parts, settling of floors, and a host of other causes.

Time is likewise a factor as corrosion forms in pipes and on vital parts, moisture seeps into electrical windings and breaks down insulation, and dirt gradually finds its way into many types of equipment. To arrest or counteract the effects of all these diseases in its equipment, the only wonder drug at industry's disposal is proper maintenance.

Scope of Maintenance.—Industrial maintenance activities generally cover building exteriors, interiors, installations, and servicing equipment; yards and yard equipment; power-plant and power-transmission equipment; electrical equipment; and productive equipment. Also functions of the maintenance department are the stocking of repair parts, piping, wiring, and other materials of maintenance; the introduction or installation of measures to reduce factory waste (*e.g.*, self-closing water faucets, proper dispensers for powdered soap, heat exchangers to permit reuse of cooling water); the responsibility for maintaining safe working conditions for plant employees (to be discussed later on in this chapter); and the guidance or education of plant supervision on ways of reducing the maintenance required in their respective departments.

It might be noted that, whereas at one time maintenance may have been a job for persons with strong backs and weak minds, it is today a job for specialists skilled at their respective trades. Modern industry abounds with automatic and semiautomatic machines, complicated processes, intricate wiring, electronic devices, hydraulic and pneumatic actuators, delicate controls and inspection devices, air-conditioning units, and filtration devices. Thus the old-time maintenance man without competent engineering supervision now is simply a bull in a china shop.

Most large maintenance departments today have one or more specialists skilled in each of the maintenance trades shown in Fig. 110. Smaller plants usually hire outside tradesmen for specific maintenance jobs, principally building repairs and painting, laying roofs, and cleaning windows. These tradesmen operate under the supervision of the maintenance supervisor or all-round handy man, depending on the size of the plant.

Even the larger plants possess some complicated equipment which must be serviced by outside specialists. Automatic elevators with their self-closing doors and various safety devices often call for the attention of trained elevator servicemen if they are to function properly. Complicated office equipment, such as calculators and payroll machines, likewise defy diagnoses by regular maintenance men. Many manufacturers of such equipment offer contractual arrangements for periodic servicing by trained specialists.

Planned Maintenance.—Planned maintenance—sometimes termed "premaintenance"—is an organized attempt to prevent mechanical break-

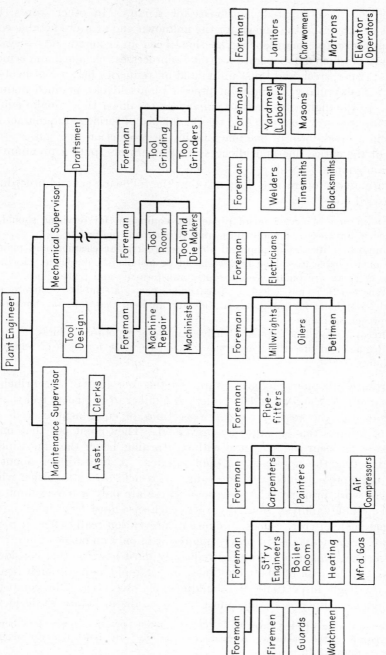

Fig. 110.—Organization chart showing the plant engineering department in a large plant.

downs and unanticipated shutdowns for repairs. In other words, the aim is to substitute the known for the unknown and at a predictable cost.

Such preventive maintenance has long been an economic necessity for enterprises which must operate continuous processes: chemical and cement plants; paper, steel, and brass mills; and oil refineries because of heat-up costs. Today many intermittent-process plants invoke planned maintenance, as the high rates paid to employees for down time [1] make equipment failures very costly. Also the prevalence of serialized manufacture, wherein a breakdown of one machine in the production line causes stoppage of the entire line and idleness of all operators, puts a premium on premaintenance.

Continuity of operations demands that the following general procedures be carried out:

1. Down time of each item of production equipment for servicing should be planned in advance, and the maintenance department notified.

2. Important items of equipment that require regular cleaning and maintenance or are liable to sudden failure should be installed in duplicate. Included in this category are pumps, compressors, transformers, and power lines.

3. Where (2) is not possible, spare units, parts, assemblies, controls, etc. should be at hand for rapid substitution for an item that fails or shows signs of approaching failure.

4. Records should be kept and analyses made of repetitive failures.

5. Regular and prescribed inspections should be made for signs of approaching failure.

Virtually all plant engineers agree on the first four of the principles defined above; the fifth is debatable. A number of engineers feel that in the long run the cost of regular inspections of equipment exceeds the cost of failures that are thereby prevented. They point out that many breakdowns occur suddenly and without warning, hence the impossibility of predicting the approach of such failures. A transformer about to blow up, a press die about to break, or a soda-acid fire extinguisher which will not work properly when inverted—these are only a few examples of unpredictable failures. Actually, then, each case must be weighed on the balance scale of cost. Does an ounce of prevention really effect a pound of cure, or does a pound of prevention result in only an ounce of cure?

Of course, economic reasoning frequently must bow to other considerations. In the case of plant buildings, for example, only through regular and thorough inspections can buildings be preserved. No competent maintenance supervisor waits until the roof falls in before he decides to

---

[1] Period during which a machine is "down," or not operating, for reasons beyond the control of the operator. A guaranteed hourly rate is customarily paid to operators during such periods.

fix it.   Furthermore, inspection can often prevent equipment failure that may be serious from the standpoints of both physical damage and safety. Consider, for example, the property damage and bodily harm that can result from an elevator failure or from an explosion attributable to improperly grounded electrical equipment.   Yet regular inspections would generally detect evidence of such failures before they occur.

The frequency of inspections will depend upon the nature of the facility or item being checked, its importance to the continuity of operations or to the safety of the plant and employees, and the time interval from the first indication of trouble to the actual failure.   Safety guards on productive equipment are customarily checked at every setup and at the start of each shift.   Certain items of plant fire equipment are checked daily or, at the very minimum, once a week.   General inspection of machinery can be scheduled at intervals of perhaps 3 months.   Building exteriors generally receive a going-over in the spring and fall of each year.

The technique of maintenance inspection may be described by the familiar admonition of the railroads: "Stop, look, and listen" but with the addition of "Feel and sniff."   The maintenance inspector searches for *predictors*, or indications, of approaching failure.   Chatter tells of potential bearing failure.   A hot motor is advance warning of a breakdown of insulation and subsequent trouble.   If a heater coil on a motor overload relay "kicks out," there is prima-facie evidence that the machine is overloaded.   Water stains down an outside building wall indicate an inadequate or stopped-up drain.   These are just a few common predictors discernible to the senses.   However, the maintenance man frequently must resort to predictor instruments such as those registering temperature, pressure, humidity, liquid or gas flow, timing, speed, light, vibration, presence of chemicals, etc., to test equipment for evidence of old age.   In order that no point of inspection is missed, it is good practice to furnish the inspector with a check-list sheet.

No planned maintenance program can be completely successful unless both maintenance and operating personnel are educated as to the job-priority problems of maintenance.   Many maintenance men fail to appreciate that their prime function is to furnish service to the rest of the plant and that their work must give preference to important jobs and dovetail into the manufacturing schedules.   Manufacturing supervisors, on the other hand, sometimes fail to appreciate the technical and scheduling problems of maintenance.   They invariably feel their jobs "should come first."   If both groups can be made to realize that the fundamentals of production scheduling apply as well to maintenance work and that service is a principal objective in both fields of endeavor, a much smoother relationship will result.

Long-term Maintenance.—Machine-tool manufacturers in recent years have begun to meet industry's demand for machines that require but little maintenance or at least are easy to maintain over a long period of time. The moving parts of many machines are now covered with "streamline" metal housings or covers, for not only is such equipment safer to operate but also dirt is prevented from finding its way into working parts. Removable panels and maintenance openings with doors that hinge or snap in place facilitate the work of repairmen. More and more machines are equipped with semiautomatic or fully automatic lubricating equipment, either that making use of pressure-feed oilers or simply "splash" lubricators. Some bearings and other moving parts are prelubricated for life and require absolutely no attention. Furthermore, motors, controls, and auxiliary equipment often can be standardized with that already in the plant so as to keep down the variety of spares required.

Attacking long-term maintenance costs from an entirely different angle, maintenance supervisors frequently plan routine maintenance work and inspection for slack periods. Not only does such a practice minimize interference between machine operators and maintenance men, but some employees who otherwise might be laid off can be kept busy.

REPLACEMENT OF EQUIPMENT

The second function of the plant engineers in the operation of the enterprise, the establishment of a sound program for the replacement of equipment, is one that has attracted considerable attention from management as well as government circles in recent years. It is a function that any concern interested in maintaining or bettering its competitive position cannot possibly overlook.

Depreciation and Obsolescence.—Any discussion of equipment replacement is all wrapped up in the subjects of *depreciation* and *obsolescence,* and these should be considered first. Depreciation may be defined as an annual charge reflecting the decline in value of an asset due to such causes as wear and tear, the action of the elements, obsolescence, and inadequacy and influenced also by tax factors, the capital structure of the enterprise, and changing price levels. Instead of charging off the cost of an expensive piece of equipment to one year's expenses, the charge is spread over a number of years during which the equipment is giving service. It is thus an arbitrary figure entered as a part of the cost of doing business each year, designed gradually to "write off" the financial investment in the plant's assets.

Obsolescence is the depreciation of existing equipment due to the invention of new and better processes or equipment. It is thus a measure in dollars and cents of the declining productivity and efficiency in relation to that of more recently developed equipment. Machine-tool manufacturers and other industrial-equipment producers are constantly improving the mechanisms available to the industrial enterprise. The development of a single piece of manufacturing equipment or the modification of but one industrial process may render an entire factory obsolescent. The textile industry of New England was undercut [2] not so much by the lower wage scales of its Southern competitors but by the high-speed textile machinery installed by the Southern operators. At one stage in brass casting, methodology advanced from hand crucibles over a charcoal pit fire to oil- or gas-fired furnaces to electric-heating furnaces to electric-induction melting furnaces in the short space of 2 years.

Industrial owners or conservative controllers often hesitate to junk obsolescent equipment on the economic theory that the machinery still retains a considerable amount of its useful life or that on the company's books the equipment has not been fully depreciated. The tendency is rather to put off buying new equipment until the old falls apart. This is borne out by the claim that the average period for writing off machine tools is 20.74 years whereas the average period of use before their obsolescence is between 7 to 10 years.[3] It should be noted also that in normal times many companies buy new machinery only if the machinery has a good chance of paying for itself within a period of 3 years. We then have the situation of the average piece of industrial equipment paying for itself in less than 3 years, becoming obsolete in 7 to 10, and yet not being fully depreciated or actually replaced for at least 20 years! How, then, does this come about?

The answer is multifold. Small depreciation figures are favored by some companies as the way to show greater annual earnings on their books—for the short-term period at least. Likewise a slow rate of depreciation is favored by the Federal government because the higher company profits mean higher annual taxes. Some companies do not keep records to know how fast they actually are replacing equipment. Other shortsighted managements oppose modernization simply because the old equipment still yields a profit. Semimonopolistic conditions sometimes retard the introduction of new processes and equipment.

Furthermore, in responding to the desire for expansion and modernization, industry usually awaits a period of prosperity and just before the inevitable recession decides to buy equipment. Apparently industry has to be firmly convinced that a business boom is really here before it loosens

[2] See *TNEC Report*, Part 30, Hearings, 76th Cong., 3d Sess., Pub. Res. 113, 75th Cong.

[3] From the bulletin "New Profits through Sensible Depreciation," published by the Kearney & Trecker Corp., Milwaukee, Wis.

up its exchequer. Yet such a period is one of high prices and delayed deliveries, and the chance to use the new equipment once it arrives is likely to be of short duration before the recession hits. Were equipment needs filled during periods of recession when machine-tool builders are hungry for orders and when prices are down, both purchaser and vendor would benefit.

From all the foregoing it would appear that in the past, industry, taken as a whole, may not have formulated a properly realistic policy for replacing its equipment.

Criteria for Equipment Replacement.—A proper policy must of necessity start with the factors which affect the useful life of a machine and hence its proper rate of depreciation. These are the factors of (1) work, (2) wear, and (3) obsolescence.

From the standpoint of the work factor alone, the life of a machine is a long one. Most machine tools are built to produce for many years. Breakdowns require repairs, but when these are made, the machine continues to run as before. Only in boom or war periods when two- or three-shift operation increases the utilization rate of the machine is its work life materially shortened. The wear factor is of greater importance as the operating conditions of operator neglect or carelessness, improper lubrication, overloading, vibration, dirt, and the like can substantially decrease the life of the machine. Finally, obsolescence, as we have seen, depends on the relative productivity of the machine in question vs. that of newly perfected equipment. Or it may hinge on changes in styles or in public fancy, which render products, and the machines that make them, obsolete. In this regard obsolescence is an elusive and somewhat unpredictable yet very important factor.

In application, the work factor alone might call for 20 years of useful machine life, or a depreciation rate of 5 per cent. The wear factor might reduce this life to 10 years and would raise the depreciation rate to 10 per cent. Anticipated obsolescence perhaps would further reduce the life to 7 years and thus being the critical factor would indicate that a realistic depreciation rate of about 14 per cent be used.

The equipment-replacement policy that is really effective will include the following additional criteria: How long will it take for the equipment to pay for itself?[4] Will the new equipment permit more production per unit of time, better quality, or lower operating costs? Will it reduce the costs of handling the product, be more economical to service and repair, improve the plant working conditions, be safer to operate? Does it have

---

[4] Good rule of thumb for stable processes: within 3 years; for processes involving yearly or other regular model changes: one-half to three-quarters of the model period; for nonrepeat orders: one-half to three-quarters of the length of the run.

greater flexibility (perhaps do the work of several existing machines)? Also, Internal Revenue Department rulings on allowable depreciation may adversely influence a decision to buy new equipment, as would a poor cash position of the enterprise itself. Any one or all of these considerations may tip the balance scale for or against equipment replacement.

Of course, a fine balance must be maintained by progressive management to obtain the maximum of use from already purchased equipment while not falling too far behind the march of technological progress. Often, "bugs" present in all new equipment are worked out during the period of initial adoption by an industry or company, and those enterprises which delay installation slightly obtain more satisfactory equipment in the long run and at lower over-all cost than do firms that pioneer in equipment adoptions.

The facts needed for an intelligent policy of equipment replacement can usually be determined only if *individual machine cost records* are maintained. Such records, which are fully as important to effective cost control as are records of labor costs, usually include data as to initial machine cost, depreciation charges, usage in terms of actual production, maintenance costs, and the like (see Fig. 111). Such a record may well prevent the all-too-common practice of making a machine do as long as it will run, or the equally wasteful practice of purchasing a new machine simply because it "looks nice and modern" in the plant.

PLANT SAFETY

The plant engineer in his preoccupation with plant buildings and installations, productive equipment, tooling, and maintenance cannot forget the human side of these operations: the safety and health, morale and comfort of the work force so necessary to the operation of the facilities. Just as the research design of a product may need to be standardized and simplified to create the best possible production model so does the plant engineer have to check all his operations to see that they are not only efficient but also safe and as comfortable as the processes involved allow. Reduced fatigue, hence more sustained production, and a heightened will to work may more than pay for the workplace improvements needed. Often changes introduced to take the danger or backbreaking toil out of the industrial job result in the greatest efficiency.

Today's industrialists look back on much of the original development of the factory system and often wonder how the creators of the enterprise could have been so thoughtless of the worker. The comforts of the workingman seemed often to have been a last consideration. Beauty in the factory seemed impossible. Lost in the folds of even recent history, however, is the fact that the industrial housing of the factory worker has

RECORD OF MACHINES

Name of Machine _36" Lathe_

Factory No. _21_ Location _Mill_   Section _7_   Date _8-10-42_

Date Purchased _4-27-29_   New or Used _New_

Cost of Machine _$1250.00_   Installation Cost _$60.10_   Total Cost _$1310.10_

	Maintenance					Production Record				
Date	Cause	Lost Hrs.	Cost		Total	Date	Employee	Pcs.	Cost	Total Cost	
1/3/40	Brk. down	31	27	90	27	90	1/2/42	W. Erb	1600	5	60	5	60
3/6 "	"	22	19	80	47	70	1/3 "	"	1520	4	82	10	42
5/20 "	"	15	13	60	61	20	4/1 "	E. Potts	1601	5	60	16	02
6/10	Sm. Repair	4	3	60	64	80	4/2 "	"	1200	4	20	20	22
8/21	Brk. down	28	25	20	90	00	5/7 "	W. Erb	1610	5	63	25	85
11/15	" "	41	36	90	126	90	5/8 "	"	1500	5	25	31	10
1/4/41	" "	33	29	70	156	60	5/9 "	"	1600	5	60	36	70
1/7	" "	27	24	30	180	90	8/10 "	"	1200	4	20	40	90
4/27	" "	21	18	90	199	80	8/11 "	"	1000	3	50	44	40
8/20	" "	42	37	80	237	60	9/1 "	"	1500	5	25	49	65
8/24	" New Pt.	52	78	21	315	81	9/2 "	"	1499	5	25	54	90
9/3/42	Brk. down	31	27	90	343	71	9/3 "	"	210		73	55	63
		347			343	71							

REMARKS _Prod. Record based on Pc. Wk. at 35¢ per 100, the lowest rate obtainable_

By _E. M. K._ _____ Cost Dept.

PROPOSITION FOR NEW MACHINERY

For Dept. _Mill_   No. _2_   Date _8-20-42_

Name of Proposed New Machine _55 F 30" Automatic Turning Lathe_

From Whom to be Purchased _Blank Mch. Works_

For Manufacture of _P. J. 7 Rounds_   Part No. _P. J. 7_

Operation _Turn_

Present Method _#21 Mch._   Hours Lost _347_
Cost Per Pc., Day Work _on Pc. Wk._   Dates of Lost Time _1-3-40 to 9-4-42_
Proposed Cost, Day Work _____   Cost Per Pc., Piece Work _.0035_
Expected Savings Per Year, D.W. _____   Proposed Cost, Pc. Work _.0013_
Based on Production of _160900_   Expected Savings Per Yr. _$3540.00_
Cost of New Machine _$1800.00_ Frt. _100.00_   Installation _60.00_ Total _1960.00_
Allowance for Old Machine _150.00_   Net Cost _1810.00_

- SUMMARY -

Savings Per Year _$3540.00_   Suggested By _J. C. Knapton_
Net Cost of New Machine _1810.00_   Compiled By _E. M. K._ Cost Dept.
Savings Per Yr. over Total Cost _1730.00_   Approved By _J. Ardus_ President.

REMARKS _____

FIG. 111.—The machine-record form (top) shows cost of maintenance and the production record of a particular machine, thus indicating its cost of operation. Bottom form is used for initiating machinery replacement. Note not only that the present machine is responsible for high upkeep costs, but also that considerable saving can be expected from the new machine. (_From Mill and Factory, August, 1945, p. 141._)

often been better, safer, more comfortable, and with greater regard for human values than his private housing and vastly above his public housing.

Safety, a Cooperative Undertaking.—The plant-engineering department calls upon many other departments to assist in achieving its objectives. Since the industrial-engineering department often prepares plant layouts, recommends methods changes, and assists in the development of new productive equipment, it also tempers its judgment with safety cautions and may remind plant engineering of overlooked safety features. The employee training in safe work methods by means of classes, safety committees, posters, awards for safe work, etc., are the industrial-relations department's contributions. The treatment of injuries, analysis of type of injury to isolate risks, industrial health problems, and classification of employees in terms of physical capacity to perform specific tasks are actions of the plant hospital. Each of these departments may head up safety and health work in specific plants. In those cases the plant engineer must still contribute his technical guidance.

Industrial Housekeeping and Sanitation.—Keeping the workplace clean and orderly is commonly called "industrial housekeeping," and the success of a production foreman is measured as much by his ability in this function as by his mechanical ingenuity and personnel-handling skill. The introduction of industrial vacuum cleaners and floor-scrubbing equipment which literally "dry-cleans" the production floor has greatly improved the dingy grease-packed floors of a decade ago. Regular maintenance crews using this type of equipment periodically clean all work areas, while sawdust, dust layers, and oil absorbers help maintain best conditions between cleanings. The provision of stack bins and tote-pan racks for work in progress helps keep the working area orderly. Workers' pride in their surroundings can often be raised by the intelligent use of posters and the suggestion system. The Ford management reports that its expenditures on housekeeping, which are high by usual factory standards, are more than repaid by the improved attitude of Ford workers toward their work. The worker in a clean plant is said to exercise greater care and pay closer attention than the worker in a disorderly plant.

Sanitary facilities ranging from toilets to wash-up rooms and showers are improving in modern factories. Whereas much of the equipment being sold emphasizes group use, the trend is definitely toward individual facilities, simply because the industrial worker demands more and better sanitary facilities. An abundant supply of pure cooled water is usually considered necessary. Salt tablets and occasionally glucose wafers are provided where sweating is excessive, to help prevent heat exhaustion.

Considerable care should be given to the safety hazards of sanitary facilities. For instance, electric-light sockets and unguarded heating pipes are particularly dangerous in shower rooms. State safety and sanitary codes in the chief industrial states often specify that lockers must be provided for workers to change clothes. Efforts are commonly made to prevent eating while the hands are still coated with metal dust. For this reason wash-up periods are paid for. Wash-up time is of little use, however, unless the methods-planning engineer in his layout of the workplace considered the relative use-load and provided adequate washing facilities.

Safety Engineering.—Safety begins on the drawing board and is continuously developed through every modification of the flow of work, manufacturing layout, or improvement of operational method. In the original design of a set of tools or the layout of a workplace, accident hazards may be built in or eliminated, depending on whether or not the design and methods engineers are "safety-minded." A safety-minded building designer will make adequate provisions for aisle and local storage space to minimize materials-handling hazards, will locate control and fuse panels where they can be reached safely, will install permanent ladders for all overhead controls, will insulate all surfaces heated above 200°F. and screen high-pressure heating areas, and will adequately guard belting and line shafting even if it is normally inaccessible. A safety-minded machine designer will include in his specifications limit switches, overload devices, overspeed tripping mechanisms, dead-man controls, gear guards, and whatever positive-action safety devices seem indicated to protect the operator. A safety-minded layout engineer or methods man changing a process will permit no unsafe process to be used, will provide workplace protective clothing and equipment where necessary, will consider work-movement hazards, and will specify mechanical handling in the safest form.

The safety engineer is the representative of management that is primarily interested in safety and secondarily in production or costs. He should have a sound mechanical engineering background to enable him to hold his own in the arguments for job reengineering. He may report to the production superintendent or plant manager but, because of the training and human relations aspect of his work, is often a part of the industrial-relations department. For full success he needs, as do all staff men, the absolute confidence and enthusiastic support of top management. His field of work is far more extensive than may be suggested by the term "safety" to the uninitiated.

Development of the Safety Movement.—The first employer's liability laws in the United States were passed in Alabama (1885) and Massachusetts (1887). Their chief weakness was that they required the employee to start legal action with no assurance that the award would justify the costs. Employers fought these cases legally and by barring from further employment employees who sued. The arguments of *contributory negligence* and *carelessness of fellow servant* were commonly introduced.

In this country the state of Maryland passed the first *workmen's compensation law in* 1902. The chief feature contributing to the success of workman's compensation laws was the removal of "fault" as the basic consideration. The newer concept did not attempt to fix responsibility or require an employee's suit to collect. If the employer was to pay damages to the injured workman, provided only that he was injured while pursuing his job, it clearly behooved the employer to take definite steps to eliminate accidents. Profit-minded employers also took steps to insure themselves against the unpredictable expenses of such liability. The insurance companies graduated premiums according to accident experience and gave further incentive to accident prevention. Insurance inspectors began rendering advisory service to their clients for accident prevention and the safety engineer was born.

Although advances greater than were believed possible have been made in providing safe working conditions, largely through the efforts of the National Safety Council, a nonprofit association founded in 1913 for the promotion of safe work practices, much remains to be done. The NSC program includes free factory inspection, a national magazine, bulletins, and educational safety slide films and movies.

When the state of Mississippi passed a workman's compensation law in 1948, the parade of state laws was complete. Each of the 48 states' compensation laws are carefully modified to fit local industrial conditions in a way no single Federal statute could be. Workman's compensation is at once a demonstration of the possibility, the advantage, and a defect of handling labor legislation at the state instead of at the Federal government level.

Costs of Accidents.—Cost reductions alone should be lure enough to increase safety efforts. The Bayuk Company over a 5-year period reduced insurance premiums by $90,000 in, at that time, the safest plant of the safest industry. In 1949 the Martinsville, Va., nylon plant (1,300 employees) of duPont Co. broke the National Safety Council record by completing 7 years without a single lost-time injury.

Insurance costs, lost time to the injured worker, and compensation payments are not the only cost of accidents. It is popularly accepted that these direct costs represent only one-fourth of the direct costs of an accident.[5] Such items as machine stoppage, spoilage of materials, possible

[5] See HEINRICH, H. W., "Industrial Accident Prevention," 2d ed., 1941, for an explanation of these higher indirect costs.

machine damage, idle time of men on near-by machines, time consumed in taking man to hospital for treatment, low production and possible material spoilage by the substitute for an injured man, legal costs, and time of supervisory help involved in compensation hearings, etc., can all add to the cost of a single accident.

Safety is no longer hard to sell to management, although the initial compensation laws were greeted with cries that industry could never bear this tremendous new expense without increasing the prices of finished goods unreasonably, and statements that accidents were inherently impossible to prevent. Today's managers know that safe working conditions are good business.

As has been indicated, a considerable portion of safety work has to do with promotion of employee health, prevention of occupational diseases such as silicosis and lead poisoning, and with fire prevention. State and municipal attention is commonly given to fire hazards, while organized labor has waged successful battles against various industrial health hazards. Most states now have departments devoted to the control of occupational disease.

Safety Devices.—Safety devices are included in modern equipment by the manufacturer but sometimes must be added to out-of-date equipment by the user. Where mechanical guards cannot be added, or for non-machine hazards, special protective clothing may be supplied by the employer to the employee. Examples are protective eyeshields or goggles, rubber boots, aprons, and gloves. An example of the range of safety devices which can be applied to a single problem will be provided by considering the power press used in metalworking, where a hazard to the operator's hands is created through the need for serving the machine by putting metal sheets or cups under the punch or die, which then descends. The original safety device was a sweeping arm which brushed the operator's hands aside. More recently positive-action "safety handcuffs" have been used. With these the operator straps his wrists to a cable, which in turn is fastened through pulleys to the mechanism so that, whenever the punch descends, the operators' hands are withdrawn. A similar result is obtained by requiring the operator to press two operating levers simultaneously, one with each hand. The RCA Victor Division at Camden, N.J., has successfully employed an electronic safety guard on presses.[6] A curtain of light, reflecting across the front of the machine and returned to the phototube by means of two mirrors, automatically—

---

[6] For further information on electronic control both for safety and for faster machine activation, write RCA, General Electric, and Westinghouse Electric; or see Electronic Intrusion-Detection Systems, *Electronics,* Vol. 15, pp. 38–45, or Industrial Applications Involving Electronics, Vol. 16, pp. 129–133.

if interrupted—locks the controls of the machine in the safe "off" position.

A different solution to this problem, which eliminates the operator's placing his hands under the tools, involves track or slide feeding devices powered by air or hydraulic propulsion and air ejection of completed parts. Air ejection is not only safer but since it actually saves one opera-

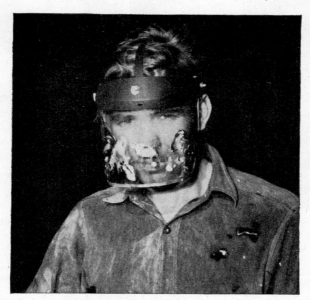

FIG. 112.—Splashes of hot metal tell the story of what might have happened without the protection of a face shield. (*Courtesy of Lockheed Aircraft Corporation.*)

tion—removing work from die—has much to commend it to industrial-methods men where simple drop delivery proves difficult (see Fig. 113).

The Accident-prone Worker.—Study of accident statistics reveals that certain workers have had many minor accidents. They seem to be repeaters. Such workers to whom accidents constantly happen are said to be "accident-prone."[7] Often uncorrected defective eyesight is to blame.

Fire Protection.—Modern factories are highly fire resistant. The material worked on, however, is often inflammable. The garment workers'

[7] From a chance distribution of accident occurrence we should expect most operators to have the average number of accidents, with some tailing off to the two extremes of no accidents and many accidents. Actual results show a skewed distribution with too many individuals on the high side and some individuals several standard deviations too high. See A Re-examination of the Accident Proneness Concept by Alexander Mintz and Milton L. Blum, in *Journal of Applied Psychology*, Vol. 33, No. 2, p. 195, June, 1949.

Fig. 113.—Typical power-press hookup utilizing air in production. Shows how a machine may be set up to blow the finished work down a chute into a pan as the ram leaves the die. Previously the operator had to feed the work and *remove* it from the die—now he *feeds only*. (*Courtesy of Schrader Division, Scovill Manufacturing Co., Brooklyn, N.Y.*)

fire in New York City, which resulted in the death of a score or more of young women a number of years back, attracted a good deal of attention. The girls died jumping from upper-story windows because no fire escapes existed from their workplace. The Garment Workers' Union diligently polices present-day establishments to prevent a repetition of this tragedy. Regular fire drills and emergency equipment are usually supervised by fire inspectors enforcing municipal fire ordinances. Few employers intentionally risk fire, but careless supervisors often permit the blocking of fire doors, exits, fire escapes, and passageways. Regular inspection is necessary to prevent such careless acts.

WASTE CONTROL

The control of industrial waste is accomplished most effectively by a twofold program of (1) *waste prevention*, which endeavors to eliminate or reduce waste at its source, and (2) *salvage*, which attempts to utilize or dispose of all waste that does occur. In organization, scope, and procedure these two functions are separate realms of endeavor. Waste prevention is a hydra-headed program in which everyone in the manufacturing organization from plant manager to sweeper engages. In spite of their efforts, as we shall see below, processing of material inevitably brings a variety of waste which must be disposed of so as to bring the greatest financial return—or least financial loss—to the enterprise. Here, then, lies the *raison d'être* of the salvage function. Contrasted with waste prevention, this function is generally the responsibility of a single section or department reporting to the plant engineer or allied with the maintenance function.

Waste Prevention.—Types of industrial waste include the following:

1. *Defective Production Material.*—This material, known in shop parlance as "junk" or "scrap," generally results from such causes as errors in engineering and drafting; defective purchased materials; improperly made or sharpened, worn, or wrong tools; defective or poorly set-up equipment; poor workmanship; damage in handling and transporting; and surplus, spoiled, or obsolete materials. In all the above the element of carelessness stands out as the prime cause. Since to err is human, it cannot be entirely eliminated, but it can be minimized by the application of controls. For example, a system for the careful checking of engineering drawings, the systematic inspecting of purchased materials, proper inspection controls of in-process material, improved handling techniques, and better production- and inventory-control methods—these are indicative of the ways in which industry can overcome human failings and reduce its defective production materials.

2. *Residue Material from the Process.*—This category includes "skeleton scrap" or filigree metal remaining from punch-press operations, "butt ends" or short pieces of the original material, as well as chips, turnings, remnants of fabrics and plastics, and other items left from production processes. While much of this waste can be classed as legitimate, some residue materials can be kept to a minimum by altering the process so as to reduce the resultant waste (*e.g.*, die-cast to size instead of sand-cast and machine to size), specifying purchased material sizes to leave a minimum of waste (*e.g.*, slit sheet-metal and cut-fabric widths to leave a minimum of edge waste), improving layout usage of material (*e.g.*, "nest" irregularly shaped designs on a metal sheet to obtain the maximum number of blanks per sheet), and checking product design for changes which reduce waste (*e.g.*, design for standard mill widths, thicknesses, and lengths of wood).

3. *Dormant Equipment.*—Here we consider worn-out, obsolete, or broken machine parts, tools, dies, fixtures, jigs, and gages as well as plumbing and electrical parts, partitions, conveyors, and the like. Careful usage and maintenance and controlled issuance and storage are typical of the preventive measures which prolong the life of such items. Once

worn out, they should be relegated to the scrap pile and not allowed to clutter up the plant interior.

4. *Supplies.*—As in the spoilage of production material, carelessness also dominates the wastage of shop supplies. The answer to this type of waste is generally to be found in educational and control measures which militate against carelessness and neglect by employees.

5. *Power and Fuel.*—Unnecessary use of lights and failure to shut down motors or machinery not in use are two common ways in which power is wasted. Steam, gas, or air leaks likewise are sources of waste. Here the solution is prompt detection and correction of the condition. Other wastage results from technical difficulties or poor engineering of equipment. For example, improper combustion in the plant's boilers and failure to counteract boiler-scale-producing salts are common sources of wasted fuel. Also, oversize motors installed on machines and power-distribution systems with excess line losses contribute to the amount of power wasted.

Many of the foregoing examples of waste may seem to be of such minor importance as to fit into the "penny wise, pound foolish" tradition and hardly to be worth the attention of a busy management. Yet consider for a moment a story told about the late John D. Rockefeller. During one of his visits to a large Standard Oil refinery, Mr. Rockefeller is reported to have stopped and watched an intricate machine solder the tops of filled oil cans. He was seen to be counting the drops of solder used by the machine on each can. Why, he asked, did the machine use 39 drops each time? Had a test been made to ascertain if this were the correct quantity? No, nobody had done so, but a test was made at once. It turned out that 37 drops were inadequate, but 38 drops would hold the cover as securely as 39. Mr. Rockefeller made some quick calculations and pointed out that to the Standard Oil Co. it was worth $50,000 a year! Thus the plant manager who feels he is trifling his time on waste would do well to consider first whether it might be a tremendous trifle.

Salvage.—The functions ordinarily assigned to the salvage department include

1. Collection of scrap from the plant and storage in suitable locations.
2. Separation and segregation of collected scrap where necessary.
3. Preparation of scrap for disposal.
4. Transfer of prepared scrap for reuse if possible.
5. Search for other uses in the plant for waste material.
6. Consideration of whether damaged or rejected material can be repaired for reuse.
7. Organizing of remaining scrap for sale to outside organizations.

For the proper salvage or disposal of most plant waste, it must be segregated according to type of scrap, *i.e.*, material, specification, grade, physical sizes, etc. It is of particular importance that metals be carefully segregated, for the price obtainable for mixed scrap metals may be only a fraction of that obtainable for the same grades properly segregated. The same need for segregation also applies in the use of scrap paper, glass, abrasives, and a host of other waste items. Thus segregation or grading at the source of the scrap is economically profitable.

Many plants use a color code to keep waste materials separate. For example, scrap containers, chip bins, and even sections of the originating machine can be painted to identify the type of scrap. The basic color black, for instance, might indicate steel, with black and white for high-carbon steel, black and yellow for nickel steel, etc. Orange might represent aluminium; gray, rubbish; etc.

Not all waste items can be segregated at the source, however. Material dropped by production operators is swept up; items in a load overturned by a trucker become mixed; operators are unable to keep materials separate, perhaps for technical reasons. Or materials may be mixed during the process, as, for example, oil is mixed with chips during turning operations, and grinding sludge consisting of minute steel and abrasive particles results from grinding operations. In such cases, salvage of the material requires a separate sorting or segregating operation.

Mixed-alloy steels can be identified and segregated by simple spark or chemical tests. Where the size of mixed items is different, mechanical means, such as a rotating drum of perforated metal or a simple screening process, can be used to separate smaller from larger items. Ferrous particles can be segregated from dirt and other contaminating materials by magnetic separators or by the familiar mining process of flotation. As a last resort hand sorting may have to be used to sort and classify some materials.

Disposition of Waste.—Properly segregated waste at the salvage depot can then be earmarked for (1) utilization, (2) reclamation, or (3) disposal.

Shipping cases and containers from incoming goods offer a good example of waste items which can be utilized "as is." If care is taken in opening such containers, many of them can be reused for outgoing shipments or at least for in-plant handling, collection of waste, dormant storage, etc. Every plant-layout change is likely to be accompanied by the removal of electrical conduit, wiring, switches, piping, valves, conveyor sections, shelving, and a host of other items. If each installation is carefully dismantled and the parts segregated, inventoried, and stored, much of it can subsequently be reused. Production material sorted from sweepings, chips, or other waste frequently can be returned to the production flow.

Slightly off-standard production material not readily correctible may be sold as "seconds" (see page 397).

The reclamation of waste involves those items which can be repaired, reworked, reprocessed, or otherwise restored for further use. In metal-working plants oil found in chips generated by machining operations can be reclaimed by a centrifuge extractor. Petroleum solvents are reclaimed by running the used solvent through settling tanks and filters to eliminate dirt and by removing the oil content in a distillation process which leaves the used solvent chemically pure and ready for reuse. Broken tools, dies, fixtures, gages, and the like frequently can be welded or brazed for further use. Old records, correspondence, and orders can be used for "scratch" paper or shredded for use as fill in packing cases. Waste rags required by employees for wiping and cleaning can be collected, washed, and reused. Similarly, dirty work gloves and greasy leather belts can be dry-cleaned.

Another type of reclamation occasionally encountered is that of materials damaged from fire or water. Where the plant area affected contains a high concentration of material, as would be the case in a warehouse, the value of damaged materials may be very great. In such cases, prompt and proper measures can prevent further damage and permit a high percentage of recovery. Insurance engineers and firms specializing in salvage work frequently must be called in for advice as to the best restoration procedure for the material involved.

Before leaving the subject of reclamation, it should be noted that some industries, notably metals, rubber, and paper, reclaim and reuse scrap as one of their basic raw materials. Their production processes are established on the practice of mixing a percentage of scrap with the virgin material. Particularly in the rubber industry, entire plants with special processing equipment are devoted to the mass reclamation of scrap.

Disposal is the next alternative if a plant is unable to utilize or reclaim its scrap. This may involve returning it to the vendor, selling to a scrap dealer, burning, or dumping. Generally the course of action is determined by the price obtainable through sale and whether that price exceeds the cost of preparing the scrap for shipment and of transportation.

Sometimes a plant can command a higher price for scrap if it is prepared for more economical shipment. For example, if metal chips are compressed in a briquette press, the resultant metal briquette is easier to handle, saves storage and shipping space, and facilitates remelting. The baling of waste paper achieves similar economies. In both cases the increment in price for the scrap thus prepared usually exceeds the cost of the additional preparation.

The sale of waste material is not limited to scrap of the type purchased by scrap dealers. For example, oil drums, if not returned to the vendor or used for in-plant containers, can be sold to drum-reconditioning firms. Burlap bags from incoming goods can be either returned to the vendor or sold to other bag users. Grinding wheels worn down may be sold to users of wheels of smaller diameter or sold to other users who break them up for the "charge" in tumbling barrels.

Finally, certain items must be burned. But even this method of disposal is not without a return—provided waste is burned in the plant boilers or if an incinerator is so connected as to make use of the generated heat. Also items which cannot be burned may be used as fill or as a last resort placed on the public dump (if you can make your peace with the city fathers).

SUMMARY

In addition to playing an important role in organizing the plant facilities, the plant-engineering department is charged with keeping those facilities operating at a minimum of cost. We have seen how the plant and equipment maintenance, replacement of equipment, plant safety, and waste control all are customarily involved in the operating program of the plant engineers.

It should be especially noted that throughout its work, the plant-engineering department is concerned with preventing or eliminating *hidden waste*. Costs resulting from an inefficient boiler, from equipment that should be replaced by faster equipment now on the market, from compensation paid to an employee injured on an inadequately guarded machine, from scrap produced by improperly made tools—these are hidden costs impossible to isolate on a profit-and-loss statement.

Most plant-engineering work is highly technical, and some of it may well be beyond the knowledge of even the most capable top management. Thus top management must rely on the technical advice of its plant engineers as to the location and correction of operating problems centering about plant and equipment—problems that in many cases may not even be obvious to top management.

CASE PROBLEMS

Obsolescence

CORPORATION X [8]

Corporation X is a metalworking firm of fair size and with an established financial reputation in the metals industry. The major share of its investment in equipment lies in its machine tools.

[8] Adapted from two booklets, "Today's Men and Yesterday's Machines" and "New Profits through Sensible Depreciation," both published by the Kearney & Trecker Corp., Milwaukee, Wis.

After the first 7 years of successful operations, the nature of the company's business began to change. Old customers faded out; new ones entered the picture with different work requirements. With the company facing new operation problems, the chief plant engineer advised his superiors that $100,000 in new machine tools should be purchased to handle the new production on a low-operating-cost basis.

However, the controller of the company argued that the existing machines were being depreciated at the rate of 5 per cent per year and were supposed to be good for 20 years. He presented figures as follows:

Original cost of existing machines.................................	$80,000
Current book value at 5% depreciation rate for 7 years..........	52,000
Estimated secondhand-market value of machines if they were to be sold..	20,000
Difference between book and market value or loss on existing equipment	$32,000

Of course, in a profit year, the loss on the sale of the old equipment could be deducted from earnings for the year as an expense, but, the controller insisted, a $100,000 investment in new equipment plus a $32,000 loss on the old was a $132,000 transaction.

As a result, no new machines were purchased and the company no longer made the same profit. During years when the old equipment had been profitable, the low rate of depreciation served to keep down the cost of doing business and thereby increased the profits and hence the dividend payments to stockholders.

Now again, several years later, the character of the firm's business has changed. This time new machine-tool equipment is a "must." However, in view of the fact that the high profits of the earlier years have gone largely into dividend payments and the profits of recent years have been low, no cash reserves are available to buy the needed equipment. Efforts to borrow money now have failed because the company's equipment is too old to justify a loan. The company finds itself in the position of having either to raise new capital or declare bankruptcy.

Preparatory Question

What was wrong with the policies of Corporation X?

Safety

Circular saws are a particular safety hazard in furniture manufacturing, lumbering, plastic sheet cutting, etc., not only because the operator may be cut but because the saw may "explode" upon hitting a hidden nail or the material may "ride up" the saw, fly and hit the operator. Suggest ways to protect the operator in a specific industry operation.

CHAPTER XIX

PRINCIPLES OF INDUSTRIAL RELATIONS

DEFINITION AND BACKGROUND

Industrial relations is the cooperatively arranged control or management of the man power of an organization. Such management is commonly exercised in three simultaneous directions: (1) labor relations, or the management of those problems largely identified as employee grievances and characterized by collective bargaining and union representation; (2) employee relations, or the recruiting, selection, hiring, and maintenance of the employees as such, epitomized by the employment office and recreation program; and (3) public relations, or the handling of company contacts outside of the working force, or of contacts with employees when not chiefly identified as employees or potential employees. These three parts are not mutually exclusive. Every one of the functions listed on page 465 has aspects that relate to each one of the three parts. Any industrial-relations activity must be integrated with every other part of the complete program.

This treatment of industrial relations can endeavor to present only what seems to be best practice in this field without explaining all the different ways of attaining the same end advocated by various companies, but this should not be taken as evidence that there is only "one best way." In employer-employee relations, any honestly conceived method that works may be recognized as desirable. The controversial nature of much of the subject matter of personnel study is indicated by the variety of names assigned to this field by different managements.

Although industrial relations is the preferable name for these activities, it is by no means universal. Department stores, banks, and governmental agencies particularly call the field "personnel administration" and the department in charge, the "personnel department." Some businesses use personnel management, industrial-relations management, labor supervision, employer-employee relations, employee personnel supervision, employment department, and even service department as terms interchangeable. In most cases, however, where a term less general than industrial relations is used, the activities of the department involved are somewhat restricted and do not include all three aspects. Not every manufacturing establishment has an industrial-relations department, although all have industrial-relations problems. In the smaller company particularly, personnel functions are often performed along with other duties: sales, traffic, accounting, office management, or industrial engineering.

Sound Industrial Relations and Competitive Position.—An enterprise must look to its industrial relations to help maintain its competitive position. The *money* market is open to all. Anybody can promote a company. In the American economy practically all companies have access to the same *materials* and *markets,* since monopoly and cartels are taboo. The short life of patents on inventions, cross-licensing requirements, and the volatile nature of work simplification enable all companies to utilize almost the same *machines* and processing *methods.* Research gives only a short-term advantage. *Man power* offers the best opportunity for competitive advantage over the long pull. *Management* must search out the best people for all levels of the organization and give them the best training, guidance, supervision, tools, etc. Then the enterprise can hold its own in any competition. Competitors may have more money, may buy out material supplies, may by aggressive sales and advertising efforts gain temporary control of distributive channels. Since people alone among these are unique, to gain and hold better people offers management its golden opportunity. Attention given to industrial relations in the last two decades indicates that advanced managements know this.

Cooperative Control.—Industrial relations is said to be cooperatively arranged control or management, because its work is most generally advisory to other operating executives or supervisors. Effective decisions in industrial relations cannot be made away from the firing line. Personnel policies cannot be converted into practice except where employees come into contact with their apparent employers at the workplace or machine. Cooperatively arranged control is also coming to have the meaning of "arranged after talking it over with the employees or their representatives." Cooperative or "consultative" management is nowhere more important than in industrial relations. Consultative management is beginning to include not only the shop foremen and lower-level supervisors, but the employees themselves. The *participation* of employees in the "thinking side" of business is increasing. Labor leaders are voicing their demands louder and louder for a part in management, and the nature of their demands points toward a share in the actual control of enterprise. Government agencies enter more and more into daily employee supervision.

No part of management, no department or division in which any person is employed, can function successfully without sound industrial relations. This fact has often been overlooked by system-minded executives who tried to solve all personnel problems by setting up a personnel department and charging it with the establishment of sound relations. No amount of good selection, careful induction training, and morale building can overcome the effects of the foreman who says, "Oh yes, you're the new girl who was hired for that machine down there on the end where my best operator lost her fingers last week."

Changing Viewpoint of Industrial Relations.—Organized programs of industrial relations are relatively new to business.[1] Labor relations became possible only a little over 100 years ago with the overruling of the "conspiracy concept" of the nature of unions. The training schools and welfare rudiments which developed into personnel management were radical innovations half a century later. There has been increasing emphasis in the last 30 years. Unionization became national policy with the New Deal only 15 years ago. Some of the twists of public relations growing from a broader concept of management and modern research were new only yesteryear. The industrial-relations movement had its most rapid growth in the years during and between the two world wars, when centralization of responsibility for employee problems became widespread. It is today the center of national politics and government social programs.

For the manager of today, industrial relations is primarily a matter of viewpoint.

The personnel viewpoint is influenced by three main considerations: individualized thinking, policy awareness, and expected group reaction. Individualized thinking will require the administrator to consider the entire situation surrounding the individual affected. Policy awareness emphasizes consistency of treatment and the precedent value of any decision management makes. The expected group reaction balances what we know of human nature in groups against the individual's situation in the light of policy. Throughout, reality

---

[1] That newness is reflected in the lack of a national professional association. Although the American Management Association was founded as a personnel group and other groups such as the Society for the Advancement of Management (mainly industrial engineering), the National Office Management Association, and the several professional associations gave personnel subjects attention, membership groups remained local until 1949, when the American Society for Personnel Administration was launched in Cleveland. This followed an unsuccessful earlier attempt to establish a National Association of Personnel Directors in Chicago and several regional federations among local clubs. The Industrial Relations Research Association, consisting mostly of professors of industrial relations and economics but accepting business and labor members and stressing an impartial position, was formed in 1948. Several "invitation fraternities" of prominent industrial-relations practitioners have existed for years.

requires all these to be considered at once in terms of present, past, and future. This viewpoint is taken by all levels of management from top to bottom in all parts of the line and staff.[2]

This developing viewpoint reflects the eclectic background of industrial relations, which borrows from many fields, as an applied social science. In its control of the employee relationship it is made up of parts taken from economics, anthropology, sociology, psychology, statistics, law, and government. Of particular interest is its relationship to cultural anthropology, to industrial sociology, and to industrial engineering. From an-

FIG. 114.—This shows stages in the industrial evolution which is eliminating the man in fabrication and replacing him with machinery. Man has progressed from a source of muscle energy to a race of skilled adjuster-builders and machine supervisors. (*Based on an idea from George Friedman, Automatism and Industrial Work, Appl. Anthrop., Vol. VII, No. 3, pp. 7–15.*)

thropology has been borrowed the *cultural concept*—that any individual personality is largely the product of the society in which it is found.[3] Industrial sociology has contributed an ultimate faith in the correctness of group decisions [4] and a respect for the organization as a cooperative system. Industrial engineering and industrial relations trace their origins back to common ancestors: Robert Owen, Taylor, Gantt, the Gilbreths, the scientific-management movement.

Another aspect of industrial engineering combines with industrial psychology to consider the human factor, *i.e.*, the biomechanics of human

[2] STACKMAN, H. A., "Personnel Administration." See also PIGORS and MYERS, "Personnel Administration: A Point of View and a Method," New York: McGraw-Hill Book Company, Inc., 1947, and SCOTT, CLOTHIER, and SPRIEGEL, "Personnel Management," 4th ed., New York: McGraw-Hill Book Company, Inc., 1949.

[3] For examples see ELTON MAYO, "The Social Problems of an Industrial Civilization," Cambridge, Mass.: Harvard University Press, 1945, and "Industry and Society," edited by W. F. WHYTE, New York: McGraw-Hill Book Company, Inc., 1946.

[4] For a defense of this position see W. E. MOORE, "Industrial Relations and the Social Order," p. 207, New York: The Macmillan Company, 1946.

physical functioning. Many factories still have certain machines which were so poorly designed that "it takes a contortionist to run 'em." Human engineering makes studies of human physiology, average sizes and strengths, sensory powers, and disabilities in an effort to make machines for which men may be efficient *servomechanisms, i.e.,* machines requiring attention, speed of reaction, strength, etc., within the range of human capacity. Where such design is impossible, electronic tubes may be substituted for human senses, microswitches for fingers, and compressed air or electric motors for muscle power (see Fig 114).

Studies have been made to find out what kind of an instrument dial face a man can read most accurately. Other studies sought to discover what kind of links—visual, auditory, tactile—between the man and his machine provide the best control. A whole new therblig system was developed to study differences between static reactions (where the body member is held fixed in space), positioning reactions (where body members are moved to a specific position accurately), and movement reactions at given speeds along specific paths.[5] This consideration of the human factor[6] makes for better industrial relations.

Labor Relations Function.—Labor relations is primarily a line supervision problem (see Chap. VI for a discussion of line and staff relationships) concerned with plant discipline, collective bargaining, and union relations. Day-by-day problems of labor relations must be met by the line executive personally. Staff service in contract negotiation, matters of law, and procedure are usually provided, but ultimately the line executive himself must solve the labor problem. This is true to an even greater extent for labor relations than for other industrial-relations functions where a representative can sometimes be sent. When Joe Workman thinks the big boss is a "stuffed shirt," only the "stuffed shirt" himself can disillusion Joe.

Plant discipline is seldom openly challenged by the individual worker during times of normal operation. Hidden disobedience, such as stealing a smoke or producing inferior work, are relatively common. Quantity as well as quality often suffers when men are driven instead of led. Discipline is difficult to maintain, if the rules governing conduct at the workplace have not been soundly conceived and realistically explained to

[5] MEAD, L. C., A Program of Human Engineering, *Personnel Psychology,* Vol. 1, No. 3.

[6] In England the term "human factor" is used primarily in connection with extensive studies in worker health, fatigue, and industrial psychology. In the United States it is also used in another sense to remind us that employees also are people. One large manufacturing concern is reported to have spent 14 million dollars to learn this. See Rothlisberger and Dickson, "Management and the Worker," Cambridge, Mass.: Harvard University Press, 1939.

the persons affected by them. Newly organized workers will sometimes openly break company rules, feeling that they can no longer be fired for such infractions. Possibly one of the greatest tasks of the modern industrial-relations department is training first-line supervisors to maintain discipline in the shop under present-day conditions when the rule of force and the threat of firing no longer keep men in line.

Collective bargaining is occupying an increasingly greater part of the operating executive's time since, under almost all formal or informal grievance procedures, employee dissatisfactions work their way up along the lines of authority established in the company. Under individual bargaining each employee made his own agreement with his employer regarding wages, hours, and working conditions. Ultimately under collective bargaining the conditions and hours of work, as well as pay rates, may be established once a year between negotiators representing the unions in an industry and a trade-association executive representing the individual companies in the industry. Negotiations may be policed and final conditions of settlement established by a government agency. At the present time collective bargaining is in a transition stage between these two extremes, with some employees striking individual bargains, a large number having some of the conditions of employment established for them by union representatives, and bargaining in small groups or individually for the remainder, and relatively few employees working under industry-wide contracts established with governmental supervision.

Employee-Employer Relations.—This is an expanding group of staff services to employees that has grown from early welfare work, the company school, and the employment office. Prior to 1900 there was almost no centralized, organized employment work in American industry. The shop foreman did his own hiring and firing by whatever means he chose, established whatever working conditions appealed to him, paid such wages as he had to, often on a contract basis with the factory ownership which made him virtually a subcontractor with the employees working directly for him, kept no employment records, paid no compensation to men injured on the job, and obtained questionable obedience by means of methods described as "Treat 'em rough and tell 'em nothing."

The first glimmerings of present-day personnel work took the form of employee-welfare programs established by paternalistic top managements providing improved employee housing, hospitals, company stores and schools, restaurants or lunchrooms, and dismal meeting places described as recreation halls. These reforms were very well intentioned and were so great a departure from practice at that time that they were roundly condemned by other managements. They were well received by some employees and contributed to industrial peace in their day. In most cases, however, these welfare activities did not have the support of the first-line supervisors, covered only a part of the need, and were severely curtailed during times of economic storm. Employees commonly took the attitude, "Put the money in our pay envelope and we'll buy our own welfare." Employees' ungratefulness caused great mental distress among the paternalistic owners who realized that distributing the cost of such welfare activities as were then common among the employees would provide only a few cents per year per man. In some few cases employee participation in planning and control was invited, and the programs succeeded.

As factories increased in size, the need for centralized employment became apparent. Foremen were spending entirely too much of their time at the factory gate "hirin' on help." The same misfit was hired and fired by different foremen time and again. The first central hiring windows established to meet this need were almost as bad as the methods they replaced but did contain the seeds of central control.

Medical service, elementary first aid, and employee-safety training developed, as severe industrial accidents called attention to the hazards of employment. Workman's compensation laws established employer responsibility for workplace injuries. The complex nature of factory activities resulted in training programs designed to improve apprenticeship methods and provide semiskilled factory labor. Somewhat later the need for foreman training was felt and programs provided. Growing union activity high-lighted the need for company-wide labor relations. As the general public became aware of the larger corporations in their midst, *public relations* was considered worthy of special attention. No one company added these functions in exactly this order, and the functions mentioned seldom started exactly as we know them today. Rather, gradual experiment and hesitant addition were the rule, with certain concerns years ahead of others in some areas, and years behind in others. Not all industrial-relations programs are complete even today. Completeness may be better judged by the way the integrated program meets a specific company's need than by the number of activities involved. Many companies boast all the activities listed on page 465 or shown in Fig. 117, but because those activities were forced on the organization from without instead of growing from within, their program is deficient.

As these additional functions were included, the defects of paternalism became apparent, and most of the dominating actions were dropped altogether, while some of the more desirable welfare activities were retitled as "employee service" and put on a voluntary basis. At the same time the practical business value of sound personnel methods began to become apparent as production per man-hour increased. Today very little paternalism exists in industrial relations, although a few die-hard managements are still trying to treat employees as slightly simple-minded children for whom "papa knows best."

Concepts of Labor.[7]—Paternalism, common in the first years of the twentieth century, was only a stage in the changing concept of labor which started with the Industrial Revolution and changes still. Although actual slavery was not found in early manufacturing as it was in agriculture and mining, a kind of serfdom founded originally upon military conquest and later upon "station-to-which-born" was common. The trip hammers and water-power presses of the armor factories of the Heraldic Knights in 1010 were operated by relatively free artisans who still had a claim for protection upon the masters they served. The English steel, glass, and textile factories upon which the Industrial Revolution, as we know it, originally impinged were operated in the thirteenth and fourteenth centuries by free handicraft workers banded together into craft guilds. The chattel concept of labor based on human slavery and serfdom is best represented in the United States by the bond servant who did occasionally work in factories.

Concepts of labor common in the industrial North at the time of the War Between the States included the machinery concept and the commodity concept. Under the former, the employer seemed to regard his employees as mere productive machines—only men did not need to be so well cared for as machines! Under the latter, the laws of supply and demand were found operative, and labor prices were fixed on a shortage basis.[8] Labor has been conceived at various times since then as part of one big happy family, as a natural resource of the country to be protected by legislation of working conditions, as individual human workers with human rights, as citizens in an industrial democracy, and most recently as customers of the business. Progressive industrial-rela-

[7] These historical concepts of labor are largely those of economists applied to employers—few employers were articulate enough to phrase a "concept." Radical worker groups held the "wage slave" concept. They denounced "wage slaves"— those whom manufacturers called "free workers"—because workers had only the "freedom" to work at manufacturers' dictated conditions or starve. These workers felt they had nothing to sell but labor in what they called a buyers' market. The ownership of the means of production (plants, tools, machinery, etc.) made factory owners dominant, workers dependent.

[8] Leaders of organized labor have been especially violent in shouting, "Labor is not a commodity!" In their own actions they reflect, nevertheless, an awareness that wages can be raised by artificial curtailment of supply through restrictive apprentice rules, immigration limitation, 3-day work weeks, or fake demand generated by "featherbedding."

tions thought today combines all of these viewpoints, but stresses: (1) the cooperative teamwork of employer and employee which enables the enterprise to provide the greatest good for society as a whole and (2) the advancement of the specific enterprise in competition through the quality of its personnel and their faith in the ultimate fairness and democratic purpose of the business.

Scope of Personnel Work.—An idea of the scope of present-day personnel work can be obtained from the breakdown of the field used in personnel-worker classification. The National Roster of Scientific and Specialized Personnel Technical Check List for Personnel Administration contains the following 20 main personnel worker activities:

1. Administration, including over-all organization and coordination of industrial-relations policies and programs.
2. Liaison between outside groups and personnel office as well as with various levels of management.
3. Legal, including drafting regulations, rules, laws or orders, and construction and interpretation.
4. Position classification, including over-all direction of job analyses, salary or wage administration, wage surveys, and pay schedules.
5. Recruitment and employment of employees.
6. Employment testing, including intelligence tests, mechanical aptitude tests, and achievement tests.
7. Placement, including induction and assignment.
8. Training, including apprentices, production workers, foremen, and executives.
9. Performance reports or merit rating.
10. Employee counseling on all types of personal problems, such as educational, vocational, health, behavior, and indebtedness relations.
11. Medical and health service.
12. Safety service, including first-aid training.
13. Group activities, such as group health and insurance, housing, cafeteria programs, and social clubs.
14. Suggestion plans and their use in labor-management production committees.
15. Employee relations, especially collective bargaining with representatives, and settling grievances.
16. Public relations.
17. Research in such fields as occupational trends, employee attitudes, and analysis of turnover.
18. Employee records for all purposes.
19. Controls through operation surveys, fiscal research, and analysis.
20. Benefit, retirement, and pension programs.

These are the major specialties only; actually provision is made in the roster for registering more than 250 different fields of activity.

Because so many different industrial-relations functions exist does not mean that every enterprise should immediately install all of them. Activities should be included only if they fit into the management pattern already set in each particular case. "The existence of every section of personnel must be justified by its helpfulness in advancing the purpose of the enterprise." [9]

Public Relations.—What the public thinks of an enterprise has such an important effect on its employee relations that developing public opinion is the third leg on the industrial-relations stool. Influencing public opinion is an important activity. It has grown from advertising and publicity roots to a company-wide effort requiring major attention from the chief executives. Often the company's efforts are assisted by some of the several hundred public-relations consultants who function as do advertising agencies. Sometimes the same vice-president heads up both public relations and industrial relations as at U.S. Rubber, General Motors, International Harvester, and Pullman Company. In other companies public relations is an independent function with its head hardly speaking to the head of industrial relations. Some practitioners, while recognizing the extreme importance of good employee relations to successful public relations, consider employees as simply another "public." [10] These group it along with stockholder relations, board-of-director relations, community relations, trade relations, and the like. Such departments (as are private consultants) are apt to be inordinately concerned with press relations, media, and "campaigns." They are also apt to overlook the fact that a more intimate relationship exists between the employer and his employees than is possible with others. Treating employees as simply another public may obtain results akin to treating them as a commodity simply because they supply a service (labor) indispensable to operation. More organization-minded companies place the industrial-relations manager at the head of all "relations" and charge him with making top executives, all levels of supervision, and employees aware of the importance of the "publics" to the success of the enterprise.

There is no actual conflict between industrial relations and public relations. Rather, it is a matter of emphasis upon *the reasons for* or *the means of* building good will for the enterprise. Neither is there any conflict between public relations and advertising, although they often use the same tools. Advertising is always an adjunct to sales, present or future. Public relations may be concerned with the same people, but chiefly in nonselling situations. Advertising problems are treated in Chap. XXVII.

[9] CURTISS, A. C., "Fundamentals and Scope of Personnel Administration," Silver Bay Conference, New York: Association Press, 1948.

[10] For a discussion of this point see REX F. HARLOW and MARVIN M. BLACK, "Practical Public Relations," p. 62, New York: Harper & Brothers, 1947.

The Public Relations Program

Programs	Representative activities included	General purpose of program
Attitudes surveys	Opinion polls, "Why I Like My Job" contests, door-to-door check, public complaint meetings	To find out the causes of employee dissatisfaction, supervisory ineffectiveness, or public lack of good will
Employee communication	Plant magazines, letters to employees, employee meetings addressed by president, annual reports to employees, posters, pay-envelope stuffers, handbooks, booklets, public-address system, dramatization	To supply adequate information to employees, to counteract false rumors heard elsewhere, to give employees a sense of "belonging" and of their importance to the enterprise, *i.e.*, to build team spirit and develop morale
Civic activity	Reports to community on jobs furnished, products bought, or taxes paid; plant tours for civic leaders; company speakers at local club meetings; public exhibits	To gain understanding of neighbors, voters, and elected representatives in plant locations; to improve tolerance of noise, smoke, and necessary wastes; to lessen excessive charity demands
Press relations (including all types of magazines, trade journals)	News releases; photographs; cartoons; personal contacts with editors, reporters, columnists; interviews; arrangements to answer all critical editorials, "Letters to the Editor," etc.; informative "ads"	To keep newspaper readers and, indirectly, employees informed; to combat false charges; to increase "friendly" news, limit derogatory stories, by furthering understanding by editors and reporters of industry
Radio-television Films	Paid programs, include news commentators as "press," industrial film shorts, educational film strips, recordings, plays	To improve understanding through visual aids and auditory effects in contacts with employees and public, to treat "new" outlets like "press"
School programs	School library, research units, teaching guides, exhibit booths, trade class "samples," booklets, films, company speakers, plant visits, annual schoolday; sponsor clubs, sports, contests, scholarships	To give teachers full story, counterbalancing misinformation; to prepare new employees in advance; to attract future managers, engineers, and skilled workers; to build future community understanding
Employee family contacts	Open-house programs, family picnics, father-son nights, recreation centers, children's clubs and programs, home-improvement campaigns, gardens	To "let family know what Daddy does," to build job pride; to add to family acceptance of necessary overtime, dirt, nightwork; to lessen radical influence
Professional group communication (clergy, lawyers, physicians, dentists, pharmacists, etc.)	Plant tours, welfare cooperation, informative brochures, "questions and answers," suggested sermons, safety and health literature, "gift" decorations, personal contact of company "professionals"	To provide additional employee information indirectly through community "thought leaders," to counteract false information, to crystallize acceptance of social responsibility and company position

Fig. 115.—Showing public-relations program activities and purposes. (*Based on analysis of campaigns conducted by American Iron and Steel Institute, Society of American Florists, U.S.V. Pulpwood Campaign, and New York, New Haven, and Hartford Railroad Co.*)

Public relations in action proceeds by three fundamental steps: *research, policy,* and *words.*[11] As stressed by James W. Irwin, formerly public-relations executive of General Motors, Monsanto Chemical, and Ford, the chief cause of unrest today in industrial relations and elsewhere is *misunderstanding.* The corrective element is *communication of ideas.*[12] Public relations is the means for the adequate conveyance of accurate ideas which lead to better understanding. By *research* the true facts are sought. Facts about the organization, the people who operate it; statistics about finances, sales, or engineering; its history, attitude, and contributions are sought. These facts are not twisted to prove a case but form the basis of *policy* for the enterprise. Sometimes the facts force a change in previous policy, but once the objective or target of the enterprise is set, all its *words* must be judged in the light of that objective. The words of a public-relations program struggle through all the mazes of semantics to reach better understanding. All the word-manipulation techniques of propaganda and the advertising copywriter are used. Every medium of publicity is used to say the right words in the most effective place. The only restriction is the audience to be reached. A company's plan for selling the facts behind its policies in the right words, at the right time, and in the right place becomes its public-relations program. Techniques commonly used are shown in Fig. 115.

Labor unions, too, use such public-relations methods as pamphleteering, press releases, teaching kits, visual aids, economic reports, and appearances before public bodies in their efforts to rally public opinion behind their negotiation demands, strike efforts, and legislation. In communicating with the members, union leaders use all the devices used by employers, including their own newspaper comic strips, air shows, sound films, and original techniques of their own. Recently the American Public Relations Association presented one of its annual "Oscars" for the most successful program to the C.I.O.

The benefits of a sound public-relations program are very evident in the other aspects of industrial relations. More applicants of all kinds hear about the company. Better applicants are more apt to seek work at the "good" company. Applicants do not feel so frightened or mystified at the prospects of employment if they have heard of the company. New employees stay long enough to "season." Expensive turnover is reduced. Employee morale and, hence, productivity are raised. Union relations are apt to be on a higher plane. Strikes and unrest are

[11] BAUS, HERBERT M., "Public Relations at Work," p. 109, New York: Harper & Brothers, 1949.

[12] *Ibid.,* p. viii.

reduced. Investigators for government agencies believe that apparent violations of the letter or spirit of regulations may be unintentional. Customers sign fewer restrictive sales contracts. Suppliers are more attentive. All parts of the company work together better in improved understanding. The greatest gain, however, is often the completely objective review of company policies and procedures which must precede turning on the spotlight of publicity. Since public relations cannot "whitewash" poor practice, it often results in more constructive company aims, rules, and efforts.[13]

FUNDAMENTALS OF INDUSTRIAL RELATIONS

The functional principles of industrial relations may be stated as: (1) sound labor policies enunciated and believed in by top management,

Fig. 116.—Training future supervisors in leadership by means of conference discussion with top executives has replaced the old "sink or swim" method in industry. (*Courtesy of Scovill Manufacturing Company.*)

(2) adequate employment practices developed by professionally minded staff assistants, and (3) effective personnel methods applied by every level of supervision. This application of the policies and practices of an organization to specific problems of individual employees may well be

[13] For a discussion of the management of public relations in business, government, labor, and social institutions see J. H. WRIGHT and B. H. CHRISTIAN, "Public Relations in Management," New York: McGraw-Hill Book Company, Inc., 1949.

guided by the advice of a centralized industrial-relations department using established techniques. The industrial-relations staff may even occasionally render direct functional assistance with specific problems or at the research and developmental level with new programs, but it cannot run a successful personnel program for a company's supervisors from some remote office. New foremen sometimes do not understand that the industrial-relations department is part of the functional staff—only advisory and regulatory within established policy. These foremen bemoan the quantities of personnel work left to the foreman. Wiser and older supervisors understand that nine-tenths of supervision is personnel work in the broader sense of the term. Even some of the more cost- or production-minded take a greater interest in their personal personnel duties when they realize that the largest part of modern manufacturing cost is made up of direct-labor costs—often estimated at 80 to 90 per cent of the total manufacturing expense when the labor costs of raw materials are included.

Labor Policies.—Dale Yoder in his "Personnel Management and Industrial Relations," [14] has defined labor policies as "simply the group of principles which guide administrators in their relationships with labor in seeking to secure the maximization of labor efficiency."

Labor policies have been defined elsewhere as statements of top-management philosophy. Not only must executive management take a position on labor problems and let that position be known, but its members must also take an active interest in seeing that those policies are carried out by line supervisors. One of the greatest defects in industrial relations today is the progressive dilution of well-conceived policy by ill-conceived decisions in practice on the part of lower-level supervisors. Too many company policies, particularly of the unwritten variety, are badly misunderstood or even unheard of at the working level. A first fundamental, then, of successful personnel administration is *top management interest* in the well-being of that program.

Hugh W. Wright [15] wrote about his company's labor policies:

The American Rolling Mill Company was the first industrial organization to publish and distribute its basic policies. However, this was not done hurriedly. Beginning with the basic thoughts of confidence, good will, and a square deal, almost 20 years of practical experience were consumed in the development of these policies to the point where they could be stated in written form. They were published in full after being officially approved by resolution of the Board of Directors on December 12, 1919.

[14] Prentice-Hall, Inc., New York, 1942, p. 22.
[15] *Factory Management and Maintenance,* Vol. 95, No. 5, p. S382, May, 1937.

The two outstanding effects of publishing and distributing company policies are:

First, it tends to create greater consistency upon the part of the supervisory organization in making decisions affecting people. . . .

Second, it provides those who are not supervisors with certain standards of treatment they have a right to expect. . . .

Space does not permit the publication of ARMCO Policies. They constitute a fairly large booklet of themselves. However, we do include a summary of the planks on organization for they are the foundation of all personnel relations at ARMCO:

1. *A Square Deal:* To insist on a square deal always to everyone.

2. *Compensation:* To provide not only fair remuneration, but the best compensation for service rendered that it is possible to pay under the changing economic, commercial, and other competitive conditions that exist from time to time. It is ARMCO's ambition to develop an organization of such spirit, loyalty, and efficiency that it can and will secure results which will make it possible for individual members to earn and receive better compensation than would be possible if performing a similar service in other fields.

3. *Incentive:* To provide every possible and practical sound incentive to best effort, as it is the great mainspring of all human accomplishment.

4. *Opportunity:* To provide every possible opportunity for advancement as it is the ladder on which the individual hopes to reach his ultimate goal. . . . It is a fixed ARMCO policy to provide such training opportunities as will aid the individual in his advancement.

5. *Working Conditions:* To create and maintain both good and safe working conditions. ARMCO believes that good and safe working conditions, in the fullest sense of the expression, are absolutely essential to industrial efficiency and progress. For that reason, concerted effort is continually being made to provide equipment such as will make for cleanliness and orderliness and safety, and such training as will reduce to a minimum the possibility of accidents.

6. *Living Conditions:* In every possible way to encourage good living conditions. . . . ARMCO believes that individually and collectively, we are the product of the environment in which we live and work. It believes that clean, orderly approaches and mill yards help us to walk straighter, think clearer, and feel finer than do uncared-for premises, and that a good environment is the foundation of the home. . . . It is the responsibility of the community to create such conditions as will eliminate human unrest and unhappiness and to deal sympathetically and helpfully with the emergencies and tragedies of life. . . . Industry should, therefore, support every sound and constructive agency established in the community in an effort to make civic conditions respond to the highest needs of its citizens.

7. *Mutual Interest:* To encourage such organizational activities as will clarify and enlarge the mutual interests of all who are working with the management of the company.

The labor policy of Bird and Son, Incorporated, of East Walpole, Mass., is stated as follows: [16]

The basic principle which has guided the management from the very beginning has been that the Bird Organization is made up of Men and Women and the continued observance of this principle has caused the business to be conducted in a manner fair to those who work within the organization, fair to the stockholders, and fair to the customers who purchase the goods we manufacture.

We believe that the skill, loyalty, and security of our workers are the foundation rocks upon which this business has been built, and that their good will is our most valuable possession.

One of the chief values to be derived from the formulation of a stated labor policy is the education of both top management and line supervisors in the actual problems, methods, and desirable solutions of the existing business. This value has in some companies been extended to the employees by having them participate in the formulation of the policies of a company. Sometimes this participation on the part of the employees takes place without management's intention during collective bargaining and union contract negotiations. Indeed the first policy statements that a good many companies have are part of their initial union contracts.

Most managements in America today agree that all employees should be treated alike. Few advocate or indulge in open nepotism and favoritism. Even the best intentioned managements, however, cannot guarantee equal treatment to every employee under the same circumstances without a set of rules to guide its several supervisors in their treatment of personnel problems. Even a single executive finds it impossible to maintain consistency from case to case under pressure without stated policies. Some companies upon investigation have found wide opposition and misunderstanding of long-stated personnel policies among even the higher levels of its executives. A second fundamental of good industrial relations can thus be seen to be *clearly stated personnel policies!*

No policy can be said to be clear until it is understood and followed by all levels of management. The industrial-relations department has the function of systematizing policy and developing necessary practices. In addition, it must be ever alert to detect any departure from established policy. No company-minded organization member can continue to violate the stated rules of company conduct once he understands them. Superintendents, foremen, and line supervisors need to be trained, there-

[16] See "Examination of the Personnel Program," Metropolitan Life Insurance Company, Policyholders Service Bureau, New York.

fore, in company policy, intention, and methods. Ideally, this training starts with the chairman of the board or the president of the company instructing his vice-presidents or general managers in his own beliefs. Each of these men then passes the information along to his subordinates as fully and as carefully as it was relayed to him. The subordinates in turn pass company decisions down the line until they reach the employee body. Any intelligent, fairly experienced employee should be able to state in his own words the outstanding features of the company policy and should know the reasons for those policies. In too few companies is this true today. Rather the carefully prepared executive decision is passed along with inadequate information as to its true meaning and reasons, and loses vitality at every transmission until, when it reaches the employee, it has all the cooperative spirit of a "Keep-off-the-grass" sign.

This training of the executive to carry out the stated policies of the company in his daily practice is not something added to an already over-full duty roster. Rather, an intelligent fulfillment of management intention in every man-to-man contact is the main function of the modern supervisor who must lead rather than drive or push. He has become the daily embodiment of the missing soul of the corporation. He makes the organization live. He supplies the lost personal contact. His personal contacts are kept uniform and in step with those of other supervisors by means of established policies and by training in those policies.

Certain companies, such as General Motors Corporation, Westing-house Electric and Manufacturing Company, and Western Electric Company, have found a detailed organizational manual, outlining the function and expected responsibilities of every supervisory position, of great assistance in such training. Fig. 118 shows an organization unit from such a manual. It is included for several reasons: (1) to show how one modern personnel department is organized (in looking at the parts we are apt to forget the integrated whole); (2) to indicate the broad scope of information that modern management feels its supervisors must have; (3) to show clearly the parts in an organizational manual write-up including a description of duties and responsibilities, establishment of measures of performance on the job, statement of relationships with others in the organization, and the limits of authority; (4) to indicate how a functional staff department operates within the established policies and assigned authority of the company organization. It should be apparent, that even on those matters where this manager has *full authority,* *e.g.,* discharge of personnel and execution of labor agreements, effective coordination with the rest of the organization requires discussion with others and a pooling of judgment. Similarly on matters where he has

ORGANIZATIONAL UNIT:.
Personnel Department

K KOPPERS

TITLE:
Manager

NO. 37

DATE ISSUED Jan. 1, 1947

DATE REVISED Apr. 15,1948

PAGE NO. 1 OF 3

JOB SPECIFICATION

BASIC FUNCTION:

      Determination of Company personnel and labor relations policies and recommendation of such matters for approval of management. Development of plans and procedures to apply approved Company personnel policies to the actual operation of its business. Study of the personnel aspect in over-all management of the Company's business, following trends and providing realistic means of meeting them. Developing controls and measurements to audit results. Over-all direction and general supervision of the department's staff activities and its relationships with other units. General supervision of operating personnel functions for the Company's general offices. Labor relations assistance and advice to Operating Divisions, and preparation of surveys and reports on conditions and trends in and outside the Company.

SCOPE:

      The duties and responsibilities delegated to this position are company-wide in scope as regards determination and recommendation of policy and general study of the personnel aspect of the Company. Responsibility for operating personnel activities is confined to the supervision of this work for the Company's general offices. Labor relations service and auditing of results of the personnel program are company-wide in scope.

DUTIES AND RESPONSIBILITIES:

1.   Development of personnel policies designed to provide the Company with a means of obtaining and maintaining an efficient and cooperative group of employees, and for dealing with those employees in a just and fair manner. Recommending these policies to general management for adoption. Preparation of specific plans and procedures for use by all units of the Company in carrying out these policies.

2.   Research and study of the general relationship of personnel to the problems of Company operations. Determination of the most effective policies, methods and procedures used by the Company and by outside organizations, and dissemination of helpful information and advice to other units on personnel and labor relations matters. Analysis of each objective of personnel management to insure that plans and programs are developed to attain these objectives.

3.   Constant review of the Company's personnel program and the manner in which it is being administered, through measurement of the effectiveness with which plans and procedures are being used by other units and the results being secured through use of such plans. Introduction of new objectives and programs to strengthen the Company's position regarding the quality and quantity of employees, the manner in which they are trained, measurement of their efficiency and worth, and of the manner in which they are reimbursed for their services.

Fig. 118.—A statement of job specification for the personnel department. (*Taken from the organizational manual of the Koppers Koke Company, Pittsburgh, Penn., by special permission of the company.*)

4.   Cooperation with the Public Relations Section in the development of programs to increase employee morale and respect for the Company, and to further complete understanding of the Company and its objectives by all employees.

5.   Supervision, in a general manner, of the assignment of duties to members of the department. Providing an organization plan for the department to cover all of the necessary functions of personnel management.

6.   Delegating responsibility and authority to section heads of the department staff.

7.   Preparing and presenting a budget of operating expenses for the Personnel Department.

8.   Preparing and presenting reports to General Management covering personnel activities and results.

METHOD OF MEASUREMENT:
        The position of the Company with respect to its employees, including wage and salary levels, good employee relationships, satisfactory relationships with labor, and the success of personnel policies and procedures in providing the Company with sufficient employees of desired quality will be a measurement of performance of these duties. General cooperation with other units will be an additional method of measurement.

RELATIONSHIPS WITH OTHER UNITS OF THE ORGANIZATION:

1.   The Manager, Personnel Department, will be responsible to the President for proper performance of these duties.

2.   The following subordinate positions will be responsible to the Manager, Personnel Department for performance of assigned duties:

        Assistant Manager
        Personnel Administrator
        Wage and Salary Administrator
        Labor Relations Administrator
        Personnel Supervisor, General Office

3.   In the course of performing the duties of this position, the Manager will develop general policies and procedures for use by other units of the organization in performing personnel work in field offices. Such matters will be referred to the President for approval and issue, and will be complied with by all other units when so approved.

4.   As a member of the Operating Committee, the Personnel Manager will be jointly responsible for consideration and recommendation of any matters within the scope of this committee.

5.   As Chairman of the Personnel Committee, the Manager will be responsible for preparing agenda, conducting meetings of the committee, consolidating the ideas of members, and presenting committee recommendations to the President.

FIG. 118.—*Continued.*

no authority, *e.g.*, in public relations, which at Koppers is a separate department, he may make recommendations or be consulted by the departments who have authority.

The complete manual from which this figure is taken contains over 270 such job specifications. Companies who use such manuals feel that

ORGANIZATIONAL UNIT:
Personnel Department

TITLE:
Manager

NO. 37

DATE ISSUED   Jan. 1, 1947

DATE REVISED

PAGE NO. 3 OF 3

JOB SPECIFICATION

LIMITS OF AUTHORITY:

	NO AUTH	FULL AUTH	AUTHORITY LIMIT	RECOMMEND TO POSITION SHOWN IF AUTHORITY IS LIMITED
Hiring Additional Employees	x			President
Approving Salaries			$7500/Yr.	"
Granting Salary Increases			to$7500/Yr.	"
Acquiring Capital Equipment			$500	Appropriations Committee
Acquiring Expensed Equipment		x		
Authorizing Travel		x		
Donations and Subscriptions	x			Director of Public Relations
Authorizing Paid Overtime		x		
Using Professional Services	x			President
Requisitioning Office Supplies		x		
*Approving Travel Expenses		x		
*Approving Entertainment Expense		x		
Leasing Property or Equipment	x			Operating Committee
Acquiring Property or Land	x			Appropriations Committee
Approving Excused Leave		x		
Sale of Property & Equipment	x			Operating Committee
Transfer of Personnel		x		
Promotion of Personnel		x		
Repairs to Capital Assets			$500	Operating Committee
Use of Telephone, Wire & Cable		x		
Discharge of Personnel		x		
Special Price Discounts	x			President
Assignment of Company Cars	x			Traffic & Trans. Department
Retaining Pensionable Employees	x			Pension Committee
Special Credit Arrangements	x			Treasurer
Expense for Employee Activities	x			President
Advances to Employees	x			Manager, Finance Department
Moving Expense of Employees		x		
Execution of Labor Agreements		x		
Expenditures for Advertising	x			Director of Public Relations
Approving Price Quotations	x			President
Accepting Orders	x			"
Approving Purchase Commitments	x			"
Opening Bank Accounts	x			Treasurer
Approval of Budgets		x		
Social Membership Dues	x			President
Trade Membership Dues	x			Public Relations Section
Professional Membership Dues	x			President
Petty Cash Expenditures		x		

*Except expenses personally incurred.

FIG. 118.—*Continued*.

the first step in training is deciding what is to be known. They have also adopted policy statements and circulate appointment registers giving the name, former position, and general duties of every man. The detailed procedures to be followed—daily "paper work" for timekeeping, leaves of absence, accident reports, etc.—are distributed as shown in

Fig. 119. It is on the basis of this available information that supervisory training proceeds. A third fundamental of effective industrial relations, then, is *detailed training of all levels of supervision in the practices necessary to carry out company policy.*

Even the most farsighted and comprehensive personnel or labor poli-

STANDARD PRACTICE INSTRUCTION	Page 1 of 2	Class. Number 2.A.5
Subject EMPLOYEE IN-PLANT PASS	Date Issued 10/12/50	By Order Of S.T.W.Gen'l.Manager
	Supersedes -	S.P.I. 3/12/45

* * * CONTENTS * * *

I. - GENERAL - A. Plant Medical Department; B. Cafeteria; C. Union Business.
II. - PROCEDURE   * * * * * *

I. - GENERAL
    No employee shall be absent from his own department during working hours, without the permission of his Department Head or Assistant. Maintenance and Repair Workers, Messengers or other employees whose work would ordinarily carry them to other departments, are exempt from this ruling.

A. - Plant Medical Department. In accordance with the procedure outlined in S.P.I. 2.C.1, "Plant Medical Department and Treatment of Injuries," an employee who sustains an injury, no matter how slight, must report the injury to his Department Head, who shall, in the case of a Minor Injury, fill out an "Employee In-Plant Pass," giving same to the employee and instructing him to report immediately to the Plant Medical Department.

II. - PROCEDURE
A. - Whenever it is necessary for an employee to leave his department, the Department Head or his Assistant shall issue an "Employee In-Plant Pass," in duplicate, listing:

    1. Employee's name   4. Reason for visit
    2. Department-Clock Number   5. Date and Time of issuance
    3. Check - Department to be visited 6. Signature of issuing Supervisor

    The employee shall be given the Original copy, and the Duplicate shall be retained in the department.

FIG. 119.—Showing S.P.I. used in loose-leaf policy manual to state rules, give directions for use of forms, etc., as a part of supervisory training in better industrial relations.

cies cannot stand by themselves without having "tools of management" or systems and techniques provided for their execution. It is at this stage of development that the professional personnel administrator is most apparent as he establishes working rules, regulations, and procedures for carrying out the policies established by top management and taught to supervisors. Most of the chapters in the rest of this section will recount these personnel tools. All that is needed here is to sound a general warning against red tape, excessive forms, innumerable records, and too many rubber stamps. Oddly enough too much personnel system can be worse than too little, although that too is a common shortcoming. When forms and procedures are too detailed, in personnel as in other phases of management, they begin to duplicate each other and become ends in themselves completely disguising defects in the industrial-relations systems of which they are a part. A fourth fundamental of industrial relations is, therefore, *a system of procedures extensive enough to effectuate the planned program, yet flexible enough to adapt to changing conditions.*

A fifth fundamental of industrial relations is the necessity of a *policing of personnel practice* and an *evaluation of personnel policies* through the use of control devices administered by a central staff authority reporting directly to the highest company authority. This policing is made necessary by several considerations, among which are the natural human resistance to change which makes new methods difficult to introduce; a common attitude among branch operating men of larger organizations, which might be expressed as follows, "Don't fuss while the head office representative is here, we'll forget what he says when he goes away"; and the reflection of an attitude often common among opportunistic business leaders that all personnel methods are merely false cloaks behind which to hide undesirable worker exploitation. It seems needless to point out to a student of practical business that any attempt to steal the benefits of industrial-relations methods without sound company policies is predestined to failure.

LABOR RELATIONS

The problems of collective bargaining, employee grievances, and union representation result chiefly from a lack of mutual confidence between those negotiating, a great deal of misunderstanding of each other's position, and the conflict between the natural urge of the employee to have a voice in matters that affect his livelihood and the normal management need and desire to make its own decisions in running a business for profit. Much of the distrust built up over a period of time could be removed if managements would be willing to take workers into their confidence, let them know what decisions are being made, and give them a chance to object before a public announcement is made. Workers have often opposed management actions when that opposition reacted to the workers' disadvantage, solely because they did not understand *why*.

The natural result of the increasing technology developing since the Industrial Revolution, and particularly since the corporation builders, has been a preoccupation of top management with problems of finance and technology, while employee problems were relegated to the lowest supervisory level. Modern management is changing its approach in this respect and is now hiring research brains to deal with the technological progress and trying to get back to the small-shop familiarity with employee problems. "Essential to the use of this type of approach is a philosophy by top management that dealing with human resources is the most important job of the executive and supervisory personnel." [17]

Prominent executives recognize this and have put it into reports to their stockholders. Only recently one report stated that the continued success of the concern over many decades was a result of the competence of the personnel, which competence management sought to perpetuate by "the realization on the part of executives and supervisors that their 'Number 1 Job' is dealing with people."

Many of the grievances presented by employees are much more a matter of attitude than of fact. In negotiations workers make statements regularly revealing their emotional bias. In dealing with employees, what they *believe* to be so might just as well be so, whether factual or not, as far as any final settlement is concerned.

The basic urge of the modern industrial worker to know and to be known by his bosses, by the top management of his company, is a natural result of the democratic way of life. As such it is wholly desirable. Contacts between employers and employees over the bargaining table or in settling grievances may serve no logical function and yet may increase profits by giving a higher rate of production per man-hour worked simply as a by-product of greater worker satisfaction.

Control of Labor Relations.—The need for granting the employee at least partial participation in decisions affecting him in his daily work if he is to give his best effort is present whether he belongs to a union or not. If he is a member, however, the ways of *granting the employee that participation instead of only representation* are so closely walled in by union and government controls that realization is difficult. The labor [18] structure of America in the A.F. of L., C.I.O., and independent unions is detailed in Chap. XXIII. That structure is sustained by a host of Federal and state labor laws, some of which are also outlined there. It has been repeatedly demonstrated at home and abroad that while government aid increases labor-union effectiveness, it also holds great dangers for labor, industry, and the economic system. In the United States since the New Deal days of the mid-1930's that aid has increasingly taken the form of control over both the employer and the union in the

---

[17] APPLEY, L. A., Emergence of a New Management Era, *Personnel,* May, 1949.

[18] All employees (including the hired manager) are "labor" in the broad sense. As the term was used when the U.S. Department of Labor was founded, all wage earners were included. In "social-status" language all who work with their hands are covered. Until recently "labor" was intended to mean "industrial wage earners" as contrasted to white-collar or clerical, professional, service, financial, and agricultural workers. As used by union leaders and increasingly by the public press, "labor" means "trades union members." The latter is the sense intended here.

collective-bargaining relationship. Some of the implications of that growing government control are given in Chap. II. Employers have felt its effect in wartime and peacetime plant seizure and the action of legal and extralegal government boards and commissions. Unions have felt control through government injunctions, through legislative investigations of labor-union monopoly, such as the 1949 investigation of the Senate Banking and Currency Committee, and in other ways.

It has been increasingly pointed out by disinterested students [19] of the labor scene that the power of employers and the matched power of unions is so great, their disagreement so bitter, and the public influence of their inability to get along so sharply felt, as virtually to invite government control. To avoid complete governmental dominance, both parties must change. Management must learn the nature of union leadership and must make constructive use of it in better employee relations. Unions must learn the functions of business management and must temper their political leadership with an acceptance of responsibility akin to the authority they already exercise.

Government Influence.—The influence of the Federal, state, and local governments on management in its industrial relations is exerted in two ways. One has been indicated as the support of unions in their dealings with employers. This began with the War Labor Board of World War I and lapsed after that war (except for railroad employees) [20] until revived as a part of the social legislation of the 1930's and embodied in the Norris-LaGuardia Anti-injunction Act (7 Stat. 70) and the National Labor Relations Act (Wagner Act), (49 Stat. 449). This act declared the public policy of the United States to be "encouraging the practice and procedure of collective bargaining." This policy was strengthened by action of the National War Labor Board during World War II and reaffirmed in the Taft-Hartley Act. State laws and local ordinances followed the approximate path blazed by Federal acts. Unions recognize this encouragement.

Unions have come to expect Federal intervention when an industry-wide strike affects the general public. This, in fact, has become an essential part of union strategy, since, when there is a complete stoppage of the production

---

[19] See SEIDMAN, J., "Union Rights and Union Duties," New York: Harcourt, Brace and Company, 1943; SLICHTER, SUMNER H., "The Challenge of Industrial Relations," Ithaca, New York: Cornell University Press, 1947; BAKKE, E. W., "Mutual Survival," New Haven, Conn.: Yale University Press, 1946; DULLES, F. R., "Labor in America," New York: The Thomas Y. Crowell Company, 1949.

[20] The Railway Labor Act of 1926 (44 Stat. L. 578, Pt. 2), growing out of government operation of the railroads during the war, specified the right of railroad employees to organize.

of a basic commodity, the strike is in reality a strike against the general public (including the workers indirectly affected), quite as much as against employers.

Federal intervention has become so much a part of present strategy in the settlement of labor disputes that the influence of labor leaders is often measured by their ability to deal directly or indirectly with the White House or the President's advisers.[21]

The second way in which government influence is felt by management is in the necessary compliance with other laws not having to do with unionism but affecting the employer-employee relationship. These are legion. Examples include workmen's compensation laws mentioned in the safety section, wage and hour laws, the Social Security Act of 1935, and the Employment Act of 1946. In addition many state and local ordinances, such as sanitary codes and fire laws, are controlling. In specific circumstances regulations of the Interstate Commerce Commission, Civil Aeronautics Board, Federal Communications Commission, Maritime Commission, and the Federal Bankruptcy Act must be followed.

As has been indicated, the problem of legal compliance can no longer be left to the company lawyer or to top management except in the small company. Each department head throughout the organization must know and comply with the regulations that govern his operations. Thus the employment manager must set up procedures for obeying such laws as unemployment-compensation regulations, minimum working-age laws, and the antidiscrimination codes found in some states. The plant hospital and safety engineer must know state sanitary codes, rules governing the handling of explosives, workman's compensation, etc. The company social-service workers must know Social Security and local "poor laws" and coordinate with the operations of local welfare departments. The wage administrator must keep the company in compliance with minimum-wage laws, the Fair Labor Standards Act, Walsh-Healey Act, and equal-wage-for-equal-work requirements. The list is so long, the coverage so great, and the growth of administrative interpretations so uncertain that no industrial-relations department can be sure it is always in step with the law, but the conscientious try to be.

An example of the problem faced can be found in experience with the Fair Labor Standards Act (wage and hours law) of 1938. The original act was intended to "spread the work" by making it expensive to work employees long hours and to improve labor standards. The act covers workers (see exceptions) engaged in interstate commerce or in the production of goods which move in interstate commerce and provides minimum wages and maximum hours. Wage minimums moved

[21] METZ and JACOBSTEIN, "A National Labor Policy," Washington, D.C.: Brookings Institution, 1947.

progressively upward from 25 cents in 1938 to 40 cents in 1945, and to 75 cents in 1950. Higher minimums have been set for many industries by action of the administrator and industry committees. Hours are not limited as they were under the Federal 8-Hour Statute of 1912, but time and a half must be paid for more than 40 hours in a week. Children under 16 cannot be employed, and at dangerous occupations not under 18. The act is enforced by the U.S. Department of Labor and provides for a fine up to $10,000 or, on second conviction, imprisonment of 6 months, or both, plus double back wages due employees.

The following employees are exempt from this act: executives; administrative and professional workers; outside salesmen; outside buyers; persons engaged in local retail-selling or retail-manufacturing establishments; employees of retail or service establishments (such as laundries), the greater part of whose business is intrastate; employees of air lines, street railways, local motor busses, switchboard operators of small telephone exchanges, local telegraph agencies, and small weekly or small daily newspapers; fishermen, seamen, and agricultural workers engaged in farming or processing within the area of production.

Two separate occasions have arisen when court interpretation of the long-existing Fair Labor Standards Act threatened a large segment of industry with bankruptcy. The "portal-to-portal" dispute arose over the payment of workers for time spent walking from the plant gate to the workbench and getting ready for work. Employers suddenly found employees' accumulated claims for millions of dollars back wages supported by the U.S. Supreme Court. Nation-wide business liquidation was avoided only by emergency passage of the Portal-to-Portal Act of 1947 (Public Law 49, c.52, 80th Cong., 1st Sess.) which provided for retroactive limitation of employer's liability and for payment of employees only for "customary working time." The "overtime-on-overtime" controversy assumed industry-wide significance when the U.S. Supreme Court sustained suit by longshoremen against stevedoring companies. Here the issue involved including such premiums as those paid for Saturday, Sunday, holiday, and night work in the regular rate for overtime-pay calculation. Acting on the advice of the wage and hour administrator, employers had been accustomed to offset such premium payments against overtime due under the law and to disregard payments for not working, such as for idle holidays, vacations, sickleave, or for showing up when no work was available. All this was questioned. Again, 11 years' liability for double back wages plus the clerical problem of recalculation threatened business stability. This time (July, 1949) the 81st Congress, 1st Session, amended the Fair Labor Standards Act with Public Law 177 banning overtime-on-overtime payments retroactively and providing that in the future employers could not be held liable for acting under administrative interpretations of the Federal wage and hours administrator.[22]

SUMMARY

The field of industrial relations in its three major aspects, labor relations, employee relations, and public relations, represents today a major segment of industrial management. The human aspects of business are coming more and more to the fore. Money, materials, machines, and markets are important. Without men and management, however, they are only empty credits and stagnant warehouses. It takes dynamic management to operate in industrial economy. Today's dynamic management is recognizing its social responsibilities and the increasing profit opportunities that result from the development of human cooperation and willing participation.

Individual techniques, procedures, and methods will always be important. Any manager must at least be acquainted with the activities listed. Growing pressure through government participation must be met. An awareness of measurable public opinion provides guidance. Industrial relations is increasingly becoming one of top management's most important jobs.

CASE PROBLEM

1. Recent debates on Federal labor laws have stressed the following issues:

a. Opposition to union radicalism: the non-Communist affidavit for union leaders.

b. Establishment of financial responsibility of unions: financial reports of expenditures, right to sue unions for damages.

c. Limitation of political force of unions: collecting and spending union funds for political campaigns.

d. Protecting public health and safety: advance notice, government intervention and injunctions.

e. Regulation of strikes *not* threatening the public health and safety: right to strike, wildcat strikes, peaceful picketing, mass or violent picketing, settlement of disputes without strikes.

f. Regulation of union and management unfair labor practices: employee coercion, right of free speech, duty to bargain in good faith, secondary boycotts.

[22] The Overtime-on-Overtime Act of June 20, 1949, and portions of the Portal-to-Portal Act, were added to amendments to the Fair Labor Standards Act of June 25, 1938, which became effective in January, 1950.

g. Limiting so-called union security: closed shop, union shop elections, checkoff of dues.

h. Establishment of collective-bargaining units: status of independent unions, crafts, foremen, guards, professional employees, industry-wide bargaining.

i. Certification of representatives through election: right to use NLRB, frequency of elections, decertification, employer rights to ask election.

Discussion Questions

1. Select any three of the above issues and state your position for or against its inclusion in Federal labor law. Give the advantages and disadvantages from the viewpoint of unions, management, employees, and the public.

2. The public welfare can be endangered by (1) subversive infiltration in unions, (2) interruption of essential services, (3) hazards to safety or health through strikes and violence. Which of the above issues provides the best controls protecting the public from these dangers?

3. Considerable issue has been made of an employee's right *not to join* a union now that union organization and collective bargaining have become national policy. Should there be such a right? Why not, or if so, how can it be assured?

CASE PROBLEM

2. Employee morale is apt to be very low in an industry which is believed to be dying. Public-relations campaigns of reeducation may be successful in their effects on customers but are apt to neglect the employee. The phonograph was made obsolete by the radio, the bicycle by the automobile, the ice industry by the electric refrigerator. All "came back" technologically and sold themselves on a service and pleasure basis. The ice industry reached its all-time production peak in 1945, yet the iceman remains the butt of public ridicule. He and his product are relegated to the days of gas lights and horse-drawn trolleys. His employment quadruples in the summer months, languishes in winter.

Discussion Questions

1. If the ice industry is able to continue its comeback, how can its importance to public health be used to improve the iceman's morale?

2. Outline the employee-relations steps, including public-relations means to be used, for getting a better class of applicants, improving worker satisfaction, and smoothing labor relations.

3. Select some other nearly obsolete industry which "came back." Suggest what part public-relations activities could play in better industrial relations for that industry.

CASE PROBLEMS

3. The employees of the Hook Chemical Company [23] organized a soft-ball team and challenged other industrial teams in the area, eventually winning the city industrial championship. This inspired them to fence in the sand lot on which they played and charge admission to their games in order to buy uniforms worthy of champions.

President Slocum of Hook Chemical Company felt justly proud of his employees but did not relish the paid admissions. He, therefore, had a grandstand erected beside some vacant land he owned and leveled a playing field. When he presented the team with Hook uniforms upon completion of this field, he took occasion to state that he was making this gift so that all games in the future might be free to all. Suggest how the employees reacted to this generosity.

4. The 89 employees of Smith Bottoms, Inc.[23] were being organized by an international union. As their relationship with the owner-manager was very friendly, the employees asked the "boss" what he thought of the speech being made by the organizer at the factory gate. The employees listened to his reply and gathered around until he found himself making a speech to the general effect that he knew of no good that had come of unions and that the specific organization in question had a bad record of sit-down strikes, etc. Assuming that the statements he made were true, was he justified?

5. The Allis-Chalmers organization chart of their industrial-relations setup (see Fig. 117) shows major departmental breakdowns, and some 95 or 100 separate functions. Consider in the light of present-day problems, how this division of the company could be reorganized under four department heads, consolidating such functions as seem to require it. Suggest additional functions.

[23] Fictitious name.

CHAPTER XX

PERSONNEL MANAGEMENT

Although the term "personnel management" is used by some companies to cover all of what we refer to as industrial relations, this chapter on personnel management will be devoted to the more limited field represented by the work of the employment office. This is perhaps the most common centralized activity in that third of industrial relations which we have labeled employee relations. We should not forget, however, that it is only one such function parallel in importance with others such as training, morale building, and social services. Personnel management includes the development of a labor market from which employees may be hired; problems of selection using interviewing techniques, application blanks, and employment testing; and a study of employee records. A final section will deal with problems of labor turnover and the stabilization of employment.

Development of a Labor Market.—One of the chief problems involved in the development of a stable employment market is the wide variation in employment activity from time to time. The employment manager seems always to live in a land of feast or famine; either there is a labor shortage and he cannot hire enough people, or there is a labor surplus and people must be turned away with an uninjured opinion of the company while the relatively few hired must be the best available. Both conditions may exist at the same time, since a labor shortage is usually only a shortage of workers possessing a specific skill.

A few applicants appear voluntarily at the factory employment office or are sent to the employment manager by other members of the organization. The majority of desirable applicants, however, must be sought out through the initiative of the employment manager. One of the most acceptable, as well as the most economical, sources of applicants is the employment service maintained by the several states. At various times these employment offices have been under Federal supervision. The United States Employment Service (USES) still supplies funds, technical service, and interoffice clearance. The state unemployment-compensation system is usually a parallel organization, often sharing offices with the employment service. Federal funds are supplied through the Bureau of Employment Security formerly of the Federal Security Agency and now of the Department of Labor. Many employers are reluctant to use

486

the services of these public-supported employment agencies.   When they were first started, the employers claimed that not enough care was given to the selection of applicants for a specific opening.   As the democratic principles of the Fair Employment Practices Committee were forced upon

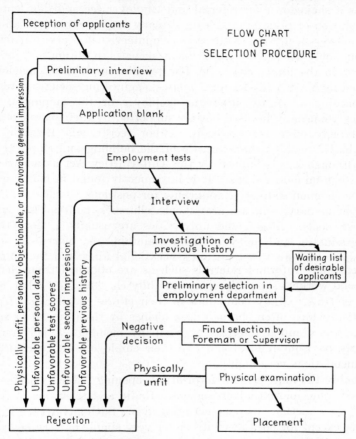

FIG. 120.—This shows the steps in selection procedure as an applicant is either rejected or passed along to the next screening action.   The placement is not completed, however, until it has been followed up by checking supervisory and employee satisfaction.

the local offices of the employment services, many employers who did not want to hire Negroes, Jews, and other minority groups found employment service applicants increasingly unsatisfactory.   Reynolds and Shister (see bibliography) present details of a study of the many problems connected with employment service.

Most private employment agencies are operated on a fee-charging basis and are licensed by the municipality in which they operate. The most common fee is one week's salary paid by the employee during the first month of employment. In some occupations, where a labor scarcity exists, the employer pays the agency's fee. Although occasional abuses, such as a shakedown for referral and employer fee splitting, enter into the operation of private agencies and many employees can ill afford the fee, employers feel that a better selective interviewing service is rendered, and commonly use private employment agencies to fill unusual jobs, particularly in the larger cities. A few private employment agencies are operated by YMCA's, settlement houses, engineering societies, etc., without charging a fee to either the employer or the employee. These agencies are usually licensed but are supported by their parent organizations largely on a service basis. Labor recruitment through "union hiring halls" remains characteristic of the building and shipping industries, although it was banned by the Taft-Hartley Act as a part of the general ban on closed shops. It is infrequently found in manufacturing.

Other common sources of applicants for positions which the alert employment manager will use are schools, churches, political and national clubs. Schools, colleges, and universities are usually anxious to place their graduates, and many of them maintain free placement services, considerate of both the applicant's vocational aims and the employer's requirements. Informal referrals such as are obtained from clergymen and social workers should be more carefully checked than other employment referrals. Many companies in their efforts to get away from the favoritism which often characterized hirings by the foreman or superintendent have limited referrals by company members. Other companies regularly pass out referral cards to their employees and consider these recommendations very highly.

Probably the most general form of job-opening publicity is the newspaper or trade-journal advertisement. Radio and television advertising "spots" are sometimes used as recruiting aids. Such advertising is seldom effective except for positions with either very simple or very complex requirements. A much condemned form of classified advertising is the "labor pirating" advertisement by out-of-town employers for highly skilled workers. Usually these advertisements request employees with specific skills to get in touch with a Mr. Smith at a local hotel. Smith turns out to be a labor scout who offers high wages, unlimited overtime, moving expenses, bonuses, etc., to encourage labor migration. Neither all labor scouting nor all migration is undesirable. When recruiting from distant points is intelligently limited to the selection of only excess workers, such as exist in areas depressed by technological change, or is aimed at discovering workers who are not employed at their highest skill, its results are socially desirable however much it may be condemned by provincial interests. College-student scouting is highly desirable from both the viewpoint of the employer and employee since it quickly places the newly qualified graduate in a position where the greatest contribution can be made.

The oldest of all applicant encouragements is the posted "Man Wanted" sign. Job-opening notice posters are sometimes used inside the factory to invite promotional requests from qualified employees. Information that such a notice is posted travels quickly by way of the employment grapevine throughout the labor market area. If definite job specifications are included, desirable applicants will appear. Small companies particularly find the factory-gate notice effective.

Employment Policies.—Before an employment manager can start hiring for the openings in a company, he must know both the written and unwritten employment policies of that company and its various divisions. Does the company attempt to maintain a balance of the minority groups in the community in its company population? Does the company employ all religious groups? Is the particular opening suitable for members of all races? Are the sexes considered equal? Are there promotional policies that make physically or mentally handicapped individuals unemployable? Are left-handed or glasses-wearing employees subjected to unusual safety risks? Must the oil-allergic or chemical-sensitive be limited to specific departments? What about the color-blind? The illiterate? The foreign-speaking only? The answers to these and similar questions constitute a company's employment policy.

Personnel Department Physical Layout.[1]—The actual layout of the plant section in which employment work is performed will depend upon the size of the company and its attitude toward employees. The employment office may range all the way from the bare minimum of an interviewing chair beside some part-time manager's desk to complex arrangements as shown in Fig. 121 for medium and large factories. Careful organization of the actual working space with flow charts of the applicant's route will save needless direction giving and speed up the hiring process. Large waiting rooms can be used, during dull hiring periods when no applicants are present, for general training and social meetings of employees.

Employment Office Functions.—The basic purpose of an employment office is to hire desirable employees for specific company openings. A good employment interviewer does a lot of public-relations work in "selling the applicant the company if not the job" and may even give surprisingly good vocational guidance, but basically he is trying to find

[1] See *Factory*, Vol. 101, No. 9, for treatment of this topic by C. T. Tucker.

the best man for an existing job as promptly as possible. "Best" quality depends not only upon aptitude and experience qualifications for the present job but also upon potentiality for growth into possible promotions. The selection and placement of the new employee, following the steps in Fig. 120, are the first opportunity for a company to start to forge ahead of its competitors by having better man power.

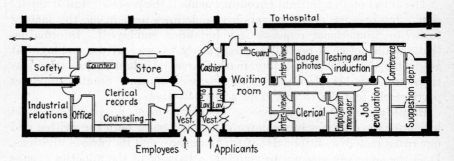

FIG. 121.—In the layout for a large plant, the personnel department is split into two halves—one for the regular employees, the other for applicants. (*Adapted from Factory, September, 1943, pp. 154–155.*)

Most modern employment offices make use of formal application blanks. There has been a deplorable tendency among many companies to copy established application blanks and to include numerous insignificant and prying questions. In states [2] having antidiscrimination laws questions having to do with race, color, religion, or national origin cannot be asked until after the employee is hired.

If the application blank is used intelligently, and not merely as a public-relations gesture and filed in the waste basket, valuable waiting lists of qualified employees can be built up during periods of slack for subsequent labor shortages. Because of inherent difficulties in keeping applicant files up to date, because job matching by record alone is difficult, and because communication with absent applicants is time consuming, many employers use the waiting room instead of the waiting list. A wiser policy is to use both, filling unskilled jobs with applicants who happen to show up in the waiting room and skilled jobs by promotion from within or from applicant waiting lists.

Employment Interviewing.—Employment men have great faith in the interview although the validity of interviewing results have been questioned by many industrial psychologists, who point out that different interviewers get different results from the same job applicants. Employ-

[2] Including Connecticut, Massachusetts, New Jersey, New Mexico, New York, Oregon, Rhode Island, Washington.

APPLICATION FOR EMPLOYMENT

KNOX STANDARD FORM NO. 1

DATE

IDENTIFICATION

FULL NAME (PRINT—DO NOT WRITE)			ADDRESS			
TELEPHONE NUMBER	SOCIAL SECURITY NO.		AGE	DATE OF BIRTH	WHERE WERE YOU BORN	
SEX	HEIGHT	WEIGHT	COLOR OF EYES		COLOR OF HAIR	
COLOR RACE OR NATIONALITY			CITIZEN OF WHAT COUNTRY			

PERSONAL HISTORY

MARITAL STATUS (SINGLE MARRIED ETC)	GIVE NAME OF HUSBAND OR WIFE (WIFE'S MAIDEN NAME)		LIVE WITH (HUSBAND WIFE PARENTS ETC)
HOW MANY DEPENDENT CHILDREN	NAME OTHER DEPENDENTS WHICH YOU MAY HAVE		
NO YEARS AT PRESENT ADDRESS	DO YOU OWN YOUR HOME, RENT, BOARD ETC		
DESCRIBE ANY PHYSICAL DEFECTS IN SIGHT HEARING HERNIA ETC		DESCRIBE ANY RECENT SERIOUS ILLNESS	
IN CASE OF EMERGENCY NOTIFY		ADDRESS	
TELEPHONE NUMBER		RELATIONSHIP TO YOU	
DESCRIBE MEMBERSHIP OR PARTICIPATION IN ANY MILITARY ORGANIZATION		SELECTIVE SERVICE CLASSIFICATION	
WHAT ARE YOUR HOBBIES OR FAVORITE RECREATIONS			

EDUCATION AND TRAINING

SCHOOL	NAME OF SCHOOL	WHERE IS IT LOCATED	NO YEARS ATTENDED	DATE LEFT	GRAD- UATED	MAJOR COURSES	DEGREE
GRADE OR GRAMMAR							
HIGH OR PREPARATORY							
COLLEGE OR UNIVERSITY							
BUSINESS OR TRADE							

WHAT OTHER SPECIAL SCHOOLING OR TRAINING DO YOU HAVE

WHAT OTHER SPECIAL QUALIFICATIONS DO YOU HAVE

JOB WANTED

WHAT JOB OR POSITION DO YOU WANT WITH THIS COMPANY

WHAT SALARY OR WAGE DO YOU WANT	WHEN COULD YOU START	IF YOU ARE NOW EMPLOYED WHY DO YOU WANT TO CHANGE

EMPLOYMENT EXPERIENCE

JOB	PRESENT OR LAST JOB HELD		SECOND TO LAST JOB		THIRD TO LAST JOB	
DATES HELD	FROM	TO	FROM	TO	FROM	TO
COMPANY						
ADDRESS						
TYPE OF BUSINESS						
JOB OR POSITION HELD						
SALARY OR WAGE						
WHY DID YOU LEAVE						

REFERENCES

Do not give relatives or former employers as references   Check here if you do not want us to contact former employers

NAME	ADDRESS	TELEPHONE NUMBER
NAME	ADDRESS	TELEPHONE NUMBER

GIVE YOUR NAME HERE IN YOUR USUAL SIGNATURE (DO NOT PRINT)

Do not write below this line INTERVIEWED BY	DATE	Interview and reference records on other side of this form

COPYRIGHT 1942, FRANK M. KNOX CO., INC.

FIG. 122.—Application for employment. (*Courtesy of Frank M. Knox Company, Inc., Personnel, American Management Association, November,* 1942, *p.* 543.)

ment tests offer only a supplement to interviewing, however, and so far no adequate substitute has been found. The interview will, therefore, probably continue to be widely used. Efforts have been made and must continue to be made to increase the interview's effectiveness by obtaining more information, by weighting that information properly in relation to job success, by standardizing the interview, and by carefully training interviewers to use sound recordings of their performance, round-table discussions of decisions, and follow-up of results. Accuracy of interviewing is improved by using objective data—past records, tests, physical examinations—wherever possible.

Interviews must still be used for rough screening with groups too small for the development of more scientific procedures and to measure certain subjective items. Even then the interviewer must be thoroughly trained. Uhrbrock recommends

. . . interviewers be trained first in conducting exit conferences; secondly, in making employee attitude surveys, using conversational methods; and finally, by participating in the actual hiring of new employees. A series of stenographic, phonographic, or dictated reports should be provided for analysis and criticism. As these reports are discussed with personnel and operating heads, improved phrasing of questions will be agreed upon. Coaching of the novice by an experienced interviewer should aid in developing 'social wisdom' in interpreting the facts revealed by skilled questioning.[3]

Employment interviewing, in common with all other face-to-face human contacts, has certain fundamental characteristics which can be most easily given in survey as a set of interviewing rules.[4]

1. The employment interview should be conducted in private. Privacy may be provided in crowded quarters by railings, glass partitions, or by a wise use of space.
2. The employment interviewer should discount his own prejudices, try to know the interviewee, and practice taking the interviewee's point of view.
3. The employment interviewer should try to make a friend of the interviewee and help him to feel at ease and express himself. This aim is served by permitting the interviewee to become accustomed to his surroundings, by being pleasant, by starting the interview with something of interest to him, and by letting him talk, while the interviewer listens intelligently. This attitude is known as getting *en rapport*.
4. The employment interviewer should keep control of the interview and keep it on the subject, should neither dawdle nor rush, and should watch for additional information through casual remarks by the interviewee at the close.
5. The employment interviewer should try not to preach or teach during the interview, should avoid asking leading questions, and should record all data as soon as possible.

[3] UHRBROCK, R. S., The Personnel Interview, *Personnel Psychology*, Vol. 1, No. 3.
[4] Adapted from BINGHAM and MOORE, "How to Interview," New York: Harper & Brothers, 3d rev. ed., 1941.

6. The employment interview will be improved if the interviewer works from a prepared interviewing outline, holds important questions in mind only long enough to get answers to them checked off, and makes the interview as factual as possible by interpreting answers as given and giving the interviewee opportunity to qualify his replies.

These principles of interviewing apply equally well to all of the various stages of employment interviewing: (1) preliminary sorting, (2) ability diagnosis, (3) final selection, (4) employee counseling, (5) leaving interview.

Preliminary sorting interviews, usually without permanent record, are used to screen out those individuals unfit for employment in the factory involved. *Ability diagnostic interviews* are used to discover, often with the aid of performance or ability tests, which employees, among the group of acceptable employees, are best qualified for what job openings. *Final selection* includes communicating the interviewer's decision to the applicant and selling the available job. When the supply of applicants greatly exceeds the jobs available, as during an economic depression, this interview will include explaining the company's reasons for not hiring. *Employee counseling* on an informal or formal basis involves a discussion of the employee's problems in such a way that the solution becomes apparent without the company or the interviewer dominating the employee's private life. Counseling is often combined with a follow-up interview by the placement interviewer to aid both the new employee's adaptation and the interviewer's future selections for similar jobs. The *leaving interview* is seldom as extensive as the hiring interview, although the possibilities of benefit to the company are much greater. Employees will often reveal situations with regard to supervision defects and working conditions when they are on the way out of a company which could not otherwise be discussed. Since the release slip given to meet certain state unemployment insurance requirements must give a reason for the termination, the leaving interviewer often originates this form. Often the employee must be interviewed by the employment manager before he can receive his last pay due from the company. This provision enables the employment manager to discourage hasty and ill-considered quitting by solving individual employee transportation, family, or financial difficulties. Leaving interviews help protect the company from NLRB charges such as that a specific foreman discharged a certain employee for union activity. They also prevent layoff of qualified employees in one department of a large company at the same time that other employees are being hired in other departments.

Interviewing Objectivity.—The most promising innovation in interviewing is a "personality measure" offered by a group of Harvard anthropologists.[5] They simply time an applicant's response to questions, pauses, interruptions, and friendly overtures during a standard interview. By computing adaptability, activity rates, and tempo as well as differences between them, evidence is obtained as to an applicant's adaptability in social situations, his ability to listen and to express himself, his dominance, initiative, flexibility, etc. This method has been used in offices, factories, foundries, and shipyards and most successfully at Gilchrist's department store in Boston. There, not only were salespeople found to have time values different from production and clerical workers, but salespeople in different merchandise divisions had different time values. Millinery saleswomen differed from hosiery girls; hardware salesmen from furniture experts. Employment interviewers have known this in a subjective way all along. This complex timing device is only one element in the trend to substitute objective measures for the interviewer's subjective judgment in employment work.

Other methods are used to give objectivity to interviewing. Application blanks on which specific items are weighted according to job-success experience, standardized interviews with check lists of replies, pooling of impressions from several interviews, subjection of applicants to observation in a social situation such as a conference with other applicants, "buddy ratings," or evaluation of promise by associates, all contribute a basis of judgment. Measurement of the social class or "situation" in the community is an important consideration in proper placement. An applicant who cannot "act like the job" regardless of his background cannot succeed. The interviewer is well situated to apply scientific determinants of social characteristics to an applicant.[6]

Employment Testing.—Employment tests have been used by American industry for some 40 years as an aid to the employment interviewer. Industrial testing received a boost from the use of tests by the Army in World War I. Too much was expected of them, however, and many users were disappointed. Industry still looked askance at testing when World War II results [7] vindicated the original usage. Most large enter-

[5] CHAPPLE, ELIOT D., The Interaction Chronograph, *Personnel*, January, 1949, p. 295.

[6] This is not a suggestion for snobbishness. "All of us are trained to know and cherish the ideals of democracy. . . . None of us is taught to know and understand the American status system which is an important part . . . and often makes the success story a brilliant reality." L. WARNER, "Social Class in America," Chicago: Science Research Associates, 1949. This book suggests determinants of social characteristics.

[7] See extensive reports of military experience such as the AAF Aviation Psychology Program Research Reports in 19 volumes edited by associates of J. C. Flanagan and the Navy Bureau of Personnel Reports edited by Stuit.

prises and many smaller ones accept the employment test as a useful management tool proved by research to make for more efficient placement, more rapid training, more satisfied employees, and more profitable business operations.

For example, at the Reliance Electric & Engineering Company a battery of tests was tried for selecting stator winders. One of the best predictors

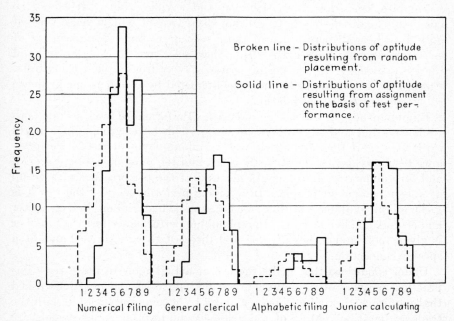

FIG. 123.—This shows improvement over random assignment obtainable by using a battery of tests administered for four clerical jobs at Prudential Life Insurance Company. It is assumed that employees are hired before testing. Tests are used to place them in the job for which they show the greatest aptitude within the limits of jobs available. Even better results could be obtained if tests were used to eliminate some of the applicants. (*Source: R. B. Selover and J. Vogel, Value of a Testing Program, Personnel Psychology, Vol. 1, No. 4, p. 455.*)

was a modification of the Minnesota Paper Form Board. Those who did well on this test showed an average production rate 5 per cent higher than the group of trainees as a whole during 17 weeks of training. In terms of money that meant a gain of $43 at the average training rate as contrasted to a cost of $200 expended on the average unsuccessful stator-winder trainee before termination or transfer.[8]

Figure 123 illustrates the step-up in placement quality obtained with

[8] For full details see E. H. LOOMIS, Do Aptitude Tests Help? *Mill and Factory,* Vol. 45, No. 2, August, 1949.

tests. With the enterprise's competitive position dependent upon its people and any subsequent training, etc., depending upon their initial selection before hiring, the importance of any method which can add accuracy to interviewing selection is apparent. In addition, testing can sometimes reduce hiring costs. During severe labor shortages it is appreciated that tests—other than the humorous suggestion "if they feel warm hire 'em"—lose both selection and savings value. It is not so commonly realized that tests will not decrease but will increase costs if only a very small percentage of those seen are hired. The accuracy of selection remains high even with a low selection ratio, however, and there is evidence that poor performers stay away from a plant using tests. Conversely, better applicants may be attracted by tests [9] as one evidence of progressive industrial relations.

Employment tests are of several types. Performance tests include both trade tests and clerical achievement tests. This latter group, particularly typing tests, are the most widely used of all employment tests. Performance tests are also the most easily given and the most objectively scored, and for validation require only a measure of the performance of a group of known competent people. In a typing performance test the typist is given a limited amount of time to copy strange material on the typewriter and is scored on her success. In a plumbing performance test the plumber is given tools and pieces of pipe and directed to cut, thread, and fit a specific connection.

Under conditions that make the use of actual tools in trade tests impractical or too costly, pictures are sometimes used and questions asked that require a working vocabulary and a basic acquaintanceship with the trade in question. Most of the achievement tests given in schools are performance tests since they require a demonstration of ability to think in the vocabulary of and manipulate the ideas learned in a specific school subject. Performance tests measure a specific ability acquired by an individual through learning and practice.

Personality tests are sometimes used in selection for such positions as salesman or receptionist, but are more commonly used in employee counseling where the employee's desire for help impels him to give honest answers. Personality tests are particularly susceptible to false answers since they consist of a great many questions such as these taken from Bernreuter Personality Inventory.[10]

   1. Yes No? Do you day-dream frequently?
   2. Yes No? Do you get stage fright?

---

[9] See E. L. STROMBERG, Testing Programs Draw Better Job Applicants, *Personnel Psychology,* Vol. 1, No. 1, for a report of just such experience.
[10] Copyright by Stanford University.

3. Yes No? Do people ever come to you for advice?
4. Yes No? Do you like to be with people?

Aptitudes are inborn tendencies to perform well in a particular field of endeavor; they are factors that make it easy for the musically inclined to play the piano or for the natural mechanic to fix broken machines and gadgets. Aptitude is usually measured by measuring knowledge or performance after what is assumed to be uniform exposure to the problem requiring solution or the apparatus by which the solution is effected. The most common aptitude measured in industry is mechanical aptitude. This is necessary for success as a machinist, toolmaker, or other tradesman. Since these trades usually require a 4-year training period paid for by the employer, care is used to select apprentices who will, through their basic aptitude, perform well in the trade when trained. Mechanical aptitude is measured by requiring the applicant to work mechanical puzzles such as the Johnson O'Connor wiggly blocks, a three-dimensional jigsaw assembly test, or by asking a prepared set of questions requiring mechanical knowledge above the average. The finger dexterity of prospective assembly workers and the eye-hand coordination of machine operators are also measured. The greatest difficulty in measuring true aptitude is the segregation of achievement or learning in a given performance (see Chap. XXI for example).

Intelligence Tests.—According to modern intelligence tests, the average person achieves adult intelligence during his late teens. General intelligence is an index to adaptability, and individuals approach a saturation point in the matter of adaptation. This saturation point is never quite reached, nor is it the same for all individuals. Since this is true, it is important to determine the general intelligence of the applicant or the employee, to determine whether his interests are chiefly in things social, academic, or mechanical, as well as to determine his specific aptitudes. All these should be considered in relation to the duties and responsibilities which the employee may be called upon to exercise on his job. When all such factors are taken into consideration, the intelligence test becomes one of many tools that the personnel office can employ in the selection of shop and clerical as well as supervisory employees.

Psychologists are not agreed upon a single definition of intelligence, indeed have not determined whether it is really a general ability or a group of generalized abilities. Factor-analysis research projects have suggested that regardless of any general ability there are several primary mental abilities, some of which are designated as: (1) *spatial*—visualization of geometric figures in space, (2) *perceptual speed*—quick noting of details, (3) *numerical*—quickness of arithmetical computations, (4) *verbal*—meanings of word ideas, (5) *word fluency*—speed in dealing with single words, (6) *memory*—facility in memorizing words and numbers, (7) *deduction*—reasoning ability, and (8) *induction*—ability to extract a common rule. Within each primary mental ability there may be subdivisions; *e.g.*, intentional memory seems distinct from casual memory.[11] Primary mental abilities are found in different intensities and combinations of intensity in different individuals. The amount of any one ability an individual possesses bears little relationship to the amount of other abilities he possesses. Mental-ability patterns of different sorts probably account for such things as musical aptitude and for the mental differences between salesmen, mechanics, and professors commonly credited with having social, mechanical, and academic intelligence, respectively.

Among the best-known intelligence tests are the Otis Self-administering Tests of Mental Ability published by the World Book Company, Revised Beta Examination published by the Psychological Corporation of New York City, and the O'Rourke Survey Test of Vocabulary by Dr. L. J. O'Rourke of the Psychological Institute of Washington, D.C. This last is included as an intelligence test because vocabulary is generally accepted as the best single measure of general intelligence. A portion of this vocabulary test is reproduced:

After each sentence or expression there are five words. Write on the line at the right, the number of the word that *means* the *same* as the word in capital letters.

1. CLOSE the door. (1) shut (2) hold (3) find (4) see (5) touch ———

2. The LITTLE ball is red. (1) big (2) soft (3) small (4) hard (5) round ———

39. He tried to AVERT it. (1) support (2) overcome (3) prevent (4) deny (5) explain ———

80. We must SIMULATE interest. (1) pretend (2) develop (3) destroy (4) obtain (5) protect ———

97. A FATUOUS person. (1) insincere (2) disagreeable (3) noble (4) stupid (5) energetic ———

---

[11] For methods see L. L. THURSTONE, "Multiple Factor Analysis," Chicago: University of Chicago Press, 1947; for discussion of results, see L. L. THURSTONE, *The American Psychologist,* Vol. 3, No. 9. For a more extensive report, see J. P. Guilford (Ed.), "Printed Classification Tests," AAF Aviation Psychology Program Research Reports, Report No. 5, Washington, D.C., Government Printing Office, 1947. This study found some twenty-seven separate factors significant for pilot-training selection. Not all of these can be designated as intelligence components, but one of them (judgment) seems an important addition to the eight above.

Test Evaluation.—There are hundreds of psychological tests.[12] Not all tests available to industry have satisfactory reliability and validity. Test results cannot necessarily be transfered from company to company. Current practice stresses the use of tests developed by industrial psychologists for particular company needs. A warning against expecting too much of tests is sounded by Lawshe.[13]

Tests are not a cure-all for all personnel ills. They cannot be used to clean up the results of mismanagement and supervisory bungling. They will not always work in every situation; and when they do work, they will not yield perfect results. The adequacy of a test or a testing program is evaluated, not in terms of perfection but in terms of batting odds. A particular test should not be criticized because it resulted in the hiring of one or two bad employees but rather should be evaluated in terms of whether or not it selected fewer bad employees than the previously used technique.

How a Test Is "Tailor-made."—When an industrial psychologist starts out to build a test for a specific industrial application, he follows seven simple steps. (1) He finds out what job is to be filled, *e.g.,* an operator, or a setup and operate man. (2) He determines how management tells how well that job is done. This is the problem of *criteria* and may involve production records, foreman gradings, customer reports, etc. (3) He studies the present job holders, seeking to identify characteristics which differentiate good performers from poor performers. He may use standard tests for this or build special new ones. (4) He seeks to hire more people with the characteristics of the good producers and avoid those with the characteristics of the poor producers. (5) He follows up the performance of those so hired to see if those in the new group with the desired characteristics also give good results on the job. (6) If the good performers are alike, he recommends to management the future use of the selection device. (7) If the good performers in the new group do not have the characteristics of the good performers in the old group, he repeats the process, thinking, "What went wrong?" Perhaps the criteria are faulty. Maybe some item on the application blank already differentiates. Is there some standard test that was not tried? Can a new test be developed with greater similarity to the job? Possibly a finer statistical treatment will yield results.

[12] "The Third Mental Measurements Yearbook" edited by Oscar K. Buros, New Brunswick: Rutgers University Press, 1949, lists some 633 commercially available tests and does not consider those tailor-made for specific programs. This excellent volume also evaluates each test.

[13] LAWSHE, C. H., JR., "Principles of Personnel Testing," New York: McGraw-Hill Book Company, Inc., 1948.

As an example of how this works, suppose a company wants to select salesmen. It studies its present salesmen and tests their reactions to a multitude of theoretical sales situations. It then "weights" the answers of the good salesmen and contrasts them to the answers of less successful salesmen. The answers typical of good salesmen become the correct answers for future sales applicants. Often these "correct" answers do not make sense to the outside observer or even to top management of the company. They may indicate that the successful salesman is irresponsible and negligent and borders on insubordination. Nevertheless, if you wish to select new salesmen with the characteristics of your present successful men, you cannot insert your own idealism or some popular idea of what constitutes a sales "type." You must follow the results found by research.

Experience Evaluation.—Although the previous experience of the applicant should be the most significant consideration in selection, not all the claims made on the application blank can be taken at face value. Large employment offices usually do investigate both educational claims and previous experience claims, and, in spite of the common warning "false information means dismissal" on the application blank, find a great deal of misinformation listed. Some of these errors may be unintentional, since few employees can accurately recall a hiring date 5 or 10 years previous; and indeed few employers have accurate records that far back.

Personal references are equally unreliable, since some good can be said about even the worst character, and no one likes to keep another man out of a job. Because references carried by the applicant are of small value and requests for critical information made by the employer are seldom honored by mail—a telephone call is often more revealing—both credit agencies and private detective services have recently established an investigative service for employers. Employers with established employment managers seldom find such reports of value, but the small concern may use such investigators in lieu of the employment manager.

Physical Examination.—The medical or physical examination of employment applicants is one part of the selection procedure which is commonly rendered to the employment manager on a service basis by the industrial hospital. In some factories the physical standards of employment are set by the plant physician or industrial surgeon in consultation with the safety and health engineer. The employment interviewer attempts to select applicants who look healthy and who have an employment record indicative of the physical stamina required. The interviewer's judgment is checked by an examination and medical-laboratory testing of indications of general health; by a carefully established medical and health history; and by specific tests of ability to lift heavy weights, read at usual distances, identify colors, hear normally, and for any requirements particularly applicable to the job in question, such as oil allergies or chemical sensitivities. Entrance examinations are given applicants for their own protection so that they will not be required to do work for which they are not physically equipped, for the protection of present employees and the product from contagion and contamination, and for the protection of the company from compensation court claims because of subsequent injury or disablement.

In addition, the entrance physical examination may be a prerequisite for admission to a group insurance plan or mutual benefit association. Many employers in states that permit such action require employees with physical disabilities to sign waivers for existing disabilities. These waivers are filed with the state compensation commissioner for reference in case the employee is injured. Waivers provide limited legal protection for an employer and may prove to be a moral deterrent to suit by an unscrupulous employee.

EMPLOYEE RECORDS

An important function of the employment office is the maintenance of accurate and adequate employment records. First among the employee records collected is the application blank used by the interviewer in the initial selection. In some organizations there may also be collected during the hiring process employment test scores, interviewers' report sheets, foreman acceptance sheets, hospital or medical record, induction training record, and receipts for employee handbook, identification, keys, etc. All these records are kept in a central file of personnel records, often in a special personnel-record envelope or folder which also contains a master record card to which is posted a running record of employment history as it occurs through promotion and transfer.

Unless some such centralized record as this exists, pertinent facts about the individual's work history are apt to be lost even in a small organization, as supervision and company methods change. Payroll and time records constitute a bulky part of the employee's record, which, though important, are usually kept only temporarily (2 to 7 years). Usually these are filed separately from the remainder of personnel records, often on microfilm. In order that at least a summary of earnings status may be added to the employee's permanent record, many firms send a carbon of all rate changes, transfer slips, etc., to the central personnel-records file.

The variety of employment-office records which an establishment will maintain depends upon its size, the nature of the employment it offers, and the importance the management attaches to facts about employees. Plants employing largely unskilled labor will need records different from plants employing many precision machinists. Companies with large office and sales groups will need records showing employee experience in those fields. Union seniority clauses and pension plans require a careful accounting of employee service. During wartime, draft and alien status

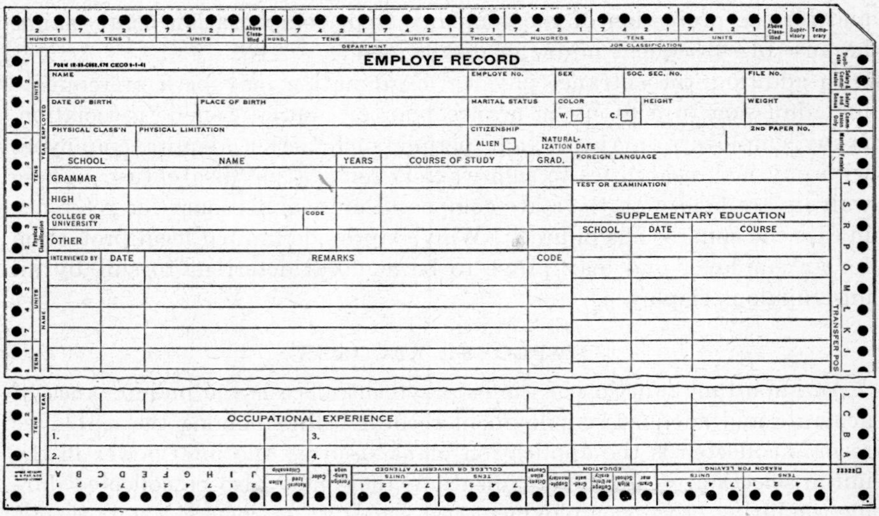

Fig. 123a.—This shows a cumulative employment record using the McBee Keysort patented-edge marking. Data posted is keyed around the margin by V-punching the card edge. Sorting-needles pushed thru the indicated holes of a packet of cards hold back the cards with solid edges, but permit cards with perforated edges to drop out. Speedy sorting in all four directions soon identifies the employee with desired characteristics. The back of this card provides space for the service and job classification posting.

becomes important. Frank M. Knox estimated the needs of different-sized organizations for 11 basic employment records as shown in Table IV.

Types of Records.—Job-performance records or merit ratings are discussed in Chap. XXV. Even though an employer does not maintain a formal system of merit rating, he will usually find it expedient to maintain two closely related employee records: (1) *disciplinary and warning records* and (2) *promotional or advancement records*. Discipline records are maintained largely to provide a record of previous warnings in case of dismissal for violation of company rules. Almost the only defense an employer has, when charged with dismissal of an employee for union activity, is proof of a "bad record." In recent decisions it has been stressed that proving the dismissed employee has a bad

TABLE IV.—BASIC EMPLOYMENT RECORDS

Personnel forms	Small companies	Medium-sized companies	Large companies
1. Application for employment	Necessary	Necessary	Necessary
2. Interview record	Not needed. Will be included on application for employment	Optional. May be included on application for employment	Necessary
3. Reference inquiry	Not needed. Inquiry will be made by telephone or on company letterhead	Optional. Inquiry may be made by telephone or on company letterhead	Necessary
4. Reference record	Not needed. Will be included on application for employment	Optional. May be included on application for employment	Necessary
5. Notification of employment	Optional. Notification may be given verbally or by memorandum	Probably necessary for good record-keeping	Necessary
6. Employee record	Necessary	Necessary	Necessary
7. Order for change of status	Optional, but makes for better records	Necessary	Necessary
8. Clearance for termination	Not needed	Probably not needed unless employees are entrusted with considerable company property	Necessary for all types of companies where employees have company property
9. Employment termination notice	Optional. Probably not necessary in smallest companies	Necessary	Necessary
10. Employee rating, merit and progress	Not needed	Probably not needed	Necessary if such a program is used in the company
11. Requisition for personnel	Not needed	Optional—depending on turnover of personnel	Necessary

Courtesy of Frank M. Knox Company, Inc., *Personnel*, American Management Association, November, 1942.

record is not enough. The employer must also prove that other retained employees have a "good record" and that the offending employee has been adequately warned. A carefully kept record of all disciplinary action taken makes such a defense possible.

Promotional records, of course, form the basis on which the promotion of the most qualified individual is justified. The employer must be able

PERSONNEL RECORD NOTICE

TO PAYROLL DEPT.: DATE __________, 19___

TO EMPLOYMENT DEPT.:

EFFECTIVE AS OF __________ (DATE) 19___, PLEASE RECORD THE STATUS

OF __________ (NAME), CLOCK NUMBER ______ AS CHECKED BELOW:

- ☐ ADD TO PAYROLL AT ______ PER ______ ☐ ORIGINAL EMPLOYMENT ☐ RE-EMPLOYMENT
- ☐ CHANGE RATE FROM ______ TO ______
- ☐ TRANSFER FROM ______ DEPARTMENT TO ______ DEPARTMENT
- ☐ RECLASSIFY FROM ______ TO ______
- ☐ PROMOTED FROM ______ TO ______
- ☐ CHANGE EMPLOYMENT STATUS* FROM ______ TO ______
- ☐ CHANGE CLOCK NO. FROM ______ TO ______
- ☐ LAY OFF TEMPORARILY
- ☐ LEAVE OF ABSENCE UNTIL ______ (DATE)
- ☐ CHANGE ADDRESS TO ______
- ☐ CHANGE PHONE NUMBER TO ______
- ☐ CHANGE SPELLING OF NAME TO ______

REASON FOR CHANGE ______

SIGNED ______ (FOREMAN) APPROVED ______ (SUPERINTENDENT)

*EXAMPLES: PART TIME OR TEMPORARY TO FULL TIME OR PERMANENT; 1ST, 2ND, 3RD OR OTHER SHIFT; MINOR OR TRAINEE TO OTHER CLASSIFICATION; ETC.

NMTA-P-4
144

FIG. 124.—Showing an employee record form used by the department foreman to notify the payroll department and the employment office of change of status. Many employment offices use a separate form for each type of change of status in place of this consolidated record form. (*Courtesy of National Metal Trades Association.*)

to prove to himself as well as to any employee who may feel qualified for the open position that he has considered all candidates and selected the best. Hiring employees from outside the organization and over the heads of equally qualified present employees is not conducive to sound employee relations. Any savings that may result from not having to train several people in a chain promotion are lost through disgruntled performance. The problem of finding the man for the job inside the company, to carry out a policy of promotion from within, is greatly simplified by an understudy system and by keeping up-to-date records of employees' preferences and outside training. Any night school or correspondence courses the employee may complete should be entered on his master record card for consideration in promotion. In companies that have an effective system of understudies, every man above the entrance jobs, such as office boys and machine operators, may be viewed as holding three jobs as outlined by Taylor under Scientific Management: (1) Each man has his own present job in which he is expected to be all-sufficient, for instance, as assistant foreman. (2) He is understudying his immediate superior so that he can learn the next job on his ladder, in this case, foreman. (3) He is a valuable reservist in case of emergency, who can step back down to a shift supervisor's job from which he was promoted and with which he keeps in touch to remain abreast of any new developments in it.

Simple Employment Systems.—Cardinal principles of any work with office forms and systems are keeping them simple, active, and useful. These rules apply to personnel systems as well. A periodic review of all personnel forms should be made regularly to determine whether any duplications may be eliminated or if any portion of the system in use may be abandoned. One form of abandonment should be avoided, however, *i.e.*, the elimination of basically sound and useful records on the grounds that maintaining them is a needless luxury since almost no promotion or hiring is occurring. Systems thus dropped always cost more to reconstruct during periods of increased employment than they do to continue through the lull in anticipation of an upswing that is sure to come.

MAINTAINING THE LABOR FORCE

The personnel problems posed in maintaining a labor force once it is established are usually considered in the negative, as the prevention of a high labor turnover and absenteeism.

Some labor turnover is inevitable as older employees die and the especially skilled move on to greater responsibilities. Since absenteeism is ordinarily defined as unnecessary absence, however, and would not include absence due to unpreventable illness and similar causes, it can never be considered normal, although perhaps a minimum residue can be expected.

Since it costs from $50 to $500, depending on the complexity of the operation,[14] to find, select, hire, and train a new employee and since an average of $5000 to $10,000 capital outlay lies idle while a replacement is being found, it is very much in the interests of economy to keep labor turnover down. The individual employee also loses by frequent job changes, not only in wages and family convenience but in satisfaction and a sense of identification. The community also finds short-resi-

[14] A report in *Sales Management*, Vol. 63, No. 2, July 15, 1949, gives the cost of recruiting, hiring, and training salesmen as $400 each, even though 85 per cent of those hired lasted less than 4 months.

dence citizens undesirable and objects to supplying school facilities, police service, fire protection, and other tax-purchased benefits for those who have not helped pay those taxes. Employers are given an additional impetus to lower turnover by industrial merit rating (experience rating) common under many of the state unemployment insurance laws. Under these laws an employer with a good record of low turnover will pay a tax of 1 or 2 per cent of his total payroll while an employer with a bad record will pay 3 or 4 per cent.

Labor Turnover.—Although personnel managers differ as to the proper mathematical formulas for calculating labor turnover, the methods of the U.S. Bureau of Labor Statistics are most widely accepted. One such formula is

$$\text{Labor turnover} = A + S \div \left(\frac{P_1 + P_2}{2}\right) \times \frac{365}{M}$$

A equals *accessions* or hirings and additions to the payroll; S equals the total of all *separations* for whatever reason, including quits, layoffs, discharges, deaths, permanently disabled, retired on pensions, etc.; P_1 equals the total number on the payroll at the beginning of the month; P_2 equals the total number on the payroll at the close of the month; and M equals the number of days in the month for which the figures were obtained.

Accession rates, separation rates, quit rates, replacement rates, and layoff rates are also sometimes separately calculated, usually on the basis of 100 or 1,000 employees. During periods of depression and in long-established companies, labor turnover is relatively low. During boom periods and in nonprogressive companies, labor turnover may equal 1,800 to 2,400 annually per 1,000 employees.

Absentee rates, sick rates, and accident rates are commonly calculated in much the same manner.

Reduction of Lost Time.—Not all of the problem of working force maintenance is represented by absolute separation from the payroll. Of equal significance from the employee, employer, and public viewpoints is time lost unnecessarily while the employee is still ostensibly on the payroll. One portion of such time loss may be charged directly to employees, as absenteeism and lateness, and combatted through morale building, health promotion, fatigue elimination, and careful attention to shift scheduling and transportation problems. A second portion of such lost time may be charged jointly to employees and employers, as, for example, strikes. The largest portion of such lost time, however, may be charged directly to the employer and is represented by seasonal variation in employment. Although nearly all employers agree that a stabilization of employment is desirable, many feel that their business is different and that they must successively hire and lay off 200 employees to maintain a year-round average of 75 in a specific plant or department.

What can be done by the employer to reduce seasonal variation in the working force and create job stability? Besides centralization of employment and personnel work, much can be done by plant super-

Fig. 125.—This shows pictorially the theory of stabilized income. (*From G. E. Commentator, July 1, 1949. This is a weekly folder of economic information sent to employees' homes.*)

vision to lend workers from one job to another and to consider all possible transfers before layoff. A policy of seniority may either aid or hinder such transfers, depending upon whether it permits "bumping" a newer employee off the job to make room for an employee with more seniority. Often a part of the employment slack can be taken up by work sharing, *i.e.*, putting all employees on a shorter work week or workday before laying off any employees. If this policy is combined with considerable increase in overtime during rush periods, greater employment stability is obtained, although employers object to paying high overtime rates instead of simply hiring new straight-time workers. Employees with greater seniority also object to the reduced week's "take-out" necessary under short time, particularly if foremen and supervisors are demoted to bench or machine work in order to save them for future expansion. This is commonly done both with and without seniority, and wage workers are given fewer hours of work to make room for the demotees. There is a reasonable limit below which hours of work cannot be reduced by work sharing. This is usually stated as the number of work-hours that will yield at least two-thirds of the normal week's pay. If the wage worker receives less than this over any prolonged period of time, he becomes extremely dissatisfied and the purposes of the work sharing may fail.[15]

A slightly different attack on the problem of seasonal employment was made by the Marshall Field Company of Chicago in cooperation with a lithographing concern and a number of lake-shore summer hotels. It was found that the employment peaks in each of these businesses occurred at a seasonal slump of the other two. By carefully selecting workers qualified for each of these lines, employees were assured of a maximum of employment throughout the year. This variant of the familiar coal and ice business has provided a highly reliable pool of seasonal labor. Something of the same sort has been developed by certain of the large New York department stores that feature their own name brands. The same light factory labor which packaged pharmaceuticals, assembled toys, and manufactured clothing under the store name is used during rush sale periods to sell. After the sale is over, the temporary sales clerk returns to the factory.

SUMMARY

Personnel management through coordinated recruitment, scientific selection, controlled interviewing, and the maintenance of the labor force is the most commonly recognized aspect of industrial relations. Even the most uncentralized management usually has an employment office. Many well-known industrial-relations departments have grown by successive additions to the employment department until top-management status was reached. Even in organizations that have made definite efforts to humanize their industrial-relations activities, however, the employment office sometimes still remains painfully impersonal.

The record-keeping functions of the employment office are also commonly in need of reform. Too often the employee record system "just grew." The basic principles of sound business records apply to employee records as well as to all others. Specific problems of the working force, such as labor turnover and absenteeism, relate directly to the employment record problem.

CASE PROBLEMS

1. In view of the employment forms described in this chapter, suggest any improvements you can in the following system: Employment for 400 employees is centered in the hands of the sales manager of the Amer-

---

[15] The Hormel plan and the methods used by Procter and Gamble and other managements in attempting to stabilize employment are described in some detail in Chap. XXIV.

ican Pipe Company,[16] as a part-time function. All employed data except rate of pay information is posted on a 5 by 8 card from the employee's verbal statements during or shortly after the interview. Employment requisitions are by telephone; changes in addresses, married names, and other changes of employee record are written on prepared individual forms by the room foreman where the employee works and filed in 5 by 8 envelopes. The employee's name and address are posted on the outside of the envelope and the "active" envelopes constitute an alphabetical employee file. Changes in rate of pay are sent by the foreman directly to the paymaster. The employee's earning record and the several necessary financial statements are maintained by the paymaster who also keeps a record of hours worked.

2. On an enlarged tracing of the employment-office floor plan mark the path of an employee coming in from outside and going through the several steps of the employment procedure. Study this chart according to the principles established in Chap. X discussing flow charts for materials. Suggest any rearrangements.

3. Prepare two lists of the questions you would ask applicants for jobs during the employment interview. Consider hiring first an unskilled factory worker and second an industrial engineer. At each point where your questions differ on the two lists, explain why the specific question is desirable in one case but not in the other.

4. Assume that you are an employment interviewer empowered to hire an office manager. Out of a busy week's interviewing you have two candidates. Which would you recommend to the controller for employment?

James Olsen: Age 26, married, no children, good health. A graduate of Boston College with special classes in accounting. Employed during summer vacations as a clerk in a department store, camp counselor, and as a switchboard operator and night clerk in a hotel. Has worked two years as a clerk for a railroad station agent and is now employed as a chief clerk in a smaller company with 16 subordinates.

William White: Age 46, married, three grown daughters, no education beyond grammar school, but presents a cultured appearance and has a high normal intelligence upon testing. He worked in a local factory for 10 or 12 years before opening his own office-supply service store, which was successful and still operates although he is no longer active in this business. For the past seven years he has been employed in the purchasing department of a large manufacturing plant in town. He has been disemployed because of a merger of ownerships and comes highly recommended by his former employer.

[16] Fictitious name.

5. The employment interviewer is interested more in the functions an applicant performed in his past jobs than he is in job names. Many application blanks are poorly designed to point up functional experience. Write down all the experience you have had, including part-time jobs, hobbies, club leaderships, etc. Translate this into functional terms, *e.g., organized a ball team and as playing coach won city championship.* Pick out the three facts that would be of greatest use to you if you were being interviewed for a new job. If you need help, see "Pick Your Job and Land It!" by Edlund and Edlund.

CHAPTER XXI

EMPLOYEE TRAINING

Industrial Training Is Important.—It aims to strengthen an existing organization and to develop present employees, making them qualified for and satisfied with their present work and capable of moving into more important work.

It has been stressed that the enterprise's competitive position depends upon its personnel. Employees, no matter how promising and willing, cannot attain success without training. In prewar years, in the war effort, in the reconversion period, and through the turns of the economy since, training has proved its worth.

Industrial training is especially important in modern industry because of the great increase[1] in semiskilled factory labor. Today's industrial workers are hired without specific skill and trained quickly to perform definite industrial operations. As a changing technology changes industrial processes, those same workers are trained in different, often unrelated operations. Without effective training, today's factories could not operate. Much of industrial training is actually retraining older[2]

---

[1] In 1922, 29 per cent of male workers in manufacturing were unskilled; just before Pearl Harbor 19 per cent were; by 1948, only 18 per cent were unskilled. This reduction was accompanied by a decrease in skilled workers also, as job breakdown provided semiskilled substitutes for work once requiring skilled mechanics. Data from *Management Record*, Vol. 11, No. 8, August, 1949.

[2] Those older employees *are* able to learn! The old saying "You can't teach an old dog new tricks" is untrue. According to the differential psychologists, human abilities of all types do decline with age, but the reduction is not so early and not so great as popularly believed. Different abilities decline at different rates. Speed of reaction and motor skills decline earliest from a peak reached at perhaps eighteen to twenty-nine years. Learning ability declines very slowly, holding almost to a plateau from thirty to fifty. Learning at any age is more difficult if it interferes with established habits. Information- and vocabulary-test scores seem to increase steadily with age up to about fifty. (The prevalence from fifty on of high blood pressure, which cuts down the blood supply to the brain, may be significant.) The amount of decline occurring even up to seventy and eighty is much less than the range of difference between individuals of the same age; *i.e.,* even with the decline, a seventy-year-old who had college-level ability is still more intelligent and learns faster than a twenty-year-old who had only grade-school ability. For further discussion see W. R. Miles, Stanford Later Maturity Study, *American Journal of Psychology,* Vol. 44, pp. 44–78, 1932, or E. L. Thorndike, "Adult Learning and Adult Interests," New York: The Macmillan Company, 1935.

employees in newer methods and in original subject matter developed after those employees were out of the schools. New laws, new technology, new machines, tools, and methods make continuous retraining necessary.

Besides meeting the moral obligation of the employer to provide employment for those technologically unemployed by industrial advance, employers train their own help because no other source exists that can provide mature workers with knowledge meeting the needs of a specific business quite so well. There is an increasing understanding of industry's needs by professional educators. The vocational guidance and training programs of many cities and states are slanted toward the needs of the possible employers. Industry is benefiting from this. Industry was also permanently benefited by the four Training-within-Industry programs and the short-term college-level courses given by Engineering, Science and Management War Training under the auspices of the U.S. Department of Education. The 12 million man-hours [3] devoted under TWI to Job Instruction Training, Job Methods Training, Job Relations Training, and Job Safety Training made employees and supervisors better trainers and "conference members." The thousands of ESMWT evenings devoted to the study of drafting, electricity, metallurgy, production control, work simplification, and the like not only exceeded by three times prewar college enrollment but turned out a backlog of graduates and instructors to carry on the interest in management education which then reached its peak after the industrial-school movement of 40 years ago. An industrial training program may include as many distinct activities as are shown in Fig. 126 for the National Cash Register Company.

Organizing for Training.—The type of organization that should be established within a company for dealing with employee training will depend upon two main considerations: (1) whether the company itself has a formal or informal, a centralized or decentralized type of management and (2) what the company training policy is, *i.e.*, why the company is interested in employee development. Many companies have attempted to copy training programs developed by other successful managements. This is a mistake. Each company must build its own program to fit its own needs.

A common organization for training places the responsibility for conducting training classes on the industrial-relations department; but the responsibility for covering the proper material and turning out the correct number of trained sales representatives, lower-level supervisors, and

[3] The TWI program officially trained 1¾ million supervisors in 16,511 plants. Its work is now carried on by the Training-within-Industry Foundation, Summit, N.J.

productive employees rests on the line organization. Top management must be behind the training program, and all levels of management must participate. It does little good, for instance, to instruct foremen in the proper methods for dealing with their men, if top management does not set an example in dealing with the foremen.

A training committee is often used as an aid to efficient selection of trainees, to realistic adaptation of training to company needs, and to evaluation of results.[4] In small organizations particularly, the training committee may substitute for a full-time training director. Such committees often consult with "cooperative" training colleges in adapting the college course to specific industrial needs.

A training committee made up of three to five operating executives will study a company's training needs and instruct the training director to fill them. Such a director (full- or part-time) will write a training course in cooperation with experts in the field to be treated, or with a "cooperative" college possessing the facilities and technical staff essential to a basic attack upon the training problem. The training course is then approved by the training committee and taught by discussion methods to selected employees also approved by the training committee. If only a few trainees are available, the company may combine its students with others in a city-wide or area study group. If company size justifies it, a full-time training staff may be used and departmental leaders developed to assist in passing the material on.

Evaluating the Results of Training.—Although the cost of industrial training to the employer may be considerable, involving cost of the participant's time lost from production plus the cost of the leader's time, plus the cost of any purchased materials, very little effort is made by industry to evaluate the results. Such evaluation is practical at several levels: (1) Immediate learning can be measured by reports and examinations, preferably of a practical demonstration or check-list nature. (2) Intermediate results can be determined objectively by attitude surveys. (3) Long-term results can be measured by reference to improvements obtained. Objective sampling will determine improvements in dealing with people in industrial and public relations. Improved job performance is obvious. Suggestions received from the group during and after the training are fair indications of progress. Promotional records of participants, measuring increased utility, are an ultimate test of good training over the years.

Characteristics of Industrial Training.—The identifying features of industrial training are the adult students and the job significance of the subject. Adult students do not differ greatly from any others. The

---

[4] See Chap. VI for a discussion of the use of committees.

TRAINING PROGRAM OF THE NATIONAL CASH REGISTER COMPANY*

Place in organization	Participants	Number	Subject	Method	Leadership	Material	Number of hours and frequency
Management	1. Top executives	28	Management problems	Conference	President	Special	1 hr., weekly
Direct supervision	2. Supervisors Foremen Job foremen	285	Departmental responsibilities and company policies	Lecture and visual aids	Supervisors	Slides and Charts	2 hr., monthly
	3. Supervisors Foremen Job foremen	285	Job relations	Conference groups of 12	Training department instructors	Special	8 hr., each, 6-mo. period
	4. Supervisors Foremen Job foremen	285	Management information bulletins	Mailed to office of foremen	Published by Elliott Service Company	Four-page bulletin	Weekly
	5. Supervisors Foremen Job foremen	175 in community group of 1,650	Foremanship	Club speakers, plant visitation	Club officers	Monthly magazine *Supervision*	Monthly, evening meetings
Nonsupervisory: Production	6. University of Cincinnati	14, about 4 a year	Work coordinated with college course	Series of jobs; written reports	Line supervision, staff and school coordination	Written reports by students	7-wk. periods, 5 yr.
	7. Dayton Parker Vocational H.S. students	83	Same as 6	Same as 6	Same as 6	None	2-wk. periods for 2 yr.
	8. Apprentices	11	Toolmaking Tool design Metal pattern making Foundry Modelmaking Engineering General mechanics	a. Routed through a series of jobs b. Public school classes c. Company evening school classes d. Apprentice discussion groups	a. Line supervision, staff coordination b. Teachers in school c. Company teachers d. Apprentice supervisor	a. None b. Standard texts c. Company texts and standard texts d. Written reports by apprentices	a. 4 yr. b. ½ day each week c. 2 hr. a week, Oct.-Apr. d. 1½ hr. each week
Nonsupervisory: Service	9. Servicemen in Company school	About 150 a year graduated	a. Repair of machines b. Theory of construction of product	a. Work in service school repairing machines b. Service school classes	a and b. Service school instructors c. Service and evening school instructors	a, b, and c. Standard texts and company texts and slide films and models	a. 6-12 mo. b. 2 hr. a day in training c. 5 hr. a week in training

Nonsupervisory: Sales	10. All servicemen	1,400	c. Elements of salesmanship in service work; All phases of servicing	c. Classes in service and evening school	Sales and service training staff	a. Bulletins; b. Questionnaires	a. Weekly; b. Four times a year
	11. New salesmen before going to training school	....	Basic sales training	a. Study course based on sales manual; b. Supervised selling	a. Branch manager assisted by sales instructor; b. Branch manager and sales instructor	a. Sales Manual and outlines	Study and practice until training school period—varies with selling position
	12. New salesmen in training school	Range, 130–240; Average, 200	Need for product, knowledge of product, selling methods	Classes and discussion groups in central school	Sales Training department (sales instructors)	Detailed coordinated outlines of instruction	44 hr. per week for 5 wk.
	13. Salesmen on job	a. 20–50 per group; b. 5–50 per group	Current subjects	a. Division conferences; b. Branch office conferences	Branch managers, division managers, sales instructors, and company exeutives	Detailed outlines of procedure	a. Varies with need; b. Varies with size and type of branch office
	14. Veteran salesmen in training school	110–140 per group	Advanced subjects	Same as 12	Same as 12	Same as 12	44 hr. per week for 3 wk.
All employees	15. Instructors in evening school	24 in one group	Elements of teaching	Lecture, demonstration, and project	State board of vocational education representative	None	1 hr.—weekly
	16. Those who choose to enroll	1 yr., 1,250 enrollments; 1,040 individuals	36 detailed courses	Scheduled classes, lecture, and laboratory	Part-time teachers	Standard texts and company texts	1–3 two-hr. sessions per week
	17. All employees	7,000	All company activities	Printed material	Editorial staff	Company magazine	Monthly
	18. All employees who choose	1,900 books used by 1,200 persons a month	Varied	Library	Library staff	Books: company or public library	
	19. All employees who choose	Average 2,200 per day	Drama, comedy, newsreels	Moving pictures	Industrial-relations staff selects films	Films from all studios	45 min. daily at noon

FIG. 126.—National Cash Register training program.

*Courtesy of the National Cash Register Company.

essentials of adult pedagogy are: Treat adults as adults; *i.e.*, teach informally, don't talk down, avoid meaningless frills and mannerisms, and keep the learner's interest at all times with fresh examples, daily-life tie-ins, and alert discussion. Psychologists are not agreed on just what happens when we learn.[5] It is not essential to know what happens, however, in order to go about learning or teaching effectively. In industrial training the job significance of the class material usually keeps the learning laws of *intensity, frequency, primacy,* and *recency* functioning. All are subject to *effect.* That which makes the strongest pleasant emotional impression is learned most readily. Within any stratum of experience with equal emotional importance, what is experienced most often is learned, first impressions are lasting, our most recent experiences are best remembered, and we tend to repeat actions which reward us while only more slowly learning to avoid those which punish us.

Much of the training of production and inspection employees; inventory, quality-control, or production-control clerks; and lower-level supervisors is on a "how-to-do-it" basis. An increasing amount of internal company training for foremen, industrial engineers, accountants, salesmen, and executive employees stresses the basic principles developed by research. For example, some supervisory training courses stress background facts from anthropology, psychology, and sociology as part of the principles of human relations.

Industrial training does not end when the production worker knows one job. Many companies have accepted *multiskill training* as a means of increasing employee interest in and understanding of the job. Such training reduces turnover, absenteeism, and upset in production schedules resulting from these. At the Bristol-Myers Company, Hillside, N.J., girl packagers work in teams to learn new jobs.[6] One girl may be trained in as many as 175 jobs, receiving a wage increase for each 12 learned. The group spirit provides social stimulation, and the variety lessens monotony. Multiskill training can be used in any industry where jobs are repetitive but where the types of jobs are numerous.

METHODS OF TEACHING ADULTS

The material to be presented or taught will often dictate the teaching method, but where a choice exists, a method should be chosen that permits

---

[5] See HILGARD, E. R., "Theories of Learning," New York: Appleton-Century-Crofts, Inc., 1948. This book surveys ten current theories of learning. See also Ellis C. Maxcy, How People Learn, *Personnel,* Vol. 19, No. 6, for an excellent treatment by an industrial personnel man.

[6] For pictures of some of the jobs in this application see *Modern Industry,* Vol. 18, No. 2, Aug. 15, 1949.

learning by doing. It has been estimated that an individual remembers about 90 per cent of what he does, about 50 per cent of what he sees, and only about 10 per cent of what he hears. Teaching methods may be evaluated from the learner's viewpoint with this in mind.

Lecture Method.—The lecture is used to speak to large groups about a general topic, but it will seldom result in more than a modicum of adult learning. If the lecturer restates many of the same things the listeners have already learned in other ways, he is adjudged to have "delivered a good lecture." If he does not, he is "difficult to follow." Seldom should new material be presented by lecture to adult groups. Most lectures could be improved by better preparation, by being shortened, and through the use of more and better examples.

Recitation Method.—Although somewhat better for adult groups than the pure lecture, the question-and-answer technique often smacks of the classroom and tends to become a parroting of either the textbook or the instructor. Questions are good if the discussion can be kept at a forum level. When a small group is being taught, the recitation method does provide an excellent measure of what has been learned and indicates weak spots requiring additional attention.

Demonstration Method.—The demonstration is commonly used in laboratory or scientific instruction and has the advantage of added realism but still lacks participation. A project method is often combined with the demonstration so that class members alternately put on demonstrations. Then the demonstrators, at least, learn. Interest of the group is often stimulated by the activity.

Conference Method.—The conference method of directed group discussion is by far the best method of exchanging information and ideas among adults. Discussion may often seem to be time-consuming, especially if some group members tend to monopolize the discussion, but more may be learned in the typical "bull session" than in the same length of time listening to a carefully prepared lecture. Conference-method advocates point out in defense of the method's slowness that it takes 3 weeks of carefully controlled warmth to hatch a chicken from an egg. If you speed up the process (apply more heat), you can get a hard-boiled egg but no chicken! New ideas incubate in much the same way.

The ability to lead a conference is an important skill. The conference method is increasingly used for training at all levels—from production employees through executives. Aside from training, conferences are used for business meetings, civic hearings, and all sorts of joint action. The same skills that make a good conference head yield leadership in any human situation. In industry, training conferences are often used to get supervisory thinking started. Then the conference merges almost imperceptibly into a method of operation. It is important for the leader to recognize when his training function for the group becomes outmoded by the conferee's own development.

The Kinds of Conferences.—There are five types of conference, and the results desired dictate the type a leader will use.

1. *Exploratory conference* such as might be held between management and a union committee preliminary to collective bargaining or between a supplier and customer before discussing a long-term contract or merger. Such a conference has the purpose of "sounding out" the viewpoints of those present, learning what possible agreements and disagreements there may be without committing anyone, "getting acquainted," and setting the framework for serious negotiation.

2. *Creative conference,* in which the proposals and wild ideas of one member strike sparks from another member for more ideas, which in turn may spark a third member to suggest a notion which the whole conference immediately accepts. Osborn calls this "brainstorming" and calls it typical of an advertising agency developing a campaign, a radio or motion-picture-story conference, or author collaboration. In contrast to other types, a creative conference jumps around, stops only *to capture ideas not to evaluate them,* and frowns on premature expressions of judgment.[7]

3. *Informational conference.* The leader of this type supplies information or has specialist members of the group do so. The leader enters with definite ideas and conclusions which he wants the group to understand and accept. This is also known as the "directed conference" or the "determinant discussion." It differs from a lecture in that group reaction and acceptance of the conclusion are sought. It differs from the next type because the leader takes an active part, contributing his own beliefs and opinions.

4. *Developmental conference.* This type is also called the "indeterminant" or "pure" conference. All conference members are expected to reach full understanding and 100 per cent acceptance of the group's decisions. The leader's function is to act as a suction pump for the ideas of the group, not to contribute ideas of his own.

5. *Reconciliation conference.* This type integrates differences in viewpoint from which members will not swerve or compromise. The leader tries to reconcile the conflicting interests by discussion. The reconciliation conference uses the two preceding types. In its initial discovery of points of difference it is like type 4. The integration is like type 3. Its distinction is the members' refusal to accept each others' reasoning and the leader's efforts to mediate.

How to Lead a Conference.—Just as the results desired indicate the type of conference, so does the type of conference dictate the leader's role. In one he *spars,* in another he *ignites,* in a third he *informs,* again he *suctions* out group experience, or finally he *mediates.* In any case he *trains* and does so by the same methods of leadership that are effective in all human relationships. We can mention only a few of the things a leader will do. As an example, take the developmental conference. This usually takes place with the conferees around a table and the leader

[7] Osborn, Alex, "Your Creative Power, How to Use Imagination," New York: Charles Scribner's Sons, 1948.

standing at a blackboard or wall tablet. In preparation he has planned the conference considering the experience of the group. He first "breaks the ice" by introducing and perhaps name-carding each conferee, giving some plausible reason (such as their aggregate years of experience) why group judgment is superior to individual judgment. With a totally green

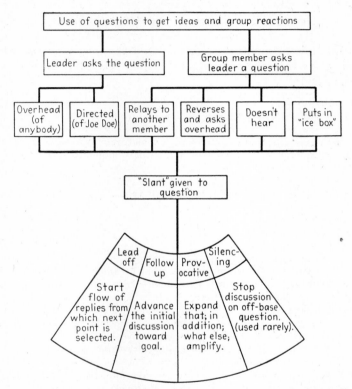

Fig. 127.—This chart shows how the leader of a conference controls discussion. (*From E. S. Hannaford, "Conference Leadership in Business and Industry," New York: McGraw-Hill Book Company, Inc., 1945.*)

group he may have them develop the procedure to be followed; with experienced men he mentions rules: his own function, sportsmanship, complete agreement, listing of conclusions, anonymity of results, and confidential or "privileged" nature of all discussion. He then throws out an "overhead" or general question or makes a statement and asks similar experiences. He directs questions from one member to another,[8]

---

[8] Figure 127 diagrams the ways in which the leader may use different types of questions for different purposes.

t·rns the discussion inward upon itself, reverses direct questions, uses humor to sooth ruffled feelings, follows up the original topic when discussion gets sidetracked, and eventually reaches both a statement of the problem and a conclusion with which the group agrees. This may be a statement or the outline of a course of action. The conference is then ready to consider its next discussion topic.

Headaches for the Leader.—Some individual conference members are slow to learn the new method and make progress difficult. They must be brought into line without antagonizing them or losing their contributions. Fern [9] suggests that the individual members may be controlled in the following ways:

1. The talkative type:
    a. Get the group to "sit on him."
    b. Politely suggest others may have something to say.
    c. Ask him questions that he cannot answer and which will show his weaknesses.
    d. Suggest, in private, that he should help draw others out instead of talking so much.
    e. If absolutely necessary, tell him frankly that he is monopolizing the time.
2. The argumentative type beyond the point of value:
    a. Tell a story.
    b. Call a recess.
    c. Ask if the board can be cleared.
    d. Try to get them laughing.
3. The final authority:
    a. He must be given opportunity to tell what he knows, or he will lose interest.
    b. Steal his thunder if he becomes too domineering.
    c. Ask questions he cannot answer.
4. The silent person:
    a. Commend him and build up his confidence. He may be oversensitive.
    b. Lead the discussion to a point where he can participate.
    c. Interpret his points for him if he has difficulty clarifying them.
    d. Try to find the reason; he may recently have been demoted.
    e. Make him feel he has a contribution to make through asking questions.
    f. Ask him to list his jobs so they can be analyzed.
    g. Try to get acquainted with him.
5. The high-strung person:
    a. Be calm with him.
    b. Come to his rescue if he cannot "give and take."
    c. Have a private visit with him; find out his problem and try to help him.
6. The chronic critic or disgruntled person:
    a. Get the group to challenge him.
    b. Determine his real interests.
    c. Get him to feel he has a constructive contribution to make.
    d. Let him criticize, then open his remarks to criticism.
    e. Explain the difference between constructive and destructive criticism.

[9] FERN, G. H., "Training for Supervision in Industry," New York: McGraw-Hill Book Company, Inc., 1945.

7. The theorist:
  a. Ask him to differentiate between theory and practice.
  b. Analyze one of his theories, getting him to participate.
  c. Ask for substantiation of his theories.

Visual Aids and Industrial Training.—Although there has been a great deal of discussion of visual aids as a teaching method, such aids are only a valuable adjunct to the other methods, particularly the *conference method,* as we have been using the term. A common conference pattern has been the presentation of a 16-millimeter movie film or a 35-millimeter slide film (see Fig. 128 for example) with or without sound effects on the subject of the conference. This presentation is then followed by a discussion on the theme set by the film [10] with special attention to an application to the specific plant concerned or industry involved.

Wall charts, mammoth slide rules, giant blueprints, posters, blackboard drawings, stereopticon slides, and sample demonstrations may also be considered visual aids to training and should be used wherever possible.

Case Studies and Role-playing.—These two training methods are used especially with supervisors to stimulate interest and promote a feeling of reality. In the case method some actual shop experience is detailed and discussion invited. Members agree upon the best solution to the problem involved, often listing management principles. In role-playing,[11] a shop situation is acted out and one member in unrehearsed dialogue gains experience in handling the problem. The performance is then criticized, perhaps by a member who shows how he would have done it. This is not only a training method but often an excellent release of mental tensions and group conflicts.[12]

TYPES OF TRAINING IN DETAIL

Viewed broadly, much of the employee-relations program is educational. Just being on the job provides new experiences which are educational whether planned as training or not. That part of the industrial-relations program usually dubbed "training" is of four types:

[10] An excellent presentation of visual-aid training films used by 100 companies such as Warner & Swasey, General Motors Corporation, General Electric Company, and Western Electric Company is found in NICB, Studies in Personnel, No. 49. Planned conference series are available through the Jam Handy Organization (2821 E. Grant Blvd., Detroit, Mich.), Vocafilm Corporation (424 Madison Ave., New York, N.Y.), and Commercial Films (1800 East 30th St., Cleveland, Ohio) as well as most projector manufacturers.

[11] See "Role-playing as a Method of Training Foremen" by J. R. P. French, Jr., in "Human Factors in Management" edited by S. D. Hoslett, Parkville, Mo.: Park College Press, 1946.

[12] As such it is closely related to J. L. Moreno's "Sociodrama." See *Sociatry,* Vol. 2, pp. 67–68, 1948.

Announcer: This case of Joe and Bob occurred in an Armstrong Cork Company plant . . .

. . . Two machines have been down for nearly two hours because order 642 was not delivered on time. . . . Joe decides to find the reason for the delay. He enters department A, which was to send the order . . . . . . and finds Bob the foreman, engaged in talking to two employees. Without waiting . . .

Joe: Say, Bob, where is order 642 that you should have had in my department two hours ago?

Bob: We've been tied up with two specials and we haven't been able to get the stuff out for you.

Joe: Always an alibi! It's your fault, and believe me the boss will be told where the trouble lies.

Announcer: With that, Joe turns his back on Bob, and stalks off to his own department . . .

. . . Put yourself in Bob's place. Think it over carefully and then you decide. If you were Bob . . . .

Fig. 128.—This shows part of a slide film used in supervisory training. (*The original is copyrighted by Armstrong Cork Co. These frames are from Factory, Vol. 107, No. 7, July, 1949.*)

(1) programs on company time; (2) after-hours courses sponsored by company; (3) printed media specifically developed to inform employees, following the fundamentals suggested by Heron in his book "Sharing Information with Employees"; [13] (4) extramural activities, such as community programs, Junior Achievement clubs, and cooperative projects with schools, churches, and local clubs which reach the employee only indirectly. Of these, only direct company programs,[14] can be discussed. The National Cash Register chart lists many of the separate programs used in supervisory, production-employees', and sales-training activities.

Orientation or Induction Training.—Induction training, or the initial time spent in acquainting the new employee with the rules, physical aspects, and company policies involved in his job (as distinguished from job instruction) originated primarily in the necessity of having legal protection against violations of company rules. It has now been adopted as a ready way of creating a good first impression of the company. Many managements understand that supervisors are often too busy with production problems to give adequate attention to the new employee, and have therefore appointed induction trainers whose sole purpose is to answer questions for the new employee, show him around, introduce him to a few workers, and follow up his adaptation in the new job. This orientation may be part of the hiring procedure or may require several days at a later date. Besides giving the new employee confidence and possibly inducing him to stay on a job that would otherwise scare him away, the induction aids in the process of identifying the new employee with the company. This identification is the first step in "belonging"— that all-important social acceptance of mutual personalities, which is furthered as the induction trainer says, "*We* XYZ Company employees ring *our* clock cards like this and wear *our* identification badges here."

Preemployment Training.—In activities requiring extensive preparations or learning connected with large machines, employers sometimes make use of formal preemployment training lasting from a few weeks to several years. Sometimes local vocational high schools give such training. In some cases fee-charging institutes give short-term training in specialized fields, such as Diesel engines, welding, air conditioning, or more recently plastics, television, and chemurgy. Many such schools will not bear investigation, but a few have done notable work especially with G.I. training. Some employers have hired unskilled workers and sent them at company expense to either public or private vocational-training centers. Such a program has the advantage of earmarking especially

[13] Stanford University Press, 1942.

[14] For a complete review of employee education see *Studies in Personnel Policy*, Nos. 15, 18, 26, 37, and 89, National Industrial Conference Board, Inc., on the subject.

well-qualified candidates for future openings. It has the disadvantage of being relatively expensive, since the earmarked employees are usually paid while learning but may never actually report for work. Preproduction employment training applies, on a short-term basis, many of the same principles discussed in the next paragraphs.

Apprentice Training.—Apprentice training is long-period trade training. Generally 3 or 4 years are used in intensive mechanical experience and related classroom work. A written agreement—called an "indenture contract"—is strongly advocated by the several apprenticeship committees.

Some of the most successful and effective apprentice programs do not use written agreements, preferring to adapt the training to specific needs as these develop. A statement of the conditions of apprenticeship in written form, whether signed by the parties or not, does offer a means of avoiding misunderstandings.

Industrial training developed from apprentice training, but the apprenticeship process has not changed much. Although the 4-year apprenticeship now served by toolmakers, machinists, millwrights, and other skilled tradesmen is much more reasonable than the 7- and 12-year indentures served by candlemakers and tailors at the time of the American Revolution or the even longer European training times starting in early childhood, even that period seems too long today. Some of the periods of instruction customary during normal times, when one of the purposes [15] of apprenticeship is to reduce competition by limiting the entrance of new talent, were greatly shortened under pressure of manpower shortages. This has been a continuation of changes in apprenticeship standards started in 1918 and emphasized in 1936 with the establishment of the permanent Federal committee on apprenticeship training under the auspices of the U.S. Department of Labor. Working with state and local committees the Federal committee has established industrial standards for apprenticeship such as a minimum starting age of sixteen, a standard number of outside instruction hours, and a definite graduation date. These conditions are those normally embodied in the apprentice agreement.

Certain employers such as General Electric, Caterpillar Tractor, and Scovill Manufacturing Company regularly include a limited number of older college-graduate apprentices in their training courses. These men are usually members of an advanced training group, such as is discussed

[15] Elton Mayo pointed out in "Social Problems of an Industrial Civilization," Cambridge, Mass.: Harvard University Press, 1945, that apprenticeship also taught a "pattern of life" and enabled a boy to fit himself into an "established" society. It is not so useful in our "adaptive" society today.

in a later section, who will specialize in supervision of the mechanical aspects of the business.

Improving Apprentice Training Programs.—Apprentice training has been improved in recent years to the greater satisfaction of management, skilled-labor representatives, and the apprentices themselves. Management complained that apprentice training was expensive because the learners did little productive work, wasted the time of highly paid experts, and quite often failed in ability or interest after having received considerable instruction. Representatives of skilled labor complained that more skilled workers were being trained than were needed, while skilled mechanics, already trained, were unemployed. Unionists also charged management with using "learners" as low-paid help to do productive work. The apprentices themselves felt that they were often kept overlong at simple tasks and given no opportunity to acquire general all-round versatility. The formalization of training effort, coupled with a more careful selection of candidates with proper mechanical aptitude to master the trade being considered, and a recognition of the need for competent instructors have answered most of these criticisms.

The mechanic who is capable of teaching a trade to the unskilled apprentice is much more rare than the craftsman able to do the job himself. But teaching ability alone is not enough. For this reason many employers have first selected respected craftsmen as instructors and then taught these instructors how to teach. When the craftsmen-instructors are qualified, this training may be given in regular vocational-training colleges. Under other conditions the training of instructors becomes another personnel function.

Not every boy who asks to learn a trade is qualified to do so. It is better to eliminate those who will eventually fail before the start of the training than halfway through the course. As variations in natural aptitude become more widely understood, such selection tests as the Johnson O'Connor Wiggly Blocks, the Minnesota Manual Dexterity Test, MacQuarrie's Test for Mechanical Ability, O'Rourke's Mechanical Aptitude Tests, and Stenquist Mechanical Aptitude Tests are more widely used to weed out the unpromising. In addition, the Kuder or the Strong Vocational Interest Blank and other indicators are used to estimate probable satisfaction in the trade selected.[16] Family background, while not a completely reliable criterion, is also commonly used as an indicator of possible vocational satisfaction.

Most apprentices are expected to work at minimum wage standards

[16] See BINGHAM, WALTER VAN DYKE, "Aptitudes and Aptitude Testing," New York: Harper & Brothers, 1937, for an explanation of these tests. See also the discussion of tests in Chap. XX.

and produce at least some regular work "to pay their way" when they are privately taught. When this necessity is removed, instruction can often be greatly speeded up. In view of the relatively small differential that exists between the earnings received by semiskilled factory workers and craftsmen, it may be questioned whether the lower learner's rates can be justified. Indeed, it has long been felt necessary to pay a considerable bonus, sometimes amounting to a half year's pay, to apprentices upon graduation in order to induce them to remain for the last year or so of apprenticeship. During these final months the young craftsman is apt to realize that his talents are salable at much higher rates than he is receiving and leave prematurely. Employers say these last instructions give the final polishing to the trade.

Special Job Training.—Of greater and growing importance in industrial training, by sheer weight of numbers if nothing else, is special training of semiskilled and unskilled factory labor for production jobs. A strong disagreement exists among industrial trainers as to whether it is better to train the new industrial worker in the regular workroom or in special instruction rooms known as "vestibule schools." Surely training in the production shop is more realistic, more apt to stay current in content, and surer to stress actual job requirements of both speed and quality. In addition, no extra training in the differences between classroom and shop is necessary, if the shop is the classroom.

On the other hand, the vestibule school, while often in close proximity to the production shop, usually has more favorable surroundings for learning and fewer interruptions of the teaching process. Because instruction is the full-time job, better instructors can be made available. Since production as such is not the object, the green learner will not interfere with necessary production but will have ample time to practice. Possibly the greatest contribution of vestibule schools during periods of manpower shortage and rapid turnover lies in keeping the new worker on the job past the initial "heart-break period" by encouragement and by increasing immediate earnings.

Public Vocational Training.—Although public high schools still continue to graduate college preparatory students, 90 per cent of whom do not enter college, and more than three times as many commercial students as there are white-collar jobs each year, gradually increasing attention is being given by both public and private schools to vocational education. In more progressive communities technical training is keyed into local industrial needs on a quota basis, so as to provide a maximum of occupational placements. Such vocational training has been objected to by organized labor on the basis that it tends to intensify class distinctions, inasmuch as workingmen's children are more apt to be so trained than are the children of business and professional people. Need exists for special job training in specific industries. The New York City vocational schools, for instance, teach many of the semiskilled operations necessary in the needle trades.

Coordinated Cooperative Industrial and Technical College Training.—As colleges approach the industrial training problem, work-study programs are being developed to provide opportunities for post-high-school study on an "earning while learning" basis. Industries are coming to view the costs of training technical and engineering personnel, as well as skilled workers, as one of the necessary costs of production, while the institute type of college is coming into its own as a practical educator for today's industry.

Such cooperative training usually takes one of two general forms. Either a program of "6 months college–6 months work" is developed, often with two or more students filling the rotating school-shop shifts, or the students work full time and are guided by the company in night-school work. The University of Cincinnati and Stevens Institute in Hoboken, N. J., have well-known programs wherein the students alternate study with practical work. Among those providing successful programs of either part-time or cooperative courses are the following:

New Haven YMCA Junior College	New York University (N.Y.C.)
University of Akron	Northeastern University (Boston)
Armour Institute (Chicago)	Northwestern University (Evanston, Ill.)
Drexel Institute (Philadelphia)	University of Pittsburgh
Fenn College (Cleveland)	Southern Methodist University (Dallas, Tex.)
Georgia School of Technology	
M.I.T. (Cambridge, Mass.)	Rochester Institute of Technology

The identifying characteristic of such cooperative-training programs as distinguished from regular night-school work is the effort made by the school to relate its training to the job of the employee, and the assignment by the company of occupations for training purposes related to the course of study. Such training is not confined to the undergraduate level. Pratt and Whitney Aircraft Company, for instance, has financed masters' degrees in aeronautical engineering for college-graduate cadet engineers on a cooperative basis. Several of the college-graduate recruiting courses provide advanced degrees upon completion of the company training program as a partial recompense to students who may not be kept after training.

Whereas some companies make no provision for financing such advanced education other than providing leaves of absence where necessary, most companies make some provision for at least partial repayment to the student for tuition, books, and transportation costs. Scholarship grants are also common, some of them, as at Fenn College, on a trust-fund basis.

Supervisory and Executive Training: Consultative Supervision.— As industry enlarged in size, as the individual workers changed from skilled craftsmen to semiskilled machine operators, and as governmental rulings created policies favorable to organized labor, the problem of the first-line supervisor became more and more complex. Industry recognizes this fact by providing an ever-increasing amount of foremanship training. Since the higher levels of management honestly expect to learn through the conference from the lower levels and since company policies are formulated and sold in these conferences, this method of training has come to be an important part of "consultative supervision."

The old-school "boss" demanded obedience, ordered cooperation, and rode roughshod over the feelings and rights of the employees to enjoy a personal sense of superiority; the new-style industrial leader considers his personal "face" last, takes a human interest in those under him, respects the rights of others, solicits opinions from subordinates, and obtains intelligently guided cooperation from his fellow workmen because they understand the reasons for their (and his) actions.[17] This does not mean that he is a "softy." It does mean that the worker is given every chance to succeed before being dismissed, and also that the supervisor receives genuine respect and admiration from his men. Many foremen who were themselves poorly supervised continue to pass along the mistakes of their superiors in much the same manner as a newly advanced sophomore group mistakenly continues to pass along to freshmen the "hazing" the sophomores received as freshmen from present juniors.

Personnel problems occupy a considerable part of the foreman's time, not because production, costs, and technologic guidance are not important, but because production is increased, costs are lowered, and profits expanded by intelligent handling of the human problems of workers. A cheerful, hard-working operator who understands what he is doing requires less supervision than the "mad" worker who thinks the special tolerances or specifications are "some fool idea" of the bosses. It is to the supervisor's selfish interest, therefore, to do his supervising in the modern way, since it makes his job easier. Under present labor laws a company is responsible for the acts of its supervisors. In a recent case the courts held that a company must give a wage increase promised by a now-

---

[17] W. B. Given, Jr., the president of American Brake Shoe, Inc., calls this "bottom-up management." See his book published by Harper & Brothers, New York, 1949. He contrasts this spread of responsibility to the usual organization where all authority, ideas, etc., come from the top down.

dismissed department head even though he had no authority to grant the increase in the first place.

Department-head and superintendent training, *i.e.*, instruction of those executives above the first line of supervision but below top management, is often neglected on the theory that these men have attained their advancement by their supervisory ability. This is seldom true. The hold of the general foreman over his lower-level foremen is greatly weakened when they see him violating management principles which they have been taught and which they may often respect as tried-and-true tools of their own supervision. Middle management may not need training as intensive as at lower levels but does need conference training for instruction in company policies and company-wide dissemination of information. Such conferences or management committee meetings are often the only means top management has of keeping in close touch with actual shop conditions.

Top-executive conferences are held both for training and for consultation with the lower levels of management prior to policy making. Sound consultative supervision demands that all levels of management consult with those affected by its orders and keep information flowing both upward and downward through the pipe lines of the management structure.

A recent development in executive training has been provided by the Vick Chemical Company which has had for a number of years a complete cadet-training program under the Vick School of Applied Merchandising. A separate training program has been set up under its own director for the exclusive training of the chairman of the board, president, vice-presidents, and general managers.

Many "canned" foreman and executive training courses may be purchased. These systems are better than no training at all but, if at all possible, should be rewritten to apply to the specific company involved. Sound management principles are the same in any industry; the examples and illustrations of any prepared course must necessarily be too general for ready application. Often such courses can be personalized by a good conference leader, but such a leader could also write an individual course for the specific company.

Management, particularly in large companies, is too apt to think that providing a supervisory training course will solve all supervisory problems. Training is not a "one-shot proposition." It must be continuous. The teachings must be a part of the everyday operation of the enterprise—as they will be if consultative supervision is practiced.

Unions, too, recognize that leaders must be developed. Each summer thousands of local union officers spend a week at typical family vacation spots attending daily classes in leadership, economics, and political action conducted by national headquarters. What they learn is brought back to conferences at the local union hall for stewards and shop leaders. Local leaders and committeemen are given special courses in collective-bargaining techniques, how to get along with foremen, and dealing with the membership. Slide films, motion pictures, role-playing outlines, and the like are often supplied by the federations.

Supervisory and Executive Training: College-graduate Training. —Many of today's "elder statesmen" among business leaders came up from the ranks of the workers, gaining their training through a series of happy accidents. Most of them readily admit that there have been times in their careers when a college training would have been useful. A few even point out that *they* were rough men in competition with rough men— relatively equal—but that their successors must expect to meet an entirely different competition. Peter Drucker determined in his study of General Motors that the greatest need of the large corporation is to find a training method which will produce future leaders—superintendents, general managers, vice-presidents, etc.[18] Most of today's leaders "grew up with the business" and gained their broad experience as their business expanded. Giant corporations are too big to offer similar experience today—yet will need tomorrow even "bigger leaders" to maintain their position among rising newcomers. To help in this, many managements are turning to planned recruitment and training of college graduates.

College-graduate trainees, often called "cadets" or "flying squadron" men, are selected by visits to the campuses. A campus interviewer, working through the college placement service, will interview and may hire outstanding applicants on the spot. Actual placements are usually made after interviews at the company by line supervision. Such trainees are often under the direction of a training coordinator who guides their progress from training job to training job. One of the year-round duties of such a coordinator is to "sell" the value of the college trainee, while assuring noncollege foremen and experienced mechanics in the organization that their own future advancement is not impaired. This is sometimes done by admitting a quota of night-school-trained or aptitude-possessing untrained regular employees to the executive training squad.

College graduates are commonly trained over a 6-month to 4-year period for specific jobs in sales engineering, supervisory production, general administration, research, or office management. Specific company objectives guide each course so that no general pattern can be formulated. What classwork is given is linked closely to work experience. It may be observed that trainees are being given real responsibility and no longer asked merely to stand around and observe regular workers. Line super-

[18] See for a partial report, P. F. Drucker, "Concept of the Corporation," New York: The John Day Company, 1946.

visors are given the chief responsibility for training the students who are put in the same work situation as regular employees. The chief difference is that they are transferred from job to job at fairly regular intervals and given individual instruction as needed to point up their all-round develop-

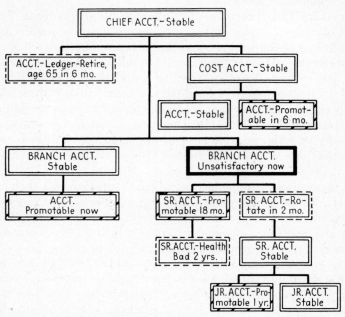

Fig. 129.—Forecasting chart showing the probable vacancies in the accounting department within the next two years. The blocks may be colored to highlight "problems."

ment. After the "cadets" graduate, they are moved around intentionally from sales to engineering to research to accounting to production, etc., partly to give the broad experience their predecessors had through company expansion, partly to overcome "the young man's desire for express trains," and partly to throw responsibility on them and see how far they can go. In these positions they may supervise small units, act as "shadows" to high executives, or strike out independently in new company ventures.

Executive Inventory Control.—A special problem is determining the size and nature of the executive-training need in any specific company. The Navy Department management engineer [19] studied the practices of

[19] "Personnel Administration at the Executive Level," Annapolis: The United States Naval Institute, 1948. The essence of this report is also given in *Modern Industry*, Vol. 16, No. 4, pp. 112–122.

53 selected enterprises such as American Cyanamid, Proctor and Gamble, Swift, and U.S. Steel. His report of industry's solution to this problem recommends the following five-step procedure for creating reserves of trained executives:

I. *Executive Organization Analysis.*—This is a two-pronged analysis of the existing jobs and men to determine the requirements of each present position in relation to the rest of the organization and the qualifications necessary to fill each position in terms of technical knowledge and the ability to work with others.

II. *Executive selection* of supervisors with the ability to handle people and with *potentiality, i.e.,* promotion growth possibilities. This is determined by multiple interviews in which at least three personal talks, assisted by formalized tests, estimate a man's growth potential.

III. *Executive evaluation* of current performance, growth achieved, and remaining potential by means of periodic multiple judgment (merit rating), discussions with the employee, continuous follow-up including a recording of progress in the personnel record file, and such objective checks as attitude surveys of what his employees think of his supervision.

IV. *Executive-development* guidance through job rotation in special trainee positions, and academic and in-service training to correct experience deficiencies in order that the man will be ready for promotion when he is needed.

V. *Executive inventory control* or systematization of the replacement process by forecast of future needs. This systematization has seven parts: (1) *Executive job audit,*[20] a summarization of the first step which designates each job as filled "unsatisfactorily" or "adequately" or by a man who is "promotable" from the job he now holds. Those for whom no present decision is reached are "indefinite." (2) *Job-replacement schedule,* which forecasts dates by which action will be taken on unsatisfactory conditions and estimates how soon expected job vacancies may occur through promotion. This makes possible a planned promotional process rather than the usual hectic scramble. Figure 129 shows parts 1 and 2 in graphic form adapted from the Navy report. (3) *Man-replacement schedule,* which summarizes the first three steps for the individual. It may use a color code and the man's picture on an organization chart to present the human strength of the enterprise visually. (4) *Promotional-sequence designation,* which determines at least the direction of each man's progress; (5) *promotional time schedule,* which determines in connection with step 4 when a man may be ready for promotion; (6) job pool, or *promotional backlog file,* of individuals who may be considered understudies for each job. Each job "pool" contains men in direct line of promotion at various stages of readiness, but it also includes promotables presently operating elsewhere in the organization. (7) *Consolidated report* of the preceding six parts. This may be kept in book form, on a scheduling board, or graphically as shown in Fig. 130.

Sales Training.—Possibly the most debated area of training lies in the sales field. Old-line sales managers held that "salesmen are born,

---

[20] For a detailed presentation of executive development see the May, 1948, and the January, 1949, issues of *Personnel*. In the latter, authors B. J. Muller-Thum and M. E. Salveson state, *"No program will really produce results until every superior recognizes and discharges his personal responsibility for developing the people entrusted to his care."*

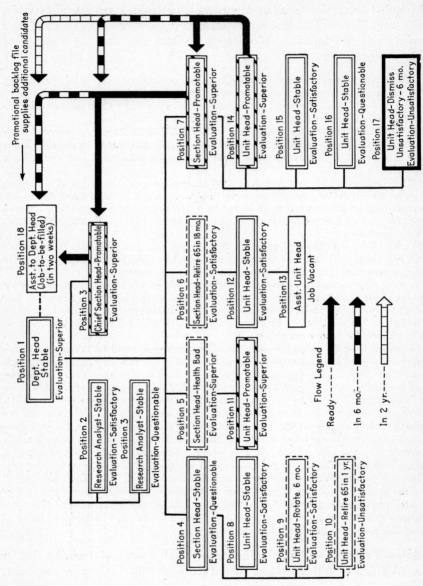

Fig. 130.—A replacement flow chart showing probable moves to fill the vacancies in newly created position 18.

not made." It was felt that the science of human behavior was too un-developed to be applied practically to the work of the salesman. In addition, salesmen were themselves individualists who resented stand-ardization. As the distributive function is conceived in modern business, however, careful sales training is a natural and logical necessity. Results obtained in the sales field have carried back into much of the training practice of large organizations. The use of new college graduates origi-nated in sales work. The effectiveness of the sales presentation is easily measured in terms of sales made. Modern sales workers are actually educating their purchasers constantly and are, therefore, more willing to be themselves educated, particularly when the results show at once in terms of sales made.

Today's sale managers are beginning to accept that *all* personnel re-cruited for sales should be trained and that *training should never end.* Each company has its own peculiar requirements for successful selling, which must be taught even to experienced salesmen: background of the company, its production methods and limitations, its products, its services, and its sales policy and procedures. A new salesman will need even more training, including basic fundamentals. His development must be nur-tured with selected experiences over a period of time—often as long as 4 or 5 years—experiences in the plant and in the field that will build the neces-sary confidence, enthusiasm, and skill.

More careful selection and planned personnel development have yielded rich rewards to management and salesmen as well. Extensive labor turn-over has lessened. The salesman has become a public-relations am-bassador for *his* company. Unit sales per sales-contract have increased. Distribution costs have dropped phenomenally. Service rendered by tech-nically trained sales engineers in fitting a company's products to the customer's needs has raised the social value of those products.

In the final analysis, inasmuch as the same raw materials, processes, and markets are available to all competitors under the democratic sys-tem, the competitive position of an enterprise in an industry and among industries depends on the quality of the employees of that enterprise. Nowhere is the value of "best" employees more apparent than in the sales field. Many problems of sales training, as with problems of all training, remain to be solved by the alert management. Closer coopera-tion with educational institutions and scientific experimental research in developing effective training procedures will mark the successful enter-prise of tomorrow.[21]

Training Women in Industry.—During both World Wars I and II women workers were taken into production work in far greater numbers

[21] See Chap. XXVI for further discussion of sales training.

than was previously customary. Women continue to a greater extent than formerly to work in industry. No special problems are involved in their training, except that like all new employees women workers must be trained in what is expected of them: to accept supervision, to stifle emotion, to meet production standards, and to work with the group. The important induction-training process has been discussed.

Fig. 131.—Women are especially adaptable to precision work such as that of the inspection department shown here in a plant manufacturing watches and precision instruments. (*Courtesy of Bulova Watch Company.*)

It may be briefly stated that women are doing and have done all types of industrial work but should in general be assigned to new jobs in keeping with their strength (about two-thirds of a man's), not lifting over 35 pounds in weight, seldom exposed to industrial poisons (especially benzene, TNT, dinitrobenzene, sulphuric ether, carbon disulphide, lead, mercury, arsenic, and silica dust) nor to intense and sustained heat, and should be given adequate rest periods and occasional help with heavier parts of the job. A gradual introduction with opportunity to overcome any "fear of the machine" together with detailed safety instruction should also be provided on new jobs.

Typical jobs in which women work are inspecting, assembly, packing, light machine work, drill-press operation, punch-press operation, grinding and burring operations, and clerical work of all kinds. Women seem to outproduce male workers, when the jobs are within the range of a woman's physical strength and where finger dexterity, eye-hand coordination, and close attention to details are required.

Such jobs as women have some difficulty performing seem largely to be training-problem jobs, *i.e.*, fields of work in which women do not normally receive instruction or fields in which they seldom practice. For instance, most girls experience some difficulty with fractions and decimals; so do men who never use them. Mathematical principles can be easily taught, although it will usually be necessary to "start training women further back" in all phases of mechanics. Because of their lack of mechanical familiarity, women require special instruction in the need for oiling and greasing machinery but will usually keep the workplace cleaner. Factory vocabulary often requires some clarification. What girl would expect a "dolly" to be alternately a low-wheeled table or a short bar of metal used behind rivets when flattening?

Summary.—Training in industry, largely through work experience and apprenticeship, is one of the oldest phases of industrial relations. Industrial training is very different from traditional "schooling," although it uses the methods of the growing field of *adult education*. The importance of man power in relation to competitive position has been stressed, and selection designated as the funnel. Within reasonable limits, regardless of variations in selection techniques, the quality of employees available to different enterprises is constant: All hire the same portion of genius. To an increasing extent, however, success and failure of the individual enterprise in competition with other enterprises are dependent upon the successful training of average individuals.

For this purpose industry uses an increasing range of training methods, courses, and training aids. The conference method is of growing importance, and employees must be taught how to lead conferences as well as to participate in them as members. Attention is now directed not only to the lower levels but most intensively to the executive level, where executive audit and development methods team with slide films and role-playing to perpetuate the enterprise.

CASE PROBLEMS

1. Assume that a training program is to be installed in the Carbide Steel Company.[22] This is a 4,700-employee metalworking plant turning out chiefly metal stampings; 4,200 men and 200 women production workers are employed. Supervision is centered in an owner-president, a treasurer, and a plant manager. No formal training has existed, al-

[22] Fictitious name.

though employees are alert, cooperative, and interested.   Plan the organization of a training committee, set up the agenda they will discuss, and recommend a course of action.   Include the number and nature of training courses, possible instructors, and enrollment.   Suggest possible relations with local educational institutions.

\2. Describe a course of training that would enable the Vimal Corporation [23] to fill the positions of office manager and sales manager 10 years from now.   Assume that the present incumbents are satisfactory and will continue so but reach retirement age in 10 years.   Vimal is a 12-million-dollar organization selling skin creams and lotions on a national basis. Twenty field salesmen contact drugstores directly to take orders and promote sales.   No accounting-department employee is of controller quality.

3. Prepare a list of the educational facilities of your community that might cooperate with industry at the various levels of training, including apprentices, production workers, and supervisory, sales, and clerical employees.   Indicate to the best of your knowledge which of these educational institutions are now cooperating with industry in meeting industrial-training problems.

4. The role-playing method of training is very useful in some circumstances.   In others it is difficult to get the participants to accept the reality of the situation.   Even when burlesqued, as it often is, however, the contrast between a "right" and a "wrong" performance is very impressive, and many details are brought out that would otherwise be missed.   With these facts in mind, select four situations in which role-playing might be used for effective training.   Sketch what would be done in each drama.

THE ROLAND ATWOOD CORP.[23]

The engineering department of the Roland Atwood Corporation has expanded from 300 to about 1,400 employees in 2½ years.   The supervisory staff of the department has increased from 25 to about 75 over the same period of time.   Of this group about 25 per cent are young men, inexperienced from the standpoint of supervision; about 50 per cent are men who have grown with the company, are what you might call "of the old school," and are still living in the past.   In ordinary times they would never be made supervisors.   The rest of the group are older men but experienced supervisors.   They recognize the emergency and adopt methods to meet it.

Close supervision of the engineering work is essential because the company must employ many engineers who are inexperienced.

[23] Fictitious name.

Management recognizes the need for training, as evidenced by their recent expenditure of large sums of money for a supervisory training course purchased from an outside agency. Whereas this was a good course and should have met with considerable success, it was not well received by the supervisors. They attended only because management requested it; and because of this pressure from management they are not in a receptive mood toward further training. Yet there is ample evidence supporting the contention of management that the engineering supervisors are badly in need of training on such topics as job evaluation, induction procedures, and methods.

The problem of training engineering supervisors is somewhat different from that of training shop foremen or supervisors. The engineer's mind has been developed to analyze problems, to get the facts, and to use those facts to solve the problem. This must be considered when organizing programs that involve engineers.

Preparatory Questions

1. Suggest a possible approach to the continuation of training for the engineering supervisors of the Roland Atwood Corporation, recognizing that *effectiveness* is dependent upon voluntary *acceptance*.

2. Should the old and the new supervisors be trained by the same methods and in the same classes?

3. Suppose you were leading the classes for the purchased training course. What means would you use to gain better acceptance of the course? How would you get participation? What problems might you meet? List three "overhead" questions which you might use to get the discussions started on each of the topics mentioned.

CHAPTER XXII

THE SOCIAL ASPECTS OF
EMPLOYEE–EMPLOYER RELATIONS

The morale or *esprit de corps* of the workers in a production plant has a direct effect on output. When workers are happy, obey the rules, and want to work, output is high; when workers are grumpy, resentful, and suspicious of management, output is low, no matter what the product or what the wage. The Western Electric Company undertook an experiment under the sponsorship of the National Research Council with the guidance of a group of Harvard scientists [1]

the aim of which was to determine the relationship between intensity of illumination and efficiency of workers, measured in output. One of the experiments made was the following: Two groups of employees doing similar work under similar conditions were chosen, and records of output were kept of each group. The intensity of the light under which one group worked was varied, while that under which the other group worked was held constant. By this method the investigators hoped to isolate from the effect of other variables the effect of changes in the intensity of illumination on the rate of output.

In this hope they were disappointed. The experiment failed to show any simple relation between experimental changes in intensity of illumination and observed changes in rate of output. The investigators concluded that this result was obtained, not because such a relation did not exist, but because it was in fact impossible to isolate it from the other variables entering into any determination of productive efficiency. This kind of difficulty, of course, has been encountered in experimental work in many fields. Furthermore, the investigators were in agreement as to the character of some of these other variables. They were convinced that one of the major factors which prevented their securing a satisfactory result was psychological. The employees being tested were reacting to changes in light intensity in the way in which they assumed that they were expected to react. That is, when light intensity was increased they were expected to produce more; when it was decreased they were expected to produce less. A further experiment was devised to demonstrate this point. The light bulbs were changed, as they had been changed before, and the workers were allowed to

[1] "Fatigue of Workers and Its Relation to Industrial Production," by National Research Council, published by Reinhold Publishing Corporation, New York, 1941. These experiments are described in detail in E. Mayo, "The Human Problems of an Industrial Civilization"; T. N. Whitehead, "The Industrial Worker"; Roethlisberger and Dickson, "Management and the Worker"; F. J. Roethlisberger, "Management and Morale."

assume that as a result there would be more light. They commented favorably on the increased illumination. As a matter of fact, the bulbs had been replaced with others of just the same power. Other experiments were made, and in each case the results could be explained as a "psychological" reaction rather than a "physiological" one.

This discovery seemed to be important. It suggested that the relations between other physical conditions and the efficiency of workers might be obscured by similar psychological reactions. Nevertheless, the investigators were determined to continue in their course.

As the experiments continued over a period of years, more than $14,000,-000 were expended to reach the final conclusions that the social aspects of the job, the beliefs and sentiments of the worker, the attitude of the informal group leaders were of great importance to production.

As a result of its experiments at Hawthorne, the Western Electric Company developed the counseling program whereby a "listening interviewer" was assigned to the task of having a talk with every employee at least twice a year—not to condemn, not to advise, not to censor supervision, indeed without any supervisory authority, but simply to give the worker a friend to whom he could talk. That management is certain the system has benefited greatly by this activity. Many of the workers express a great liking for the interviews and oppose their discontinuance. Although it is now more than 20 years since the Western Electric experiments, few managements have made constructive use of the *informal organization* or of worker *sentiments* which were proved so important.

The Mainsprings of Morale.—What is this thing called "morale"? How is job enthusiasm created? Why did Westinghouse Electric maintenance workers choose to work 16 hours in intense heat, blowing live steam away with high-pressure air hoses to repair a steam leak instead of making the repair in the simple way after shutting down the entire Westinghouse plant for four shifts?

Job enthusiasm is something more easily detected than created.[2] When a stranger steps into a plant where employees are not prompt in complying with orders, where they are disrespectful of superiors and their rules, and where production jams constantly occur, he knows morale is low. Similarly, when he steps into a plant where the employees obviously feel that the jobs they are doing are important, where they identify themselves as part of the organization, where discipline is spontaneous, and where employees are smiling and cheerful on the job, he knows job enthusiasm is great. The stranger or new worker senses the morale level easily; the plant executive is often too engrossed in the problems of the

---

[2] See HEYEL, CARL, "How to Create Job Enthusiasm," New York: McGraw-Hill Book Company, Inc., 1942, from which much of the following treatment is taken.

business, too much the "boss," to know how the workers feel about their jobs.

Since enthusiasm is a matter of emotions—something that goes on inside of people—it is not always susceptible to the forces of logic. The workers themselves cannot always put their real grievances into words.

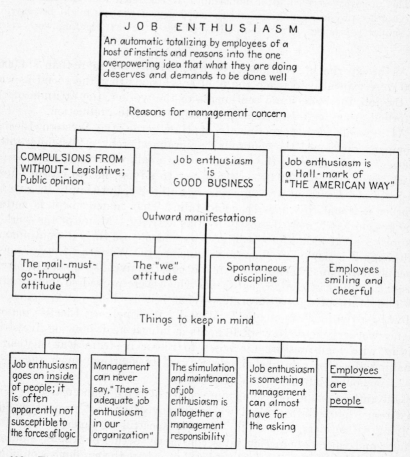

FIG. 132.—Five things to keep in mind. (*From Carl Heyel, "How to Create Job Enthusiasm," p. 53, 1942.*)

The things workers ask for when they strike are not always the things that upset them. Management can improve morale and can do it very simply. Any organization can be greatly benefited by increased job enthusiasm. But the best of managements cannot improve morale simply by certain automatic benefits or services. The maintenance of morale is an important part of the industrial-relations program. Morale is conditioned by the *whole* program—by the spirit which lies behind it as much as by the specific employee-relation actions or public-relations methods used. All levels of management must constantly strive to maintain enthusiasm among employees and guard particularly against any policies and actions on management's part that disturb enthusiasm. *Employees must be treated as people.* Their wants, desires, emotions, sentiments, and wholly unjustified beliefs must be respected and dealt with by management in a democratic fashion.

The usual personnel department activities directed at morale building can help create identification or the "we" attitude. The "we" attitude is gained by increasing the perspective of the job and by promoting employee cooperation and the management partnership idea. A better perspective is obtained by "stretching" the employee's mind beyond his immediate job, perhaps by inspection tours, product displays, or statements concerning the use of the part in the completed product or the importance of the product. Employee cooperation is stimulated by encouraging employee suggestions and by dramatizing the importance of waste control and cost reduction. True management partnership is evidenced by (1) employees "in the know" about the company's business success and future, (2) recognition of employee ambition and ability, and (3) a reasonable degree of security for employees.

A professional approach to the job can be stimulated and a special sense of responsibility nurtured by showing in bulletins, house organs, etc., that the well-being of many people throughout the organization depends on the individual job well performed. Aids to this feeling are (1) allowing workers to use as many of their skills as possible and creating a sense of growing skill, (2) appealing to the creative instinct by showing the end results of good work, (3) minimizing worker anonymity by identifying individuals and their crafts, and (4) enhancing the "social acceptance" of the job by special privileges, special status, etc. All these activities may be greatly aided by a spontaneous self-discipline, such as is diagramed in Fig. 133.

A part of the recognition of employees at all levels of authority as "people" revolves around a relieving of internal stresses and strains and an injection of human warmth into the work relationship. The attitudes and actions of management toward employees and other management members must reflect an appreciation of employees as human beings. Organized induction procedures must be provided for making the new employee feel at home. Those little "extras" that help make life on the job pleasant have a value far beyond their cost. Practices that have proved their worth in public relations can be applied within the organi-

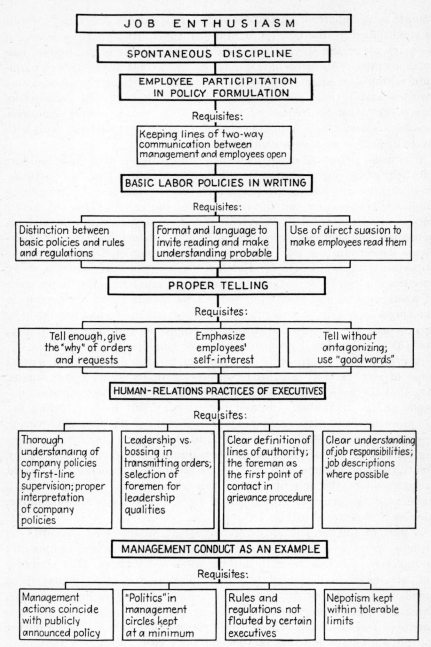

Fɪɢ. 133.—Spontaneous discipline. (*From Carl Heyel, "How to Create Job Enthusiasm," p. 209, 1942.*)

zation to emphasize courtesy. Management has definite responsibility for appreciating the tremendous importance of "face" among all classes of employees, for respecting the informal organization present in every working group, and for avoiding stimulation of unfounded fears and "jitters" on the part of employees whenever possible. The lower levels of management, especially the foremen under rapidly changing conditions, must also be afforded these protections.

Why Do We Act Like People?—If we hope to build morale—to motivate human action—we should try to understand the query that heads this section. How people are supposed to act, hence, how *we* act is entirely a product of the society in which we live. Culture makes the individual! We live up to the customs and rituals of the groups to which we belong.[3] This is the *cultural concept* which is the basic concept of social anthropology. Our American culture makes us write a meaningless "Dear Sir:" at the head of our letters but taboos one man's kissing another; French culture uses "Monsieur" and includes a male kiss with a man's medal for bravery.[4] Psychologists explain that the human animal at birth is equipped with only certain "drives," or *physiological necessities,* such as the need for food, water, air, and warmth plus a few reflex actions. Some, such as the sexual drive, mature later. The baby, forced by an overriding "drive to live," learns from experience how to satisfy his physiological needs. As learning progresses, the primary drives may be supplemented with secondary learned drives, which assist the primary satisfaction. Many of these used to be labeled *instincts.* They remain important determiners of social behavior, although psychologists cannot explain in mechanical terms just how they originate. Adult human nature, then, with which the industrial-relations worker must deal to build morale, consists of certain physiological necessities which are satisfied through socially acquired cultural habits. Let us consider why we do not all acquire the same habits—why people in the same culture have different personalities. The chief reason is that we do not have the same experiences. Our physiological make-up differs slightly. In addition we are each subject to a different environment.

The psychoanalysts explain our socialization, most of which occurs in the first three, four, or five years of life, by reference to the unconscious, to a three-part regulating system consisting of *id, ego,* and *superego,* to personality habits formed at different stages in infancy, and to "defense mechanisms." Psychoanalysis is too complex and controversial to treat

---

[3] Saying "Good morning," although it is raining is a custom; tipping one's hat a ritual. Sociologists call things like this folkways or mores.

[4] For further examples see A. L. KROBER, "Anthropology," rev. ed., New York: Harcourt, Brace and Company, Inc., 1948.

here.   Habits do persist, however, as many a broken New Year's resolution testifies, and it is possible that babyhood habits of cooperation, aggression, resistance, and affection govern much of adult life.   Certainly we see defense mechanisms in action every day.   Some of these are

1. Sublimation—channeling primitive energy into socially approved activity. (Kicking the scrap box or slamming the door instead of punching the boss's nose.)

2. Rationalization—explaining plausibly (although incorrectly) to ourselves why we think, feel, or behave as we do.   (Saying we eat at Ptomaine Pete's because we like the food when it is really the waitress or because we are too lazy to walk two blocks to the YMCA cafeteria.)

3. Projection—assigning to other persons, perhaps in disguised form, the wishes and fears we cannot admit openly that we have.   (Insisting that a man we fired is "no good" because secretly we have a guilty feeling he may have been right.)

4. Conversion—forcing threatening impulses into functional disorder.   (Sudden blinding headaches in the face of unadmitted fear, momentary stuttering or loss of voice under stage fright.)

Neither the sociologists nor the social psychologists today believe in a "group mind" existing outside individual minds, but we can all agree that minds act differently in groups from the way they act alone.   A mob has a different spirit from 200 individual citizens.   People in a group are more suggestible, impulsive, and irrationally emotional than they are alone.

In addition to the general behavior patterns of our country, region, state, city, church, and neighborhood, we all follow the customs and rituals of innumerable other groups to which we belong.   Work groups, for instance, have customs and even vocabularies of their own, which must be understood in dealing with them.   This is the reason for including "group expectancy" in the personnel viewpoint.   Students of social relations have pointed out that, while different groups have different characteristics, groups as such have identifiable common features. Groups, for instance, tend to solve the problems of individual members by group action; *e.g.* a group of pieceworkers will restrict production to protect a "weak sister."   Groups show memory for group experiences; *e.g.* young unionists rant about yellow-dog contracts dating from the 1920's.   Groups retain habits of characteristic action in spite of continual turnover of membership; *e.g.* printers wear square paper hats or machine-shop workers send novices for left-handed monkey wrenches.   Groups exercise a choice of membership, admitting or rejecting those who approach them, *e.g.* the "ribbing" a newcomer to an established department takes upon his acceptance.   Some have even proposed that the group has a "personality" closely parallel to the personality of its members.[5]

[5] R. B. Cattell, in *Psychological Review*, Vol. 55, No. 1, names this "syntality" in his discussion of group-personality characteristics.

This excursion into the social sciences that underlie industrial relations should make it clear that there is no cut-and-dried explanation for any human action. It should also make it clear that every man, being human, is not automatically, therefore, an expert at "human relations." There is still a vast field to be explored and understood before we can reduce personnel work to the exactitude of metallurgy or applied mechanics. None of us are able to *understand fully all* the things *we feel,* think, or do. If we cannot explain ourselves, how can we explain others? Human motivation remains obscure. We may appeal to a man's pocketbook and hurt his job pride, as when we ask a craftsman to hurry up for a bonus. On the other hand mere attention may get the results reported in the Western Electric experiment. To achieve the latter result rather than the former we must honor each man's needs: (1) For wholeness—the whole man must take part in the job. (2) For participation—he must have a voice in deciding the vital things that affect his work life. (3) For consistency—his position must not contradict itself. We can do this and build morale through attention to each man's leadership, motivation, and identification.[6] Good supervisors through *leadership,* consideration for the employee, and personal interest win confidence. That same leadership, along with information on how to do the job and the reason for doing it well, produces a *motivation* toward the job which we have called job enthusiasm. *Identification* occurs as the members of the group develop a social consciousness—the "we" attitude—a unity of purpose which minimizes personal inconvenience and makes the worker more satisfied with his lot.

Failure in Morale-building Efforts.—Many well-intentioned efforts of management to increase morale have had exactly opposite results. Nowhere is paternalism easier to create; nowhere can paternalism have a worse effect. Paternalism, as the term is used in personnel work, is the tendency common to old-line managements of wanting to do things for the employees without permitting them to have a voice in what is to be done—a sort of benevolent despotism wherein the workers are considered as little children incapable of knowing what is good for them. This is a natural outcome of much of the earlier welfare-movement type of industrial relations.[7]

When Hershey Village at Hershey, Pa., was opened, it provided better housing, schooling, hospitalization, and shopping facilities than most of the Hershey workers had yet enjoyed. Prices were not high. It was not a "company town." Yet workers refused to move into its modern

---

[6] For a brief treatment see MENNINGER, W. C., "Psychiatry," Ithaca, N. Y.: Cornell University Press, 1948.

[7] See also Concepts of Labor, Chap. XIX.

attractive homes and continued to crowd into slum areas because they felt the company was trying to dominate them. Many other examples of highly illogical, emotionally conditioned worker actions can be given, as well as some long-term industrial-relations programs, such as those at the American Rolling Mill Company or at Endicott-Johnson Shoe Company where, although the management does make advantageous conditions available, it does not force those conditions upon anyone.

Another common mistake managements make when morale building is to buy a "canned program" and use it without adequate adaptation to specific plant needs. Pointing out the mistake of "canned programs" is not a condemnation of printed posters, manufactured suggestion systems, or good advertising-copy slogans. Rather it is a warning that such personnel aids cannot be used automatically.

Modern advertising agencies commonly make use of "customer consultants." These "average customers" report on the appeal value of advertising effort. Factual information is substituted for artistic temperament. The personnel department employing advertising methods in its bulletins, handbooks, and posters might well copy this idea and make liberal use of "employee consultants."

The Personnel Audit.—This term has three meanings in personnel work: 1) A recapitulation of the strengths and weaknesses, ages, training, and experience of the people on the payroll. In this sense it resembles the first step of executive inventory control extended enterprise-wide. (2) An internal audit of the practices, methods, and organization in the industrial-relations department. As such it is a management survey aimed at detecting possible shortcomings. (3) An attitude survey of the employees to determine how they feel about their treatment in the organization.

This last merits discussion. An opinion poll is a matter for experienced social scientists, careful preparation, and skillful interpretation. A statistical morale index for the company as a whole and for each department may be developed.[8] This will show up "sore spots" in need of correction and "short-circuited" employee-relations activities. Such trouble zones may develop because of unskilled supervision, because of faulty company policy, because of ineffective employee-relations service, or because of peculiarities in the specific work group.[9] Figure 134 shows

---

[8] See a description in DEWEY, C. S., A Method for the Analysis of Employees' Appraisal of Management, *The American Psychologist,* Vol. 4, No. 7, p. 281.

[9] The weakness of political election polls are not found in employee-attitude surveys, since no forecasts are made; the whole work group is surveyed, not just a sample; a range of answers is provided; and opinions on specific matters, not questions regarding future action, are asked.

the deviation on such a survey. The survey form used is shown in Fig. 135.

One method of making a survey is to hire an outside consulting firm to conduct a poll by means of interviews and questionnaires anonymously submitted. The Armstrong Cork Company circulated to each of its

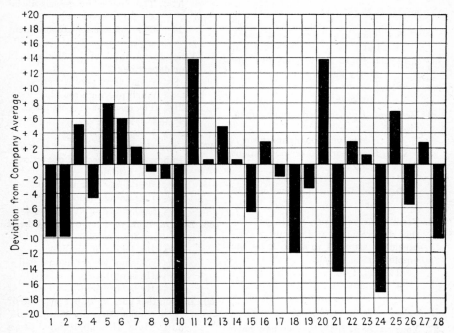

FIG. 134.—This shows how a morale survey reveals "trouble spots" by comparing individual department responses to company-wide results. The numbers across the bottom represent different departments. (*From Factory, Vol.* 106, *No.* 8, *p.* 86.)

employees a booklet entitled, "How Do You Feel?", asking for criticisms of the employee-service programs of that company. Owens-Illinois Glass Company has checked one activity at a time.

A promising development in the field is the employee letter-writing contest. Several have been held, but the most complete was the General Motors "My Job and Why I Like It" contest. In competition for 5,145 prizes including automobiles, Frigidaires, radios, etc., 174,859 employees (59 per cent of those eligible—several divisions had 100 per cent participation) wrote their feeling about their jobs. Opportunity was also provided for constructive criticism. They produced some of the most human documents in print [10] and mentioned some 69 themes. These are regrouped as

---

[10] These are available in "The Worker Speaks," General Motors Corporation, 1948.

1. What do you think of your job?
- 2% I do not like it
- 13% I am not very well satisfied
- 51% I like it pretty well
- 34% I am very well satisfied

2. What is your reaction to such social activities as the Christmas party?
- 1% Such things are a waste of time
- 8% They may be good for others, but I don't care for them
- 23% I think such activities are pretty good
- 68% I think such activities are excellent

3. How would you describe your supervisor?
- 4% He is a very poor supervisor
- 12% He doesn't know much about being a supervisor
- 54% He's a pretty good supervisor
- 30% He's the best I've ever worked for

14. From what you hear, would you say that the president and executive vice-president are well thought of by the employees?
- 2% No, I don't think they are
- 4% They aren't too well thought of
- 43% They are pretty well liked
- 51% They are very well liked

27. Your company feels that we now have one of the best group insurance programs in this part of the country— what do you think?
- 1% I don't like the program
- 17% The program seems to be O.K.
- 72% I think it is a fine program
- 10% Frankly, I don't understand enough about it to express an opinion

47. Do you think this company is well managed?
- 2% No, I do not
- 10% It is not very well managed
- 56% It is quite well managed
- 32% It is very well managed

55. Do you feel the company offers you the opportunity to get ahead?
- 11% Opportunities for advancement are very poor
- 22% It's pretty hard to get ahead here
- 53% The chances for getting ahead are fairly good
- 14% The chances for advancement are excellent

56. What do you think of the discipline in your department?
- 8% It is very poor; there's too much playing around
- 21% The discipline is just fair
- 48% It is quite good
- 23% It is very good

57. Do you think your company is trying to improve its methods of operation?
- 1% No, I do not
- 19% It is doing just a fair job
- 55% It is doing a good job
- 25% It is doing an excellent job

58. Do you think your top divisional head is qualified for his job?
- 5% No, he is not qualified
- 10% He is not very well qualified
- 52% He is quite well qualified
- 33% He is very well qualified

59. Do you feel your work is appreciated?
- 6% No one cares about my work
- 33% My work is appreciated just a little
- 47% My work seems to be appreciated quite a lot
- 14% My work is appreciated very much

60. In the absence of a company store, do the vending machines throughout the plant satisfy your needs?
- 31% Not at all
- 31% Only a few of my needs
- 24% Most of my needs
- 14% All of my needs

There follows a blank page headed "Comments." 81 per cent of employees used this page.

Fig. 135.—This shows some of the sixty questions asked by Standard Register Company, Dayton, Ohio, in its attitude survey. The percentages shown are the distribution of the answers given. (*From Factory, Vol. 106, No. 8.*)

TABLE V.—THE WIDE RANGE OF THINGS WHICH MAKE UP EMPLOYEE MORALE.

Vote for the five most important factors to employees in NICB check-list survey of six companies in 1944. The morale factors on the check list were based on the opinions of labor leaders and managers.

Themes selected by G-M employees in "My Job, and Why I Like It" letter writing contest in 1948. Subjects were freely selected by 174,854 employees, and coded by personnel analysts after winners were announced.

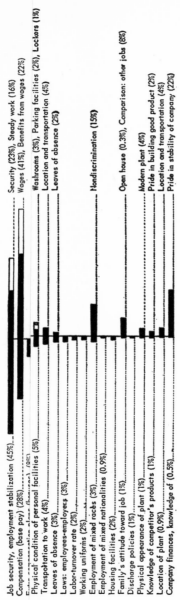

Job security, employment stabilization (45%)
Compensation (base pay) (28%)

Physical condition of personal facilities (5%)
Transportation to work (4%)
Leaves of absence (3%)
Laws: employees-employers (3%)
Labor-turnover rate (2%)
Working uniforms (2%)
Employment of mixed races (3%)
Employment of mixed nationalities (0.9%)
Housing facilities (2%)
Family's attitude toward job (1%)
Discharge policies (1%)
Physical appearance of plant (1%)
Knowledge of competitor's products (1%)
Location of plant (0.9%)
Company finances, knowledge of (0.5%)

Security (23%), Steady work (16%)
Wages (41%), Benefits from wages (22%)

Washrooms (3%), Parking facilities (2%), Lockers (1%)
Location and transportation (4%)
Leaves of absence (2%)

Nondiscrimination (15%)

Open house (0.3%), Comparison: other jobs (8%)

Modern plant (4%)
Pride in building good product (2%)
Location and transportation (4%)
Pride in stability of company (22%)

Genuine Human Dignity
nature, status, and importance.

These may all be grouped into the four areas shown, but no one factor is outstandingly important to *all* employees. Most of the factors have both a positive aspect, contributing to morale for some employees, and a negative aspect, disturbing morale for others; all must be in balance. No one factor can substitute for others; all must be in balance. (*Source: National Industrial Conference Board, Studies in Personnel Policy, No. 85, and Personnel Psychology, Vol. 2, No. 2, p. 220; and "Partners in Production," 20th Century Fund, N.Y.C.*)

shown in Table V. This table also shows the contrast between the occurrence of freely chosen themes and the factors that were assigned first importance in a NICB survey of employee morale.

What the Worker Wants from His Job.—Several research organizations and many private managers have studied the basic "wants" or "needs" of the industrial worker. What satisfactions does he want? What are his fundamental demands? Apparently industrial workers need to know and be known by the "big boss" as well as by the fellow at the next bench. This fact accounts for the good employee relations that commonly exist in the small shop where all the workers call the owner-manager "Bill." Many small-shop managers are astounded to discover, when once they have expanded beyond the one-man management stage, how quickly they can lose contact with the working force.

Above all else, today's industrial worker wants a share in the management of the enterprise of which he is a part. The same may often be said of nonpolicy-making levels of management. This *sharing,* this mutuality of interests, is what the worker is really after in his attempts to know the boss. Oh, yes! He likes the feeling of "being somebody." He gets a kick out of association with the great. He wants someone in authority who will listen sympathetically to his human troubles and problems. (That's why the counselor policy succeeds.) He wants all that. But, he wants *something more* as well.

In the old days when the worker dealt with "Bill," the small-shop owner-manager, he felt he was *in* on things. He shared "Bill's" problems, too. The confidences were mutual. He knew Bill's wife, heard when Bill's kid got measles, sympathized with Bill when the bank called a loan unexpectedly, *worked out with Bill* the cost and sales prices of products. In other words, in the small shop, the worker was a participating member of the team, as well as a fellow human being and friend of the boss. No gap existed between boss and worker. This was a status that allayed distrust.

Today, there is a gap, a wide gap, between impersonal corporate owners and employees. This is understandable. There is no excuse for a gap, however, between the hired manager and the worker. Too often the worker is regarded impersonally. He has no sense of fellowship with the boss, no companionship, no confidences, and no pride in the final product because he makes only part No. 758. He does not *participate* in the enterprise.

The worker today is seeking, often subconsciously and perhaps without himself ever having been a member of a small-shop family, the old familiarity, the old sense of belonging, the full confidence of participation. That is what the worker wants. That is the desire that management is trying to satisfy with dead committee memberships, with collective bargaining at arm's length, with canned morale builders, with empty counseling, and with welfare activities. So long as these pale imitations alone are offered, so long will the worker remain mysteriously dissatisfied. So long as management does not go the second mile, so long as the worker does not have that sense of full sharing, that sense of responsibility in the enterprise as a whole, just that long will there be suspicion, distrust, and trouble between workers and management.[11]

EMPLOYEE SERVICE ACTIVITIES

What are the service programs and activities common in industry? The pattern varies from company to company. Possibly the most common service activity is recreation. Benefits which industry expects from a well-rounded recreation program include improved employee morale, attitude, and health, as well as necessary relaxation from the pressure of work.[13] One of the most effective service activities is the employee-suggestion system or LMC discussed in Chap. XVII. Once employees understand that their ideas are considered and adopted—that they have a chance to change the conditions and methods of the daily job—their enthusiasm makes them effective partners in the enterprise. The most costly service activities are benefit plans (such as pensions and group insurance) when paid for entirely by the employer. The employee-relations service activities may be grouped into four classes: (1) those having to do with employee communication, such as employee magazines, handbooks, posters, and management letters; (2) benefit and health programs including group insurance, pensions, employee hospitals, salt tablets, etc.; (3) recreation activities covering hobby clubs, outings, dances, etc.; and (4) outright services such as industrial cafeterias, counseling, parking

[11] Some industrialists feel that workers, particularly organized groups of workers, have not demonstrated that they really desire to participate in management, i.e., workers do not show a willingness to study problems of production and marketing, understand comparative financial statements, nor be realistic in their economic demands. Those who hold this view state, "Workers don't want to take over the management of a plant, don't want the headaches and problems. They only want to be assured that their interests are considered." Certain union leaders feel much the same. Thus the "U.E. Guide"[12] says in effect: *Management's job is to run the plant. The local union's job is not to be drawn into management problems but to protect the interests of its membership.* Neither of these views considers the broad desire of the individual worker to identify himself with his work and find it interesting, purposeful, and worthy of his effort.

[12] "Wage Payment Plans, Time Study and Job Evaluation," United Electrical, Radio, and Machine Workers of America, at that time, of the C.I.O.

[13] Statement of A. C. Curtiss, vice-president, Scovill Manufacturing Company before the 1942 Congress of the National Recreation Association.

space, and cooperative purchasing. Figure 136 shows the prevalence of some of these personnel practices in industry.

Summary.—Management recognizes the profit possibilities hidden in improving employee morale and uses all the methods of industrial relations to seek that improvement. Morale building is good business, but

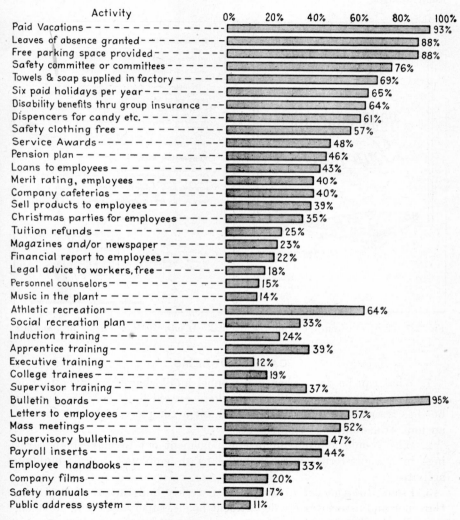

Activity	
Paid Vacations	93%
Leaves of absence granted	88%
Free parking space provided	88%
Safety committee or committees	76%
Towels & soap supplied in factory	69%
Six paid holidays per year	65%
Disability benefits thru group insurance	64%
Dispencers for candy etc.	61%
Safety clothing free	57%
Service Awards	48%
Pension plan	46%
Loans to employees	43%
Merit rating, employees	40%
Company cafeterias	40%
Sell products to employees	39%
Christmas parties for employees	35%
Tuition refunds	25%
Magazines and/or newspaper	23%
Financial report to employees	22%
Legal advice to workers, free	18%
Personnel counselors	15%
Music in the plant	14%
Athletic recreation	64%
Social recreation plan	33%
Induction training	24%
Apprentice training	39%
Executive training	12%
College trainees	19%
Supervisor training	37%
Bulletin boards	95%
Letters to employees	57%
Mass meetings	52%
Supervisory bulletins	47%
Payroll inserts	44%
Employee handbooks	33%
Company films	20%
Safety manuals	17%
Public address system	11%

FIG. 136.—This chart shows the prevalence of certain personnel administration services and activities. (*Source: National Industrial Conference Board data from Vacation and Holiday Practices, Studies in Personnel Policy No. 75, and Personnel Practices in Factory and Office, Studies in Personnel Policy, No. 88.*)

much social research must be completed before its operation is automatic. Meanwhile job enthusiasm depends on company-supervisor-employee cooperation in satisfying employee wants and removing irritations disclosed by attitude surveys, employee-discussion and suggestion systems and upon management's success in providing leadership, motivation, and identification.

Fig. 137.—Extracts from an employee manual. (*Courtesy U.S. Time Corporation.*)

CASE PROBLEMS

1. What can be done when a personnel audit shows employee morale to be low in a specific department where an old-line "boss" is overage but has trained no assistant? Answer for a company with and without an industrial-relations department.

2. Why should a profit-minded management out to make high earnings in a short-term existence bother with employee morale-building activities?

3. From *Management Information*, a weekly bulletin edited by Glenn Gardiner and associates for department heads, supervisors, and foremen, the following is taken:

Realizing the importance of improving methods and cutting costs, one foreman known to us decided to take his men into partnership.

"We can all help in improving methods and reducing costs," he told them. "Our factory costs include raw materials, supplies, repairs, upkeep of buildings and equipment, heat, light and power, and wages per unit of our product. Any one of us who will help to cut these costs will be doing something to help protect his own job."

Then he told them of his plan to post each week on the bulletin board an itemized statement of the cost per unit of product so that all could see just what they were accomplishing.

Then this foreman put up a suggestion box on the wall and invited his men to contribute their ideas on ways to improve methods and cut costs. At the end of the week the items suggested were posted on the bulletin board. Here are some of them:

Use brass punchings for tool checks.

Punch small washers from waste punchings.

Turn off light and power when not needed.

Install drinking fountains nearer workers.

Better layout of work to reduce "short ends" and wasted punchings.

Furnish a "move man" to bring materials to men and remove finished items.

By interesting his men in working for improved methods, in their own interest as well as in the interest of the company, this foreman has brought about a spirit of partnership with his men which is helping greatly to cut costs at many corners.

How can the suggestions received be increased and their quality improved?

4. Consider any working group of which you have ever been a part. Write down in detail the working rules of the group, which were not established by the boss but by the working group itself. Pay particular attention to those rules the violation of which was particularly common among new employees before they really began to *belong* to the group. Identify the unofficial work leader as distinct from lines of business organization if you can.

5. List three examples of culturally conditioned conduct in any working group or club to which you have belonged. Tell how the group showed disapproval of the behavior of a member who "misbehaved."

CHAPTER XXIII

JOINT RELATIONS AND COLLECTIVE BARGAINING

The problem of joint relations in industry is the heart of labor relations. Joint relations contrast to "individual bargaining," in which conditions of employment are arranged between the employer and each employee—one at a time. Contact between the employer and groups of employees occurs at three major levels: at the *organizational* level, where an employee group attempts to obtain recognition as representatives of and spokesmen for the employee mass; at the contract *negotiation* or collective-bargaining level, where the rules governing the work relationship are established; and at the *employee-grievance* level, where individual-worker complaints are settled. Joint relations at all three levels may exist either with or without union representation of employees. "Collective bargaining," since Federal control was established in 1935–1937, can legally exist (in businesses engaged in interstate commerce) only between an employer and the freely selected representatives of the employees—usually a union group certified by the NLRB. Although collective bargaining can occur only with a union, better than two-thirds of the nonagricultural workers in the United States are not members of unions. For these, informal representation plans provide the only participation. Some efforts such as the Labor Management Committee (LMC) reported in Chap. XVII and the multiple-management approach explained in this chapter exist both in unionized and in unorganized plants.

The bulk of industrial wage earners are employed by a small number of very large firms. Viewed from the employers' side, only 25 per cent have as many as 10 employees and only 10 per cent have more than 30. From the employees' side, a full twelve per cent work for the 20 largest employers in groups of 10,000 or more, and one-fifth of those employed work for the 100 largest employers. While 1 per cent of the employers have 48 per cent of the employees, 70 per cent of the employees work for only 5 per cent of the total employers. The size of the employment unit varies within industries as well as between industries. The wage earners of one large steel company (in that industry the four largest producers employ close to 50 per cent of the employees) may outnumber the total employment in such industries as cigarettes, refrigerators, or rayon manufacturing.[1]

In certain industries at least, the day of relations between the independent, individual worker and the small-shop owner is rapidly passing. Large blocs of workers, acting through vigorous labor organizations, have taken their place. In a great many other industries, however, the small shop still prevails. Individual relations between worker and small-shop owner predominate, but the status of such labor is increasingly becoming a problem to both small-shop owners and to the large labor unions.

The attitude of American society toward unions has been derived from English common law. In Great Britain during the sixteenth and seventeenth centuries the state regulated wages and conditions of labor as well as prohibited unions.[2] During the eighteenth century many of the controls fell into disuse, but trades unions were still viewed by the courts as conspiracies to raise wages and combinations in restraint of trade. American courts held to the view that unions were conspiracies until about 1840. During the quarter century until the war between the American states, unionism grew gradually with many radical and utopian offshoots. The foundations of the present trade-union movement were laid during and just after that war, when the Knights of

TABLE VI*

Year	Total labor force, in millions	Nonagricultural civilian employed, in millions	Total union membership in millions	Per cent of union membership to total labor force	Per cent of union membership to nonagricultural civilian employed
1930	50.08	35.14	3.63	7	10
1935	53.14	32.15	3.73	7	12
1939	55.60	36.14	8.98	16	25
1941	57.53	41.25	10.49	18	25
1945	65.29	44.24	14.80	23	33
1948	62.65	51.26	15.60	25	30

* Source: See Fig. 140 for listing.

[1] Data from TNEC Hearings, Part I, pp. 97*ff.*, "Economic Prologue," by Dr. Willard Thorp, and National Resources Committee Report, Part I, p. 270, "The Structure of the American Economy," by Dr. Gardiner C. Means. Both may be obtained from the Superintendent of Documents, Washington, D.C.

[2] "Industrial Relations Handbook," London: Ministry of Labour and National Service, 1944. Earlier acts and the Combination Act of 1800 prohibited all unions. They remained illegal until 1824.

Labor emerged. This was a social-reform group with a strong crusading spirit that enrolled all liberals and became a nation-wide union. It was gradually replaced by the American Federation of Labor, organized in 1881. Through a period of growth that reached its peak during World War I and a severe decline thereafter, the A. F. of L. followed a policy of "business unionism." Unions kept out of politics,[3] tried to make the "best deals" possible on wages for their members, and fought employers.

Industries	Percent covered by union contract	Total employed (in millions)
Manufacturing - steel, rubber, electrical, auto, meat, packing, glass, clothing	80 to 100%	3.6
Railroads and trucking	80 to 100%	3.2
Construction and mining	80 to 100%	2.7
Textile - cotton, rayon, silk	20 to 40%	.65
Service - hotel, restaurant, maintenance	20 to 40%	2.2
Clerical	1 to 20%	5.0
Government	1 to 20%	5.8
Retail and wholesale	1 to 20%	8.0
Agricultural	Less than 1%	2.2

FIG. 138.—This shows employment and per cent covered by union contract in some major "industries." Although in the total American labor force, only one in four is a union member, in manufacturing about seven out of ten production workers are unionized. (*Source: Fortune, February, 1949.*)

American trade-union membership rose from around 791,000 in 1900 to about 15,600,000 by 1948. As shown in Fig. 140 the growth has been larger in numbers, however, than as a percentage of the total or of the non-agricultural civilian labor force. The approximate doubling in union

[3] Except for the principle of using votes "to reward your friends, punish your enemies" regardless of political party.

membership during the war years occurred at a time when the labor force was increasing greatly. A comparison of totals is shown in Table VI.

The percentages shown in Table VI grossly understate the situation in specific industries. For instance, the building trades, printing, mining, railroad transportation, and the clothing industry have long been almost completely unionized. Since the 1935 drive, oil refining, meat packing, trucking, and the mass-production industries of steel, automobile, rubber, glass, and electrical manufacturing have been to a large extent organized. Figure 138 shows the pattern for some major segments of American enterprise.

The American Federation of Labor.—The A. F. of L. is the largest as well as oldest of the two chief federations. It is, as its name implies, a "federation" of about 105 national and international (to cover some Canadian locals) unions. Control of the Federation is in the hands of the largest member unions shown in Fig. 139. Each of the 105 national and international unions exercises a high degree of control over its own

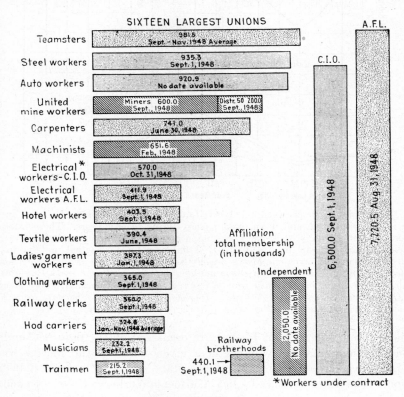

Fig. 139.

affairs, making its own agreements, controlling its membership, and calling strikes. Most of them are organized on the *craft* principle—the workers in one craft such as carpenters, electricians, or plasterers having their own union. The specific trade is the basis. But there are also

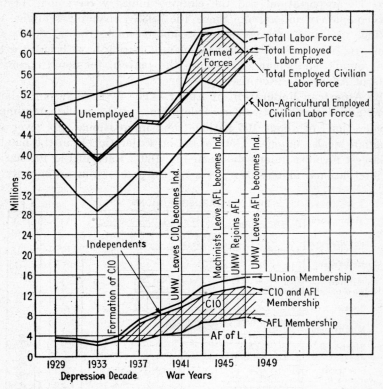

Fig. 140.—This chart shows total labor force, unemployed, armed forces, non-agricultural employed, and union membership during twenty years. These internal values are not mutually exclusive, *i.e.*, a union member may be unemployed or carry his civilian card while in the armed forces. Total labor force is "actual" not "normal." Federal non-armed forces employees are civilian. (*Source: Labor force totals and divisions from U.S. Bureau of Census adapted by National Industrial Conference Board. Federation membership from Bureau of Labor Statistics, A. F. of L. and C.I.O. national convention procedures. Independent union membership from National Bureau of Economic Research, Bureau of Labor Statistics.*)

unions within the A. F. of L. that are organized on the *industrial*-union basis, meaning that all workers in a given industry (no matter what their trade or what work they perform) are joined in a single industry union. The International Ladies' Garment Workers' Union is such a union.

Craft organizations are by far the most numerous in the A. F. of L.

Each of the national and international unions is, in turn, composed of local unions, and in some cases where there are no national unions, the local unions may be connected directly with the federation. In many areas local unions cooperate through city or central labor councils. The individual worker is thus a member of a local union, and through it he is affiliated with the national (or international) union and the over-all federation. The federation undertakes to keep the whole together, setting jurisdictional lines among the constituent unions, acting upon matters of common labor policy, etc. Since its organization, the total membership of the A. F. of L. has fluctuated with the times (see Fig. 140). In testimony before a committee seeking to rewrite the Taft-Hartley Act in 1949 William Green, president of the A. F. of L., claimed 8 million members.[4] The tendency of labor unions is to claim as large a membership as possible so as to enhance their bargaining power. The guesswork will not be taken out until some standards are set up for counting who are and who are not members and until such figures are systematically audited and published.

The Congress of Industrial Organizations.—The other large federation is the C.I.O., consisting of about 38 national and international member unions. It was formed in 1935 through a split in the ranks of the A. F. of L. over the principle of industrial vs. craft unions and because dissatisfaction arose over the lack of vigor displayed by the A. F. of L. in organizing workers in many industries.[5] While the C.I.O. sought to organize whole industries on the industrial union principle, it

[4] Hearings before the Senate Committee on Labor and Public Welfare, 81st Cong., 1st Sess., p. 1836.

[5] The C.I.O. was formed by some seven national unions, formerly affiliated with the A.F. of L., under the leadership of John L. Lewis, president of the U.M.W.A. For several years prior to the open breach, there had been dissatisfaction in the leadership of the A.F. of L. Some of the reasons advanced were apparent stagnation of growth, failure of the A.F. of L. to take full advantage of the encouragement toward labor organization afforded by the favorable political conditions created by the Roosevelt administration, failure to meet the changing industrial conditions which were held to demand industrial rather than craft unions, and general dissatisfaction with the managing bureaucracy or hierarchy (executive council). The dissenting unions under the Lewis leadership were first suspended and later expelled from the A.F. of L. Before expulsion these unions had grouped themselves under the title of *Committee* of Industrial Organizations, but subsequently this was changed to *Congress* of Industrial Organizations when they stood independently of the A.F. of L. Immediately after the split, the Lewis group proceeded vigorously to organize workers in the mass-production industries such as steel, automobiles, rubber products, and electrical equipment. This led to frequent clashes in policies, jurisdiction, and activities with the A.F. of L. and its affiliates which were equally aroused to action by the turn of affairs. Many efforts to reunite the two groups failed, although they often cooperated. The United Mine Workers under Lewis returned to the A.F. of L. early in 1946 but "disaffiliated" again Dec. 12, 1947.

also organized workers in groups that are certainly comparable to the crafts in the A. F. of L. The Newspaper Guild, an affiliate of the C.I.O. consisting chiefly of newspaper writers, is close to such a type. In short, although each of these large federations actively championed one basis of union organization, craft or industrial, both were willing to include and do include labor groups organized on the opposite principle. In the brief period between 1935 and 1939, the C.I.O. had considerable success and by the latter year had organized about 4 million workers, with further increases during World War II. Figure 139 shows 6.5 million C.I.O. members in 1948 as reported by the individual unions to the NICB. The official claim has been 6 million members at each annual convention since 1945. A minority spokesman at the 1948 convention put the dues-paying membership at 4.2 million. The *C.I.O. News*, publishing excerpts from the first financial report filed under the Taft-Hartley Act, estimated *per capita* worth in such a way as to suggest approximately 5.9 million C.I.O. members in 1950.

The C.I.O. in 1949 began a "purge" of some of its more left-wing units. These were brought up on charges of refusing to follow the directions of the National Executive Committee. When a unit is expelled the C.I.O. charters a new group to organize the field or merges the leaderless locals with a strong affiliate. Thus U.E. was declared disbanded and a charter granted to the International Union of Electrical Workers. On the other hand, the agricultural workers were merged with U.A.W.

The independent unions are those not affiliated with the two large federations, although they may have affiliates among themselves. The two largest, since the Machinists rejoined the A. F. of L. in 1950, are the U.M.W. and a federation labeled as a left-wing group and expelled by C.I.O. The most influential group, in addition to those already mentioned, are the operating crafts on the railroads: the engineers, firemen, brakemen, and conductors. There are also many smaller independent unions, including some affiliated with such defunct federations as the International Workers of the World (I.W.W.), Trade Union Unity League, and the Knights of Labor. Many independents are organized on a single-plant basis. The 16 largest unions, both federated and independent, are listed in Fig. 139.

Public Interest in Unions.—As labor unions have grown in numbers and influence, they have become increasingly important to the economy. The power of an organized minority is felt in national politics, in social legislation, and in public opinion. The public-relations activities of unions reach the school, press, pulpit, and screen. When an industry-wide strike is called in a major industry all other workers soon feel the pinch. The successive rounds of wage increases after World War II added to the inflationary spiral and was felt in every pocketbook. Unions today are too big, too powerful, too dynamic for the common man to ignore.   John Q. Public has an interest in the unions.   He wants strong unions, but he also wants them responsible.   As stated by Carroll Daugherty,[6]

What the majority of this country's citizens, union or otherwise, would like to see . . . is peace between the A. F. of L. and the C.I.O.,—a resolution of their organizational and operational antagonisms, so that employers and the public will suffer no longer from this sort of destructive competition; membership in unions open to all employees, regardless of their color, sex, national origin, political affiliation, or financial status; the making of job opportunities controlled by unions democratically available to all members; participation in all union affairs open to all members, so that democracy may be available where it means the most to employees; democratization of union constitutions and by-laws, particularly, with respect to the nomination and election of officers, decisions on special issues (including the levying of special assessments and the appropriation of funds for special purposes such as contributions to political parties), the right of expressing minority views within the union, and the availability of detailed accounting of all income and expenditures; opportunity for appeal from arbitrary disciplinary actions by union executive bodies; a serious and determined effort to drive racketeers out of the woodwork of labor's house; a great increase in the quantity and quality of workers' education; abstention from violent, mass picketing in labor disputes; abstention from the use of imported, non-employee pickets; abstention from picketing an employer when union membership is a minority of employees, particularly after a labor board election has established the fact of minority; abstention from strikes arising out of jurisdictional disputes; a willingness, such as that shown by the railway unions for many years, to utilize, before striking, all peaceful means of dispute settlement, including acceptance of the mediatory efforts of government agencies during a moderate cooling-off period of, say, fifteen days and including, in certain basic industries such as coal and steel, the submission of unmediated issues not to a board of compulsory arbitration but to special boards of investigation and publicity appointed by the President or by his designee; a willingness to support certain sanctions against those who engage in certain unfair union practices; and active, public-spirited participation in community projects which require the support of various kinds of organizations.

The Legal Background.—The present era in Federal labor law [7] started with the Sherman Anti-trust Act of 1890, which illegalized every

---

[6] Address delivered before the National Economic Association and National Political Science Association, at Washington, D.C., Jan. 23, 1944.

[7] The student will want to consult the loose-leaf publications of Commerce Clearing House, Prentice-Hall, Inc., *Washington Daily Reporter*, etc., for a current treatment of the Federal labor laws. The complex range of state laws, too detailed for treatment here, are also covered by those services as well as by publications of trade associations, the chamber of commerce, and management service groups.

Original date	Amended	Action	Purpose or function: "What it did"
1884		Creation of Bureau of Labor Statistics in the Department of Interior	To collect labor information, wages, hour data, etc.
1890	1911, 1937	Sherman Antitrust Act	Declared illegal every combination in restraint of trade or commerce among the states to protect against monopolies
1892	1912, 1913, 1917, 1940	Federal 8-hr. law	Prohibited laborers and mechanics working more than 8 hr. per day on public works. Suspended during war for specific projects upon payment of overtime, and relaxed in 1940 provided overtime is paid beyond 8 hr.
1907	1916, 1935, 1939, 1940	Hours of railroad employees (common and motor carriers)	Limited hours of railroad labor to 16 in 24 hr. work, 8 hr. used to pay; motor carrier drivers to 10 in 24 or 8 off duty
1908	1939	Federal Employers' Liability Act	Provided workmen's compensation for railroad employees in interstate commerce
1912			Creation of Children's Bureau to investigate among other things employment of children, dangerous occupations, health and accidents
1913			Creation of U. S. Department of Labor with cabinet rank from bureaus in other departments. Secretary given power of mediation in labor disputes, injunctions
1914		Clayton Antitrust Act	Exempted unions from antitrust laws in carrying out legitimate objects, but permitted injunctions to individuals from Federal courts.
1920			Granted permanent status to Women's Bureau in Dept. of Labor; first set up as wartime agency 1918.
1925	1943, 1947	Federal Corrupt Practices Act	Original barred political expenditures by corporations and national banks; Smith-Connally included unions in ban during war (1943–1947); unions included in peacetime by Labor Relations Act of 1947, Public Law 101, 80th Cong.

FIG. 141.—See description on page 566.

Original date	Amended	Action	Purpose or function: "What it did"
1926	1934, 1936	Railway Labor (Disputes) Act	Established adjustment board and national mediation board to settle railway employee disputes in order to continue railway service. Recognized unions, refused closed shop, required arbitration. Air transport added 1936
1931	1935, 1940	Davis-Bacon Act	Provided for the payment of "prevailing" wages determined by Secretary of Labor on public works
1932		Norris-La Guardia Anti-injunction Act	Forbade injunctions issued by Federal courts in labor disputes, freed unions and members from responsibility for acts of agents, first declaration of public policy favoring unionization
1933	1935	Wagner-Peyser Act (USES)	Established Federal aid to help states set up employment service, later merged with Social Security Unemployment Compensation
1934		Copeland Anti-kick-back Law	Forbade return of part of wages paid on public works
1935	1947	National Labor Relations (Wagner) Act	Established public policy of collective bargaining, National Labor Relations Board, representation elections, union certification, and barred employers' unfair labor practices
1935	1939	Social Security Act	Established 10 separate welfare programs such as old-age and survivors' insurance, unemployment compensation, aid to needy, etc., all but first administered by states with aid of Federal funds obtained by a graduated payroll tax on employers' and employees' payroll
1936	1938	Byrnes Act (Interstate transportation of strikebreakers)	Prohibited interstate transportation of persons to interfere with self-organization, collective bargaining, or picketing
1936	1940, 1942	Walsh-Healey Public Contracts Act	Provided for payment of minimum wages, overtime over 8 hr. in one day, 40 hr. per week, on government contracts over $10,000

Fig. 141.—*Continued.*

Original date	Amended	Action	Purpose or function: "What it did"
1938	1947, 1949	Fair Labor Standards Act (Wages and Hours Law)	Established minimum wage at 40¢ per hr. (by 1945), required overtime for over 40 hr. per week, prohibited child labor. Recent additions are "portal-to-portal" and minimum increased to 75¢ by 1950
1946		Coercive practices affecting radio broadcasting (anti-Petrillo)	Amended Federal Communications Act so as to prohibit featherbedding, stand-by labor, excessive crews at radio stations
1946		Antiracketeering Act, Amending Act of June 18, 1934	Originally directed at criminal rackets, the 1946 amendment directed this act at stand-by labor and substitute crews
1947		Labor Management Relations Act 1947 (Taft-Hartley Act)	Amended the Wagner Act. First peacetime legislation aimed at restricting unions. Increased union responsibility, provided protection for the employee against unfair labor practices of both employer and union, reestablished government injunctions in interests of public health and welfare

Fig. 141.—Some Federal labor legislation in the last 60 years. The U.S. Supreme Court attempts to interpret all previous laws in the light of subsequent legislation. This list is not complete. It does not contain expired laws or wartime regulations. A compilation of Federal laws by the House Document Clerk may be obtained from the Superintendent of Documents. Parallel state laws may be obtained from the specific state labor department.

contract, combination, or conspiracy in restraint of trade. Other legislation came slowly but followed a pattern which with the Clayton Act in 1914 granted union status, with the Norris-La Guardia (1932) Act and the Wagner Act in 1935 lent moral support to unions, and with recent legislation attempted to force union responsibility. The most important of this legislation is listed in Fig. 141 along with the main function of each part. State laws generally paralleled these.

All these laws and orders have been freely interpreted by their administrators, but the courts do not always agree with these interpretations. As was described in Chap. XIX in connection with the "portal-to-portal" and "overtime-on-overtime" cases under the Fair Labor Standards Act, this sometimes requires explanatory amendments. The

Federal court decisions, administrators' interpretations, and case-by-case applications make an impressive legal library for each law. Only the most general statement of the underlying principles of two recent laws can be given here as examples.

The National Labor Relations (Wagner) Act was passed July 5, 1935, to grant employees [8] the right to organize unions and select representatives of their own choosing to bargain collectively. When declared constitutional by the Supreme Court two years later, it was followed by a rash of "little Wagner Acts" to cover employees in commerce within the states, but the Federal act was so widely applied as to limit the application of these. For example, the Wagner Act was held to cover even charwomen and elevator operators in buildings used by the general public. It did not cover agricultural laborers, domestic servants, and certain other employees generally covered by other acts. The act was administered by a three-man National Labor Relations Board appointed by the president through regional offices in major cities. The board's initial function was to decide the appropriate bargaining unit and hold representation elections upon petition of employees or unions. Employers could petition only if two or more unions contested. After the growth of unions was well started, emphasis shifted to the investigation and prosecution [9] of unfair labor practices. The board was empowered to obtain enforcement of its orders through the appropriate circuit court of appeals but usually obtained voluntary compliance from employers to "cease and desist" any of the specific unfair labor practices.[10]

[8] In any industry, plant, or establishment where labor disputes might have the effect of obstructing interstate commerce. Railroad employees and other carriers were not covered by either the Wagner Act or the Taft-Hartley. They were already under the Railway Labor Act of 1926.

[9] By means of contempt-of-court proceedings. In addition the Department of Justice could institute suit for interference with any agent under penalties of $5,000 fine and one year's imprisonment or both.

[10] 1. To interfere with, restrain, or coerce employees in the exercise of rights guaranteed (self-organization to bargain collectively through representatives of their own choosing).

2. To dominate or interfere with the formation or administration of any labor organization or to contribute financial or other support to it.

3. By discrimination in regard to hire or tenure or conditions of employment, to encourage or discourage membership in any labor organization.

4. To discharge or discriminate against an employee who has filed charges or given testimony under the act.

5. To refuse to bargain collectively with representatives of employees designated by the NLRB as exclusive bargaining agents of an appropriate unit.

During this period, the board held the following, among others, to be unfair labor practices: (1) employing labor spies; (2) bribery of union members, agents, or officers; (3) general antiunion meetings, pamphlets, or publications; (4) formation of

Between 1935 and 1947 the National Labor Relations (Wagner) Act (Public Law 198, 74th Congress) controlled labor relations. This act was amended by the Labor Management Relations (Taft-Hartley) Act (Public Law 101, 80th Congress, 1st Session). Many of the Wagner Act provisions were carried forward, however, so that it remained of interest.

The Labor Management Relations Act, 1947 (Taft-Hartley), was passed in response to growing public demand for restraint of the power of unions. This demand had been growing for 12 years as unions moved from an underdog position to one of dominance and prestige in the economy. The failure of the National Labor-Management Conference, called by President Truman to seek a peacetime successor to labor's wartime "no-strike pledge" set the stage. The President requested labor-regulating legislation in 1945. Pressed by utility, coal, and railroad strikes in 1946 he demanded reinstatement of emergency injunctions and the right to draft strikers into the Army. The House agreed, but the Senate refused. Congress responded to the earlier request with the moderate Case bill, which the President vetoed. With almost 5,000 strikes costing 116 million man-days, 1946 was the most turbulent year in labor history.[11]   Union leaders refused to admit any need for changes in existing law. After extensive hearings the Labor Management Relations Act of 1947 was passed, vetoed, and passed overwhelmingly over veto by a coalition of Republicans and Democrats. The LMRA, 1947, kept most of the NLRA, 1935, restrictions on employers and added restraints on union leaders for the protection of employee-members and the general public. No complete treatment of the law can be given, but historically it had the effects listed on page 569.

----

citizens' committees, back-to-work movements; (5) use of individual contracts of employment (yellow-dog contracts) to defeat organization; (6) company dominance of company unions; (7) discouraging membership in rival unions; (8) refusal to employ (except under a closed-shop agreement) a worker because he belongs or does not belong to a labor organization; (9) discriminating in layoffs, furloughs, or assignment of work; (10) refusal to reinstate an employee in case of a strike (the right to strike being specifically preserved) or layoff for union activity; (11) failure to pay back pay ordered by the Board; (12) limiting bargaining to members of the union instead of all employees in the collective-bargaining unit; (13) not showing a willingness to negotiate during bargaining; (14) refusal to sign an agreement after verbal acceptance of its provisions; (15) calling for an employee vote on proposals; (16) seeking to discredit the union by changing conditions of work; (17) making a unilateral determination of the conditions of employment.

[11] *Monthly Labor Review*, Vol. 64, No. 5, p. 790. The first of the pattern wage increases (18½ cents in 1945–1946) settling those strikes started a wave of inflationary price increases which were blamed on the unions.

1. Increased the membership of the National Labor Relations Board from three to five and separated administrative from judicial functions within the Board by creating an independent "general counsel" who takes over all but the judicial function. (An old NLRB trial examiner Robert N. Denham was appointed and set up procedures much like the old field offices. He resigned in 1950.)

2. Forbade the closed shop (making union membership necessary before employment) [12] but permitted the union shop (workers must join union after hiring) or maintenance of membership (once joined must stay) after a secret ballot, and/or checkoff of dues if approved by the employee.

3. Required labor organizations before using NLRB to register with the Secretary of Labor, to furnish financial reports to members, and to submit affidavits signed by its officers that they were not Communists.

4. Protected the employer's right of free speech provided he made no threat of reprisal or promise of benefit for joining or not joining a union and permitted him to petition for a representation election by the board.

5. Permitted a union to sue and be sued (but not the members personally) for violation of its contract or for damages through boycott or jurisdictional strikes (for which a settlement commission was provided).

6. Provided a "cooling off" period of 60 days before strikes but expressly protected the right to strike except for Federal employees, or as secondary boycotts, jurisdictional strikes, and featherbedding walkouts.

7. Attempted to limit featherbedding and racketeering by barring payments for work not performed, discharge for any reason except nonpayment of dues in a union shop, and payments to union representatives or to welfare funds not carefully restricted (unless the funds were established before the law). Decertification petitions were permitted once a year if employees found a union no longer representative. Foremen could form unions, but employers were not required to bargain with them. Guards could not be included in a production workers' bargaining unit, and professional workers only with their consent.

8. Protected public health and safety in emergency cases by permitting Federal injunctions for 80 days while a special board investigated and required an employee vote on the employer's last offer.

9. Applied the same limitation on union political expenditures as had applied to corporations for many years.

10. Required the union as well as the employer to bargain in good faith but did not compel agreement.

11. Added unfair labor practices which coerce the employee to those already prohibited if performed by an employer and made these subject to injunction by NLRB application, thus protecting employees from both employers and unions.

12. Created an independent Federal Mediation and Conciliation Service, abolishing that formerly in the Department of Labor.

---

[12] Even without Federal ban, the closed shop was barred by several state laws. Closed-shop contracts were illegal (1949) in Arizona, Arkansas, Florida, Georgia, Iowa, Nebraska, North Carolina, North Dakota, South Dakota, Tennessee, Texas, and Virginia. A similar ban was repealed in Louisiana in 1948 and New Hampshire in 1949. Voters refused to ban the closed shop in Maine, Massachusetts, and New Mexico in 1949. In Delaware and Maryland closed shops are against public policy. In Colorado, Kansas, and Wisconsin workers must approve a closed-shop contract. Other states may be expected to pass state laws dealing with union membership.

How Did the Taft-Hartley Act Work Out?—The answer to this question depends upon the point of view taken (of labor, of employers, of employees, of the public, etc.), but certain observations can be made. The adoption of LMRA in 1947 was the most comprehensive national labor legislation in United States history and represented the second step (the Full Employment Act, 1946, discussed in Chap. II was the first) toward a complete peacetime control of the economy by government. Labor leaders called it a "slave-labor law" because they resented limitations on their power and because they feared that Federal injunctions could be issued forcing men to work. Union liability was increased, and union rights restricted deliberately for the first time [13] in United States history. The law put organized labor in rough balance with industry in the matter of regulations, restrictions, and responsibilities. During the first year of the law's existence, however, union membership increased (though at a slower rate), wages rose, and disputes with employers were settled with fewer work stoppages than before the act. Major labor leaders, nevertheless, demanded a return to the Wagner Act. Employers who did not like the law pointed out that it continued the public policy of favoring unionism enunciated in the Norris-La-Guardia Act and the original Wagner Act but accepted the principle of building a structure more acceptable to both employers and labor on this foundation. Managements accepted the independent Conciliation and Mediation Service headed by Cyrus Ching, a former industrial-relations man, much more readily than they had accepted the same service from the Secretary of Labor. Employees and the public did not notice any great change brought about by the law and often wondered "what the fuss was all about." The government took on the biggest control job ever essayed in labor relations but with the larger board and independent general counsel made surprising progress.

The "watchdog" committee established by the LMRA (1947) made and was expected to continue to make recommendations for necessary changes in the law shown up in operation. Congress is attempting to spell out in legislation many of the matters left to highly variable administrative interpretation under other labor laws. The initial committee criticisms [14] of LMRA (1947) operation covered five areas: control of collective bargaining, ban on the closed shop, ban on secondary boycotts, legal liabilities of unions for performance of contracts, and

---

[13] In peacetime. Wartime restrictions had affected unions. The War Labor Disputes Act (Smith-Connally) provided imprisonment and fines in 1943 for encouraging strikes in government-seized facilities.

[14] See Senate Report 99, Parts 1 and 2, 81st Cong., 1st Sess.

injunctions. Future labor law must show statesmanship, not partisanship, in dealing with these.

In addition to formal law and administrative interpretations, the government has influenced industrial relations through various reports, public appeals, and boards of investigation. Examples are the hearings before Senate and House public-welfare and education committees, White House and Congressional wage-settlement recommendations, and the wage boards in steel, coal, meat packing, and automobiles. Wage-board recommendations in 1946 started the series of "pattern" postwar wage increases.[15] The recommendations of the steel fact-finding board in 1949, under Chairman Carroll R. Daugherty, stopped the fourth yearly round of increases and substituted for it the board-recommended pattern of social insurance and pensions.

Labor Relations: Organizational Stages.—The opening paragraph of this treatment stated that labor relations had three stages: organization, collective bargaining, and grievances. The organizational stage history has been sufficiently sketched in the explanation of how the present unions came to power. The organization campaign for a specific plant resembles any sales campaign. Leaflets and handbills are passed, corner speeches made, meetings held, and members signed up.[16] In some cases, the enthusiasm of untrained organizers suggests violence, threats, and intimidation, but these actions are much more typical of a strike situation unless the employer actively resists organization by these means. Before the Wagner Act union organizers, who believed they had obtained a large enough following to justify the claim, usually requested a meeting with the employer. When this was denied or demands made during the meetings were refused, the organizer called a strike. Other unions boycotted the employer. Economic warfare raged. If the employer felt he could not afford a strike or if he decided the strike called was hurting his business, he often agreed to collective bargaining with the union representative or with union employees. The strike threat naturally hung over all subsequent relations. If the employer felt that he could weather a strike, he often stole the show by "locking out" union employees before they could strike. Such actions seldom

---

[15] Fact-finding boards are required in railroad strikes under the Railway Labor Act. They were appointed in an effort to prevent or end strikes in oil, General Motors, meat packing, etc., in 1945–1946. The President himself proposed the 18½ cents settlement to U.S. Steel president Fairless and C.I.O. president Murray at the White House.

[16] See Practical Strategies, *Advanced Management,* January–March, 1945, for an organizer's story of just how he works. See same in "The Labor Leader" by Eli Ginzberg, New York: The Macmillan Company, 1948.

contributed to improved employee morale. The strike still remains a respected weapon of economic warfare but is now used less often to compel recognition (see Fig. 142 for a picture of the causes and results of strikes).

After the Wagner Act, the organizer requested the NLRB to certify his union as exclusive bargaining agent for the appropriate unit. Some-

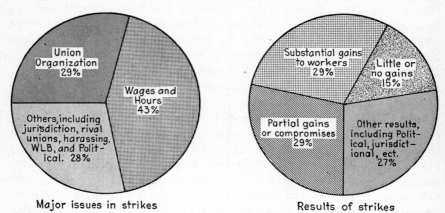

Major issues in strikes   Results of strikes

FIG. 142.—This shows the major issues and results of strikes involving some 17 million strikers during ten full years under the NLRA. Sufficient experience not accumulated to assess LMRA. (*Source: Bureau of Labor Statistics data. Charts original.*)

times the employer would agree to a "consent" election, but more often the union had to present sufficient authorization cards from employees to indicate the probable outcome before the election was held. If no contender among several unions received a majority of votes, a "runoff" election was held.

As long as the regional attitude and "national climate" is favorable to unions, the organization of the individual plant seems almost automatic unless the employer has convinced his employees that they are already "partners" in the enterprise. So much depends upon the "gains" and "benefits" which the union organizer is able to promise that plant experience with organization varies.

Labor Relations: Collective Bargaining.—"Collective bargaining is the term applied to the process of carrying on negotiations concerning the terms of employment between the representatives of organized employees and their employers, which, if successfully consummated, result in a written collective labor agreement." [17] As soon as the employer has accepted, formerly through strike or strike threat and now commonly

[17] LIEBERMAN, ELIAS, "The Collective Labor Agreement," New York; Harper & Brothers, 1939.

through election, the agent representing the employees, the second level or negotiating stage of joint relations is reached. Here again, there has been a distinct change in process since the Wagner Act. Previously, the labor agreement lasted only as long as the strike threat remained effective. Now the collective bargaining contract may be carried on from year to year with only minor changes. The Wagner Act also outlawed "company unions," as well as outmoding many employer-originated plans for joint relations, as discussed later in this chapter.

The Negotiation Meeting.—Possibly the most concrete aspect of collective bargaining is the negotiation meeting, *i.e.,* management-union discussions aimed at reducing to writing the union agreement, or working contract of their relationship. Negotiation initially occurs as the first or basic union agreement is drawn up. When additions are to be made or when the initial contract expires (usually after one year), negotiation continues for contract amendments or renewal. A description of the negotiation process in the abstract will fall as far short of actual negotiation as a description in the abstract of the process of making a sale falls short of the action of an outstanding salesman overcoming sales resistance. Conditions of collective bargaining vary widely. There is no standard rule of procedure. Many negotiations will fit the following hypothetical pattern:

Assume that an organizational drive has resulted in an NLRB certification of a specific local of an international union as the "exclusive bargaining agent" for an appropriate unit—in this case the entire work force of a given plant. What takes place between that certification and the signing of a contract? First, the union usually holds a meeting of its members to select negotiators and decide upon the provisions it wishes to advocate. A union negotiating committee of several members (often 10 to 20) is commonly captained by one or more international representatives who act as spokesmen. Standard union provisions, often standard clauses suggested by the international union headquarters, and specific demands on management to meet local needs are incorporated. The union proposal is usually presented for management's signature, perhaps with a suggestion that meetings be held with the negotiating committee to discuss alternative provisions. Management selects several of its members to meet with the union negotiating committee and a meeting time is arranged. If meetings are held during business hours, management arranges for such employee negotiators as would normally be working to have time off, but may or may not pay them for the time lost. Early negotiating meetings are usually held on the premises of the employer, although sessions requiring mediation and arbitration are commonly held in public buildings, hotels, etc. Meetings are commonly

held biweekly but may occur as often as daily. The closing time of
meetings may be set in advance, or successive negotiation sessions may
be broken off at logical stopping points. Final agreement meetings are
sometimes continuous and may run 24 hours or longer.

When the initial negotiation meeting is assembled, the chief company negotiator usually acts as chairman and outlines a suggested negotiation procedure. In active negotiation, the union's proposals are considered one by one. A common procedure is to read a suggested contract
clause and then discuss its merits. Often management will make a coun-
ter-proposal to the provision or present arguments to prove that the request is undesirable at that meeting or later. Agreement may be reached,
provision by provision, or the entire contract may be kept open until
over-all agreement is reached. When a provision is acceptable to both
parties, it may be initialed by the chief negotiators, or the stated agreement may be incorporated into either summarized or verbatim minutes.
Where minutes are kept, management commonly provides them and
furnishes a copy to the union. As negotiations progress from week to
week, the union negotiation committee reports to the union membership
and the management negotiators report regularly to those management
members apt to be affected by the provisions tentatively agreed upon.
When all but a few points have been agreed to, the final "hoss tradin'"
phase of negotiations swings into high gear. The union may suggest that
it can withdraw some one of its demands if others are granted. Management may suggest that other demands be dropped in return for granting
some union favorite. Agreement on the final provisions of the contract is
usually reached eventually. Where disagreement is prolonged, conciliation, mediation, or arbitration may enter to influence the final results.

When the final form of the contract is agreed upon, the union negotiating committee calls for adjournment, so that it may present its agreement to the union membership for ratification. The local contract is
usually reviewed by a national or international contract committee at
this stage also. Sometimes the union membership will repudiate its negotiating committee and negotiations must be started anew. More often
only a few minor changes will be requested before ratification. After
union ratification, a final negotiating meeting is held to sign the contract.
The negotiating committee, which commonly includes the union local
president or the business agent, signs for the union. The chief negotiator signs for management, often in conjunction with the company president or other company officer.

Common Contract Provisions.—The common provisions that are
found in union agreements may conveniently be broken into seven main
headings: general provisions, union-management relations, wages and

hours, overtime payment, vacations and holidays, seniority, and grievance procedure. Included in the *general provisions* are such specific points of agreement as "coverage" or eligibility for union membership (certain groups such as supervisors and clerks are usually excluded from membership in the factory workers union); duration of agreement (usually one year); renewal provisions; and provisions for termination or amendment. *Union-management relations provisions* commonly name the type of union coverage; outlaw strikes and lockouts for the duration of the agreement; settle whether union memberships can be solicited and union dues collected on company time and property; and provide for specific limitations on the various functions and prerogatives of management. Common limitations concern the right to hire, fire, promote, and transfer, as well as establish the rights the union enjoys with respect to time studies and incentive plans. Provisions are often included providing that the company shall continue to guard health and safety of employees, shall continue benefit or bonus plans in operation, and shall provide bulletin boards for union notices.

Wage and hour provisions of the union agreement often state the minimum wage to be paid, and some include the entire wage scale. Where general wage increases are provided by the agreement, they are stated in this section. The regular work period is stated (usually 8 hours per day, 5 days a week, 40 hours per week). Provisions are also commonly included to provide the amount and method of payment in case of temporary transfer, shift differentials, or when no work is available (breakdown or call-in pay).

Overtime-payment provisions call for penalty payments for work beyond the regular schedule. Time and a half is commonly paid for work beyond 8 hours per day or 40 per week. Double time is often paid for work on holidays, Saturday, or Sunday. *Vacations and holidays* are commonly mentioned in union agreements.

Seniority provisions state that men with long service in the company or department shall be laid off in reverse order of length of service and often grant consideration for promotion in order of length of service. Ability to do the job available is a common condition. Union stewards are often granted "top seniority," and management may also exempt a few exceptional workers. Many problems arise in the application of seniority rules, for there is a natural conflict between the employees' desire for advancement by merit and the union effort to prevent discrimination and competition among members. There is also conflict between the interests of older and younger workers, craftsmen and unskilled, employees in a specific department and those transferred from other parts of the plant.

Labor Relations: Grievance Procedure.—When the working rules of the enterprise have been established by negotiation or by employer statement of policy, individual employees may have complaints of various kinds. These complaints are called "grievances" and the established method for their settlement is a grievance procedure. Good grievance procedure is an essential of sound labor relations whether or not a plant is organized.[18] The grievance machinery enables management to discover and correct the sore spots in working conditions and employee relations. If no system exists for bringing complaints to the surface, management may permit small grievances to grow unknowingly. When the inevitable explosion does come, production schedules are shattered and morale is permanently injured.

A well-devised and well-conducted grievance procedure provides: [19]

1. A channel or avenue through which any aggrieved employee may present his grievance.

2. A procedure assuring the systematic handling of every grievance.

3. A method whereby the aggrieved employee can relieve his feelings.

4. A means of assuring promptness in the handling of grievances. This is important from the union point of view. There have been many charges of stalling on grievances which have led to union insistence on the inclusion in contracts of definite grievance-handling procedure, with time allowances for rulings and for the various steps in appealing decisions carefully specified.

The grievance procedure is controversial at both the first and the last step. Employers have generally insisted that the first step should be for the aggrieved employee to go to his foreman (immediate supervisor), thus affording opportunity for local settlement (see Fig. 143 for pattern). Under management-originated plans for joint relations or where there is no union representative, this is the inevitable first step, although some management plans provide that the aggrieved employee may select another employee as spokesman if he so desires. Unions, on the other hand, contend that the aggrieved employee should go to his union steward [20] before speaking to the foreman. Interpretations under the Wagner Act, and specific wording in the Taft-Hartley provided that individual employees could present their grievances direct to management, provided the union was given opportunity to be present at the settlement, which

---

[18] See, Settling Plant Grievances, *Bulletin* 60, U.S. Department of Labor, Division of Labor Standards, 1943, from which much of the following is taken.

[19] ARMSTRONG, T. O., Grievance Procedure—an Aid to Production, *Management Record,* Vol. III, No. 8, NICB.

[20] The term "union steward" is used to designate the lowest level of union authority—a worker in a department or work section who collects dues, posts union announcements, solicits new members, and speaks for other workers to management. He may also be called "chairman" or "committeeman."

was not to be inconsistent with the union agreement.   Certainly the well-trained foreman, given adequate authority and knowledge of management policies, is in a position to solve fairly a large number of employee grievances as they initially arise.   His position of leadership in the department is thus strengthened, higher-level management time is saved,

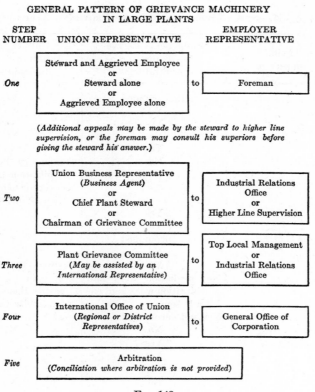

GENERAL PATTERN OF GRIEVANCE MACHINERY IN LARGE PLANTS

STEP NUMBER	UNION REPRESENTATIVE		EMPLOYER REPRESENTATIVE
One	Steward and Aggrieved Employee or Steward alone or Aggrieved Employee alone	to	Foreman

(Additional appeals may be made by the steward to higher line supervision, or the foreman may consult his superiors before giving the steward his answer.)

STEP NUMBER	UNION REPRESENTATIVE		EMPLOYER REPRESENTATIVE
Two	Union Business Representative (*Business Agent*) or Chief Plant Steward or Chairman of Grievance Committee	to	Industrial Relations Office or Higher Line Supervision
Three	Plant Grievance Committee (*May be assisted by an International Representative*)	to	Top Local Management or Industrial Relations Office
Four	International Office of Union (*Regional or District Representatives*)	to	General Office of Corporation
Five	Arbitration (*Conciliation where arbitration is not provided*)		

FIG. 143.

and the employee benefited by a speedy, just decision on his complaint. Conversely, a poorly trained foreman with only a hazy notion of policy can make many sour decisions.   The union holds that the worker needs someone who is not afraid of the boss to represent the worker's side of the argument.   Workers themselves may prefer to have a union steward take their grievance up with management.   This is usually because the union has done a good job in selling its services and getting results, because the worker either fears or dislikes his superior, or because the worker realizes he cannot present his own case convincingly.

Labor Relations: Mediation-Conciliation-Arbitration.—Assistance from outside the management-employee group in the settlement of matters of joint relations may be voluntarily sought by the parties or may be enforced. Aid may be obtained from the Federal or state mediation and conciliation services (see Table VII for a summary of these). The agreement between the parties may call for arbitration by the American Arbi-

TABLE VII.—STATE MEDIATION SERVICES PROVIDING ARBITRATION*

States having mediation service	Same persons serve as mediators and as arbitrators?	Outside panel of arbitrators utilized by state board?
California.................	Yes, not encouraged	Yes
Colorado..................	Yes	No
Connecticut..............	Yes	No
Georgia..................	Yes	No
Illinois..................	Yes	No
Indiana..................	No	Compulsory Public Utility Arbitration Act requires governor to appoint panel with 20 members
Kentucky................	Yes	
Maine...................	Yes	No
Massachusetts...........	Yes, not encouraged	Yes
Michigan................	No	No
Minnesota...............	No	Yes; paid by state
New Jersey..............	No; mediation work and arbitration work kept entirely separate	Yes; paid by state where parties themselves do not pay arbitrator
New York...............	Yes, not encouraged	Yes
North Carolina...........	No	Yes
North Dakota............	Yes	No
Oklahoma................	Yes	No
Oregon..................	No	No
Pennsylvania............	No	No
Rhode Island............	No	Yes
South Carolina...........	No	No
Washington..............	No	Yes
Wisconsin................	Yes, not encouraged	No
Alaska..................	Yes	No
Hawaii..................	Commission of labor and industrial relations: Yes, but not encouraged. Employment relations board: No	No
Puerto Rico..............	Yes, but not encouraged	No

* Source: New York State Board of Mediation.

tration Association, professional arbitrators, or a permanent umpire. What is the difference between mediation, conciliation, and arbitration?

There is little difference between conciliation and mediation. Conciliation is the act of a third party bringing together the two parties in dispute for a negotiation for settlement of that dispute. Mediation, on the other hand, is the process whereby the third party not only brings the two parties together, but actively participates in the negotiation, generally consulting with each of the parties separately and, by persuasion, effecting a compromise acceptable to both. Arbitration, however, is a judicial process. The arbitrator is a judge. The parties are required to submit evidence and each is permitted to cross-examine the evidence of the other. Upon the evidence submitted, the arbitrator makes his award, which by prior agreement of the parties, is final and binding upon them.[21]

Workers' Grievances.—The individual worker's grievances, which arise whether there is a union bargaining agent, a management works council, or no representation whatsoever, follow a fairly definite pattern. Management must settle these if it expects good worker morale, sound employee relations, and a high rate of production per man-hour. Typical examples are:

1. Concerning wages:
   a. Demand for individual adjustment; worker feels he is underpaid.
   b. Complaints about job classification; worker deserves upgrading, or job is underrated.
   c. Complaints about incentives; piece rates too low or too complicated. Piece rates cut when production has been increased.
   d. Mistakes in calculating pay.
2. Concerning supervision:
   a. Complaints against discipline; foreman picks on him; inadequate instruction on job.
   b. Objection to a particular foreman; foreman is playing favorites; foreman ignores complaints.
   c. Objection to general method of supervision; there are too many rules; regulations are not clearly posted; supervisors do too much snooping.
3. Concerning individual advancement:
   a. Complaint that employee's record of continuous service has been broken unfairly.
   b. Complaints that seniority has been abused; wrongly calculated; younger workers promoted ahead of older.
   c. Charges that disciplinary discharge or layoff has been unfair; penalty too severe for offense; company wanted to get rid of him.
   d. Request for transfer to other department or shift based on dissatisfaction with work or odd shifts.

[21] BRADEN, J. N., Voluntary Labor Arbitration, *Management Record,* Vol. 4, No. 10, NICB, 1942.

4. General working conditions:
   a. Complaints about facilities and services; toilets inadequate; lunchrooms lacking or dirty.
   b. Complaints about working conditions; dampness, noise, fumes, and other unpleasant or unsafe conditions could be corrected; overtime is unnecessary; he loses too much time waiting for materials.
5. Collective bargaining:
   a. Company is attempting to undermine a union; has it in for worker who belongs to union; contract violated; company stalls on union grievances.
   b. Company will not let supervisors settle grievances.
   c. Company disregards precedents and agreed-on action.

Employee-representation Plans.—Employee-representation plans are found in three areas of joint relations: company unions, nonunion grievance procedures, and consultative management programs. *Company unions* may be management-originated devices for preventing the organization of "real" unions, or they may be of the *Whitley council* type.[22] Company unions dominated by the employer were barred by both the Wagner and the Taft-Hartley Acts. This ban threw out both good and bad representation plans indiscriminately. Most of the unwieldy *industrial democracy* plans (patterned after state government with a workers' house of representatives, foreman's senate, formal bills, and vetoes) could not be converted. Some *works councils* became independent unions under the NLRB representing the employees vigorously. They continued as *shop committees* with elected representatives discussing grievances and making final decisions on work rules.

Most employers do not have a union and receive employee grievances via the "open door." This means that an employee can take his gripe "right up the line to the company president." Employees rarely do this except where the over-all tone of industrial relations in the company provides mutual respect and confidence. Some companies, such as Eli Lilly of Indianapolis, have *personnel representatives* in the operating departments who assist the foremen in establishing good relations with their employees. The personnel representatives also accept and attempt to settle grievances.[23] Other nonunionized companies[24] establish formal

[22] So called after the 1916 British report under the chairmanship of the Speaker of the House of Commons, J. H. Whitley, which recommended employee representation, saying, "What is wanted is that the work people should have a greater opportunity of participating in the discussion about and adjustment of those parts of industry by which they are most affected. . . ." Following this report such councils were set up all over the world.

[23] This procedure is described in NICB, *Management Record*, June, 1949.

[24] For a discussion of grievance procedures in 61 nonunionized companies see *Studies in Personnel Policy*, 1950, National Industrial Conference Board, Inc.

grievance procedures of four, five, or six steps sometimes ending in arbitration. Such plans exist in both large and small companies in all types of industry. More than half reduce the grievance to writing. Many provide for review by a committee of fellow employees who may reverse management decisions. Such plans often settle more grievances than many unionized companies receive. Both supervision and employee morale is improved.

Consultative management is necessary to give employees a sense of participation in the affairs of the enterprise. Only then can they pull their full weight. It may be used in either unionized or nonunionized plants. In nonunion plants, to avoid "decertification" by the NLRB as a dominated company union, such plans must avoid matters of collective bargaining. This type of employee representation [25] is supplemental to collective bargaining in the same sense that state government is supplemental to Federal government. Both provide "government by consent of the governed," but at different levels.

Perhaps the best known example is the "multiple management" of McCormick & Co.,[26] Baltimore spice manufacturers. This plan provides for several subordinate boards of directors composed of employees originally appointed by management and since then perpetuated by election of promising members by the existing board. These discuss production, distribution, and sales problems and recommend solutions to management. Tenure on the boards and advancement from junior to senior boards are by vote of the board members twice a year. These boards look at all company records. Almost all their suggestions are adopted by the company. Monthly reports are made by the regular board of directors to employees at factory-wide meetings. A profit-sharing trust plan has operated at McCormick & Co. since 1932, with an extra share for employee board members. Most of the present top-management group was trained on the employee boards. The essence of the McCormick representation plan is *full information to employees,* who are given a *substantial voice* in company operation, from the success of which they benefit. Many other companies have adopted modifications of this representation plan.

The importance of consultative supervision is widely recognized. The Hoover Commission included among its multitudinous recommendations

---

[25] For a pre-Wagner Act defense of employee representation see Tead and Metcalf, "Personnel Administration," New York: McGraw Hill Book Company, Inc., 1933. For a current discussion of the need of employee participation, see A. Heron, "Why Men Work."

[26] For a full discussion of this plan, see "Multiple Management" by C. P. McCormick.

for improving Federal-agency employee efficiency and morale one requiring the agency heads to provide for employee participation.[27]   A suggested means was through the establishment of supervisor-employee councils patterned after those in the Federal Communications Commission, TVA, and Bonneville Power Administration. The expectation was that suggestions would result which might materially reduce the time, money, and personnel expended in perpetuating "red tape." Such councils are particularly needed in government because Federal employees are not permitted to bargain collectively or strike, but they are equally useful where there is a union.

The National Planning Association has published a series of case studies of the "Causes of Industrial Peace," *i.e.*, why some companies have a lasting history of good industrial relations. The first was Crown Zellerback (Pacific Coast pulp and paper producer). Among the reasons for success were found: (1) The company has used the constructive potential of unionism—it has invited union participation on a consultative basis, (2) the foremen and shop stewards have become effective conduits of upward and downward communication, and (3) the union has felt institutionally secure and has respected management's basic control over hiring, firing, promoting, directing the labor force, and making improvements.

What Does Management Seek through Joint Relations?—Except where collective bargaining is only a legal gesture, management has cer-

---

[27] This idea is presented as Recommendation 21, "Report to Congress, Personnel Management." It is based upon "Programs for Strengthening Federal Personnal Management" by the Personnel Policy Committee, which made recommendations to the Commission on Organization of the Executive Branch of the Government. In a statement of additional views Commissioner James K. Pollock emphasized the significance of this suggestion by concluding (p. 59): "In my opinion the report of the Commission fails to uncover and identify the real weaknesses . . . a complete and unmistakable decentralization must take place. It is even more important that a revolution in the philosophy and practice of personnel management be consummated. Preoccupation with mechanical and legalistic procedures must give way to genuine concern and attention to the human relations aspects of management." This means (p. 51) "The employee must be made to feel that he belongs in the organization, that he is creatively, not passively participating, and that he is contributing to its total effort . . . we must develop a personnel program which has more concern with people than with procedures; which gives more attention to motivation, incentives, and morale than to refinements of written examinations, pay plans, and service ratings. In short, the modern approach implies less preoccupation with the apparatus of personnel transactions and more concern with results measured in terms of the quality, morale, and performance of personnel." The report may be obtained from the Superintendent of Documents, Washington, D.C. An abridgment has been published by McGraw-Hill Book Company, Inc., under the title "The Hoover Commission Report."

tain very definite aims in its joint relations. One of these is the improvement of worker morale. Small irritations, long unsettled, easily convince workers that the employer is not interested in their well-being. Disgruntled workers are poor producers. It was the desire to enhance worker participation in the enterprise that led to most of the works councils developed by management before unions became powerful.

Management may also have grievances that can be settled jointly. Only a few managements recognize the grievance procedure as one that they can use. It seems too indirect a solution to disciplinary problems that have long been management's sole province, to talk the matter over with employee representatives. Yet the slow indirect approach is often conducive of better long-term solutions than quick-fired action. Some of the matters that are taken up by management through the grievance procedure, particularly in an effort to live peaceably with a union, are the following:

1. Dissatisfaction with individual worker.
    a. Complaints concerning discipline: disregard of plant rules, safety regulations, or supervisor's orders.
    b. Complaints concerning work: slowing down for time studies, loafing, poor work.
2. Dissatisfaction with unions' use of the grievance procedure.
    a. Complaints concerning attitude: lack of good faith, failure to give stewards authority to make concessions.
    b. Complaints concerning use: failure to obtain facts before presenting grievance; stewards spend too much time on grievance work.
3. Complaints concerning organizing efforts of union: organizers irresponsible, misrepresent management.

Most employers take a passive attitude toward union demands, receiving them and attempting to grant those found feasible. Some of the larger employers such as General Motors, Ford, and General Electric have made active demands of the union.

Unions have regarded management attempts to force union responsibility as "union busting" and resent it.[28]

What Do Union Leaders and Union Members Seek?—The somewhat divergent interests of union members who enjoy the higher earnings and union leaders who remember historical abuses in the matter of incentive pay have been discussed. The conflict between ambition and

---

[28] For a discussion of management rights in collective bargaining see *Factory,* Vol. 107, No. 8, August, 1949. For a management statement of a course of action see Hill and Hook, "Management at the Bargaining Table, New York: McGraw-Hill Book Company, Inc., 1945. For a union organizer's viewpoint see *Advanced Management,* Vol. 19, No. 2, p. 72.

seniority was mentioned. An equal chasm often exists between leaders and members over joint relations. The driving interest of the employee in his job, his workplace, and participation in his management has been stressed. The leader naturally has no such personal identification with the various plants wherein his members work and finds his own self-expression in the leadership of those members. The worker is inclined through mental inertia or lack of information concerning better conditions to accept working conditions considerably less satisfactory than those demanded for him by his leaders. Since the greatest social and economic pressure during strikes falls on the worker, he is also less inclined to continue the strike beyond the primary "day-out-of-school" stage, although he may, through lack of adequate experience in labor relations, be more inclined to threaten to strike or actually stop work initially against his leaders' wishes. The worker convinced through day-to-day association is also more inclined to think he has a "good boss."

The International Ladies' Garment Workers' Union [29] has published its views on this matter as follows:

Generally speaking it is more difficult to organize people in a long-established factory where the employer has built up loyalties than in a factory newly established. It is (then) necessary to point out, sometimes very tactfully, that the boss is not really so good; that even though their particular boss is less rapacious than some, he can be so because the union has established certain conditions nationally and that his workers have benefited without belonging; further, the union can help the boss to establish better conditions by fighting employers worse than he is.

Besides the expected general benefits of unionism as such and a greater part in the management of the enterprise, the union leader usually seeks for the worker certain specific benefits. These will vary from shop to shop. Local conditions create local demands. The I.L.G.W.U. states its program as follows: [29]

Such demands usually include stipulations as to wages—either an increase on a general percentage basis or specified rates for the different classes of work; as to hours with provision for length of the work-day and total hours per week, including higher rates for overtime; as to conditions—improvements in lighting, ventilation, toilet facilities, drinking water, etc. Most important among the demands, of course, is that the employer shall deal with his workers through the union.

In addition to objectives sought by the union leader in the interests of the specific local's members, broader aims influence him. The future

[29] "Trade Union Methods," Educational Department, International Ladies' Garment Workers' Union, New York, N.Y.

success of the organized labor movement of which he is a part is often an important consideration. Labor unions regularly maintain national and state "lobbies" to influence legislation favorable to the organized labor movement. The individual personal power and influence of the labor leader himself is sometimes a consideration.

Union-Management Relations.

It has frequently been noted that union-management relations follow a fairly typical course of historical change. When a union is first organized in a plant, the relationship is likely to involve a high degree of suspicion and conflict. Usually this "fighting stage" gradually disappears and is followed by a relatively neutral stage characterized by a decrease in suspicion, a growth of mutual understanding, and in general a mildly friendly atmosphere. This is the stage of successful collective bargaining. Where circumstances have been favorable, a third stage in union-management relations emerges. This is a stage in which suspicion and conflict have disappeared, and in which the atmosphere is one not alone of acceptance, but of constructive joint efforts to solve mutual problems. The term union-management cooperation has been applied to this third stage of the historical process.[30]

This growth will always be slow and arduous, will advance at different rates of progress in different parts of the company and on different subjects, and may be stopped or reversed by untoward action at any stage.

Unionists have insisted that this cooperation stage is never reached unless a closed shop and checkoff of dues are attained, but do nevertheless recognize the growth process. Golden and Ruttenberg state:

The attitudes and actions of management largely determine the degree of co-operativeness of union leadership.

The time lag in the growth of constructive union leadership, after management ceases its opposition, varies with the extent to which labor assumes responsibility for the development of its leaders.

The leadership requirements and responsibilities of management increase under union-management relations.[31]

Union-management co-operation tends to make management more efficient and unions more cost-conscious, thereby improving the competitive position of a business enterprise and increasing the earnings of both workers and owners.[32]

In reviewing this book for the American Management Association, Sumner H. Slichter said:

[30] KNICKERBOCKER and McGREGOR, Union-Management Cooperation: A Psychological Analysis, *Personnel,* November, 1942.

[31] GOLDEN and RUTTENBERG, "The Dynamics of Industrial Democracy," Chap. III, New York: Harper & Brothers, 1942.

[32] *Ibid.,* Chap. IX.

The chapters on union-management cooperation illustrate vividly both the improvements in output which union-management cooperation makes possible and the numerous obstacles and difficulties which it encounters. The authors dispose effectively of the idea that thinking is a prerogative of management. The preposterousness of this notion is evident when one remembers that probably one-third or more of the men who will be the presidents of enterprises or the managers of plants 20 or 25 years from now punched a time clock in some plant this morning. A high proportion of the ablest men in industry have always come from its ranks, and many of the industrial leaders of the future are in the ranks today. This means that many a foreman and many a plant manager has under him men who are far abler than he is and who will rise far higher in industry than he will ever go. It is one of the responsibilities of management to discover these extraordinarily able men as soon as possible and to get ideas from them. . . . Nor is there anything in union-management cooperation which limits management's authority to make innovations on its own initiative.

What Are the Major Difficulties?—The solution to the difficulties of joint relations seems a simple one of giving the individual worker a greater active part in the management of the enterprise. Many difficulties arise, however, in attaining this simple end.

The problems of collective bargaining have been treated throughout this section. They may be summarized as problems concerned with workers' grievances, wages and labor costs, and employers' objections to union desires in "principle." A sound grievance procedure ending with some positive device for resolving the dispute meets the first need. Other final dispositions are possible, but arbitration is the most common.

Certain demands are for increased wages or for benefits that are indirect wage increases. Vacations, shorter hours, increased overtime, higher minimum wages, work spreading before layoff, are all elements that increase labor costs. Since labor costs are an appreciable portion of the costs of doing business, the employer tries to keep these down. Union leaders are not consciously trying to increase costs but in their search for more benefits may unknowingly do so. When union activities contribute to the increase of costs in a union plant over the costs of a non-union plant through barring new machinery, entrance to the trade, retention by ability vs. seniority, normal work loads and piecework, they place the union employer in an unfortunate position in the competitive market.[33] Their extra burden on the union employer may, therefore, bring insecurity instead of security to union members.

The economic disadvantage thus inflicted on the union shop will ultimately force it out of existence unless constructive action is taken to

[33] See Sumner H. Schlichter, "Union Policies and Industrial Management," Washington, D.C.: Brookings Institution, 1941, for an excellent discussion of this subject.

attain greater productivity. A monopoly of product or extreme shortages, such as in 1945–1948, will enable the higher labor costs to be passed on to the consumer, as will industry-wide price fixing, difficult under anti-trust laws. If union workers produce more per wage-dollar, their higher wages need not result in a higher unit cost. Unfortunately, some of the union "featherbedding rules," [34] or clinging to outdated methods, actually restrict production. Some union workers, on the other hand, do work harder than nonunion workmen and, by ingenious application, help management to keep production costs below selling price. Instances are on record where union employees took pay cuts voluntarily in order to keep from "organizing a shop out of business."

Most efforts necessary to remain in a competitive position while still meeting union wage demands, however, are dependent upon the employer. His management must be more efficient, his methods must be more advanced, his inventive genius must keep the plant's producing costs down in spite of increased labor costs. Future business success of union shops depends upon management's success with this problem. Unions recognize this and a few are beginning to take an active part through labor-management cooperation in solving the problem of worker productivity. Current limitations are both union disinterest and management's reluctance to share its problems—especially the profit problem of production and distribution cost vs. selling price. This reluctance springs from: (1) a fear of destroying competitive advantage through indiscriminate discussion of costs, (2) a feeling that many union leaders know more about mass psychology than they do about modern business administration, and (3) a stand on "principle."

Management, when forced by unionization to justify its actions for the first time, often takes strong stands on controversial issues as a matter of "principle." This stand sometimes represents an innermost conviction of right and wrong. Whole business philosophies may be built on "principle." More often the stand taken simply represents an inability to explain reluctance to change from traditional ways. No attempt will be made to resolve these "principles." Rather, illustrative examples of the clash of "principles" will be listed with the statement that certain successful managements insist on their inviolateness while most unions

[34] "Featherbedding" is the practice of requiring excess workmen in attendance, not needed to perform productive work. An example might be the rail union's requirement that an unnecessary fireman, outmoded by the passage of the steam locomotive, be carried on Diesel engine locomotives. Unionists say this is a safety precaution but have no similar defense for considering a crack express run made in 6 hours as 3 days' work because it passes outdated trip-length limits. A practice against which Congress attempted to legislate was the musicians' union requirement that a stand-by professional musician be hired whenever amateurs appear publicly.

and some equally successful managements accept the inevitability of the change in practices.

Clash of "Principles."—Three representative issues are union shop, discharge review, and the checkoff.

Unions inevitably demand what is called *union security*. The closed shop (where applicants must be union members) is still demanded, although the Taft-Hartley law permitted union shops only where applicants join after hiring. Only by requiring all employees to be union members does the union gain full control of the working force. Union members resent the "free riders" who benefit by union action without paying dues. Employers desire an open shop where both union and nonunion members may work, and stand on the "principle" that no employee should be forced to obtain and retain membership in any organization to work for the employer. Modifications include the "preferential union shop," where preference in hiring and retention is given to union members, and the "agency shop," where nonmembers must pay the union a "service charge" equal to dues. (This is an equivalent to the "maintenance of membership" for union members.)

The right to discharge workers has been a leading cause of bitter labor struggles. Before Federal and state labor legislation prohibited such activity as an "unfair labor practice," the practice of discharging workers for union activity was common. Employers now stand on the "principle" of their right to be the sole judge of worker fitness and desirability. Unions insist that safeguards against favoritism, nepotism, and unjustifiable discharge be established. A common compromise is to list a series of specific causes for discharge: incompetency, misconduct, insubordination, loafing, and breach of reasonable rules.

The checkoff system requires that the employer deduct, from the employee's wage, union dues and remit them to the union. Not all unions desire the checkoff, since it gives the employer a constant measure of union membership, but unions where it is difficult to contact the workers on the job or at a central point, often request it. Employers object on the "principle" that this deduction makes them agents for the union. The deduction does place the employer in a position of strengthening the union he may not relish. Objections that the deduction places a financial burden on the employer have been met by the union's paying the employer from the dues collected for any clerical expense incurred.

Problems of Joint Relations.—The mere statement of the disagreement on "principle" possible in these specific matters illustrates the magnitude of the problem presented by the future of joint relations. Can leadership be found, in unions and in industry, capable of bearing the new responsibility? Is the government in labor relations to stay?

Is there any limit to the widening area of bargaining subjects? Will organized labor continue direct political action or return to the "reward your friends" approach? Has management any undeniable "rights," prerogatives, functions? Can unions succeed in providing satisfactions to the members other than monetary advantages? Can public interest be protected? Is there an unlimited "right to strike," even against the government? Can collective bargaining be made an educational process for both union and management? Can the politically elected leadership of even the local unions make an honest effort to find the best solution, rather than make the biggest gain? Will stockholders permit management to accept a trustee relationship to employees and customers as well as its legal responsibility to them? Can management accept unionism as a constructive force? Can the interests of the employee as an individual be protected in the three-cornered fight for power now going on between union leaders, management, and government for control? Can management take a realistic and constructive approach to negotiating without protests from unionists and others? Can union leaders persuade members that the right to negotiate on a subject does not always result in getting what is wanted? Can union demands be tempered to economic reality? Can the old personal relationship of the small shop be regained by supervision? Can racketeering, undemocratic practices, and subversive influences be eliminated from the union movement? Can union leaders join management in increasing productivity by eliminating waste, restrictive rules, and incompetence wherever demonstrated throughout the enterprise? Can the standard of living for all groups be raised? Can lack of discrimination and equality be legislated? Can the *golden rule* replace the *rule of force* for all parties to industrial relations?

Summary.—In the field of labor relations the present and the past determine the future to a large extent. Present-day joint relations reflect the colonial concept of "conspiracy unionism." All the labor laws have grown out of prior abuses. Two-thirds of industry's workers are not members of unions; many are without an adequate sense of participation in workplace decisions so necessary to job morale. Government's intervention has made management and unions legal antagonists rather than partners in the leadership of the industrial worker. Public opinion seems convinced that only the government can protect its interests. The whole future of our economy is involved in the constructive solution to the problems suggested in the preceding paragraph.[35]

[35] For those who view this as crying "wolf!" unnecessarily, we may point to our near neighbor, Mexico. There the 30-year Diaz dictatorship was overthrown in 1910 by a revolution against *los científicos* who were applying scientific-management tech-

CASE PROBLEMS

1. The Texas Brass Works [36] has never had a union contract, although employee relations have not been disturbed. After a whirlwind organizational campaign the International Metalworkers [36] have won an NLRB election by a 7 to 1 majority. Among the contract provisions requested by the union negotiating committee are the following. Should management accept?

a. The company recognizes and will abide by the principle of collective bargaining and recognizes the union as the exclusive collective bargaining agency for the employees of the company, who shall present grievances only to union stewards.

b. The union, for the purpose of effectively representing such employees, may appoint for each plant of the company, and the company will recognize and deal with, one or more members of the local union in each department of each plant to act as stewards in the department for which appointed.

c. The company will, in the event of layoffs and rehirings, promotion and upgrading, apply the principle of seniority on a plant-wide basis. A shop steward shall, during his term of office, in the event of layoff, have top seniority.

As counterproposals, management has suggested the following clauses. Should the International Metalworkers accept?

a. The company has, and will retain, the unquestionable right and power to manage the plant and direct the working forces, including the right to hire, suspend, discharge, promote, demote, or transfer its employees for just cause.

b. The company shall have the right, when necessary, to hire, recall, or retain any person, regardless of seniority status, because of exceptional or necessary skill, ability, knowledge, or supervisory experience.

c. The parties agree that they have identical interests in increasing productive efficiency, in improving skills, abilities, processes, and equipment, in training new employees, and in reducing waste and scrap. Both parties will support discipline for any interference with these objectives.

---

niques according to the emerging pattern of its American counterpart. Mexican industrial advancement ceased, and the ferment continues to this day. In the labor-relations field it is symbolized by the still effective Federal Labor Law of 1932. This law operates to provide among other things (1) dismissal compensation equal to 3 months plus 20 days for every year of service, (2) business shutdowns only with government approval, (3) payment of all wages during a strike or shutdown.

For an account in English of management under such conditions see Dale Purves, The Substance of Management, *Journal of the Franklin Institute,* Vol. 248, No. 2, pp. 105–112, August, 1949.

[36] Fictitious name.

2. Assume that you have been called in as a mediator or conciliator in a labor dispute arising during the foregoing negotiations. Substantial agreement has been reached on all provisions except point *b* in the company's proposal. What suggestions would you make to bring the parties together?

THE BLUERIDGE BOX CO. [37]

On a Monday morning the president of the Blueridge Box Co. asked for a meeting with the executive committee of the union. When the committee had assembled, he pointedly stated, "Boys, I have been turned across a barrel and severely spanked by the board of directors of this company. Our competitors are running us out of business. Unless we can get a 10 per cent reduction in our labor costs, we must close our doors. Therefore, I am asking you as the representatives of the laboring force of this company to approve a 10 per cent reduction in wages. I would like your answer Saturday morning."

The president of the union spoke up after a moment of hesitation, "There's no need to wait until Saturday; the answer's 'No.' "

"Well, you think it over. I want you to realize what this means. Unless this reduction in cost is approved, the whistle will blow on Saturday for the last time. You fellows talk it over and let me know on Saturday."

On Saturday morning the union committee reported that the answer was still "No." "You're not kidding us," said the spokesman, "this plant is not going to close."

Two points were perhaps paramount in the thinking of the union in the refusal of the 10 per cent reduction in wages: (1) they stood on the principle of a "fair and living wage"; and (2) they thought the president of the company was bluffing.

1. What weakness in management and union relations is apparent in this situation?

2. Suggest the possible action of both parties, (1) if the company president was bluffing, (2) if he was not bluffing.

THE GALE SHOE CO.

The 200 employees of Gale Shoe Co. were glum. They had just been told by their leaders that their vacation was apt to be permanent if they took it this year. It seemed that their employer's machinery was not the right type to turn out women's shoes in the current style. Unless a way could be found to get new machinery, no business was available. The union leaders now proposed that the workers authorize them to go to the Gale management and waive vacation rights if management would

---

[37] A true case, but a fictitious name.

use the money to buy new equipment and reopen the plant as soon as possible. It was estimated that the $25,000 vacation fund would be a sufficient down payment, that business in the new styles was available, and that the new equipment could be used on other business to come.

QUESTIONS

1. Would real union leaders have made such a suggestion?
2. Should the workers give up their vacations?
3. Do you think Gale management would accept? Why?

CHAPTER XXIV

WAGE AND SALARY ADMINISTRATION

The payment of wages in industry originated with the beginnings of industry itself. The earliest written records of man in the Chinese, Arabic, and Egyptian civilizations stress work and earnings.[1] The specialization of product, concentration of workers, and mass production started by the Greeks and Romans in the sixth and seventh centuries B.C. also extended the practice of wage payment. All through history the problems of wages have been difficult ones.

As described earlier, if natural resources, accumulated money, and labor are combined in just the right way by intelligent management, more capital or wealth is created. What is created is divided among the parties concerned. A portion in the form of rent goes to those who supply the land, or land and buildings. Another portion goes as interest to those who lend money to the enterprise. Dividends and the benefits of ownership go to those who have supplied the equity capital. In most manufacturing enterprises the major portion goes to workers as wages. A portion also goes to hired management as salaries. There is no fixed rule for apportioning the shares among the parties. It is axiomatic, however, that labor must receive at least a minimum living wage plus desirable rewards for additional skill, responsibility, etc. If this takes more wealth than is created, the enterprise is insolvent. If income exceeds the claims of rent, interest, wages, salaries, and certain arbitrary taxes [such as a real-estate tax] pure profits exist. These belong to the equity owners of the enterprise. Part are subject to additional profits taxes. Part may be used for the expansion of the business or kept in liquid form for emergencies. Part may be turned back to consumers by lowered prices. Periodically, extra dividends may be declared. From profits, realized or anticipated, extra inducements may be paid to attract exceptional management ability.

Industrial management, although usually itself hired labor, makes most of the decisions concerning the shares. In recent years, the rest of labor, through collective bargaining, has been gaining a greater voice both in the division of earnings and in other management functions. Not only fellow employees are checking on management, but the leaders of organized labor are doing so. Public officials also are concerned with

[1] See VITELES, MORRIS S., "The Science of Work."

wage problems.   In the growing pattern of government control are such things as minimum-wage laws and workmen's compensation.

Socioeconomic Problems in Wage Policy.—Among the most important policies which an enterprise establishes are those having to do with wages.   The wage level in relation to production is both the essen-

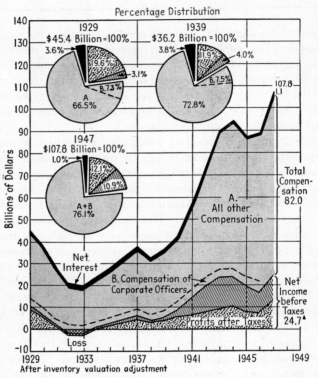

Fig. 144.—National income originating in corporate business (*Source: National Industrial Conference Board, Inc.*)

tial element of competitive position among enterprises and the essence of the employer-employee relationship.   Under either collective bargaining or individual dealing, wage matters constitute the major portion of the contract.   The procedural side of the problem is solved by wage administration, to be described shortly; the philosophical or socioeconomic aspect remains unsolved.   Many of management's wage problems have broad economic implications.   The sweep of these is indicated in Chaps. I and II. Examples follow of specific problems which a management must consider, whether it recognizes them as economics or not.

Distribution of income among the several groups who receive income from industry is a problem that constantly snarls wage negotiations. Figure 144 shows that employees already get the major share of that half of the national income originating in corporate business. In collective bargaining, however, the demand is always for more. Employees rarely understand that manufacturers spend 65 to 70 cents of every sales dollar received to buy raw materials, utilities, etc., and another 25 cents for employees' wages. Just how small a share of income is represented by officers' salaries and profits is also apparent in Fig. 144.

Many union leaders have claimed that workers can be benefited by raising money wages. Economists point out that increased wages can only raise prices unless productivity is also increased. They stress that the workers of all industry are the main consumers of the products of each industry. In the final analysis, therefore, all that can be exchanged among the various segments of the economy is hours of work.[2] If one segment gets high wages for their work hours, the other segments must work more hours to purchase the output. If the low-wage segments refuse, the first group has simply "priced itself out of the market." The 1949 recession seems to have been started in this way.

That there has been little proportional gain for wage earners as related to others is shown by Fig. 145.[3] Through the swing of the economic cycle the percentage of national income represented by employee compensation has averaged around 65 per cent. The dollar value of that same percentage has increased as the national income increased; *i.e.*, wage earners continued to receive two-thirds of a larger pie. Certain segments of the wage-earner group have gained, *e.g.*, miners, steelworkers, and automobile workers. Some of this gain came from top-income brackets, but the comparative aggregate from these is so small (only 3 per cent of national income to those receiving over $25,000 a year) that most of the gain seems to have been at the expense of other groups of

---

[2] This theory assumes that technology, machines, and methods are constant at any one time. The benefits from advances in these would then go to the whole population, not to the specific group where the improvement occurred. Workers on an improved job often feel they personally should benefit from technological change, and management may increase their wages to assure acceptance.

[3] The labor income shown in this table may be understated. The U.S. Chamber of Commerce estimates nonwage income in the form of benefits, services, etc., at $400 per year for the average worker. ("The Hidden Payroll," Washington, 1949.) Total wages and salaries may also be understated, since, as prepared by the Department of Commerce, the table does not include wage disbursements made in households and institutions, etc. Other authorities have estimated the portion of national income attributable to employee compensation in one form or another at from 80 to 95 per cent. A letter from Charles R. Hook to the stockholders of American Rolling Mill states that, when consumer costs are traced to their source, "at least 92 per cent of those costs are represented by compensation for human effort."

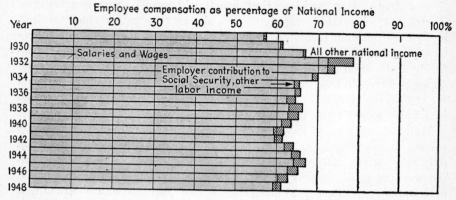

Fig. 145.—Total compensation of employees decreased from 50,786 millions of dollars in 1929 to 29,330 in 1933, and increased thereafter to 51,786 by 1940, 122,908 by 1945, and 133,800 by 1948 (estimated). During these years its relation to the total of national income from all sources remained about the same. (*Source: U.S. Department of Commerce.*)

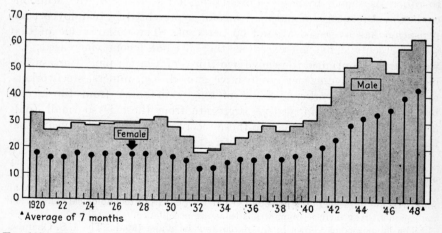

Fig. 146.—This shows average weekly earnings in dollars per week for male and female production workers in 25 manufacturing industries, 1920–1948. Between 1920 and 1948, men's *hourly* earnings (not shown) climbed 134 per cent from $0.62 to $1.50; women's *hourly earnings* (not shown) rose 163 per cent from $0.41 to $1.09. Despite the substantial reduction in hours worked (not shown) weekly earnings climbed 92 per cent for men and 136 per cent for women between 1920 and 1948. (*Source: National Industrial Conference Board, Inc.*)

wage earners such as schoolteachers, clerks, municipal employees, and service workers, who have lost in "real" wages by receiving smaller wage increases than factory workers.

Wage economists point out that in normal times the majority of workers are in the lower income classes. With the labor shortages of World War II and the steady employment of the next few postwar years a considerable change in income-class distribution arose, as shown in Table VIII. In part this was also an effect of the *inflationary spiral*

TABLE VIII.*—DISTRIBUTION OF FAMILIES AND SINGLE INDIVIDUALS LIVING ALONE BY INCOME CLASSES, IN PER CENT†

Income class	1910	1935–1936	1943	1948
Under $1,000	69.4	46.5	17.6	11
$1,000 to $1,499	20.9	22.1	12.7 ⎫	15
$1,500 to $1,999	4.5	13.1	12.5 ⎭	
$2,000 to $2,999	2.6	11.2	20.7	20
$3,000 to $3,999 ⎫ $4,000 to $4,999 ⎭	1.5	4.6	21.5	⎰ 20 ⎱ 12
$5,000 to $7,499 ⎫ $7,500 and over ⎭	1.2	2.3	15.1	⎰ 14 ⎱ 8

* Source: KING, WILLFORD I., "The Wealth and Income of the People of the United States," NICB, Federal Reserve Board.

† The increase in recent years is caused by higher wage rates and steadier employment but is also influenced by the presence of more workers employed per family.

touched off by the rounds of increases in wage rates without a corresponding increase in consumers' production. The extent to which wages increased in different industries is shown by the 1940 and 1948 averages by industries in Fig. 148 and by the top curves of Fig. 147.

One claim of the labor economists, that wages have not kept up with the cost of living, is refuted by Fig. 147. Workers' *real wages, i.e.,* what dollars will buy in pork chops, furniture, socks, etc., have been rising over the years. In the last hundred years real weekly earnings (in 1923 dollars) have increased from about $17 to over $40, while hours of work per week decreased from 65 to under 40. Today's worker spends only half as many labor hours as his father spent to buy food and clothing.[4] The remainder of his working hours he spends for an increased *standard of living* and for automobiles, electric refrigerators, radios, television sets, better housing, more luxurious furnishings, more nourishing food, better education, better medical care, and luxuries his father never knew. Since the start of World War II "real" weekly earnings increased 34 per cent

[4] "Studies in Labor Statistics," No. 3, National Industrial Conference Board, 1950.

in 1939 dollars. Since the low of 1932, average weekly money earnings, as shown in Fig. 146, have increased three and one-half times. It is not intended to imply that this is undesirable or that industrial workers and farmers should return to former living standards. Labor economists rightly hold that our mass-production economy depends on the mass

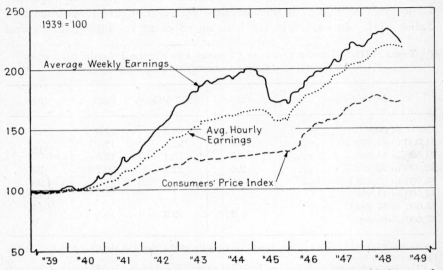

FIG. 147.—This shows the comparative increase between factory workers' indexes and the consumers' price index. This last was known as the cost-of-living index before it was attacked in 1946 by organized labor. Several investigations determined that the index was statistically accurate but was misnamed. Real wages are determined by dividing wages received by the consumers' price index. (*Source: Bureau of Labor Statistics. Reprinted by special permission of the National City Bank of New York.*)

market of the highly paid factory worker and farmer. The point here is that the worker's "flat pocketbook" results from his buying more things as well as paying more for the same things.

Figure 146 also highlights the problem of differences between *wages paid to men and women*. Women generally do lighter, less skilled work than do men, but sometimes they are paid less for the same work.[5] While they are on less skilled work, they are on a par with *unskilled male wage earners*, who also average only about three-quarters of the wage paid to skilled workers.

[5] Wage stabilization required *equal pay for equal work* between the sexes, but this regulation lapsed, and the states took up the cudgels. New York established the most complete enforcement, using time-study procedures. Illinois, Massachusetts, Michigan, New Hampshire, and Washington had laws by 1949, when California and Connecticut passed laws.

Different *segments of the labor force* vary in their income. Miners receive more money than farmers; storekeepers more than sailors; airplane pilots more than bank clerks. In that one-quarter of the labor force employed in manufacturing, *weekly income differs widely by industry* as shown in Fig. 148. Printing, steel, and automobiles are high-

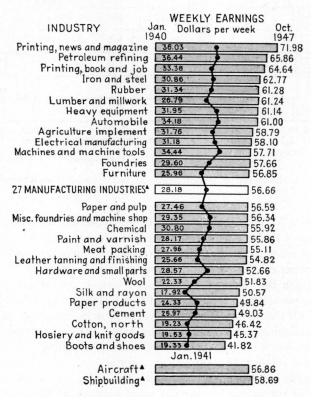

FIG. 148.—Weekly earnings of production workers in 27 manufacturing industries averaged $28.18 in January, 1940, and $56.66 in October, 1947. Since January, 1941, the base date of wartime wage-stabilization efforts, average weekly earnings have risen 85 per cent. (*Source: National Industrial Conference Board, Inc.*)

pay industries. Textiles, shoes, and cement are low-pay industries. Within industries there are wide differences in *occupational group income* as shown in Fig. 148a. Regardless of occupation there are *regional wage differentials*, although these seem [6] to depend upon differences in *size of community, productivity per employee,* and *degree of investment* as much as upon location of industry in the North, South, East, or West.

[6] See *The Management Review,* April, 1948.

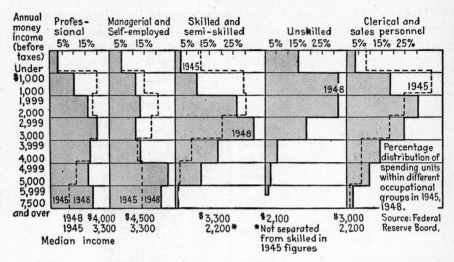

Fig. 148a.—This shows the wide differences in income within and between occupational groups.

Regional costs for goods and services differ to the extent shown by Table IX. The mere listing of the problems met suffices to show that management cannot set wage policy without considerable socioeconomic wisdom.

Management of Wage Administration.—Regardless of the economic problems which the payment of wages may pose, operating management reduces the problem to a series of logical steps: (1) job analysis, or finding out all the facts about the several jobs in industry; (2) job rating, or establishing a hierarchy among jobs; (3) job pricing by means of wage surveys, wage policy, and collective bargaining on wage schedules; (4) task setting, or establishing standards of performance in terms of time, quality, and behavior, through time study for some workers and through merit rating for others; (5) wage control, involving a system of wage records, systematic means of changing wage rates, timekeeping, and the work of the paymaster. In effective operation all these steps are interrelated. No fine line is drawn where one begins and another stops. Although the term "wages" is used throughout, the same procedures are used in connection with salary payments. The wage-administration functions of management may be centralized, or the several steps may be distributed among the controller, sales or office manager, industrial engineer, and personnel administrator. As long as top management has established explicit wage policies and sees that those polices are administered uniformly throughout the organization, "who performs what" is unimportant. We shall describe job analysis, job rating (job evalua-

TABLE IX.—RELATIVE DIFFERENCES IN THE COST OF GOODS AND SERVICES IN THE CITY WORKER'S FAMILY BUDGET, JUNE, 1947.* (WASHINGTON, D.C. EQUALS 100)

City	Total	Food	Clothing	Housing	Other
Atlanta................	92	100	90	82	92
Baltimore..............	95	101	90	89	95
Birmingham............	93	102	92	81	97
Boston.................	96	102	91	85	102
Buffalo................	90	100	94	73	95
Chicago................	95	101	98	91	91
Cincinnati.............	91	96	96	79	94
Cleveland..............	93	101	99	77	98
Denver.................	92	100	94	79	96
Detroit................	96	102	96	82	103
Houston................	88	99	87	71	93
Indianapolis...........	90	97	89	77	94
Jacksonville...........	91	100	90	77	98
Kansas City, Mo........	88	98	89	70	94
Los Angeles............	94	101	92	75	106
Manchester.............	91	102	89	77	94
Memphis...............	94	101	92	84	96
Milwaukee.............	96	99	100	88	99
Minneapolis...........	95	99	103	89	93
Mobile................	94	101	90	89	93
New Orleans...........	88	102	92	65	93
New York..............	97	105	102	90	90
Norfolk...............	94	101	94	81	99
Philadelphia...........	92	102	94	79	93
Pittsburgh.............	96	102	98	82	100
Portland, Maine........	93	103	90	82	95
Portland, Ore..........	92	98	90	77	100
Richmond..............	93	98	90	89	94
St. Louis..............	94	100	91	88	96
San Francisco..........	95	102	97	78	105
Savannah..............	92	102	85	83	93
Scranton..............	92	101	98	76	95
Seattle................	98	105	99	84	105
Washington, D.C.......	100	100	100	100	100

* Source: Bureau of Labor Statistics.

tion), and merit rating in the next chapter. Those are the functions closest to personnel management. The more common industrial-engineering functions will be given later in this chapter. Those functions related to accounting and office management are treated in a separate chapter under those titles.

Motivating the Worker.—Employers in our economy pay wages to motivate employees. Ricardian economists postulated an "economic man" who directed all his activities by economic logic. Such a man worked for wages alone. This view is now outdated. Employers today recognize the facts of human motivation pointed out in the chapter on morale. The actions of men at work, as in everything else, are motivated by certain fundamental drives. These psychological drives may be conditioned (perhaps initially by experiences in infancy now lodged in the "unconscious") to give almost any response. The workers' drives for such needs as food and shelter have been conditioned to the acceptance of money wages. This acceptance has not eliminated other motivations.[7] A desire for participation, for recognition, for partnership was stressed in Chap. XXII. Employers have provided many incentives besides wages.[8] The "fringe benefits"—holidays, vacations, pensions, and welfare—are not wages, but they are costly to industry. The Associated Industries of Cleveland, Ohio, in a survey of the average cost of fringe benefits in its area, found that some 20 benefits cost small employers about 18 cents, medium-sized employers about 19 cents, and large employers (over 1,000) about 23 cents additional in indirect wages for each hour of the employees' time paid for directly. Bargaining on these matters will increase as a result of the Supreme Court's holding in the Inland Steel case that they were a proper subject for bargaining, even if long established at the time of unionization. The 1949 steel fact-finding board said, "Social insurance and pensions should be considered a part of normal business costs to take care of temporary and permanent depreciation in the human 'machine' in much the same way as provision is made for depreciation and insurance of plant and machinery." [9] The demands of collective bargaining discussed in Chap. XXIII as well as basic human nature will require these efforts to be continued and extended. The present section, however, will deal only with money motivation of the employee.

Methods of Employee Payment.—Methods of employee payment in common use at the present time may all be included in one of two major classes: those based upon satisfactory performance of duties during a

[7] In some parts of the world, force—whippings, starvation, imprisonment, torture— is still used to compel work.

[8] H. Moore in "Psychology for Business and Industry" lists (1) major financial incentives—piecework and profit sharing; (2) minor financial incentives—savings, stock-purchase, and pension plans as well as such health-promoting services as free lunch, salt tablets, and vaccines; (3) unorganized, nonfinancial incentives—policies providing knowledge of progress, commendation, and competition; and mutual trust, removal of fears, freedom of self-expression; (4) organized, nonfinancial incentives— suggestion systems, employees' publications, recreation programs, etc.

[9] DAUGHERTY (chairman), ROSENMAN, and COLE, "Report to the President," Superintendent of Documents, Washington, D.C.

lapse of time, and those based upon the successful completion of a unit of work. Time-payment methods are still commonly called "daywork," although the most usual time interval used for calculation is now the hour of working time. Time wages may be figured by the week as is customary for lower paid clerical and sales employees, by the month as for higher ranking supervisory and governmental employees, by the term of three or six months as for teachers and seasonal workers, or by the year or a longer contract period for managers and technicians. In any event, the actual earnings are customarily delivered weekly or bi-weekly.

Employers customarily pay different employees different wages. The greatest part of the difference is because of varying duties. The wage administrator uses job analysis, job evaluation, and wage surveys to set these gross differences. Within the same job, however, different rates may be paid to different employees. If they are paid incentive rates, their wage rises and falls day by day (even hour by hour or minute by minute) as their productivity changes.

If employees are paid on a daywork basis they get the same rate from week to week. Changes are made through merit rating, which provides an incentive for increased efficiency and production. Often the merit-rating system is so subjective and informal as to be nonapparent. Then employees claim that wage increases are given for "apple polishing" or to "break the union" through favoritism. As an alternative some union leaders have proposed *automatic progression*. Under this system all employees are hired at the same rate, receive wage increases after stated lengths of service, and are paid the same daywork wage regardless of productivity. Many workers feel that this system of automatic advancement, in effect, discourages effort, stifles ambition, and foreshortens opportunity.

Although daywork is the simplest method of paying wages, it may be more costly in the long run. The clerical expense of careful production, time, and earning records necessary for incentive payment is saved. The salaries of incentive engineers are saved. Less supervision may be needed. This is not all gain. The records kept for incentive payment are so useful for other management-control purposes that they may have to be kept anyway. The industrial engineers necessary to an incentive system may improve operations in general through scientific management, especially methods improvement. The more numerous supervisors may be better supervisors—more competent technically, better able to enlist employee cooperation—and, under greater pressure from the employees, may do well management's job of planning, scheduling, and controlling. In addition productivity of operators may be increased from 20 to 50 per cent, with consequent higher earnings and lower unit costs.

Working shifts provide another source of differences in wages. The employer may pay a higher wage to attract workers to odd-hour shifts or to compensate them for the unnatural hours of work. Many operations, as in the chemical, metal-alloying, and papermaking industries, are more economically performed on a continuous basis because of the long preparation, warm-up, or make-ready time. Any industry requires less machinery and equipment for the same production if it is able to run that equipment more hours per day. Overhead costs per unit produced are lower with increased production. For these reasons many factories operate a second shift between 3 (or 4) in the afternoon and 11 (or 12) o'clock at night. Some operate a third shift from then until the usual morning starting hour of 7 or 8 o'clock. A premium wage of 5 or 10 cents per hour worked is paid shift workers. This may be expressed as a percentage of earnings.

Wage Policy.—The establishing of a company's policies is a function of top management. Public-relations, employment, labor, and wage and other policies are all established in this way. In companies where wage policy remains unpublished, however, the wage administrator or personnel manager may through research and consultation with line management reduce desirable action to writing for top-management publication. Many considerations such as productivity, supply of labor, cost of living, living standards of employees, climate, and cultural factors will enter into the determination of a company's wage policy. A company may have a policy of making quick adjustments to changes affecting wages, or it may choose to act relatively slowly. Where industry and regulatory standards permit and where better workmen may be attracted thereby, a company may have a policy of paying higher than average rates.

A. L. Kress [10] has established a set of desirable wage policies which, in addition to the payment of prevailing wages according to job-evaluation classifications, include:

1. Individual or group effort should be rewarded wherever possible through use of an incentive method of wage payment.
2. Fair standards of performance should be set which can be reasonably and consistently attained.
3. Employees should be compensated for waiting time due to reasons beyond their control.
4. A reasonable normal work week should be adopted (with provision for

[10] See National Electrical Manufacturers Association, *Industrial Relations Bulletin* 19.

seasonal and other emergencies) including shift arrangements which permit a maximum of normal living.

5. Full information should be given to any employee regarding the wage-payment policy or plan.

6. Complaints arising from operation of the wage-payment plan should be investigated promptly and adjusted in accordance with the facts.

An important consideration in a company's wage policy is the union relationship—with the employees' union if there is one or with other unions in the industry and economy. Other important items to be covered by wage policy include wage changes upon promotion, demotion, or job-duty changes; training-period increases; instructors' wages; maintenance of a satisfactory relationship between the earnings of production workers, supervisors, and clerical workers; the spacing of periodic wage reviews; and responsibility for wage schedules, records, and control. Since worker morale is quickly and seriously affected by disruption of previously accepted wage relationships, most managements go to considerable effort to keep informed of conditions inside and outside the company that are likely to affect wages.

Job Pricing.—Perhaps the most important step in wage administration is pricing the job. Consistency within the company (like pay for similar jobs and defensible reasons for different pay on dissimilar jobs), and comparability in the community (the payment of prevailing wage rates), are the two most influential elements in the employees' acceptance or rejection of a company's wage scale. Both are considered in *job pricing*. The problem of pricing the wage scale is entirely distinct from the problem of rating jobs. A job-evaluation rating scale is usually constructed on a logical direct-ratio basis. Equal increments of skill, effort, and responsibility required by the job result in equal increments of job-rating value. Although some job analysts have advocated [11] that this logical 1:1 ratio should carry over into the wage scale, community surveys often reveal the actual relationship to be otherwise.

Instead of a 1:1 ratio, the logically related jobs that are arranged along the base line will have to be priced according to the laws of supply and demand (often assisted by organized labor) in the specific community in which the wage scale is set. In theory, the wage curve for a group of jobs, arranged equally distant along a base line according to their importance to the company, should be a straight line rising evenly from a low base (usually the legal minimum) to the highest rates the community can pay for its most skilled workers. Actually, organized pressures may have distorted this line. During labor shortages, men

[11] See Eugene J. Benge, "Job Evaluation," National Foremen's Institute, Deep River, Conn., for such an advocacy.

just will not work in the simpler jobs for as little as the jobs are worth; during labor surplus periods, employers may not pay as much as skilled jobs are worth. Therefore, a somewhat parabolic curve is common (see Fig. 149 for example).

Wage Surveys.—Many efforts have been made to standardize wage surveys. These are usually sponsored by local trade associations, al-

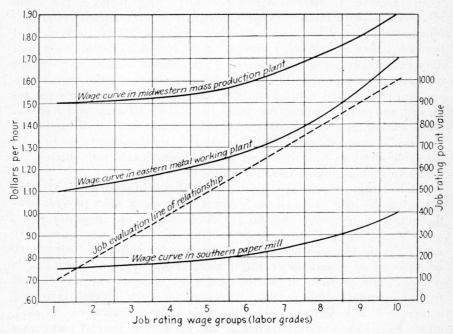

Fig. 149.—The difference between the straight-line relationship of job evaluation broken into evenly spaced wage groups, and three parabolic curves of the type found by actual wage survey of these groups in industries and areas. These curves demonstrate the necessity of a wage survey in pricing the job-rating scale.

though they may be conducted by private concerns. The Bureau of Labor Statistics regularly makes surveys for its established indexes as well as at the request of other government agencies. The essential features of the wage survey are (1) a fixed period of time to be surveyed, usually one week during a specific month or other pay period; (2) an agreed-on basis of pay, usually the straight 40 hours' earnings without bonuses (other than piecework or production bonuses) or night-shift extras; (3) a set of job definitions to be considered, usually called "key jobs"; and (4) a reporting form that will enable the variable factors (such as male and female employees doing the same work or daywork

Instruction printed across the chart head: OPPOSITE "A" IN EACH OCCUPATION ENTER THE EACH EARNED RATES PER HOUR (INCLUDING INCENTIVE) AND DIRECTLY BELOW, OPPOSITE "B," THE NUMBER OF EMPLOYEES AT EACH RATE. DESIGNATE IN THE LAST COLUMN BY "P" IF EARNINGS ARE PIECEWORK OR BY "D" IF EARNINGS ARE STRAIGHT DAY WORK.

MALE OCCUPATIONS — MANUFACTURING

Occupation	Description	P or D	Avg. Rate / Total Emps.	Earned rates (A) and number of employees (B)
PACKER & BOXER	STANDARD PACKING OF ONE OR MORE ITEMS IN CARTONS OR CRATES. MUST BE FAMILIAR WITH STANDARD PACKING METHODS AND MATERIALS USED. RESPONSIBLE FOR ACCURACY OF WORK.	P	1.11 / 314	A: 108 110 113 115 116 117 119 122 125 128 130 134 137; B: 17 18 15 17 12 26 31 12 12 9 14 5 1
TOOLROOM DIEMAKER GROUP I	REQUIRES A MAN WITH DIVERSIFIED DIE-MAKING EXPERIENCE, CAPABLE OF DEVELOPING BLANKS USED IN MAKING DIES, LAYING OUT AND MAKING MOST COMPLICATED DIES WITH LITTLE OR NO SUPERVISION. MUST BE ABLE TO CALCULATE ANGLES, OPERATE MACHINE TOOLS OF ALL TYPES, BE EFFICIENT IN USE OF SPECIAL TOOLS, AS SINE BARS, ETC. RESPONSIBLE FOR ACCURACY OF FINISHED DIES. MAY HAVE LESS EXPERIENCED DIE MAKERS WORKING UNDER HIS DIRECTION.	D	1.85 / 145	A: 140 150 160 165 170 175 180 185 190 195 200 205 210 215; B: 3 1 3 1 5 26 20 28 22 19 9 1 4 3
TOOLROOM DIEMAKER GROUP II	A MAN IN THIS CLASS MUST POSSESS ALL-AROUND DIE-MAKING EXPERIENCE CAPABLE OF LAYING OUT AND MAKING COMPLETE ORDINARY BLANK, PIERCE, AND FORM DIES. DRAW AND FORM DIES WITH VERY LITTLE DEVELOPMENT. MUST BE ABLE TO OPERATE ALL TYPES OF MACHINE TOOLS, HAVE SOME KNOWLEDGE OF CALCULATION OF ANGLES. MUST BE CAPABLE OF MAKING ALL NECESSARY REPAIRS ON ORDINARY DIES. RESPONSIBLE FOR ACCURACY OF FINISHED DIES.	D	1.63 / 116	A: 115 120 125 130 135 140 145 150 155 160 165 170 175 180; B: 2 1 1 1 2 2 3 3 10 19 25 33 13 4
POLISHER HAND GROUP I	POLISHES FOR PLATE OR EXTREMELY HIGH FINISH. AN ALL-AROUND EXPERIENCED OPERATOR WHO POLISHES A VARIETY OF IRREGULAR SHAPED PARTS. HIGH INSPECTION REQUIREMENTS. SKILL REQUIRED IN APPLICATION OF PROPER PRESSURE TO REMOVE IMPERFECTIONS AND DIE SCRATCHES IN METALS WITHOUT SPOILING PART AND OBTAIN HIGH POLISHED SURFACES. USES FINE GRADE OF EMERY COVERED WHEELS. HAZARD OF DUST, PARTIALLY ELIMINATED BY BLOWERS.	P	1.61 / 70	A: 105 110 115 120 125 130 135 140 145 150 155 160 165 170 175 180 185; B: 1 1 1 1 1 2 2 3 6 2 1 9 3 20 14 3 2
TRUCKER INSIDE, HAND & ELECTRIC	OPERATES TRUCKS USED TO MOVE PRODUCTION MATERIAL WITHIN OR BETWEEN DEPARTMENTS. REQUIRES CARE, SKILL IN HANDLING TRUCK IN CONGESTED AREAS, KNOWLEDGE OF FACTORY LAY-OUT.	D	1.15 / 57	A: 95 100 105 110 115 120 125 130; B: 1 1 4 23 3 4 12 7

FOUNDRY

Occupation	Description	P or D	Avg. Rate / Total Emps.	Earned rates (A) and number of employees (B)
COREMAKER	MAKES SAND CORES USED IN MOLDS TO FORM HOLLOWS OR HOLES IN METAL CASTINGS.	P	1.30 / 19	A: 120 130 131 132 133 134 135; B: 5 1 1 2 2 2 6
CUPOLA TENDER	OPERATES A CUPOLA FURNACE. RESPONSIBLE FOR TEMPERATURE OF METAL. WORKING UNDER SUPERVISION AS TO ANALYSIS.	D	1.48 / 3	A: 145 150; B: 1 2
MOLDER BENCH	DIVERSIFIED MOLDING WITHOUT SPECIAL EQUIPMENT, DIFFICULT CORE SETTING. WOOD OR METAL PATTERNS.	P	NONE	
MOLDER FLOOR	LARGE OR MEDIUM FLOOR WORK. LITTLE REPETITIVE WORK. REQUIRES ABILITY TO WORK WITH LOOSE PATTERNS AND INTRICATE CORING. WOOD OR METAL PATTERNS.	P	1.76 / 11	A: 155 160 170 175 180 181 182 185; B: 1 1 1 1 1 1 2 3
SANDBLASTER	CLEANS CAST WITH HOSE IN SMALL ROOM OR SHOP. WEARS RESPIRATOR HELMET.	P	1.52 / 10	A: 125 130 133 135 137; B: 1 1 2 3 1

FIG. 150.—Wage-survey chart. (Courtesy of Southern New England Telephone Company.)

and incentive-paid earnings) to be separated if desired. A typical wage-survey form is shown in Fig. 150. Hypothetical data have been supplied.

The wage survey makes the establishing of "prevailing wage rates" possible for a given community. These prevailing rates may be used by the company to establish a community wage curve for use in formulating its own wage schedule. Wage blocks might be constructed by calculating values for each labor grade (or classification of job) 10 per cent above and 10 per cent below the community average rate. These values would then represent a rate range from minimum to maximum to be paid for any job in a specific labor grade or classification.

Wage blocks may be constructed to be above or below the community average, depending on company policy. They may overlap, meet end-on, or have gaps between grades. In some cases company wage policy may dictate the same minimum starting rate for all jobs and calculate only the maximum from wage-survey data. When the actual wage schedule is established from the wage survey, the job-pricing operation is complete. Union actions, both within (if the plant is organized) and without, influence pricing. There is some evidence (see Reynolds and Shister) that workers themselves actually have very little information about comparative wage rates between plants. They do not select their jobs systematically on the basis of wages and conditions of employment but do become very disgruntled, sometimes years later, when they discover discrepancies.

Naturally, the wage schedule, job by job after pricing, will not agree in every respect with the company wage pattern before such study. In a typical installation [12] the total of 1,200 employees were covered by some 250 jobs. About 29 per cent of the jobs covering some 18 per cent of the wage earners were found out of line. Managements using job evaluation agree, under such conditions, to bring the underpaid up to company standards but *not to reduce those paid more* than the proper rates. These individuals are permitted to remain overpaid for the job, but no other employees are paid above the job-rating value. Sometimes those whose rates are frozen above the wage scale are promoted into jobs worth the rate received or are held stationary during a period of general increases so that the wage scale is permitted to catch up to them.

---

[12] See REDWAY, A. S., Putting Job Rating to Work, *Executives' Service Bulletin*, Vol. 18, No. 7, Policyholders Service Bureau, Metropolitan Life Insurance Company, New York.

TIME–STUDY [13] METHODS AND PRACTICE

The discussion of methods analysis in Chap. XVII and of incentive wage payment thus far in this chapter has stressed the following conditions which are essential to the success of wage incentives:

1. Management must establish a sound wage policy for the guidance of its members in wage matters.

2. The company wage structure must be established by logical means such as job evaluation and community wage surveys.

3. Standard conditions and procedures must be established for the performance of each operation. These procedures must be in keeping with the best of modern methods study.

4. Careful time studies must be made by intelligent trained observers, devoting sufficient time to each study for recording an accurate performance standard. Where elemental data are available, the timing may be set synthetically, but even greater care is then required (see discussions).

5. These time-studies must be uniformly translated by simple understandable methods into rates permitting worker earnings in keeping with established wage policies.

The interdependence of the several scientific-management functions has been emphasized in earlier chapters. We may reiterate the origin of modern industrial engineering in efforts made to install piecework.

For example, when the setting of piece rates was considered at Midvale, it was found that the major factors governing productivity and quality were beyond the workers' control; that these were, in fact, functions of management. To obtain fair standards which would be equitable to the different workmen and to the same workmen at different times and on different jobs, it was necessary first for management to bring these factors under control.

It was therefore found necessary to plan the work systematically so as to eliminate lost time waiting for work; to provide the workman with proper tools; to show him the experimentally determined proper speeds for his machine; to standardize the belting to drive at the required speeds without breakdown; to work out with the workman the best method of performing each operation; to develop standards of method and mechanism; to institute research in procedure and equipment; to analyze materials; to develop specifications; and finally, to

---

[13] Although the terms have an exact meaning, *time study* and *rate setting* are commonly used to mean "putting a price on a job" by means to be discussed. In the same way *piecework* is used to mean any method of pay which gives the employee more money for more production, including production *bonus plans* and other *incentive systems*. The specialist in this field is known variously as an *industrial engineer, time-study engineer, incentive engineer, rate setter, time-study man,* or *standards man.* The results are *standards, timings, studies, incentives, prices,* or *rates.* A day's work is a *quota, load,* or *bogey.*

develop the methods of determining standard times of performance through the use of elementary or unit times as distinguished from over-all times.[14]

Rate setting is, therefore, seen to be the godfather of many of the practices that mark successful management today. It is to be regretted that not every piecework installation has carried with it all the other management tools necessary to its success.

Who Makes the Timing?—Fixing the time required for a given task is the chief function of the industrial engineer, but since not every company employs one, his work may be performed by any member of management. In the last few years, union time-study stewards have assisted in setting rates in a few plants.[15] In many of the original incentive installations, particularly in small plants, outside consulting engineers were hired at $75 to $150 a day to make the timings. The use of such outsiders has the advantage of providing a fresh viewpoint and of making better men available than the small company can afford to employ full time. It has the disadvantage of making all regular employees somewhat distrustful of the "human" elements of the installation. The daily upkeep and making of new timings on new jobs make a resident time-study engineer highly desirable. In many small plants the general manager may make observations and set rates. In the early days of time study the foremen were sometimes given this responsibility. Since the day-by-day supervisory problems of the foreman are greatly eased by "loose" timing [16] and since few foremen have adequate training in time-study methods, few managements today continue this practice. Instead, they delegate the responsibility to a central department or individual who can apply uniform standards to the whole plant. Such an individual usually reports to the plant manager, but where the organization contains a wage-administration section in the personnel department, he may report to that department. Correctness of work method in time study is more important than the question of "who reports to whom."

Time-study Practice.—How are piece rates set? No matter who may set the rates, the same observational tools are in common use. First

---

[14] History of Scientific Management in America, *Mechanical Engineering*, September, 1939, pp. 671–675, prepared under the chairmanship of Stanford E. Thompson.

[15] See Murray Corporation "Production Standards," C.I.O., Local 2, U.A.W., Detroit, Mich.

[16] Piece rates which are so set that workers easily earn a high rate of pay in a short time are said to be "loose," while piece rates upon which close and continuous application to the job is necessary to earn even minimum amounts are said to be "tight." Naturally, labor costs are increased by loose timings. Management generally favors a middle ground where timings are neither loose nor tight.

is an observation sheet (see Fig. 151). This may be supplemented by detailed study sheets, job-layout sketches, and even workplace photographs. Such records are of great value in proving the work method in use at the time of the original investigation should a restudy ever be necessary. Second is the time-study clip board, shaped especially for ease of recording while standing, with a special holder for keeping the stop watch in an easily read and operated position. The stop watch is commonly used in time study, but any recording device may be used. Motion pictures can be used, either by including a clock or "wink counter" in the picture or by using a constant-speed camera and counting the frames.

Time-study engineers now agree that a decimal timer is to be preferred to the usual seconds-and-minutes stop watch used in sporting events. Ease in adding and subtracting times more than compensates for any initial difficulty in reading the decimal timer. A similar controversy has raged over whether the watch should be left running continuously and observations or readings taken at regular intervals or whether the watch should be stopped and started with each observation in the "snapback" technique. Greater accuracy is claimed for observations made by the latter method, since the watch can be stopped at a precise point without removing the eyes from the worker, and an exact reading taken at leisure.[17] Most time-study engineers today seem to favor the continuous running watch since it makes possible the correction of erroneous watch readings. Impossibly fast or illogically slow performances may be disregarded if a sequence record is obtained. Clerical-recording errors may thus be avoided.

Analysis: First Step in Time-Study.—An initial step in time study is a thorough study of possible ways of improving the operation. Present-day industrial engineers conceive such improvements as major aims of time study. Lowry, Maynard, and Stegemerten [18] have stated these aims:

To subject each operation of a given piece of work to a close analysis, in order to determine the quickest and best method of performing each necessary operation; also to standardize equipment, methods, and working conditions; then, and not until then, to determine by scientific measurement the number of standard hours in which an average man can do the job.

Unless an operation or job has been running for a considerable period of time, improvements are bound to occur in workplace, in layout, in

[17] See Norman Bailey, "Motion Study for the Supervisor," for a simple treatment favoring the snapback technique.

[18] LOWRY, MAYNARD, and STEGEMERTEN, "Time and Motion Study," New York: McGraw-Hill Book Company, Inc., 1940.

tools, and in workers' skill. Often the initial timing is made before the job is ready to be timed, and management experiences considerable embarrassment in getting a proper timing on it subsequently.

After all possible improvements have been made in the job, the time-study engineer standardizes the production method, sometimes by issuing standard practice instructions which describe in detail exactly how the job is performed. In plants where standard practices are not used, the time-study itself may list sufficient detail to make the work method clear.

Recording Data: Second Step.—Many different forms for recording observed data, varying from blank paper to complex code-recording systems, have been developed.

The time-study record sheet (face and reverse in Fig. 151a and b) was compiled by a committee of Scovill Manufacturing Company time-study engineers to meet the need for (1) presenting greater detail of record and (2) instructing new time-study engineers in a typical industrial plant using incentives. Hypothetical data have been supplied to show the use of the form.

A form such as this protects the time-study engineer from hasty studies on which important data are lost because of pressure for quick results. Important preliminary data will include a sketch on cross-sectional paper of the workplace layout and any special tools used. Accurate identification is essential.

The division of the operation to be timed into its elements, or steps, depends on the nature of the process itself. Lathe operation has steps different from punch-press operation. Both differ greatly from assembly or plating. The selection of natural "break points" between steps, such as reaching for new work or pressing operating lever, will greatly improve the accuracy of recorded observation. These "parts of a job" should be as short as possible and should carefully differentiate between "worker-paced" elements, which the operator can speed up or slow down, and "machine-paced" elements, the duration of which is not controlled by the operator. Actions that occur every work cycle should be kept separate from those which occur only once in several work cycles. Each break point should be recorded on the report form in advance of the study.

The worker to be studied should be selected with care. Since it will usually be necessary to decide from the observations made what can be expected of an average operator, an operator whose performance is as close to average as possible should be selected. The purpose of the study should be explained to the operator and his cooperation gained. Many workers object to being time-studied since they feel that fellow workers will blame them for setting too fast a work pace.

Leveling Performance: Third Step. Speed-Rating or "Normalizing."—It will not always be possible to make observations on an average operator nor will the operator always work with equal diligence. To correct for minor variations in observed performance the time-study engineer "levels" the performance, *i.e.*, he adjusts the actual time to what he believes the average time of the normal worker should be.[19] This is done either on an over-all basis for the operation as a whole or by elements of the operation. The over-all rating is often called "speed-rating," while the element-by-element process is more commonly known as "leveling." The term "normalizing" is sometimes used when the time-study engineer makes allowances to reduce the performance he witnesses to normal factory performance. The rating or leveling may be made unsupported or it may be subdivided into such factors as skill, effort, surrounding conditions, and consistency of performance during the observation period. This rating factor is then applied to the recorded times to bring them to the level of performance expected of the average operator over a considerable period of time.

Points are often used in this procedure and a "60-point performance" taken as average. Points are typical of the Bedaux system of incentive payment in which a "point" or "B" is the total of (1) a fraction of a minute of effort and (2) a fraction of a minute of allowance or rest time. Both together always equal one full minute. Sixty points is thus a normal hour's effort plus a normal hour's recovery allowance for a normal factory worker. Good workers readily produce 70 to 80 points per clock hour and expert workers occasionally 100 points.

The process of leveling is one of the most commonly criticized[20] procedures in time-study. Charges of arbitrariness seem justified in many cases. If all time-study engineers are consistent, however, in their speed-rating activities, their arbitrary judgments are at least usable. Because no two men ever speed-rate exactly alike, training sessions are commonly

---

[19] Statistically, such an "average performance" might be obtained by studying each member of a large group for a period of time long enough to determine his average performance and then finding the mean of this sample array of observations. Practically, because workers commonly hold back when being studied for piece rates and because management does not feel the added research expense to be justified by the increased accuracy, considerable use of judgment is made instead of adequate sampling. Some of the work with synthetic timings discussed later does establish such averages.

[20] For such a criticism see "A Trade Union Analysis of Time Study" by William Gomberg, director of Management Engineering Department, International Ladies' Garment Workers' Union (A.F. of L.), published by Science Research Associates, Chicago, 1948.

conducted by large time-study departments to equalize errors of judgment and arrive at what may be known as a "company standard performance."

The Society for the Advancement of Management has attempted, by rating clinics, by the circulation of motion-picture films of activities such as walking, and by the collection of intercompany data, to reach industry-wide performance standards. To date, the result has been to emphasize the wide differences in performance and judgment existing.

Time-study Allowances: Fourth Step.—The time standard set for an operation should permit the normal employee to work on that operation regularly without exceptional fatigue and perform the task set in the standard time. This standard must include, therefore, all the elements that enter into the operation plus time for personal needs, delays, and overcoming fatigue. Sometimes all allowances are combined, but better practice lists the length of time put into the timing for each of the foregoing considerations.[21]

The usual industrial practice is to allow from 2 to 4 per cent of the workday for personal needs. Women are allowed slightly more personal time than men. Dirty jobs that require considerable washing up are allowed more personal time than clean, light jobs. Resting time allowed on heavy jobs is usually called "fatigue allowance," although there is considerable evidence that this is a misnomer.[22]

Unavoidable delays are usually considered the result of bad management. Some lost time may result from machine breakdown. The appropriate amount of allowance time to be entered in any specific case is usually determined by studying actual shop experience over a considerable period of time. Any excessive amount of machine down time may require management attention before a timing can be established. Where a low base rate and high earnings are desirable, an allowance called "incentive" is sometimes used. In theory, this is actually additional personal time which is used by the low-earning employee for loafing. In practice, the incentive allowance may be abused by foremen out to make a good cost showing and, if used, the operation of the system should be watched carefully.

Calculating the Timing: Final Step.—After the job is running right, an adequate observation is made of an average operator, the necessary allowances are made, and the timing is calculated. The steps in this calculation may be more easily followed by reference to the time-study record sheet in Fig. 151a and b.

[21] This practice is advocated by Ralph M. Barnes, "Motion and Time Study."

[22] For a discussion of "time fatigue" see Bartley and Chute, "Fatigue and Impairment in Man," New York: McGraw-Hill Book Company, Inc., 1947.

Synthetic Time Standards: Alternative to Stop-watch Recording.
As a substitute for recording times actually taken by operators and the
first nine steps discussed under Fig. 151, averages from many previous
observations may be used. In any industry where the same operation is
repeated many times on different products, elemental timings may be
used to build synthetic time standards which will be of considerable use
in estimating, production and cost control, and under circumstances
where a timing cannot be made, as on a single casting in a job foundry.
The essential steps in establishing synthetic time standards are: (1) make
accurate time studies in the usual fashion over a considerable period of
time, exercising care to select elements of like nature whenever timings
are made of similar operations, (2) accumulate data from separate time
studies on the same element into a statistical table, (3) evaluate the
several contributing parts and arrive at an average time value for the
element, (4) test this average time value statistically and in practice to
determine its usefulness. Finally, if the average time values prove
statistically sound, they may be used to make synthetic studies. The
average time values for different elements common to the plant are
usually presented in the form of tables, rules, and formulas. Graphic
presentation will often save considerable explanation and aid understanding. The special conditions or extra time allowances should be
listed with each table of values.

Two viewpoints exist as to the length of the elements for which time
values are collected. One school uses operation steps or elements such
as are shown in Fig. 151a; the other breaks the operation down to
therbligs or even finer. The latter school feels that the length of time
for an average person to perform an elemental motion should be fairly
constant. If those constant values are determined, any new motion
pattern can be constructed synthetically. Confidential collections of
therblig time values have been prepared by several large manufacturing
companies. Consulting management engineers have circulated "for
clients only" time values for a number of years. Perhaps the most extensive published source of such values is the Methods Engineering Council
(a consulting company), which has combined a further detailed breakdown of the original therbligs with a list of time values for those elements
into a system known as methods-time-measurement (MTM). That
methods-time-measurement system they have successfully taught to a
number of clients.[23]

Some advocates of synthetic timings claim that using them makes a
stop watch unnecessary. (For that reason the method is popular where
the stop watch is banned, as in government installations.) A synthetic

[23] For discussion of MTM in popular terms see *Fortune Magazine,* October, 1949.

FIG. 151a.—Time-study record sheet.

Step 1: Obtain elapsed time by subtraction from continuous watch readings. This provides the values in columns 1 to 5.

Step 2: Summarize these values to obtain total time spent on each element during the study. Foreign elements such as A are discarded in this summarization (shown in bottom quarter of page, top line, under Summary).

Step 3: Count the number of usable recordings of each element (second line under Summary).

Step 4: Calculate average time by dividing values obtained in steps 2 and 3.

Step 5: Record minimum time for each element. Observe this in columns 1 to 5. If this time is illogically different from the average, some foreign elements may not have been caught, and certain readings may have to be discarded. If this is done, steps 1 to 4 must be repeated. Discarding readings without recorded reasons is undesirable, and if it occurs often, the whole study must be repeated. This is a matter for the judgment of an experienced time-study man.

Step 6: Repeat step 5 for the maximum time recorded. Workers will object vehemently to the discarding of "long times."

Step 7: Calculate the level factor. This is obtained by totaling algebraically the successive judgments under "skill," "effort," "conditions," and "consistency," with regard to the specific time-study observation made. In Fig. 151 we wish to add 6 per cent, so the level factor is 1.06.

Step 8: Level the average time found in step 4 by multiplying each average by the level factor. Record this leveled time.

616

Fig. 151b.—Reverse side of Fig. 151a.

Form contents (Fig. 151b):

2315 PRINTED IN U.S.A.

CARD NO. 2192   PART NO. 745-77   OPERATION Assemble

DEPT. Radio   DATE March 15, 1944   OBSERVER H.A.S.

Radio base, flare base, inspect, wrap and pack

ARTICLE Aircraft Radio connector base

OPERATOR Ⓔ Mary Jane   CHECK NO. 145576

M   MUST STAND ☐   CAN SIT ☒

SERVICE Floorman brings work in pans to left side of press, wrapping tissue and boxes to right side; removes finished work from pile to operators right. Operator fills own work holders, polishes punch once each day. No other maintenance.

MACHINE DATA	
TYPE	Horton
	Bench Press
NO.	89
SAFETY	Horton 2 hand
	and sweep
DRIVE	Belt
R.P.M.	168
FEED	Hand
LUBRICANT	None

TOOL DATA	
TYPE	Single action
SIZE	1/8 × 6 × six

PROD. DURING STUDY 36 pcs.
EARNINGS DURING STUDY $.064 or $6.88/hr.

TOTAL CYCLE TIME .7157   MIN. PER unit

PERSONAL TIME 5 %   Polish

MACHINE DOWN TIME 1 %   punch

FATIGUE 2 %   %

ADJUSTED %   100 − 8 = 92 %

ADJ. CYCLE TIME .7157 × .7779   MIN. PER I

INCENTIVE 92 % 20 %

FINAL ALLOWED TIME .9335   MIN. PER unit

STD. PROD. 64.27   PER HOUR

STD. HRS. 15.56 *   PER 1000

CODE 23-40

DISPOSAL DATA	
Packed after wrapping in	
dozen box. Left piled	

MATERIAL DATA	
ALLOY	706-pins
FINISH	Nickel-pins
TEMPER	✓
GAUGE	✓
SIZE	1/8 × I

DATE EFFECTIVE 3-15-44

PERMANENT ☒   TENTATIVE ☐

OLD STD. HRS. None   DATED ✓

REMARKS Initial order in this size

REFERENCE RATES
See 745-75
745-76

* 15.56 × 65¢ base rate = $10.114 per 1000 on
.010114 each

(Diagram labels: Belt drive; Hand trip; Incoming work; Horton Bench Press 89; Fixture; Fibers-Pins; OPERATOR Tissues; Hand trip; Boxes Incline feed on boxes; Completed work; Box in process of packing piled else where on skid after filling)

Step 9: Record the number of times each element occurs in production cycle. Note that element 3, "cover," (which in its use of the next box top to close the previous box is a good example of work simplification) occurs only three times in 36 complete readings—only one-twelfth of a time per cycle.

Step 10: Find elemental time per cycle by multiplying leveled time by occurrences per cycle.

Step 11: Total the values found in step 10 to record total cycle time. Turn over sheet and enter this in center column.

Step 12: Decide and record allowances to be made for personal time, machine down time, fatigue, etc.

Step 13: Total allowances and subtract from 100 per cent to obtain adjusted percentage.

Step 14: Multiply total cycle time by adjusted percentage to obtain adjusted cycle time. This is the time it takes an average operator to assemble, wrap, and pack the radio connector base when we consider necessary time lost.

Step 15: Apply the "incentive" (necessary only if a low base rate is used and high earnings are expected) to arrive at the final allowed time.

Depending on the incentive system used, the timing calculated may be carried through several alternative final steps. Standard production per hour standard hours per thousand, price per thousand, price each, or expected earnings per day may be used to express the final value.

timing is faster to make than a stop-watch time study and can be prepared away from the job or even in the absence of the equipment to be used. Since it uses predetermined values, the selection of an average operator or leveling to an average performance is unnecessary. This may make it more acceptable to employees and labor unions. A more thorough methods analysis is made, and all the values of methods study may be by-products. Results obtained by different rate setters are apt to be more similar, and less time may be required for the training of new time-study men.

Those who wish to retain the stop watch point out that the accuracy of a synthetic standard depends upon the accuracy of the original values collected. It also depends upon the availability of data on a complete range of possible elements, many of which differ almost imperceptibly but influence the time required. The correctness of the particular therblig breakdown (where judgment enters into deciding just what elemental motions are involved) is another influence. Finally, many people believe that each department or factory has its own work pace which may be faster or slower than the pace of a "true average," even if that were obtainable. A time study should be made, therefore, in light of where the work is to be done. Several college foundations have recently turned their attention to a study of the actual time taken by the various possible human motions and to the differences among individuals in this respect.

Incentive Control.—Much of the groundwork for present-day methods engineering is laid by time-study work. Employee relations, cost and material control, and general management can be improved by a sound program. In this connection Phil Carroll, Jr. says,

Management often overlooks the fact that it has certain responsibilities to fulfill in the operation of an incentive-control plan. The application of a wage incentive plan makes many demands upon an executive's time and attention, and after it is functioning as a method of control, even more analysis and executive action are needed. . . . Quite often an incentive scheme is *tried out* just to relieve the burden of costs that are high when compared with the selling price. As soon as the pressure is removed, the management heaves a sigh of relief, and the incentive plan runs along as best it can. . . . The executive who is afraid of hard work, or who would rather not know some of the weaknesses of his organization, should use daywork or some incentive that puts the whole burden of proof on the operator, and should by all means avoid the mirror of modern control methods.[24]

One of the most difficult problems in wage-control work is the relationship between daywork and piecework earnings on the same job. Since

[24] CARROLL, PHIL, JR., "Timestudy for Cost Control," 2d ed., pp. 253–254, New York: McGraw-Hill Book Company, Inc., 1943.

production is usually greater among pieceworkers than among dayworkers, earnings of pieceworkers are customarily higher. But how much higher? One proposed solution is to consider the normal range between minimum and maximum paid for a given labor grade (usually about 25 per cent) as indicative of similar differences in the "merely attending" worker and the consistent high producer. Pieceworkers, then, would be expected to earn the maximum of the labor grade.

However, since individual differences [25] in ability, training, and application will result in differences in earnings for two workers on the same job under piecework, it is not expected that all pieceworkers will earn exactly the maximum. Some will earn below the maximum. A few exceptionally gifted may earn well above. So long as the average for all workers approximates the expected earnings level, incentive control may be held to be reasonably successful.

Incentive Control Aids Objectives of Employer and Employees.

The principal objectives of the employee are to secure maximum earnings commensurate with the effort expended, while working, insofar as conditions will permit, in a healthful and agreeable environment. Time study has contributed immeasurably toward the attainment of these objectives for the employee, because thorough time-study analysis brings to light undesirable and improper working conditions and methods and establishes a fair time value for every job. These time values, when used with a proper incentive system of wage payment, enable the employee to increase his earnings by increasing his output.

The employer's objectives are, briefly, to secure a maximum output of standard quality at a minimum cost per unit. Progressive employers recognize the proper application of time-study methods as being one of the most important factors in modern industrial management which tend to bring about the accomplishment of their objectives. Such obvious benefits to the employer as having a better satisfied working force, resulting in a minimum labor turnover, and getting what he pays for are alone sufficient to command his cooperation and support.[26]

Prevalence of Incentive Wage Plans.[27]

There is considerable variation in the extent to which incentive-wage plans have been adopted in the different industries (see Table X). This may be

[25] For discussion of individual differences see BURTT, H. E., "Applied Psychology," New York: Prentice-Hall, Inc., 1948; HUSBAND, R. W., "Applied Psychology," rev. ed., New York: Harper & Brothers, 1949; SCOTT, CLOTHIER, and SPRIEGEL, "Personnel Management," New York: McGraw-Hill Book Company, Inc., 1949.

[26] LOWRY, MAYNARD, and STEGEMERTEN, *op. cit.*, pp. 6–7.

[27] The following paragraph and table are taken from Fred Joiner and Van Dusen Kennedy, "Incentive-Wage Plans," Bureau of Labor Statistics. Report prepared under the direction of Florence Peterson, chief of Industrial Relations Division, U.S. Department of Labor.

due to the nature of the work performed in the several industries or trades, to the diverse attitudes of management, or to the resistance or lack of resistance to incentive wages by the workers and their unions.

During World War II incentive pay systems received a considerable boost. Extreme pressure for production and the ban on universal wage increases caused many managements to install incentive systems to give

TABLE X.—PREVALENCE OF INCENTIVE METHODS OF WAGE PAYMENT AMONG
PRODUCTION WORKERS IN SELECTED INDUSTRIES*

Slight	Moderate	Substantial	General
Building	Aircraft	Electrical equip-	Clothing
Chemicals	Ammunition	ment	Coal mining
Explosives	Automobile	Flat glass	Gloves
Nonferrous smelting	Leather, luggage,	Steel	Hats and millinery
and refining	belting, etc.	Textile	Hosiery
Printing and publish-	Machinery		Rubber
ing	Machine tool		Shoes
	Meat packing		
	Nonferrous mining		
	Pulp and paper		
	Shipbuilding		

* Excludes clerks, maintenance and repair men, inspectors, designers, packers, truckers, and other special workers in occupations incidental to production. The term "incentive methods of wage payment" includes piecework as well as the more complex premium or bonus systems.

increased wages for increased productivity. These had varying success. The average range of increase in production ran from 0 to 130 per cent.[28] Many of these incentive systems were based not on time study but on past performance records, ratio of labor to over-all sales, etc. Most were of the "group incentive" variety and some included the entire plant personnel in the group. Most of these incentive installations were abandoned after the war when wage stabilization lapsed. The need for lower unit costs caused an increased interest in incentives on the part of management with the downturn in business in 1949. Unions then often renounced incentive systems as "speed-ups."

INCENTIVE SYSTEMS

Popular Piecework Plans.—Many different kinds of incentive systems have been used by American management. Lytel[29] analyzes some 25

[28] Speech by John W. Nickerson, director of the Management Consultant Division, WPB, before American Society of Mechanical Engineers, Dec. 1, 1943.

[29] LYTEL, CHARLES W., "Wage Incentive Methods," New York: The Ronald Press Company, 1942.

major plans and many minor modifications for paying workers a variable wage related to production. Only four representative plans will be outlined here: the "straight" piecework system, the Halsey 50–50 constant sharing plan; the Gantt task-and-bonus plan; and the measured standard day-work plan.

Straight Piecework.—Under this system, management establishes a price that it will pay for each unit of production, say, $\frac{1}{10}$ cent for each hole drilled. Then for drilling 10 holes the worker gets 1 cent, for 100 holes 10 cents, and for 1,000 holes $1. For a day's pay of $8, the employee would drill 8,000 holes. It is customary to guarantee at least a minimum hourly earning rate, usually much below the average incentive earnings.

In rate setter's parlance such a minimum guarantee is often called a "Manchester guarantee" after Manchester, England, where the practice originated. Because of minimum wage laws, the practice of paying workers only what they earn at piece rates with no minimum guarantee has now been virtually abandoned under all incentive systems in the United States. If the difference between the average earnings expected of the average worker—called the "task rate"—and the lowest wage customarily paid for the type of work involved—called the "base rate" [30]—is large, the system is known as a low-base system; if it is small, as a high-base system. In terms of incentive wage theory, the low-base system, which requires continuous application to approximate usual earnings, provides the greater urge to the worker to sustain production. In practice, it is sometimes found that a worker who gets off to a bad start or for some reason is delayed in his work is discouraged by the large gap between his usual earnings and the earnings he may then receive.

The standard hour system of calculating costs is often used with straight piecework, and then the employee earns hours (possibly 10.5 hours in an 8-hour day) at a standard rate instead of money per piece, but it makes little difference to the worker who invariably figures the price he will be paid as so much per 1,000 pieces or dozen work pans.

The straight piecework system has been called the highest type of incentive and certainly has many advantages to both the employee and employer. Any objections that may be made to it are summarized later under labor objections to incentives in general. Certainly straight piecework is the fairest of all incentive plans and often appeals to workers for

---

[30] "Base rate" may in some cases be below the "guaranteed minimum" especially in old piecework installations that have been modernized piecemeal. In such cases the base rate is only a mathematical factor used in calculating expected earnings. Workers in factories having incentive systems often confuse "base rate" and "task rate."

this reason. Ambitious workers are able to earn high wages and are equally repaid at all steps of effort. Straight piecework stimulates a sense of fair treatment and simplifies record keeping and earnings explanation. Production output is more constant, and cost or scheduling planning may be done more accurately. Cooperation is furthered both between workers and between management and workers.

Inasmuch as overhead costs remain relatively fixed, the employer benefits through lower over-all costs per piece produced, although his unit labor costs remain the same. Because payment is the same for each unit produced, straight piecework is called "100 per cent premium" or "100 per cent sharing plan." This contrasts with plans such as the Halsey plan described below.

Halsey (50–50) *Constant Sharing Plan.*—This type of incentive developed from independent work at the Yale and Towne Manufacturing Company and at the Rand Drill Company and has also been known as the "Towne-Halsey gain sharing plan" or, in England, the "Halsey-Weir plan." Its chief value is the sense of partnership which it sponsors, since increased profits through greater production are supposed to be split.

Another advantage is the possibility of establishing expected production levels by estimate without time study. (Note that time studies *can* be used with constant sharing plans, but originally were not.) Thus, the foreman or rate setter judges the time necessary to complete a given task and offers the dayworker a premium over his day wage for completing the task on time, or ahead of time. The premium offered is commonly 50 per cent of the time saved because that appeals to the worker as an equal and just partnership. If expected production were set at 24 pieces per 8-hour day for a $6 per day wage, about 25 cents would be paid for each piece produced at that level. If 48 pieces were produced in an 8-hour day, the production rate would be 200% and would result in a saving of 8 hours. The saving is shared with management 50-50, however, and a $9 wage is paid. This is about 19 cents paid for each piece produced. Here a constant sharing plan contrasts most sharply with a straight piecework plan. In defense it should be noted that it often pays a greater per piece price at lower production levels than can be justified by selling price, and makes up the loss by the lesser price per piece paid at higher production levels.

The owners gain more from a production increase under a Halsey plan than under straight piecework, since under straight piecework 100 per cent of the gain goes to the worker. This feature has been attacked by labor but, since production tasks are usually low and workers do get higher wages, the plan sometimes works. For the initial lift from lower production, a premium plan is usually more generous than piecework to the operator, but it soon loses its generosity as higher production levels are reached.

A Halsey premium plan often pays a portion of the gain to foremen and supervisors. This has the effect of interesting these men in increasing production and thereby the earnings of their subordinates. A premium payment plan is especially well adapted to job manufacturing (and to indirect labor or maintenance jobs) since premiums can be set on the basis of estimates. Bickering is apt to develop through workers' efforts to be assigned to jobs on which generous estimates have been made. Many of the varieties of incentive payment have developed through modifications of straight piecework and premium systems. Common modifications include: (1) the introduction of bonus steps instead of the smooth ratio curve relation between production and earnings and (2) various plans for accelerating or retarding the slope of the earnings curve at various levels of production.

Gantt Task and Bonus.—H. L. Gantt, an associate of Taylor in the development of scientific management, who showed a great appreciation of the human problems involved, developed what has come to be called the "task and bonus" system of incentive payment. It differs from other incentive systems in three main particulars:

1. It pays the employee a high relative hourly rate which he gets whether he makes his time on the job or not.

2. It pays him a higher rate if he does complete the job in the time allowed and continues this higher rate just like straight piecework for all work produced beyond the standard.

3. As originally developed by Gantt, the plan provides for showing the employee graphically and daily just where he stands in relation to other workers, his own previous records, and the standard set.

An early advocate of much that has become standard in personnel management, Gantt stressed the worker's individuality and pride of achievement. He stressed the "habits of industry" to be ingrained in the worker so that he always made a high rate of pay. The combination of a high guarantee and of nonsharing increment makes this plan a particularly good installation where an old piecework system is redone.

In terms of application, suppose the "task," or the expected production, had been set at 24 pieces per day for which $7.20 would be paid. Then, for 14, 16, 18, 20 or any number up to 24 a wage of $6.00 might be paid. For 27.4 pieces (a saving of 1 hour of production time) $8.22 would be paid, and for 32 pieces (a saving of 2 hours production time) $9.60 would be paid. Note that labor cost per piece decreases until the task is achieved and then holds constant for all succeeding production.[30a]

[30a] Earnings below task are hours worked times rate; at task bonus of 20 per cent is added; above task bonus is 20 per cent of standard hours earned.

Measured Daywork.[31]—Considerable attention has been attracted recently by the rise in popularity, particularly among production men, of a partial incentive payment plan called "measured daywork." In theory, all workers should be motivated to their best efforts by any incentive system. In practice, workers themselves seem to feel that great differences in production between workers on the same job should not occur. In part, this feeling stems from a fear gained through bitter experience that any job on which a worker earns excessive wages will be cut, *i.e.*, more work will be required of all workers for the same pay. In part, it stems from a social feeling on the part of operators that no one worker should "show off" by doing more work than his fellows are able to do, and also from an effort to protect the "weak sister" from management attention and possible dismissal. In any event factory workers do control their production. Workers who could easily outstrip their fellows hold back. New and inexperienced workers are warned by the "old hands" not to "work too hard and kill the job." Where lax management makes it possible, excess work completed by one worker is taken from him and credited to a slow comrade. Lower levels of management are aware of all this.

Management efforts to recognize differences in incentive workers, as differences are regularly recognized among hourly workers, has led to measured daywork.[32] One chief feature of the system is the use of job evaluation to establish the base rates to be paid for different types of factory work. (See Chap. XXV for a discussion of job evaluation.) Thus the relative skill, effort (mental and physical), responsibilities, and working conditions of the job may be considered as compared to other jobs in the same plant. Once the jobs are arranged in order of their possession of these factors, their money value may be established by means of a wage survey and a wage curve. Then a series of several base rates may be established, one for each labor grade or class of work. Many other incentive systems have adopted this feature.

In its second chief feature, measured daywork resembles the usual daywork system more, for by means of a merit rating of the individual worker an extra compensation rate is set which awards versatility, dependability, and other characteristics valuable alike to the worker and to management (see Chap. XXV for a discussion of merit rating). This recognition of factors other than production is, of course, a departure

---

[31] The term is often used erroneously, as indeed most incentive system titles are, to describe some company-sponsored modification of a step-bonus or premium-payment plan, as well as to indicate "production pacing" such as is common in conveyor line work.

[32] See Howell, William R., Measured Day Work, *SAM Journal,* Vol. 3, No. 1.

from usual incentive methods but represents an effort on the part of management to humanize the incentive payment plan somewhat. Rositzke,[33] while claiming that mechanical improvements can be installed more easily with measured daywork than with other types of incentives, because the change does not violate the worker's "personal property" right in his guaranteed rate, states,

Measured daywork provides a balanced plan of rating a worker's value by considering four factors. It fixes hourly wage rates by setting uniform base rates by jobs and giving added inducements determined separately for each employee on the basis of his productivity, quality, service, dependability, and versatility, measured over a relatively long period.

Each worker thus has in effect his own base rate which will reward him for both productivity and good service. His rate is changed if his work changes at one- to three-month intervals. The base rate of the job and, therefore, the earnings level of the individual remain constant from review period to review period. Possibly it is this feature of leveled-out earnings over a considerable period of time that appeals most to workers. Because of this leveling out, however, the system depends for its incentive effect partly on the periodic readjustments of rate. A higher grade of supervision is essential. Somewhat detailed records of worker performance are necessary to the success of the plan, but clerical work is much less than is common with other systems.

The periodic possible downward adjustment of wage rates (at least the time-paid portion can come down; piecework prices cannot be cut) gives measured daywork its greatest advantage over simple merit rating. Increases granted under merit rating can rarely be rescinded, even though the quality of the work for which the increase was given deteriorates. It is thus a "one-way street" offering positive rewards only.

Stated Union Opposition to Piecework.—Individual workers in many cases react favorably to the idea of payment varying in amount with individual productivity. Employees experienced in piecework payment say that they find it easier to learn a new job and to attain a high productive level if urged along by wage increases geared to the speed of production. The leaders of organized labor in 1911, reacting both to abuses of the then developing scientific management movement and to unemployment, condemned all incentive payment.[34] Since that time many

[33] ROSITZKE, R. H., *Factory,* Vol. 95, Nos. 2 and 6, and *NACA Bulletin,* Sept. 1, 1938.

[34] Labor sought Federal support and in 1914 obtained passage of the "Anti-Stop-Watch" law, a rider attached to Federal appropriation acts forbidding expenditure of any of the money appropriated for time-measuring activities, motion study of

changes have occurred in labor's attitude, but as a matter of policy the national conventions of the A.F. of L., the C.I.O. and most independents have repeatedly condemned all payment by the piece. Some unions allow individual locals freedom to continue preexisting incentive-wage plans, but new installations are generally frowned on. Unions that have had experience with incentives say that only the abuses need control. The United Electrical, Radio and Machine Workers, then C.I.O., issued a 127-page guide to its members on wage-payment plans and time study. This stressed the union's policing function and the protection of its members from rate cutting and speed-up. The Murray Corporation of Detroit's time-study stewards have U.A.W.–C.I.O. backing. The I.L.G.W.U. has organized a management-engineering department with union time-study engineers and the following objectives: [35]

1. To assist in improving the manufacturing techniques and operating methods of all branches of the industry with which our workers' earnings are intimately bound. This will be done through plant inspections by department representatives, followed by specific recommendations.

2. To serve as a central information agency:
   a. To determine the level of "fair" piece-rates.
   b. To record the production system and manufacturing techniques under which these rates are paid.
   c. To assist in training shop members and committees in distinguishing bad time-study practices from good time-study practices in the determination of rates.

Why Do Workers Distrust Piece Rates?—There is sound reason why workers object to incentives. The abuses of this useful tool by sweatshop managements were legion. Faulty interpretations by dictatorial foremen of top-management wage policy have given many workers personal knowledge of the arbitrary possibilities. The objections of workers include a generalized distrust of any system that treats workers mechanically and four specific charges: (1) rate cutting, (2) speed-up and stretch-out, (3) fooling workers with complex systems for calculating earnings, and (4) condemnation of the gains-sharing principle.

Rate Cutting.—In the early days of scientific management when many engineers did consider workers impersonally—almost as a part of the machine—many piece rates were "cut." These rates had unstandardized operations so that retiming was inevitable, but no one then explained

---

employees, or premium wages. This limitation has been reenacted with every Army, Navy, and Post Office appropriation between 1914 and 1949. It was dropped largely through the influence of John W. Nickerson.

[35] See GOMBERG, WILLIAM, The Relationship between the Unions and Engineers, *Mechanical Engineering,* Vol. 65, No. 6, p. 425.

this to the workers. Even fair-minded employers, pressed by competition from sweatshops, spiraled new timings and rate cuts. Workers found themselves working much harder and, when the spiral went too high, working for less than their old day rates before the advent of piecework. Modern managements do not change piece prices once established unless some recognizable change occurs in the method, tools or materials. Workers are convinced, nevertheless, that if they earn too much on the job the price will be lowered. In many instances workers restrict their output to keep from earning enough to attract attention.

Speed-up.—When changes in tool steel, machine tools, and manufacturing methods resulted in a faster working tempo and greater daily production, workers naturally realized they were doing more work. When they felt they were being made to work too fast, they called it a "speed-up." A fear stated was the early burning out of the worker and a shortening of his productive life. A hidden fear was that the fast worker was keeping someone else out of a job or perhaps working himself into unemployment. Especially condemned were efforts of employers who had not installed the new equipment to remain in competition by getting more work out of employees. The faster work pace possible when accumulative fatigue was reduced through a shortening of the working day from 14, 12, 10 hours to the 8-hour day lent color to the charges of speed-up. When methods improvements, automatic safety stops, hopper feeds, etc., made it possible to reduce the number of machine attendants and enabled one operator to tend several machines, the worker, thus spread over a larger area of less intensified attention, called it a "stretch-out." This charge was the basis of the 1949 Ford strike over production quotas.

Complexity.—Workers are greatly confused when they cannot calculate their earnings. A simple price per piece they can understand. Any other plan is viewed with suspicion. When strange terminology such as "Manit" or "*B* hour" is introduced, the confusion grows. Whenever management requires mathematical tables for determining the worker's earnings, as they do in some premium systems, their very necessity destroys a direct relationship between work and pay. Clinton S. Golden, when vice-president of C.I.O.'s Steelworkers, stated, "One important test, by no means the only one, is that a fair incentive scheme should be simple and clear. Usually, complications are necessary only to conceal the real effect of a plan and its unfair distribution of the benefits of increased productivity." [36]

Gains-sharing.—The original partnership idea intrinsic in all the "gains-sharing" incentives systems is desirable but hardly fits the modern factory. The worker with only a meager investment in tools and only

[36] Address before New York Chapter, SAM, Nov. 20, 1943.

his time to sell realizes he is not on an equal footing with the $6,000 to $10,000 worth of machinery furnished him. He does not, however, feel that he should share the gain in his production wage with the machine. Rather than have management pay him more than his work is worth at lower levels of production and less at higher levels in order to break even, he prefers to be paid a constant price. Anything else he calls the "take-away curve." In his mind some of his earnings for working harder are taken from him and given to management which has not worked any harder.

How Can Incentive Plans Be Made to Succeed?—Certain simple rules for the success of incentive systems can be written from a study of these worker objections to incentives. Perhaps the most important rule is to provide easily available grievance procedure [37] through which the workers may state their disagreements, and to answer those grievances promptly and factually on the basis of thought-out wage policies. Considerable care should be exercised in selecting men with production experience to operate the incentive system, since many peculiarities of the job will be noticed only by production men. Since one of the workers' pet hates is the "young college engineer," [38] rate setters should be chosen for their maturity and seasoned judgment.

These production-minded rate setters, guided always by a personnel man's emphasis on the worker as an individual, will be greatly assisted by the following desirable incentive policies:

1. The incentive system chosen should be superimposed upon fair guaranteed hourly base rates which will provide the workers with at least their earnings previous to the installation of piecework.

2. Production standards should be based upon carefully detailed time studies of sufficient duration to represent the job adequately.

3. Provision should be made for changing the production standards, without charges of "rate cutting," whenever sufficiently significant changes occur in conditions of the job, *i.e.*, methods, material, tolerances, or equipment.

4. There should be no restriction of production by either management or workers purely to keep earnings in line.

5. Except for temporary timings installed to cover transitory conditions which should be kept at a minimum, no production standard should be reduced while conditions remain the same, *i.e.*, piece rates should be guaranteed until the method changes.

6. Straight piecework, avoiding the gains-sharing principle, should be used wherever possible and in as simple a fashion as possible. Other

---

[37] Grievance procedures are found in both unionized and nonunionized enterprises.
[38] What's Itching Labor, *Fortune Magazine*, November, 1942.

systems adapted to special circumstances may be used but should be fully explained to all workers.

7. For greatest incentive lift, the incentive should be applied to individuals or small groups where a directly observable relationship exists between effort and results.

8. Indirect workers should be included in the incentive whenever possible, but only where their efforts actually contribute to production.

9. Where there is a union, its leaders as well as the workers, and in all cases the employees who work under the incentive system, should understand, have confidence in, and agree in advance to changes in the incentive system.

10. The incentive system should not be used in an effort to compensate for management ineptness or unscientific methods. When incentives are used, every modern means should also be used to raise the standards of efficiency of the business as high as possible, to stabilize fluctuations in employment as much as possible, and to establish the future of the organization on as firm a base as possible.

RECENT DEVELOPMENTS IN WAGE PAYMENT

Many managements have seen fit to establish a more direct contact between top-management's wage policies and the wage earner by way of the personnel department. Since those most commonly charged with wage matters, the rate setters, have not always succeeded in gaining the worker's confidence, this is a natural reaction. There is a place in wage-work for both industrial engineers and personnel workers. A judicious combination of the merits of both is necessary to successful wage administration. Particularly in companies having job evaluation, the personnel department is apt to have a voice in time-study work. This will be doubly true if the grievance procedure provides for an appeal from incentive standards.

Annual Wages.—Workers are as interested in security of employment as they are in any other thing (see Chap. XXII). Although the advocacy of a minimum annual wage, strongly supported in British social-security thinking, is still new to American industry,[39] many efforts have been made to avoid the peaks of boom hiring and valleys of dull layoffs that formerly characterized manufacturing. Market research and distribution planning from a master sales budget for the year have helped. Plans for long-range expansion, or for diversifying and simplifying the line manufactured, fit in here. Customer purchasing habits have even been changed to avoid rush sales periods. In addition to minimizing

[39] The Chicago Convention of the C.I.O. in 1944 voted the annual wage as one of its national aims. Union pressure has been continuous since then.

the effects of technological changes by introducing new equipment slowly, many managements have planned for annual wage stability.[40]   Among them are Armstrong Cork, Berkshire Knitting Mills, Nunn-Bush Shoe Co., Spiegel mail-order house, and the Visking packing company.

One of the earliest guaranteed employment plans still in use was started by Proctor and Gamble Company of Ohio in 1923.   This plan embraces all hourly paid employees with 2 years' service and effectively provides 48 weeks of employment per year.   Transfers and temporarily shortened work-weeks help make this possible.   The Geo. A. Hormel meat-packing plant at Austin, Minn., started its 52-week guarantee plan in 1931 but covers only those departments which petition for annual wages.   About 90 per cent of those employees eligible work under the following plan.   A labor budget is established for a year in advance. Those hired under this budget are paid regular weekly amounts in 52 installments but work the number of hours required by packing production.   Any overtime remaining at the end of the year is paid as a bonus. A deferred-distribution profit-sharing plan is also included.   Normally an indebtedness exists at the end of the year.   This indebtedness is paid off with the first overtime of the next year.   Special provisions of the Fair Labor Standards Act of 1938 make this possible.

Private industry recognizes the desirability of income stability but finds its temporary efforts to stabilize employment more effective than its permanent guarantees.   Company plans of income assurance fail in a depression.   Of plans started before 1929 only the Procter & Gamble guarantee plan has lasted, and it required revisions during the 1930's.[41] Only four active company plans are over 20 years old.   Abandonment has been caused by union antagonism; by uncertainties in the business situation, including greatly expanded employment during the war years; by Federal and state legislation; and by company failure.   The Employment Act of 1946, discussed in Chap. II, represents a Federal effort to provide stability where private industry has not done so.

Profit Sharing.—This is one of the most controversial ways of supplementing payments to both workers and executives.   Plans are adopted to increase efficiency, lower turnover, provide a more flexible wage struc-

---

[40] See Annual Wage and Employment Guarantee Plans, *Studies in Personnel Policy*, No. 76, National Industrial Council Board, Inc., for details of plans found in 1946.   For an extensive study see "Guaranteed Wages" by Murray W. Latimer (available from Superintendent of Documents, Washington, D.C.).   This 1947 report concludes that guaranteed-wage plans coordinated with unemployment insurance are entirely practicable, although individual plant adjustments must be made and most industries are not yet ready for them.

[41] The Seaboard Airline Railway plan, which also lasted out the depression, applies to only a minimum maintenance force.

ture, and improve employee-employer relations. New attention has been given in the last few years to this oldest of wage incentives. The trend of interest is away from the older *current-distribution* type, under which payments are made in cash at regular intervals, toward the *deferred-distribution* plan.[42] Under this, profits are paid into a trust fund to be distributed in the future when needed for disability, retirement, or death. This is often a part of an extensive insurance and benefits program.

The Johnson Wax Company, Racine, Wis., started its current-distribution plan in 1917 and feels that the plan has stimulated employee productivity and an understanding of business risk. Leeds and Northrup, Oneida, Ltd., and the Quaker Oats Company use this type of profit sharing. Current-distribution profit sharing also provides the large annual bonuses at Lincoln Electric Co.[43] On the other hand, Gruen Watch, Hormel (see above), Nunn-Bush, and Sears, Roebuck have the deferred-distribution type.

Eastman Kodak Company has shared profits since 1913 by declaring annual "wage dividends," based on employee earnings, whenever stockholder's dividends go above a minimum level. Congoleum-Nairn, Sheaffer Pen, and Pitney-Bowes use this plan. The president of Pitney-Bowes defends wage dividends thus: "The worker does risk a part or all of his working life on the success or failure of an enterprise . . . isn't it fair and reasonable to pay the worker some 'risk' dividend on his year's work?"[44]

Employer experience with profit sharing has not been good, especially when profits are slim. More than half of the older plans in America were abandoned in the 1930's. A survey in 1936 of British plans showed 62 per cent discontinuances. The Bureau of Internal Revenue (which must approve profit-sharing trust funds for tax purposes) reported[45] that only 2 per cent of manufacturing and nonmanufacturing establishments had plans. Employees tend to take profit-sharing plans for granted. They fail to see the connection between their own efforts and profits. The year-end payment seems too distant to induce increased effort. Union leaders oppose[46] profit sharing, not necessarily in principle but as

---

[42] In its 1948 *Studies in Personnel Policy*, No. 97, Profit-Sharing for Workers, NICB reports 60 per cent of the 167 active plans found were deferred-distribution plans.

[43] See "Lincoln's Incentive System," New York: McGraw-Hill Book Company, Inc., 1946.

[44] *Fortune Magazine*, January, 1949, p. 21.

[45] Extent of Nonproductive Bonuses, *Monthly Labor Review*, October, 1947, p. 451.

[46] For a statement of union opposition, see *The Iron Age*, Vol. 163, No. 16, pp. 92–94, Apr. 21, 1949.

operated.   They claim profit sharing is merely a way to cut wages when profits go down.   They say it destroys stability of earnings, often because of management mistakes in buying materials, engineering, or selling the product.   Local unionists who understand the operation of a particular plan may accept profit sharing as they accept incentive wages.

SUMMARY

The industrial worker regards the enterprise first as a source of wages, second as a way of life which he hopes will give him security and satisfaction.   Although money wages are usually considered when incentive payment in industry is discussed and payment for production has probably contributed more to the leadership of American industry in the world economy than any other single factor, money wages are not the only incentive.   The worker is motivated by his desires for recognition, self-respect, and confidence as well.   His basic driving forces are present in the work situation as well as elsewhere in life.

The chief problems of wage administration remain, nevertheless, problems of techniques and methods.   The hundreds of piecework payment systems developed by industrial engineers represent, as yet, an unsuccessful effort to find an ideal wage-payment method.   Knowledge of proper tools is more widespread than is proper use.   Measurement of the effort put into work by the average employee and variations in the establishment of expected performance remain major weaknesses.   Possibly the severest handicap to overcome is the lack of confidence of employees in the integrity of complicated wage-payment systems.   Any evaluation for the future must consider the burden of an unfriendly union attitude.   The greatest contribution may yet be found in the by-products of methods improvement and the establishment of standard practices as prerequisite to establishing the time standard.

CASE PROBLEMS

1. When Bill McGuire, the yard storage boss, decided he needed the space occupied by a pile of pig iron, he instructed Mike and Joe to carry it over to a pile by the fence.   As they didn't seem to be making much progress the second day, he put them on piecework at 3 cents a 100-pound pig.   They had almost completed the move with fair increased success when the factory superintendent found what they were doing and ordered the pig-iron pile moved over to the foundry shed.   Mike and Joe walked off the job.   Why didn't this work and how could the desired results have been obtained?

2. A company that has a well-established and sound job-evaluation system with wage-administration provisions of a maximum and minimum for boring-mill operators finds itself unable to find a skilled boring-mill

man to hire and has already upgraded all candidates. Finally, after a week's search, a man who seems able to do the job is found, but he wants 10 cents an hour more than the maximum of the labor grade to go to work. This is more than any men presently on this job receive. Should he be hired, and at what price?

3. William Gomberg, director of the Management Engineer Department, I.L.G.W.U., quotes Prof. R. F. Hoxie's 1911 criticism of time study as a science, indicating six variables greatly influenced by the judgment of the time-study man: [47]

1. The extent to which the working method has been simplified and standardized before the study is taken.
2. The method of measuring and recording the raw data.
3. The particular statistic derived from the raw data.
4. The allowances for personal needs, rhythmic variation, and fatigue.
5. The method of reducing time-study data to normal data.
6. The allowances added for down time, setup time and clean-away.

Mr. Gomberg asks two questions:

A. How much progress has the (time-study) profession made in reducing these variables to uniform treatment?

B. To what extent does the factor of human judgment still influence the measurement of the variables listed? [47]

4. Figure 147 shows the increases in earnings and prices. From that figure Table XI gives the earnings of factory workers before the war,

TABLE XI.—CHANGES IN ACTUAL WAGE EARNINGS OF FACTORY WORKERS AND COST OF LIVING AT THREE DIFFERENT TIMES*

	Average hourly earnings, cents	Average weekly earnings	Consumers' price index 1939 = 100	Real hourly earnings, cents	Real weekly earnings
1939 average.........	63.3	$23.86	100.0	?	?
1945................	104.4	47.42	127.7	?	?
Per cent change.......	?	?	?	?	?
1945 average.........	104.4	47.42	127.7	?	?
1948 average.........	137.6	55.01	172.4	?	?
Per cent change.......	· ?	?	?	?	?
1939 average.........	63.3	23.86	100.0	?	?
1948 average.........	137.6	55.01	172.4	?	?
Per cent change.......	?	?	?	?	?

* Source: Bureau of Labor Statistics.
NOTE: 1945 first quarter average, 1948 December.

[47] GOMBERG, *op. cit.*

at its end, and at the peak of inflation in December, 1948. Calculate real hourly earnings and real weekly earnings. Calculate how much actual earnings, the price index, and real hourly and weekly wages went up during the war, between 1945 and 1948, and in the decade.

5. In Table IX pick out the city nearest your home. List those of the 34 cities having higher costs of goods and services in 1947. Is yours a high-cost or low-cost area? Which makes it so: food, clothing, or housing?

6. Notice Fig. 144, national income originating in corporate business. Explain how it was possible for corporations to show a loss in 1932 while still contributing 20 billions of dollars to national income.

7. Notice Fig. 146, earnings of male and female production workers. On the average, in the 20 years before World War II, what appears to have been a week's pay for the average male and female production worker? Compare this with money wages during and after the war.

8. Consider Fig. 145, employee compensation. In what three years was the employee-compensation portion of the national income greatest? How do you account for this?

CHAPTER XXV

JOB EVALUATION AND MERIT RATING

Origin of Job Evaluation.—Job evaluation, as one of the useful tools of modern management, was taken over from the field of public administration. Job classification began with efforts at Civil Service reform as early as 1871. Modern job analysis and formal rating were not added until 1910 in Chicago. As used in public administration, job evaluation is one element of a *merit system* (civil service) for improving public service and explaining to the taxpayers why the salaries paid are justified. As industrial management was called upon by stockholders, employees, union leaders, and government representatives to justify the wages and salaries it paid, it turned to job evaluation. Job evaluation is now an integral part of industrial engineering, but its refinements were developed by personnel administrators, not by Taylor and the early followers of scientific management. In the early days rate setters were satisfied to "grab their rates out of the air," *i.e.*, to work backward from expected earnings to arrive at the necessary base rates.[1]

Business management has always used the principles of job evaluation shown in Fig. 152, but only recently has clearly stated them. The first industrial job evaluation was installed in the Commonwealth Edison Company shortly after 1910. The practice spread slowly to manufacturing, where early installations were made at the United States Rubber Co. by 1922, and in the electrical industry by the late 1920's. Job evaluation was stimulated by industrial cooperation under the short-lived National Industrial Recovery Act, and by employers' reactions to the C.I.O. drive to organize the mass-production industries, starting in 1935. During World War II selective-service manning tables introduced many industrialists to job classification. Wage stabilization made systematic wage administration essential. During these years management, union leaders, and employees accepted job evaluation as an alternative less objectional than an absolute wage freeze. After the war the growth of job evaluation continued, with particular attention to salesmen and clerical workers. In the keener competition starting in 1949, job evaluation was used as a systematic tool for control of wage costs and continues to contribute to greater worker satisfaction with wages, and better union

[1] See LYTLE, C. W., "Job Evaluation Methods," p. 10, New York: The Ronald Press Company, 1946.

relations. The Socony-Vacuum Oil Company,[2] has stated its purposes for engaging in job evaluation as follows:

To secure a complete, accurate and impersonal description of the work done by each employee. This is the basis for all further considerations.

To determine the relative value of the various positions (or kinds of work done) in a department, and to line up similar jobs in different departments.

To define lines of organization, and to determine responsibilities and channels of authority.

To furnish full information in convenient form for the use of the employment office in connection with both initial employment and transfer possibilities.

To determine fair minimum and maximum salaries for each position (or kind of work done) throughout the organization, including initial salaries and wages for new employees.

For use in making salary adjustments, to learn whether or not any employee's salary is decidedly above or below the limits set for the kind of work he does, and why.

To establish a basis of comparison when checking company salaries with those paid generally for the same kind of work in the community.

To facilitate recognition of merit and promotion to positions of larger responsibilities, thus stimulating ambition.

To facilitate setting lines of job progression so when an employee attains a position of high responsibility his experience background will be as rounded as possible.

To furnish a basis for training employees for greater efficiency and for positions of greater responsibility.

Common Terms in Job Evaluation.—*Job rating*, or wage determination, is in general confined to the problems of wage earners—those non-clerical employees paid by the hour, the day, or the unit produced. *Salary rating* covers any other employees in clerical, technical, and supervisory jobs. Salary rating in a few instances covers all occupations up to the chairman of the board, although it is the more common practice to evaluate only those paid a salary up to $7,500 or $10,000 a year—usually about the level of major department heads.

Both wage determination and salary evaluation deal only with the job and not with the individual employee. When consideration is given to the human being filling the specific job, that process is known as "merit rating." It is discussed in a later section. A job may be either a whole trade, such as carpentry, or some portion of a trade, such as hand nailing, depending upon the assignment of duties to the individual common in the industry. An occupation is normally the calling pursued by the individual rather than the specific job performed in a specific factory. In this sense a man who is, by calling, a machinist may be on the job of

[2] "Job Analysis," Socony-Vacuum Oil Company, Inc.

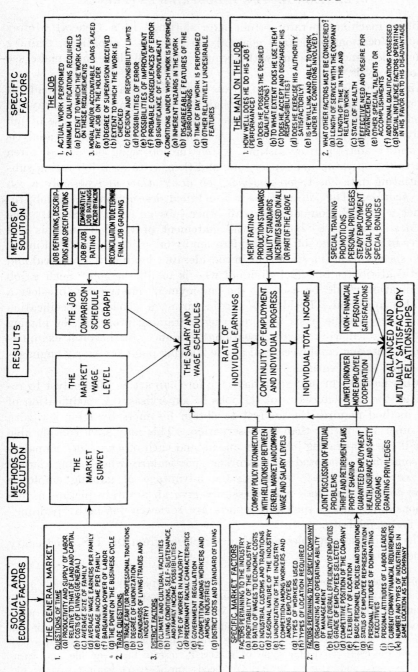

FIG. 152.—The why of job evaluation.   (*Courtesy of R. H. Rositzke, Paper Trade Journal, March 20, 1941.*)

"milling machine operator—front axle slotting" in a General Motors plant. Vocational guidance generally deals with occupations, training with trades, and job rating with specific jobs. All three may make use of job analysis.

Any evaluation, or rating, of a job requires that a study be made of the activities of the employee on that job. There are several ways in which this can be done. One of the most effective is by the use of job analysts. The job analysts, who have been especially selected for analytical ability and reporting instinct, watch the job being performed, often talk to the operator and supervisors, and then write up a job-rating substantiating data sheet, *job analysis, job description,* and possibly a *job specification.* The *job analysis* is a detailed description of the job, together with such comparisons with other jobs as seem pertinent. The *job description* is a "boiled-down" statement of the job analysis and serves to identify the job for consideration by other job analysts. Finally a *job specification* is a statement in considerable detail of the physical and mental attributes of any individual who is to fill the job. Such a job specification would be used by the employment interviewer to select a suitable applicant. Besides its use in hiring, a good job specification might serve as the basis for preparing a training program, for placing partly disabled workers, for vocational guidance, for hospital examinations of entering employees, and as the starting point for safety engineering or job simplification.

Other methods of job rating have the foreman act as job analyst to report on the characteristics of the jobs he supervises. A modification of this method requires the analyst to obtain his facts by interview with the supervisor rather than by observation. This may save considerable time if the cooperating job raters understand each other. Questionnaires are sometimes circulated to the workers, particularly when rating clerical and supervisory jobs. This has the advantage of gaining employee understanding but does not necessarily give an accurate picture of job responsibility unless such self-reports are reviewed for both "padding" and undue modesty.

The following examples are job descriptions from the U.S. Dictionary of Occupations.

Do-All Saw Operator (machine shop) 6-78.610. Operates an electrically powered band-type sawing and filing machine known by the trade name of Do-All, to cut and file irregular shapes from various metal materials; receives parts premarked or may mark them from templates with a scriber; turns selector dial on machine and reads indicator for the proper saw blade or file and speed to be used for each particular type of material; inserts blade or file and turns variable speed indicator to prescribed speed; pushes part against saw or file, and guides it along marked lines by hand, or may use pedal to operate a hydraulically controlled feeding device; for internal sawing, cuts or drills a starting hole in part, breaks saw or file blade and welds it together with an automatic butt welder built into the machine; turns valve to regulate a stream of air that keeps part clean during the process.

Guide, Factory (any industry) 2-36.31. Conducts visitors and observers about an industrial establishment; leads the way to the site or process to be observed; explains operation of various processes and machines; answers questions and supplies information on the work of the departments visited.

Rigger (IX) (aircraft manufacture) 7-03.512. Installs the cables that connect airplane cabin controls to ailerons, rudders, and fins; connects one end of cable to flying control by hooking cable eye to clamp on control; threads cable through pulleys in wings and fuselages; connects free end of cable to central control column with clamps or links; adjusts length of cables by setting controls at neutral and tightening the cable turn-buckles to equalize the tension on the control cables; tests adjusted cables with a tensiometer. May install pulleys in wings and fuselages, locating them according to blueprints and drilling and threading the necessary holes.

Methods of Job Rating.—The term "job rating" is used to describe the process of assigning a location in the hierarchy of jobs to a specific job as it might be performed by *any* person. The actual assignment may be made by a job analyst working alone, but more commonly a job-rating committee is formed to pool judgment. The local union is sometimes represented on this committee. Union representatives at U.S. Steel (Pittsburgh), Sperry Co., and Chase Metalworks are reported to have made the job-evaluation installation more acceptable to the employees.[3] The division of responsibility between the job analyst, the committee, and the foreman is shown diagramatically in Fig. 153.

Job rating has been formalized into a number of systems or methods. Possibly the most common method, and certainly the simplest although not necessarily the most satisfactory, is the *job-to-job comparison* or ranking method. Another common rating method, which has much to commend it, is the *factor-comparison* method. Most defensible seems to be one of the various *point systems* of job rating. Few companies confine themselves to only one method. Most installations use all three methods as checks and counterchecks. Recent writers have offered original combinations of all three. Figure 154 illustrates one such merger.[4]

[3] For a discussion of selling these methods to union representatives see Patton and Smith, "Job Evaluation," Chicago: Richard D. Irwin, Inc., 1949.

[4] From JOHNSON, BOISE, and PRATT, "Job Evaluation," New York: John Wiley & Sons, Inc., 1946. See also SMYTH and MURPHY, "Job Evaluation and Employee Rating," p. 66, New York: McGraw-Hill Book Company, Inc., 1946.

Job-to-job Comparison.—The old-fashioned way of rating a job was to compare that job in its entirety with all other jobs without putting any details of the comparison in writing except the final conclusion. The records would then show "what" but could not show "why." In a small

(*Read down*)

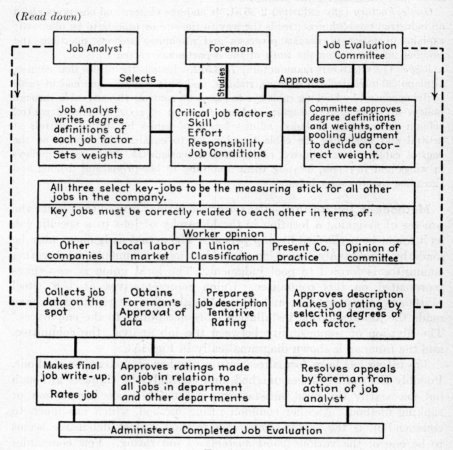

Fig. 153.

plant accurate results are possible with this method, although it is usually difficult to find a rater or committee of raters who know all the details of any considerable number of jobs. One method is to list the highest and the lowest jobs to be considered, then to pick out several jobs of average difficulty to place in the middle of the list. Each job to be rated is then compared with the jobs on the list. As the list becomes longer, more and more comparison is necessary to locate successive jobs accurately. Ease of arrangement is sometimes increased by putting the job titles on individual cards. An airframe manufacturer made the original job evaluation in his plant by moving such cards up and down on an

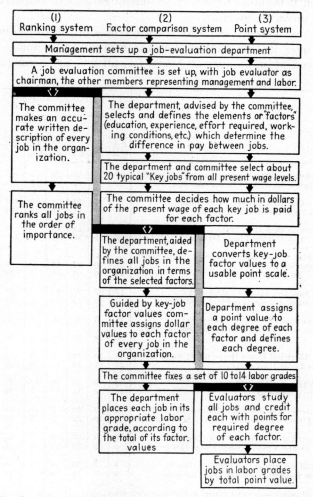

Fig. 154.—Showing steps in the operation of three kinds of job-rating systems. (*Source: Johnson, Boise, & Pratt.*)

ordinary production-scheduling rack until the committee making the job rating agreed. Photostats then preserved the record. Satter put each job on a card with every other job and had management judges pick the one rating highest. The votes were then totaled, and jobs arranged in order of comparative position.[5] Ratings made by job-to-job comparison are difficult to explain or justify should exception be taken to them.   It is especially difficult when new jobs must be added to an already approved list or when it becomes necessary to defend ratings to employees, stockholders, or union representatives.

Factor Comparison.[6]—Some of the directness of job-to-job comparison is carried over in this method, but the comparison is made factor by factor instead of on an over-all basis; *i.e.,* all jobs are arranged in order

JOB	POINTS						Base Class	Hrly. Rate at 1.05 Conv.
	Mental Effort	Skill	Phys. Effort	Responsibility	Work. Cond.	Total Points		
Toolmaker Leaderman (Working gang-pusher) (Daywork)	27	37	16	22	5	107	106	$1.11
Gyroscope & Marine Instrument Repairman (Daywork)	28	34	17	19	7	105	106	1.11
First Operator—Pipe Still Battery (Shift work)	24	24	16	24	14	102	103	1.08
Ethyl Blending Plant Operator (Daywork)	19	21	21	22	21	104	103	1.08
Toolmaker, Machine Shop (Daywork)	24	34	19	17	5	99	100	1.05
Bricklayer, 1st Class, Outside Plant (Daywork)	17	28	30	14	11	100	100	1.05
Flying Squad. Man (Comb. pipefitter, boilermaker, rigger, welder) (Daywork)	23	20	27	14	10	94	94	0.99
Shop Machinist, All-Around (Daywork)	21	29	24	15	5	94	94	0.99
Pipefitter, 1st Class, Outside Plant (Daywork)	17	22	27	15	10	91	91	0.96
Operator, Pipe Stills, Stabilization Plant (Shift work)	22	19	16	19	15	91	91	0.96
Operator, Sodium Plumbite Plant (Shift work)	17	16	20	16	17	86	85	0.89
Automobile Painter—Finisher, Striper & Spray (Night work)	16	24	25	12	9	86	85	0.89
Asst. Engineer, Electrical Power House (Shift work)	14	19	19	17	9	78	79	0.83
Tool Checker & Tester (Daywork)	28	11	19	15	6	79	79	0.83
Ship Loader, Wharves (Shift work)	4	8	33	10	16	71	70	0.74
Tester, Viscosity (Daywork)	18	20	15	11	6	70	70	0.74
Boilermaker's Helper, Outside Plant (Daywork)	6	7	33	5	10	61	61	0.64
Sample Room Attendant, Research Dept. (Daywork)	14	10	23	9	6	62	61	0.64
Common (Heavy) Labor, Outside Plant (Daywork)	3	3	37	3	9	55	55	0.58
Induced Draft Engine Tender, Boiler House (Daywork)	6	8	23	12	7	56	55	0.58
Janitor, Pipe Still Battery & Pump House (Daywork)	4	3	30	4	9	50	49*	0.52
Stencil-Cutter & Shipping-Tank Gauger (Daywork)	8	6	19	8	6	47	49*	0.52

*Jobs totaling 50 points and under placed in minimum-rate class

Fig. 155.—Examples of detailed rating and grading of plant hourly rated positions. (*From S. L. H. Burk, A Case History in Salary and Wage Administration, Personnel, Vol. 15, No. 3, 1938.*)

[5] For a report of this see G. A. Sattery, "Method of Paired Comparisons," *Journal of Applied Psychology,* Vol. 33, No. 3.

[6] This method is described in Burke, Hay, and Benge, "Manual of Job Evaluation."

of their possession of certain characteristics such as skill, effort, responsibility, and working conditions.   Points are assigned to each factor, and the factors are then totaled and converted to a money scale.   The points are assigned in a continuous series by one-digit steps, which results in easy recognition of slight variations between jobs.   This system, in common with other point systems, is subject to a basic difficulty in weighting the several factors equitably.   If a toolmaker ranks first in the skill factor but far down the list in undesirable working conditions and a coal-car unloader ranks first in undesirable working conditions but equally far down the list in skills, how are the two factors to be added together to a logical summation?   This is the problem of weighting (see Table XII).

Comparison among large numbers of different jobs for even one factor is a laborious process.   The factor-comparison method seldom defines exact degree steps.   Those who use this system establish the degree steps by the use of key jobs, as is shown in Fig. 155.

When a rating is made subsequent to the initial ranking, a key job-rating list makes it more nearly possible to recreate the rating mood that prevailed at the time of the initial rating.   In effect, new jobs to be rated are compared to the key job list and rated in relation to that list.   Whereas this facilitates ratings by management members, other than the original rating committee, it requires either an acceptance on faith of all that has been done or an involved redoing of the key job rating.   To recreate the key job rating is difficult because work sheets explaining the decisions made are seldom to be found.   When employees or union leaders challenge the job ratings, therefore, a defense is difficult.   Because of the direct relationship between the points and money value, a conversion factor must be used in pricing the rating scale anytime the general wage level changes.   It should be noted, however, that a factor-by-factor check is commonly made by analysts using other point systems.

A statement of the detailed divisions of one factor-comparison system has been given by R. H. Rositzke: [7]

Mentality: This is calibrated in terms of prerequisite schooling. It does not imply that an employee will not be eligible for a job if he does not possess such schooling. It does, however, mean that a job requires learning comparable to a certain amount of schooling. This in no way hinders or influences the progress of self-taught or self-made employees. Used in this sense, it aids ambitious employees to select the type of home or other study which will improve their eligibility.

Skill: The measurement of this job characteristic or requirement is broken down into three considerations: (1) the length of training required for an average employee to reach acceptable proficiency, (2) the variety and complexity of the

[7] *Paper Trade Journal,* Mar. 13, 1941.

operations or activities of the job, (3) the dexterity and manual skill necessary to perform the job satisfactorily.

Mental Application: This factor is gauged on the basis of concentration of attention (tension), intensity, and frequency of thought necessary.

Physical application gages fatigue, the laboriousness of the job, and its posture requirements.

Responsibility is judged by the possible and probable product-damage value the job is responsible for, the equipment damage possible or probable, the tool and fixture damage, and the responsibility for safety of other employees.

Working Conditions: Requirements of the job are gaged on the basis of work location. (Is it inside, outside, etc.?) Is the work in a damp, wet, or very wet location? What are the conditions of working temperature, noise involved, eyestrain, physical contact with oil, accident hazard, and health hazard due to dust or fumes?

Point Systems of Job Rating.—The most commonly used method of job rating employs one of the several different point-system scales. These point systems presuppose that a descriptive scale can be prepared for each job-rating factor. The entire range from the least amount found in a factory to the greatest amount probable is broken into approximately equal degree-steps. Definitions are written for each degree, and sometimes key jobs selected as typical of the degree. Equal point values are commonly assigned to each degree-step of a factor. Some systems assign an exact point value to each degree; others provide a range. In the point system originated by General Electric for job rating, a basic 400 points is assigned for general human values and the first degree-step carries a value of zero. In most other systems, the first degree carries a real point value, and every job rated is evaluated not less than the first degree-step of the factor. Jobs to be rated are compared with this established scale instead of with each other. Thus any error in rating stands alone. It is not carried over into subsequent comparisons between jobs. This check-against-a-scale feature of point rating makes it easy to explain the results obtained.

The point values derived from the degrees selected for each factor are customarily grouped into brackets called "labor grades" or "wage groups" for ease of administration. Thus all point values from 110 to 130 might be grouped into one labor grade. This grouping partly destroys the false sense of accuracy which the use of numbers in the rating imparts. Job rating, by whatever means, cannot become mathematically accurate. It is only a semiscientific procedure of controlled judgments or educated guesses. Point systems, because they regularly put in writing the basis for all decisions and have a logical appeal to workers, have been readily accepted by some unions. The U.S. Steel Company in its Pitts-

JOB RATING—SUBSTANTIATING DATA

Job Name_____ Lathe Operator—Engine (Up to 30″) _____ Class___ A ___

FACTORS	DEG.	BASIS OF RATING
EDUCATION	3 (42)	Use shop mathematics, charts, tables, hand book formulas. Work from complicated drawings. Use micrometers, depth gauges, indicator gauges, protractors. Knowledge of machining methods, tools, cutting qualities of different kinds of metals. Equivalent to 2 years high school plus 2 to 3 years trades training.
EXPERIENCE	4 (88)	3 to 5 years on wide variety of engine lathe work, including diversified set-ups.
INITIATIVE AND INGENUITY	4 (56)	Wide variety of castings and forgings of complicated form. Close tolerances. Difficult set-ups of irregular shaped parts. Considerable judgment and ingenuity to plan and lay out unusual lathe operations, select proper feeds and speeds, devise tooling, for varying materials and conditions.
PHYSICAL DEMAND	2 (20)	Light physical effort. Set-ups may require handling of heavy material mounting on face-plate. Machine time greatest part of cycle. Most of time spent watching work, checking, making adjustments.
MENTAL OR VISUAL DEMAND	4 (20)	Must concentrate mental and visual attention closely, planning and laying out work, checking, making adjustments. Close tolerances may require unusual attention.
RESPONSIBILITY FOR EQUIPMENT OR PROCESS	3 (15)	Careless set-up or operation, jamming of tools, dropping work on ways, jamming carriage, may cause damage seldom over $250.
RESPONSIBILITY FOR MATERIAL OR PRODUCT	3 (15)	Careless set-up or operation may result in spoilage and possible scrapping of expensive castings, forgings, shafts, etc., *e.g.*, machining below size, inaccurate boring of diameter and depth. Probable losses seldom over $250.
RESPONSIBILITY FOR SAFETY OF OTHERS	3 (15)	Flying chips may cause burns, cuts or eye injuries. Improperly fastened work may fly from face plate or chuck. May injure another employee when setting work in machine.
RESPONSIBILITY FOR WORK OF OTHERS	(5)	None.
WORKING CONDITIONS	2 (20)	Good working conditions. May be slightly dirty, especially in set-ups. Some dust from castings. Usual machine shop noise.
UNAVOIDABLE HAZARDS	3 (15)	May crush fingers or toes handling material or from dropped tools or clamps. Possible burns, cuts or eye injury from flying chips and particles. Finger or hand injury from rotating work.
Total	311–4	

Fɪɢ. 156.—Some 350 master sheets like this have been developed to expedite the actual task of rating jobs. When a specific job is rated, any one of three things can happen: (1) The master can be used "as is" or (2) adapted; or (3) a new one can be worked up. (*Courtesy of Factory, Vol. 97, No. 10, October,* 1939.)

burgh plant developed a complex point system with the C.I.O. steel-workers, which has been applied successfully. A point system having wide acceptance is that advocated by the National Electrical Manufacturers Association and the National Metal Trades Association. The essential steps in this application [8] are

1. The job rating based on point values. The weighting used is that of plan 4 in Table XII. Each of the 11 factors is broken into five degrees.

2. A job-rating substantiating data sheet shown in Fig. 156.

[8] Kress, A. L., *Factory Management and Maintenance*, Vol. 97, No. 10.

TABLE XII.—COMPARISON OF FOUR MEASURING STICKS: SKILL, EFFORT, RESPONSIBILITY, AND JOB CONDITIONS*

Major element from plan 4	Plan 1	Relative weight, per cent	Plan 2	Relative weight, per cent	Plan 3	Relative weight, per cent	Plan 4	Relative weight, per cent
Skill	Mentality	12½	Skill, dexterity and accuracy	23	Basic education	18.5	Education	14
	Skill	50	Education or mental development	10	Experience required	18.5	Experience	22
		62½	Experience and training	12	Aptitude	23.0	Initiative and ingenuity	14
				45		60.0		50
Effort	Mental application	6¼	Mental effort	10	Physical application demand	7.4	Physical demand	10
	Physical application	6¼	Physical effort	6	Mental application demand	7.4	Mental or visual demand	5
		12½		16	Visual application demand	7.4		15
						22.2		
Responsibility	Responsibility	12½	Responsibility	24	Responsibility for equipment	4.6	Responsibility for equipment or process	5
					Responsibility for product	4.6	Responsibility for material or product	5
					Responsibility for safety of others	4.6	Responsibility for safety of others	5
						13.8	Responsibility for work of others	5
								20
Job conditions	Working conditions	12½	Working conditions	10	Unusual features NOTE: In this plan "job conditions" is a supplementary factor added after the above factors are evaluated	3.7	Working conditions	10
			Fatigue	5			Unavoidable hazards	5
				15				15

* National Industrial Conference Board, *Studies in Personnel Policy*, No. 25, Job Evaluation, p. 6.

NOTE 1: Most job-rating systems use from 2 to 50 rating factors, weighted by pooled judgment of supervisors and personnel men, although there is no evidence that *anyone knows* how many cents of a dollar in wages should be assigned because of skill, effort, or job conditions. It seems evident, however, that different factors on which jobs might be compared have different values between themselves and in different labor markets.

NOTE 2: Some plans with many factors depend on repetition of highly similar factors (unweighted) to have the effect of weighting an area of comparison. If weights are not used, the differences between factor values are assigned by chance and by the frequency with which the several degrees are assigned in differentiating fashion to different jobs. Since the several degrees do not occur with equal frequency, the true weightings may be far different from the assigned weightings listed.

NOTE 3: There has been very little effort to scale factor weights by statistical methods. Some comparisons with wage-survey data by one of the authors suggest that the weights established by pooled judgment may not be fully defensible. In any event, the separate pricing operation may correct any errors in weighting but does not serve the main function of job evaluation, which is to fix a fair price on the rare job which cannot be priced in the wage survey.

NOTE 4: Among the factors added are originality of problems, teamwork, public contacts, and expense to the operator for clothes or tools he furnishes. All these are in different words in the measuring sticks above.

3. An over-all comparison between jobs on a labor grade basis which determines that the points assigned a given job bear a logical relationship to all other jobs (see Fig. 157).

4. A correlation chart, presenting graphically the relation between job-rating points and wages earned. This enables management to spot quickly any jobs that may be out of line within the company. This chart resembles the wage curve shown in Chap. XXIV.

Job-rating Problems.—It has been pointed out that competition among the different job-rating systems is being removed by merger. Four other problems deserve mention: (1) the number of factors to be used, (2) weighting the factors (see Table XII), (3) training job raters, and (4) continued maintenance after installation. Ever since Merrill R. Lott established the first thoroughgoing plan for weighting separate characteristics in 1924, the tendency has been to have many rating factors. Recent factor-analysis work at Purdue University seems to indicate that fewer factors may be needed.[9] Such commonly used factors as "safety of others" and "mental and visual demand" seem to contribute very little to the over-all rating. Job analysts are apt to continue to use such factors, however, because they appeal to employees and supervisors. The *weighting problem* is treated in Table XII.

A third problem is the *training of job raters* so as to standardize their judgment. Each rater must mean the same thing by his degree values. In a small plant one man's consistent judgment may be used; the larger plant must correlate judgments closely. This is achieved by training new raters in close association with experienced raters. Outside engineers commonly teach these standards to company employees doing job rating for the first time.

The final problem mentioned has to do with keeping the job-rating system running after it is once installed. A rating system cannot be left to run itself—it must be *administered and controlled*. In study of the success and failure of job evaluation programs Princeton University found four conditions essential to successful operation: (1) a carefully established plan, *i.e.*, one "sold" to employees and supervisors; (2) full approval of all members of management; (3) union acceptance—if there is a union; and most important (4) adequate administrative controls. These include centralized coordination, systematic evaluation of new or changed jobs, and regulation of rate changes in accordance with job rating.[10]

[9] For example, see LAWSHE *et al.*, "Studies of Job Evaluation," *Journal of Applied Psychology*, Vol. 32, No. 2.

[10] BAKER and TRUE, "The Operation of Job Evaluation Plans," Industrial Relations Section, Princeton University, 1947.

JOB RATING SUMMARY BY LABOR GRADES
PRODUCTIVE JOBS—MACHINE SHOP

OCC. CODE NO.	OCCUPATION	CLASS	LABOR GRADE	TOTAL POINTS	SKILL: EDUCATION DEG.	EDUCATION PTS.	EXPERIENCE DEG.	EXPERIENCE PTS.	INITIATIVE AND INGENUITY DEG.	INITIATIVE AND INGENUITY PTS.	EFFORT: PHYSICAL DEMAND DEG.	PHYSICAL DEMAND PTS.	MENTAL-VISUAL DEG.	MENTAL-VISUAL PTS.	RESPONSIBILITY: EQUIP. OR PROCESS DEG.	EQUIP. OR PROCESS PTS.	MATERIAL OR PRODUCT DEG.	MATERIAL OR PRODUCT PTS.	SAFETY OR OTHERS DEG.	SAFETY OR OTHERS PTS.	WORK OF OTHERS DEG.	WORK OF OTHERS PTS.	JOB CONDITIONS: WORKING CONDITIONS DEG.	WORKING CONDITIONS PTS.	HAZARDS DEG.	HAZARDS PTS.
	Labor Grade 2																									
104	Layout-Out Man	A	2	347	4	56	5	110	4	56	2	20	4	20	2	10	4	20	3	15	1	5	2	20	3	15
55	Boring Bar-Horizontal	A		343	3	42	5	110	4	56	3	30	4	20	3	15	3	15	3	15	1	5	2	20	3	15
45	Assembler-Group Leader	A		341	3	42	4	88	4	56	3	30	4	20	2	10	2	10	3	15	5	25	3	30	3	15
	Labor Grade 3																									
85	Inspector-Mechanical	B	3	335	4	56	4	88	4	56	2	20	4	20	3	15	3	15	3	15	3	15	2	20	3	15
122	Set-Up Man-Welding	A		331	3	42	4	88	4	56	3	30	4	20	2	10	2	10	3	15	3	15	3	30	3	15
125	Sheet Metal Worker	A		331	3	42	4	88	4	56	3	30	3	15	3	15	2	10	3	15	1	5	4	40	3	15
103	Lay-Out Man	A		327	4	56	5	110	4	56	2	20	4	20	2	10	2	10	2	10	1	5	2	20	2	10
76	Grinder-External	A		326	3	42	4	88	4	56	3	30	4	20	3	15	2	10	3	15	1	5	3	30	3	15
78	Grinder-Internal	A		326	3	42	4	88	4	56	3	30	4	20	3	15	2	10	3	15	1	5	3	30	3	15
97	Lathe Operator-Turret	A		326	3	42	4	88	4	56	3	30	4	20	3	15	2	10	3	15	1	5	3	30	3	15
116	Planer Operator	A		326	3	42	4	88	4	56	3	30	4	20	4	20	3	15	3	15	1	5	2	20	3	15
58	Boring Mill Operator	A		321	3	42	4	88	4	56	3	30	4	20	3	15	3	15	3	15	1	5	2	20	3	15
91	Lathe Operator-Engine	A		321	3	42	4	83	4	56	3	30	4	20	3	15	3	15	3	15	1	5	2	20	3	15
90	Lathe Operator-Engine	A		316	3	42	4	88	4	56	3	30	4	20	3	15	2	10	3	15	1	5	2	20	3	15
96	Lathe Operator-Turret	A		316	3	42	4	83	4	56	3	30	4	20	3	15	2	10	3	15	1	5	2	20	3	15
108	Milling Machine Operator	A		316	3	42	4	88	4	56	3	30	4	20	3	15	2	10	3	15	1	5	2	20	3	15
109	Milling Machine Operator	A		316	3	42	4	88	4	56	3	30	4	20	3	15	2	10	3	15	1	5	2	20	3	15
	Labor Grade 4																									
130	Welder-Arc	A	4	314	3	42	3	66	4	56	3	30	3	15	2	10	4	20	3	15	1	5	4	40	3	15
56	Boring Bar-Horizontal	B		307	3	42	4	88	3	42	3	30	4	20	3	15	3	15	3	15	1	5	2	20	3	15
105	Lay-Out Man	B		306	4	56	4	88	3	42	2	20	4	20	2	10	3	15	3	15	1	5	2	20	3	15
83	Heat Treater	–		305	3	42	3	66	3	42	3	30	3	15	4	20	3	15	3	15	1	5	4	40	3	15
67	Frill Press Operator-Radial	A		302	3	42	4	88	3	42	3	30	4	20	3	15	2	10	3	15	1	5	2	20	3	15
113	Miller—Worm Thread	–		300	3	42	3	66	3	42	4	40	4	20	3	15	2	10	3	15	1	5	3	30	3	15
110	Milling Machine Operator	B		299	3	42	3	66	4	56	3	30	4	20	3	15	3	15	3	15	1	5	2	20	3	15
120	Punch Press-Set-Up Man	B		296	2	28	3	66	3	42	3	30	3	15	3	15	2	10	4	20	3	15	4	40	3	15
126	Sheet Metal Worker	B		295	3	42	3	66	3	42	3	30	3	15	3	15	2	10	3	15	1	5	4	40	3	15
86	Inspector-Mechanical	C		294	4	56	3	66	3	42	2	20	3	15	3	15	3	15	3	15	3	15	2	20	3	15

FIG. 157.—When all the jobs in a department have been rated, they are summarized and graded according to total scores. All ratings are then carefully checked and compared. (*Courtesy of Factory Management and Maintenance, Vol. 97, No. 10, October, 1939, p. 62.*)

Clerical and Salary Evaluation.—Evaluation of clerical, technical, professional, and supervisory jobs is handled by most companies as a function independent from the evaluation of production jobs. It requires a different approach to the collection of information about the job and a different classification and control. Production employees are usually studied from without; other employees usually assist in their own job rat-

Job title	Skill					Responsibility				Conditions		Total points
	Education	Special knowledge	Experience	Learning time	Personal capacity	Responsibility for supervision	Responsibility for company property	Responsibility for company operations	Responsibility for safety and welfare	Working conditions	Public contact	
Maximum points for factor.......	10	8	12	8	15	25	8	12	5	8	8	119
Group leader—traffic dept......	6	5	9	6	11	3	1	5	1	1	2	50
Senior schedule clerk..........	4	3	6	4	10	0	0	5	0	1	0	33
Senior order-service clerk..........	4	0	3	4	6	0	0	3	0	1	8	29
Stenographer......	4	3	3	2	5	0	0	1	0	1	0	19
Typist..........	4	2	0	2	3	0	0	1	0	1	0	13
Messenger........	2	0	0	0	2	0	0	1	0	3	0	8

Fig. 158.—Evaluation of six key-salaried jobs.

ing either by filling out questionnaires or by answering questions about the job. Items such as "analytical complexity" and "confidential information" must often be added to the clerical rating, while such factors as "physical effort" and "hazards of the job" lose their significance. Different point weightings must be used.[11] Office progression from starting job to supervisor is usually much more identifiable than are similar lines of progression from factory job to foreman. Office ratings are harder to maintain, because most office operations are unstandardized and may add or subtract functions periodically.

The clerical-job evaluation is an extremely useful tool of *office manage-*

[11] For a discussion of the development of rating scales in two Middle Western paper-mill offices by factor comparison and by scoring items on a job-analysis blank, see G. A. Sattery, *Journal of Applied Psychology*, Vol. 33, No. 3, p. 218, June, 1949.

ment. It is usually supervised by the office manager. Clerical supervisors are generally evaluated as part of the clerical force, while shop foremen are usually evaluated as part of management. Figure 158 shows point values on jobs in the salary system used by The Norton Company, Worcester, Mass. (abrasives and grinders). The guide chart for one of the factors is Fig. 159.

Examples of Special Knowledge	Points
Adding machine, ditto machine, checking, or proofreading	1
Filing, comptometer, bookkeeping machine, typing, telephone switchboard	2
Blueprint reading, stenography, bookkeeping, detail drafting	3
Printing, motion-picture projection, librarian, physical education	4
Accounting, sales, layout drafting, traffic, machine-shop practice	5
Credits, time and motion study, advertising, sales engineering	6
Patent law, personnel management, mechanical engineering	7
Ceramics, plant physician	8

Fig. 159.—Guide chart for evaluation of special knowledge.

The Future of Job Evaluation.—Job rating can hardly continue growing at the rate it has in the last 20 years, but the toehold it has in industry seems permanent.

It should also be apparent that job evaluation techniques are not scientific in the true sense of the term but are systematic only. When this systematic procedure is applied through the pooled judgment of a number of trained individuals the results approach, as nearly as possible, those that will be obtained by the scientific procedures of the future.[12]

The current criticisms of job evaluation stem from two sources: industrial psychologists and union leaders. In the first group Dr. Lawshe's criticism of the number of factors used has been mentioned. Dr. Otis and Dr. Leukart,[13] have condemned the subjective judgments made, and Dr. Viteles [14] has listed the following criticisms:

1. Job evaluation gives a false sense of accuracy and there is a great deal of chaos yet to be eliminated by careful research.
2. Too many rating factors are used. There should never be more than 5 or 10.
3. Definitions of factors and degrees are not so accurately made as they could be in terms of action patterns and objective situations.
4. Too wide a range of factors is assumed and too many degrees are defined.
5. Too great a controversy is raised over method and not enough attention paid to results.

[12] Johnson, Boise, and Pratt, "Job Evaluation," New York: John Wiley & Sons, Inc., 1946.
[13] Otis and Leukart, "Job Evaluation," New York: Prentice-Hall, Inc., 1948.
[14] *Personnel*, Vol. 17, No. 3.

6. "Mental set" of raters is allowed to influence results.

7. Since workers who feel that they are paid on the basis of merit will tend to be happier and more productive than those who have reason to question the wage scale, more job evaluation is needed, but it should be better job evaluation. It might be made better if common sense and a due regard for the scientific method were followed.

Union Views on Job Evaluation.—Many considerations of modern management are influenced by the views of the labor organizations. Job evaluation is one of these. Whereas some unions will not agree to any handling of wage matters in an impersonal way, many leaders recognize in job evaluation a logical answer to problems of differences in pay raised by their membership. Ex-C.I.O., United Electrical, Radio and Machine Workers have issued a 127-page manual on the subject. This treatment favors a simple job-classification system of job evaluation. It condemns the "mumbo jumbo" of point-rating systems as apt to substitute scientific methods of determining wage differentials for collective bargaining. Specifically to be sought by the local union as part of the protection for its members are opportunities to use the companies' job-rating systems to show up the jobs that are "out of line." Where job-evaluation systems are being installed, this manual urges the local union to seek guarantees that no rate shall be cut because of them. The research director of the Steel Workers, C.I.O., on the other hand, has assisted in the development of an elaborate point-rating system now in use by several large steel companies. In an address before the New York chapter of the SAM [15] he further stated that such a system could be as useful to the unions as to management. A debate in print on the subject between William Gomberg and Solomon Barkin is found in "A Labor Union Manual on Job Evaluation," [16] which gives the I.L.G.W.U.–A. F. of L. position in favor and the Textile Workers position against these methods.

MERIT RATING OF EMPLOYEES

The origin of merit rating is credited [17] to Robert Owen, the Scottish millowner who in the early nineteenth century kept "character books" for his employees and displayed a colored block indicative of merit on each worker's bench. Development was halting until the rise of the personnel movement a hundred years later. Its growth was sporadic then but a NICB survey [18] found 11 plans started by 1918 and 16 more

[15] Society for Advancement of Management, wage conference, Hotel Pennsylvania, New York, Jan. 15, 1942.

[16] Labor Education Division, Roosevelt College, Chicago, 1947.

[17] See SMYTH and MURPHY, *op. cit.*, p. 174.

[18] *Studies in Personnel Policy*, No. 8.

by 1923. Most of these have continued, and hundreds are added yearly. A 1948 survey [19] found that 55 per cent of those companies employing 5,000 and over used merit rating and 33 per cent of the companies employing under 1,000 reported employee-rating plans. The most common rating interval was semiannually, with quarterly ratings next most popular. New employees are frequently rated at shorter intervals. Employees usually know they are rated, and many companies permit employees to challenge the ratings.

Why Merit Rate?—Merit rating is most commonly used to justify wage increases, but it has many other industrial-relations uses: [20]

1. Merit ratings are used as a part of the *selection* process itself in deciding whether probationary employees are to be retained by the company or not.

2. Merit ratings are used for the purpose of *guiding* new employees by identifying their defects. This kind of merit rating forms the basis of supervisory inspirational conferences with the employee for the employee's benefit.

3. Merit ratings are valuable as aids to the analytical study by the supervisor of the employee for purposes of correct *job placement* in line with the individual employee's personal peculiarities.

4. Merit ratings help in the identification of *promotional* and *transfer* candidates. Such ratings are an excellent tool for determining those individuals who are not making a success of their present assignment and therefore would benefit by a substitute assignment or for selecting those individuals most deserving of additional opportunities.

5. Merit ratings may be used as a *criterion* by the employment office to judge the effectiveness of its own selection of new employees. They may be used in the same way by the industrial-relations director as a measuring stick of employment-office-selection effectiveness.

6. Merit ratings (considered for the benefit of the employee previously) may also be a useful tool for the *benefit of the supervisor*, who learns through rating the employee more about his own job.

7. The quality of the merit-rating job that the supervisor does may form the basis for *rating the supervisor* himself in terms of his supervisory capacity.

8. The merit ratings may be used as part of a seniority system for *layoff purposes*. Where ability is considered along with length of service as a part of seniority, a defensible selection between two individuals for layoff may be made on the basis of merit ratings. This type of record will be different from the usual increase or promotional merit ratings.

9. Merit ratings may be used as a part of the employee's *disciplinary record* to protect the employee, the supervisor, and the company from discrimination, favoritism, or charges of such unfair labor practices. It should be remembered in this connection that a given individual can be proved "bad" by a merit rating only to the extent that other merit ratings prove other employees to lack the defects and therefore to be "good."

10. The merit-rating record of an employee may be collected simply as part of the whole background story about the employee. No immediate use may be at once apparent. Future uses are sure to develop. In this sense, merit rating is

[19] *Studies in Personnel Policy,* No. 88, National Industrial Conference Board, Inc.

[20] Information from STACKMAN, H. A., JR., "Application of Merit Rating," p. 90, Silver Bay Industrial Conference Proceedings, New York: Association Press, 1946.

actually *a "standby" record* which by its existence tends to improve employee morale. The regular collection of merit ratings will also help to systematize the handling of all personnel matters.

Methods of Merit Rating.—For whatever reasons merit rating is used, the rating method is developed to assist the supervisor in formulating his opinon of the work performed by his employees. One of the most complete classifications of rating methods is shown in Table XIII. Common

TABLE XIII.—OPERATIONAL CLASSIFICATION OF RATING METHODS*

Operations of scale construction by experimenter	Operations of scale use by rater	Name of method
Compiles list of names of ratees for the use of the rater	Ranks individuals on list from best to worst	Rank order
Compiles pairs of names or ratees in which each name is paired with every other name	Determines which ratee is the better of each pair	Paired comparisons
Determines and defines separate traits to be rated and constructs a continuum or several discrete intervals for each trait, placing "guideposts" along each continuum	Determines where ratee falls on each trait continuum; may also write in reasons for his rating	Linear Alphabetic Numerical Graphic Defined distribution Behaviorgram
Determines and defines traits to be rated and directs raters to select and place five individuals at five representative points on trait continuum	Matches each ratee with one of five individuals comprising comparison standard group	Man-to-man
(1) Collects large number of behavioral descriptions applying to work ratees are doing, (2) requires group of judges to sort or rank statements using one of psychophysical methods, (3) selects final items on basis of scale value and dispersions obtained in (2)	Determines which items in the list apply to or describe behavior of ratee	Weighted random check list
(1) Collects large number of behavioral descriptions or adjectives applying to work ratees are doing, (2) obtains criterion measure of individuals who form scale standardization group, (3) selects final items on basis of their differentiating value, using criterion subgroups	Selects alternatives within each item as being most descriptive and least descriptive of ratee	Forced choice

* Source: KNAUFT, E. B., Personnel Rating Methods, *Journal of Applied Psychology*, Vol. 31, No. 6, p. 618.

examples from this will be discussed.   This emphasis on different kinds of forms used should not lead to the conclusion that merit rating is entirely a matter of paper records.   Some of the best rating plans do not use these forms.   One alternative is the *field-review method* [21] used by Eli Lilly. This is a planned conversation between a personnel representative and the employee's supervisor aimed at helping the supervisor work more effectively with the employee and also at improving the employee's performance.

Man-to-man Rating Scales.—The man-to-man rating was originated during World War I as an officer-training tool.   This method required the rater to select the man having the greatest and the least amounts of a given characteristic among all the men he ever knew and then to compare the man being rated to that scale in terms of the characteristic. For instance, the best leader is placed at the top, a normal leader in the middle, and a poor leader at the bottom, and the ratee placed as having more than one man but less than another man.   These scales are constructed from the experience of the rater and may vary as greatly as the raters themselves differ.   The factors are seldom defined and raters may differ greatly in their definitions of the thing being rated.   Comparisons between ratings made by two different raters by these methods are very difficult.

Graphic Rating Scales.—The graphic rating scale is the best method yet devised of recording briefly a great many objective judgments about an individual.   Such a scale is usually prepared by grouping adjectives in ascending order along a line with appropriate provision for checking the place on such a scale where the individual being rated falls (see Figs. 160*a* and 160*b*).   Numbers are sometimes attached to the graphic scale to facilitate summarizing, but this may result in a false sense of accuracy. Proper weighting of the point scale for each and all jobs is also very difficult.

Check Lists.—A series of statements about the individual's job performance which indicate progressively greater degrees of satisfactory performance is prepared as suggested in Table XIII.   Without attempting to say whether he is satisfied or not, the supervisor is asked to indicate the facts about a given employee by checking the statements which apply. A merit rating is then calculated centrally.   In effect, the foreman checks the facts and is told what this means.   Such statistical interpretation is needed with any rating method to overcome the supervisor's tendency to rate too high or too low.   Check lists are thought to be more objective and to free the supervisor from any preconceptions of good or bad job per-

[21] Developed by Guy W. Wadsworth, Southern Counties Gas Company of California. See *Personnel Journal*, December, 1948.

FORM 3

GRAPHIC RATING REPORT II

On Executives, Department Heads, Foremen, and Supervisors

KIMBERLY-CLARK CORPORATION

NOTICE TO RATERS: Before making your ratings, read every word on both sides of this sheet.

Person Being Rated: Name_____Job_____Mill_____

Name of person doing rating_____ Job of person doing rating_____ Date rating was made_____

Ability	Report				

I. Consider his success in winning confidence and respect through his appearance and manner.

Inspiring	Favorable	Indif-ferent	Unfav-orable	Repellent

II. Consider his success in doing things in new and better ways and in adapting improved methods to his own work.

Routine Worker	Fairly Progressive	Resourceful	Highly Constructive

III. Consider his success in winning the co-operation of his subordinates, in welding them into a loyal and effective working unit.

Frequent Friction In His Department	Fails to Command Respect	Handles Workers Well	Capable and Forceful Leader

IV. Consider his success in organizing the work of his department or unit, both by delegating authority wisely and by making certain that results are achieved.

Effective Even Under Difficult Circumstances	Effective Under Normal Circumstances	Lacks Planning Ability	Inefficient

V. Consider his success in making his department or unit a smooth running part of the whole organization; and his knowledge and appreciation of the problem of other departments.

Exceptionally Co-operative	Co-operative	Not Helpful	Difficult to Handle	Obstructionist

VI. Consider his success in improving his subordinates by imparting information, creating interest, developing talent, and arousing ambition.

Discourages and Misinforms Workers	Neglects to Develop Workers	Develops Workers Satisfactorily	Develops Workers of High Calibre

VII. Consider his success in applying specialized knowledge in his particular field, whether by his own knowledge of ways and means or through his use of sources of information.

Expert	Competent	Uninformed	Neglects and Misinterprets the Facts

(SEE OTHER SIDE)

FIG. 160a.—Graphic rating scale. (*From National Industrial Conference Board, "Studies in Personnel Policy," No. 18, Plans for Rating Employees, June, 1938.*)

FORM **3**—(*Continued*)
Supplementary Information About Person Being Rated

1. This person should be considered for promotion at the first opportunity. Reasons and suggested line of promotion: _____

_____

_____

2. He should be transferred to other work. Reasons and suggested line of work:_____

_____

3. He is ambitious to progress and should be advised how best to qualify himself for advancement. Remarks: _____

_____

4. Additional information on this employee:_____

_____

The Graphic Rating Report—What It Is and How It Works

The Graphic Rating Report is a practical method through which each employee's ability and fitness for increased responsibilities can be known quickly, with a reasonable degree of accuracy and uniformity throughout our organization.

Each mill manager, operating superintendent, tour boss, department head, etc., rates the employees immediately subordinate to him. Conversely, each employee is rated by several supervisors.

This ensures a well-balanced judgment in each instance. Where marked differences of opinion occur, the reasons are discussed to find the facts.

Because the Graphic Rating Report calls attention separately to each ability, it lessens the danger that opinions will be based upon minor points, with a corresponding disregard of important qualities. It is to the interest of all to replace snap judgments by carefully thought-out reports.

Each employee is rated periodically, every few months. The ratings are kept on file in the Personnel Department and are considered in salary increase, promotion, lay-off, etc.

All ratings are confidential. Any employee who is rated, however, may be told where he stands in order that he may improve himself if he so desires.

Instructions for making out a Graphic Rating Report are given below. If the reports are to be of the most service, these instructions must be followed word for word:

1. If you have any question about the operation of the Graphic Rating Report, be sure to have it answered before you make your ratings. A snap-judgment is an injustice not only to the employee being rated, but also to yourself.

2. Be certain that you understand what is meant by each listed ability. Study the definition carefully. Read every word on the Report.

3. Do not begin to rate the employees until you have considered each of them with regard to the abilities on the Report. Take all the time you need.

4. Consider one ability at a time and rate all the persons on that ability. Then, rearranging the order of persons at random, rate them on the second ability, and so on for the remaining abilities. Rate all your subordinates on one quality at a time.

5. Compare each employee with other employees now on similar jobs in Kimberly-Clark Corporation or elsewhere. Behavior on the job is more significant for present purposes than behavior in purely social gatherings.

6. Try to free your rating on any one ability from the influence of the other abilities of the person, and from any general impression or attitude you may have in regard to him. Try to be uninfluenced by the time you have worked with the person or the closeness of your friendship with him.

7. When judging a person, call to mind concrete instances of the behavior in question. For example, do not indicate that an employee is "lazy" unless you can call to mind several clear instances of his laziness on the job.

8. Remember that extremes of ability are rare. Measurements of abilities have shown that most people are grouped about the average and that fewer persons have the higher or lower degrees of ability. Do not, therefore, consider all the persons to be either very high or very low in ability.

9. Indicate your rating in each ability by placing a check mark ($\sqrt{}$) on the line just where you think it ought to be. It is not necessary to put the check mark directly above any of the descriptive adjectives.

10. After you have rated all the employees on each ability, turn the Reports over and give in detail the supplementary information about each person being rated.

FIG. 160*b*.—Reverse side of Fig. 160*a*.

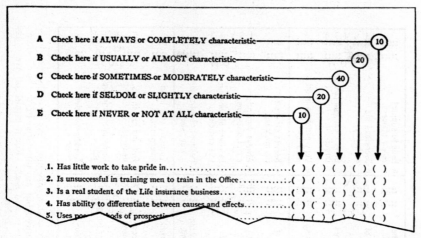

A Check here if ALWAYS or COMPLETELY characteristic —————————————————— ⑩

B Check here if USUALLY or ALMOST characteristic ————————————————— ⑳

C Check here if SOMETIMES or MODERATELY characteristic ————————— ㊵

D Check here if SELDOM or SLIGHTLY characteristic ——————————— ⑳

E Check here if NEVER or NOT AT ALL characteristic ————————— ⑩

1. Has little work to take pride in...................................( ) ( ) ( ) ( ) ( )
2. Is unsuccessful in training men to train in the Office..............( ) ( ) ( ) ( ) ( )
3. Is a real student of the Life insurance business.... ....( ) ( ) ( ) ( ) ( )
4. Has ability to differentiate between causes and effects............( ) ( ) ( ) ( ) ( )
5. Uses po—— ——ods of prospecti——   .....( ) ( ) ( ) ( ) ( )

Fɪɢ. 161.—A portion of a weighted check-list appraisal form developed by Leonard W. Ferguson, Research Section, Field Training Division, Metropolitan Life Insurance Company. This form was developed for use in the appraisal of field training instructors. It represents a significant step of progress in appraisal procedure. Mr. Ferguson suggests that such an appraisal form should be useful in selection, promotion, individual training, and salary review.

The weighted items on the form were refined from a large number of critical statements about the ratees. Each statement was given a range of replies from *always* to *never*. Scoring weights were established experimentally based on the designations of a group of raters. The numbers in the circles at the heads of the columns of parentheses are percentages and are *not* scores. They constitute a guide for the rater. For example, the 10 in the A column indicates that the rating is in the upper 10 per cent, *i.e.*, 90 to 100. Since the B rating shows 20 in the circle, it ranks 70 to 90. E, being at the lower end of the scale, ranks 0 to 10.

This promising development overcame some of the traditional difficulties by careful attention, experimentally, to what supervisors found to be characteristic of successful and unsuccessful performers. For a more detailed explanation of the procedures used in developing this appraisal method, see Leonard W. Ferguson, The Development of a Method of Appraisal, *Personnel*, Vol. 24, No. 2.

formance (see Fig. 161). The extensive statistical work necessary to weight the checked items is sometimes performed by an outside consultant.

Forced Choice.—This is the method now used by the U.S. Army. Similar scales have been prepared for airline pilots and by the Westinghouse, East Pittsburgh, plant for shop foremen. To prepare a scale such as is illustrated in Fig. 162 requires a very large number of ratings and some objective criteria of performance. Where this is available the method shows promise, since the rater does not know which of the characteristics he is checking are favorable and which are unfavorable to the ratee—hence, intentional over- or underrating is limited. Logical

READ INSTRUCTION SHEET CAREFULLY
BEFORE MARKING THIS SECTION

Section IV. JOB PROFICIENCY

1 MOST / LEAST
A. Becomes dogmatic about his authority.
B. Careless and slipshod in attention to duty.
C. No one ever doubts his ability.
D. Well-grounded in all phases of army life.

2 MOST / LEAST
A. Follows closely-directions of higher echelons.
B. Inclined to "gold-brick."
C. Criticizes unnecessarily
D. Willing to accept responsibility.

3 MOST / LEAST
A. A go-getter who always does a good job.
B. Cool under all circumstances.
C. Doesn't listen to suggestions.
D. Drives instead of leads.

4 MOST / LEAST
A. Always criticizes never praises.
B. Carries out orders by "passing the buck."
C. Knows his job and performs it well.
D. Plays no favorites.

5 MOST / LEAST
A. Constantly striving for new knowledge and ideas.
B. Businesslike
C. Apparently not physically fit.
D. Fails to use good judgment

6 MOST / LEAST
A. Cannot assume responsibility.
B. Knows how and when to delegate authority.
C. Offers suggestions.
D. Too easily changes his ideas.

7 MOST / LEAST
A. Fails to work for the best interest of all.
B. Has a high degree of initiative.
C. Never makes excuses for his mistakes.
D. Slow in accomplishing his work.

8 MOST / LEAST
A. Criticizes policies of superiors.
B. Others can't work with him.
C. If he is wrong, will admit it.
D. The men know they can rely on his judgment.

9 MOST / LEAST
A. Doesn't try to pull rank.
B. Knows men, their capabilities and limitations.
C. Low efficiency.
D. Uses a steady monotone in his speech.

10 MOST / LEAST
A. Fails to support fellow officers.
B. Oversteps his authority.
C. Gives clear and concise directions.
D. Very exacting in all details.

11 MOST / LEAST
A. Blames others for his mistakes.
B. Always demands strict discipline.
C. Excellent at constructive criticism.
D. Hesitant about rendering decisions.

12 MOST / LEAST
A. Can take over in an emergency.
B. Fair and just in his dealings.
C. Lacks interest in his job.
D. Questions orders from superiors.

Fig. 162.—Section from forced-choice rating. The rater must mark the two statements most like and the two least like the ratee among each set of four. The four items are statistically balanced but are unrelated in "surface" value. This system was developed to overcome the rater's tendency to rate everyone too high. For a report of Army experience see Colonel J. C. Fry, All Superior Officers, *Infantry Journal*, Vol. 43, No. 1.

selection is prevented because half the items are neutral, counting neither for nor against a man. The Standard Oil Company (New Jersey) uses thirty such groups of "most descriptive" and "least descriptive" statements in its forced-choice system.

Shortcomings of Merit Raters.—Although merit rating is one of the oldest as well as one of the most widely practiced personnel procedures, it has many unsolved problems, including (1) *halo effect,* or the tendency of raters to rate a man who is high on one trait high on all others; (2) *different standards* among raters resulting in a tendency to rate low or, more commonly, to rate high; (3) *lack of spread* so that the rating does not distinguish between employees, commonly resulting in everyone being rated as "exceptional"; (4) *lack of agreement* as to the same employee's value because different raters have seen him perform under different conditions; (5) *failure to predict* success or disagreement between the rating and some criteria of effectiveness, such as earnings or production records. The rating methods just discussed have been combined with an effort to train raters more effectively and statistical controls to overcome these shortcomings, since there is great promise in merit rating despite its failures. Ratings of the future will require more accurate job analysis to determine job requirements. They will start with identification of *critical incidents* [22] making for success or failure rather than of assumed traits of people. These "critical incidents" will be built into a rating system which raters can use in practical supervision to provide the strongest possible incentive for employee performance and growth. Successful merit rating can be an aid to improved employee-employer relations. As commonly used it may be a detriment.[23]

SUMMARY

As more and more industrial engineers, business administrators, and labor leaders become acquainted with the principles of job evaluation, this function of industrial relations assumes increasing importance. The performance and promise of an individual employee will never be completely separated from job rating, but man rating or merit rating [24] as a

[22] See description of technique in "Current Trends in Industrial Psychology," Job Requirements, chapter written by John C. Flanagan, Pittsburgh: University of Pittsburgh Press, 1950.

[23] See the Personnel Management Report to Congress by the Commission on Organization of the Executive Branch of the Government, February, 1949, p. 33, which recommends a shift in emphasis on merit rating from being the basis for such personnel actions as pay increases or order of layoff to being a basis for a personal conference with the employee to facilitate his future progress.

[24] The term "merit rating" as used here should not be confused with "merit rating" used to refer to the practice in many states of assessing unemployment tax rates

management tool is also becoming increasingly objective. Job rating based on careful analysis and an objective evaluation of all aspects of the worker in his work cannot help but contribute to better understanding. Considerable difference of opinion exists among personnel technicians and job analysts as to the exact job-rating system to be employed. Point systems and factor-comparison methods compete with over-all job-by-job comparison to the benefit of all three. All are agreed, moreover, that consistency of application and a factual approach yield desirable results. The perfect merit-rating system is still to be developed. There is conflict: merit rating to help the supervisor formulate his opinion (as on the graphic scale) vs. efforts to force the supervisor to admit that not all his men are exceptional (as on the weighted check list and forced choice). In it the basic purpose of merit rating as an aid to the individual employee's development may be overlooked. It seems probable that progressive industrial-relations departments will continue their research in this important field to the ultimate benefit of both industry and the worker.

CASE PROBLEMS

1. Prepare a job description of the duties of some job you have performed or of some worker whom you can readily interview such as elevator operator, sales clerk, or the like. Write a job specification for an individual to fill the job.

2. Study the several sets of job-rating factors given in Table XII. Select one of these as your choice, or write a new set of factors expressing your opinion. Be prepared to defend your selection. Put your defense into the form of a brief outline.

3. Prepare a graphic rating scale for the specific job selected in question 1. First select the qualities making for success in the occupation, then construct a scale of descriptive statements ranging from a small amount of the characteristic to outstanding possession of the characteristic.

4. Explain what other records an employer would find advisable in addition to the discipline-warning record illustrated in Fig. 167 of Chap. XXX.

5. A burly machinist strode in, wiping his hands on a piece of waste. The foreman greeted him, "What's the matter, Bill?" "I'm fed up! I'm

according to the employer's layoff experience. Many unions and the unemployment tax commissioner complain that this provision, which was intended to provide incentive for stabilized employment, has failed. They say that the tax reduction is often a "windfall," and in other companies excessive "short time" is used to avoid a heavy layoff and consequent higher taxes.

leaving the Jammed Machine Co.[25] and I'm leaving Bridgeport, Conn. Come Friday, I'm getting through. I'm heading west where a man can make some money. I don't blame you, John. You're paying me the rate for my classification. We only got one rate, but I been working on that horizontal boring bar for seven years. Seven long years, and still a class B operator. Why, I can do anything as good as any man in the shop. Bar none! Is there any job you can't give me?

"No, Bill, there isn't, but before you walk out you better let me call a job analyst."

The analyst found in consultation with the foreman that the work Bill had been doing justified another degree of *initiative and ingenuity,* for it was very complex. That called for one more degree of *experience* —which Bill had.

Discussion Questions

1. Would these additional points change Bill's labor grade? If so how much of a raise would be justified in this single-rate plant following the community wage curve? If not, what is needed to get Bill a raise?

2. Should Bill accept any raise offered, or should he leave as planned? Who was at fault in this case?

3. As a matter of policy should men be granted increases, should jobs be reviewed, should any reclassification be made when a man has threatened to quit? *Hint:* Fig. 157 labor grades 2, 3, 4 are equivalent to labor grades 9, 8, 7 in Fig. 149.

[25] Fictitious name.

C. Selling the Products

SALES CONTROL

In early days each man was his own manufacturer. When he had surplus goods, he met with his neighbors in what came to be known as a marketplace and exchanged or bartered for other goods to serve his own needs. Today the distribution of goods is a specialty within itself.

There are at least three factors that have chiefly contributed to this specialization. First, with the Industrial Revolution came specialization in production. Instead of a man's being a producer of many things, he chose to devote his attention to a few products and at the same time to rely more upon others for anticipating his needs and producing for the satisfaction of those needs. This tendency toward specialization has formed the basis for our present system of mass production. This has meant that, where previously a man served his neighbors in his immediate community, the manufacturer of today serves an international trade. This naturally has called for expansion and specialization of sales activities.

A second factor contributing to the development of the field of selling is the ever-increasing standard of living in this country. As we developed specialization in production for human wants and as we expanded to include a national and international trade, a greater variety of products became available to all men. The cotton of the South was made easily available to the man of the North in exchange for his lumber, iron, and paper products. The products of our North American industries were exchanged for the coffee in South America and the rubber of the Dutch East Indies. This expansion geographically in the area of exchange brought to each man a greater selection of products and materials and, through this increased activity and improved methods, particularly in our own country, the general standard of living was raised to a point where previous luxuries became essentials. The automobile, the refrigerator, and the radio are only a few examples of the many items that are now considered necessities.

A third factor contributing to the expansion of the field of selling is competition. The village blacksmith in earlier days had little competition. Consequently he did not feel the need for salesmen. The quality and the usefulness of his product were its own salesmen. But when others entered his field of specialization and undertook to serve his trade, he found that inducements other than the product itself became essential for the continuance of his business. Consequently he found that he must personally devote a portion of his time to the building of trade. He studied his potential customers and sought means for improving the quality of his service to them; he added little extra services in addition to the product itself. Then came the hardware industry which transformed the whole picture of the work of the village blacksmith. As the hardware industry grew, it too found competition and followed on a larger scale the same process of expansion in selling activities.

An interesting bit of proof of the effect of competition on selling activities was witnessed in World War II when, because of the increase in demand and the decrease in availability of materials for production, competition in sales became obscure. The principal customer of American industry was the Federal government itself through its armed forces. Instead of attempting to cover a world-wide market, industry had only to concentrate on one customer, or, if on a subcontract basis, with perhaps six or eight customers. Once a contract was obtained, the principal activity became one of production, allowing, of course, for the continuation of research and engineering to meet the demands for the improvement of the product. Salesmen were called in from the field and were placed on production jobs or in the expediting of materials for production.

FUNCTIONS OF THE SALES DEPARTMENT

The functions of a sales department may be classified under five headings: (1) planning for sales, (2) advertising and promotion, (3) selling, (4) inquiries and orders, (5) servicing.

Planning for Sales.—It is only in times of a business decline that the importance of the customer is fully realized. During periods of prosperity when industrial goods are in demand for industrial expansion, a manufacturer tends to assume more of an attitude of independence. He receives more orders than he is able to fill, and his attention is directed almost wholly to the problems of production. But when the cycle of business turns and he suddenly awakens to the fact that orders are not running his plant to capacity, then he turns his attention to ways in which he can obtain additional orders by the cultivation of old customers or the development of new ones. The wise manufacturer recognizes that to wait until the depression occurs may be too late. He, therefore, seeks means during periods of accelerated business activity for cushioning the effects of the period of declining business activity.

There are, of course, many ways by which a manufacturer may plan during periods of prosperity for periods of recession. Among the more obvious is to cultivate the customer through studying his probable future needs, as has been described in Chaps. VII and VIII, and through the extension of services to the customer as an instrument of good will.

Failure in maintenance of service during and immediately following World War II was the cause of painful regret by manufacturers and retailers, who struggled to regain their customers when the tide turned. By 1950 business emphasis on service had reached an all-time high.

Although the nondurable goods market is highly competitive, it has the advantage of greater stability over durable goods. For example, for the year 1929 the durable goods index shows a production figure equal to 120 per cent of the long-term trend. In 1932, the depth of the depression, production was at 33 per cent. On the other hand, nondurable goods attained a peak of only 108 per cent in 1929 and dropped to a low of 79 per cent in 1932.[1] In recognition of the value of stability, many manufacturers of durable goods attempt to develop lines of nondurable goods that can be depended upon in low periods.

Another means for cushioning the shock of declining business activity is to plan for the prevention of an oversupply during periods of prosperity, the idea being to spread the period of demand over a greater number of years. For example, automobile manufacturers have discovered that there is a growing tendency for automobile owners to buy new cars every three years. An unusually heavy volume of sales in any one year will have a tendency to repeat itself three years hence, all other conditions being equal. Through research, manufacturers are able to catalogue the potential buyers of automobiles. It stands to reason that, if an undue number of automobiles is produced and distributed in any one year, this will be balanced through a decline in demand in other years, allowing, of course, for the fact that new automobile users may enter the field of demand. Peaks and valleys in the distribution of automobiles disrupt the production efficiency of automobile manufacture. During the lull, or valley periods, manufacturers have plants and equipment lying idle. Highly skilled personnel must be laid off. Those that find employment elsewhere may never return to the original employer. When the peak periods come, the production facilities and personnel are taxed beyond the point of normal and anticipated operation, and perhaps beyond a point of maximum efficiency. Ideally, the manufacturer seeks to level out these peaks and valleys, at least partly, through the planning and control of distribution.

[1] See *The Economic Almanac,* National Industrial Conference Board, for additional information relative to variations in production and in distribution.

The problem of planning and control of distribution becomes difficult, and in some instances impossible, unless there is cooperation between competitive enterprises. Manufacturer *A* would be reluctant to curtail distribution and production in any given year if he knew that manufacturer *B*, his chief competitor, was pushing for the highest possible volume through the introduction of new models and special price incentives that would entice potential customers. Recognizing the mutual benefits to be obtained from controlled distribution, manufacturers through their trade associations have been able to develop cooperative planning to varying degrees in different types of industry. This cooperative planning has been carried into cooperative research, cooperative advertising, and many other special activities, such as planning for the introduction of new products or improvements in existing products.

To be most effective, cooperative planning should extend beyond the bounds of a limited group of closely related manufacturers. In a society that is knit together by modern transportation and communication, individuals and enterprises assume a closer interdependency. People must earn to buy and they must work to earn. A sudden flood of goods on the market in any particular period has a tendency to exhaust the demand; sales decline; production is curtailed; earnings decrease; and so on through a vicious circle of declining business activity and the lowering of standards of living.

This brings us to the problems of economic and social planning which are too elaborate and complicated for adequate coverage in this chapter. The significant point presented here, however, is that distribution and production must be planned together, and they, in turn, must be based on the buying power of the users of consumer and industrial goods. And this buying power is dependent on the enterprises that provide avenues for earning.

Some of this planning must be on an international, cooperative basis, some on a national basis, some within a group of related industries, and some left to the individual enterprise—all limited, of course, by provisions of our anti-trust laws.

Advertising and Sales Promotion.—Advertising and sales promotion form a highly specialized field which is usually set apart from the other sales activities but comes under the sales manager. The object of this function is to stimulate a desire on the part of potential customers. This function will be discussed in detail in Chap. XXVII.

Selling.—In a sense, all activities of the sales department may be considered selling. However, this particular function refers to the work of the salesman, which is the oldest approach to the customer and is still rated as one of the most effective. Once the plans and policies for the manufacture and distribution of products have been established and the advertising material has been distributed through various media, it becomes a responsibility of salesmen and branch sales offices to make the personal contact with customers. This personal appeal seems to have no substitute that is fully adequate. It is recognized that, with so many competitive articles on the market, many customers will make their choice of products in terms of their liking or dislike for the salesman. They value his personal interest and the little services which he is able to make available to them. The customer may grow to consider the salesman an advisor on the choice of products to serve his particular needs. In many instances, the salesman becomes a personal friend as well as counselor.

For this same reason, an enterprise that serves a large geographical area considers it wise to establish branch sales offices that will give at least some semblance of the home-town enterprise and will provide a better opportunity for continuous contact with customers.

Inquiries and Orders.—A significant function of the central and branch sales offices is the handling of inquiries coming from customers by mail, telephone, or telegraph. These inquiries request information regarding a particular product, the date on which delivery can be made, points regarding installation and maintenance, complaints, and many other points of a similar nature. The sales offices usually designate responsibility for this function to a group of specific individuals, frequently referred to as sales correspondents. They must become familiar with the products manufactured and the sales policies pertaining to the distribution and servicing of those products, in order to deal intelligently with inquiries received. It is expected that technical questions must frequently be referred to the engineering department for an answer. However, the person receiving the inquiry may assume responsibility for following it through to completion. Many of the inquiries will be directed to a branch office or to a salesman in the field for a more personal follow-up. In other instances, the sales correspondent may respond to the inquiry, sending a copy of his response to the salesman assigned to that particular territory.

Frequently the sales correspondent will be responsible for the actual handling of the order. On the other hand, some companies establish a separate order division. The advantage of the correspondent's handling the order is that it centralizes contact between the office and the customer in the checking of specifications, establishing credit, setting delivery dates, and other special problems that may be peculiar to the order. These matters will require clearance with many different departments, such as engineering, manufacturing, credit, and shipping. From the standpoint of efficiency and customer relations these clearances must be centralized.

Servicing.—Industry is rapidly adopting the principle that service is an essential part of the sale itself. A manufacturer of production machinery finds it essential to see that his products are properly installed. This not only is a service to the customer but is protection against complaint and general dissatisfaction on the part of the customer, which in the end would operate to the detriment of the manufacturer and his products. Once the equipment is installed, the manufacturer may assume responsibility for instructing the maintenance crew of the customer in the proper care of the equipment. He may also provide a maintenance service over a designated period of time through his special maintenance staff located either at the home office of the company or through its network of branch offices.

At times it is possible for a manufacturer to provide this maintenance service through his salesmen if the product is not so complicated that an unusually large amount of skill is required. For example, typewriter salesmen are frequently trained as repairmen. Manufacturers' sales offices of typewriters may extend a 12-month service with each machine sold. Any repairs required during this period are usually minor in nature and can be made by anyone familiar with the parts of the machine. It has been found that customers appreciate the continuity of service on the part of the salesman and the personal interest that he demonstrates through service after the sale.

In the case of more complicated machinery, it is a common practice for a manufacturer to maintain a staff of skilled engineers and mechanics who serve the customer through making necessary repairs and adjustments at the point of installation.

CHANNELS OF DISTRIBUTION

A channel of distribution may be defined as the route by which a product passes from producer to consumer. A channel of distribution may be either direct from the manufacturer to the consumer or through intermediary trade, generally known as middlemen, who in general are specialists in the resale of products to the consumer. The choice of a channel of distribution is influenced greatly by the nature of the product and the market to be served. In the case of consumer goods, a manufacturer will rely upon resale agencies almost exclusively. In some instances, he may have a limited number of retail stores operating under the name of the company. But in reality these divisions may be considered as resale units and for all practical purposes are handled in much the same way as an outside agency. On the other hand, capital or industrial goods that have a smaller turnover and require servicing by specialists are frequently sold direct to the business or industrial purchaser.[2]

As noted in Table XIV, a large proportion of goods is sold by the manufacturer to the intermediary or wholesale trade. Wholesalers are of many different types. Included in this group is the industrial distributor whose purpose is to serve manufacturers through the supply of a limited number of items in large quantities. These items are standard products, such as chemicals, lubricants, and various types of equipment and supplies used in manufacturing processes.

TABLE XIV.—SUMMARY OF SALES OF MANUFACTURERS [*]
(In millions of dollars)

Consumers	$ 2,100
Exporters	3,100
Utilities	3,100
Institutions	2,000
Retailers	6,400
Intermediary trade	31,800
Manufacturers	20,800
Extractive industries	300

* Adapted from AGNEW, JENKINS, and DRURY, "Outlines of Marketing," p. 35, New York: McGraw-Hill Book Company, Inc., 1942.

Manufacturers' agents, another type of wholesaler, may either devote attention exclusively to the sale of products of one manufacturer, or may also carry companion products purchased from other sources. This enables the agent to extend a more complete service to the purchaser and results also in increased benefit to the agent and his supplier, the manufacturer.

Brokers usually carry no stock but operate as a medium through which contact is established between the manufacturer and the consumer or the retail store.

Manufacturers' branch offices for purposes of sales are commonly classified as wholesale outlets. These branches are owned and operated by the manufacturer in order to facilitate the distribution of his products through direct contact with the industrial purchaser or the retailer or consumer. The sales branch may have its own warehouse, or several branches may be served by one warehouse or directly from the plant.

Various other types of wholesalers may be found, operating in a man-

[2] The committee on definitions of the National Association of Marketing Teachers define industrial goods as those which are used in producing consumer goods, other business or industrial goods and services, and/or in facilitating the operation of an enterprise. They include land and buildings for business purposes, equipment (installation and accessory), operating supplies, raw materials, and fabricated materials.

ner found most suitable to the distribution of the products that they handle and the customers whom they serve. Among these are auction houses, cooperative sales agencies, delivery agencies, importers and exporters, commission men, and mail-order houses that serve either the retail or the manufacturing trade.

There are many factors of distinction between the distribution of consumer and industrial goods. Many of the consumer goods, especially those of the luxury class, are purchased not on the basis of need but more by whim or fancy. Selling to this market is considered the job of specialists. The product must be dramatized and demonstrated; a desire for the product must be created since it is not prompted by need. To accomplish this, direct personal contact is an important advantage. Also, the market for consumer goods may be as large, potentially, as the population itself. To contact this vast market, the manufacturer who is first a specialist in production usually prefers to rely upon other agencies for distribution. Needless to say, capital investment is also an item that must be considered in attempting a direct channel between the consumer and the manufacturer. Where volume and inventories are large and prices irregular, manufacturers may wish to free themselves of this financial uncertainty.[3] Table XIV shows that manufacturers sell 76 per cent of their products to other manufacturers and to intermediaries and only 24 per cent to the six other classifications of buyers. Note that only 3 per cent are sold direct to consumers and that 30 per cent are sold direct to other manufacturers.

A difficulty of long standing that has been encountered by manufacturers who are selling through resale outlets is the question of building good will among the actual users of the products. Manufacturers are anxious, naturally, to be informed of any expressions of dissatisfaction about the product in order that they may make adjustments and that they may perhaps make changes in future products to overcome these difficulties. This at times becomes difficult when working through wholesalers whose interests are divided among many different products and who may not be in possession of the special knowledge regarding the product that would enable them to overcome objections on the part of the user or to pass on to the manufacturer an accurate description of the difficulty.

This problem of relations with wholesalers or agents becomes especially significant during periods of declining consumer demand, when the manufacturer feels the need for an "all-out" effort on sales yet can-

[3] See Agnew, Jenkins, and Drury, "Outlines of Marketing," pp. 26–28, for a discussion of these and other problems characteristic of the distribution of consumer goods as distinguished from capital or industrial goods.

not exercise exclusive control over the efforts of the agents. He may put his own representatives in the field to work with and assist the agents. He may step up his efforts in advertising and new sales promotion. But inevitably in these periods he often repeats the wish that he might have more complete control. In other words, when a manufacturer sells through a resale outlet, he may gain many advantages but he may find that he sacrifices the values to be attained through direct contact with the user.

THE SALES ORGANIZATION [4]

The organization of the sales department will vary, as do other departments in an industrial enterprise, in terms of the nature of the product, the size of the company, and the availability of personnel. In some instances, the head of the sales department reports directly to the president or executive vice-president of the company. Under him will come the various divisions relating to the functions, such as advertising and sales promotion. In some instances, advertising may be a division of the sales-promotion department. This is determined largely by the volume of work to be performed in any one of the stated functions. That is, if the company is one that engages in a large amount of advertising, the advertising department may be set up separately to avoid over-loading the manager of the sales-promotion department. On the other hand, if the manager of the sales-promotion department is an especially capable person, the company may wish to obtain the benefit of his executive ability in the management of both the advertising and sales-promotion functions.

The use of branch offices by large manufacturers, as previously mentioned, is becoming an accepted practice owing to the fact that it facilitates contact with the customer and supervision of salesmen or other distributive outlets. It is frequently advisable, particularly in instances where a company maintains a number of branch offices, to set up a manager of branch sales offices with a local manager in each branch. Each local manager will have his personnel of salesmen and general office people.

Some manufacturers make a further division in the organizational structure of the sales department by separating the sales personnel in accordance with the different lines of products manufactured. The real advantage of this division is that it permits the sales personnel to become specialized in their particular lines. This is all the more important in companies manufacturing mechanical products or items of a highly technical nature. Naturally a salesman may become more familiar

[4] See organization chart, Fig. 5.

with the technical details of the product if he is permitted to specialize in one or a few of the products. His task becomes more simple and he is better able to keep up with changes in design and variations in uses to which the product may be applied. Where branch offices are maintained, the various sales managers in charge of specialized lines will each work with the managers of the branch offices in order to obtain the acceptance of their particular lines.

Service Departments.—Practice varies in different companies in the placement of service departments in the organizational structure. Because of the very close relationship of service to sales, the service department is frequently placed under the supervision of the head of the sales division. In cases where branch offices are used, servicemen are placed in those offices under the supervision of the branch managers. If branch offices are not maintained, a separate service department may be set up parallel with the other departments of the sales organization at the home office. In some instances, the service department may be set up entirely separate from sales with the head of the service department reporting directly to the chief executive of the organization, to the works manager, or possibly to the chief engineer or other appropriate executive in a particular situation.

Case Example of Organization for Sales.[5]—The Apparatus Sales Department of the General Electric Company is presented as an example typical of the distribution organization of a product division of a large industrial enterprise. This department is concerned with the sale of electric apparatus to the following classes of customers:

1. About 10,000 large and 20,000 small industrial customers (manufacturing establishments, mines, quarries, and institutions). Also contractors, consulting engineers, etc.

2. About 2,500 large and 3,000 small central stations (private and municipal).

3. About 1,000 large and 1,500 small steam railroads and urban and interurban transit systems.

4. Government and war agencies (Federal, state, and municipal).

Electric apparatus ranges from turbine generators and water-wheel generators for the production of electricity; through transmission and distribution equipment as represented by transformers, lightning arresters, and switchgear; to products like motors and control in a customer's plant.

The chairman of the apparatus sales committee is the administrative head. He is assisted by the apparatus sales committee of 14 members.

[5] Adapted from the General Electric lecture series, summer–fall, 1942, by special permission.

Subject to the approval of the advisory committee, the sales committee determines general commercial policies, approves special types of sales contracts, approves certain expenditures and leases, and generally supervises the operations of the general office sales departments and the district offices.

The vice-president in charge of the apparatus sales department has a small staff, taking care of general functions serving the entire sales organization. The *manager of special contracts* takes care of sales contracts with certain of the affiliated companies and coordinates activities with them.

The three major sales departments are the central station, industrial, and transportation. The *industrial department* is responsible for those products which are most frequently used by industry such as motors, welding equipment, control equipment, and industrial heating equipment. In addition to seven product sections, the department has customer sections serving certain classes of customers who buy, for resale or for their own use, equipment that include items from two or more of the product sections.

The organization of the *central station department* closely parallels that of the industrial department. There are line sections, each responsible for products most frequently purchased by central stations such as generating and conversion equipment, turbines, meters, lighting, wire and cable, transformers, and switchgear. The *customer division* is concerned with sales made to holding companies and educational institutions.

The *transportation department* is responsible for sales to transportation companies generally of such products as electric and Diesel-electric locomotives, railroad electrification equipment, mining locomotives, street and rapid-transit cars and buses.

There are two specialized office sales departments. The *Federal and marine department* is primarily responsible for ship-propulsion equipment and for apparatus sales to the different departments of the Federal government. On account of the special requirements for bidding, adherence to specifications, inspection, and acceptance, characteristic of government business, this department has been set up to conduct this highly specialized work.

The second specialized department is known as the *Graybar-Western Electric department*. The General Electric Company has for many years sold large volumes of equipment to the Western Electric Company and the Graybar Electric Company. In order to facilitate servicing the orders received from these two companies, it was mutually agreed that this department would handle all commercial relations.

The *publicity department* is classified as a general department and serves all the apparatus sales divisions in preparing advertising and sales promotion campaigns for both GE salesmen and dealers. This department will be explained in more detail in Chap. XXVII.

The *distribution department* is responsible for maintaining adequate stocks of apparatus at distribution centers in the United States, operation of six regional warehouses, and supervision of finished stock on hand at the apparatus works. At four locations, this department also furnishes warehousing service to appliance and merchandise distributors and to affiliated companies.

The United States is divided into 10 districts with apparatus and supplies *district sales offices* located in Boston, New York, Philadelphia, Atlanta, Cleveland, Chicago, Dallas, Denver, San Francisco, and Portland. In addition to these, there are 71 other cities in which sales offices are maintained; 28 resident agents are located in still other cities. Warehouses are maintained as a part of the district sales office organizations in 26 cities, and service shops operate in 21 of them.

With the addition of accounting, financial, and order service sections, the organization of the district personnel parallels that of the principal general office sales departments. There are transportation, central station, and industrial salesmen organized along departmental lines in every district.

The *commercial engineering department* is responsible for the many orders that require special engineering owing to the size of the orders involved, to the fact that several works must contribute to the equipment ordered on the one requisition, to the fact that special designing engineering work is involved, or because of special installation work and service guarantees.

In each of the sales districts there is a *district engineer* responsible for engineering, installation, and construction in the field. These men assist the salesmen in solving the engineering problems that are constantly arising and in putting requisitions in such form that the factories can build the apparatus that will satisfy the customer's requirements.

The *district service shops* are under the supervision of the district engineers. These service shops are really small GE factories established to give quick repair service and, in many cases, to carry on special manufacturing operations and assembly work. One of their main values to the company is the fact that they are flexible to meet local needs and offer a convenient method of developing unusual apparatus applications for customers without incurring heavy engineering development expense. In addition to the regular service shops, certain of the factories maintain service shop sections in order to supplement their facilities.

The *contract service department* has the responsibility of coordinating engineering and manufacturing work for the following:

1. To circulate the working copies of domestic contracts to obtain credit, engineering, commercial, and legal approval.

2. To follow the progress of customers' orders in the engineering and manufacturing departments in order to keep the commercial and district offices informed of the status of orders.

3. To handle complaints concerning apparatus in customers' hands as intermediary between the district engineers and the works engineering departments.

4. To supervise the operations of the district service shops, receive and assist customers' inspectors, and obtain passports for General Electric people traveling abroad.

Foreign construction work is also done by this department for the International General Electric Company. Domestic installation and construction are carried on by the district engineering departments with assistance as needed from the contract service department.

Typical Zone Distribution Organization.—The following description of a General Motors *zone organization* is typical of the small unit of a large corporation operating under a decentralized plan of distribution.

Each car division has its own sales department and field organization; the parent corporation has a distribution staff which functions only in a policy-forming and advisory capacity.

Figure 164 shows the distribution organization typical of one of the car divisions under normal conditions. Indicated on the chart are the various functional activities carried on by a zone office which operates under a regional office and controls considerably less territory than a region. For instance, a car division may have 4 or 5 regional offices and probably 20 to 25 zone offices, each region handling 5 or 6 zones. The particular organization depends not only on geographic considerations but also on the total volume of business.

There are many variations of the zone office organization, depending on the volume in a particular zone and on whether business conditions are normal; for instance, in some cases the car distribution work and office management function are combined under one head; also, the parts, accessories, and service departments may be handled by one man.

It is important that the field organization be held flexible for adjustment to the size of the territory and volume and to the ability and aptitude of the personnel available.

That part of the chart above the direct dealer represents what General Motors terms the "wholesale" organization, while that part starting with the direct dealer is the "retail" selling organization. Dealerships

are independently owned and operated and, in some territories, especially in the rural sections, the direct dealer may have an associate dealer operating under him in a smaller near-by town. As in the case of the zone office organization, the functional departments shown under the direct dealer may vary according to the size of the dealership. For instance,

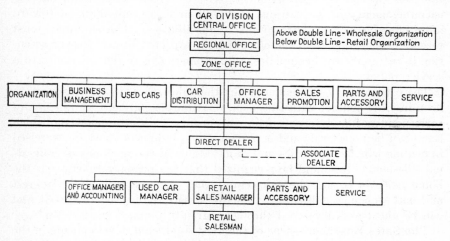

Fig. 164.—Typical distribution setup of a General Motors car division. (*Courtesy of General Motors Corporation.*)

parts and service may be handled by one manager and in a number of cases the new-car sales manager is also responsible for the used-car business.

Responsibilities of the Sales Manager.—It is not difficult to visualize the scope of the problems of coordination and management of any one of the variations of sales organizations just described. Effective selling requires that all activities of a sales organization be synchronized in the general sales plan. Advertising and sales promotion must be properly timed with the delivery of merchandise to the distributing agent in order to avoid confusion, misunderstanding, and complaint on the part of both customer and distributor. Salesmen's quotas must be established. Complaints of customers must be analyzed and adjusted. Means must be established for the detection of changing customer demands and the development of new products to meet those demands. Sales budgets must be established as a basis for the development of operation schedules for the entire company including production, financing, and personnel.

Perhaps the most important function of the sales manager is to exercise supervision over the personnel of the sales organization. This job becomes especially difficult owing to the fact that the personnel of the organization may be scattered throughout the world. Naturally the sales manager must depend largely upon the delegation of supervisory responsibility to the managers in branch offices and the various divisions of the sales organization. The sales office, however, plays a very important role through its correspondence with salesmen in the field, offering encouragement and suggestions that will urge the salesman on toward more effective performance of his responsibilities. The salesman must receive cooperation from the office if he is expected to give proper attention to the analysis of complaints of customers and to the adherence to a service policy.

There is apt to be a tendency for the sales office, in its eagerness to keep in close contact with salesmen, to require a burdensome amount of correspondence and reports from salesmen. This is a point on which there can be no set rule and is one on which judgment must be exercised in dealing with personalities and observations of the reactions of individual salesmen. It should be recognized that the primary function of the home office is to aid the salesman rather than control him. Interest and enthusiasm, a salesman's principal assets, should be protected and can be aided and developed through carefully planned supervision.[6]

The Sales Engineer.—One of the most significant developments in the marketing of industrial goods during the past twenty-five years has been the development of the sales engineer. Lester defines sales engineering as the art of selling equipment and services that require engineering skill in their selection, application, and use.[7]

The sales engineer must be both a salesman and an engineer. There are still some executives who feel that a satisfactory combination of these two in one individual cannot exist except in rare instances. This skepticism, however, is rapidly being dispersed by the performance of young men, trained through our engineering colleges, who were entering the field of industrial marketing in large numbers prior to World War II. Such companies as General Electric, American Steel and Wire, Crucible Steel, the brass industries, the machine-tool industries, and many others now depend extensively upon men trained as sales engineers in the marketing of their industrial goods.

The rapid growth of this idea is not at all surprising in consideration of the fact that the salesman of industrial goods is dealing with customers who are production and engineering specialists. The ordinary salesman who is not trained in engineering finds difficulty in gaining the respect and

---

[6] See Richard P. Crisp, "How to Reduce Distribution Costs," pp. 4–7, for an excellent description of questions that come from salesmen in the field.

[7] Reprinted by permission from Bernard Lester, "Sales Engineering," p. 3, New York: John Wiley & Sons, Inc., 1940.

confidence of this type of customer. He becomes totally ineffective in representing a job-order industry where products are developed in accordance with the customer's specifications. It is considered the function of a salesman to assist the customer in drawing up these specifications. As a matter of fact, the seller has a legal responsibility for checking the appropriateness of the use to which the product is to be applied. For example, a steel company that is asked to provide steel for an aircraft structure must check with the aircraft manufacturer in the verification of specifications that will allow for the necessary margins of safety. Failure to take reasonable precautions in the checking of specifications makes the supplier liable for damages resulting from the failure of his product. The sales engineer is particularly valuable in discovering adaptations of the product to new uses. This frequently requires some change in structure or design but may add to the uses of the old product or aid in the development of a new product. In World War II, Johnson's Wax salesmen became active in assisting production men and plant engineers in solving difficult finish problems, such as rust-inhibiting waxes for metal, water-repellent finishes for army uniform cloth, carton waterproofing, and rifle-bore cleaner for government arsenals. Here was a case where the company was attempting to make rapid changes in serving new needs. Direct contact with the customer through qualified sales engineers and chemists became a powerful aid in this adjustment.

Selection of Salesmen.—There may be special characteristics which we frequently observe in salesmen, but it is erroneous to refer to a sales *type*. Each person is a combination of characteristics which by their interaction make him an individual different from others. Therefore each person must be analyzed as an individual and not be given a "rough" classification. A salesman may be successful with one product and a failure with another. He may hit top and bottom with two companies handling competing products. He may be a good salesman in North Dakota and a failure as a salesman in New York City. There are too many factors peculiar to success in selling a particular product for a designated company to a selected group of customers in any one region to assume that there can be an over-all salesman type.

Acceptance of the principle expressed in the preceding paragraph establishes the basic pattern for the selection of salesmen; *i.e.*, each company must determine what characteristics in salesmen are important for the selling of each of its products to customers of each geographical region. It does this by studying its present salesmen.[8]

[8] See also Paul H. Nystrom, "Marketing Handbook," Sec. 16, pp. 645–693, New York: The Ronald Press Company, 1948, for a good and complete description of techniques used in the selection of salesmen. This reference also gives numerous examples of forms used.

The acceptable method of selection attempts to make a job analysis of the work expected of the salesman, using the principles and procedures outlined under Job Evaluation, Chap. XXV. From this analysis an interpretation is made of the personal characteristics necessary to do the job. Selection then follows in the regular manner as explained in Chap. XX.

The selection of salesmen today is giving emphasis not alone to the volume of sales within a given period but also to the reduction of turnover in sales personnel and the building of permanent favorable relations with customers. Turnover in personnel can be costly. There is the expense of original recruitment, training, and lower return on salary investment while in the beginning stage. But there is also the costly interruption of relations with the customer that may result in the long-term loss of business.

Training of Salesmen.—It is becoming the accepted principle that *all* personnel recruited for sales is in need of training. If we accept the fact that each company has its own peculiar requirements for successful selling, then we should conclude that each company will have something to teach. Even if the company found the rare individual who possessed all the developed abilities which they sought in a salesman, there still would be the job of endowing him with an understanding and appreciation of the background of the company, its production methods, its products and processes, its services, and its sales policies and procedures.

Most new salesmen in most companies will need even more training than in those items listed in the preceding paragraph. If he is inexperienced in selling, he will need to learn the basic fundamentals mixed with the opportunity to "break the ice and get his feet wet." His development must be nurtured with selected experiences in the plant and in the field that will build the necessary confidence, enthusiasm, and skill. Some companies may take as long as 4 or 5 years in this initial training period. A long period of training is especially necessary in the preparation of sales engineers, whose work was described earlier in this chapter.

Sales training may be classified generally into three types:

1. *On-the-job training.* Such training involves regular assigned work on a selection of jobs in the plant, in the office, and/or in the field. To be most profitable, jobs must be assigned under interested supervision capable of effective individual instruction.[9]

2. *Home office or branch schools.* These schools are used where there are sufficient numbers to be trained and where it is found that there is

[9] See Fig. 165 for an illustration of selected job experiences.

a common body of information and skills applicable to the needs of a group.

3. *Related education in outside schools and colleges.* The thinking of training directors seems to be moving in the direction of greater utilization of community schools and colleges in providing basic education and

	A SALES ENGINEERING WORK-STUDY PLAN	
	Individual Courses in College	Job Experiences in Company
1st Year	English Math. Physics Economics	One to two months in each of following: Factory crib, trucking, etc. Tagging wire, checking specs. Cable Dept. Tubing Dept. Service Dept. Crib at plant
2nd Year	Math. Mechanics Electricity Applied Psychology	One or more months in each of following: Insulating Dept. Planning Dept. Braid Dept. Shipping Dept. Scheduling Dept. Research and Testing Lab.

3rd Year	Senior Problems
	Marketing and sales
	Electricity
	Personnel
	  Administration
	Industrial
	  Organization
		Final year in Sales Dept. Writing specifications, checking orders and contracts, analyzing complaints, correspondence, follow-up on orders, etc.

FIG. 165.—An illustration of a coordinated plan of on-the-job training in the company and related education in the community college.

highly specialized subject matter for which the colleges are equipped with faculty and laboratories more adequate than can be provided by most companies.[10]

Usually a company will find it advisable to use a combination of two or more types of training in the preparation of its salesmen. It should also be borne in mind that the initial training of salesmen is only a part of the sales-training function. Actually, training should never end. If the sales force is to be kept alive and in step with changes in products,

[10] See Fig. 165 for an illustration of a coordinated plan of on-the-job training in the company and related education in the community college.

processes, personnel, customer wants, competitive developments, and improved sales methods and promotion, all the training techniques will be needed in a program of continuous training.[11]

CONTROL OF SALES COSTS

The Twentieth Century Fund in 1939 published a report of its research on the subject of distribution costs.[12] This report showed that in 1929 the cost of commodity distribution was 38.5 billion dollars, or almost 59 per cent of the total cost of the product. One-third of this distribution cost was for retailing, and one-fourth for distribution by the manufacturers.[13] A report prepared by Marvin Bower for the American Management Association in 1945 suggested the probability that the portion of total cost chargeable to distribution was then even higher.[14]

The cost of distribution is made up of such items as advertising and general sales promotion, transportation, packing charges, overhead expenses of various sales offices, service costs, installation costs, and the salaries, commissions, and expenses of salesmen. Up to a few years ago, little attention had been given to the analysis and reduction of distribution costs as compared with the work that had been done in the improvement of methods for the reduction of production costs. Since distribution does comprise such a large part of the sales dollar, it is worthy of careful attention and study. Perhaps one reason that more progress has not been made in reducing the costs of sales is that sales people have been considered "show" people. They were given a rather free hand in expenses as long as they were able to bring in the volume of business. Advertising men, who were strong believers in their power to sway the minds and buying incentives of people, felt that every possible means of getting before the public was of merit if it would sell the product, and that cost should be a factor of incidental consideration.

Today, however, management faces a cost problem that is far from academic. No longer is the problem only one of answering the public cry regarding distribution costs. The big issue now is how can we reduce our total costs in order to bring the price of our product within the reach of a larger market. Competition is pressing in with the decline in the backlog

---

[11] Further information regarding training principles and techniques may be found in Chap. XXI. See also Nystrom, *op. cit.*, Sec. 27, for an especially good discussion and illustration of sales-training plans.

[12] "Does Distribution Cost Too Much?" New York: The Twentieth Century Fund, Inc., 1939.

[13] *Ibid.*, pp. 117–118.

[14] "Reducing Distribution Costs," Marketing Series 58, New York: American Management Association, 1945.

of wartime demand. Customers are again price conscious. When a top executive takes a look at total costs, his eye dwells on the distribution portion because it represents one of the larger portions. He knows that for many years the plant has been driving hard toward the reduction of labor costs through methods improvements. It has made improvements in materials for cost reduction. Has it made the same scientific approach to the reduction of distribution costs? Too frequently the answer is "no." Here then lies opportunity.

One of the first steps taken by management is an attempt to educate sales people to the development of scientific steps in the analysis of consumer demand and in the planning of the cost and probable return from sales activities.

Through analysis, the more profitable areas geographically have been selected for concentration in the sales effort at the exclusion of those areas which would yield a smaller proportion of profit. The classification of potential customers as to income, profession, vocation, etc., has aided in the direction of sales effort and consequently in the reduction of sales costs. Sales departments are put on a budget which is arrived at cooperatively between the sales department and the central budget committee of the company. Through salesmen's meetings each man plays a part in the planning of sales activities and the budget to carry on those activities. By this procedure he is aided in the development of an appreciation of costs. It is one thing to make a sales cost budget, and it is quite another thing to live within it. To assist in the control of the sales cost budget, the sales manager together with the heads of the various divisions of sales should develop definite analysis and report procedures whereby costs may be compared for each division, each branch office, each sales activity, and so far as is possible the cost incurred by each member of the sales personnel participating in that activity.

As industry enters a highly competitive market, the necessity of careful analysis of distributive costs may become more pressing. If the company adopts a price policy based on distinction in quality with relatively small volume, cost becomes secondary, and advertising ingenuity may be given an almost free hand in any expenditure of money that will improve the quality appeal of the product. However, if competitive price becomes one of the principal sales appeals, cost becomes primary. It is then that the sales department must look to possible distribution economies. For example, it may be found that special promotional containers and wrappings may be replaced with a less expensive standardized container; printing on cartons may be simplified, using one color instead of two or more; free samples may be eliminated; catalogues and promotional pieces may be simplified and distributed more conservatively;

shipments of goods may be grouped with some reduction in the speed of delivery but also considerable reduction in transportation costs; salesmen may be discouraged from the practice of overloading a customer with stock, a large part of which may be returned with resulting expense to the manufacturer; credits may be reviewed more carefully for the reduction of debt losses and undue collection expenses; and billing may be centralized, permitting the elimination of separate billing departments in the branch sales offices for the improvement of efficiency and the reduction of billing costs. American industry is now at a period of development in the system of marketing where ingenuity in these and other economies may mean the difference between business growth and business failure.

SUMMARY

Efficient sales departments, through their planning and operations in the distribution of goods, become the backbone of industrial prosperity and independence. The extent to which they are able to distribute needed goods at the proper time and place determines the value of the industrial contribution to the society in which they operate. This requires organization. The organization for sales represents the machinery for efficient planning and control of distribution. Through efficient organization a sales department is able to extend the influences of an enterprise to all parts of the world, yet operate with much of the effectiveness of a small and local enterprise.

As industry faces what may be a new world era of social economic life, it is called upon to look at several related problems for which it must chart its course of action:

1. Can industry of a free-enterprise system provide as much security and as good a standard of living for all people as some would have us believe can be provided through the expansion of control by government regulations?

2. Special services accompanying products have been increasing because of stimulation by competition. This has added to an already burdensome cost of distribution. Pressure by consumers and government are demanding that this cost of distribution should be lowered. What can industry do in a competitive market to curtail services and other special items of distribution costs without thereby suffering an undue loss of business?

3. With the growth of big business a hierarchy of distribution agencies has developed which has not only added to the cost of distribution but has also removed the manufacturer from contact with the actual users of products. As a substitute for this direct contact through sales, the manu-

facturer has resorted to special marketing research devices as a means of determining customer needs and desires and as instruments of good will. These research devices are not only expensive but are in some ways poor substitutes for direct personal contact. What alternatives can be devised to reestablish the producer-consumer contact?

CHAPTER XXVII

ADVERTISING AND SALES PROMOTION

Advertising and sales-promotion activities are important parts of our present-day industrial system. Through advertising a manufacturer is now able to bring his products to the attention of an audience of world-wide buyers. The daily newspaper, the popular and technical magazines, outdoor signs, the radio, and various other media have become a part of the lives of our people. Through these media, the manufacturer is able to enter the lives of the people and bring to them pertinent information regarding the products they buy. Through this information he is able to provide them with a basis of comparison and selectivity in their purchases. In this respect advertising as a means for the dissemination of information is a service to the public.

Dr. Hans Zeisel, associate director of research, McCann-Erickson, Inc., reported in June, 1949, that the total advertising expenditure in the United States in 1948 was $4,830,700,000. This was an increase from $1,980,400,000 in 1939 and almost a 100 per cent increase over 1943.[1] These figures impress upon us the fact that not only is advertising a big business within itself but it is rapidly growing larger.

In addition to the more common forms of advertising, manufacturers carry on a great variety of other sales-promotion activities to aid in bringing their products to the attention of the buyer and to improve the service of the product to the buyer. Installation and servicing, hints on adaptability of the product to different uses, special exhibits, and information on the care of the product are only a few of the many activities that buyers have grown to expect.

ECONOMIC AND SOCIAL VALUES

In 1927, Stuart Chase and Frederick John Schlink wrote "Your Money's Worth," which presented to the consumer a critical and comparative analysis of "name" products. It sought to show that a highly advertised name did not necessarily carry a high value in product. In 12 years, more than 100,000 copies of the book were distributed. In 1933 Hallet and Schlink wrote "100,000,000 Guinea Pigs," which sold over 250,000 copies in six years. This too was an attempt to prove to the public that it had been gullible to advertising propaganda. Soon after

[1] *Printers' Ink,* June 17, 1949, pp. 27–29.

the publication of "Your Money's Worth" consumer clubs were organized all over the country for the further study of the comparative ratings of products. Then came various national product-rating services which in 1939 claimed 135,000 subscribers and four or five times that number of regular readers. These rating services classified products into three categories: *recommended, intermediate,* and *not recommended,* or under similar classification headings. Unfortunately, these various rating services were not always able to agree in their ratings. But nevertheless, they served to develop a consciousness on the part of the consumer relative to the comparative value of products. Many national organizations, such as the National Congress of Parents and Teachers, the American Nurses Association, the Federal Council of Churches of Christ in America, the American Association of Adult Education, the National Woman's Relief Society, and others have either conducted consumer study groups, assisted in formation of consumer cooperatives, or have taken an active part in the furtherance of Federal regulation over advertising and food and drug legislation.[2]

INDUSTRY'S SOCIAL RESPONSIBILITY

In days when consumer products were simple and choice limited, the rule of *caveat emptor* (let the buyer beware) was at least within the bounds of reason. It was considered appropriate that in a free economy each man should be his own judge of the relative merits of competing products.

Today the complexities inherent in the technical development of modern products are beyond the knowledge of the average layman. All sorts of mechanical gadgets have been added to automobiles, radios, refrigerators, and other consumer products as a means of vying with competition in the field. But how is the average consumer to judge the relative merits of this or that addition?

Not only are products more complex but the number of brands or makes in a product field are more numerous. Consider, for example, the problem that the consumer faces in shopping for an electric refrigerator. What features should he observe in making his choice from among the dozen or more popular names in the field? He probably recognizes that, at least, the refrigerator must have a good motor. But, since the manufacturer knows that the consumer will be unable to judge a good motor from a bad one and may throw it out of adjustment through needless tinkering, he seals the motor and tells the consumer that he, the manufacturer, will assume responsibility for the quality of the motor. The

[2] See *Business Week,* Apr. 22, 1939, pp. 40–52, for a concise history of the consumer movement and a selected bibliography on the consumer and his problem.

consumer needs only to place his faith in the reputable name of the manufacturer. And so the consumer goes from point to point, attempting to judge relative capacity, operating cost, efficiency, etc. But in all cases he finds that he must rely solely upon what the salesman tells him. As the consumer goes from one dealer to another, he becomes more and more confused since each dealer proves, to the satisfaction of the consumer, that his particular make is superior to any other. Finally, the consumer finds a personable salesman who is a friendly and appealing individual and who offers to "throw in a set of refrigerator dishes," and the decision suddenly becomes easy.

It is because of the plight in which the buyer finds himself that he turns for aid to the research laboratories of the Federal government and consumer organizations. Since industry does not seem to cherish this tendency of the consumer, what alternative can be suggested?

If industry is willing to stand on the merits of its products, it should be willing to shoulder its rightful responsibility for giving the consumer a fair and intelligent basis for judging competing products. It should be able through its advertising to make the consumer aware of significant points of quality and to provide simple tests to be used in judging that quality. It is not enough to invite the consumer to "look at all three."

The manufacturer must tell him *what* to look for and, most important of all, *how* to look. If the manufacturer is willing to place his faith in the basic intelligence and good judgment of free people in a free enterprise, he should be willing to sacrifice some of his ballyhoo about the good name of the company and the fancy but meaningless "dressings" of his product and devote some advertising space to the fulfillment of its proclaimed function—the dissemination of pertinent information.

TYPES OF ADVERTISING

Advertising may be divided into two principal types: advertising intended to promote the sale of a particular product and advertising intended for the promotion of an idea. The first type is the one most commonly used over a period of years. It is the type that conveys information regarding quality, price, and general desirability of a named product. It is a direct approach to the customer in an attempt to induce him to buy. This type of advertising is particularly important in introducing a new product to the market. The U. S. Department of Commerce found that it requires twice as long under ordinary conditions to sell a new product as it does to sell an equivalent product that has been adequately presented to the consumer through advertising by the manufacturer.[3]

[3] PYLE, J. F., "Marketing Principles," p. 590, New York: McGraw-Hill Book Company, Inc., 1936.

The second type of advertising which proposes to promote an idea is a more indirect approach to the customer. In many instances it may be intended as a means of keeping the name of the company before the public. Some have termed it "good will" or "institutional" advertising; others call it "publicity"; while the more severe critic may call it "propaganda."

Arthur Kaufmann, executive head of Gimbel's, said before the Poor Richard's Club in 1943, "The time to sell your business to the public is every day, and all the time—not once in a while when you get a hunch you should drop a large institutional ad in the paper—but every ad should say something about your institution in it."[4] Thus he was saying that the promotion of a name, an idea, or an institution is an important element in the building of an institution and of gaining its acceptance on the part of the public at large, recognizing that any institution, industrial or otherwise, is a part of our total social structure, and that to live and prosper it must become a valued part of that social structure. Through this type of promotion an industry prepares the way for and strengthens the more specific product advertising that may follow.

Many companies have built large special services departments to carry on this kind of work. Lecturers are sent out to appear before women's clubs, service clubs, and various groups of community and business organizations to speak on topics of general interest, content if the only advertising that they get is the announcement that the lecturer is a member of the X Manufacturing Company. Many large organizations, including railroads, the General Electric Company, General Motors, and others, have carried on this type of advertising very extensively for the past number of years. World War II, however, brought about a notable increase in this type of advertising. The restrictions on the production of consumer goods brought a scarcity of consumer products. The demand greatly exceeded the amount the manufacturers were able to supply. Consequently there was little point in the development of extensive product advertising. One might have expected that, with this condition, the volume of advertising would decrease. However, in the February issues of industrial periodicals, advertising volume was 10,983 pages in 1943 as compared to 9,157 pages in 1942.[5] There were two factors of probable greatest influence in this particular situation: (1) Taxes were high. Some companies were paying as much as 80 or 90 per cent on excess profits. Under Federal regulations, a "reasonable" amount of advertising could be justified as a part of the cost of production and consequently could be charged to war contracts. (2) Perhaps more important, manu-

[4] *Printers' Ink,* May 28, 1943, p. 19.
[5] *Industrial Marketing,* March, 1943, p. 110.

facturers were concerned lest the public would forget the company and its products owing to the absence of the products from the market during the period of war. Consequently, Nash Kelvinator ran a long series of ads conveying the idea that we must preserve the traditions of our American democracy to insure a lasting peace. Oil-burner manufacturers advertised the home of tomorrow and in some instances provided architects' drawings as a special service feature. The hope of the manufacturer was that by this service he would draw the attention of the potential home builder, and that, when peace came and housing construction began to flourish, the individual homeowner would think of this particular company in purchasing an oil burner.

But even after World War II when industry had returned to production for consumer use, other necessities for this type of advertising arose. Both wages and prices were spiraling. Industry found it necessary to justify to the public and particularly to its immediate community its resistance to spiraling wages on the one hand and the reasons for increase in prices on the other. Then in the late 1940's when public pressure came for the reduction of commodity prices, industry made extensive use of advertising space to inform the public of its efforts in the "war on inflation."

Institutional advertising of this sort becomes an important part of the total public-relations program of the company. It is an avenue of communication. Institutional advertising may originate anywhere in the plant. It may come from the industrial-relations department if the topic is one that is directly related to the work of that department. It may come from product development or from the finance division in cooperation with the department in charge of public relations. The job of the advertising department is to aid in the preparation of copy and layout and in acting as a clearinghouse in contact with the media.

ADVERTISING MEDIA

The selection of media for the promotion of an idea or product is a highly technical matter that should be based on careful, scientific research. Consideration must be given to the geographical area to be covered, the type of buyer to be reached, his habits and customs, and his psychological reactions. Because of its complications, the selection of the media usually requires the services of special research organizations which are equipped with experience and special facilities. Each medium has its special advantages. Newspapers, being a daily custom of the mass of people, are excellent avenues for obtaining immediate action. Consequently they are especially good in the advertising of consumer products such as food and clothing, these being items that are bought frequently and with relatively limited forethought. Magazines, as contrasted with newspapers, hold the attention of the reader and potential buyer for a longer period of time. Consequently they are more appropriate for idea advertising where sustained thought on the part of the reader is required. Outdoor advertising is favored for its geographical selectivity in that it automatically comes to the attention of all people who pass it.

The radio has gained wide favor during the past few years as a medium for idea or institutional advertising, since through entertainment the manufacturer may create good will and consequently develop future buyers. He reaches the listener through no pressure but instead entirely at the choice of the listener who tolerates the "commercial," which in better practice is very brief, in order that the entertainment portion of the program may be received. Thus, the promoter of a good radio program builds in the mind of the listener respect and admiration for the company as well as its services.

Various other media, such as direct mail, motion pictures, industrial exhibits, and instructional booklets, each have their particular advantages and may have a part in the total advertising campaign.[6]

THE ADVERTISING AGENCY

As previously mentioned, advertising and sales-promotion activities require the assistance of specialists skilled in the techniques of research and promotion within their particular fields. To serve this need, agencies have been organized consisting of groups of specialists—specialists in research, in the preparation of copy, in art, in production, in the selection and contact with media, in radio, and in other specialized functions. To the agency, the manufacturer delegates all or a part of the responsibility of his advertising and sales-promotion campaign. Needless to say, no specialist can properly carry on an advertising campaign for a manufacturer without obtaining close and continued cooperation from the personnel of the various departments in the manufacturing enterprise. Usually the manager of the advertising department in the company acts as liaison officer between the company and the agency. He provides for the services that must come from the engineering department regarding the technical phases of the product to be advertised, from the production division regarding process and operations through which the product passes, and from other departments that can supply specific information needed by the agency to make its work most effective.

In addition to acting as liaison between advertiser and media, the

---

[6] See Weiss, Kendall, and Larrabee, "The Handbook of Advertising," pp. 78–113, New York: McGraw-Hill Book Company, Inc., 1938, for a more complete yet concise discussion of media.

modern agency renders services of both a creative and advisory nature. These services, standards, and ethics are considerably advanced from the original advertising agencies, which were principally dealers in advertising space. In those days the agent merely bought space from the media and sold it at a higher rate to the advertiser. In fact the form of agency compensation in use today, whereby the agent draws a commission of 15 per cent from the media, is a carry-over. This usually represents his full compensation except where special advisory services are involved. In the latter case a special fee is arranged between the agent and the client (the advertiser).

The agency in most cases assumes responsibility for the selection of media, the preparation of copy, the making of engravings, arrangements for radio programs and talent for those programs, and all other special technical phases.[7]

COOPERATIVE PROMOTION

The growth of big business, the increase in competition, and the discovery of substitute materials and products have tended to bring about a greater spirit of cooperation between manufacturers within particular industries. The common practice in cooperative promotional activities is for manufacturers of an industry to organize an association to conduct a campaign for the welfare of the industry as a whole. Pyle reports that "the greeting-card manufacturers increased their sales 400 per cent in six years; the Oak Flooring Bureau increased the sales of its products 800 per cent in a period of a few years; the American Face-Brick Association expanded the combined sales of the manufacturers two-and-a-half times in four years."[8] These associations may carry on other activities as well, such as cooperative research as exemplified in the rubber industry.

FUNCTIONS OF THE ADVERTISING DEPARTMENT

Recognizing the valuable specialized service that may be obtained from an advertising agency as explained in the previous pages, one might be led to question whether the function of an advertising department can be justified. However, most advertisers go on record proclaiming that an advertising department is an essential for efficient operation. Hepner cites a study by the National Industrial Advertisers Association [9] where

[7] See ERBES, P. H., JR., Agency Service Is Expanding into Broader Range of Marketing Functions, *Printers' Ink*, Mar. 9, 1939, p. 13. See also Rochester Industrial Advertisers, "Practical Advertising Procedure," Chap. 24, The Advertising Agency, pp. 407–422, New York: McGraw-Hill Book Company, Inc., 1948.

[8] PYLE, *op. cit.*, p. 607.

[9] HEPNER, H. W., "Effective Advertising," p. 24, New York: McGraw-Hill Book Company, Inc., 1941.

they found that 40 per cent of industrial advertisers have both an advertising department and an agency; 20 per cent use an agency but have no advertising department; 14 per cent have neither an agency nor an advertising department; and 26 per cent have an advertising department but no regular agency service. These figures reveal that a total of 66 per cent of industrial advertisers have an advertising department.

The general functions of an advertising department have been listed as follows: [10]

1. Determining the appropriation.
2. Budgetary control of the appropriation.
3. Liaison with the agency.
4. Supervising advertising and marketing research.
5. Keeping in touch with representatives of important media.
6. Cooperation with the sales department and with other departments.
7. Distribution of advertising material.
8. Production and supervision of sales-promotion material.
9. Supervision of copy.
10. Merchandising the advertising.
11. Administration.

One other function has gained sufficient importance to seem to warrant inclusion in the list:

12. Participation in the preparation of materials intended for the improvement of employee relations.

Determining the Appropriation.—The preparation of any budget or part thereof should be a cooperative undertaking on the part of all departments affected and the personnel of those departments. In this sense the budget may become a coordinating influence—a goal toward which the personnel of an organization may direct their efforts with greater understanding and unification of purpose. The spread of participation will of course vary among companies and among departments within the same company. In better practice among larger departments a minimum requirement would be an appropriations committee within a department to work in cooperation with a central budget committee of the company or corporation.

Furthermore, it should be understood that the preparation of the budget appropriation is not merely an allocation of funds to be expended on advertising or sales promotion, but what is more important it is the planning of the production within the department and the approximation of expense essential for this production. Management views the allocation of funds in terms of what it is intended to produce. The budget must, of course, be held flexible to meet unanticipated contingencies in

[10] Weiss, Kendall, and Larrabee, *op. cit.*, p. 170.

the plans of the department and in the change in the requests that may be made upon it from other departments.

Budgetary Control.—It is expected that some special procedures should be established in terms of the peculiarities of the advertising department. For example, campaign plans are budgeted as to media to be used, material to be prepared, meetings to be scheduled and promoted, etc. Each phase of each campaign will have a financial budget allotment. This may be broken down even further by dividing the appropriation or budget allowance into geographic areas and making each branch office responsible for its particular area. As previously mentioned, it is to be expected that changes will be necessary as new developments occur. The control procedures are established in order that the purposes and the limitations of the budget may be adhered to and that the needed flexibility will be made possible. The control of the budget, as in the case of the preparation of the budget, is a cooperative undertaking and should be fully appreciated and participated in by the department as a whole.

There are, of course, many sundry expense items, such as office supplies, traveling expenses, rentals, and telephone, that will enter into the administrative expenses of the department. McMillan reports that a figure drawn up by the Association of National Advertisers in 1935 revealed that the administrative expense of advertising departments, including salaries, averaged 7.72 per cent. Even though this is a relatively small percentage of the total budget, it should be controlled and reported with the same care as the larger accounts.

It is expected that routine reports will be made to the central budget committee at designated intervals, usually each month. It is also expected that special reports on the budget will be prepared at the conclusion of specific projects.

Liaison with the Agency.—The exact nature of the function of the advertising department in its relations with the advertising agency will depend upon several factors. (1) If the product is of a highly technical nature requiring the interpretation by either an engineer or some other specialist with a technical background, it is to be expected that the advertising department will need to keep in close contact with the work of the agency. (2) The variety of products manufactured will influence the extent of cooperation that will be required between the agency and the department. Many other factors will enter into the picture, such as the volume of business, the number and type of media, and geographical coverage.

In most instances, the head of the department will assume major responsibility for liaison with the agency, calling upon his specialists within the department for various phases of technical detail. However, it should be remembered that the primary purpose in securing the services of an agency is to obtain knowledge and skills of specialists. Therefore, the principal function of a department in working with an agency would be the clarification of plans and policies of the company and the offering of special assistance on points of difficulty.

Supervising Advertising and Marketing Research.—Considerable attention has been given to organization for research in Chaps. VII and VIII. Because research is a highly specialized function, companies of medium size have grown to depend more and more upon outside agencies and trade associations. However, in the case of large companies, such as the General Electric Company, large marketing research organizations are maintained. In some instances, this function is sufficiently large in scope to justify a separate department within the company. More frequently, however, in companies of average size it is made a function of the advertising department. In such case, one or more individuals within the department should be given the specific responsibility of testing and research for the purpose of improving and evaluating the advertising carried on by the department and of improving the channels through which sales pass.

In many instances certain forms of advertising research are carried on by the media or the agency as, for example, in radio in the checking of program audiences to determine who listens and at what hours and the popularity of different types of programs. This, of course, is part of the broadcasting company's own research activity carried on as a means of improving its own business. But at the same time it provides a service for the client in the selection of programs and hours of broadcast to reach the potential buyers of a specific product. In the case of radio this research or testing is carried on principally by direct mail questionnaires, by telephone, or by personal interview. It is to be expected that an agency or the medium is in a better position to carry on this highly specialized research.

There are times when an advertising agency or an advertising department within a company may wish to carry on its own testing or research as a check on the report of the media agency or as a promotion device for the introduction of new products. For example, the Crane Company in 1943 issued a booklet describing its prewar bathroom fixtures. Accompanying this booklet was a consumer questionnaire asking what the consumer wanted in postwar fixtures. Did he want a bathtub with a side-seat? Did he want a connecting shower? And if so, how much additional would he be willing to pay? Did he want a square tub or a rectangular tub? How deep should the tub be, etc.? This questionnaire really served two purposes: (1) it supplied the Crane Company with information regarding the desires of the consumer, (2) it stimulated interest on the part of the potential buyers and caused them to look with anticipation upon improvements that might be forthcoming in postwar days. This type of contact with the consumer may be carried on either by the advertising agency or directly by the advertising department in the company. In either case the advertising department must assume an important role since it is in a position to know the possibilities for future development, and also because it should be in a position of contact with the consumer which is sufficiently close to feel his wants, desires, and dissatisfactions.

Contact with Media.—Although the advertising agency may have been given the responsibility for space buying with the approval of the advertising department, it is frequently considered advisable for the advertising department to maintain some contact with the media. Two purposes can be achieved by this direct contact. First, it gives the advertising department an opportunity to keep in touch with trends and developments. Frequently, through these direct contacts, suggestions may develop which only the company man who is familiar with the product of the company can visualize.

A second purpose in direct contact with media is the furtherance of good relations with the media. Media representatives feel, and rightfully so, that it is a part of their job to keep themselves informed regarding the companies that they serve, even though they may be serving them through agencies.

The advertising manager may feel that he should assume chief responsibility for this contact with media representatives. However, if the company is large, the number of media representatives calling upon him will make personal contact with the advertising manager almost prohibitive, except in a restricted sense. In this case, the advertising manager may well appoint a media man within his department to be responsible for maintaining the contact and relieving the advertising manager of at least some of his responsibility.

Coordination with the Sales Department.—Special mention should be made of the necessity for close coordination between the advertising department and other departments of the distribution division. This has been a problem within industries for many years. In fact, it may almost be considered a stage through which a department passes in its growth or development. Eventually, if the distribution division is under wise administration, there will develop a realization on the part of the personnel of all departments within the division that they are working toward a common cause, that their efforts if coordinated will complement each other, and that if their efforts lack coordination, a part of the effectiveness will be destroyed. For example, it is recognized that advertising aids the salesman, but it is also important to realize that the salesman may increase the effectiveness of the advertising if he is kept informed about the advertising schedule and is able to assist the dealer in the coordination of his local advertising efforts with the efforts of the advertising department and the agency of the company. The salesman is also in an excellent position through his direct contact with the buyer to detect grievances and to obtain evidence regarding the reception of advertising copy. If a good cooperative relationship exists between the sales department and the advertising department, salesmen can become valuable to the advertising department in assisting in the planning and follow-up of advertising campaigns. Similarly, the advertising department can be of great value to the salesman in doing everything to assist him in improving his service to the distributor or to the consumer.

There is perhaps no other department in the company that has more responsibility for service throughout the company than the advertising department. It is through this cooperation that the advertising department is able to obtain its material for the preparation of copy and for the organization of advertising campaigns. It is expected that the advertising department will be called upon to perform special promotion jobs for various departments. This it must plan to do as a part of its assigned responsibility. Means of control and coordination in the cooperative functions of the departments will be discussed in a subsequent chapter.

Sales Promotion.—Sales promotion as a specialized function may be established as a separate department or it may become a part of the advertising department. The scope of the function itself may vary greatly between companies. For example, in some companies the sales-promotion function may include specialized service and maintenance, or the handling of complaints and adjustments. In other companies where the amount of such service is large, a separate department may be established.

Usually sales-promotion materials are thought of as special booklets for distribution to customers, window and counter displays for dealers, and souvenirs and samples. In some instances companies may find it advisable to seek the services of outside agencies for some of these highly specialized materials. This will depend somewhat upon the volume produced and the availability of specialized personnel. In the case of special promotion booklets where copy is the important element, it is almost imperative that it be prepared by the advertising department. The Johns-Manville Corporation, for example, prepares instruction books for customers. The material for these booklets must necessarily come from the engineering department working in cooperation with the advertising department. The Cleveland Rock Drill Company produced at one time a small booklet answering questions regarding trouble experienced in operating tools. This is an effective means of attempting to train the users of the tools in proper care and maintenance, thus avoiding complaint and dissatisfaction and consequently promoting future sales among satisfied customers.

Many customers consider it a sales-promotion responsibility to assist dealers in providing service for customers. For example, in 1942, the General Electric Company, recognizing that the ability of their dealers to service refrigerators might make it possible for these same dealers to continue in business during the period of the war, organized special training classes for 3,300 dealers in 115 cities. Later, other courses on the repair of washing machines and electric ranges were organized. The company also maintained its own service depots to which the dealer could send special repair problems. In such case, the dealer was allowed a handling charge.

The automobile industries have, for many years, conducted training courses for repair mechanics. Other companies, particularly those dealing in the manufacture of production machinery, have developed special courses for the purpose of training the maintenance and engineering staff in the proper use and care of the equipment.

The advertising department may carry full responsibility for its sales promotion, or it may share in it as a cooperative undertaking. For example, in the case of training courses for dealers, the advertising department may have the responsibility of preparing the instruction manual for use in the courses, while the sales department may carry the responsibility for the actual conduct of the courses.

Supervision of Copy.—Some mention has already been made of the responsibility of the advertising department in the preparation of copy. This is particularly true in the case of producer goods, where the product is of a highly technical nature. Practical technicalities in the copy will require that the advertising department obtain much of the material from the engineerng and research division of the company. In the case of consumer goods of a nontechnical nature, much of the responsibility for the preparation of copy may be delegated to the advertising agency.

Merchandising the Advertising.—Mention has been made under Sales Promotion of the necessity for coordinating advertising with the activities of salesmen and dealers. This function is one of planning and follow-up which may be easily overlooked and which carries great significance in determining the degree of effectiveness of the advertising and, consequently, of selling. Usually, some one individual within the department will be given responsibility for working with the sales department in the promotion of coordinated activities.

Administration.—The function of administration in the department will be given special treatment in the section on Departmental Organization (page 699). It will suffice here to say that, regardless of titles and relative position, each function should be carefully delegated with appropriately defined lines of responsibility and authority.

ORGANIZATION OF THE ADVERTISING AND SALES PROMOTION DEPARTMENTS

Organization for advertising and sales promotion must necessarily be varied among companies in terms of the nature of the products manufactured, the number of different products, the variety of media used in advertising, the relationship with the advertising agency, and finally the factor which shows itself in the organization of all departments, namely, the qualifications of available personnel.[11]

McMillan reports that, in the examination of 262 national manufacturers, he found that in 105 of them the head of the advertising department carried the title of advertising manager. In one company the head of the department was called "assistant to the president." In 55 companies the head of the advertising department was placed in the rank of vice-president, although usually the vice-president was also in charge of the entire distribution division of the company.[12] It seems safe to say that in most instances we shall find the advertising manager responsible to the head of the distribution division, although there has been a strong attempt on the part of advertisers to encourage the establishment of a separate advertising division with the advertising manager reporting directly to the president or the general manager. The reason given is that the functions of advertising are expanding to the extent that it includes functions pertaining, not only to the sale of goods, but also to other activities such as the promotion of better employer-employee relations and the improvement of the coordination of personnel throughout the internal organization of the company. The advertising department is also being given a great amount of responsibility in public relations. The extent to which the advertising department is given the responsibility in areas other than the direct promotion of sales will carry a direct influence in the decision as to whether the advertising department should be a section of the distribution division, whether it should establish direct contact with

[11] See Chap. VI, for a discussion of organization in terms of availability of personnel.

[12] McMillan, G. S., Organizing the Advertising Department, in Weiss, Kendall, and Larrabee, *op. cit.*

the policy-making group, and whether it should be in a more independent position to work with the various departments or divisions of the company.

In the organization of the advertising department it is important, so far as possible, to separate the work according to functions, placing indi-

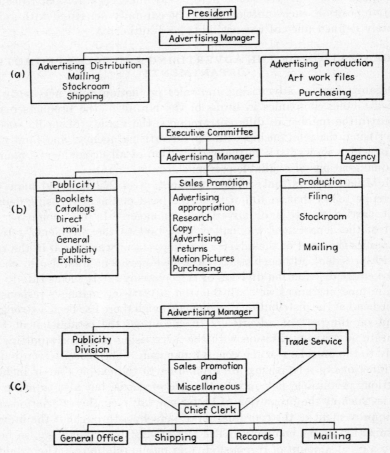

Fig. 166.—Advertising department organizations.

viduals in charge of one or more functions. A few illustrations will show how this division and assignment of functions may vary. Figure 166a makes a very simple division between advertising distribution and advertising production. Figure 166b groups the functions into three divisions: publicity, sales promotion, and production. It will be noted that in this figure the advertising agency makes its contact directly with the advertising manager. This is true in most companies, except in cases where the department is so large or the contact must be so frequent that an assistant to the advertising manager may carry the function of liaison between the company and the agency as his sole responsibility, or in conjunction with other functions of the department that may be assigned to him.

Figure 166c makes a somewhat different division of functions. Here the division is made in terms of publicity, sales promotion and miscellaneous, and trade service. The trade-service division assumes responsibilty for working with dealers and jobbers and for all special exhibits and industrial shows. Serving all three of these divisions is a centralized division operating under a chief clerk and broken down into four subdivisions: general office, shipping, records, and mailing.[13]

Centralization vs. Decentralization.—Where a company manufactures a variety of products, the problem always arises as to whether the department should be *centralized* or *decentralized*. In cases of this sort, the sales department is frequently divided according to product. If advertising is decentralized, it would be organized under each of these product divisions, *i.e.*, the divison handling a product would assume responsibility for the advertising of that product. If a centralized department is used, it is set up as a separate unit, serving all product divisons. The Hercules Powder Company is an example of a company that uses a centralized advertising department. This department assumes responsibility for all advertising, sales promotion, public relations, market research, certain employee services, and the operation of a printing plant. The department acts as a service agency to all departments of the company in any advance communication of facts or ideas. Naturally, a department that sets itself up in a position such as this may expect to be flooded with a great variety of jobs. However, this at times may be less irksome than to follow a policy that creates a new department every time a new job arises. Theodore Marvin, advertising manager of the Hercules Powder Company, enumerates some of the specific duties of their advertising department, which are reprinted here as an example of the variety of work that a centralized department may be expected to perform.[14]

1. Co-operates with sales departments in the planning and selection of sales promotion and merchandising avenues.

2. Prepares general and specific advertising compaigns which further the use of Hercules product, utilizing trade paper advertising, direct mail, publicity, personal contact, movies, or a combination of these media.

[13] See McMillan, *ibid.*, for a description of these and various other examples of departmental organization.

[14] Advertising Department Functions as Independent Unit, *Printers' Ink,* Apr. 9, 1943, pp. 46–50.

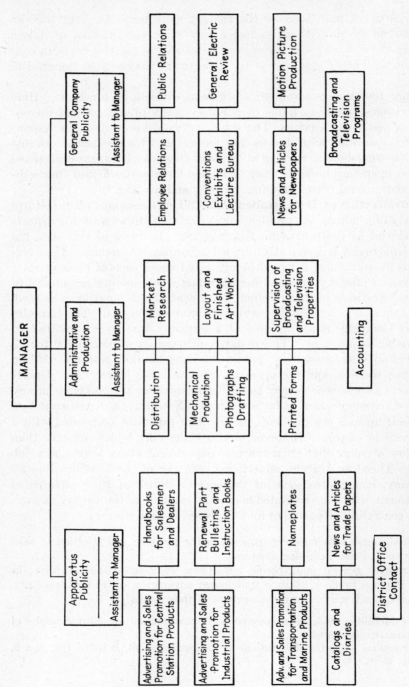

Fig. 167.—Publicity department organization. (*Courtesy of General Electric Company.*)

3. Produces and distributes booklets, manuals, handbooks, folders, leaflets, and calendars which promote use of Hercules products or which aid the purchaser in the application of our products. It reprints and distributes technical and service articles prepared by our technical men.

4. Through motion pictures, exhibits, house publications, and public-relations releases, it strives to increase industry's knowledge and esteem of Hercules Powder Company and its products and personnel.

5. It functions in an advisory capacity, obtaining information about advertising, merchandising, and distribution.

6. It fosters the company's family tradition by publishing "The Hercules Mixer," which is dedicated to the welfare of all our employees. It maintains jurisdiction over plant newspapers, checking on costs, printing efficiencies, and the work of the editors.

7. Its circulation division serves, besides its own activities, other home office units such as treasurers.

8. Its members, who belong to trade and technical associations, often serve on committees and present papers at meetings, thereby increasing company contact with a large number of consumers of our products, and gaining first-hand information for themselves of possible markets.

SUMMARY

Advertising and sales-promotion activities have reached a point of influence in present-day society where they draw significant attention from the manufacturer who sees in them a means for widening the area of distribution for his products. He sees in them also a constant threat since they may be used to even greater advantage by his more powerful competitors.

Advertising and sales-promotion departments in cooperation with outside advertising agencies have become specialized business within themselves. As such, they are service organizations to all departments of their respective companies and also are departments serving their own primary function, *i.e.*, the dissemination of information regarding products.

In considering the present status and possible future of advertising and sales-promotion activities, several basic issues stand out and seem worthy of careful study and deliberation:

1. Critics of advertising claim that advertising increases the cost of distribution and consequently increases the price that must be paid by the consumer; that advertising is an uneconomic practice from a broad social point of view; and that, if the cost of advertising were converted into the improvement of quality of the product or if the cost of advertising were eliminated with a resulting reduction in the price of the product, the consumer would benefit and the manufacturer would gain through increased sales.

Advertisers contend that history does not support these claims of the critics. They point to instances where advertising has over a period of years increased volume with a resulting decrease in price.

Both of these opposing points of view appear logical, but how can they be reconciled if true? Can other means be suggested for the dissemination of information that will promote the necessary volume in the sale of products but with less economic waste?

2. Advertisers point with pride to the fact that advertising has changed "the habits of a lifetime" and transferred products from the luxury to the necessity classification. This power may be beneficial and even essential to mass production of specific products. However, some people contend that this same power is a danger which threatens the economic and social stability of a nation whose people have already been "oversold." What restraints can control these possible harmful influences without undue disruption of the processes and progress of free enterprise?

3. Responsibilities assigned to advertising and sales promotion continue to increase in number and variety. Observe, for example, the attention which the advertising departments have given to the improvement of general employee morale, public relations, employer-employee relations, the development of training programs, etc. Where can we draw the line on this allocation of functions? Will the advertising department eventually be required, because of its ability in writing, to assume responsibility for all written correspondence between the company and outside contacts? Is it to be asked to take over an even larger portion of the original functions of the personnel department such as safety education, health education, employee recreational activities, and the recruitment of new employees? How can the logical functions of an advertising and promotion department be limited and defined?

4. In consideration of the huge advertising appropriations of larger companies, how can a small company hope to compete for attention in the presentation of its name and its products to the public? Will advertising eventually eliminate the small manufacturer? Is it possible that advertising of "name" products may hinder the introduction of new competing products? What recourse does the small manufacturer have against this possible development?

5. Does industry have a social responsibility for providing the consumer with a fair and intelligent basis for judging competing products? Can industry afford to give up its instruments of emotionalism and depend upon the exercise of intelligent judgment by people who are given adequate bases for judging?

CASE PROBLEMS

WATER-PUMPING EQUIPMENT AND ALLIED PRODUCTS [15]

In February, 1944, it was reported in *Sales Management* that only 17 per cent of the rural homes in the United States had running water. Manfacturers of pumping equipment and allied products considered this situation an opportunity for a huge postwar business. An analysis at that time of sales of electric water systems is shown in Table XV.

TABLE XV.—SALES OF ELECTRIC WATER SYSTEMS

Year	Units sold	Year	Units sold
1929	123,000	1937	182,000
1930	102,000	1938	175,000
1931	76,000	1939	220,000
1932	50,000	1940	260,000
1933	57,000	1941	347,055
1934	77,000	1942	239,072
1935	109,000	1943	155,000*
1936	149,000		

* Estimated.

It will be noted that in 1935 there was a decided increase in volume of sales of electric water systems. Manufacturers of equipment for water systems attributed this increase to a 5-year plan of promotion which was inaugurated in 1934. It will be noted that the increase in sales continued until 1943 and at that time was curtailed on account of the unavailability of material because of the war. The results that were obtained from this 5-year promotion campaign convinced manufacturers that it should be possible to develop further the source of potential customers in rural areas.

It was proposed that the new promotion campaign should be on an industry-wide basis in order to obtain the best results. Manufacturers of many different types of equipment would need to make plans to insure adequate supply for distribution. It was recognized that benefits to be derived from promotion would accrue to all related manufacturers.

Preparatory Questions

1. List the various kinds of equipment and services that might be involved in this plan for the promotion of rural water systems.

[15] Adapted from Pump Industry Sees Huge Post-war Volume Potential in U.S., based on an interview by L. C. Colby with H. C. Anster, taken from *Sales Management,* Feb. 1, 1944, pp. 98–102.

2. Comment on the appropriateness of each of the following types of media for use in this promotion campaign:

a. Magazines.

b. Newspapers.

c. Radio.

d. Outdoor advertising.

e. Rural associations.

f. Direct mail.

THE CLEARWATER CORPORATION [16]

The Clearwater Corporation is engaged in the manufacture and sale of building hardware. In a business such as this the sales forecast is very essential to the planning of materials and production, and of other items that must be budgeted in advance. The quota is arrived at cooperatively between the sales manager and the salesman involved. As a general rule, this quota is set on an annual basis but, during unusual periods of expansion or curtailment, budgets are constructed on a quarterly basis. Even then it is found that it is practically impossible to estimate sales within any reasonable degree of accuracy. A sales quota and control sheet for each salesman is kept as shown in Fig. 168. This forms a running account of the activities of each salesman.

The sales manager has found that during periods of unusually high business activity quotas have a negative psychological effect on salesmen. If sales in general are rising in excess of anticipation, the salesman is either inclined to "let down" or to become unduly optimistic, depending upon sales to come in automatically rather than through efforts which he might exert toward obtaining them. On the other hand, if sales are declining, quotas become an instrument of dissatisfaction and discouragement. In consideration of these negative effects the sales manager is proposing that quotas be set by a sales committee without the assistance of individual salesmen; furthermore, he suggests that salesmen should not be informed of their individual quotas.

Can you list positive elements that should accrue from individual participation in sales budgeting and that should be considered by the sales manager? Comment on his suggestion of a revised procedure for the construction and use of sales quotas. Can you make alternative suggestions?

THE COLES MANUFACTURING COMPANY [16]

The Coles Manufacturing Company for many years has been engaged in the manufacture of electrical appliances for the consumer trade. During World War II the company converted 100 per cent to the manu-

---

[16] Fictitious name.

SALES QUOTA AND RESULTS

Representative _____   Sales Territory _____

	Total sales	Floor trucks	Lift trucks	Racks	Platforms	Reports			Reports		
						New	Old	Total	New	Old	Total
January											
February											
March											
Total											
Quota											
April											
May											
June											
Total											
Quota											
July											
August											
September											
Total											
Quota											
October											
November											
December											
Total for year											
Quota for year											

FIG. 168.

facture of various types of insulated wire under subcontracts with manufacturers of aircraft and communications equipment.

With the close of the war the company returned to its appliance business to take advantage of the pent-up consumer demand. However, its product-development division has continued to experiment in the development of new manufacturing processes and with new materials that might reduce the cost of production of insulated wire. As a result of this developmental work the company is now ready to return to the wire business with the announcement of a new product which it feels can undersell the market.

Distribution of electrical appliances manufactured by the company has been entirely through a separately owned and separately organized distributing organization specializing in electrical appliances of several different manufacturers. The Coles Manufacturing Company is now faced with the necessity of decision regarding the distribution of insulated wire to the manufacturing trade on a job-order basis.

Preparatory Questions

1. What, if any, changes in channels of distribution would be necessary in the marketing of insulated wire as contrasted with the line of electrical appliances?

2. What new selling and service functions would be introduced?

3. What variations in advertising methods and media would be necessary?

D. Managing the General Offices

CHAPTER XXVIII

OFFICE AND ACCOUNTING CONTROL

Developing with the growth and modernization of American industry, office functions now have a new significance in the total organization of an enterprise. No longer can one think only of the more common activities of the accountant and the stenographer. Office work now plays an important part in the planning and control activities throughout the industrial organization. This development represents a challenge to specialists in office organization and management. Dependent on the ingenuity and efficiency of the office manager and his staff lies much of the future of modern industry. If industry is to continue to move forward in its increase of production with decreasing unit costs, continued improvements in methods of coordination and control are imperative. Industry is now loaded with a burden of paper work, much of which might be eliminated through further mechanization and simplification of office routines. The office manager must take his place with other staff specialists in the drive for improved efficiency in production and distribution geared to a new national and international economy.

The Function of the Office Manager.—In a large enterprise the office functions throughout the enterprise may become the responsibility of the office manager. In the smaller plant the function will probably be added to the work of the treasurer, controller, or chief accountant. The office manager is a specialist in charge of the organization of office functions, the designation of office personnel for specific functions, and the procedures for their performance. His duties should be approached just as scientifically as any other function of the enterprise. This means (1) job analysis for the purpose of determining a detailed description of the work to be done, (2) a selection of methods for performing the work and, where at all possible, standardization of methods to facilitate uniformity throughout the organization, (3) the selection of personnel best fitted to perform the job in question, and (4) training the personnel in the proper methods for performing the work. Each division of work, including correspondence and transcribing, materials follow-up, production follow-up, accounting, duplicating, filing, and messenger service, calls for specific analysis and for personnel with special qualifications.

707

Some people are better suited to calculating and recording functions, while others adapt themselves better to the correspondence and interviewing classifications that require direct contact with people.

Centralization vs. Decentralization.—The old controversy of what functions should be centralized and what should be decentralized occurs in the organization of office work as in all other management functions. The problem is one that requires careful analysis of each service in terms of the degree of skill required, necessary variations between departments, turnover of service personnel, the efficient use of equipment, standardization of forms and procedures, the efficient use of the time of executive personnel, and other factors entering into the problems of any specific enterprise.

Perhaps the most common form of centralization in industry provides for centralization of control but decentralization in the physical layout of workplaces. This permits the functional location of office operations, yet provides a measure of specialized supervision. This plan of centralization incorporates the principal functions of the office manager as previously stated, *i.e.*, the organization of office functions, and the designation of personnel and procedures to perform those functions. Applying this, for example, to the supervision of engineering clerks, an engineer might designate *what* is to be done, but a special office supervisor will designate *who* and *how*. This form of centralization also affords a compromise more satisfactory to the executive who insists on the assignment of specific individuals to his work.

Office Equipment.—As industry moves toward the division of labor for the performance of specialized functions, it may also benefit from the selection of special equipment to serve those special functions. For example, it would be unreasonable to expect that a standard, 6-foot, kneehole desk of the executive type would be equally adaptable to the work of all clerks, stenographers, and executives. Similarly, book-keeping machines must be selected and adapted to the needs of the particular enterprise. Manufacturers of this equipment now maintain large service departments for the purpose of assisting the purchaser in analyzing the equipment requirements of the various office functions in his company. Once this analysis has been completed and agreed upon, ideally the department then seeks to suit the equipment to the job. Unfortunately, at times it is not always possible to make the necessary equipment adaptations. Then the purchaser must either seek to meet his needs elsewhere or change the requirements of the job.

Accounting Control.—Any well-managed industrial enterprise must establish procedures for regular and prompt reporting of its operating conditions. These reports are basically historical in that they present an account of operations over a given period of the past and, therefore, reveal the conditions of the present. There are two basic financial reports: (1) the balance sheet, which is a statement of assets (what the company owns in cash, inventory, notes receivable, accounts receivable, etc.) and the liabilities (what the company owes in notes payable, accounts payable, etc.). The difference between the assets and the liabilities represents the net worth of the enterprise.[1]   (2) The profit-and-loss statement reports the income from the sales of goods and services for a given period and the expense incurred through the production and distribution of the goods and services. The difference between the income and the expense represents the profit from operations.

These two basic financial statements are the key reports prepared for the guidance of top management. Naturally, a large number of additional reports are prepared in terms of the requirements of a particular enterprise. It has been said that they report the operations of the past and the conditions of the present. Yet, perhaps their primary purpose is to aid management in projecting plans for the future. Through the analysis of these statements, management constructs guideposts for the development of policies and procedures for future operation.

The necessary data for these reports can be obtained only through a well-organized system of records. These records should be as simple as the specific requirements of the enterprise will permit. It is true that there may be certain basic principles more or less generally applicable to any enterprise. Yet variations are so numerous that they greatly outweigh any principles that might be called general. Several very good studies have been conducted over the past ten years in an attempt to establish guiding principles in accounting which would be generally applicable to all types of industrial enterprise. The Haskins and Sells Foundation sponsored such a study in 1935.[2] Generally speaking, the financial records must provide procedures for the recording of all transactions which add to or subtract from the capital of the enterprise and those transactions which add to or subtract from the income or earnings of the enterprise. An internal check for accuracy must be provided which will serve to assure accuracy of records and which will make possible a verification at least annually for the benefit of the interests of the enterprise and of the stockholders.

---

[1] Financial statements are discussed more in detail in Chap. XXX.

[2] MacDonald, John H., "Controllership: Its Functions and Technique," New York: Controllers Institute of America, 1940. A summary of these principles is given on pp. 69, 70. On p. 70, MacDonald also reports a summary of a paper presented by Charles B. Couchman, read before the Finance Conference of the American Management Association, in January, 1940, pertaining to the same subject.

These records must, of course, go further in the arrangement of transactions in such a way that they will lend themselves to analysis. For example, the records showing the purchase of equipment must be arranged so that the value of each type of equipment may be readily ascertained and that its depreciated or *book* value may be identified. The book value of a given piece of equipment is determined by deducting from the purchase price an amount estimated for general depreciation and obsolescence. Any system established for the purpose of recording financial information regarding the operations of an enterprise is generally known as *bookkeeping*. The most acceptable form of bookeeping system uses a double-entry record procedure. The principle of double-entry bookkeeping is based on the two opposing phases of the balance sheet: assets on the one hand and liabilities on the other. For example, an entry showing the purchase of equipment would add to the equipment account, an asset. If the equipment was purchased for cash, the other half of the double entry would record a reduction in cash, another asset account, which means there was simply a change in assets with no change in the net worth of the enterprise. However, if the equipment was purchased on account, no reduction would be made in the cash account but a liability account would be set up, an account payable. In this latter case, the liability entry would balance the asset entry, again resulting in no change in the net worth of the enterprise. Assume, however, that an entry is being made for the depreciation of equipment. Here, one-half of the entry would deduct from the equipment account, an asset, while the other half of the entry would add to the depreciation expense. Here we have had a decrease in the asset, equipment, with no corresponding decrease in liabilities. Thus, the net worth of the enterprise has been decreased by the amount of depreciation recorded.

The Function of the Controller.—The controller of an industrial enterprise is responsible for the records and reports of internal finances. In a large enterprise he is usually responsible to the chief operating executive. However, practice relative to the line of responsibility varies greatly. In some companies the controller may be responsible to the president. the treasurer, the board of directors, or a finance or executive committee. In a small organization, the treasurer will usually assume the controller function.

C. E. Knoeppel in an address to the Chicago chapter of the Controllers Institute of America in 1935 defined controllership as the coordinating, planning, and control of profits. According to him the controller should be in an investigative and advisory position on sales and production control as they relate to the finances of the business. The controller has been referred to by many people as the right hand of management and the chief adviser on all internal financial affairs. On many occasions he is the budget officer, a position through which he may exercise the breadth of function advocated by Mr. Knoeppel.

The Controllers Institute of America has developed a standardized statement of specific duties that may be outlined in a by-law when a corporation desires to set forth the controller's duties in detail. [3]

The Controller is specifically charged with the following duties:

1. The installation and supervision of all accounting records of the corporation.

2. The preparation and interpretation of the financial statements and reports of the corporation.

3. The continuous audit of all accounts and records of the corporation, wherever located.

4. The compilation of production costs.

5. The compilation of costs of distribution.

6. The taking and costing of all physical inventories.

7. The preparation and filing of tax returns and the supervision of all matters relating to taxes.

8. The preparation and interpretation of all statistical records and reports of the corporation.

9. The preparation, as budget director, in conjunction with other officers and department heads, of an annual budget covering all activities of the corporation, for submission to the board of directors prior to the beginning of the fiscal year. The authority of the controller, with respect to the veto of commitments or expenditures not authorized by the budget, shall, from time to time, be fixed by the board of directors.

10. The ascertainment currently that the properties of the corporation are properly and adequately insured.

11. The initiation, preparation, and issuance of standard practices relating to all accounting matters and procedures and the coordination of systems throughout the corporation, including clerical and office methods, records, reports, and procedures.[4]

12. The maintenance of adequate records of authorized appropriations and the determination that all sums expended pursuant thereto are properly accounted for.

13. The ascertainment currently that financial transactions covered by minutes of the Board of Directors and/or the executive committee are properly executed and recorded.

14. The maintenance of adequate records of all contracts and leases.

15. The approval for payment (and/or countersigning) of all checks, promis-

---

[3] *Ibid.,* pp. 7, 8. See also Rautenstrauch, Walter, and Raymond Villers: "The Economics of Industrial Management," New York: Funk and Wagnalls Company, 1949, p. 4.

[4] It should be noted here that in a large organization the office management function is usually delegated by the controller to an office manager.

sory notes, and other negotiable instruments of the corporation which have been signed by the treasurer or such other officers as shall have been authorized by the by-laws of the corporation or from time to time designated by the board of directors.

16. The examination of all warrants for the withdrawal of securities from the vaults of the corporation and the determination that such withdrawals are made in conformity with the by-laws and/or regulations established from time to time by the board of directors.

17. The preparation or approval of the regulations or standard practices required to assure compliance with orders or regulations issued by duly constituted governmental agencies.

The Auditing Function.—Most large companies maintain an internal audit procedure as a function of the general accounting department or in a separate department under the controller. This function includes the checking of payroll, inventories, and the general books of the enterprise. The importance of this function is emphasized where the enterprise maintains a large number of branch plants and subsidiaries scattered over a wide geographical area. Traveling auditors provide a check on accuracy but perhaps their most important function is to promote the standard accounting practices that have been adopted by the enterprise. Naturally, in such matters as payroll and inventory, a check of a sample of not more than 50 per cent is practical. In the case of payroll, the auditor checks the worker's account card, which shows the number of hours worked, against time-clock readings, wage payment, etc. He also checks on alterations within the wage system, and the time studies which may have been used as a basis for such changes, in his attempt to verify the adequacy of method and the results obtained.

The internal audit is entirely a company proposition as contrasted with the annual audit by an independent firm of accountants, which is for verification of the financial records of the enterprise in the interests of its stockholders.

Payroll Department.—The work of the payroll department has become greatly expanded during recent years with the introduction of Federal wage regulations, deductions for Social Security, group insurance, union dues, and various taxes collectible at the source of income. These regulations and deductions from payroll complicate the mechanics of the payroll department not only through the increased volume of bookkeeping but also because of special reports that must be prepared. Each employee is entitled to know the amount of each deduction from each pay check at the time that he receives it. The Federal regulatory bodies require both individual accounts and group summaries arranged in such a way as to facilitate a periodic audit.

When a new employee enters the enterprise, the employment office prepares a record which is routed through the payroll department where information pertinent to that department is recorded.[5] An individual record for the employee is then set up in the payroll department. This becomes his permanent record for the recording of all pay checks and deductions. If the employee is on an hourly rate, a clock card is issued. This card becomes the source of information for the recording of hours worked and the calculations of pay. There are various supplementary records, such as work orders, which may be used as a cross check for the verification of time worked.

Figure 169 gives an illustration of a payroll summary. A copy of this summarization is sent to the accounting department where entries must be made to the various deduction accounts, such as union dues, taxes, and insurance.

If the employee is paid by check, a statement of deductions may be attached as shown in Fig. 170. This becomes the employee's own record for verification and future reference. This report to the employee becomes particularly important where the amount of pay will vary from week to week, owing to variations in the amount of overtime work, and consequently the amount to be deducted for taxes and other items.

In a large enterprise, the work of the payroll department may be greatly facilitated through the use of special machinery, such as tabulating and recording machines, addressographs, and other equipment.

The actual details of the records of the payroll department will naturally vary with the enterprise and in terms of variations in wage systems. Payroll records maintained under incentive payments systems, as described in Chap. XXIV, are more complex than records necessary when the plant is paid in terms of time spent on the job. For example, if the enterprise is operating on a piecework basis, record forms would have to be altered for the procurement of information relative to the production of each employee and consequently the amount of pay that he is to receive. Each enterprise will have a group of salaried employees whose pay does not vary with overtime or the volume of production. These employees would be handled either through separate record forms or forms specially earmarked so that they will be excluded when calculating variations in the weekly payroll.

The responsibility for the payroll department is usually delegated by the controller to a *paymaster*. In a large enterprise the payroll department is subdivided in terms of various functions, such as timekeeping, payroll calculation, and payroll reports. A supervisor is appointed for each function and is responsible to the paymaster. Even though em-

[5] See illustrations of employee record cards in Chap. XX.

DEPARTMENT__________ SHEET NO.________

PAY ROLL NO.__________

LOCATION__________

PAY ROLL FOR PERIOD 19 TO 19

REMINGTON RAND INC.— MADE IN U. S. A. FORM NO. 50-5010

	DEPT. OR CLOCK NO.	SOCIAL SECURITY NUMBER	EMPLOYEE NAME	HOURS OF WORK									TOTAL DAYS	RATE OF COMPENSATION	COMPENSATION				EMPLOYEE PAYROLL DEDUCTIONS				NET PAYROLL	
					S	M	T	W	T	F	S	TOTAL			REGULAR PAY	OVERTIME PAY	OTHER	TOTAL	FED. O.A.—%	OTHER	MIS'CL DEDUCTIONS A/C NO.	MIS'CL DEDUCTIONS AMOUNT	AMOUNT	CHECK NO.
				O.T.																				
				REG.																				
				O.T.																				
				REG.																				
				O.T.																				
				REG.																				
				O.T.																				
				REG.																				
				O.T.																				
				REG.																				
				O.T.																				
				REG.																				
				O.T.																				
				REG.																				

FIG. 169.—Payroll record by department. (*Courtesy of Remington Rand, Inc.*)

FIG. 170.—Pay check with deduction slip attached. (Courtesy of Standard Register Company and Liquid Cooled Engine Division of The Aviation Corporation.)

ployees of the payroll department may be scattered throughout the plant, it is important that they should be directly responsible to the paymaster for the standardization of payroll procedures.

The Tax Department.—Accounting for taxes has become one of the major functions of the controller. In a small company, this is handled in the general accounting department; in the larger company, a special department is organized, as shown in Fig. 15. It is the responsibility of this department to calculate all taxes on the basis of the general accounting records, including reports of payroll deductions for taxes, the taxable earnings of each employee, the excess profits tax of the corporation, and all other taxes or deductions subject to state or Federal regulations. A significant part of the function of the tax department lies not only in the mere recording and reporting of taxes but in advising the controller relative to action that should be taken in anticipation of taxes.

For example, Federal regulations permit a company to purchase insurance for employees with a maximum premium equal to 5 per cent of the net earning of the employee. If the company is paying a tax of 75 per cent, the net cost of such insurance to the company would be only 25 per cent of actual premiums. Management might well consider that present and future values of such action are well worth the relatively small investment. As another example, contracts with educational institutions for the organization of training programs for the company can be purchased covering a period of several years, yet arranged in such a way that payment chargeable to operating costs can be made in one year, since the value of benefits in subsequent years cannot be calculated. Projects such as these not only are permitted but are expected of a progressive management that looks toward continued improvement in benefit to the enterprise and the society in which it operates.

Credit Department.—Practically all sales in an industrial enterprise are made on a credit basis as contrasted with over-the-counter cash sales of a retail establishment, thus emphasizing the role of the industrial credit department. The credit manager in charge of the department is responsible for the establishment of policy and procedure which will enable the enterprise to maintain and possibly expand in sales volume, yet at the same time to avoid unnecessary losses through bad accounts and to avoid an undue drain on working capital. This means that the credit department must establish effective sources of information regarding the financial status of its present and potential customers. It also means that it must work very closely with the sales department and with the financial heads of the enterprise.

There is a natural tendency on the part of enthusiastic salesmen to urge the approval of credit arrangements with customers. The salesman is interested in volume and, if he is a good salesman, he should also be interested in extending every possible service to his customers. He may be unappreciative of the fact that when he oversells a customer he may be doing him a disservice, *i.e.*, if through the overpurchase of inventories and equipment, the customer is forced into a strained financial condition, he may lose his credit rating and actually face business disaster. It should be the responsibility of the credit department to work with the salesman in determining the amount of credit that should be extended to the customer, both in the interests of the company and of the customer.

There are numerous sources of financial information regarding customers. Financial houses, such as Dun and Bradstreet, publish listings of credit ratings and, upon request, will prepare special reports regarding a specific enterprise. Trade associations may also maintain a credit bureau as a service to their members. The salesman is perhaps one of the most valuable sources of information. Through his contact with the customer he can obtain pertinent credit information, such as a copy of the current balance sheet, profit-and-loss statement, and other financial statements which may reveal the current operating status. Care should be taken to view such statements critically, making sure that they present an accurate picture of the present, since the financial condition of an enterprise may change rapidly. If the salesman is receiving a large order, he may ask the customer to prepare a special statement of specific information of existing liabilities, advance production orders, etc.

The amount of sales that can be tied up in accounts receivable must naturally depend somewhat upon the amount of working capital available for this purpose. An enterprise with a good financial policy will attempt to avoid the maintenance of an undue amount of working capital which would lie idle. Yet there is danger of overconservatism. It is possible that an enterprise would be so cautious in the administration of its credit policy that good credit risks would be refused certification with a consequent loss of business. This problem can be solved only through the careful preparation and administration of a flexible budget and through advance preparations for expanding financial resources. For example, where credit volume threatens to exceed the financial resources of the seller, it is possible for the seller to request from the customer a negotiable acknowledgment of the indebtedness. This is commonly termed a "credit instrument." It may be used by the seller to obtain credit from financial houses in order that he may pay his own bills.

There is a very close relationship between the certification of credit and the administration of collection procedures. Care in the first step will greatly facilitate the second. Customers may be classified roughly into three groups: (1) those who always pay their accounts promptly when due, (2) those who are considered good risks but are slow in payment, and (3) those who are questionable or poor credit risks. Unfortunately, it is not easy to classify an enterprise into any of these three groups and be assured that the classification will remain permanent. Circumstances beyond control may force the customer into a situation where it is not possible to meet accounts promptly. There are always those customers who appear to sway back and forth between two classifications. These are the customers who require the careful and personal attention of the credit department, lest misjudgment result in the loss of a potentially good customer or overconfidence in him result in a loss through a bad account.

Cash discounts are usually allowed to customers for payments within 10 days of the date of sale. This is a special inducement for prompt payment, thereby reducing the credit risk and also the drain on working capital.

It is the responsibility of the credit department to develop regular follow-up procedures for the collection of overdue accounts. A follow-up immediately after a due date would be nothing more than a routine reminder. Each successive step thereafter becomes more pointed and drastic, finally resulting in the placement of the account in the hands of a collection agency, which approaches the account from a purely impersonal and unsympathetic point of view. Most companies prefer to have this last step handled by an outside agency rather than to be forced to insert unpleasant procedures into its own collection policy that might have a negative effect upon public relations. At times a company may establish its own collection agency to administer this final step with difficult accounts. In such case, the agency usually bears a different name in order to minimize its relationship to the parent company.

COST CONTROL

Cost accounting is a part of the total accounting organizational procedure. It concerns itself with the accumulation of facts pertaining to expenses of the enterprise which are chargeable to a particular period of operation, to a given department, to a specific product, or to a single manufacturing operation. No attempt will be made in the brief space allowed in this chapter to offer a description of the cost accounting processes. Attention will be confined to an explanation of the elements that comprise the costs of a manufacturing organization and an introduction to the means for their control.

Purposes of Costing Procedures.—There are three primary purposes of costing procedures. Such procedures serve as

1. An important element in determining the selling price of a product.

2. A measure of the efficiency of operation.

3. A check on whether certain lines of products are profitable to the operations of the enterprise.

It has been stated that the primary purpose of an industrial enterprise is to make a profit. That profit is interpreted as a return on the investments of the stockholders. Stated another way, a manufacturer sells time of buildings, equipment, and personnel. This time is used in transforming material or products into items of greater utility to the buyer. The cost of the time allocation to a particular product plus a reasonable profit determines the selling price of the product. It, therefore, becomes apparent that the manufacturer must have some means for determining cost in order that he may determine selling price.

Any information that may be obtained from previous experience on similar products will naturally be of value in the preparation of cost estimates for the new product. Such factors as the amount of material required, the amount of labor involved in the manufacturing operations demanded by the product, and special items such as die costs and tooling setup charges are of special consideration. Added to this must be a proportionate amount of the general or overhead expenses of the enterprise that can be charged to the product. In serialized production, manufacturing standards may be established for a broad line of variation in the parts of the product, these variations being necessary to meet customer demands. From experience, the manufacturer determines cost involved for each part variation. When the order is received from the customer, the cost of the parts required in product specifications are added together to make up the price quotation. However, in a job plant, where the customer's order may call for specifications that have not been experienced by the manufacturer in previous orders, the problem of estimating becomes much more difficult. The only basis available is to analyze previous jobs for at least some elements of similarity. To facilitate this comparison of the new job with previous jobs, some job plants arrange classifications depending, of course, upon the complexity and number of operations required for manufacture. Each classification is given a unit cost estimate, *i.e.*, cost may be estimated in terms of the weight of the product, its rectangular area, or some other distinguishing factor which will provide the best possible measure of cost variation. These classifications, however, form only a rough estimate and may prove inadequate where the margins of profit tend to become smaller through the influence of competition.

Once the selling price is quoted the manufacturer must find means of controlling his costs in order to keep them within the bounds of his price quotation. He must obtain data on the waste of material which may be occurring through spoilage, poor planning of operations, faulty workmanship, or many other possible circumstances that may increase costs and consequently reduce profits. He must develop a continuous source of factual information regarding the man-hour efficiency of personnel—is production conforming to the man-hour requirements that have been previously estimated or experienced through previous periods? And so we might go on through all the elements of costs, showing that for each there must be a means for control if the enterprise is to operate efficiently and profitably.

It may be that an analysis of cost data will show that a given product or line of products is unprofitable to the enterprise. This may be due to the price of material, competition of other companies manufacturing a similar product, or other circumstances peculiar to this particular product. In such case the manufacturer must consider the total advisability of continuing the product at a loss or comparatively small profit, or discontinuing it from production. Other factors that should be considered in making this decision have been discussed in Chap. VII.

Organization for Control of Costs.—Ideally, the cost department is one of several departments coming under the controller. However, in actual practice we find that the cost department may be a part of the production-control department, industrial-engineering department, or methods department, or it may be set up as an entirely separate staff department reporting to the general manager or executive vice-president. The reasons for variations in organization which were cited in Chap. VI are applicable to this variation as well. There is still another factor that has contributed largely to the separation of the function of cost control from the general accounting offices in many industrial organizations. For as long as industry has existed there has been the problem of misunderstanding and conflict between the man of the shop and the man of the office. In years past they have been men of different backgrounds. They developed different methods of work and of handling people. The man of the shop spoke a language of machines, material, and production. The shop foremen developed a reputation for their hard disciplinary procedures and the no uncertain manner in which they dealt with workmen, especially in those moments of rage that called forth all a good foreman possessed in the way of a self-styled vocabulary.

Place beside this shop foreman a man who has been brought up with books, ledgers, and the virtues of a white collar and clean fingernails. The latter was the man of the front office. From the moment that he started in as office boy he learned the courtesies of office routine, the idiosyncrasies of the chief executives, the irate customers, and slippery salesmen, but he also learned to keep out of the shop. That was another world all its own. It is to be expected, therefore, that when the need for detailed cost information regarding the operations of the shop was recognized by management means were sought that would not require the intermingling of these contrasting personalities. Fortunately at that time perhaps, it was found that this information could be obtained efficiently through the establishment of a separate control unit in the shop with responsibility for cost records subsidiary to the central accounting records.[6]

Although much of the conflict between the man of the office and the man of the shop still exists, a definite attempt has been under way for some time to correct it. Men from the shop have been transferred for training to the accounting office, and vice versa. Committee organization has brought the foreman and the accountant together for the discussion of mutual problems. Accountants have been put through orientation programs in the shop where they spent from six months to a year on a number of jobs. Progress has been made to the extent that the shop man is more accounting-conscious and the accountant knows his way about the shop. So today it is not uncommon to find the cost department located in the middle of the shop with direct responsibility to the controller or chief accountant in the executive wing.

Organized Efforts toward Cost Reduction.—Pick up almost any industrial publication today, and you will find at least one article devoted to means toward cost reduction. Such emphasis usually is the result of declining buyer demand, increased competition, uncontrollable increases in specific costs such as labor and material, or the anticipation of any of the three. A manufacturer is constantly faced with the problem of meeting the demands of three groups:

1. The buyer, who requires quality, service, and a favorable competitive price within the limits which he can afford to pay.

2. The worker, who demands wages commensurate with the changes in the cost of living and community wage standards.

3. The stockholder, who expects a reasonable return on his investment.

In facing a necessary decline in price the manufacturer must choose between lower profits or reduction in costs. In granting an increase in wages he must accept a decline in earnings, an increase in selling price, or reductions in other costs. The result is that he searches constantly for present or possible future opportunities in each of the alternatives.

In seeking opportunities for cost reduction, consideration must be given to the division of responsibility for costs. A manufacturing organiza-

---

[6] Kimball and Kimball, "Principles of Industrial Organization," 6th ed., p. 329, presents an effective diagram showing the flow of labor and material and the way in which subsidiary cost records may be established for accounting and control.

tion seeks to bring together customers' orders, land, buildings, equipment, materials, and labor. The efficiency and consequently the effectiveness of the organization are dependent upon its ability to bring these elements together with the least possible time utilization and the greatest possible customer satisfaction.

Management has learned that the utilization and consequently the cost involved in each of the elements of manufacturing must be the joint responsibility of labor, staff personnel, and management. Buildings may be planned for durability and low maintenance costs, but such planning in one plant did not anticipate that workers would throw hammer heads through partitions. (In this instance the union finally stepped in and called a halt to these unnecessary costs.) Worker suggestions of improved operating methods with resulting savings in costs do not anticipate increased mountains of unnecessary paper work inflicted on the operation by one of the staff departments to offset savings with increased clerical expense. We could go through each department and each function and show that a program of cost reduction must be a "team" effort by each member of the entire organization, all working toward a common goal.

Effective participation in cost reduction has its beginning in a spirit of *knowing* within the personnel of the organization—knowing the conditions of business within the company, its problems, its pressures, and consequently *why* cost reductions are essential for the immediate and the long-term future. Only with this knowledge of *why* can an attitude of *assistance* be enlisted. The building and maintenance of knowledge and attitude are ever-continuing jobs. They require effective organization and carefully planned communication techniques. Heron refers to this as the "understanding unit." [7] He emphasizes that the regular line organization of the company must provide for small groups, each capable of becoming an "understanding unit" in the total operation of the company. This will be discussed more fully under internal coordination, Chap. XXXI.[8]

Cost Control in a Multifactory Organization.—In order to accumulate cost data and provide controls for more than one factory of an organization, it becomes necessary to distribute accounting personnel into various plant offices which are sometimes referred to as *cost sections* or *factory-control sections*. It is the function of these control sections to accumulate the cost data and make reports to the central cost department

[7] HERON, ALEXANDER R., "Sharing Information with Employees," pp. 195–204 Stanford University, Calif.: Stanford University Press, 1942.

[8] Methods improvement, a significant factor in cost reduction, has been discussed in Chap. XVII.

at the home office. This involves an accounting of labor costs through the keeping of time cards, the keeping of a perpetual inventory system for the control of materials and their charges to the costs of products manufactured, and waste and salvage control records and other special factors that enter into the total cost of the factory. A factory cost section may also be given other responsibilities such as the accumulation of employment information for foremen and supervisors, or any other information that must be obtained through detailed recordings within the factory. All cost and payroll information is summarized on central forms and forwarded to the central cost department of the home office where it becomes a part of the total accumulative cost data.

The same principle of organizational responsibility of cost personnel as described in a previous section applies to the multifactory organization. A cost section is merely a division of the central staff department of the home office. This procedure, of course, leads to difficulties at times between the superintendent of the factory and the supervisor of the factory cost section. These difficulties sometimes make it necessary to vary from the ideal of organization and place the cost section under the superintendent of the factory or even under some subordinate of the superintendent. Here again, the factor of personalities may dictate the form of organization. In any event, there must be a clear line of communication and control between the cost department of the home office and the separate factory division.

Elements of Cost.—The costs of an industrial enterprise may be divided into three principal elements: (1) material, (2) labor, and (3) expense (see Table XVI). These elements vary in terms of their application to a chargeable cost unit—product or service.

The cost of material may be either *direct* or *indirect*. If the material in question is used in the manufacture of a specific product and becomes a part of that product, it would be considered a direct material charge. Material which does not become a part of the product but which is essential to the manufacture of the product is considered indirect material. This classification includes such items as sandpaper for the sanding of the brushes of electric motors, fuel oil for the operation of heat-treating furnaces or for the heating of the plant, and chemicals for the cleaning of water-heating units. These are materials essential to the operation of the equipment which manufactures the product but are difficult to allocate to a specific product unit.

Labor costs are classified in much the same way as material costs. Labor which is applied directly to the manufacture of a product and which changes the shape, form, or nature of the product is considered *direct labor* and is charged directly to the product unit. Labor which has a more general and less direct application is considered *indirect*. Salaries of janitors, carpenters, electricians are usually considered indirect labor charges.

As in most rules of classifications, there are instances where it is difficult to determine whether a cost should be considered direct or indirect. For example, material used in a finishing or plating operation may become a part of the product and actually change its appearance. Yet it is dif-

TABLE XVI.—ILLUSTRATING THE CLASSIFICATION OF COST ITEMS

Direct costs	Indirect costs		
Direct material	Factory expense	Administrative expense	Selling expense
Direct labor	Superintendents Salaries of foremen Factory office salaries Wages of maintenance staff Material and parts for repair of plant and equipment Factory supplies Insurance on plant and equipment Depreciation Light, power, and heat	Salaries of chief executives General office salaries Office supplies Professional fees (general) Telephone, telegraph, and cable Loss on bad accounts Depreciation of office equipment Insurance on office equipment	Salaries and commissions of salesmen Salaries of service and installation men Salaries of sales office clerks Advertising Rent on branch sales offices Traveling expenses of salesmen

ficult to measure the exact cost of this material that is used in one particular product. Many different products may pass through the same vat or spray. Many factors may operate to bring variations in the amount of material used per product. In such case it may be considered more appropriate to make a proportionate indirect charge instead of attempting to calculate the exact charge that should be made direct. The same principle applies to labor. A member of the maintenance staff may be assigned exclusively to the cleaning and repair of equipment that is used in the manufacture of one product. In such case his salary would be chargeable directly to the cost of that product. In general it may be said that where the amount of material or labor that has gone into a given product can be precisely identified, it should be considered a direct charge to the cost of the product. Otherwise a proportionate indirect charge should be made.

Costs other than labor and material are classified as expense, frequently referred to as *overhead* or *burden expense*. Items such as taxes, interest, rent, utilities, depreciation, and insurance are included in this classification. A portion of the total of these expense items is charged to the cost of a given unit.

A division of expense is usually made in terms of (1) factory expense composed of items wholly chargeable to the actual operation of the factory, (2) administrative expense which includes such items as general office salaries and professional fees, and (3) selling expense including advertising, salaries of salesmen, and other expenses connected with distributing the product.

Classification of Costs.—Costs may be classified further under four headings each representing a step in the breakdown of the total cost of the product:

1. Prime costs: direct labor plus direct material.
2. Factory costs: prime costs plus factory expense.
3. Manufacturing costs: factory costs plus administrative expense.
4. Total cost: manufacturing costs plus selling expense.

This classification may vary with individual enterprises. For example, there is variation in practice in the classification of packaging costs. Some manufacturers may include these costs as a part of administrative expense to be included in the cost of manufacturing, while others will charge them to the cost of distribution (selling expense). The nature and purposes of packaging may be contributing factors in determining the classification—costs of elaborate packaging for sales appeal may be considered an appropriate charge to distribution, while mere protective boxing may be a legitimate charge to manufacturing.

Expense Distribution.—The distribution of expense to cost units is a complicated matter. Circumstances surrounding a particular enterprise or a given product cause many variations in practice. The aim is to make a fair and equitable distribution of the overhead or burden charges to the various items produced. However, this usually cannot be done through a simple mathematical division in terms of proportionate volume. Consideration of a few of the factors that should be given attention in the distribution of expense will illustrate the complications that may be involved.

Competition—How Much Can the Competitive Price Carry?—In considering the factor of competition, management is faced squarely with the question of pricing the product in line with competing products in the field and at the same time attempting to retrieve a reasonable portion of the general factory expenses. The decision may be to withdraw the product from production because the competitive price will not permit the product to carry its full share of the burden of expense. If the product is withdrawn, the machines may remain idle, but expense such as taxes, insurance, depreciation, etc., will continue. If a new and more profitable product can be substituted without undue costs of conversion of plant and equipment, the situation will, of course, be relieved. If this is not possible, however, management must accept "half a loaf" in the return of expenses in preference to no return at all.[9]

Distinction between Primary and By-products.—It is said that the modern packer uses all of the pig except the "squeal." The primary product in the packing industry is meat, yet the company manufactures soap, glue, fertilizer, gelatine, and an endless line of by-products. The cost of the direct material going into these products is negligible considering that it would otherwise be classified as waste with little or no sale value. These by-products may become the manufacturer's principal source of profit. Or, figured in another way, it may be found that a major portion of the factory expenses can be charged to the by-products thus reducing the burden charges to the primary product. Again the fundamental issue is "How much can the product carry?" There are, of course, actual additions to cost which must be allowed for in the charge-up to by-products.

Off-season Production Orders.—The ideal production schedule is one that avoids high and low periods or "peaks and valleys" in volume. As an aid to attaining a more even production schedule, some manufacturers offer incentive prices to customers who will place orders for off-season production. Such a policy has existed for many years between the foot-wear divisions of the U.S. Rubber Company and Sears, Roebuck & Company. Thus Sears Roebuck obtains a reduced price, and U.S. Rubber is able to cover at least a part of its burden costs during otherwise low production periods of the year.

Methods of Expense Distribution.—There are four principal methods used in the distribution of factory expense. Each method purposes to base the expense-burden rate on a factor that is common to all products and varies in direct proportion to the amount of the burden that should be charged to any one of the products. One hundred per cent accuracy can, of course, never be attained universally over all the products. For this reason most companies have found it more practical to use different methods in different departments or with different products.

The Direct-material Basis.—This method charges a burden rate commensurate with either the weight or the cost of the direct material going into the product. This method is limited in its application to companies or departments of a continuous-process type, and where the material and method of manufacture are common to all products. If, for example,

[9] Pricing is discussed in more detail elsewhere in this chapter.

either of two materials (steel or aluminum) is used in the manufacture of the products in a company, it might be relatively simple to chart the expense-burden rate in terms of the variation of weights and manufacturing operation of each material. In a job-order plant, however, variations in materials and production operations would limit the practicability of the method to those operations which were of a repetitive nature for most production orders.

The Direct-labor Basis.—This method uses the cost of direct labor charged to a particular product as a basis for setting the expense-burden rate for the product. Based on past experience, if the total direct-labor payroll of the plant is $50,000 as compared with $10,000 general factory expense for the same period, the expense-burden rate would be 20 per cent of the direct-labor charge. Therefore, if the direct-labor charge on an order is $5,000, the expense burden would be $1,000.

The chief fallacy of this method is that it ignores variations in equipment used in different production operations. Thus, a highly skilled filing operation requiring only hand tools might carry a heavier burden rate than a hydraulic-press operation requiring large and expensive equipment. Under normal operating conditions this method might be quite satisfactory. Assume, however, that the trend of production orders results in an increase in semiskilled machine operations and a reduction in skilled hand operations. Expense distribution will at once be thrown out of balance and an undistributed expense balance will remain to be deducted from profits at the end of the period.

The Man-hour Basis.—Variations in pay that cause confusion in the direct-labor cost basis are eliminated in the man-hour basis. By this method hours instead of cost of direct labor form the basis for determining the expense-burden rate. It still does not recognize variations in type and size of equipment.

The Machine-rate Basis.—The machine-rate basis attempts to base the expense-burden rate on a study of the actual overhead expenses of the equipment used. Factors such as capital investment, average maintenance and repair expense, depreciation, proportionate charge for floorspace, and power consumed are calculated.

A burden rate is then established on an hourly basis. A product is charged in terms of the number of hours of operation required on each of the various machines.

It can readily be seen that this method is applicable to a larger number of different situations than the methods previously described. There are, however, two principal criticisms: (1) considerable additional record keeping is required and (2) the accuracy of the method is dependent upon the accuracy of predetermined estimates of the hours of operations for each of the various machines. Estimates are very difficult to make in abnormal times; yet these are the times when accuracy is needed most.

Manufacturing-expense Absorption.—Any of the methods for distributing expense is dependent upon estimates of time, volume, quality of production, and many other factors which may affect the number of units passing through the plant within a given period and to which a portion of the expenses may be attached. It also depends upon estimates of the total amount of expense that will be incurred during a budgeted period.[10] It is to be expected that either a plus or minus balance will remain in the manufacturing-expense accounts at the close of the periods. If the expense has been overestimated or if the volume of production has been underestimated, a balance will remain in the manufacturing expense accounts which has not been charged off to the costs of the products manufactured. On the other hand, if expenses have been overestimated or if production volume has been underestimated, the manufacturing expense will show a credit balance. Means for caring for this plus or minus balance has been termed "manufacturing-expense absorption."

There are two principal means of effecting this absorption: (1) it may be apportioned to the cost of the products manufactured and in turn be reflected in the profit or loss on the products, or (2) it may be applied to the surplus account. The latter method is favored because it forms a more stable basis for the fixation of burden charges to each product, from one period to the next, that are not disturbed by temporary variations in the general or manufacturing expenses. Also, a special report of unabsorbed expense that is to be withdrawn from surplus will draw the attention of the management. This special attention may cause steps to be taken to correct the causes in order that similar results will not occur in future periods. It may be that poor planning resulting in idle man and machine hours has contributed to the situation. Undue waste of materials or other factors previously mentioned may be in need of study and correction. It is true, of course, that these factors could and should be studied if the unabsorbed expenses were charged to the products manufactured. There would be a tendency, however, for them to become lost in the total cost picture.

Standard Costs.—From the data procured through cost accounting of past performance, most companies are now able to establish cost standards in much the same way as they establish material standards or engineering standards.[11] In other words, an analysis of previous experience makes it possible to establish a normal cost for material, labor, and over-

---

[10] This will be discussed in Chap. XXIX.
[11] See Chap. VIII.

head or general expenses for a product or for a production unit within the organization. The establishment of cost standards has two principal benefits:

1. It reduces much of the need for detailed and continuous cost analysis, procedures which are time-consuming and which have a tendency to slow up the avenues of control and correction. Standard costs tend to bring about a more systematic and thorough analysis of costs and discourage reliance on separate job-by-job studies as a basis for cost estimates on new products.

2. Standard costs have a tendency to reduce to a minimum the variations in price or job quotations. Once costs are thoroughly studied and selling price is established in terms of cost standards, only major changes in circumstances, such as cost of material or labor, should necessitate a change in the selling price.

It is to be expected that standard costs would operate best in serialized production of standard products where there is a continuous flow of materials from one operation to the next and where there is a minimum of variation in operations required on different production orders.[12] Standard costs become less applicable as diversification of production orders increases. Companies operating on a job-order basis are usually organized on a functionalized department or production-center basis. In cases where the operations of a department or production center are the same for all or most of the production orders passing through that department, it may be possible to establish cost standards for that department. On the other hand, in departments where operations vary greatly, an attempt to establish cost standards must be considered a waste of time.

It is possible at times to establish standards for the elements of costs that are constant in a given operation. This is quite frequently true in departments engaged exclusively in the processing of materials. Usually basic material of a type that would be processed within a department can be placed in one of a few classifications as to grade, quality, etc., in the raw stage, and also as to processing required. For example, compregnated wood used in many industrial products is made by compressing wood under a very high pressure and impregnating it with urea or other chemicals that soften the gluey lignin and make it resistant to oil, water, and fire. Added strength can be obtained by making it into a plywood of crisscross grain, the layers glued with a resin glue of tremendous strength. Classifications are established in terms of such requirements as strength and pliability. The standards of each classification form the basis for processing. Naturally, variations in the requirements of processing will vary the costs. By careful analysis of the process required of

[12] See Chap. VIII.

each classification it is possible to segregate the basic cost elements of direct material and direct labor and establish cost standards for them.

Many job-order plants make a special effort to establish cost standards for direct labor. There are two purposes to be served through the establishment of standard labor costs or time standards: (1) it is a check over the quantitative efficiency of labor and (2) it forms a basis for the scheduling of production orders through the plant.[13] Because of this second purpose, the planning department usually keeps a record of the time requirements of all types of operations. This record becomes the basis for the establishment of time standards on specific operations. When a production order is written up, specifying the operations to be performed, the standard time is marked beside each operation for which standards have been established. If the details of the operation are different from any previous operation ever performed in the department, a time estimate is indicated. The operator may be paid a bonus for performing the operation in less than the estimated or standard time, thus providing an incentive for the improvement of efficiency. Time standards must, of course, be subject to change, especially on relatively new operations. The aim, however, is to avoid frequent fluctuations after a period of thorough analysis and experience with the operation. Recognizing that actual costs will vary from standards, special variation accounts are used for under and over amounts, finally being cleared into the profit-and-loss statement. If a consistent variation persists, the job must be restudied and new standards established, or the causes of excessive cost eliminated.[14]

Fixed and Variable Costs.—As a further means of control, especially in estimating or budgeting costs, a classification is made in terms of the extent of variability of cost items.

There are two interpretations of the terms "fixed" and "variable" costs. One interpretation considers a fixed cost as one that is constant in total amount for a given period, while a variable cost increases or decreases in proportion to the volume of production. The second interpretation defines a fixed cost as one that is constant in amount per unit of production but varies in total, while a variable cost changes in amount per unit but remains constant in its total amount for a given period.[15] It will be noted that these two interpretations are directly opposite in their meanings. The classification as described herein assumes the ac-

[13] See Chap. XIV.

[14] See Chap. XVII for a more detailed discussion of time study and the establishment of time standards.

[15] See LAWRENCE, W. B., "Cost Accounting for War Production." Lawrence prefers the application of the second interpretation in the classification of fixed and variable costs.

ceptance of the first interpretation. Salaries of major executives, capital taxes, depreciation, etc., remain fixed regardless of the volume of production. These are known as fixed costs. Other items, such as direct labor and direct material vary almost in proportion to the amount of production and are termed variable costs. Most costs are subject to some variation. Cost of light may be considered relatively constant but even that will vary with extreme changes in volume of production which may require changes in the length of the working day or in the number of working shifts. Therefore, in some enterprises, a third classification of *semifixed costs* is added.

Let us consider for purposes of clarification the application of this classification to a nonindustrial enterprise, an educational institution. Cost items such as library materials, printing, telephone, salaries of the president and deans, and interest on borrowed capital remain constant whether there are 4,000 or 5,000 students registered in a given academic year. These would be considered fixed costs. There are other items, however, that would be reduced with a variation of 1,000 students. One or more residence halls might be closed thus effecting a saving in light, heat, janitorial and maid service. A number of class sections might be eliminated, thus making it possible to reduce the instructional staff. Assistant deans might be dismissed during the period of low registration. These are the variable costs that can be varied in terms of volume.

It is not to be expected that variable costs will change in exact proportion to volume of business. Referring to the illustration of the educational institution, if 100 students were added to the school of engineering, instructional costs might remain the same provided the increase was somewhat evenly divided through the four classes. However, if the 100 students were added to the sophomore class alone, it would probably necessitate the increase of instructional expense. The same principle applies to an industrial enterprise. For example, as production volume within a given department or plant increases, there are some variable costs that may decrease per production unit. This may be due to advantages gained through price discounts on increased volume of material purchases or through the decrease of loss resulting from idleness of men and machines. For this reason variable costs are usually charted to show change in terms of variations in the volume of production. The tabulation and use of variable cost data will be discussed in more detail in Chap. XXIX.

RELATIONSHIP OF COST TO PRICE

The accounting department, if it is a centralized department, is responsible for the accumulation and determination of cost information pertinent to price setting. This does not mean that accounting sets price or that cost plus the addition of the desired margin of profit are the sole determinants of price. Many other factors must be taken into consideration. Most of these have been mentioned in early discussions but will be reviewed in this section in order to assist in the integration of the total price picture.

Fundamentally, price is set through the joint consideration of expected *volume at designated price levels* and the *cost per unit* at each level. The market survey, as described in Chap. IV, is expected to supply information regarding the first part, *i.e.*, how many items can be sold at different price levels such as \$14.95, \$16.95, \$19.95, or \$24.95. Competition, of course, is a significant factor. A strong *quality* competitor may make the lower price field more attractive. Or the survey may show strong competition in both the \$14.95 and the \$24.95 fields but a gap of supply in the middle- or medium-price bracket. In the latter case the survey may show a demand for a product better in quality than existing lower priced competition but yet at a lower price and consequently lower quality than the existing higher priced products.

The company is interested not only in the fact that a demand exists but the extent of the demand, *i.e.*, how many it can sell at this price in contrast to either a higher or a lower price.

The accounting department is responsible for the second part of the basic consideration of price, namely, the cost per unit at designated volume. Figures 172 and 173 in the next chapter on budgetary control show that cost per unit may be affected by volume. The company has indirect costs, explained in preceding pages, which in general would be expected to reduce per unit as volume increases. Direct cost of labor per unit may be decreased through methods improvements if justified by increased potential sales volume. Substitution of lower quality material required by the lower or medium-price bracket should cause reduction in direct material costs per unit.

Distributing costs, as discussed in the chapter on Sales Control, may comprise 50 per cent, more or less, of the selling price. The market survey may show the percentage of the selling price which must be allowed as a margin for the wholesaler and retailer. Such margin will include customary discounts.

The more common forms of discounts are (a) quantity discounts, legal under the Robinson-Patman Act when provable savings from the quantity order result; (b) trade discounts, where differentiation is made between classes of dealers such as wholesalers, agents, and retailers; (c) cash discounts, established by the credit policy and influenced considerably by competitive practice; and (*d*) special discounts, usually in the form of "extra" goods or for distributor advertising. Such discounts must be for a specific and justifiable purpose.

The manufacturer's distributing costs, including advertising, sales promotion, sales office expenses, sales service, and other expenses connected with getting the product into selected trade channels, must be added as a part of the unit cost.

From these and other considerations the accounting department is able to report the expected cost per unit at each of the quality and quantity levels in question. These are then translated into profit per unit multiplied by expected volume. All other things being equal, a unit profit of $1.00 with an expected volume of 500,000 units is to be preferred to a profit of $1.50 for 250,000. The purpose of the survey and analysis is to show at what point of quantity, quality, and price the company may expect the largest net return.

Aside from these fundamental price considerations, other factors have been mentioned which in the end might be the determinants in the selection of price level. The survey may show that dealers are unreceptive to the lower price brackets because of lower dealer profits per unit. They may prefer to handle competing lines where returns per unit are larger. In such case the manufacturer must either establish new outlets, perhaps his own, or resurvey the project for possible adjustments better calculated to meet dealer demands.

The manufacturer may consider that the new product at the lower price may be injurious to some of his other products in the line.[16]

The long-term forecast of economic conditions may provide warning of risks that make inadvisable the capital investment needed for increased production.[17]

These are only a few of the many considerations that at times may cause the manufacturer to select a price bracket which to the casual observer would not appear to be the most profitable.

SUMMARY

Many factors have developed in recent years to give added significance to the role of accountancy. The tremendous increase in the regulatory functions of Federal and state governments have imposed an endless array of records and reports. The transition from the small enterprise to the huge industrial organizations of our day has carried with it the necessity

[16] See Chap. VII, Developing the Product—Research and Engineering, Effect on Other Products in the Line.

[17] See Chap. IV, Industrial Risk and Forecasting.

for the redesign and expansion of financial records. Inherent too in this movement, an interpretative function has developed—interpretation of financial records in a way that will convey their meaning to groups of stockholders and employees.

From the financial records of an industrial organization, two basic financial reports are prepared: (1) the balance sheet, which is a statement of assets and liabilities, and (2) the profit-and-loss statement, which reports the income from the sale of goods and services and the expense incurred through the production and distribution of these goods and services. The value of these statements as control devices is apparent. Yet the primary purpose, and one that is frequently overlooked, is to assist in the preparation of plans for the future activities of the enterprise. The degree to which the accounting department is able to prepare and interpret the financial information to those charged with the responsibility of over-all management of the enterprise will greatly influence the extent to which the enterprise will be able to adjust itself to changing conditions—changes that seem to accelerate as time goes on.

It is to be expected that with the surge toward the acceptance and adaptation of scientific management procedure to our system of free enterprise, techniques for the control of cost would gain particular attention. Accurate cost information for the production of goods for a competitive market is essential not only to the determination of selling price but also as a control over the efficiency of operation. The values of efficient costing procedures have become so widely recognized that it is now expected that every member of the administrative and supervisory personnel of an organization will have at least an elementary understanding and appreciation of the elements of cost and the means toward the control of cost within their respective departments. Costing is considered a cooperative function that brings the man of the shop and the accountant together in the furtherance of their mutual interests.

Of the many improvements in costing procedures, two are of special significance: (1) the development of cost standards and (2) the systematic accumulation, analysis, and charting of costs of job-order production which may be used as a guide in the preparation of cost estimates for purposes of pricing. These two related developments have done much to take the guesswork out of costing. Furthermore, they have tended to reduce time-consuming analysis procedures which otherwise would have a tendency to retard the flow of cost information. These techniques tend to make the great mass of procurable cost information more meaningful and workable to the point where they become effective as a means of control over operations.

CASE PROBLEMS

THE P & B COMPANY[18]

The P & B Company manufactures bags, envelopes, and paper cups. Approximately 40 per cent of the orders are made to customer specifications. The folding department consists of eight machines which die-cut paper blanks and fold them into open-end envelopes. The machines are of three sizes: one H–O machine for large envelopes, three L–O machines for medium sizes, and four S–O machines for the smaller sizes. All machines are adjustable within certain limitations. For example, a 9 by 12 can be run on either the H–O or the L–O machines. The limitations of adjustment are shown in the following figures:

The H–O machine manufactures sizes 8×11 to 15×18.

The L–O manufactures sizes 7×9 to 9×12.

The S–O manufactures sizes 2×3 to 6×9.

Burden rates for the department are calculated on a machine-hour basis. The rate is varied in accordance with the size of the machine, *i.e.*, the burden rate for the L–O machine is less than the H–O. Normally, a 9 by 12 envelope would be folded on the L–O machine, owing to the fact that the L–O carries a lower burden rate. There are times, however, when the L–O machines may be fully scheduled on long runs, while the H–O machine may be idle or in a series of short runs. In order to avoid the costly interruption and temporary change-over of an L–O machine, a rush 9 by 12 order is run on an H–O machine. All orders are based on advance quotations of from one day to four weeks. Quotations for a 9 by 12 envelope include the burden rate of the L–O machine. The company operates in a very competitive market, and consequently quotations must be as low as possible. Therefore, when a 9 by 12 size order is run on an H–O machine, the excess burden charged against the order will cause the records to show a smaller margin or even a loss on the order. This naturally results in considerable confusion and friction between the cost and production departments.

Preparatory Question

How would you reconcile the difference between the estimated and actual costs? How should actual costs be calculated in this situation? State all your assumptions.

THE ROCKLAND MANUFACTURING COMPANY [18]

A department of the Rockland Manufacturing Company operated on a man-hour basis of indirect cost allotment. This was used as a type of

[18] Fictitious name.

budgetary control. Sheets listing budgeted and actual indirect charges, and also direct labor charges, were issued to each department monthly. If the actual indirect charges exceeded the allowable budget for the month, the balance was noted as a loss. If budget exceeded actual, the balance was a profit.

Owing to the acquisition of an additional plant it became necessary to hire and train a large number of women at the starting hourly rate given to male help. This program was started three months prior to the date at which it was expected the personnel would be depleted by transfer to the new plant. For the first month the training program cost was charged to an expense number which incorporated this as an indirect cost. As expected by the department head, the sheets for that month indicated a loss. During the next month, however, the women were put on production. The department head knew from reports from the production department that the degree of expected increase in production from added labor had not been attained. He knew also that the cost per unit of production had increased owing to a decreased efficiency.

Preparatory Question

Would the departmental budget sheet for the second month show a profit or a loss? Comment upon the weaknesses of this budgetary control procedure and how they can be corrected.

Cost Estimates of Forging Designs [19]

DOUGLAS AIRCRAFT COMPANY

The Douglas Aircraft Company has sought to develop procedures that will enable it to predetermine with reasonable accuracy the relative future cost of new forgings on any particular order. These forgings are formed on forging machines equipped with dies. The metal stock is placed on the stationary portion of the die. The machine then advances the movable half of the die under great pressure to form the metal into the desired shape. The total direct cost per piece is made up of three main elements: die costs, tooling set-up charges, and material and labor costs per unit of the finished product.

Forgings made by Douglas Aircraft are either of aluminum alloy or steel. Forgings vary greatly as to size, shape, and general contour. Some are I sections, others bulbous parts, round sections, T sections, deep cone-shaped parts, shallow parts, etc.

---

[19] Adapted from an article by O. A. Wheelon, methods analysis engineer, Douglas Aircraft Company, Inc., *Product Engineering,* November, 1942, pp. 641–643.

The following factors have been found to be pertinent to the analysis of cost variation.

1. The size of a forging dictates the dimensions of the die block. In general, the larger the die block, the greater becomes the cost of preparing the die. In examples 1, 2, and 3, Fig. 171, the dimensions and actual cost of three representative dies are as follows:

	Rectangular area, sq. in.	Die cost
1	361	$1,000.00
2	59	163.43
3	162	448,75

2. Some forgings require a warped parting plane, adding 50 per cent to the cost, as illustrated in example 4.

3. V-type forgings add 200 per cent, U-type forgings add 300 per cent, as illustrated in examples 5 and 6, respectively.

4. Shallow forgings reduce cost by 50 per cent, as illustrated in example 7.

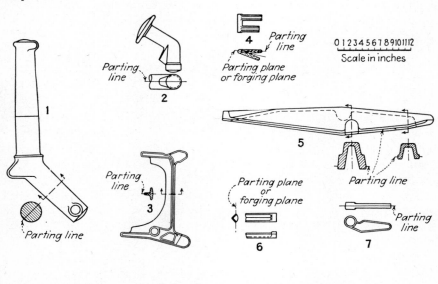

Example	1	2	3	4	5	6	7
Rectangular Area (Sq. Ins.)	361	59	162	12	154	5	13

Fig. 171.—Examples of variations in forging design.

From experience it has been shown that variations in setup charges correspond in reasonable proportion to the variations in the sizes of the forgings. Setup costs for the forgings shown in examples 1, 2, and 3 are as follows:

	Rectangular area, sq. in.	Setup cost
1	361	$70.00
2	59	11.44
3	162	31.41

Preparatory Questions

1. Develop some workable bases, such as formulas, charts, or graphs, which might be used by Douglas Aircraft for estimating that portion of their forging costs represented by (a) the preparation of their dies and (b) the cost of setting up the machine for each run of forgings.

2. What would be the die and setup costs for the forgings shown in examples 4, 5, and 6 (Fig. 171)?

CHAPTER XXIX

BUDGETARY CONTROL

The budget is an instrument used by management in planning its future activities. It is a means whereby management charts its course for any given period of one month, six months, one year, or five years. It includes an estimate of sales, of production, and of the expense that will be involved. It takes cognizance of the requirements of the period, including working capital, buildings, equipment, material, and labor.

Management that is able to look ahead and predict, on the basis of available information, a trend in business activity is better able to prepare itself for one of two courses of action: (1) it can adjust itself to the acceptance of the developing trend or (2) it can seek means for cushioning the impact of the trend on its activities. If it seems apparent that the trend of business activity is upward, preparations can be started early that will enable the enterprise to take advantage of the opportunity for increased profits through increased production. Arrangements can be made, at least tentatively, for additional space and equipment. In anticipation of a scarcity of materials, a program of research may be started for the development of substitutes. A program of training may be inaugurated for the attainment of increased numbers and flexibility of skilled personnel. New products may be pushed in their development in order that they may be introduced at the point of favorable customer demand.

Contrary to the preparation for the upward trend, management must at times prepare for the acceptance of a period of low business activity. It avoids long-term contracts for equipment and material. It reduces to a minimum the inventories of raw material and finished products. Employment policies may be changed in anticipation of the needed reduction of personnel. The announcement of new products may be withheld in anticipation of a declining demand.

A second type of action which has been mentioned is that which attempts to alter what appears to be a developing trend in business activity. This is the type of action frequently chosen by aggressive management that is described as "not knowing the meaning of defeat." This is the management that studies probable customer demand and prepares to serve those demands which will be least affected by the declining business trend. It dares to challenge the trend by marketing new products and enlarging the advertising program.[1]

These are some factors of change forming the policies on which budgets are based. However, wise management views budgeting as a continuous activity that must function during periods of "normal" production as well as in the "abnormal." This introduces a second function in addition to planning, namely, *control*. Budgets are yardsticks for the measurement of the efficiency of operations. They form the bases for comparing actual production and its accompanying costs with estimates taken from past experience. When the course has been charted and expressed through the medium of a budget, means must be found that will enable the enterprise to hold its course as planned or, if need be, to make orderly changes in its plans in accordance with changing and developing circumstances. This has been termed the "operation of the budget" or "budgetary control."

The Historical Background of Budgeting.—Budgeting for the industrial enterprise developed as a part of the "scientific management" movement of the past quarter of a century. The use of budgets in nonindustrial organizations, however, dates back as far as the eighteenth century. Sinclair states that in England

the annual accounting report to Parliament, by the Chancellor of the Exchequer, was known as the budget, and included:

A statement of the past year's expenditures.

An estimate of the coming year's expenditures.

A schedule of taxes and recommendations as to methods of levying the taxes.[2]

Similarly in the United States, but not of particular significance until the early part of the twentieth century, budgets were first used by institutional and governmental organizations. Use was limited, however, to the allocation and control of expenditures. Income from taxation was relatively fixed from year to year in the case of local, state, and Federal governmental organizations. On the basis of this anticipated income, budgets of expense were authorized for the various divisions. These budgets served as instruments for control of expenditures for the designated periods of operation. Institutions such as churches, hospitals, and private schools adopted a similar budgeting procedure.

The use of the budget in industry also was applied first as a means for the systematic authorization of expenses. We find that budgets were constructed for the allocation and control of the expense of advertising, supplies, and maintenance. The more extensive use of budgets to include

---

[1] See Chap. IV on industrial risks for a more detailed discussion.

[2] SINCLAIR, PRIOR, "Budgeting," p. 3, New York: The Ronald Press Company, 1934.

sales and production came with the movement toward a more systematic analysis and control of production operations and costs. With the coming of the crash year of 1929 the use of the budget was fully established in industry as an aid to management in planning and control. Thus we see that the industrial budget has served a complete cycle of business trends from the prosperous years of the twenties, through the depression of the early thirties, and the peak years of World War II.

Purposes of Budgets.—Stated briefly, the purposes of budgets are:

1. Planning: A systematic and unified plan of activities for designated periods of operation.

2. Control: A standard of measurement of results against which variations from previous plans become evident.

3. Coordination: Activities become a part of a plan for the enterprise as a whole. Democratic processes basic to the construction and operation of a budget tend to bring understanding and unification of departments and personnel.

Planning through the Budget.—The construction of a budget forces the formation of policies on the part of management. Through the budget, management is committing itself at least tentatively to a plan of action. This action requires decision regarding scope and sequence of future activity. It brings to the foreground such fundamental problems as quantity vs. quality of products to be manufactured. Is the company to place its emphasis on the manufacture of an article of superior quality even at the sacrifice of volume, or is it to manufacture a "competitive" product in large volume but of less quality and directed toward a specific price range of customer demand? This and other problems of planning previously mentioned are forced to the foreground for decision through the necessity for the construction of a plan of action.[3]

Control through the Budget.—It should be understood that a budget is a means toward an end and is not an end within itself. Budgets are made to be used. They are tools of management. They are standards against which every executive and supervisor in the organization may measure the results attained. They establish goals to which each department and each workman within a department must contribute his designated share in terms of the unified plan. This leads toward precision and confidence. A department head knows what is laid out for his department to accomplish. He knows what is expected of him. He knows when he has done a good job or when and where he is falling behind. Thus, much of the worry of uncertainty is eliminated.

Through the recording of actual against the estimates of the budget, reports are constructed that reveal the points of difficulty and danger—

---

[3] See the introduction of this chapter for other problems requiring planning.

the points which must be analyzed and improved upon. Management operating on the "exception principle" may pick up these points of variation and devote attention to them.

Coordination through the Budget.—Budgets should be constructive aids to all departments within an organization in achieving their common goals. Unfortunately, however, this purpose is frequently misunderstood. The early emphasis given to budgets as controls of expenditures established in the minds of subordinates the attitude that budgets were negative controls only—devices to limit expenditures. This led to the "padding" of departmental budgets, the idea being for each department to get as large an allotment for expenditures as possible. When all budgets were assembled and reductions were deemed essential, each department felt that it was the subject of discrimination. Thus, the budget became a "sore spot" and a factor of disintegration within the personnel of the organization.

This attitude toward industrial budgets as negative controls may be compared to the attitude of a housewife or a son or daughter who looks upon the family budget merely as a means for dad to save his money. They may not realize that a budget can be a means toward achieving the desired ends of all concerned. The budget may include both the necessities of life and some of the luxuries as well. Perhaps dad (or management) may be somewhat at fault too in this misunderstanding. Perhaps he has not been fair in the past in the distribution of savings. More frequently, however, he has failed to bring the family in on the planning of the budget that they might have a part in establishing the goals and selecting the means toward attaining them.

Without planning, an enterprise will operate with irregularity in volume and with resulting overexpansion and contrasting curtailment. Additional personnel will be hired in large numbers during a peak period only to be laid off during the period of recession. Under these conditions employees develop a feeling of insecurity and look forward to the day when they may join the ranks of the unemployed.

Budgets, properly constructed and operated, may have a constructive influence on the personnel of an organization. Budgets may serve as a means for bringing about a realization on the part of the personnel of the common goals of all who belong to the organization and all who serve it. In this capacity the budget serves as a coordinating influence—one that brings unity to the organization.

Types of Budgets.—There are two principal types of budgets: the *static*, or fixed, budget and the *variable*, or flexible, budget. The static budget depends upon ability to predict income, sales, or shipments with at least a reasonable degree of accuracy. Using this prediction as a base, fixed sums are allocated for expenditures with a fixed budget of production operations for the period in question. The variable budget recognizes the unreliability of income or sales predictions and makes provisions in advance for variations in production and expenditures in accordance with variations in sales.

The Static Budget.—Industry inherited the static budget from governmental and institutional organizations. This type of budget served a

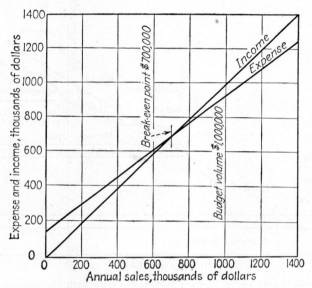

Fig. 172.—Profit graph for one department of the Stanley Manufacturing Company, Dayton, Ohio. Graph based on fictitious figures.

valuable purpose in the planning and control of certain fixed types of expenditures. The inadequacies of such a budget, however, were soon felt when industry moved into the period of mass production where margins of profit per unit of production were small and planning and control over all operations became more essential. Through study it was found that costs per unit change at different levels of production.[4] The degree of change varies on different products and on different operations involved in the manufacture of the same product. Figure 172 is a simplified illustration of the relative variation in expense in one department of the Stanley Manufacturing Company of Dayton, Ohio. An annual sales volume of $700,000 was required in this department in 1941 in order to

[4] See material on Cost Control, Chap. XXVIII.

pay the expenses. This is known as the "break-even point." Beyond this point unit costs decline as sales increase.[5]

The Variable Budget.—The variable budget is constructed in anticipation of variations in sales. It provides in advance for orderly change in the volume of production and in expenditures. The fixed, semifixed, and variable costs are tabulated and charted at different levels of pro-

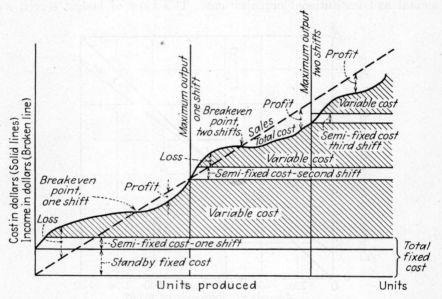

Fig. 173.—Typical cost curve showing how cost varies with the volume of production. Note the effect—on the cost elements and on the profit—of adding a second and a third shift.

duction. This tabulation is based on the recording of costs of previous periods or on the standard costs that have been established through study and experience.

Figure 173 is a simplified version of a typical cost curve intended to show the variation in costs as volume increases. Note that three types of cost are illustrated: fixed or stand-by costs representing those items of overhead which must be met even though the plant is closed down; semifixed costs; and variable costs.[6] Actually, however, the semifixed costs do not usually follow a straight line but form more of a curve upward as volume increases. For purposes of simplicity and clarity the rise in semifixed costs is indicated at points where the rise is more pronounced, *i.e.*,

[5] Taken from *Factory*, October, 1942, p. 99.

[6] See material on Cost Control for a description of types of costs.

at points where it becomes necessary to establish additional shifts with the addition of foremen, sweepers, extra maintenance crews, etc. The same effect would be obtained at points where additional buildings have to be opened for increased volume of production. The greatest variation in costs, however, is in those items which are classified as variable costs, such as material and labor. These are the items of greatest concern in budgeting because they are flexible and must be controlled and adjusted as volume increases or decreases.

Holding to the principle of variable budgets, variations in form of budgeting procedure may be established to meet the peculiar needs of a specific enterprise. In general, we may say that simplicity in budgeting should be held as a primary virtue. Detailed clerical work involved in the preparation and operation of a budget should be held to a minimum. This principle not only leads to the elimination of unnecessary costs in budgeting but in general promotes ease in the interpretation and control of the budget. In a small company where costs are easily identified and controlled or in companies where there is little variation in production volume, a very simple type of budget becomes more practical and appropriate. As an enterprise increases in size and variability, the budget procedure must change to provide the necessary information and control.

Variable budgets are of two principal types. One is the *step budget* which is really a series of budgets set up at different levels of volume of production or sales. These steps are usually established at points in the variation in volume where pronounced changes in costs will occur, such as additional shifts, buildings, and supervisory personnel. The budget for each step recognizes a point of maximum and minimum production. Demands in excess of the maximum or below the minimum require a change in the basic budget or, in other words, the adoption of the budget which has been established for the next step.

The second type of variable budget provides an estimate of the *variable rate of cost* per unit of production or per dollar shipments or sales. Table XVII shows a listing of cost classifications. It will be noted that in this case direct material, a variable cost, constitutes 30 cents of the sales dollar. Therefore, if the sales volume is $130,000, the direct material cost would be $39,000. If volume was increased to $150,000, the direct material cost would be increased in direct proportion ($150,000 × $0.30 = $45,000). The factory burden cost, however, is divided into two parts, *i.e.*, stand-by, or fixed, cost and variable cost. The fixed cost of $10,000 remaining constant, the variable cost is estimated at 12 cents per sales dollar. Therefore, a sales volume of $130,000 would result in a factory burden cost of $25,600 ($130,000 × $0.12 + $10,000).

Any estimate of the variable *rate* of cost must recognize maximum and

TABLE XVII.—STAND-BY AND VARIABLE RATE OF COSTS

Item	Stand-by	Variable rate per sales dollar
Direct material.............	....	$0.30
Direct labor................	....	0.14
Factory burden.............	$10,000	0.12
Administrative expense......	4,000	0.02
Selling expense.............	9,000	0.04
Total operating cost.......	$23,000	$0.62

(Sales volume.................................	$130,000)
Direct material—130,000 × $0.30.................	$ 39,000
Direct labor—130,000 × $0.14....................	18,200
Factory stand-by burden........................	10,000
Factory variable burden—130,000 × $0.12........	15,600
Administrative stand-by........................	4,000
Administrative variable—130,000 × $0.02..........	2,600
Selling expense stand-by........................	9,000
Selling expense variable—130,000 × $0.04..........	5,200
Total operating cost........................	$103,600

minimum volumes. As previously stated, the rate of cost of material may be expected to decrease as volume increases, owing to advantages that may be attained through purchasing in larger lots. Greater labor efficiency, however, may be obtained from the regular force of 1,000 workers than would be realized per unit of production after an additional 500 inexperienced employees had been added to the payroll. Therefore, the variable rate of cost is calculated as an *average* rate between two points of minimum and maximum production.

The Requisites of Budget Preparation.—Stated briefly, the requisites of budget preparation are: (1) established lines of authority and responsibility, (2) clearly defined business policies, (3) information available for the forecasting of probable income, (4) adequate cost information.

Lines of Authority and Responsibility in Budget Preparation.—It has been said that the preparation and control of the budget should be a cooperative undertaking. It should become a means for attaining coordination between departments. This calls for the establishment of democratic procedures but with clearly defined lines of authority and responsibility.

Centralized responsibility and control are usually placed with a *budget committee,* which should be representative of all major departments or divisions of the enterprise.[7] The executive committee of the enterprise

[7] See material on the use of committees in Chap. VI.

frequently serves as the budget committee in recognition of budget preparation and control as one of the most important management functions. In large organizations, however, a subcommittee may be established. It is the function of the budget committee to receive and approve all forecasts, departmental budgets, and periodic reports showing comparison of actual and budget.[8] The budget committee may also request special studies of deviations from the budget and consider revisions of budget to meet changed business conditions.

Because of the scope and importance of budgeting as a cooperative function, a budget officer is usually appointed to serve as coordinator or point of contact between departments. Most frequently he is the controller or assistant controller, depending on the size of the organization. However, the treasurer or the general manager may assume the responsibility of budget officer in a small organization. Here again we find the matter of personalities dictating to some extent the appointment of the officer in charge. He must be a man who works well with people. He must be able to organize work. He must know how to function under a committee type of organization. He must be able to obtain the facts regarding the operation of each department—the strengths, weaknesses, and problems. MacDonald states,[9]

the department head who says, "I would like to have the budget executive participate in this discussion because he knows our problems," is paying the budget executive a real compliment, whereas the one who says, "Never mind about him, he only looks at these things from the point of view of the figures," is clearly implying that he has no real respect for the budget executive's knowledge and opinion and in reality regards him as nothing more than a compiler of figures.

The budget officer must see that all department estimates are prepared with sufficient supporting data to provide an adequate basis for effective consideration by the committee. He has the responsibility for the presentation of these budgets to the committee and for transmitting back to the departments the recommendations of acceptance or revision. The budget officer is also responsible for the organization of a system of regular periodic reports regarding the operations of each department. He may also prepare special reports regarding points of special difficulty and recommended revisions to correct these difficulties.

The preparation of budget estimates within each department should

[8] See Sinclair, p. 30, for schedule of budgets and budgetary outline used by a manufacturer of electrical machinery, apparatus, and supplies. See also Spriegel, William R. and Richard H. Lansburgh: "Industrial Management," New York: John Wiley & Sons, Inc., 1947, pp. 403–404 for example of sales budget reports.

[9] MacDonald, John H., "Controllership: Its Functions and Technique," p. 96, Controllers Institute of America, 1940.

also be a committee proposition. This is in adherence to the same principle of *participation as a means toward cooperation*. Participation in the preparation of a budget serves to familiarize the personnel with the problems involved. With this knowledge of the problems and the feeling of having a part in setting the goals and limitations of the department, the personnel will give more effective cooperation in the operation of the budget. The head of the department may act as chairman of the department committee but, in the case of a large department, he should delegate responsibility for the gathering of details for use by his committee. In other words, he should have an organization within his own department for the preparation of the budget that follows the same general pattern as the budget organization for the enterprise as a whole. He will find that this organization not only will lead to better budget preparation but will prove especially useful in budget control.

Business Policies.—Attention has already been directed to the necessity for the establishment of business policies as a foundation for budget preparation. These policies, however, must be clearly defined and interpreted in terms of their effect on each department of the organization. These policies set the stage for the development of attitude on the part of personnel essential to good budget preparation and control. If the policies call for curtailment of production and costs, the reasons for this curtailment should be made clear. Departments should be fully aware of the over-all extent of this curtailment and their proportionate share. On the other hand, if a premium is to be placed on increased quantity of production in the months ahead, each department should recognize in advance its full responsibility.

Availability of Information for Business Forecasting.—Gardner refers to forecasting as "business acrobatics."[10] This seems to be a rather accurate description of the task that management must face in attempting to foresee its future business activities. This task is made easier and more accurate, however, if it has been anticipated and information accumulated that will show the trends of the past and the present. Considerable attention has already been given in this material to the means for the development and use of forecasting information.[11] It will suffice to say at this point that a budget can be only as good as the forecast on which it is based, and the forecast as accurate as the information from which it was derived.

Adequate Cost Information.—Adequate cost information is a prime essential of budgeting. It constitutes the foundation for the conversion

---

[10] GARDNER, FRED V., "Variable Budget Control," p. 216, New York: McGraw-Hill Book Company, Inc., 1940.

[11] See Chap. IV.

of forecast and business policy into production. Our forecast tells us how much we can sell at a given price level. Our cost information tells us how much it will cost to produce it in the volumes specified. Full realization of cost in advance of budget preparation may cause management to question the advisability of the continuance of certain lines of products or it may lead to the expansion of a particular line that is able to carry a favorable margin of profit.

Perhaps the most important advantage to be gained through the availability of accurate cost information is that budgeting can be based on facts instead of personal guesswork. The individual who is called upon to provide estimates without facts on which to base these estimates is in the long run facing trouble. Through superior personal judgment he may receive the praise of management when times are good and when production is progressing at a relatively even tempo. If he is wise he will probably allow reasonably safe margins to protect himself from the possible errors of his judgment. This he may be able to do under "normal" conditions. But invariably there will come a time when the "abnormal" occurs—when the "pressure" is put on to decrease the budget of costs in order that the business may continue to operate at a profit. Those are the times when the individual may be forced to eliminate those margins of safety. He promises to operate at less cost yet he does not have a detailed plan approved by management as to just how those costs are to be reduced. The chances are that they will not be reduced and he will be criticized, if not discharged, for poor management of his department. How much better it would be if he could supply facts regarding costs— facts that could be interpreted by any member of the management group. The individual could then relieve himself of reliance on personal judgment alone and present his estimates accompanied by systematically prepared data. Once the estimates are accepted by the budget committee, with full realization of the facts on which they are based, the committee shares the responsibility for the accuracy of those estimates.

The Sales Budget.—As previously mentioned, the estimates of future sales set the bounds of limitations for other budgets of the enterprise. There are two principal sources of data for use in the preparation of sales estimates: (1) past performance (sales of previous periods) and (2) market analysis.[12] Both sources are generally used in gaining a composite picture of the relative demand for the different products manufactured and the general changes in business conditions which are pertinent to the future sales of the products of the enterprise.

Salesmen can play a significant role in the preparation of the sales budgets. They are in personal contact with the customer. They are

[12] See Chap. IV.

able to obtain first-hand information regarding his wants, his attitude toward future business conditions, his attitude toward the services provided by the enterprise, his attitude toward the program of advertising, etc. If salesmen are trained in the importance of this information and the methods by which it should be produced, the enterprise can develop within its own organization a valuable source of market information. Many companies make the preparation of sales estimates and the introduction of new products to the market a cooperative undertaking which includes participation by vote on the part of each salesman. A by-product of this procedure is the development of a feeling of responsibility on the part of the salesman for meeting sales estimates once they are cooperatively established.

The budgeting of selling expense is a very difficult proposition especially during a period of business decline. Good management recognizes that, generally speaking, "money gets money." That is, more advertising and more salesmen in the field should develop more sales. The problem, however, is to find the point of diminishing return or the point where the increase in selling expense exceeds the increase in profit from sales. This point will naturally vary under changing business conditions or in the life cycle of a company and its products. A new company or a new product may require more selling expense than a well-established company or product that can "ride" on its reputation during an unprofitable market period. For example, in 1942, by government regulation, the manufacture of alcohol for consumer purchases was prohibited for the duration of the war. All sales, therefore, had to be taken from stock. Unwilling to drain their stocks of liquor that should be aging for future years, distillers budgeted as much as a 50 per cent cut in liquor sales for the year 1943. The more well-established distillers curtailed all advertising except a limited amount of "good-will" advertising intended as a means of keeping the name before the public. Naturally a new and little-known industry could not afford such a curtailment if it expected to be able to stay in business. In fact, a new industry might grasp at this opportunity to increase its advertising program when there would be little competing advertising in the field. Many of our now prosperous industries gained their footing during the depression of the thirties through the adoption of such a policy.

Manufacturing Budgets.—The number and division of budgets for the manufacturing division of an enterprise will, of course, vary with the size and type of enterprise and the products it manufactures. In general, it may be said that six basic budgets are needed: (1) the production budget which outlines the schedule of product units to be manufactured, (2) the materials budget which specifies the direct material needed to produce the number of units scheduled, (3) the plant and equipment budget that sets forth the requirements of space and machinery, (4) the maintenance budget, (5) the manufacturing expense budget which includes the overhead or burden charges for the period, and (6) the labor budget specifying the productive personnel needed to meet the production schedule.[13]

The production budget is taken directly from the sales estimates except that it attempts insofar as possible to spread the work evenly over the period. Table XVIII illustrates a very simple form to be used in a production budget. This budget forms the basis for other manufacturing budgets as listed above. With the aid of the materials specifications sheets for each product, the materials budget can be prepared by months for the guidance of the purchasing department. Similarly, the plant and equipment, maintenance, and manufacturing expense budgets must conform to the production budget for the various departments, not only as to *what* will be needed but also *when*.

TABLE XVIII.—TENTATIVE PLANT PRODUCTION FORECAST

(Date)

In Case Units   From_____to_____

Product Code No.	Department A				Department B					Department C			
	A2043	A5630	AI402	Total	JX242	X321	JR200	JL401	Total	B410c	B2043	BX302	Total
Oct.	300	150	535	985	85	110	90	430	715	240	300	250	790
Nov.	300	150	535	985	85	110	110	430	735	275	300	250	825
Dec.	300	150	535	985	85	110	120	430	745	350	300	250	900
Totals	900	450	1605	2955	255	330	320	1290	2195	865	900	750	2515

The direct labor budget (see Table XIX) is exceedingly important for reasons previously mentioned and also as a more systematic forecast of the need for recruitment and training. From the production estimates of each department the labor demands can be forecast for each job classification. This forecast is then compared with the roster of present per-

---

[13] Space does not permit the explanation and illustration of the various schedules required in the development of the manufacturing budgets. The purpose here is only to call attention in this division to the nature and scope of budgeting. Many excellent references are available for the student of budgeting who wishes to pursue the subject further. Attention is called particularly to Sinclair, "Budgeting," and Gardner, "The Variable Budget," each of which treats the subject of manufacturing budgets in detail and with many good illustrative forms.

sonnel. It may show a probable surplus in one personnel classification and a shortage in another. In such case the company must either discharge from the surplus classification and add to the shortage classification, or plan for the retraining of present personnel for the performance of new jobs. Plans for shifting and retraining become particularly essential

TABLE XIX.—DIRECT LABOR BUDGET

Dept._____From_____to_____

Classification	Number of operators	Estimated man-hours	Rate per hour	Total cost

when there is a scarcity of labor available for recruitment or when the company is converting to the manufacture of a new product involving new operating skills.

Owing to the interdependence of the production, plant and equipment, and direct labor budgets, all three must be constructed concurrently. In order to produce, there must be equipment for the performance of specified operations. Expansion in volume may require either the purchase of additional equipment or the establishment of shifts. If the latter course is considered, attention must also be given to the availability of personnel.

The Financial Budget.—The financial budget presents a summarization of anticipated receipts and disbursements for the budget period. Its purpose is to plan for the allocation of working capital as represented by the current assets of the enterprise. Data for the financial budget are derived from the budgets as prepared by the various divisions. The financial budget must anticipate the cash receipts by months or at other designated points of the period and make allowance for the raising of additional funds, if needed, to meet current expenses. This means that income from accounts receivable, notes receivable, cash transactions, etc., must be budgeted as accurately as possible. Expenditures may be planned in consideration of two primary factors: (1) the absolute necessities of the budgets of the various divisions, *i.e.*, monthly requirements of materials for production, payroll, etc., and (2) the limitations of available cash. It is not considered good business to have large amounts of cash lying idle during ten months of the year in order that funds will be available to meet unusually large expenditures during the other two months. Good business policy would suggest that attempts should be made either to spread the added expenses of these two months over a longer period or to borrow additional funds through short term notes. There are many problems arising out of attempted control of working capital, and there are likewise many possible solutions that may be derived to fit the needs of an individual enterprise. The significant point here is that these problems must be anticipated and avenues selected to meet them. The financial budget is a device intended to serve those objectives.

There are times, of course, when the limitations of capital may make the plans as set forth in the budgets of various divisions prohibitive. This is especially true during periods of rapid expansion when additional plant and equipment must be provided in order to meet the budgeted schedule of production. In such case the financial budget acts as a negative control over other divisions. In most instances, however, the financial budget provides a systematic and positive approach toward the attainment of the coordinated plans of all divisions.

Length of the Budget Period.—There are many factors that tend to cause variations in the length of the budget period. A short budget period naturally gives greater flexibility, it being possible to reconstruct the budget at frequent intervals in terms of changing market conditions. On the other hand, a longer budget period enables the enterprise to coordinate its immediate activities with a systematic, long-term plan, *i.e.,* the research and finance programs, for example, can be coordinated with the planned production activities. Budgets are usually planned in terms of one month, three months, six months, or a year. At times it may be advisable to construct a budget for as long a period as five years, realizing of course, that it must be subject to change.

In an enterprise manufacturing to stock it is considered advisable to construct a budget for a period that will coincide with a seasonal cycle or the turnover of stock, *i.e.,* a manufacturer of shoes may produce a heavy line of shoes for the winter market and light-weight sport shoes for the spring and summer months. If he manufactures these to stock, production for a seasonal group may be spread over a period of perhaps six months. In such case he should select a 6-month budget period to coincide with the production period, thus facilitating better planning and control.

Most companies that operate on an annual budget break it down into quarters or months. A refinement of this plan is to reconstruct the budget monthly, projecting it 12 months into the future. That is, if a budget is constructed for a period of one year extending from January 1 to December 31, it will be reviewed and revised on February 1 and extended 12 months into the future, making the termination date January 31 of the following year. This combines the short adjustment period with the long-term planning period and is particularly helpful in companies manufacturing to stock.

Budgeting for Job-order Production.—Budgeting for job-order production is a special problem in that it is exceedingly difficult to predict in advance the size and nature of orders. During peak periods it is possible to have a sufficient backlog of orders for the construction of at least a quarterly budget in terms of orders actually received. In low periods of production when the enterprise is not running to capacity, the problem becomes more difficult. Usually, however, an order is in the process of negotiation for a period of as long as 2 or 3 months. Management is, thereby, supplied with at least some evidence of production requirements. It knows the specifications of the order in general; it is able to predict the probable amount of labor, material, etc., and it has at least a "hunch" as to whether it will be able to obtain the order. Nevertheless, definite plans must be held in abeyance until the order is actually received and approved. Consequently the budget must be held open for frequent adjustment.

Operating the Budget.—Any budget, regardless of how carefully it may have been prepared, must be followed up in operation if it is to achieve its full purpose. Too frequently the budget is prepared and then forgotten until too late to remedy or remove the factors that are blocking progress as planned. Of course it is quite possible that these conflicting obstacles cannot be altered, but instead the budget must be changed in consideration of them. The important thing is for changes and variations to be called to the attention of the budget committee as soon as possible in order that their effect may be anticipated and adjustments made to counteract them.

The machinery for the control of the budget in operation is planned in conjunction with the preparation of the budget as previously explained. Each department or division is organized with responsibility allocated for the control as well as the preparation of the budget. The various divisions are then coordinated through the budget director and the budget committee of the enterprise as a whole.

Recording of Operations.—Good budgetary control requires that accounting procedures be established that will provide a recording of actual operations in terms of sales, production, income, expenditures, or other budgeted units within a department. These recordings form a basis for the authorization of operations and the comparison of actual results with those which had been budgeted. This enables the budget director and each department to have a constant check on operations. Unusual variations come immediately to the attention of the departments concerned.

Operating Reports.—Regular reports to the director of the budget showing comparison of actual and budget, and the reasons for variations are prepared for each department. Frequently the reasons for variations are not immediately explainable, but at other times they may be quite apparent. For example, failure to meet a production schedule may be directly attributable to a shortage of labor or the unavailability of material.

Variations between actual and budget and the reasons for them, however, may frequently require more thorough analysis by the budget director and his staff. He should seek to determine why the employment department has not been able to obtain sufficient labor, what methods have been used in their attempts, what other methods should be explored. Herein lie the means for control and coordination of all departments throughout the plant. Because of the inevitable interdependency of departments, all must be kept as near as possible within a point of minimum effectiveness if the total operations of the enterprise are to stay within reasonable limits of the budget as planned.

The various department reports are summarized and consolidated by the budget director in his regular reports to the budget committee. On the basis of his report the budget committee may recommend revisions in the budget. The budget director may also submit supplementary reports regarding special points of variation upon which he asks for action regarding policy and procedure.

Limitations of the Budget.—Too frequently too much is expected of a system of budgeting within a short period of time. It should be recognized that no budget is better than the people who operate it and that people cannot be changed in their habits and interests overnight. The idea of budgeting must be sold and, furthermore, it must be demonstrated. It may gain rapid acceptance and effectiveness in one department and only "half-hearted" acceptance in others. As previously mentioned, many will consider the budget as only a negative control and something to be resisted and postponed as long as possible. Some will give "lip-service" to the endorsement of the idea but know in their own minds that "it can't work in our department." The chances are that it will not work in that department until the desire to make it work has been established. That desire cannot be forced. Budgeting, as an instrument of planning, control, and coordination, must be cooperative budgeting. As such, time is an essential element.

SUMMARY

It is somewhat appalling that the development of systems of budgetary preparation and control in its broader meaning has been so slow, especially when one considers that the purposes of budgets are synonymous with management functions: planning, control, and coordination. The majority of companies, even in the early forties, still thought of the term "budget" as applying only to the financial planning of the enterprise. This, of course, dates back to the original concept of budgets as handed down to industry by institutional and governmental organizations. However, with the noticeable surge of interest in improved management techniques, stimulated by World War II, further development and refinement of budgeting as a management technique appears hopeful.

There are two distinct but closely interrelated phases of budgeting: preparation and control. Three elements of method are of special significance: (1) If the purposes of budgeting are to be fully realized, procedures of preparation and control must be cooperative. This means that there must be participation by representatives of all departments or groups throughout the enterprise. Here we have a perfect example of the values inherent in the principle of *participation as a means toward cooperation*. (2) Good budgeting procedure requires that demands shall be held flexible. Some degree of change is inevitable. That is the kind of world we live in, but the fact that the future is uncertain does not justify aimless wandering. Quite to the contrary; it increases the need for planning and requires that plans be constructed in a way to provide alternative lines of action. Various interpretations of the *variable budget principle* provide a means by which industry may plan for the uncertain future. (3) Adequate budget preparation and control require a system of records that will make available the various types of information pertinent to the subject with the least possible delay. The latter is particularly important in budgetary control. The shorter the time lag in the reporting of information, the more effective the control.

CASE PROBLEM

THE B & G ENGINEERING CORP.[14]

The B & G Engineering Corp. was organized in 1910 as a consulting firm. During the period of World War I it entered the manufacturing field for the development of a line of instruments of a highly technical nature. It has continued in the manufacturing business and has gained an international reputation for the quality of its product.

The corporation is owned by three men, all of whom are actively en-

[14] Fictitious name.

gaged in the management of the enterprise. They have a working personnel of 1,500. Like many of the old-line owner-manager type of company, all decisions relative to the operation of the business are the sole responsibility of the owners.

During the past 8 years, the company has encountered serious difficulty in its attempt to obtain and hold labor. The workers organized and became affiliated with one of the international unions. Through the efforts of the union, wages were increased, raising labor costs to a considerably higher level. General unrest and turnover of the working force resulted in contract cancellations. The company now faces the problem of building new markets in what has become a highly competitive field. Many of its competitors during this same period have developed huge industrial organizations. These large companies have moved into new levels of increased efficiency at reduced costs.

The corporation has felt that budgeting would be a needless waste of time. It has based this feeling on the following:

1. The nature of the products makes forecasts of future business totally unpredictable.

2. The company manufactures 80 per cent to *stock*.[15] As orders come in, they are filled wholly or in part from this accumulated storage. Predetermined minimums for goods in storage are set in anticipation of needs for one month in advance.

3. The company is small. Since all capital invested is held by three men, the company is free from the responsibility of justifying its operations to interests removed from the business. The company has had ample financial resources.

4. Since the owner-managers are very close to the operation of the enterprise, a formal budgetary system of control over production is unnecessary.

Preparatory Question

Do you agree with the attitude taken by this corporation toward budgeting? Would a system of budgets aid in solving any of the problems referred to? Refer specifically to factors that might be considered by the corporation in attempting to increase the reliability of sales forecasts.

[15] Goods produced and stored in anticipation of future orders.

CHAPTER XXX

RECORDS AND REPORTS

Previous chapters have pointed with emphasis to the need for records in the operation of an industrial enterprise. They are the instruments of control through which management exercises its directive influence. Records become a part of the *system* through which mass details are placed under routines that are acted on by subordinates but which at the same time reveal *exceptions* that must be called to the attention of the responsible executive.[1] When these danger signals are flashed, management then turns to its past records for information that may assist it in charting a revised course.

From material presented thus far, we can see that industry to be effective must be dynamic. It must be alive and active, changing with the turn of the times, developing its own individuality. New products developed by the research department may steer the enterprise into a wholly new field of development. A war may change it from job-order production to serialized production, or a depression may create a crisis that threatens its very existence. To become dynamic, it must have people who are active, but it must also have managerial machinery which is in tune with its needs and which enables it to pursue this shifting and turning forward movement.

A portion of this chapter is devoted to a discussion of records as a part of the dynamic machinery of an industrial enterprise. It will attempt to set forth the basic principles pertinent to the construction, operation, and continual adjustment of a system of records. Since an enterprise gradually assumes an individuality of its own and, as an individual has its own peculiar problems, no rule-of-thumb directives can be given to guide the organization of a system of records. Instead, management must look to general principles for its cues in the development of records to fit its own problems and its own needs.

The Requisites of Efficient Records.—There is a tendency to add record forms but never to discard, until the system becomes so weighty and cumbersome that a major housecleaning sweeps away the unessential. Present, too, is a natural aversion on the part of some people to the establishment of any new records that may cause any additional work. Both tendencies act to obstruct effective management.

[1] See Chap. VI for a discussion of the exception principle as an aid to management.

The Hoover Commission report revealed illustrations of waste in record keeping that, although amplified by the size of our Federal operations, are typical of conditions that also exist in business and industry.[2] For example, it was found that about 5,000 people, at a cost of more than 15 million dollars a year, are required to examine freight carloads of vouchers hauled to Washington from all over the United States. This costly system results from the law which requires administrative agencies to submit all expenditure vouchers for every individual transaction to the General Accounting Office for examination and settlement. The commission recommended that the individual examination of all expenditure vouchers in Washington should be curtailed by enabling the Comptroller General to spot-check vouchers outside Washington.

The commission also reported that at the time of its investigation the records of the Federal government would fill six buildings each the size of the Pentagon Building. About 50 per cent of the total records of the average government agency could have been transferred to a records center. The government saves about $27 a year every time the contents of one filing cabinet are transferred to a records center.

Recognizing these possible weaknesses, management of industry must be constantly on the alert for unnecessary duplication of records or, on the other hand, an inadequacy of them. Many industrialists have decried the flood of records and reports that have been required by the Federal government in the control of costs, materials, labor practices, etc. Undoubtedly, many of these complaints of the industrialists were justifiable. Yet, some of these same industrialists will admit that only through the help and pressure of the Federal government were they able to establish adequate records for the carrying on of their own managerial functions. The control of materials is a fitting example. Industrialists were dealt their first real blow in the way of compulsory records with the inauguration of the controlled materials plan in World War II. But only because of these Federal regulations was an adequate system of records established. Once in operation, their usefulness to the enterprise was quite evident. But even if the regulations had been removed, the majority of manufacturers would probably have voted for the continuation of the same or similar record procedures.

As an aid to the evaluation of records, the following principles are presented.

Is the Purpose Essential?—The test of the need of a record is to ask: How is it used? Has it been used as a basis for action? Can specific

[2] The Hoover Commission was the popular name of the Commission on Organization of the Executive Branch of the Government, created by the 80th Congress in an act of July 7, 1947.

instances be cited where this particular record became the foundation for future planning?   In reviewing the purpose of a record, consideration must be given to the attitude of people toward records.   Some people are fiends for establishing new records which they are then unwilling to operate.   They are interested only in the development of something new, while other people actually become attached to their records.   Instances have been known, particularly in small companies, where office workers would seek to continue their cherished recordings after working hours, after management had ordered their discontinuance.

There are times, of course, when facts and information should be preserved to cover the legal responsibility of the enterprise, or to present the history of an order, a customer, or an employee, even though the chances of using this particular record may be small when measured in terms of previous practice.   The questioning of how a record is used is not meant to discourage the preservation of facts and information concerning all operations of the company.   The purpose is to eliminate a multiplicity of forms which result in unnecessary duplication of information.

Could the Information Be Obtained from Other Records?—The continuous addition of records soon leads to an endless entanglement of "red tape."   Therefore, when a new record is proposed and the purpose has been found to be essential, the next question should be: Are there records now in existence from which this information could be obtained?   An essential safeguard to avoid unnecessary duplication of records is, of course, that some one person shall keep a master file of the record forms in use and shall continually review these forms and their functions, especially as new needs arise or old needs seem to disappear.   This person, in many instances, may be the controller or the office manager.   In some companies, separate records departments have been established to aid in the accumulation of information with the least amount of duplication.   It assembles this information for use by all departments.   In other instances, only a portion of the record system is put under a special records department.

Quite frequently it will be found that an existing record form does not carry the new information that is desired but does obtain its information from the same source.   In this instance it may be found more advisable to reprint the form, adding the space necessary for the new information, thus avoiding the duplication of much of the information, and thereby clerical labor, that would be involved in the operation of an additional record form.

Is the Form Consistent with Related Records So That It Will Fit Easily into Consolidated Reports?—Where a large number of different individuals are responsible for the preparation of their own record forms, unnecessary variations occur which make the consolidation of information from several records very difficult. Assume, for example, that each department desires to keep a record of the reason given by employees who voluntarily leave the organization. If the record form were left to the initiative of each department, a jumble of slightly different reasons would be recorded. Also, some departments would include more supplementary information than others. Even if all necessary items were listed on a directive to the department, the order and form in which each department would place the items on the record would be so mixed that the clerks, who would need to consolidate them into a central report to management, would encounter needless difficulties. The alternative, of course, would suggest that one record form be agreed upon by all departments with a space for special variations in terms of each department and each employee (see Fig. 174).

Does the Most Important Information "Stand Out" on the Form?—This point is important to the usefulness of the record. The information representing the primary purpose of the form should be so arranged that it is easily identified by the reader without unnecessary loss of time.

Is the Size of the Form Convenient for Handling and Filing?—The form should be constructed in terms of how it is to be used. If it is to be placed in a visible file and rarely, if ever, removed from the file, it may be placed on a small card conforming to the size of the standard filing equipment. On the other hand, if the form may be removed from the file at frequent intervals and sent to the desks of clerks or executives, a somewhat larger size may be desirable. For one thing, small cards are easily misplaced when taken from the files. If they are placed in a folder with other material, they become lost between larger sheets within the folder. In some instances, when card forms or forms of less than letter size must be removed from the files at frequent intervals, special folders or notebooks that bind the forms together by clamp or ring are provided to facilitate handling and to prevent loss of records. Naturally, the form, binder, and file would all have to be taken into consideration at the time the form was constructed.

Does the Record Routine Automatically Call Forth Exceptions?—As previously stated, records are an essential tool for the operation of the "exception principle." If the record routine is properly established, little if any executive or supervisory attention is required until a danger signal is flashed or an exception to the routine occurs. For example, as explained in Chap. XVI, regular inspection records are usually maintained as a matter of routine. Production tolerances are established which inspectors are authorized to pass or reject. However, a chief inspector or some of his designated subordinates may be called upon to

TERMINATION OF EMPLOYMENT

DATE _____

NAME _____ S. S. NO. _____

ADDRESS _____

CLOCK NO. _____ TOOL ACCOUNT _____ LAST DAY WORKED _____

WORK QUALIFIED FOR _____ BENEFIT RATE _____

REASON FOR SEPARATION (CHECK)		LAID-OFF	DROPPED

QUIT

☐ LACK OF WORK   ☐ SICK

DISMISSED   ☐ CONTINUED ABSENCE

☐ HAS ANOTHER JOB   ☐ LEAVING CITY   ☐ INCOMPETENCE   ☐ DAMAGED TOOLS

☐ WORK UNSUITABLE   ☐ TO GET ANOTHER JOB   ☐ ATTENDANCE   ☐ EXCESS SCRAP

☐ FAMILY REASONS   ☐ UNKNOWN   ☐ INTEMPERANCE   ☐ LABOR DISPUTE

☐ TO RETURN TO SCHOOL   ☐ PAY   ☐ DISCIPLINE   ☐ ACT OF GOD, FIRE, ETC.

☐ TO RETURN TO SELF-EMPLOYMENT   ☐ REFUSED TRANSFER

☐ TO RETURN TO EXEMPT EMPLOYMENT   DISCHARGED   ☐ _____

☐ GAVE NOTICE OF _____ DAYS   ☐ MISCONDUCT

☐ STATE "SEPARATIONS REPORT" FILED   ☐ WORKMEN'S COMPENSATION

PHRASE USED _____   ☐ OLD AGE BENEFITS

DETAILED STATEMENT: (MUST BE MADE AT TIME OF SEPARATION)

_____

_____

_____

_____

_____

_____

_____

SIGNED _____ APPROVED _____

SUPERINTENDENT

EMPLOYEE PROTEST—IF EMPLOYEE DISAGREES WITH COMPANY STATEMENT MADE ABOVE, HE MAY WRITE IN HERE HIS OWN VERSION OF THE REASON OF EMPLOYMENT TERMINATION. DOING SO WILL NOT IN ANY WAY IMPAIR ANY RIGHTS OF UNEMPLOYMENT BENEFITS OR INTERFERE WITH FINAL PAYMENT OF WAGES DUE. USE OTHER SIDE IF NECESSARY.

_____

_____

_____

_____

_____

_____

THE FOREGOING IS THE REASON FOR THE TERMINATION OF MY EMPLOYMENT

SIGNED _____

REPLACED BY _____ AS PER EMPLOYMENT REQUISITION NO. _____

NAME

SIGNED _____

EMPLOYMENT MANAGER

FIG. 174.—This termination of employment form is typical of the 8½ by 11 inch forms in use today. This form allows space for the departing employee to register his protest if he disagrees with the reason given for termination of employment. Employer can also present his version of why the employment is ending. (*Courtesy of Remington Rand, Inc., from their booklet, Personnel Administration Records and Procedure.*)

762

act upon those exceptions that fall within a margin of uncertainty, *i.e.*, those items which are not within the allowable tolerances or so close as to make rejection questionable. The inspection records should be so established that these exceptions are easily segregated and sent to the chief inspector automatically.

Pursuing the same inspection illustration, routines must be established to facilitate the control of scrap materials in production. A certain amount of scrap is expected and varies in terms of different operations. Clerks responsible for handling the inspection-records should, by their records procedure, be able to run a cumulative check on scrap. When the amount reaches a point where, by predecision, it is thought excessive, it is automatically referred to the executive in charge for further analysis and possible action.

Use of Committees in Construction and Review of Record Forms. As previously mentioned in this chapter, consideration should be given to the attitude of individuals toward records. Each company is filled with different personalities that must be brought together into a harmonious relationship. Each will have his own ideas regarding records that pertain to his work. Therefore, in order to obtain the acceptance and effective operation of records, every person in authority whose work pertains to the record form that is being constructed should be consulted. To consult these people individually can bring to the surface only a variety of opinions and suggestions. Little can be accomplished through individual consultation in the way of harmonizing these opinions. Preferably, these individuals should be called together to consider the proposed record form in terms of the requisites previously mentioned In this way, each may become conscious of the total purpose of the record throughout the organization. The final form that is adopted arises from group decisions. This is quite different from having the form inflicted from above or from someone in a parallel position.

Many companies have the policy of a periodic review of all records. When record forms are first constructed, a review date is set. It is expected that each individual who comes into contact with the form will accumulate criticisms and suggestions for its improvement. When the review date arrives, the blank form is circulated for notations of suggested improvements or for its elimination. Usually more than one form can be circulated at the same time and later brought before a committee for consideration of recommended changes.

A Typical Record Adaptation.—For purposes of illustration, Figs. 175 to 178 present an actual example of the adaptation of an inventory-control record procedure to a situation that involved increased volume and Federal control of materials for production. Check the original and revised record forms against the requisites of efficient records as described earlier in this chapter. It is not proposed that this revision is the only or the best form for this particular situation, but it does illustrate the kinds of improvements that can be made within given conditions.

Figure 175 shows the one and only stock record in use by the company at the time revision was being considered. This form was found to be inadequate for the accurate recording of scattered deliveries against a single purchase order. For example, according to the record, delivery of 1,000 units was completed on purchase order 2067 on Mar. 4, 1944. However, delivery was actually made in four amounts of 250 units each in December, January, February, and March. The procedure followed by the record clerk was to erase and correct the amounts in the "quantity received" and the last "balance on hand" items as each additional delivery was received. The auditor found it was impossible to verify the records.

Figures 176 to 178 present the revised forms that collectively replaced the form shown in Fig. 175. These are visible record forms designed for ease of referral. A few items were added, but for the most part the change was one of form rather than content. Note that the form contains four principal sections: ordered, receipts, issuances, balance. Each section operated more or less independently. All purchase orders were recorded in the ordered section in their proper sequence. As parts of these various orders were received, they were recorded in the receipts section according to date. Note that the purchase order number identified receipts with the appropriate item recorded in the ordered section. As materials were issued, the amounts were recorded in the issuances section with no attempt made to identify it with any particular delivery, this identification being contained in a separate record. Balance on hand was divided into two categories: free stock and earmarked. Earmarked stock is that which is applicable only to a designated job number. Note that when full delivery of an order was received, indication of this fact was made by a check mark in the last column of the ordered section. Similarly, when all the items of any particular delivery had been issued, a check was placed in the last column of the receipts section.[3]

The raw-stock control record was a folded sheet into which the detail record (see Fig. 177) could be inserted, thus having in one concise form the record summary and detail. Note that the detail record is for the purpose of identifying materials with job numbers. As many of these detail records could be inserted inside the summary record as necessary. From this record any materials recorded in either the receipts or issuances columns could be identified. Supplementing this raw-stock record

[3] This information was contained on a separate detail record.

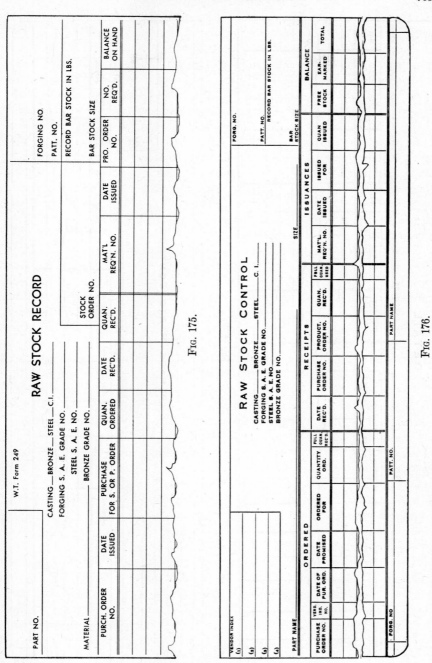

Fig. 175.

Fig. 176.

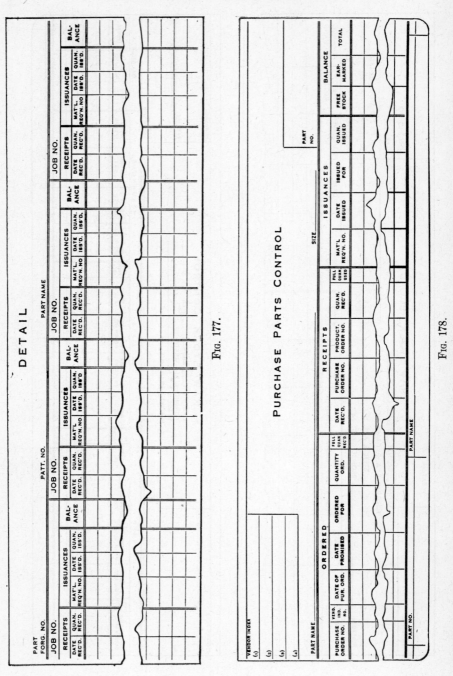

Fig. 177.

Fig. 178.

was a purchased-parts record constructed in exactly the same way and with its own detail inserts (see Fig. 178). Note that all these records are standardized as to form. This facilitates recordings and attempts to reduce clerical errors.

REPORTS

Records form the basis of action. But those records in the hands of a busy executive are worthless unless the pertinent information contained therein is summarized and directed to the problem in question.[4] A report may come as a result of records that reveal exceptions in terms of the "exception principle." It may present the findings resulting from a long period of research and experimentation, or it may merely be a segregation and condensation of material drawn from various sources but requiring not more than a half day's time to prepare. An executive may receive a long, detailed directive from a Federal agency, defining rules and regulations covering a broad field of industrial activity. For the executive who is not familiar with legal terminology or with much of the subject matter of the directive, to comb through this mass of material would perhaps take hours. While he is doing this, he is delaying other matters of business that require his attention and action. So he calls to him one of his subordinates whom he knows to be skilled in the analysis and presentation of material and says, "Look this over and tell me in one page what it means for us."

Thus we find that reports will vary considerably in scope and in subject matter. They will also vary as to type and presentation. These variations will be discussed more in detail in this chapter.

Since reports are the basis for action, the accuracy of information presented is extremely important. There is also the possibility of misinterpretation of information on the part of the person to whom the report is directed. To avoid misunderstanding and misinterpretation, a report of importance should be presented in writing. However, the slogan, "Write it down," may be carried to the extreme with a resulting waste of time and effort. There are times when a verbal discussion of the problem may be more effective. This is especially true when personalities are involved and where the attitude of the individual to whom the report is being presented should be taken into consideration during the presentation. At other times a simple "yes" or "no" without lengthy discussion either verbally or in written form is all that is required.

Types of Reports.—One of many possible classifications characterizes reports as either *periodic* or *special*. A periodic report is one that forms

[4] The reader is referred to Saunders and Anderson, "Business Reports," for further elaboration of many of the points presented in this chapter.

a part of a regular system. It may be presented daily, weekly, quarterly, or at any other regularly designated period. A monthly financial statement is an example. Sales reports may be presented daily, weekly, monthly, or quarterly. Various reports are presented by executives to the board of directors at regular intervals. These may include income statement, balance sheet, tax accruals, orders by product division this year and last, and the number of employees classified by department, by shifts, by method of wage payment, by function, etc.[5]

A *special* report is one that is presented upon request of an executive or upon the initiative of anyone in the plant. In either case it is submitted in reference to a specific problem or idea. It is based on analysis of data secured upon special investigation. Because of the nature of its purpose it usually includes not only facts but conclusions and recommendations. This may vary somewhat in terms of the position and prestige of the individual submitting the report or the dictates of the person requesting it. Special reports may arise automatically as the result of the showing of a danger signal in the accumulation of records. Examples of this are reports on the causes of excessive scrap, absenteeism, and idle time of machines.

It would be impossible to list the subjects that might be covered by a special report. The list would be endless. The report may result from a specific market analysis, an investigation of investments, facts regarding creditors, analysis of trends, a recommendation for a change in channels of distribution, a suggested improvement in production method, a recommendation for the installation of a conveyor system, etc.

Reports Prepared by the Controller.—The controller's division is responsible for the preparation of financial reports for the enterprise. These reports are issued for the guidance of management, investors, creditors, and the general public. Among the various financial reports that must be prepared, two stand out as basic summarizations which are widely used by anyone seeking to study the financial condition of an enterprise. These statements are the balance sheet and the profit-and-loss statement.

The Balance Sheet.—The balance sheet presents a statement of what the company is worth, expressed in terms of dollar value. This statement is divided into three major parts: (1) the assets (what the company owns), (2) the liabilities (what it owes), and (3) net worth (the difference between the dollar value of assets and liabilities).

The balance sheet may report the assets and liabilities of the current year only, or it may make a comparison between two or more years, listing

[5] See Holden, Fish, and Smith, "Top Management Organization and Control," for a listing of operating reports presented to boards of directors.

the assets and liabilities, and net worth, for each year or parts of years in separate columns. This is known as a *comparative balance sheet*.

Where an industrial organization is made up of more than one corporate unit, the financial condition of any one unit is dependent, of course, upon the condition of the other units. In order that an observer may obtain a financial picture of the complete organization, a *consolidated balance sheet* may be issued. This practice has become so widely established that it is considered imperative where multiple units are involved.

Figure 179 is a consolidated balance sheet for the General Motors Corporation for the years 1942 and 1941. Note that the assets are in two main divisions: *current assets* and *investments and miscellaneous assets*. Current assets are those which are fluid and easily converted into cash. Note that only short-term government securities are included in this classification, to the exclusion of long-term securities.

A significant problem in the reporting of assets is the determination of true value. As a general principle, only those assets are included in the balance sheet for which value can be accurately determined. This usually means the purchase or sale price. For example, in Fig. 179, inventories are reported at cost or less, and not in excess of market. This note is added to the inventory item in Fig. 179 in order to allay the fear that inventories have been reported at an inflated value. This same principle is observed in reporting accounts receivable and notes receivable where explanation is given regarding the reserve that has been established for "doubtful receivables."

Attention is called to the last item reported in the assets in Fig. 179: good will, patents, etc. It is usually accepted that items such as these are reported only in the balance sheet if they have been purchased. In this particular instance, General Motors is undoubtedly reporting the good will of a subsidiary company which they had purchased when the subsidiary joined the General Motors organization. Here, General Motors paid a fixed amount for good will over and above the value of other assets. This affords a reasonable basis for estimating the present value of this particular asset. It should be understood that the good will reported in this item does not represent the total value of all the good-will assets of the General Motors Corporation which, of course, cannot be determined except as a matter of opinion.

In the reporting of liabilities, it is considered good business to include even those liabilities which may be doubtful. These may be set up in the form of contingencies or reserves. For example, if the company is being sued for a patent infringement, an estimated liability should be reported if there is a reasonable chance that damages may be allowed. Observe that, in Fig. 179, an amount is set up under reserves for postwar contin-

GENERAL MOTOR
AND CONSOLIDA
CONDENSED CONSOLID
DECEMBER 31,

ASSETS

Current Assets:	Dec. 31, 1942	Dec. 31, 1941
Cash..	$ 287,282,344.81	$ 196,230,729.66
United States Government securities at cost:		
Short term...............................	—	19,997,161.53
Tax notes.................................	57,463,920.00	265,084,000.00
Accounts receivable—United States Government	391,344,591.27	71,089,940.07
Other accounts receivable, notes receivable, trade acceptances, etc. (less reserve for doubtful receivables: 1942, $1,235,888.04; 1941, $1,627,465.73)...........................	111,493,569.51	112,387,425.81
Inventories—at cost or less, not in excess of market (excludes inventories held for account of others under cost-plus-a-fixed-fee contracts:. 1942, $54,772,044.80; 1941, $7,029,526.47)........	466,265,584.86	332,826,773.77
Total Current Assets.......................	**$1,313,850,010.45**	**$ 997,616,030.84**
Investments and Miscellaneous Assets: (Schedule 1)		
Investments in subsidiary companies not consolidated..................................	$ 157,013,694.56	$ 215,913,878.18
Other investments............................	46,260,452.10	43,246,452.50
Miscellaneous assets.........................	10,987,370.62	8,722,825.41
Total Investments and Miscellaneous Assets...	**$ 214,261,517.28**	**$ 267,883,156.09**
Common Capital Stock In Treasury:		
Held for bonus purposes (1942, 41,171 shares; 1941, 211,740 shares).....................	$ 1,678,625.46	$ 4,486,510.02
Real Estate, Plants, and Equipment.................	$ 872,924,635.33	$ 858,193,530.16
Less reserve.for depreciation (including amortization of special war facilities).............	501,441,552.87	448,319,073.97
Net Real Estate, Plants, and Equipment.......	**$ 371,483,082.46**	**$ 409,874,456.19**
Prepaid Expenses and Deferred Charges.............	$ 28,261,329.73	$ 13,800,132.28
Goodwill, Patents, Etc.................................	$ 50,236,551.42	$ 50,322,686.38
TOTAL ASSETS......................	**$1,979,771,116.80**	**$1,743,982,971.80**

88

FIG. 179.—(*Courtesy of*

S   CORPORATION
TED SUBSIDIARIES
ATED BALANCE SHEET
1942 AND 1941

LIABILITIES, RESERVES, AND CAPITAL

	Dec. 31, 1942	Dec. 31, 1941
Current Liabilities:		
Accounts payable.........................	$ 146,613,940.34	$ 86,293,937.83
Notes payable to banks, under Federal Reserve Regulation V...........................	100,000,000.00	—
Due to foreign banks......................	2,423,005.16	17,980,865.05
Taxes, payrolls, warranties, and sundry accrued items............................	87,499,021.45	82,136,175.08
Due to contracting agencies of United States Government, for price reductions required under contracts providing for retroactive price redeterminations......................	104,152,102.71	—
Due to United States Government, under an overall renegotiation agreement with the Government....................................	48,661,545.11	—
Deposits on government contracts............	27,839,152.63	18,217,467.62
United States and foreign income and excess profits taxes...........................	136,049,869.41	290,491.677.43
Employes bonus (see notes).................	5,990,680.10	178.342.49
Dividends payable on preferred capital stock...	2,294,555.00	2,294,555.00
Total Current Liabilities.....................	**$ 661,523,871.91**	**$ 497,593,020.50**
Other Liabilities:		
Employes bonus (based upon cost of treasury stock distributable as bonus)..............	$ 1,639,189.05	$ 5,587,148.64
Taxes, warranties, and miscellaneous..........	39,969,075.39	18,414,160.80
Total Other Liabilities.....................	**$ 41,608,264.44**	**$ 24,001,309.44**
Reserves:		
Employe benefit plans......................	$ 6,386,933.43	$ 6,352,514.43
Employes bonus (undistributed portion of 1941 fund)...................................	—	2,477,295.87
Deferred income..........................	6,339,014.66	5,875,551.58
Post-war contingencies and rehabilitation......	40,584,959.28	16,598,644.22
Contingencies and miscellaneous:		
Allocable to foreign subsidiaries............	12,909,530.11	25,427,545.13
General.................................	16,657,110.92	39,533,717.29
Total Reserves...........................	**$ 82,877,548.40**	**$ 96,265,268.52**
Minority Interest in Preference Stock of Subsidiary Company................................	**$ 1,888.613.20**	**$ 1,888,613.20**
Capital Stock and Surplus:		
Capital stock:		
Preferred, no par value, stated value $100 per share (authorized, 6,000,000 shares; issued, 1,875,366 shares of $5 series; less in treasury, 39,722 shares; outstanding, 1,835,644 shares)................................	$ 183,564,400.00	$ 183,564,400.00
Common, $10 par value (authorized, 75,000,000 shares; issued, 43,500,000 shares)........	435,000,000.00	435,000,000.00
Total Capital Stock.....................	**$ 618,564,400.00**	**$ 618,564,400.00**
Capital surplus..........................	11,944,258.99	11,787,272.91
Earned surplus...........................	561,364,159.86	493,883,087.23
Total Capital Stock and Surplus..............	**$1,191,872,818.85**	**$1,124,234,760.14**
TOTAL LIABILITIES, RESERVES, AND CAPITAL..................	**$1,979,771,116.80**	**$1,743,982,971.80**

89

General Motors Corporation.)

gencies and rehabilitation. This item is in recognition of the probable but indefinite expenditures that will be necessary in converting to peacetime production.

The net worth section of Fig. 179 is shown under the heading, Capital Stock and Surplus. The capital stock represents the dollar value of *shares of ownership* held by the stockholders of the corporation and its consolidated subsidiaries. The surplus is divided into two amounts: *capital surplus* and *earned surplus*. Capital surplus represents original capital held by the company as a surplus; earned surplus represents undivided profits which may be distributed as dividends to stockholders.

Profit-and-Loss Statement.—The profit-and-loss statement (or income statement) summarizes the operations of the enterprise for a given period in terms of the effect on profit or loss. To do this, it reports the income for the period and deducts from that the costs of operations. This statement is particularly important in analyzing recent operations. Where the balance sheet reports the financial condition at a designated date and compares it with the financial condition on a previous date, the gain or loss between those two dates stands unexplained. The profit-and-loss statement attempts to offer explanation of this change.

Figure 180 is the companion statement for Fig. 179. In this particular statement, income is given under three classifications: net sales, equity and earnings from subsidiary companies not consolidated, and other income. Income may be derived from any number of sources, and there is no standard practice regarding the classifications under which income should be reported.

The costs of operations should be divided into at least two classifications: (1) cost of sales and (2) selling, general, and administrative expense. The cost-of-goods-sold item in a manufacturing enterprise is made up of the costs of direct material and direct labor, and the manufacturing expenses directly attributable to the goods sold.[6]

Attention is called to the distinction made between actual expenditures, as included in cost of sales and the three classifications of expense, and the provisions for future expenditures, as listed under depreciation, postwar contingencies, employee bonus, etc. These provisional expenditures are set apart in order to present an honest picture and to avoid the suspicion of hidden expenditures or reserves. This same principle applies to the listing of "income items of a special nature," as illustrated in Fig. 180. These special income items really belong to 1941 earnings but were not actually received until 1942. Because these items were doubtful in

---

[6] These costs should be itemized in separate statements, accompanying the profit-and-loss statement. Further information regarding the identification of these costs is given in Chap. XXVIII.

GENERAL MOTORS CORPORATION
AND CONSOLIDATED SUBSIDIARIES
SUMMARY OF CONSOLIDATED INCOME
FOR THE YEARS ENDED DECEMBER 31, 1942 AND 1941

	Year 1942	Year 1941
Net Sales.....................................	$2,250,548,858.53	$2,436,800,977.49
General Motors Corporation's equity in earnings (net) of subsidiary companies not consolidated (dividends and interest received amounted to $17,818,323.65 in 1942 and $19,955,336.65 in 1941).............	21,529,817.88	22,866,496.22
Other income (including dividends received of $7,003,448.77 in 1942 and $14,011,659.63 in 1941) less sundry income deductions...................	10,440,516.09	17,212,368.08
Total...............................	$2,282,519,192.50	$2,476,879,841.79
Less:		
Cost of sales (excluding provision for depreciation).	$1,832,215,524.96	$1,803,608,246.99
Selling, general, and administrative expense.......	56,196,884.53	101,480,273.85
Provision for:		
Depreciation and amortization of real estate, plants, and equipment.....................	59,162,639.91	53,161,346.73
Post-war contingencies and rehabilitation.......	23,986,315.06	16,598,644.22
Refund in connection with the renegotiation of war material contracts under an agreement with the United States Government..............	48,661,545.11	—
Employes bonus (see Note A)................	5,273,650.30	12,386,479.33
United States and foreign income and excess profits taxes—includes provision for United States excess profits taxes of $30,373,494.30 (after deducting post-war credit of $3,374,832.70) in 1942 and $171,931,085.50 in 1941.............	124,500,520.15	287,992,342.67
Total.................................	$2,149,997,080.02	$2,275,227,333.79
Net Income before Special Income Credits..........	$ 132,522,112.48	$ 201,652,508.00
Add Income Items of a Special Nature:		
Reduction in United States income and excess profits taxes charged to income in 1941 resulting from write-off in 1942 of investments in enemy and enemy-controlled territories (see Note B)........	$ 28,906,475.25	$ —
Recovery in settlement of stockholders' action (see Note C):		
Gross amount recovered......... $4,500,000.00		
Less fees awarded by Court to plaintiffs' attorneys and accountants ($795,000.00) and United States income taxes applicable to recovery ($1,482,000.00)........... 2,277,000.00	2,223,000.00	—
Total Income Items of a Special Nature..	$ 31,129,475.25	$ —
Net Income for the Year.........................	$ 163,651,587.73	$ 201,652,508.00
Dividends on preferred capital stock—$5 series......	9,178,220.00	9,178,220.00
Amount Earned on Common Capital Stock.........	$ 154,473,367.73	$ 192,474,288.00
Average number of shares of common capital stock outstanding during the year....................	43,498,457	43,366,660
Amount Earned Per Share of Common Capital Stock..	**$3.55**	**$4.44**
In 1942, the amount earned per share of common capital stock before adding income items of a special nature amounted to..........................	**$2.84**	

The notes on page 90 form a part of this statement.

FIG. 180.—(*Courtesy of General Motors Corporation.*)

1941, they were not included on the profit-and-loss statement of that year. The General Motors Corporation has now set them apart in the statement for 1942 in order to avoid giving the impression that these were part of the earnings from operations in 1942. This is particularly significant since the amount earned per share of capital common stock, even including these special income items, was considerably less in 1942 than in 1941.

Reconciliation of Surplus.—Stockholders, investors, and creditors are always concerned regarding the details of changes in the surplus accounts. To serve this interest, a special report showing a reconciliation of surplus accompanies the balance sheet and profit-and-loss statement (see Fig. 181). This report merely presents a summarization of the factors resulting in the change in the surplus between the beginning and the end of the designated period. In Fig. 181 the report first states the earned surplus at the beginning of the year, lists any special adjustments in the net income for the year as taken from the income statement, subtracts cash dividends, and shows the earned surplus as of the end of the year. The same general idea applies to the form used in the section reporting capital surplus.

Other Reports Prepared by the Controller.—Most routine periodic reports are usually the responsibility of the controller. The records maintained by his department contain the information essential to the operating reports for departments throughout the organization. These departments are usually held responsible for the control of their own budgets, adjusting their activities as necessity dictates. Therefore, it is exceedingly important that reports to department heads must come at frequent intervals of not more than a month. The kind and number of reports prepared by the controller must naturally vary in terms of the requirements of a particular enterprise. MacDonald makes the following classification of reports prepared by the controller, stating, however, that the listing makes no attempt to include all the kinds of reports but merely indicates a broad division: [7]

Daily and weekly reports, such as reports on sales, collections, and cash position.

Monthly reports, including the operating statement (with such subsidiary analyses as may be required), balance sheet, comparison of budgeted and actual results, status of capital appropriations, etc.

---

[7] MacDonald, John H., "Controllership: Its Functions and Technique," p. 99, Controllers Institute of America, 1940. The reader is referred to this book for an elaboration of the subject of controllers' reports. MacDonald presents a careful selection of excerpts from articles published in the *Controller,* illustrative of reporting practice.

GENERAL MOTORS CORPORATION
AND CONSOLIDATED SUBSIDIARIES
SUMMARY OF CONSOLIDATED SURPLUS
FOR THE YEARS ENDED DECEMBER 31, 1942 AND 1941

EARNED SURPLUS

	Year 1942	Year 1941
Earned Surplus at beginning of year..................	$493,883,087.23	$471,021,152.95
Transfer to Capital Surplus of excess of award value over cost of treasury stock distributable as bonus for the year 1940.......................................	—	7,004,057.47
Remainder................................	$493,883,087.23	$464,017,095.48
Net Income for the Year per Summary of Consolidated Income.......................................	163,651,587.73	201,652,508.00
Earned Surplus before dividends.....................	$657,534,674.96	$665,669,603.48
Less cash dividends:		
Preferred capital stock—$5 series.................	$ 9,178,220.00	$ 9,178,220.00
Common capital stock:		
Mar. 12 ($0.50 per share in 1942)..............	$ 21,749,479.99	$ 32,532,335.89
June 12 ($0.50 per share in 1942)..............	21,748,738.49	43,376,430.50
Sept. 12 ($0.50 per share in 1942)..............	21,749,236.49	43,376,435.75
Dec. 12 ($0.50 per share in 1942)..............	21,744,840.13	43,323,094.11
Total................................	$ 86,992,295.10	$162,608,296.25
Total cash dividends...............	$ 96,170,515.10	$171,786,516.25
Earned Surplus at end of year.......................	$561,364,159.86	$493,883,087.23

CAPITAL SURPLUS

	Year 1942	Year 1941
Capital Surplus at beginning of year..................	$ 11,787,272.91	$ —
Excess of award value over cost of treasury stock distributable as bonus:		
Amount attributable to 1940 bonus...........	—	7,004,057.47
Amount attributable to 1941 bonus...........	585.59	4,078,234.82
Amount attributable to 1942 bonus...........	27,425.27	—
Adjustments arising from forfeitures of prior years' bonus awards reverting to the Corporation...	33,820.57	—
Excess of stated value over cost of $5 series no par preferred stock held in treasury..................	—	704,980.62
Transfer from reserve for general contingencies of profit realized in prior years upon the sale or use of common capital stock received as a result of the operation of the employes investment fund.......	162,795.79	—
Capital Surplus at end of year.......................	$ 11,944,258.99	$ 11,787,272.91*

* Capital Surplus of $11,082,292.29 previously reported at December 31, 1941 has been adjusted by $704,980.62 excess of stated value over cost of $5 series no par preferred stock held in treasury, as a result of reflecting such stock as a reduction of outstanding stock rather than as an asset as reported at December 31, 1941.

NOTE: Earned Surplus includes $32,237,742.46 at December 31, 1942 and $28,597,778.03 at December 31, 1941 for net earned surplus of subsidiaries not consolidated; also $1,679,466.70 at December 31, 1942 and 1941 for earned surplus of companies in which a substantial but not more than 50% interest is held.

87

FIG. 181.—Summary of consolidated surplus. (*Courtesy of General Motors Corporation.*)

Annual reports to management, employees, and stockholders.

Reports to governmental bodies, including Federal, state, county, and municipal authorities and those prepared for trade associations or similar bodies.

Special reports.

Reports of public utilities.

The Glenn L. Martin Company has indicated that its

. . . accounting department prepares approximately thirty financial statements (depending upon the number of contracts in process) before the fifteenth of each month, covering the operations of the preceding month and the status at the end of the month. Most of these statements are schedules giving detailed information as to the individual items on the monthly balance sheet and statement of operations. A copy of each statement is furnished to every executive and director who has an active personal interest in the particular subject covered. We do not believe in distributing reading matter unless the recipient has specific interest in it. Hence, this selective procedure in distributing these statements. The titles of these statements are as follows: [8]

1. Balance Sheet (2 pages).

2. Statement of Surplus and Current Year Income (profit and loss statement).

3. Accounts Receivable Schedules (3 sheets).

4. Condensed Summary of Costs (one sheet for each major contract, one sheet for all miscellaneous production orders, one for open shop orders, and stores orders).

5. Statement of Property, Plant, and Equipment showing Cost, Depreciation, and Net Book Values by groups.

6. Schedule of Other Assets.

7. Schedule of Deferred Charges.

8. Schedule of Notes Payable.

9. Schedule of Miscellaneous Accrued Liabilities.

10. Schedule of Unfinished Orders.

11. Statement of Income from Operations.

12. Statement of Engineering Development, Selling, General, and Administrative Expenses.

13. Statement of Factory and Engineering Overhead Expense.

14. Statement of Payroll Summary and Distribution of Overhead.

15. Schedule of Advances Received under Terms of Contracts.

16. Analysis of Sales for the Month.

In addition to the above, columnar statements of detail shop order costs to date for each major contract are made up monthly for the executive vice-president and the vice-president in charge of manufacturing. The columnar statement shows the accumulated costs to date of the engineering labor, engineering overhead, tool labor, tool overhead, tool material, production labor, production overhead, production material, purchased equipment, and direct charges, for

[8] MacDonald, *op. cit.*, pp. 101, 102.

each shop order. Each shop order, of course, covers a particular part of the order, such as design, outer wings, control surfaces, landing gear, and so on, each contract being divided into approximately thirty-five main divisions.

The controller is the person most commonly selected as the director of the budget. Perhaps one reason for this selection is the availability of information within his department. In his administration of the budget he must present projected forecasts of volume, production, and sales, the cash that will be needed for operations during the succeeding months, anticipated receipts and disbursements, etc. These reports are prepared in cooperation with the operating departments and presented to executive officers and the board of directors.

Reports Prepared by Other Departments.—Where records are accumulated within a department, it is customary that reports on operations will be submitted at regular intervals for coordination and control. For example, the general sales executive may require periodic reports from each salesman in the field. This report may present results of each individual call upon a customer or it may summarize the results of a week or month. These reports may be in letter form or they may be on a form supplied by the department. Also, the reporting of personal expenses of the salesman is usually required at regular intervals rather than to permit uncontrolled expenses to accumulate over a long period of time. In all departments routine reports become a part of the established system for the operation of the company where personal and continuous contact of executives with operations within departments becomes impossible or impracticable owing to the size of the enterprise.[9] In some ways the report is a poor substitute for personal contact, but in many instances it is superior in that it becomes more accurate in precise details than would be possible through observation. People have a natural tendency to exercise greater care and discretion in a written report than in one that might be given orally. If the inquirer seeks to investigate for himself through his own personal observation, others frequently feel, rightly or not, that, if facts detrimental to the department are not discovered, no one is responsible for calling them specifically to the inquirer's attention.

On the other hand, for example, if it is established practice that all accidents are to be reported by the department head in writing and under specific headings, the report will tend to be more inclusive of all the facts and will show a greater regard for the truthfulness and accuracy of the factors involved. We may glibly make a statement verbally but we think twice before writing it down.

[9] Reports prepared by the manufacturing, purchasing, sales, and industrial-relations divisions have been discussed in considerable detail in other chapters. See particularly Chaps. XII, XX, and XXVI.

Progress Reports.—It is customary, especially in long investigations, for a progress report to be submitted in order that executives may be kept informed regarding developments. Quite frequently these investigations may be carried on by outside agencies; for example, market research may be carried on by an advertising agency; an organization analysis, conducted by a firm of management engineers; or a financial audit, conducted by a firm of accountants. In other instances, these same investigations might be carried on by departments within the enterprise. In either case, management is desirous of maintaining the privilege of limiting or expanding the scope of the investigation in terms of developments. If after a reasonable period little or no progress has been made, it may seem advisable to discontinue the investigation entirely. On the other hand, consultation may reveal that the scope of the investigation should be enlarged. In some instances, information obtained early in the investigation might be extremely important to management in its immediate plan. A research project being carried on by a research department might, even in the early stages, present evidence that would cause the management of the enterprise to withhold production on the old product in consideration of its possible replacement with a new and better product. A market trend might influence management in an immediate decision regarding new contracts. In most instances, progress reports are brief and present facts with little or no interpretation, unless especially requested. Generally speaking, they are regarded as tentative and subject to change when the investigation has been completed and the total facts brought together for final conclusions and recommendations.

Forms of Reports.—As previously mentioned, some reports present only the facts with perhaps some interpretation, while other reports add conclusions and recommendations. Periodic reports that are of a routine nature fall into the first classification. They are usually known as an *informational* form of report or a *research* form. Quite frequently, these reports follow definite patterns and may even be prepared on printed forms. Research engineers are continually conducting tests and experimentation for which the reporting may be essential for the mere recording of facts, but their application is quite frequently not immediate. It may be that only after years of further experimentation will the findings of today become applicable. For that reason, specific recommendations at the time of reporting are inappropriate.

The *analytical* form of report presents a complete summarization of facts with recommendations and conclusions. This is a form commonly used for special reports. The form itself will vary somewhat in terms of the scope of the subject matter and in terms of its purpose. All analytical reports usually contain the following sections: summary, text, conclusion, and recommendation. The summary at the beginning of the report presents a brief condensation of the content to follow. It attempts to focus the attention of the reader upon the more essential points involved. In a sense, it also tells him whether the report is of sufficient importance to be read in its entirety. Perhaps he will find from the summary that he should give the complete report his immediate attention. On the other hand, he may decide that it should be placed aside temporarily to make room for more urgent matters demanding his attention.

The Text of the Report.—The text or body of the report will usually include at least two divisions. The first is the introduction and contains the statement of purpose, history, or background of the situation that called forth the investigation, and the method used in accumulating and interpreting the data. It is exceedingly important that there be a clear statement of the problem showing the scope and the limitations of the investigation. It is important for the reader to be aware not only of what is intended in the way of points to be investigated or proved, but also of what is not intended. This will tend to influence the reader in confining his thinking to the specific points in question. The statement of method will sometimes include copies of questionnaires and photographs, or drawings of apparatus, etc.

The second division of the text is the statement of findings. This should be a precise statement of facts. It will include tables, graphs, photographs, and other supporting data, presented in terms of the background and interest of the reader.[10]

In the preparation of the main body of the report, it is usually advisable to arrange all data into tables, graphs, etc., and build descriptive and interpretative material around them. This aids the writer in establishing logical sequence in the presentation. Each table or graph should be referred to and interpreted, thus aiding the reader in gaining a full concept of its meaning and applicability to the points in question.

Conclusions and Recommendations.—Conclusions may be a part of the main body or text, or they may be given a separate section of the report. Conclusions should be brief and should avoid unnecessary duplication with the statement of findings. Frequently, conclusions can merely be tabulated or listed. In all instances, the reader should be referred back to supporting data in the text. It should be kept in mind that the writer is expected to base his conclusions precisely upon the evidence that has been presented.

Recommendations.—This is the opportunity for the writer to take greater liberties in interpreting his findings. It is expected that he will

[10] Variations in terms of the reader will be discussed in a later section of this chapter.

assert himself, presenting his thinking, and his ideals, and to some extent his prejudices, since in this section he is not bound to strict adherence to facts specifically proved. Here he can refer to implications that seem to appear and are important to the over-all interpretation. Because of these liberties permitted the writer, there should be a definite line of demarkation between the section on conclusions and the section on recommendations.

Care should be taken to avoid the insertion of new data which were not included in the statement of findings. It is expected by the reader that the recommendations section will set forth practical suggestions as to the application of the findings to specific policies and procedures of the enterprise. This is the point at which the reader may be expected to ask, "What is the meaning of all of this in terms of the operations of our company?"

The Detailed and Formal Report.—In the more lengthy and more formal report, which may be bound and given rather wide circulation, additional sections are added, partly to break up the report into a more comprehensible form and partly to permit the insertion of additional information which might not be necessary where the report was being prepared for only a rather restricted group of readers. Saunders presents an outline of a complete formal report which, in general, is considered standard.[11]

    I. Cover.
    II. Title page.
   III. Copyright notice.
   IV. Letter of authorization.
    V. Letter of acceptance.
   VI. Letter of transmittal.
  VII. Letter of approval.
 VIII. Table of contents.
   IX. Table of charts and illustrations.
    X. Foreword. Usually combined. Sometimes included.
   XI. Preface. In the letter of transmittal.
  XII. Acknowledgment. (Frequently combined with the Foreword and Preface and sometimes in the letter of transmittal.)
 XIII. Synopsis.
 XIV. Body.
      A. Introduction.
      B. Text.
      C. Conclusions and recommendations.
  XV. Appendix.
 XVI. Index.

[11] SAUNDERS and ANDERSON, *op. cit.,* pp. 183, 184.

Note that sections I–XII, XV, and XVI have been added; XIII and XIV are the sections described earlier in this chapter, the section on synopsis being the same as our summary section. Note in this instance that conclusions and recommendations are made a part of the body or text of the report. This is optional depending upon the degree of separation desired by the writer. Section XV contains supporting data which are too long and involved to be inserted in the text without undue disturbance to the flow of continuity in the thinking of the reader. The more technical reader will wish to study this section with great care, while others may glance at it briefly, preferring to accept the interpretations of the writer as superior to his own.

Understanding the Reader.—As mentioned at the beginning of this chapter, writing reports has assumed added significance because through them the enterprise now attempts to reach many different groups of people. In earlier industrial practice, reports were exchanged principally between people who were of a similar background of training and experience. The owners of industrial enterprises were few in number, compared to the millions of small shareholders to whom annual reports are now submitted. Where the owner was previously in close contact with the enterprise, he understood its products, its techniques, its terminology. In most instances, he was an active part of it. Today the enterprise reports to owners who are unknown except by name. These owners represent every walk of life. They vary in their training, experience, and interests. Yet the writer must attempt to understand these people if he is to prepare for them a report which will be meaningful and which will convey the message he has intended.

The function of reporting to executives within the industrial enterprise has also become more complicated for the same reason, but to a lesser degree. For example, the manager of a branch of a world-wide organization prepares reports for executives whom he may have seen but whom he does not really know as individuals. He may have no conception of their individual likes and dislikes. Yet, to be effective, he must do all that he can to understand them.

It is now recognized that the industrial enterprise must carry information to the general public. This is usually handled by the public-relations and advertising departments. In advertising, it is known generally as name advertising or institutional advertising. The public, through these reports, knows an enterprise for its ideals and its achievements. The enterprise becomes a name that carries certain connotations gathered from its reports of activities (see Chap. XXVII on Advertising).

The fourth group is the employees of the enterprise. Recent years have seen a marked development of an attempt to instill in workers an attitude of "belonging." Management seeks to break down the barriers that have existed in the past between the executive "class" and the worker "class." As one manufacturer stated, "We strive to make no distinction between the president and the janitor; they are both essential to the organization." Of course it must be admitted that this is an ideal which as yet is far from realization. But an important factor in moving toward the attainment of this ideal is the extent to which an enterprise is able to share information with its employees.[12] Note that the word "share" means a two-way passage of information. To obtain this passage, management must study workers and workers must study management. Gradually, as they learn to talk to each other, verbally and through their reports, they will come nearer to the ideal of a single operating unit.

Presentation of Data.—Instrumental to making reports meaningful to the reader, consideration must be given to the arrangement of data in a form that will attract the attention of the reader, causing him to peruse its content and at the same time to place in his thinking the pertinent points involved. The technical reader, such as the banker, or broker, the controller, or treasurer, may prefer to have his financial data arranged in table form where he can analyze them in their entirety. Because he is familiar with this type of reading, he can comprehend its meaning more quickly. Because he possesses some confidence in his ability in the field, he may wish to rely chiefly upon his own interpretations without being unduly influenced by the writer.[13] Contrast this type of individual, however, with the casual reader who may have little interest in or experience with financial reports. Yet the enterprise is anxious that he know of its financial successes or failures. As aids to the interpretation of data, charts and pictorial sketches are frequently used. They are especially valuable where otherwise it might be difficult for the reader to make a comparison. To the average reader the comparison of a million dollars and a billion dollars is rather vague. But if given a chart or a picture that will show him a comparison in terms of inches, he can more easily extract the meaning.

Terminology.—Perhaps the greatest difficulty encountered by specialists is that they drift into the use of terminology that is totally foreign to the average reader. The difficulty arises from the fact that the specialist

[12] The reader is referred to an excellent book by Alexander Heron, "Sharing Information with Employees," Stanford University Press, 1942. See also Fayol, Henri: "General and Industrial Management," New York: Pitman Publishing Corp., 1949, pp. 104–107.

[13] This, of course, is not always true. Frequently, financial executives do not wish to be burdened with detailed analyses but expect the writer to make the interpretations in concise form.

frequently is unconscious of his error. The only way in which he can talk to the average man on these technical subjects is to translate his technical terminology into everyday language, or into graphical or pictorial illustrations. Figure 182 is a reproduction of a balance sheet of Swift and associated companies. Note the simplicity of the language in this report as compared to the usual technical terminology of balance sheets. No knowledge of accounting is needed by the reader to obtain a thorough understanding of the assets and liabilities of the company.[14] This report was prepared especially for employees of the company.

Where it is impossible to translate technical terms into more common language without becoming exceedingly wordy and boresome, a report may devote a section to a definition of terms. In the February, 1943, issue of the monthly publication of the Automotive Council for War Production, an article appeared, entitled, How It's Done—No. 1—The Tool and Die Industry. In a prominent box in the middle of a double-page spread the following definitions appeared: [15]

Jigs and fixtures are holding devices. The principal variation is that a jig locates and accurately guides tools during machine operations, whereas a fixture firmly holds in place material to be machined.

Dies are metal blocks with the pattern or contour of a part reproduced on their surface. They are used in presses or forging hammers for forming identical metal parts.

Tools are the implements of machines. They do the actual work of cutting, drilling, shaving, milling, etc.

Gages are devices for accurately measuring the dimensions of manufactured parts. They determine whether or not the dimensions are within specified limits.

The prominence of the box of definitions was such that the reader would automatically observe that the definitions were there, should he have cause to refer to them in the reading of the article.

In one General Motors report [16] the writer, explaining the activity of the company in the manufacture of fighting planes, refers to the production of variable-pitch propellers which the company has developed after several years of research and experimentation. The second sentence of the paragraph explains in simple language, as follows: "A variable-pitch propeller is used in about the same way as the gear-shift in a car,

[14] Reproduced from Company Annual Reports to Employees, *Studies in Personnel Policy*, No. 47, National Industrial Conference Board, Inc., 1941.

[15] *Automotive War Production*, Vol. II, No. 2, February, 1943, pp. 4, 5, Public Relations Department, Automotive Council for War Production, Detroit, Mich.

[16] "Producing More for Victory."

Balance Sheet of Swift and Associated Companies

Listing what we own, what we owe, and what we are worth, as of November 1, 1941, when we closed our books.

Assets (What We Own)

We have cash in 700 banks in various cities, used to pay wages, to purchase raw materials and supplies, and for other expenditure .... $ 14,767,916

We have money coming to us from customers for products we sold to them 59,541,039

We have on hand meats and other finished products, raw materials and other materials being processed; also supplies such as fuel, barrels, boxes, paper, salt, and sugar 119,420,156

We have investments, largely in A. C. Lawrence Leather Company, and English subsidiaries 11,699,088

We have land, buildings, also machinery, tools, delivery equipment, fixtures, and furniture used in our operations 100,960,393

We have miscellaneous assets 7,691,889

    Total Assets   **$313,980,381**

What We Owe and What We Are Worth

Liabilities (What We Owe)

Owing to debenture holders who loaned us money .... $ 23,750,000

Payment to be made on May 1, 1942 for retirement of debentures 1,250,000

Owing to manufacturers for materials and supplies; interest payable; also for wages and salaries available to employes on their next pay day 13,874,151

Provision for income taxes 6,925,487

Provision for social security, state, local, and foreign taxes 2,913,845

Miscellaneous liabilities (including notes payable) 3,773,352

    Total Liabilities   **$52,289,835**

Shareholders' Ownership (What We Are Worth)

Shareholders have invested their savings used to buy plants, equipment, tools, and other materials to operate our business. $150,000,000

Shareholders have left a part of past earnings in the business used for the purchase of additional plants, machinery, raw materials, etc. This is known as "Earned Surplus". 93,367,779

Shareholders have left a part of their earnings in the business as a reserve for fire, contingencies, and possible declines in inventory values. 18,322,767

    Total Shareholders' Ownership   **$261,690,546**

    Total Liabilities and Shareholders' Ownership   **$313,980,381**

Fig. 182.—Balance sheet.   (*Courtesy of Swift & Company.*)

providing a means of varying the power in relation to operating needs." Note the skillful use of an analogy bringing the thinking of the reader to a comparison of the unknown with an object with which he is familiar.

Compare these two illustrations with a report prepared by the U.S. War Production Board.[17]   The first paragraph of the preface signed by Donald M. Nelson, then chairman of WPB, states that "The American people are entitled to a report on the progress of production in our first year of war."   This statement, it would seem, labels the report as intended for public consumption.   Mr. Nelson goes on in the second paragraph of the preface with a statement that gives the casual reader a quick picture of the status of production: "Today we are making as many combat weapons—tanks, planes, guns, ships—as the entire Axis. Today the United Nations together are turning out twice as many weapons as the enemy."   These are striking statements using simple terminology that would undoubtedly interest and impress even the casual reader. If the reader decides, however, that he would like to learn more through the remaining 20 pages of the report, he encounters a maze of figures and technical terminology that leaves such wide gaps in his thinking that intelligent reading becomes impossible unless he is already familiar with the subject matter.   Terms such as "vanadium," "molybdenum," "flue ash," "electrolytic refineries," "ingot production," "forging, rolling, and extruding mills," and "marginal ores," were thrown into the text with no explanation of their meaning or significance.   One pictograph in the beginning of the 21-page report was the only instance where even an attempt was made to present data through the use of charts, graphs, pictures, sketches, or diagrams.

The Length of the Report.—The casual reader cannot be expected to read a long report.   In all probability, he does not have sufficient knowledge of the subject matter to be interested in the detail of the report. Yet, the writer may feel that it is exceedingly important that his reader obtain an appreciation of the points involved.   He may feel that it is impossible to present an appreciation of the subject without becoming lengthy.   In such case, he might do well to submit several separate reports at intervals, each report dealing with only one point and presenting it in a short, concise, and easily understandable manner.   Is it not possible that it might be better for the reader to obtain an appreciation of one point than for the entire report to be wasted?

Conversely, the company executive or other technical reader might much prefer that all points be presented in one report and in considerable detail, even though the report is long.   However, even the executive who

---

[17] "War Production in 1942," issued by the Division of Information, War Production Board, Government Printing Office—War Board 2903.

should be intensely interested in the report must be attracted by a well-prepared summary or synopsis at the beginning of the report.[18]

SUMMARY

The records system of an enterprise must be a part of the moving personality that characterizes the enterprise. Each company, therefore, must construct a system in terms of its own specific needs. But the real problem is to keep the system sufficiently flexible and constantly changing to meet changing needs. Records are intended to serve the enterprise, and it is not intended that the enterprise shall become a slave to an antiquated system. To keep a system in tune with the needs requires constant vigilance by people who appreciate the real significance and purpose of records. This usually requires that the system be centralized under one individual but with the cooperation and assistance of representatives of all departments.

Records form the basis of action, but in order for records to be meaningful they must be interpreted and condensed into reports which may be issued at regular and designated intervals (periodic reports), or they may be prepared as the need arises (special reports). Both types are essential. These reports may vary in general form in terms of the nature of the situation. A report may merely present *information* without comments or recommendations, or it may be *analytical* and present an evaluation of the factors involved in the situation and recommendations for action.

The industrialist whose chief function is one of operation is frequently unmindful of the importance of the reporting function. His chief interest is in getting the work out. Telling others about his work may be viewed by him as an unnecessary burden. Yet if he neglects his reporting function, there will inevitably come a time when he will realize that he does not have the support and cooperation of employees under his supervision or the executives who are his superiors in rank. Through a system of periodic and special reports he might have been able over a period of time to have given these people an understanding, appreciation, and enthusiasm for the operations of his department.

Report writing has assumed added significance in industry because in this day reports must go to many different groups of people, people of varied interests and backgrounds. The report writer must understand his reader and must prepare his report in a manner that will be within the bounds of comprehension and in a way that will attract and hold attention. This requires much more than a technical knowledge of product operations or financial analysis. It requires a knowledge and understanding of people and an appreciation of their basic interests and desires.

[18] The summary of the report was discussed in an earlier section of this chapter.

CASE PROBLEMS

The A. B. Smith Company [19]

The A. B. Smith Company has a practice of issuing warnings to employees for inefficiency, misconduct, and other general infractions of regulations. At least one warning must be issued before an employee is discharged.

The foremen issue all warnings in writing, using the form illustrated in Fig. 183. The notice is first referred to the plant manager for review and signature before being delivered to the employee.

EMPLOYEE WARNING NOTICE

NAME			CLOCK NO.	DEPT.	PLANT		TIME ___ A.M. P.M.	DATE

WARNING AND REMARKS

DEFECTIVE WORK	SAFETY	CONDUCT	LATENESS	ABSENCE	ATTITUDE	HOUSEKEEPING	DISOBEDIENCE	CARELESSNESS

REMARKS

SIGNATURE OF FOREMAN OR SUPERVISOR	SIGNATURE OF PLANT MANAGER

REMINGTON RAND INC.

FIG. 183.—Employee warning notice. (*Courtesy of Remington Rand, Inc., from their booklet, Personnel Administration Records and Procedure.*)

The company feels that all warnings should be recorded on permanent records in the personnel department. This record would provide valuable information regarding the employee's efficiency and would be highly useful and important in dealing with the labor union regarding layoffs and dismissals.

[19] Fictitious name.

Preparatory Question

Suggest forms and procedures that might be used in the installation and operation of a system to provide cumulative individual records and at the same time retain the feature of individual written notices. Sketch any additional forms that you think may be needed. Since the foremen are now familiar with the form and procedure of the warning slip that is issued to the employee, needless change in this form should be avoided.

Reporting Progress in Railroad Efficiency

A study in 1943 of the operating efficiency of the railroads of the United States showed a remarkable improvement when compared with the war year of 1918. The following table shows that passenger traffic had nearly doubled and freight traffic had increased by 78 per cent. Yet the number of freight cars in 1943 was 26 per cent less than 1918; the number of passenger cars was 32 per cent less; the number of employees was 21 per cent less; and the number of locomotives was 34 per cent less.

TABLE XX.—U.S. RAILROADS IN TWO WARS

	1918	1943	Percentage of change
Number of locomotives.........	67,936	45,000	34% decrease
Number of freight cars.........	2,397,943	1,780,000	26% decrease
Freight traffic, revenue ton-miles	409 billion miles	730 billion miles	78% increase
Number of passenger cars.......	56,611	38,600	32% decrease
Passenger traffic, passenger-miles	43 billion miles	85 billion miles	98% increase
Number of employees..........	1,842,000	1,450,000	21% decrease

Preparatory Question

Prepare a recommendation to the American Railway Association suggesting, (1) two groups of people who should receive reports of this improved efficiency, (2) the form that the reports might take for each group, and (3) the most appropriate media by which the reports might be distributed. Where possible, make rough sketches of drawings, layouts, and other special features of the suggested reports.

Coordination of the Industrial Enterprise

CHAPTER XXXI
COORDINATING THE ENTERPRISE

Viewed as a whole an industrial enterprise is a complicated tool of production. In many respects it is like a machine even though its parts are different. It consists of land, buildings, working people, equipment, and materials, which must be combined in the right proportions to make an efficient, operating organization. Materials of many kinds and forms flow into it, are processed by the workers and equipment within the plant, and then flow out of it in different forms designed for other manufacturers to use or for consumers. Like a machine, the parts of an enterprise must be properly selected and arranged. They must fit together and operate smoothly. The object is to unify the enterprise and to make it an efficient, producing mechanism. At the same time the enterprise must be fitted to serve in the world outside of factory doors, because whatever other purposes it may have, that is the grand reason for its existence. Unifying the enterprise as a producing mechanism may be approached as a problem of *internal coordination;* fitting the enterprise into the outer world, as one of *external coordination.* Separating the problems thus for convenience of discussion should not obscure the fact that there is constant interaction and interrelation between them.

INTERNAL COORDINATION

Men set up private industrial enterprises for many reasons, but the prime motive is to gain profits.[1] Real profits come only from the production and exchange of goods and services.[2] The main object of every

---

[1] In modern economy where enterprises are operated by hired managers instead of by owner-managers, profits may take the form of high salaries, bonuses, and many collateral business opportunities opened to managers whereby they may derive personal benefits from the positions they hold.

[2] In a pecuniary economy where profits are first realized in the form of money, greater profits may sometimes be realized by a single enterprise by limiting the

industrial enterprise, therefore, is to produce and sell as much goods as possible so as to maximize profits within the framework of management's responsibilities to stockholders, labor, and the public.[3] Maximum production is best achieved if the enterprise is soundly organized and if all its parts are knit together into a smooth-functioning mechanism. Internal coordination seeks to attain this end.

The business executive is familiar with the problem in its most practical aspects. In many ways in the everyday conduct of his enterprise, the necessity of coordination is forced upon him. If, in the very beginning, he has not properly combined land, labor, plant, and equipment, he starts out with an unbalanced concern. High costs with low profit margin, resulting ultimately in financial difficulties, may be the outcome. If the production department turns out more goods than the sales department can sell, inventories pile up, costs rise, and losses set in. If sales exceed production capacity in the time set for delivery, customers may be lost. If equipment is not properly maintained and if the flow of production is not well planned, waste, stoppages, and breakdowns result. If personnel is poorly selected or improperly placed in the enterprise, disharmony and inefficiency weaken performance. If finances are not carefully planned, the enterprise may fall into distress. These and a thousand more detailed experiences may hamper efficient production and consequently cut down profits. If harmony and a sound working balance are not achieved, the enterprise will be weak and may ultimately fail. It is to avoid this that management must pay special attention to internal coordination.

Scope and Control over Internal Coordination.—Although often difficult and complex, the problem of internal coordination is a manageable one. Every industrial enterprise is something of a little world of its own. It is an independent unit, has functional completeness, and controls its own activities. Although outside forces of various kinds do affect the internal operations of an enterprise, a large degree of control

---

amount of goods produced. The resulting relative scarcity of its products raises their price and tends to increase money profits. The fallacy of limiting production so as to make greater money profits becomes obvious as soon as the economy as a whole is considered. If *all* producers limit output (the volume of money remaining the same), greater money profits would be realized by all, but everyone (including producers) would have less goods to use and enjoy.

[3] Management has gradually come to realize this threefold responsibility. Its duty to the owners of the enterprise is to safeguard their investment and to produce reasonable profits. To labor, management owes living wages, healthful working conditions, and such participation in the enterprise as will give labor a real interest in work. Management's duty to the public is to produce more goods, of standard quality, at reasonable prices.

over company operations is exercised by management. Company executives determine policies and objectives. They know that success depends upon revenues exceeding expenditures. This is the simple rule of profit and is itself a guiding hand and unifying element for the enterprise. Company executives deal with a simple operational structure—production, sales, and administrative departments; all other parts of the organization are elaborations and refinements of these. Within certain limits, executives can plan production, speed up or slow down operations, and change the quality, nature, and style of the product. They can rearrange departments and change the sequence of operations. They can change working conditions, hire better men, carry on in-factory training, and discharge incompetents. They can study the market and adapt their products to it. They can originate sales policies and advertising campaigns for the wider distribution of their product. Executives can budget finances and plan future operations. They can set up administrative and operations committees and establish a system of interdepartmental memoranda, records, and reports.

Attention to all these things is involved in the problem of internal coordination. Its essence lies in constant experimentation with all phases of company organization and operations. The object is to bring all the parts to the highest perfection possible and to weld them into a smooth-working, efficient organization of the enterprise as a whole. It can be said fairly that management is thoroughly familiar with this problem of internal coordination and that it strives constantly to solve it by study, planning, and experimentation.

The means necessary for achieving internal coordination include every tool of management and reach into every phase of industrial operation. Every chapter of this book is designed to show the best known methods for organizing and operating each department of an enterprise. Procedures for connecting each department with every other department are likewise explained. Certain chapters deal very specifically with various phases of the problem of internal coordination. One of these is Chap. VI covering the building of the internal organization. An entire section on managing the general offices (Chaps. XXVIII to XXX) and dealing with office organization, cost control, budgeting, records, and reports, has particular significance in the problem of internal coordination. Where the problem shifts to the manufacturing division, Chap. XI on production planning, Chap. XVII on methods, and the "control" chapters (XII to XVI) will be found very helpful.

Attention is called particularly to Sect. 3-B, Administration of Industrial Relations. Here emphasis has been given to the dependence on the selection, training, and continuous development and unification of personnel. Here, we have said, is by far the most significant opportunity for management to improve its competitive position. Management has learned that responsibility and authority must be *shared* through the *pooling of judgment* at all levels of personnel within the enterprise. The effective application of this principle requires the organization of the company into a network of *understanding units* built through the utilization of modern machinery of human-relations principles and practices.

Limitations on Internal Coordination.—In striving to perfect internal coordination, management has to deal with conditions and agencies that lie in various degrees outside of its control. Vast changes have radically altered the little world of the industrial enterprise. Changes in specialization, competition, science, technology, population growth, industrial expansion, the status of labor, the role of government in economic life, the markets for goods and services, and other factors of economy have today reduced the individual company to the place of an atom in a vast and complicated outer world. Independent though it may be in its own sphere, the industrial enterprise is vitally affected by these forces. Increasingly, it becomes a problem of internal coordination for the enterprise to adapt itself to this outer world. Indeed, this process of adaptation is so important, and the methods of achieving it are so different from those involved in internal coordination, that it constitutes a subject all of its own. We consider it as the problem of *external coordination* and believe that it constitutes a challenge to the best brains in industrial management today.

EXTERNAL COORDINATION

External coordination deals with problems which are generated in the world outside factory doors and which vitally affect the conduct of every industrial enterprise. No company today can be operated in disregard of the influence of labor organization. No company can remain aloof from developments in its industrial class or from the influences of the wider economy. Every enterprise must keep abreast of advances in science and technology. Industrial management today is vitally affected by government operations and by the demand that complex community life makes upon private enterprise. If management fails to understand and to take account of these forces and conditions, the success of the enterprise is likely to be jeopardized. It is the aim of external coordination to tie the individual company to its industrial group and to the national economy; to fit it into life in the community and in the nation; to bring it into contact with the international economy; in short, to provide for a two-way passage of information between the industrial enterprise and the outer world and to bring about mutual understanding of the problems in each sphere.   To do this, it is necessary to understand the complete setting in which every enterprise must function.

The Setting of the Industrial Enterprise.—In addition to his own interests, every person has interests connected with his family, his community, and the nation.   He has contacts and relations in each sphere. From each of them he receives certain benefits and to each he owes certain responsibilities.   Rarely can he live his life uninfluenced by conditions in these other spheres.   In the same way a single industrial enterprise can function only in relation to its industrial family, the community, the nation, and to other areas of thought and action.   In each of these spheres certain forces and conditions are present which differ from those in the other spheres.   For that reason and for convenience of explanation, we treat each sphere as something of a "world" of its own.   We try to see what transpires in each sphere, how it affects the industrial enterprise, and what management can do about it.

Standing at the factory door, so to speak, we see not one but many outer worlds surrounding the company.   We might visualize each enterprise to be the center of a series of concentric circles, as in Fig. 184.   Each of these circles represents a different sphere, an outer world with which the individual enterprise has relations.   Some of these worlds are close to the individual company and others seem very remote; but near or distant, what goes on in all these different worlds affects each enterprise. Suppose we look first at the picture as a whole, and later describe its parts in detail.

At the center of the picture is the company which is a small world of its own.   Internal coordination is the fundamental problem in this sphere.   Passing to the circle first removed from the company, we find the *industrial world* with which the company is closely related.   Here, we find the industry, associated industries, service organizations, and markets as spheres functionally related to the company.   The second circle is the world of the *national economy*.   The company and the industry of which it is a functional part comprise a small section of the larger field of "manufacturing," which is itself a small branch of the whole national economy.   The third circle shows the *geographical world* which is the *physical* setting for every enterprise.   Every company has some practical relation with various areas: the local community, the state, the United States regional area, the nation, the world regional area, and the international community.   In the fourth, outermost circle we find the *world of thought, ideas, and resources*.   What goes on in the many fields here influences the industrial enterprise profoundly.

The world external to the enterprise is thus not a simple, single universe, but a complex series of many worlds with which the single enterprise must maintain contact. The connecting lines binding the whole together (in the diagram) do not signify functional or organizational connection, although sometimes they may show such relationships. But they do indicate interdependence, interrelationship, and the dynamic

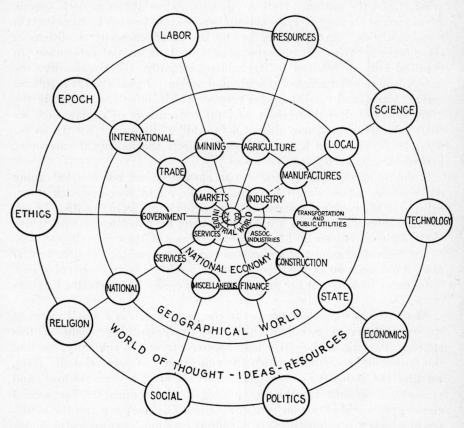

FIG. 184.—The chain of relationships between a single enterprise and the world outside its doors.

motion that connects each world with all others. The positions of the worlds in the diagram are constantly changing, and limitless patterns of association are turned up from one moment to the next in kaleidoscopic fashion. The whole makes up the world external to the single enterprise. Every company must, and does in some measure at least, coordinate its interests and activities with this outer world. No company can live by itself, in a vacuum so to speak, securely insulated from the influences of all that exists outside. Why this is so may best be seen by a closer examination of the problems that come to the factory doors from the external world.

Coordinating the Enterprise with the Industrial World.—The industrial world immediately surrounding the individual company is the world best known to it because the company is a functional part of it. Here, we find other enterprises producing the same and similar products and competing with the company. We also find the vast network of associated industries and activities which cooperate with the company and with which the company cooperates in turn. These are the material suppliers; those who sell machinery, equipment, tools, and accessories; sources which provide the labor supply; others who perform insurance, banking, engineering, research, transportation, and other services for the enterprise; and finally, those who furnish outlets for the products of the enterprise—other industries, wholesalers, jobbers, and retailers.

Although these enterprises and activities lie in an area outside of and surrounding the individual enterprise, they are so essential to it that they are, in fact, but external parts of it. The individual company cannot function without coordinating its activities with theirs. How vast a field this coordination may have to cover is best indicated by the wartime experience of General Motors which maintained relations with 18,735 subcontractors on the subject of production alone. But whether these relationships are complex as in the case of the mass production industries or simple as they would be to the small machine shop, the coordination takes place naturally and easily in the course of the ordinary business routine of the enterprise.

The production and purchasing departments of a company, for example, establish relations with those who supply raw materials, machinery, other equipment, and production services. The personnel and industrial-relations departments maintain contacts with the labor supply and with labor organizations. The sales department makes contacts with the various outlets for the products of the enterprise; and through advertising and other methods, attracts the attention of others in the industry. The shipping department coordinates its activities with transportation agencies. The managing officers of the company build up relationships with insurance, banking, and other service agencies. This natural coordinating process is aided by a large and varied literature pertaining to the industry—catalogues, directories, statistical reports, and other material issued by government and private organizations. In this manner and as a routine part of its own functions and operations, each enterprise surrounds itself with a network of coordinating lines which tie it in with others who serve and complement it. These connections are supplemented by organizations serving the particular industry in which an enterprise is classified, and by coordinating channels within the economic system as a whole.

Trade Associations as Coordinators.—Among the organizations directly serving particular branches of industry, the trade associations are by far the most important. A trade association is a voluntary nonprofit organization of business competitors established to look after the common interests of all member firms in an industry or particular branch of an industry. Business units such as corporations, partnerships, and individual enterprises, rather than individuals, comprise its membership. It does not itself produce, buy, or sell goods for profit. The trade association assists its members in matters of accounting practices, business ethics, commercial and industrial research, standardization, statistics, trade promotion, and in relations with government, labor, and the general public. It may issue periodic bulletins on these interests and often conducts a trade magazine. It arranges frequent conferences and annual conventions for members of the industry. It often represents the industry before legislative bodies and in public relations. The trade association, in short, is a powerful instrument directly concerned with coordinating the firms in a particular industry and relating them to all other industries. There are approximately 8,000 trade associations active in the United States, of which 2,200 serve manufacturers.

The textile industry provides a good example to show the interrelations of various branches of a single industry and how they are served by specific trade associations. Take the Cozy Comfort Mills,[4] a company that produces cotton blankets. This company, along with other companies making sheets, army duck and canvas, tire fabrics, etc., is part of a specific industry called the "cotton broad-woven goods" industry. The cotton broad-woven goods industry is itself one of four subgroups— the other three being the cotton narrow-fabrics industry, cotton yarn industry, and cotton thread industry—in the minor industrial group called "cotton manufacturers." Nine of these minor industrial groups— cotton; silk; rayon; woolen and worsted; knit goods; dyeing and finishing; carpets, rugs, and other floor coverings; hats except cloth and millinery; and miscellaneous textile manufactures—make up the major group of Textile-mill Products and Other Fiber Manufacturers. Twenty major groups of industries comprise the national economy.[5] The chart

[4] Fictitious name.

[5] The 20 major groups in manufacturing are foods; tobacco; textile-mill products; apparel; lumber; furniture; paper; printing and publishing; chemicals; petroleum and coal; rubber; leather; stone, clay, and glass; iron and steel; nonferrous metals; electrical machinery; other machinery; automobiles and equipment; other transportation equipment; and miscellaneous industries. See note 1, p. 1, of this volume.

Many abbreviations have been used in order to simplify the relationships between

in Fig. 185 shows how the textile industry is served by trade associations; and supplementing these are many other trade associations in other industries whose equipment and products are used in the textile industry. In the same way every one of the 20 major industry groups in the national economy is subdivided and served by other trade associations.

The World of the National Economy.—In an economy of specialization where each enterprise is dependent upon many other, widely different enterprises, coordination within each industrial group must be supplemented by coordination in the economy as a whole. The textile industry, for example, does not operate in a vacuum. It functions in connection with, and is affected by, the 20 major industrial groups that make up the field of "manufacturing." And manufacturing, in turn, has to be associated with the other major fields—agriculture, mining, forestry and fishing, construction, finance, trade, government and other professional services, and miscellaneous activities—to make up the national economy.

The problem here is to link the individual enterprise with the national economy. There are two aspects to the problem: (1) coordination for purely technical and functional reasons and (2) coordination for the purpose of handling national problems that indirectly affect every enterprise.

The need of coordinating every single company with all other parts of the economy as a functional mechanism is obvious. How could the textile industry operate without connecting links with button manufacturers, makers of dyestuffs and other chemicals, producers of looms, importers of textile fibers, manufacturers of motors and machines, sources of electric power, and the like? These are all outside the textile field but they affect every company in the textile industry. In the same way the mining of coal and iron has to be linked with industries making steel. Steelmakers, in turn, must be linked with the thousands of industries that use steel in making products for every other branch of the economy. These are examples of technical and functional coordination. How is it achieved?

Each enterprise is linked functionally with the national economy in the same way that it is connected with other enterprises in its own field, *i.e.*, through specialization. In the course of their operations, the various departments of an enterprise establish these connections because interdependence makes them necessary. At many points they utilize the

---

industrial groups that comprise the national economy. For a more detailed description see "Industry Classifications for the Census of Manufactures, 1939," U.S. Department of Commerce, Bureau of the Census, Washington, D.C., 1940.

THE TEXTILE INDUSTRY : ITS PRINCIPAL SUBDIVISIONS AND LEADING TRADE ASSOCIATIONS

THE "TEXTILE-MILL PRODUCTS" GROUP WAS THE LARGEST OF AMERICA'S 20 GROUPS OF MANUFACTURING INDUSTRIES AS TO NUMBER OF EMPLOYEES IN 1939 (SEE EXHIBIT 4). IT INCLUDED 6,400 FACTORY ESTABLISHMENTS , WITH MORE THAN 1,160,000 EMPLOYEES AND PRODUCTS VALUED AT ALMOST $4,000,000,000.

THE SUBDIVISIONS OF THIS GROUP ARE PRESENTED BELOW, TOGETHER WITH DATA FROM THE 1941 FINAL REPORTS OF THE CENSUS OF MANUFACTURES COVERING 1939. LEADING TRADE ASSOCIATIONS OF MANUFACTURERS OF TEXTILE PRODUCTS ARE GIVEN FOR EACH SUBDIVISION, TOGETHER WITH THE APPROXIMATE MEMBERSHIP OF EACH. A NUMBER OF PROFESSIONAL AND OTHER ASSOCIATIONS IN THIS INDUSTRY ARE NAMED BELOW. ASSOCIATIONS OF "APPAREL" MANUFACTURERS ARE LISTED IN SECTION 7, GROUP 23.

THIS CHART INDICATES THE TIME-SAVING INFORMATION THAT CAN BE PREPARED BY COMBINING DATA IN THIS DIRECTORY WITH PERTINENT INFORMATION FROM REPORTS OF THE CENSUS BUREAU OF THE DEPARTMENT OF COMMERCE.

No. of manufacturing employees*	SUBDIVISIONS	Number of factories	Volume of production (millions)	LEADING TRADE ASSOCIATIONS (and number of members)
323,000	COTTON BROAD WOVEN GOODS	661	$869	**COTTON Manufacturers:**
15,000	COTTON NARROW FABRICS	163	49	Cotton Textile Institute (450 members)
73,000	COTTON YARN	349	199	American Cotton Mfrs. Assn. (400)
14,000	COTTON THREAD	75	51	National Assn. of Cotton Mfrs. (400)
(145,000)				Cotton Thread Institute (50)
				Durene Assn. of America (20)
				Mercerizers Assn. of America (20)
				Middle States Textile Mfrs. Assn. (20)
				Interlining Mfrs. Assn. (20)
167,000	HOSIERY	932	416	Narrow Fabrics Institute (30)
				Webbing Mfrs. Institute (20)
				Print Cloth Group of Cotton Mfrs. (50)
				Southern Combed Yarn Spinners Assn. (60)
155,000	WOOLEN & WORSTED MANUFACTURES	659	698	**HOSIERY Manufacturers:**
3,000	CARPET YARNS, WOOLEN & WORSTED	18	20	National Assn. of Hosiery Mfrs. (400)
(158,000)				Full-Fashioned Hosiery Mfrs. of America (40)
				Southern Hosiery Mfrs. Assn. (300)
				Woolen Hosiery Institute of America (20)
73,000	RAYON BROAD WOVEN GOODS	275	278	**WOOL Manufacturers:**
7,000	RAYON NARROW FABRICS	120	21	National Assn. of Wool Mfrs. (400)
9,000	RAYON YARN & THREAD	84	30	National Assn. of Wool Fibre Mfrs. (20)
(89,000)				Hair Cloth Mfrs. Assn. of the U.S. (20)
				Pacific Coast Wool Mfrs. Assn. (20)
41,000	KNITTED UNDERWEAR	199	113	**SILK & RAYON Manufacturers:**
25,000	KNITTED OUTERWEAR (except gloves)	709	104	National Federation of Textiles (100)
12,000	KNITTED CLOTH	229	69	National Rayon Weavers Assn. (40)
6,000	KNITTED GLOVES	20	12	Rayon Yarn Producers Group (20)
(84,000)				Silk Commission Mfrs. Assn. (150)
				Textile Economics Bureau (20)
				Throwsters Research Institute (80)
				KNITTED GOODS Manufacturers:
67,000	DYEING & FINISHING COTTON, SILK, Etc.	468	271	National Knitted Outerwear Assn. (500)
4,000	DYEING & FINISHING WOOLEN & WORSTED	63	37	Underwear Institute (180)
3,000	CLOTH SPONGING & FINISHING	112	24	Associated Knitwear Contractors Assn. (100)
(74,000)				United Knitwear Mfrs. League (100)
				DYEING & FINISHING Plants:
				Brattice Cloth Mfrs. Assn. (20)
23,000	SILK YARN AND THREAD	131	64	Canvas Water Proofers Assn. (20)
11,000	SILK BROAD WOVEN GOODS	119	37	Dyers & Printers Employers Assn. (40)
5,000	SILK NARROW FABRICS	· 100	13	National Textile Processors Guild (50)
(39,000)				National Assn. of Finishers of Textile Fabrics (50)
				Textile Refinishers Assn. (40)

Fig. 185.—How the textile industry is served by trade associations.

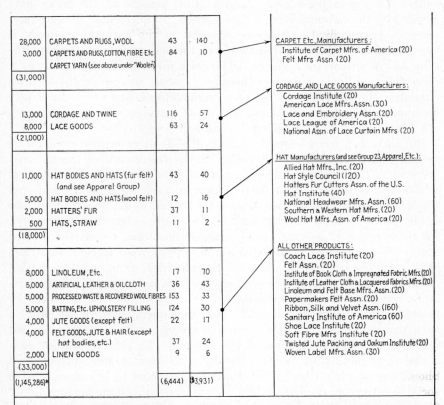

28,000	CARPETS AND RUGS , WOOL	43	140
3,000	CARPETS AND RUGS, COTTON, FIBRE Etc.	84	10
	CARPET YARN (see above under "Woolen)		
(31,000)			

CARPET Etc., Manufacturers :
   Institute of Carpet Mfrs. of America (20)
   Felt Mfrs Assn (20)

13,000	CORDAGE AND TWINE	116	57
8,000	LACE GOODS	63	24
(21,000)			

CORDAGE, AND LACE GOODS Manufacturers:
   Cordage Institute (20)
   American Lace Mfrs. Assn. (30)
   Lace and Embroidery Assn. (20)
   Lace League of America (20)
   National Assn. of Lace Curtain Mfrs (20)

11,000	HAT BODIES AND HATS (fur felt) (and see Apparel Group)	43	40
5,000	HAT BODIES AND HATS (wool felt)	12	16
2,000	HATTERS' FUR	37	11
500	HATS, STRAW	11	2
(18,000)			

HAT Manufacturers (and see Group 23, Apparel, Etc.) :
   Allied Hat Mfrs., Inc. (20)
   Hat Style Council (120)
   Hatters Fur Cutters Assn. of the U.S.
   Hat Institute (40)
   National Headwear Mfrs. Assn. (60)
   Southern & Western Hat Mfrs. (20)
   Wool Hat Mfrs. Assn. of America (20)

ALL OTHER PRODUCTS :
   Coach Lace Institute (20)
   Felt Assn. (20)

8,000	LINOLEUM, Etc.	17	70
5,000	ARTIFICIAL LEATHER & OILCLOTH	36	43
5,000	PROCESSED WASTE & RECOVERED WOOL FIBRES	153	33
5,000	BATTING, Etc. UPHOLSTERY FILLING	124	30
4,000	JUTE GOODS (except felt)	22	17
4,000	FELT GOODS, JUTE & HAIR (except hat bodies, etc.)	37	24
2,000	LINEN GOODS	9	6
(33,000)			
(1,145,286)*		(6,444)	($3,931)

   Institute of Book Cloth & Impregnated Fabric Mfrs.(20)
   Institute of Leather Cloth & Lacquered Fabrics Mfrs.(20)
   Linoleum and Felt Base Mfrs. Assn. (20)
   Papermakers Felt Assn. (20)
   Ribbon, Silk and Velvet Assn. (160)
   Sanitary Institute of America (60)
   Shoe Lace Institute (20)
   Soft Fibre Mfrs Institute (20)
   Twisted Jute Packing and Oakum Institute (20)
   Woven Label Mfrs. Assn. (30)

LEADING STATES in the Textile Industry include North and South Carolina, Massachusetts, Georgia & Pennsylvania

OTHER "TEXTILE INDUSTRY" ASSOCIATIONS (over-all, miscellaneous, professional, etc.) include :

Allied Textiles Research Society	Better Fabrics Testing Bureau	Nat'l. Council of Textile Industries
Amer. Assn. of Textile Chemists & Colorists	Houston Cotton Exchange	Nat'l. Farm Chemurgic Council
Amer. Assn. of Textile Technologists	Memphis Cotton Exchange	Nat'l. Needlecraft Bureau
Amer Cotton Cooperative Assn.	Nat'l. Assn. of Woolen & Worsted	Nat'l. Wool Growers Assn.
Amer Cotton Waste Exchange	Overseers	Nat'l. Wool Marketing Corporation
	Nat'l. Cotton Council of America	New Orleans Cotton Exchange

New York Cotton Exchange   Textile Export Assn. of the U.S.
Savannah Cotton & Naval Stores Exchange   Textile Foundation
Southern Textile Association   Textile Salesmens Association
Staple Cotton Cooperative Association   U.S. Institute for Textile Research
Textile Board of Trade   West Coast Textile Association
Textile Color Card Association   Etc.

ASSOCIATIONS OF DISTRIBUTORS : In addition to the approximately 90 associations listed above, there are a number of important national associations of wholesale and retail distributors of textile-mill products; see Section 7 (Commodity Index), Groups 403,419,50 & 51

*Includes 1,082,602 manufacturing wage earners, 54,573 manufacturing salaried employees, and 8,111 salaried officers. It does not include 18,165 distribution, construction, etc., employees of textile mill factories
Source: Trade assn. data - U.S. Department of Commerce, Trade Association Section, other data - U.S. Department of Commerce, Bureau of the Census

"Trade and Professional Associations of the U.S., 1941 Edition", U.S. Dept. of Commerce, Washington, D.C., 1942, Exhibit 6, p.12

FIG. 185.—(Continued.)

trade associations to bring about coordination where a single enterprise cannot itself gain the objects sought. But, because of the wider field covered by the national economy as a whole, supplemental channels and agencies are required. Close coordination of the national economy is brought about by the great network of finance, marketing, transportation, and other service agencies. The price mechanism also serves as a powerful coordinating agency because, among other functions, price regulates the relationship between commodities and thus indirectly coordinates the producers of goods. These, together with specialization, are among what may be called *institutional coordinators*.

But there is a second aspect in which the single enterprise needs to be coordinated with all other enterprises in the framework of the national economy. This aspect reaches beyond the technical coordination that relates the various parts of the economy to each other in a functional whole. It is the kind of coordination that would bring about alterations in the parts of the economy, and in the single enterprises themselves, for the purpose of solving broad national problems. Shall the United States raise or lower its tariff charges on imports from foreign countries? Shall subsidies be paid to assist infant industries, or to equalize the income of great sections of the economy such as industry and agriculture, or to bring about price stabilization? Shall investors in securities be protected by national regulation? How can unemployment be handled as a national problem? How can the consumer be protected against monopolistic practices? Should the consumer be protected from concealed poor quality of merchandise by a national grade-labeling law? Should the people of the United States be protected by a comprehensive social security program, and how should such a system be organized? Should the United States encourage labor organizations, and should it regulate the relations between employer and employee? These are a few samples of the limitless variety of questions and problems continually arising in the world of the national economy.

When problems like these first arise, they seem remote from the individual enterprise. Where they do touch the interests of a single company, the connection is at first only incidental. That is, the problem some day *may* affect many individual companies; but for the present, no company has to meet it in its current operations. Such problems are left to be discussed, matured, and acted upon in the country at large or in circles quite distant from the individual company. Rarely does the individual company assert a direct voice in these circles. It attempts to meet larger problems by taking out memberships in many different kinds of group organizations. Aside from the trade associations connected with specific trades or industries, these organizations include national business organizations like the Chamber of Commerce of the United States and the National Association of Manufacturers; the service clubs like Rotary, Kiwanis, and others; special-purpose organizations like the 70 commodity exchanges, the American Association of Independent Small Business, and the like. They include organizations serving business interests of a community or city; state organizations of a similar kind; and regional councils such as the New England Council. Still another group of organizations which department heads of a company may join for participation in group action are the professional associations such as the American Association of Engineers, American Accounting Association, American Management Association, and others of a similar character.[6] It is not unusual for the individual company, as such, and for its various executives to hold memberships in several different organizations.

These group organizations consider the wider problems in the economy that affect the special interests of the members in each group and also problems of a more general nature. They often adopt policies and take detailed action with reference to these problems. By acting as a single representative for a large group of individuals or single enterprises, these organizations coordinate their memberships and bring their collective power to bear upon national problems of interest to the individual enterprise. They often wield great power and, as is often the case in the exercise of power, there is danger of its abuse, as we shall see below.

The Geographical World.—Every enterprise has its place in a physical setting. By its location it is part of a single locality, the local setting. By its charter, operations, and other features, an enterprise is also part of a larger setting, the state. Through dependence upon climate, natural resources, water power, special labor supply, type of market, and particular forms of transportation, an enterprise may find itself part of a regional area such as the fish-processing plants in New England, steel mills in the region of the Appalachians, and factories producing textile-mill products along the Atlantic coastal area. The country abounds with these special regions, some of which are smaller than a state, while the great majority stretch over parts or all of several states. All enterprises have their being, of course, in the nation as a geographical area; but also because they are operating units in an integrated national economy. And, since the national economy is part of world economy, industrial enterprise has its international setting as well.

---

[6] For a complete survey and list of these organizations, see C. J. Judkins, "Trade and Professional Associations of the United States," U.S. Department of Commerce, *Industrial Series* No. 3, Washington, D.C., 1942.

The postwar years began a new era in the number and scope of international organizations. Because of its military victories, economic strength, foreign-occupation obligations, and interest in the peace of the world, the United States plays an increasing part in international activities. In the postwar years 1945 to 1949 the United States made loans, gifts, and other commitments to foreign nations approximating more than 35 billion dollars. This aid; the Marshall Plan (ERP); arms aid to west European countries; special loans to individual nations such as Greece, Turkey, China, Brazil, and others; the Truman proposal (Point Four—Inaugural Address, January, 1949) for developing backward areas of the world; and participation in the expanding functions of the United Nations—all extend the leadership, activities, and obligations of the United States in international affairs. Correspondingly, they exert strong influences on the American national economy and upon every enterprise within American borders.

Every enterprise that bears some direct relationship to its geographical setting will have problems of a special kind. They are problems of location and will cover many different subjects such as local taxation, state regulations covering corporate operations and industrial conditions, special labor problems, raw-material problems, and transportation problems. Many of the problems will involve company relationship to the social conditions of the place where it is located. Some of these problems arise locally and can be solved locally. Others require wider action. Some can be solved by the individual company; others require the combined action of many companies having like interests in the geographical area.

This means that the individual company has two approaches in meeting the problems of geographical setting. Where possible it may coordinate its activities, by its own direct action, with the geographical area in which its problems arise and can be solved. But it will also have to work indirectly through group action with other enterprises in matters that can be solved only collectively. By studying the nature of its interests in relation to the geographical setting, each company can determine how best to approach the problems that arise.

Coordination with the Local Community.—For example, take the question: How best can a company work with the local community in which its plants are located? The problems here usually have to do with local taxation; with ordinances bearing upon the conduct of business; with the health, safety, and morals of the population; with housing and community improvements; with relief of workers in time of unemployment; and with local charities. In other words, the company is a member of a local community and is expected to play a part in solving community problems. Many of these problems are shaped by the fact that the company has its place of business in the community.

There are many ways by which to bring about coordination between the company and the community. Almost every official of every department of the company finds it necessary to keep himself informed of conditions and events in the local community. In many instances, it is part of his daily routine, just as are his relations with his own industrial world. But community problems go beyond the technical relation with plant operations; and in these instances coordination has to be brought about by other means.

A wide variety of channels are open for this purpose. Officials of the company often serve in various capacities in local government bodies. They participate in community organizations which deal with general problems. They become members of local service clubs where they meet officials of other enterprises and where local problems may be discussed. They take part in political groups where most community problems are focused. They make friends in other influential quarters of the community. Many of the associations previously mentioned as coordinators in the industry and in the national economy have local branches in the community, through which company officials often work.

If a direct problem between the company and the community arises and cannot be settled by simple negotiations, company officials may utilize as many of these supplemental channels as the occasion seems to warrant. In many cases the factory is so large, and the community is so utterly dependent upon it, that for all intents and purposes the community belongs to the company. Although less conspicuous than in the earlier days of American industry, "company towns" are by no means extinct. Where they exist, actual coordination between the company and the town is less a problem than is the *kind* of coordination that results. Not all such relationships are so fine as those in Hershey, Pa. In all too many cases, the community is completely subordinated to the plant, which, to put it mildly, is not always for the best interests of the community; nor of the plant. Not only should the company seek to solve its local problems through community action, but it should strive to see these problems through the eyes of the people and public officials in the locality. This may result in some immediate disadvantage to the company, but it is likely to prove to be the best policy in the long run.

Coordination in the Larger Geographical Setting.—Bringing the company into proper relation with the larger areas of its setting—the state, regional area, nation, and the international community—is a much more difficult problem. Rarely can it be done by the efforts of the single industrial enterprise. The problems of these larger areas are too many and too varied, and the interested persons and organizations are too many, for any one company to make headway on its own. Every company can, of course, follow the trend of events and conditions in all these areas and adapt its interests accordingly. But here again, and even in greater measure than is true of the local community, the problems are political, social, and broadly economic. They affect people in the mass. They concern dozens of local communities. The interests of hundreds of enterprises are involved. And the problems themselves are so complex that they must be approached from many different angles. The differential railroad rates between the North and the South is an example of such an issue. The problem of developing the St. Lawrence River as a deep-sea ship canal and for electric power purposes is another example. Such problems can be handled only through group action, which is the form coordination often takes.

In place of direct action as in the case of the single enterprise in the local community, the company affected seeks to act indirectly by participating as a member of a group. In this case as in others previously mentioned (and as further discussed below) the group may be a trade association, a professional association, a political organization, a national manufacturers' association, a chamber of commerce, and others of the same type. In addition there are separate associations formed precisely for the purpose of dealing with problems of a specific area. Examples selected at random from among the many hundreds of these are the New England Council (sponsored by states, cities, and individual companies), the Eastern Shoe Manufacturers' Association, the Southern Commercial Congress, the Mid-West Shippers Advisory Board, the Western Petroleum Manufacturers' Association, and the Pacific Coast Steel Fabricators Association. Every individual enterprise whose interests are rooted in some special locality can find one or more organizations formed to serve the business of such local areas. In part of their activities, associations serving geographical areas link the individual enterprise with others in its own industry. In part, they tie it in with the national economy and with the still larger world of thought and ideas. But primarily they exist to serve enterprises whose interests center in a geographical region, a state, or a city. This often leads to sharp conflict when the geographical interest of the association is at variance with its interest in a special industry and with its national and broader interests. Members of the New England Council, for example, might find themselves involved in many conflicts (shipping, rail transportation, seaports, power, and distribution) whenever the question of building the St. Lawrence Seaway is raised.

The World of Thought, Ideas, and Resources.—At the outermost circle of the external relationships of the industrial enterprise lies the world of thought, ideas, and resources. Here, we find the forces of science and technology at work. Here, too, we come upon the broader problems of labor and resources. It is also the world of frontier thinking in the fields of economics, politics, social relationships, religion, and ethics. What we may call "the world of the epoch" is also to be found here. This means the pattern that stamps a particular age (or epoch) of mankind and influences all that we are and what we do. This concept becomes clearer when we look back over the past and see long periods of time classed as the "feudal system," "mercantilism," the "capitalistic age"; or, when taken from other points of view, the "wood age," the "age of iron and steel," the "power age," the "age of plastics," "electronics," and the like. The basic ideas that stamp a particular period of time create special problems that affect industry.

What goes on in this vast outer world is in some cases very close to the industrial enterprise, as are developments in practical science and technology, or the proposals that labor be given a direct share in management. In other cases the connection is very remote as in the abstract hypotheses of science and technology on such subjects as genes, atomic energy, and developments in the newly discovered field of the electron. In like manner, abstract ideas in economics, politics, social relationships, religion, and ethics circulate in this outer world but seem remote from the practical affairs of industrial enterprise. As a matter of fact, every field in this outer circle has its concrete practical aspects, which do affect the individual enterprise, and also its abstract aspects, which seem to lie beyond practical affairs.

Importance of Coordinating the Enterprise with the Outermost World.—There is not much trouble about coordinating the little world of the enterprise with the concrete aspects of this outermost world. This is because they enter the immediate world of the industry and directly touch the interests of every industrialist and businessman. Take, for example, the idea of social security. So long as this remained a dream of a world of "plenty for all," it was an abstraction to be fondled by dreamers, philosophers, and humanitarians. But when the abstract ideas began to take the concrete form of pension and retirement plans, industrial accident and health insurance, unemployment compensation, and "ever-normal granaries," through laws regulating working conditions and levying taxes for social ends, the once abstract idea became a part of the practical world of the industrialist.

It is with abstract aspects of this outer world that coordination is the most difficult for the industrial enterprise. In this world new ideas are generated, new ground is broken, and material progress is fashioned out of dream stuff. Before we ask how the single industrial enterprise can make contact with this world, a more fundamental question must be answered: Should the enterprise be expected to make contact with this field? Does not the industrialist have enough to do "to meet a payroll" and to hold his place in the stiff competitive struggle? Is not the job of coordinating production big enough for those who form and operate an enterprise? Is not this outer world of pioneering in thought and ideas too vague, too vast, too complex for the men who have tough, practical jobs to do in the workaday world?

Why is it necessary for industrialists to look beyond the practical job to the world of abstract ideas and ideals? The answer may be found partly in the relation that holds between the abstract and the practical world. Problems continually arise in the abstract world which at first seem remote from the routine conduct of business. Eventually, however, many of them take an unexpected, practical turn and affect every enterprise in a material way.

History abounds with illustrations of such developments. In the atmosphere of Wilson's "new freedom," for example, many ideas previously branded as vague, idealistic, utopian, crackpot, confiscatory, and communistic, were brought to maturity in the form of legislation that shook the world of the practical industrialist. Among them was the sixteenth amendment to the Constitution permitting income taxation, the seventeenth amendment providing for the direct election of Senators, the eighteenth amendment writing prohibition into nationwide law, and the nineteenth amendment establishing universal suffrage. There was also other, equally momentous legislation enacted in that period—the Federal Reserve Act overhauling the nation's financial system, national inheritance and estate tax laws which became permanent from that day forward, the Adamson 8-hour-day law for all trainmen engaged in interstate transportation, the Underwood tariff lowering duties on imports, the Clayton Antitrust Act affecting business combinations, the Federal Trade Commission Act giving a government agency great power over industrial and commercial practices, and the Webb-Pomerene Act providing for concerted action by American businessmen engaged in export trade.

Standing at the point of Wilson's new freedom, it makes no difference whether we turn back the musty pages of history to ancient times or look forward to contemporary times under the New Deal or the "Fair Deal," or whether we peer into the distant future of Roosevelt's "four freedoms" and Wallace's "century of the common man"—we meet the same situation. Ideas generated in the "intellectual climate" seemingly remote from practical operations bear fruits of enormous importance to practical business.

The problems thus generated are unlimited. They do not deal only with "social" questions, with political, economic, labor, and ethical problems. They are found in fields of science and technology which are certainly close enough to industrial enterprise. Long the object of discussion and experiment in the realms of scientific "dream stuff," the audion tube in the form of the radio created a revolution in the practical world. Whitney's principle of interchangeable parts was a century old in the world of technology before it flowered in modern mass production and fundamentally altered the practical world. Today's laboratory experiments in the transmutation of matter, in synthetics, plastics, electronics, and in the lighter metals and alloys, promise great changes for the world of tomorrow. In these days of rapid development, the ideas in the abstract world are much closer to the practices in the so-called practical world than we recognize.

If industrial enterprise is certain to be vitally affected by these problems, it ought to know about them, participate in the discussion and solution of them, and learn how to adapt its policies and operations to them. And it ought to do this before those problems reach the practical stage. In other words, it is a matter of long-range planning for the individual enterprise to be brought into a working relation with this distant external world where so many problems mature. It is also a matter of peace and expediency. Much needless conflict is generated because the idealists, dreamers, and professors speak one language while the practical businessmen speak a different one. The world's progress is intolerably slow and often accompanied with much violence while the barriers between the two worlds are swept away and cooperation is effected.

Coordinating the Enterprise with the Outermost World.—Means of coordinating the practical world of the enterprise with the abstract outer world are not lacking. Most of the organizations previously mentioned in other connections make it their business to keep abreast of the frontiers in science, technology, political, economic, and social developments. These would include the trade associations, business and commercial associations, and the professional societies.

In addition to these, there is also a network of miscellaneous organizations whose activities cover a wide range and have concrete bearing upon the practical industrial world. They include many different organizations under such headings as advertising clubs, agricultural associations, cooperative societies, educational bodies, foreign government agencies, foreign trade associations, charitable and research foundations, labor organizations, associations of many racial minorities, political and religious bodies, recreation and social welfare groups, and women's associations.[7]

Too often in the past these organizations represented a blur in the distance as the factory executive looked out of his office window. Interested in the technical problem of getting out a product for profit in the face of lively competition, industrialists found little time to examine the activities of nonbusiness groups. In some cases, they permitted their publicity departments to use these groups for propaganda purposes favorable to industry alone. Industrialists began to take closer notice, however, when these associations grew larger and began to line up behind such demands as those for pure food laws, workmen's compensation acts, social security provisions, protection for investors in securities, honesty in advertising and grade labeling, abolition of commercial frauds, fair employment practices in regard to women and racial minorities, conservation of natural resources, prosecution of monopolists, governmental regulation of private enterprise, slum clearance and better housing, and other matters of interest to the welfare of the people. These associations were pulling problems out of the vague outer world, giving them a practical twist, and laying them on the factory doorstep. Had factory officials maintained contact with these organizations, many conflicts over social progress might have been avoided. Businessmen have loudly complained that they have been in the "doghouse" since 1933. If that is so, it is because so many industrialists crawled into the kennel when they should have been in the main house working on the family problems.

In addition to working with scientific, commercial, and social organizations, practical businessmen might also make better use of government agencies at their disposal. Where the agency is close at hand or serving the direct functional needs of the enterprise, company officials do make contact with them. But for the most part, individual enterprises leave relations with government agencies to their group associations. By such indifference they overlook many aids that would be of distinct advantage to them.

All governing bodies, from the smallest local community to the Federal government, are organized primarily along functional lines. This means that there are government departments and officials responsible for specific activities bearing upon many phases of the private economy: such as public works, finance, industry, domestic and foreign trade, and national defense. Each of these broad fields is further divided and subdivided until we find specialists at work on every detail of problems that touch industrial enterprise. Except where political appointments have lowered standards, men in government service possess high qualifications and

[7] JUDKINS, op. cit.

gain their posts through competitive civil service examinations. It would be impossible to set forth in detail all the departments and agencies on the three government levels. It can only be pointed out that they exist, that they develop a vast amount of information valuable to industry, and that they are eager to cooperate with businessmen on the problems of the economy. Officials in charge of functional activities within the company might well maintain continuing contacts with government agencies whose work bears upon company operations.[8] By correspondence, direct personal relations, use of government literature, and by willingness to aid and to receive aid from government departments, individual companies may go a long way toward the coordination of industrial interests with those outside of factory doors.

This does not mean that a company must go to the extreme of making itself an unofficial branch of government departments. Yet the contacts between government and industry have steadily increased over the years, and the trend is likely to continue. Industry collects excise, social security, income, and other taxes for the government. In this and other connections, industry's services to government go far beyond the simple taxpaying relationships of the past. Valuable (and costly) administrative services are now being performed by industry for government for which some tangible credit ought to be allowed. During the war, industry assisted in administering gasoline rationing and transportation problems, draft deferments, war bond campaigns, air raid and other community protective activities. Without the splendid cooperation of industry on raw-materials allocations and production operations, the amazing record of war production would have been impossible. In peacetime, industry often acts as the spearhead for community chest drives, relief activities, and various community surveys.

All of this means that government and industry face the problem of closer collaboration. Here, government can be improved to work better with industry. It is not the rule, but occasionally government officials are poorly informed on the practical difficulties in the business

---

[8] Not necessarily by means of "5 per centers" (independent agents and counsel in Washington who offer representation, advice, contacts and sometimes "influence" to business firms or associations on a retainer or commission basis). The term "five per centers" gained much notoriety during the Senate investigation in August, 1949, of gifts of deep-freeze cabinets to Major General Harry H. Vaughan, President Truman's military aide, by persons alleged to have had transactions with the government. The Federal government issues an annual guide, "United States Government Manual," which explains the entire framework of departments, bureaus, and agencies. It is an invaluable aid to every enterprise in these days when the role of government is a large and active one. The manual may be obtained at nominal cost from the Superintendent of Documents, Washington, D.C.

world. Government fieldmen occasionally strut their authority and make unsympathetic associates. Better selection of government personnel and a more cooperative industrial-relations policy on the part of government would go a long way toward making industry more receptive to government contacts. What seems to be needed is a new attitude on both sides from which greater mutual benefit may be derived.

Broader Difficulties in the Problem of External Coordination.— Where problems are technical and closely connected with the functional operations of industry, the channels of external coordination appear to serve adequately. But where the problems are social; where they concern improvement in the general welfare of the people; where benefits have been sought for such groups as consumers, wage workers, the aged, and the underprivileged; or where changes have been sought in the established ways of business in the interest of full employment of man power and resources with the object of higher standards of living for all the people; in all matters such as these, the channels of coordination seem to work imperfectly.[9] That such coordination is lacking seems to be amply proved by frequent economic crises of increasing severity, by bitter controversies between industry and labor and between industry and government, and by prolonged resistance to social betterments.

Why is this so? Despite the vast network of coordinating channels, is machinery lacking for the purpose? If so, what kind of machinery is needed to do a better job? If present coordinating channels are ample, why do they fall so far short of success? Why do management and labor so often deal with each other at arm's length, with the implied threats of lockout and strike in the backs of their minds? Why is the solution of so many social problems sought by law in place of being worked out in harmony through the voluntary cooperation of industry with all other interests in the outer world? If machinery is not lacking, is there something wrong with the methods employed or with the men who operate the machinery?

Do trade associations and other coordinating organizations make the mistake of serving only as advocates of a particular interest? In place of serving as *coordinating* agencies, do they act solely as "pressure groups" out to get what they can for their own members? Most of these organizations do perform many valuable coordinating functions in their

[9] Latest in attempts at national coordination on these broad lines is the Employment Act of 1946 setting up the President's Council of Economic Advisers to study and report on the state of the nation's economy and the Joint Congressional Committee to consider the President's economic report. A regular reading of the periodical reports issued by these bodies is an invaluable aid to an understanding of the state of the national economy.

own fields and for their own members. But they appear to be weakest when it comes to problems requiring the adjustment of the interests of their members with the larger interests of the national economy and of the public. Where this is so, as it is in many cases, perhaps improvement might come from a higher type of trade association executive. Too often these executives are controversy-minded lawyers, men who have failed in business enterprise, or journalists with a flair for publicity. Sometimes they are dyed-in-the-wool reactionaries, one-track-minded idealists, or aggressive extremists. In many cases they are insufficiently educated, too inexperienced in industrial problems, and temperamentally unfitted to serve as representatives of an entire industry. Too often such executives and a few of the members of their association set up a clique within the organization for the purpose of advancing special interests. Better selection of association executives and, above all, more active participation upon the part of all members of the organization might well be a corrective of such conditions.

Much of what is observed of trade associations also applies to other organizations serving business, industry, finance, labor, farmers, the professions, and others in the economic world. The sins are not those alone of management and industry. No group is lily-white, and all of them push vigorously for the interests of their own members. In a large populous country like our own and in modern times, it is perhaps inevitable that special interest groups will be formed. That these groups disseminate one-sided propaganda and exert pressure upon government and others in order to obtain laws and conditions favorable to their members seems equally inevitable and understandable. The practice is not objectionable; each group is entitled to make the most of its special case and to protect the interests of its members. The struggle between self-interested groups is not altogether unhealthy in a free economy *if it leads to compromise and balance in the direction of social peace and progress.*

But it is precisely at that point, however, that serious objection must be entered against self-interest groups. The struggle between them does lead to compromise, but compromise is too long delayed; the price in terms of social peace is too high, and the compromise is not always in the direction of social progress. Delay in adjustments is permitted until the struggle between self-interest groups either approximates domestic warfare as in strikes and lockouts, or reaches the arena of politics and government. Either consequence is likely to be bad. Domestic, economic, and social warfare leaves deep scars on all participants, and the victory of any one group over another is a brief one before the struggle breaks out anew. If struggles in the private economy are carried into the field of politics and government, then the compromise either takes the form of a coercive law or of a transference to government of functions that might have been better performed by private enterprise.

In all too many cases, government does not work a compromise between the conflicting interests or permit them to work out the details of future action. It supersedes the private parties and substitutes government controls and operations for private ones. The innocent are punished with the guilty. This is termed "government interference" and, for the little good it may achieve, it may work far greater evil. When government becomes the arena for adjusting private interests, the price of a sack of potatoes becomes a political issue, and the rules over a poultry market shake the very foundations of the country.[10] A demand for 5 cents more per hour by railroaders, miners, steelworkers, or others sets the whole nation by the ears. In some instances, a strike or a lockout takes on all the heat and seriousness of a rebellion.[11] Government boards and agencies multiply like fruit flies as politicians seek to devise machinery capable of adjusting economic conditions throughout the country. These were so numerous and so often changed in the New Deal period (1933–1940) that only their abbreviation to "alphabet" agencies enabled the public to identify them. First the industrialist and businessman, then labor and farmers, and finally the people at large are put to winding up miles of red tape as they are increasingly compelled to grope their way through the dead passages of bureaucracy. Social conduct is dictated by raw authority rather than by reason and simple adjustment. And authority in popular government moves further away from responsibility. The door is thus opened to favoritism, bribery, and corruption. The people become bewildered and agitated. Eventually, self-interest groups become victims of the very compromises they sought through government. And when all of this leads to resentment and to flouting of the law and of government action, government responds with more laws and with more reprehensible repression. Thus, the price of governmental compromises of conflicting interests may be long periods of social strife.

Nor is it certain that government solutions of conflicts between private economic interests will always lead to social progress. It can delay social progress for long periods of time (as did the national prohibition law); or it may even turn the clock backward as history amply demonstrates. This is because what seems like a government compromise

[10] Reference is here to the decision invalidating the NRA (*A. L. A. Schechter Corp. v. United States*, 295 U.S. 495) and to President Roosevelt's statement of the implications of that decision (see "The Public Papers and Addresses of Franklin D. Roosevelt," Vol. 4, item 65, p. 200, "The Two Hundred and Ninth Press Conference").

[11] As in the sit-down strike in the automobile industry in Michigan, 1936–1937.

between self-interested groups is really not a compromise at all, but an imposition of the will of the stronger of those groups over the weaker by means of the machinery of government. Strong interests are not always on the side of progress; and when they bend government in their direction, the steps taken may be backward rather than forward. Moreover, any attempt to do by law those things which by nature must be gained only by the evolution of thought and practice is a precarious method of reform or of progress.

Thus delay, high social price, and the uncertainty of progress being made render government adjustments between private economic interests a clumsy and doubtful affair. By far the better method is for private interest groups to work out their problems *before* their differences become issues in the field of politics and government. Such adjustments are more likely to be satisfactory, socially progressive, and more enduring. New difficulties and evils that come when the door is opened to government intervention are likely to be avoided. The *place* to work out these adjustments is in the single enterprise and in and between the group associations that private interests set up for the protection and advancement of their affairs. This means that management-labor differences, as one example, should be adjusted first, between the single company and the representatives of the workers where the trouble arises. If the problem pertains to a whole industry or to a geographical area, those are the places where adjustments can be made by the parties immediately concerned. But where the problem concerns many firms in different industries, large groups of workers, and the wider public interest, its solution ought to be found by conference between such groups as the National Association of Manufacturers, the American Management Association, national labor union organizations, and similar coordinating bodies. The *process* is one of external coordination; the *technique*, that of understanding the broader point of view and the will to compromise.

The will to compromise and to adjust ought to run so strong that no stone is left unturned until success is achieved. This means more than the self-righteous attitude that concedes small things but remains hard as nails on fundamentals. It means frank and open dealing, infinite patience in seeking out and trying new proposals, willingness to admit other points of view and to see the broad public interest above the private controversy; and it means the making of concessions and real sacrifices (even, sometimes, when it seems that all the sacrifices are being expected from one side). Self-interest groups have yet to learn that a point is always reached when to press their own narrow claims further is to start upon the road to their own defeat. The danger signs are always clear to read. But self-interest groups in the headlong rush for advantage do not pause long enough to study or to note their implications. Hence they remain blind to the danger signs until it is too late.

Group organization and the machinery and methods connected with it are tools for men to work their will. It is with persons, therefore, that in the last analysis the answers to economic peace and social progress must be found. Economic and social statesmanship in the private economy is the crying need of the times. The call is addressed to industrialists, managers, bankers, labor leaders, advertising counselors, farmers, merchants, to all individuals who exert a directing hand in economic life. Unless men as individuals can rise above their own interests or, rather, unless they learn to see self-interest in its higher, broader setting, there can be no road to social peace and progress other than the road that now winds through bitter group conflict, widespread social distress, and government interference.

The Public-relations Department.—Although the problem of coordinating the individual enterprise with the external world is a much larger one than can be handled by any single department within a firm, a word here about the "public-relations department" will not be out of place. Because of their size, their widespread activities, and their recognition of the importance of controlling external contacts of the company, many large corporations established public-relations departments. In the beginning, with few exceptions, the objects were to influence and control public opinion and to counter the work of organizations whose activities interfered with factory operations, disturbed commercial relations, and interrupted profit making as most industrialists saw those things. In many cases these public-relations departments consisted of one or two individuals whose qualifications lay in the field of journalism and advertising. Patterning their activities after their employers' views and policies, these public-relations counselors became bland and blind advocates of their company's interests. Their efforts soon became stamped with the label of "propaganda," and their usefulness to the company became doubtful.

But in recent years a change has set in. Industrial executives are coming to see the real role of the public-relations department. It is not to disseminate questionable propaganda in devious ways or to act as a partisan advocate with an eye only for the firm's interests. The true role of a public-relations department is to maintain contacts between the company and the outer world, to act as interpreters and disseminators of information *both* ways, and to study the company's interests in the light of the trends in public progress with a view toward bringing the company in harmony with unfolding developments. This means that the public-relations department is as much concerned with educating the officials of the company on public demands as it is with interpreting company policies and operations to other business interests, to government, labor, and the general public. The concept of the public-relations counselor as a journalist, press representative, advertising counselor, and advocate is giving way to the highly trained educational and research specialist who is supported with a staff qualified in psychology, economics, social relations, and allied fields dealing with the wider aspects of industrial management.

Valuable though it may be, especially to large corporations, the public-relations department cannot handle all the coordination required to connect a company with the external world. Nor would it be advisable to have such a department as the sole means of contact. Coordination is best understood if conducted by the executives who have to make decisions on problems that come to them from the outer world. For this reason it will still be necessary for company executives to utilize the channels of coordination previously described. For small firms who are unable to employ a public-relations specialist, there is little other choice than to work through these group organizations.

ADAPTING THE ENTERPRISE TO CHANGING CONDITIONS

Change is the one indisputable law of the universe. With the passing of the moment, nothing remains the same as we have seen or known it. Change is growth; it is decay; it is the constant mutation of living things and inanimate matter into different forms and qualities. In some instances, change is slow and barely noticeable; in others, it is rapid and violent.

Ours is a generation of revolutionary change. Two world wars compelled the country to make the drastic shift from peace to war and back to peace again. The greatest economic depression in modern history compelled us to make the most fundamental alterations in our lives and work. The world as our fathers knew it has been completely remade by electric power, the automobile, airplane, radio, motion picture sound and visual projection, synthetics, electronics, and other products and processes. Our productivity has brought us to the brink of the greatest achievement since the dawn of civilization—the abolishment of poverty. Society has been shaken to its foundations by Nazi, Fascist, and Communist systems, by the demand of suppressed peoples, as in China and India, for control over their own destinies, and by the rising insistence upon the part of working men and women at home that things be ordered in the interest and general welfare of the many rather than of the few. A thousand times a day the meaning and effect of these great developments knock at factory doors and make themselves felt in every department of the enterprise.   No enterprise can ignore them.   How can it adapt itself to changing conditions?

The enterprise has to become as dynamic and as fluid as is the world in which it functions.   It cannot sit complacent on an established routine.   It must be ready at all times to cut, trim, and make over its organization and operations.   Many of the great changes today revolve around the problem of reconciling the freedom and interests of the individual person and enterprise with the welfare of the people generally. This means that each enterprise will have to reexamine its policies and operations to see how best it can serve all the people—stockholders, workers, consumers.   The findings of this examination may be used as a scale of values with which to handle changes.   Constant vigilance and work will be found necessary to preserve such values as are found to be worth while.   But there will also have to be alertness to initiate or assist change.   There must be the willingness to search for and accept desirable changes, and the will to reject and eliminate the undesirable. Every tool of management must be employed to appraise changing conditions and to turn them in the direction of the highest individual and social satisfactions.

One place to do this is in the enterprise itself.   A house is built with single boards or bricks; let a board be rotten or a brick be crumbly, and the house itself will be faulty.   The national economy cannot be sound and cannot serve the whole people if individual enterprises are inefficient and only self-serving.   Individual enterprises do not have to wait for government plans or "directives."   There is much that every company can do for itself now and every day to raise the caliber of its organization and performance.

Every chapter of this book is intended to show what is being done by the best firms and what can be done to bring further improvement. The best-known methods of forming and financing the enterprise, of ordering and increasing production, of conducting labor relations, and of extending markets have been described.   Where unsolved problems exist, they have been pointed out and discussed.   In direct connection with the problem of adapting the enterprise to changing conditions, a number of procedures have been described.   There is, for example, the technique of relating the enterprise to the changing body of laws and regulations (Chap. II).   Many devices for continuous research and development of new products and processes have been described (Chaps. IV, VII, and VIII).   Plant surveys and outside business barometers have been explained and their many valuable uses in the conduct of the enterprise have been pointed out.   Techniques of forecasting and of meeting business risks have been outlined (Chap. IV).   Half a dozen chapters deal with changing labor relations and problems. Budget controls to meet the all-important problem of controlling internal finance have been described. Finally, the extensive network of channels for coordinating the enterprise with the world outside of factory doors has been set forth in considerable detail because great changes are now coming to the industrial enterprise from this outer world. This entire volume, in short, is intended to bring industrial enterprise abreast of modern developments and to provide tools for adapting it to future conditions. As far as can be foreseen, what are some of the basic problems of the future that are likely to require changes in management and operations?

Problems of the Immediate Future.—Industrial enterprise, as well as the industrial world in which it moves, is only one section of the larger national economy, but it will be called upon to play a major part in the solution of a number of great national problems. Most of these problems overlap or are otherwise interrelated. All of them demand the attention of management in the operations of each particular enterprise as much as in the relations between the enterprise and the outer world. Stated another way: What can each enterprise do in detail to adapt itself to the changing conditions presented by these problems? Categorically, these problems are:

1. *How to Maintain Full Employment of Men, Machines, and Resources within the Limits of Optimum Efficiency?*—It is doubtful whether the people will ever again permit the outrageous spectacle of the Great Depression in which factories operated at half and even quarter of normal capacity while men walked the streets looking for work and while the people suffered for want of the goods these factories could have produced, but did not produce.

This is as much a problem of the individual enterprise as it is of the economy at large. In the single enterprise it means better administrative organization, constant improvement of product and process, more efficient employment of machines and labor, steady lowering of costs and prices, elimination of monopolistic practices, and a new conception of profits and service. Several of these are themselves major problems as stated below.

But there are further phases of the situation that will have to be studied and converted into terms for application within the single enterprise. By full employment, do we mean an assured job for everyone willing to work 8 to 10 hours a day, 5 or 6 days a week? If so, why not adopt the regimented systems of Germany and Russia which did achieve that kind of full employment? Or, by full employment, do we mean the assurance to everyone of a minimum standard of living in terms of maintenance, health, education, and recreation, with the further goal of progressively increasing the benefits of the minimum? If so, how can industry be operated to contribute toward that goal? What steps can be taken in the matter of wages and hours? How can social-security programs be supplemented by industrial administration? What steps can be taken within each enterprise to contribute toward the goal of full security, and by what methods can similar steps be introduced into all other enterprises?

2. *How Can a Share in Management Be Accorded to All Interests Affected by an Enterprise?*—No industrial enterprise today concerns only its owners. Its formation, its financing, the conduct of its operations, its product, its gains, and its losses affect many others as well. What you do in your own backyard may be your own business up to a certain point; but when what you do affects your neighbors, they will soon want a voice in controlling your operations. Industrial operations today are at a stage where they seriously affect others. This is the basis on which labor, government, and the consumer claim a share in management along with stockholders and hired managers. What forms can this share in management take, and by what methods can it be brought about?

3. *How Can Monopolistic Practices of All Kinds Be Eliminated; or, Where Monopolies Are Permitted for Justifiable Reasons, How Can We Be Assured That They Are Devoted to Public Rather Than Private Interests?* What can the individual enterprise do about the patents it owns to avoid censure for abuse of its privileges? How can prices be cleared of the monopolistic elements contained in them in recent years, which competition has been powerless to remove? If prices can be arbitrarily fixed (administered prices) by corporations producing the bulk of a given product, by what methods can consumers be assured that such prices are fair? How can corporations owning large national resources assure the public that such resources are being used in the public interest?

4. *How Can Essential Honesty Be More Completely Secured in Economic Life?*—Is the brand name a completely satisfactory method for guaranteeing the quality of merchandise? How can the public be protected from the confusion of like products, each one claiming to serve a need better than all others? How can deceit, fraud, and plain hokum be eliminated from advertising and selling? Is it possible for industry to plan a system of national laboratories to test products in the interests of consumers and to induce producers to improve the quality of their products? How can the wasteful use of men and resources in making useless or inferior goods be eliminated? Much progress on these lines has been made, but infinitely much more needs to be done. Can private industry police itself, or must the public turn to government aid which means government regulation of industry?

5. *How Can Trade Associations and Other Business Organizations Extend Their Usefulness to Their Own Members and to the Public?*— Trade associations are now so numerous and so advantageously placed in the industrial system that they are ideal agents for the working of reform and improvement in industry. Why do their achievements fall so far short of their potentialities? What can individual enterprises, which are the members of trade associations, do to limit the propaganda activities and pressure-group tactics of their associations and to raise the level of their work to a higher plane in the nation's service?

6. *How Can Private Enterprise Gain Greater Freedom from Government Interference and Bring About Lower Business Taxes?*—To what extent is a demand for less government interference also a demand for more extensive and more effective industrial self-government? To what extent is a demand for lower business taxes also a demand that business find ways of doing the things that government levies taxes to accomplish? While becoming aware of the disadvantages of government regulation and government operation of enterprises, can we overlook the alternatives that there must be more effective competition, or a substitute for competition when it does not function in the private economy? What new business units can be formed to carry out, by collective action in the private economy, many of those things that are now being done by political agencies?

7. *In What Ways Can the Economy Gain by Further Concentration of Production on More Efficient Methods, with Greater Standardization of Products and Increased Interchangeability of Parts?*—How may this be brought about?

8. *What New Policies Can Government and Private Enterprise Pursue in the Matter of Patents So That New Developments Will Be Utilized Quicker, at Lower Costs to the Consumer for the Products, and by a Wider Circle of Producers?*

9. *To What Extent Should Private Industry Widen Its Research in Fields Such As "Pure Science," Technology, New Production, and Administrative Methods?*—How can they work with universities, technical schools, government agencies, and other bodies now engaged in such research?

10. *How Can Industry Further Abolish Backbreaking Labor from Manufacturing Activities and Increase Efficiency through the Use of Mechanical Handling, Lifting, and Conveying Devices?*—How may the use of lighter tools and machines be increased? In what ways can heavy operating controls be transferred to mechanical devices?

11. *How Can Campaigns Be Organized to Improve Factory Surroundings and Working Conditions, Eliminate Safety and Health Hazards, Se-*

cure Better Heating and Ventilation, Eliminate Unnecessary Dirt, Fumes, Wetness, and Undue Exposure of the Worker to Fatigue?

12. *The Costs of Getting Goods from Factory Producer to Ultimate Consumer (Distribution) Are Today Considered Excessive. How Can They Be Reduced? How Can Wasteful Cross Hauls Be Eliminated? What Suggestions Can Be Offered in the Way of Coordinated Air, Water, and Land Transportation? What New Transportation Devices Offer Possibilities for Increased Efficiency and Lower Costs?*

13. *To What Extent Can Industry Cooperate to Its Own Advantage and to the Benefit of General Public Welfare in Matters of Public Health, Housing, Diet Improvement, and Education?*

CONCLUSION

These are but a few of the major problems facing industrial management in the immediate future. Each single enterprise has an obligation to do what it can toward the solution of them. The method of approaching each problem is relatively simple. Find out the precise nature of the problem. Get the facts. Break down the larger problem into its elements or parts. List the conflicting interests. Set up the desirable objectives and note the difficulties standing in the way of their achievement. Explore the means of overcoming each difficulty as far as that can be done within each enterprise. In weighing the sacrifices demanded against the advantages sought, take the long view. Put the public interest and the general welfare above the private one. Do everything possible to solve problems within the enterprise itself because that is where management exercises its most effective power. Where the problem is too large for the single management, turn to the industry's trade associations, to general business and commercial organizations, and to community bodies, private and public. Do not wait for others to attack problems or to make improvements; open the new trail yourself.

We live in a day of great opportunities. They call for a new, inspired and crusading spirit upon the part of industrial, business, and labor leaders. Instead of remaining on the defensive, these leaders must be willing to go forth and meet the great human problems of the times. That is what all this industrial organization and rationalization is for: to release management and to give it the freedom to pioneer. There is a great demand for the imagination that will take industrial management beyond the stage of self-interested corporate combination to the wider group action needed to solve problems too big for the single enterprise. There is a demand that the same zeal be devoted to public interests as has been displayed in securing private advantages. There must be a willingness to reason and to sacrifice—the ability to take the broader view, to suppress the heat over a problem, and to work on it with opposing groups. *The imperative challenge of our times is to find the way by which owners, managers, financiers, labor, government, and the general consuming public can work in harmony toward full and efficient use of our resources, factories, and distribution system with the goal of greater productivity and higher living standards for all.*

CASE PROBLEMS

Following is a complete editorial from the *Country Gentleman,* August, 1943, page 76.

A STEP BACKWARD [12]

The Washington theorists still keep trying to force grade labels on all processed foods. They attempted this scheme first through the ill-fated NRA, then through a revision of the Food and Drugs Act, and now are endeavoring to put it over through the OPA. A lot of misleading propaganda has been spread by them and it is time the public knows the real issues involved.

What these theorists propose is to have all processed foods sold under mandatory Grade A, B, or C labels with the result of probably eliminating the well-known brands and trade-marks under which these foods are commonly sold. If this were done, the consumers would lose and farmers would gain nothing. Quality would become stationary and demand would not be increased. The high quality of processed food in this country is largely the result of free, open competition among the food companies to sell their products to the largest markets possible. That means that they must offer a good product and apply unceasing research and improvement to make it better. If they don't, some competitor will and he will take the market away from the laggards.

This driving pressure for betterment, imposed by free competition in the marketplace, would be removed by grade labels. All would become laggards because there would be no necessity to be otherwise. There would be only fixed government standards to meet. Quality would be adjusted to them and would remain at dead levels. Consumers would lose the benefits of the improvement that competition now requires in the food-processing business.

Sale of goods under established brands and trade-marks is one of the main reasons why American manufactured products carry more integrity than any others in the world. The name or trade-mark on an article puts the producer back of it. If the article doesn't come up to the claims made for it, he loses customers and soon goes out of business. If it is satisfactory, the customer has an identification by which to ask for more of the same maker's products. That is the way it should be; it is the way by which the American public has constantly been able to get better goods of all kinds. Grade labeling would be a step backward.

[12] Reprinted by special permission from the *Country Gentleman,* copyright 1943, by The Curtis Publishing Company.

Preparatory Questions

1. In this problem of grade labeling what are the interests and points of view of (a) the industrial food processor, (b) the advertising media such as press, radio, and magazines, (c) the household consumer, (d) the Federal government? Wherever possible, go to original sources and quote the views found there.

2. List all the points in the editorial *against* grade labeling. Using these same points, write an editorial of your own, *favoring* grade labeling. Make your editorial comparable to the original in size.

3. In the form of an extended study or term paper, consider grade labeling as a case for external coordination.

a. Describe the principal channels of coordination that may be involved.

b. Lay out a complete program which you believe will coordinate the food-processing industry with the outer world in the matter of grade labeling, being careful to explain how each step you propose should appeal to all the conflicting interests involved, and bring them to a desirable reconciliation. (NOTE: Your program may point toward either full adoption, partial adoption, or complete rejection of grade labeling.)

4. Select some local industrial corporation. Draw a chart of its management structure showing the functional titles of the officers who manage the company. Indicate on this chart how the company and how each of the officials individually may establish contacts with channels coordinating the company with the world outside factory doors. (Government publications on "Trade and Professional Associations" may be of considerable help to you.) When the chart is completed, mail it to the head of the company with a covering letter telling what you have done, and ask him to point out your mistakes. Report the entire procedure to the class.

BIBLIOGRAPHY

The field of industrial organization and management is so broad that the selection of specific references, from the many available, is difficult. This selected bibliography is intended only as a guide to further investigation.

The first section of the bibliography presents a list of references which apply generally to many of the topics discussed in various chapters of this book. The remainder of the bibliography is arranged by chapters as an aid to the reader in the selection of material for specific topics.

It is especially important that the student of management become familiar with sources of current reference material. Articles referred to in this bibliography are only a few selected from the many that appear regularly in the periodicals. New books in the field are listed and reviewed in such periodicals as *Personnel, Personnel Journal, Journal of Applied Psychology, Factory, Modern Industry, Advanced Management, Mechanical Engineering, Printers' Ink, Industrial Marketing, Journal of Accountancy,* and others. Many colleges and universities have research centers which periodically publish reports of their studies. It is suggested that sources such as these be consulted for recent material.

Annual editions of such material as the following should be checked: National Industrial Conference Board: "The Economic Almanac," "The Management Almanac"; *The New York World-Telegram:* "World Almanac" (which has an excellent annual labor review, currently edited by Fred W. Perkins); the A.F. of L. and C.I.O. federations and various national and international unions; convention reports and releases; Commerce Clearing House, Prentice-Hall, etc.: "Labor Course" and law guides; state labor departments and U.S. Labor department: annual reports and releases; Council of Economic Advisors: Annual Economic Review; and recent publication lists of the A.M.A., N.A.M., N.I.C.B., C. of C., S.A.M., etc.

GENERAL

ALFORD, L. P.: "Cost and Production Handbook," New York: The Ronald Press Company, 1938.

ANDERSON, A. G., M. J. MANDEVILLE, and J. M. ANDERSON: "Industrial Management," New York: The Ronald Press Company, 1942.

ANSHEN, MELVIN: "An Introduction to Business," New York: The Macmillan Company, 1949.

BOGART, ERNEST L.: "Economic History of the American People," New York: Longmans, Green & Co., Inc., 1942.

BOWERS, EDISON L., and HENRY ROWNTREE: "Economics for Engineers," 2d ed., New York: McGraw-Hill Book Company, Inc., 1938.

BRADY, ROBERT A.: "Business as a System of Power," New York: Columbia University Press, 1943.

BUCHANAN, NORMAN S.: "The Economics of Corporate Enterprise," New York: Henry Holt and Company, Inc., 1940.

CLEETON, GLENN V., and CHARLES W. MASON: "Executive Ability," Yellow Springs, Ohio: Antioch Press, 1946.

823

COMAN, E. T.: "Sources of Business Information," New York: Prentice-Hall, Inc., 1949.

Committee on Economic Accord, "Handbook of Accepted Economic Definitions, Principles and Statements," New York: W. I. King.

DAVIS, R. C.: "Industrial Organization and Management," New York: Harper & Brothers, 1940.

———: "Shop Management for the Shop Supervisor," New York: Harper & Brothers, 1941.

DOANE, R. R.: "The Anatomy of American Wealth," New York: Harper & Brothers, 1940.

DOUGLAS, L., R. O. SKAR, and R. G. PRICE: "Modern Business: An Introduction to Principles and Problems," New York: McGraw-Hill Book Company, Inc., 1948.

FAIRCHILD, FRED R., EDGAR S. FURNISS, and NORMAN S. BUCK: "Elementary Economics," 2 vols., New York: The Macmillan Company.

FERGUSON, JOHN M.: "Landmarks of Economic Thought," New York: Longmans, Green & Co., Inc., 1941.

FILIPETTI, GEORGE: "Industrial Management in Transition," Chicago: Richard D. Irwin, Inc., 1946.

FOLTS, FRANKLIN E.: "Introduction to Industrial Management," 3d ed., New York: McGraw-Hill Book Company, Inc., 1949.

GERSTENBERG, CHARLES W.: "Financial Organization and Management of Business," New York: Prentice-Hall, Inc., 1939.

HOLDEN, PAUL E., LOUNSBERRY S. FISH, and HUBERT L. SMITH: "Top Management Organization and Control," Stanford University, Calif.: Stanford University Press, 1941.

KIMBALL, DEXTER S., and DEXTER S. KIMBALL, JR.: "Principles of Industrial Organization," 6th ed., New York: McGraw-Hill Book Company, Inc., 1947.

KRESS, A. L.: "Foremanship Fundamentals," New York: McGraw-Hill Book Company, Inc., 1942.

LIVINGSTON, R. T.: "The Engineering of Organization and Management," New York: McGraw-Hill Book Company, Inc., 1949.

LOKEN, R. DEL., and E. P. STRONG: "Supervision in Business and Industry," New York: Funk & Wagnalls Company, 1949.

National Resources Committee, "The Structure of the American Economy," Washington, D.C.: Government Printing Office, 1939.

PETERSEN, ELMORE, and E. GROSVENAR PLOWMAN: "Business Organization and Management," Chicago: Richard D. Irwin, Inc., 1946.

RAUTENSTRAUCH, WALTER, and RAYMOND VILLERS: "The Economics of Industrial Management," New York: Funk & Wagnalls Company, 1949.

ROLL, ERIC: "A History of Economic Thought," New York: Prentice-Hall, Inc., 1942.

ROWLAND, FLOYD H.: "Business Planning and Control," New York: Harper & Brothers, 1947.

SLICHTER, SUMNER H.: "The American Economy," New York: Alfred A. Knopf, Inc., 1948.

SPENGLER, E. H., and JACOB KLEIN: "Introduction to Business," New York: McGraw-Hill Book Company, Inc., 1948.

SPRIEGEL, WILLIAM R., and RICHARD H. LANSBURGH: "Industrial Management," 4th ed., New York: John Wiley & Sons, Inc., 1947.

"Trade Associations and Industrial Coordination," London: Sir Isaac Pitman & Sons, Ltd., 1938.

Chapter I. Fundamental Concepts

Glover, John George, and William Bouck Cornell: "The Development of American Industries," New York: Prentice-Hall, Inc., 1941.

Hoover, E. M.: "The Location of Economic Activity," New York: McGraw-Hill Book Company, Inc., 1948.

Patterson, S. Howard, and Karl W. H. Scholz: "Economic Problems in Modern Life," New York: McGraw-Hill Book Company, Inc., 1948.

Roll, Eric: "A History of Economic Thought," New York: Prentice-Hall, Inc., 1942.

Snyder, Carl: "Capitalism the Creator: The Economic Foundation of Modern Industrial Society," New York: The Macmillan Company, 1940.

Trundle, George T., Jr. (Editor-in-Chief): "Managerial Control of Business," New York: John Wiley & Sons, Inc., 1948.

Walker, James Blaine: "The Epic of American Industry," New York: Harper & Brothers, 1949.

Chapters II and III. Industrial America—Control at the Mid-Century; Basic Industrial Structures

American Economic Association, "Readings in the Social Control of Industry," Philadelphia: The Blakiston Company, 1942.

Andres, E. M., and C. D. Cocanower: "Economics and the Consumer," Boston: Houghton Mifflin Company, 1942.

Backman, Jules: "Government Price Fixing," New York: Pitman Publishing Corp., 1939.

Berge, Wendell: "Economic Freedom for the West," Lincoln, Neb.: University of Nebraska Press, 1946.

Buchanan, N. S.: "Economics of Corporate Enterprise," New York: Henry Holt and Company, Inc., 1940.

Carver, T. N.: "Essays in Social Justice," Cambridge, Mass.: Harvard University Press, 1922.

Chase, Stuart: "Government in Business," New York: The Macmillan Company, 1936.

Childs, Marquis W.: "Sweden: The Middle Way," New Haven, Conn.: Yale University Press, 1936.

Clark, John M.: "Social Control of Business," New York: McGraw-Hill Book Company, Inc., 1939.

Coons, Arthur G. (ed.): "Government Expansion in the Economic Sphere," Philadelphia: American Academy of Political and Social Science, 1939.

Dixon, Russell A.: "Economic Institutions and Cultural Change," New York: McGraw-Hill Book Company, Inc., 1941.

Edwards, C. D.: "Maintaining Competition: Requisites of a Governmental Policy," New York: McGraw-Hill Book Company, Inc., 1949.

Fitch, Lyle, and Horace Taylor: "Planning for Jobs," Philadelphia: The Blakiston Company, 1946.

Hall, Ford P.: "Government and Business," New York: McGraw-Hill Book Company, Inc., 1949.

Lyon, L. C., and V. Abramson: "Government and Economic Life," Washington, D.C.: Brookings Institution, 1940.

National Industrial Conference Board, Inc., "A Practical Program for the Coordination of Government, Labor and Management," New York, 1938.

PETERSEN, ELMORE, and E. GROSVENAR PLOWMAN: "Business Organization and Management," Chicago: Richard D. Irwin, Inc., 1946.

QUEENEY, EDGAR M.: "The Spirit of Enterprise," New York: Charles Scribner's Sons, 1943.

RUML, BEARDSLEY: "Government, Business and Values," New York: Harper & Brothers, 1943.

WRISTON, HENRY M.: "Challenge to Freedom," New York: Harper & Brothers, 1943.

CHAPTER IV. INDUSTRIAL RISK AND FORECASTING

AGNEW, HUGH E., and DALE HOUGHTON: "Marketing Policies," New York: McGraw-Hill Book Company, Inc., 1941.

BRATT, E. C.: "Business Cycles and Forecasting," Chicago: Richard D. Irwin, Inc., 1940.

BULLINGER, CLARENCE E.: "Engineering Economic Analysis," New York: McGraw-Hill Book Company, Inc., 1950.

BURNS, A. F., and W. C. MITCHELL: "Measuring Business Cycles," New York: National Bureau of Economic Research, Inc., 1946.

DEWEY, E. R., and E. F. DAKIN: "Cycles: the Science of Prediction," New York: Henry Holt and Company, Inc., 1947.

GOODBAR, J. E., and L. U. BERGERON: "A Creative Capitalism," Portland, Maine: Boston University Press, 1948.

HABERLER, GOTTFRIED: "Prosperity and Depression," 35th ed., Geneva, Switzerland: League of Nations, 1941.

LERNER, ABBA P.: "The Economics of Control," New York: The Macmillan Company, 1947.

MILLS, F. C.: "Price-Quantity Interactions in Business Cycles," New York: National Bureau of Economic Research, Inc., 1947.

NOURSE, E. G.: "Price Making in a Democracy," Washington, D.C.: Brookings Institution, 1944.

RUML, BEARDSLEY: "Tomorrow's Business," New York: Harper & Brothers, 1945.

SILBERLING, NORMAN J.: "The Dynamics of Business: An Analysis of Trends, Cycles, and Time Relationships in American Economic Activity since 1700; and Their Bearing upon Governmental and Business Policy," New York: McGraw-Hill Book Company, Inc., 1943.

STIGLER, G. J.: "The Theory of Price," New York: The Macmillan Company, 1946.

CHAPTER V. FINANCING THE INDUSTRIAL ENTERPRISE

BONNEVILLE, JOSEPH HOWARD, and LLOYD ELLIS DEWEY: "Organizing and Financing Business," 2d ed., New York: Prentice-Hall, Inc., 1942.

BURTCHETT, FLOYD F., and CLIFFORD M. HICKS: "Corporation Finance," New York: Harper & Brothers, 1948.

CHERRINGTON, H. V.: "Business Organization and Finance," New York: The Ronald Press Company, 1948.

CONANT, W. H.: "Business Administration, The Art of Management," New York: Gregg Publishing Company, 1945.

DEWING, A. S.: "Financial Policy of Corporations," 4th ed., New York: The Ronald Press Company, 1941.

GERSTENBERG, CHARLES W.: "Financial Organization and Management of Business," New York: Prentice-Hall, Inc., 1942.

MILLER, GLENN W.: "American Labor and the Government," New York: Prentice-Hall, Inc., 1948.

MOULTON, HAROLD G.: "Financial Organization and the Economic System," New York: McGraw-Hill Book Company, Inc., 1938.

SCHERMANN, HARRY: "The Promises Men Live By," New York: Random House, 1938.

WESTERFIELD, R. B.: "Money, Credit, and Banking," New York: The Ronald Press Company, 1938.

CHAPTER VI. BUILDING THE INTERNAL ORGANIZATION

ANDERSON, E. H. and G. T. SCHWENNING: "The Science of Production Organization," New York: John Wiley & Sons, Inc., 1938.

FILIPETTI, GEORGE: "Industrial Management in Transition," Chicago: Richard D. Irwin, Inc., 1946.

GULICK, LUTHER, and L. URWICK: "Papers on the Science of Administration," New York: Institute of Public Administration, 1937.

HEMPEL, EDWARD H.: "Top Management Planning," New York: Harper & Brothers, 1945.

HOLDEN, PAUL E., LOUNSBERRY S. FISH, and HERBERT L. SMITH: "Top Management Organization and Control," Stanford University, Calif.: Stanford University Press, 1941.

LIVINGSTON, R. T.: "The Engineering of Organization and Management," New York: McGraw-Hill Book Company, Inc., 1949.

SECKLER-HUDSON, C.: "Processes of Organization and Management," Washington, D.C.: Public Affairs Press, 1948.

SIMON, HERBERT A.: "Administrative Behavior: A Study of Decision-Making Processes in Administrative Organization," New York: The Macmillan Company, 1947.

TAYLOR, FREDERICK WINSLOW: "Scientific Management," New York: Harper & Brothers, 1947.

URWICK, L.: "The Elements of Administration," New York: Harper & Brothers, 1943.

CHAPTERS VII AND VIII. DEVELOPING THE PRODUCT

EDWARDS, A. L.: "Product Standards and Labeling for Consumers," New York: The Ronald Press Company, 1940.

PHELPS, D. M.: "Planning the Product," Chicago: Richard D. Irwin, Inc., 1947.

THOMPSON, JAMES E.: "Engineering Organization and Methods," New York: McGraw-Hill Book Company, Inc., 1947.

Periodical:

Product Engineering, monthly magazine covering new developments in the field of product design and engineering.

CHAPTERS IX AND X. ORGANIZING THE PHYSICAL FACILITIES

American Society of Tool Engineers, "Tool Engineers' Handbook," New York: McGraw-Hill Book Company, Inc., 1949.

CONNELLY, JOHN R.: "Technique of Production Processes," New York: McGraw-Hill Book Company, Inc., 1943.

DUNHAM, CLARENCE W.: "Planning Industrial Structures," New York: McGraw-Hill Book Company, Inc., 1948.

Henry Ford Trade School, "Shop Theory," New York: McGraw-Hill Book Company, Inc., 1942.

IMMER, JOHN R.: "Layout Planning Techniques," New York: McGraw-Hill Book Company, Inc., 1950.

Industrial Plant Buildings, *Factory Management and Maintenance,* April, 1948, Sec. B, and April, 1949, Sec. B.

TURNER, WILLIAM P., and HALSEY F. OWEN: "Machine Tool Work—Fundamental Principles," New York: McGraw-Hill Book Company, Inc., 1945.

VILBRANDT, FRANK C.: "Chemical Engineering Plant Design," 3d ed., New York: McGraw-Hill Book Company, Inc., 1949.

CHAPTER XI. PLANNING FOR PRODUCTION

HEMPEL, EDWARD H.: "Top Management Planning," New York: Harper & Brothers, 1945.

ROWLAND, FLOYD H.: "Business Planning and Control," Part I, New York: Harper & Brothers, 1947.

CHAPTERS XII AND XIII. CONTROLLING MATERIALS, TRAFFIC, AND RECEIVING

BONNELL, C. M., JR.: "Bonnell's Manual on Packaging and Shipping," New York: Bonnell's Publications, Inc., 1941.

CADY, EDWIN L.: "Industrial Purchasing," New York: John Wiley & Sons, Inc., 1945.

HEINRITZ, STUART F.: "Purchasing," New York: Prentice-Hall, Inc., 1947.

HUDSON, WILBUR G.: "Conveyors and Related Equipment," New York: John Wiley & Sons, Inc., 1944.

LEWIS, HOWARD T.: "Industrial Purchasing," Chicago: Business Publications, Inc., 1940.

STOCKER, HARRY E.: "Materials Handling," New York: Prentice-Hall, Inc., 1943.

WILSON, G. LLOYD: "Traffic Management," New York: Appleton-Century-Crofts, Inc., 1941.

CHAPTERS XIV AND XV. CONTROLLING PRODUCTION

BETHEL, L. L., W. L. TANN, F. S. ATWATER, and E. E. RUNG: "Production Control," New York: McGraw-Hill Book Company, Inc., 1948.

CLARK, WALLACE: "The Gantt Chart," New York: Pitman Publishing Corp., 1938.

KNOWLES, A. S., and R. D. THOMSON: "Production Control," New York: The Macmillan Company, 1943.

KOEPKE, CHARLES A.: "Plant Production Control," New York: John Wiley & Sons, Inc., 1949.

MUTHER, RICHARD: "Production Line Technique," New York: McGraw-Hill Book Company, Inc., 1944.

TIRANTI, D. and W. F. WALKER: "Introduction to Production Control," London: Chapman & Hall, Ltd., 1946.

YOUNGER, JOHN, and JOSEPH GESCHELIN: "Work Routing, Scheduling and Dispatching in Production," New York: The Ronald Press Company, 1947.

CHAPTER XVI. QUALITY CONTROL

DODGE, HAROLD F., and HARRY G. ROMIG: "Sampling Inspection Tables," New York: John Wiley & Sons, Inc., 1944.

GRANT, EUGENE L.: "Statistical Quality Control," New York: McGraw-Hill Book Company, Inc., 1946.

JURAN, J. M.: "Management of Inspection and Quality Control," New York: Harper & Brothers, 1945.

RICE, WILLIAM B.: "Control Charts in Factory Management," New York: John Wiley & Sons, Inc., 1947.

RUTHERFORD, JOHN G.: "Quality Control in Industry," New York: Pitman Publishing Corp., 1948.

SMITH, EDWARD S.: "Control Charts," New York: McGraw-Hill Book Company, Inc., 1947.

Statistical Research Group, Columbia University, "Sampling Inspection," New York: McGraw-Hill Book Company, Inc., 1948.

CHAPTER XVII. METHODS ANALYSIS AND CONTROL

BARNES, R. M.: "Motion and Time Study," 3d ed., New York: John Wiley & Sons, Inc., 1949.

DAVIS, LOUIS E.: Improvement of Time-Study, *Mechanical Engineering,* Vol. 71, No. 5, pp. 399–402, May, 1949.

FRY, VAUGHN: "The Office Stakes a Claim in Standards," N.O.M.A. Forum, Vol. 23, Nos. 8, 9, pp. 10*ff.*

Industrial Management Society, *Proceeding* of the Eleventh Annual National Time and Motion Study Clinic, Nov. 5–7, 1947, Chicago, 1948.

Metropolitan Life Insurance Co., Policyholders Service Bureau, "Suggestion Systems," New York, 1942.

MOGENSEN, ALLEN H., *et al.:* Carry Out a Methods Improvement Program, *Factory,* Vol. 197, No. 7, pp. 66–88.

MURPHY, M. J.: Why Unions Cry "Speed-up"—and How Management Can Answer, *Factory,* Vol. 107, No. 7, pp. 122–126.

SEINWERTH, H. W.: "Getting Results from Suggestion Plans," New York: McGraw-Hill Book Company, Inc., 1948.

STEWART, TED C.: Work Factor Analysis Takes Stopwatches Out of Time Study, *Factory,* Vol. 106, No. 5, pp. 126–128, May, 1948.

TAYLOR, F. W.: "Scientific Management: Comprising Shop Management, The Principles of Scientific Management, Testimony before the Special House Committee," New York: Harper & Brothers, 1947.

CHAPTER XVIII. PLANT ENGINEERING

BLAKE, ROLAND P.: "Industrial Safety," New York: Prentice-Hall, Inc., 1943.

BRANDT, ALLEN D.: "Industrial Health Engineering," p. viii, New York: John Wiley & Sons, Inc., 1947.

DICKIE, A. L.: "Production with Safety," New York: McGraw-Hill Book Company, Inc., 1947.

HEINRICH, H. W.: "Industrial Accident Prevention: A Scientific Approach," 2d ed., New York: McGraw-Hill Book Company, Inc., 1941.

The International Industrial Safety Movement, *International Labour Review,* Vol. 59, pp. 1–33, January, 1949.

JUDSON, HARRY H., and JAMES M. BROWN: "Occupational Accident Prevention," New York: John Wiley & Sons, Inc., 1944.

LIPPERT, FREDERICK G.: "Accident Prevention Administration," New York: McGraw-Hill Book Company, Inc., 1947.

MINTZ, A., and M. L. BLUM: A Re-examination of the Accident Proneness Concept, *Journal of Applied Psychology*, Vol. 33, No. 3, pp. 195–211, June, 1949.

MOLLOY, EDWARD: "Plant Engineers' Manual," Brooklyn: Chemical Publishing Company, Inc., 1942.

National Safety Council, Inc., *National Safety News* (monthly), *Transactions of the National Safety Congress* (annually), and "Safe Practices Pamphlets," Chicago, Ill.

Rutgers University, "The Joint Safety Program of the Forstmann Woolen Company and Local 656, Textile Workers Union of America, C.I.O.," Institute of Management and Labor Relations, New Brunswick, N. J., 1948.

Periodical:

Factory Management and Maintenance, monthly magazine one section of which is regularly devoted to plant maintenance.

CHAPTER XIX. PRINCIPLES OF INDUSTRIAL RELATIONS

American Management Association, "How to Establish and Maintain a Personnel Department," Research Report No. 4, New York, 1944.

APLEY, J. C., and E. WHITMORE: "Handbook of Industrial Relations," 3d ed., Chicago: Dartnell Corporation, 1948.

BAUS, HERBERT M.: "Public Relations at Work," New York: Harper & Brothers, 1948.

BRADLEY, P.: Special Libraries and Research in Labor and Industrial Relations, *Special Libraries,* Vol. 39, pp. 82–86, March, 1948.

Business Is Still in Trouble (Public Relations), *Fortune Magazine,* Vol. 39, No. 5, pp. 67–71, 196–200.

CASE, H. L.: Cornerstones of Personnel Administration in T.V.A., *Personnel Administration,* Vol. 11, No. 3, pp. 10–12, January, 1948.

Chamber of Commerce of the United States, Insurance Department, "Analysis of Provisions of Workmen's Compensation Laws and Discussion of Coverages," Washington, 1945.

DALE, ERNEST: When Labor Cooperates with Management, *Advanced Management,* Vol. 14, No. 3, pp. 101–106, September, 1949.

HALSEY, GEORGE D.: "Handbook of Personnel Management," New York: Harper & Brothers, 1947.

Industrial Relations Center, "The Industrial Relations Five-Foot Shelf," Minneapolis: University of Minnesota Press, 1947.

JUCIUS, MICHAEL J.: "Personnel Management," Chicago: Richard D. Irwin, Inc., 1948.

JURGENSEN, CLIFFORD E.: Personnel Administration in Small Firms, *Personnel,* Vol. 26, No. 1, pp. 24–42, June, 1949.

Princeton University, "The Office Library of an Industrial Executive," Bibliographical Series, No. 77 (revised), Industrial Relations Section, Department of Economics and Social Institutions, Princeton, N.J., March, 1946.

PIGORS, PAUL, and CHARLES A. MYERS: "Personnel Administration: A Point of View and a Method," New York: McGraw-Hill Book Company, Inc., 1947.

SCOTT, WALTER DILL, ROBERT C. CLOTHIER, and WILLIAM R. SPRIEGEL: "Personnel Management," 4th ed., New York: McGraw-Hill Book Company, Inc., 1949.

SLICHTER, SUMNER H.: "The Challenge of Industrial Relations; Trade Unions, Management, and the Public Interest," Ithaca, N.Y.: Cornell University Press, 1947.
———: "The Development of Executive Leadership," Cambridge, Mass.: Harvard University Press, 1949.
THUM-ANSCO, C. T.: A Practical Personnel Program for the Office, N.O.M.A. Forum, Vol. 23, No. 1, pp. 10–20.
WRIGHT, J. HANDLY, and BYRON H. CHRISTIAN: "Public Relations in Management," New York: McGraw-Hill Book Company, Inc., 1949.
YODER, DALE: "Personnel Management and Industrial Relations," 3d ed., New York: Prentice-Hall, Inc., 1948.

CHAPTER XX. PERSONNEL MANAGEMENT

American Management Association, "Manual of Employment Interviewing," Research Report No. 9, New York, 1946.
Are You Straightjacketed by Seniority, *Modern Industry*, Vol. 8, No. 3, pp. 51–54, Sept. 15, 1949.
BINGHAM, WALTER V.: "How to Interview," 3d rev. ed., New York: Harper & Brothers, 1941.
KITSON, H. D.: "How to Find the Right Occupation," 3d ed., New York: Harper & Brothers, 1947.
LAPP, JOHN A.: "How to Handle Problems of Seniority," New York: National Foremen's Institute, Inc., 1946.
LAWSHE, G. H., JR.: "Principles of Personnel Testing," New York: McGraw-Hill Book Company, Inc., 1948.
National Industrial Conference Board, Inc., "Personnel Forms and Records," Studies in Personnel Policy, No. 87, New York, 1948.
REYNOLD, L. G., and J. SHISTER: "Job Horizons," New York: Harper & Brothers, 1949.
THORNDIKE, ROBERT L.: "Personnel Selection: Test and Measurement Techniques," New York: John Wiley & Sons, Inc., 1949.

CHAPTER XXI. EMPLOYEE TRAINING

Acting That Teaches How to Handle People, *Modern Industry*, Vol. 17, No. 6, pp. 50–53, June, 1949.
GARDNER, B. B.: What Makes Successful and Unsuccessful Executives? *Advanced Management*, Vol. 13, pp. 116–125, September, 1948.
HENRY, WILLIAM E.: "Identifying the Potentially Successful Executive," pp. 14–20, Personnel Series No. 127, New York: American Management Association, 1949.
International Ladies' Garment Workers' Union, "A.F. of L. Report of Education Department, I.L.G.W.U.," June 1, 1946, to May 31, 1948, New York, 1948.
KATZELL, R. A.: Testing a Training Program in Human Relations, *Personnel Psychology*, Vol. 1, pp. 319–329, Autumn, 1948.
LERDA, L. W.: Recent Trends in Supervisory Development, *Supervision*, Vol. 11, No. 8, pp. 8–9.
National Association of Manufacturers, "Cooperative Education and Other Work-Study Plans (at the College Level)," New York, 1948.
Standard Oil Company of New Jersey, A Guide to Successful Conference Leadership, *Personnel*, Vol. 24, pp. 328–340, March, 1948.
STIGERS, M. F.: "Making Conference Programs Work," New York: McGraw-Hill Book Company, Inc., 1949.

CHAPTER XXII. THE SOCIAL ASPECTS OF EMPLOYEE-EMPLOYER RELATIONS

American Management Association, "Attitude and Morale of Office Workers," Office Management Series, No. 118, New York, 1947.

BLUM, MILTON L.: "Industrial Psychology and Its Social Foundations," New York: Harper & Brothers, 1949.

BLUMER, HERBERT: "Sociological Theory in Industrial Relations," *American Sociological Review* (University of Chicago), Vol. 12, pp. 271–278, 1947.

BOWLER, EARL M., and FRANCES TRIGG DAWSON: "Counseling Employees," New York: Prentice-Hall, Inc., 1948.

BRADSHAW, F. F., and H. E. KRUGMAN: Making the Most of Morale Surveys, *Personnel,* Vol. 25, No. 1, pp. 18–22, July, 1948.

DUGGINS, G. HERBERT, and FLOYD R. EASTWOOD: "Planning Industrial Recreation," Purdue University, Lafayette, Ind., 1941.

FLANAGAN, JOHN C.: "Personnel Psychology," in Dennis, W., "Current Trends in Psychology," pp. 138–168, University of Pittsburgh, Pa., 1950.

GARDNER, BURLEIGH B.: "Human Relations in Industry," Chicago: Richard D. Irwin, Inc., 1945.

HERON, ALEXANDER R.: "Sharing Information with Employees," Stanford University, Calif.: Stanford University Press, 1942.

———: "Why Men Work," Stanford University, Calif.: Stanford University Press, 1948.

HOSLETT, SCHUYLER DEAN: "Human Factors in Management," Parkville, Mo.: Park College Press, 1946.

LEWIN, KURT (edited by Gertrude Weiss Lewin): "Resolving Social Conflicts, Selected Papers on Group Dynamics," New York: Harper & Brothers, 1948.

MAIER, NORMAL R. F.: A Human Relations Program for Supervision, *Industrial and Labor Relations Review* (Cornell Quarterly), Vol. 1, No. 3, pp. 443–464, April, 1948.

MOORE, W. E., *et al.:* Industrial Sociology: Status and Prospects, *American Sociological Review,* Vol. 13, pp. 382–400, August, 1948.

PIGORS, PAUL: Making Two-Way Communication Effective, *Advanced Management* (S.A.M. Quarterly), Vol. 14, No. 2, pp. 68–72.

Dartnell Corporation, "Planning and Preparing Employee Manuals," Report No. 585, Chicago.

ROSS, MALCOLM: "All Manner of Men," New York: Reynal & Hitchcock, Inc., 1948.

TIFFIN, JOSEPH: "Industrial Psychology," 2d ed., New York: Prentice-Hall, Inc., 1947.

WARNER, W. LLOYD, MARCHIA MEEKER, and KENNETH EELLS: "Social Class in America," Chicago: Science Research Associates, 1949.

CHAPTER XXIII. JOINT RELATIONS AND COLLECTIVE BARGAINING

Arbitration Awards and Their Effect on Labor-Management Relations, *Mill and Factory,* Vol. 43, pp. 93–98, November, 1948.

AHERN, EILEEN: "Collective Bargaining in the Office," Research Report No. 12, New York: American Management Association, 1948.

BAKKE, E. WIGHT: "Mutual Survival, the Goal of Unions and Management," New York: Harper & Brothers, 1946.

BARBASH, JACK: "Labor Unions in Action," New York: Harper & Brothers, 1948.

CHAMBERLAIN, NEIL W.: "The Union Challenge to Management Control," New York: Harper & Brothers, 1948.

Cooke, Morris L., and Philip Murray: "Organized Labor and Production," New York: Harper & Brothers, 1940.

Daugherty, C. R.: "Labor Problems in American Industry," 6th ed., Boston: Houghton Mifflin Company, 1948.

Gardiner, Glenn: "When Foreman and Steward Bargain," New York: McGraw-Hill Book Company, Inc., 1945.

Golden, Clinton S. and Harold J. Ruttenberg: "The Dynamics of Industrial Democracy," New York: Harper & Brothers, 1942.

Green, William: "Labor and Democracy," Princeton, N. J.: Princeton University Press, 1939.

Heron, A. H.: "Beyond Collective Bargaining," Stanford University, Calif.: Stanford University Press, 1948.

Hill, Lee H., and Charles R. Hook, Jr.: "Management at the Bargaining Table," New York: McGraw-Hill Book Company, Inc., 1945.

Keller, A.: "American Arbitration," New York: American Arbitration Association, 1948.

Labor Relations at Work, *Fortune Magazine,* Vol. 40, No. 3, pp. 102–108.

Lapp, John A.: "How to Handle Labor Grievances," Deep River, Conn., National Foremen's Institute, Inc., 1945.

Millis, Harry A., *et al.:* "The Economics of Labor," 3 vols., New York: McGraw-Hill Book Company, Inc., 1945.

Mills, C. Wright: "The New Men of Power; America's Labor Leaders," New York: Harcourt, Brace and Company, Inc., 1948.

Nadell, M.: Labor Leaders and Industrial Values, *Sociology and Social Research,* Vol. 33, pp. 107–112, November-December, 1948.

National Planning Association, "Causes of Industrial Peace under Collective Bargaining," Washington, D.C. (15 case studies).

Princeton University, "A Trade Union Library," Bibliographical Series No. 80, rev. ed., Industrial Relations Section, Department of Economics and Social Institutions, Princeton, N.J., June, 1949.

Quigg, M. T.: The Law of Labor, *American Affairs,* Vol. 3, No. 4, pp. 283–296, Autumn, 1946.

Rowe, E. K., and A. Weiss: Benefit Plans under Collective Bargaining, *Monthly Labor Review,* Vol. 67, pp. 229–234, September, 1948.

Selekman, Benjamin M.: "Labor Relations and Human Relations," New York: McGraw-Hill Book Company, Inc., 1947.

Tead, O.: Labor Management Relations and the Public Interest, *Advanced Management,* June, 1947, pp. 48–52.

Chapter XXIV. Wage and Salary Administration

Bankers Trust Company, "289 Retirement Plans," New York, 1948.

Clague, E.: The C.P.I. (Consumers' Price Index)—A Summary of Its Essential Features, *Monthly Labor Review,* Vol. 67, pp. 8–11, July, 1948.

Council of Profit Sharing Industries, "Profit Sharing Manual," Columbus, Ohio, 1949.

Curle, A.: Incentives to Work: An Anthropological Appraisal, *Human Relations,* Vol. 2, No. 2, pp. 41–47, 1949.

Dallin, David J., and Boris I. Nicolaevsky: "Forced Labor in Soviet Russia," New Haven, Conn.: Yale University Press, 1947.

Ferguson, Leonard W.: "Clerical Salary Administration," New York: Life Office Management Association, 1948.

GALTON, L.: Small Business Can Pay Pensions, *Nation's Business,* Vol. 37, No. 9, pp. 29*ff.*, September, 1949.

GOMBERG, W.: Union Attitudes on the Application of Industrial Engineering Techniques to Collective Bargaining, *Personnel,* Vol. 24, pp. 443–454, May, 1948.

GOTTERER, M. H.: Supervisory and Executive Wage Incentives, *Modern Management,* Vol. 9, No. 1, pp. 17–19, January, 1949.

HOFFMAN, P. G.: "Management's Responsibility to Capitalism," New York: Committee for Economic Development, 1947.

Institute of Industrial Relations, "Wages, Prices and the National Welfare," University of California, 1948.

LITTAUER, S. B., and A. ABRUZZI: Experimental Criteria for Evaluating Workers and Operations, *Industrial and Labor Relations Review* (Cornell Quarterly), Vol. 2, No. 4, pp. 502–526, July, 1949.

LOUDEN, J. K.: "Wage Incentives," New York: John Wiley & Sons, Inc., 1944.

LYTLE, CHARLES W.: "Wage Incentive Methods," rev. ed., New York: The Ronald Press Company, 1942.

O'NEILL, HUGH: "Modern Pension Plans," New York: Prentice-Hall, Inc., 1947.

REYNOLDS, LLOYD G.: "Labor Economics and Labor Relations," New York: Prentice-Hall, Inc., 1949.

SAMUELSON, PAUL A.: "Economics: An Introductory Analysis," New York: McGraw-Hill Book Company, Inc., 1948.

SHISTER, JOSEPH: "Economics of the Labor Market," Philadelphia: J. B. Lippincott Company, 1949.

SLICHTER, S. H.: "The American Economy," New York: Alfred A. Knopf, Inc., 1948.

STEWART, BRYCE M., and WALTER J. COUPER: "Profit Sharing and Stock Ownership for Wage Earners and Executives," New York: Industrial Relations Counselors, Inc., 1945.

U.S. Department of Labor, "Guaranteed Wage Plans in the United States," Bureau of Labor Statistics, *Bulletin* 925, 1948.

WHYTE, W. F.: Incentive for Productivity: The Case of the Bundy Tubing Company, *Applied Anthropology,* Vol. 7, No. 2, pp. 1–16, Spring, 1948.

CHAPTER XXV. JOB EVALUATION AND MERIT RATING

BALDERSTON, C. CANBY: "Wage Setting Based on Job Analysis and Evaluation," New York: Industrial Relations Counselors, Inc., 1940.

BENGE, EUGENE J., SAMUEL L. H. BURK, and EDWARD N. HAY: "Manual of Job Evaluation," New York: Harper & Brothers, 1941.

BITTNER, R.: Developing an Employee Merit Rating Procedure, *Personnel,* Vol. 25, pp. 275–290, January, 1949.

COHEN, L.: More Reliable Job Evaluation, *Personnel Psychology,* Vol. 1, pp. 457–464, Winter, 1948.

FERGUSON, LEONARD W.: The Development of a Method of Appraisal, *Personnel,* Vol. 24, No. 2, pp. 127–136, September, 1947.

GOMBERG, WILLIAM: "A Labor Union Manual on Job Evaluation," Chicago: Roosevelt College, Labor Education Division, 1947.

HALSEY, GEORGE D.: "Making and Using Industrial Service Ratings," New York: Harper & Brothers, 1944.

JONES, P. W.: "Practical Job Evaluation," New York: John Wiley & Sons, Inc., 1948.

KNAUFT, E. B.: Construction and Use of Weighted Check List Rating Scales for Two Industrial Situations, *Journal of Applied Psychology,* Vol. 32, pp. 63–70, February, 1948.

MAHLER, W. R.: "Twenty Years of Merit Rating," New York: The Psychological Corp., 1947.

Metropolitan Life Insurance Company, "An Introduction to Job Evaluation," New York, 1947.

OTIS, JAY L., and RICHARD H. LEUKART: "Job Evaluation, A Basis for Sound Wage Administration," New York: Prentice-Hall, Inc., 1948.

PATTON, JOHN A., and REYNOLDS S. SMITH, JR.: "Job Evaluation," Chicago: Richard D. Irwin, Inc., 1949.

U.S. Department of Labor, U.S. Employment Service, Occupational Analysis Branch, "Industrial Job Evaluation Systems," Washington, D.C., 1947.

Western Reserve University, "Handbook of Job Evaluation for Clerical, Supervisory and Administrative Jobs," Cleveland: Personnel Research Institute, 1948.

CHAPTER XXVI. SALES CONTROL

AGNEW, H. E., JENKINS, and J. C. DRURY: "Outlines of Marketing," p. 35, New York: McGraw-Hill Book Company, Inc., 1942.

CRISP, RICHARD D.: "How to Reduce Distribution Costs," New York: Funk & Wagnalls Company, 1948.

NYSTROM, PAUL H.: "Marketing Handbook," Sec. 16, pp. 645–693, New York: The Ronald Press Company, 1948.

PHILLIPS, CHARLES F., and DELBERT F. DUNCAN: "Marketing Principles and Methods," Chicago: Richard D. Irwin, Inc., 1948.

LESTER, BERNARD: "Sales Engineering," New York: John Wiley & Sons, Inc., 1940.

Periodicals

American Management Association, "Reducing Distribution Costs," *Marketing Series,* No. 58, 1945.

National Industrial Conference Board, Inc., "The Economic Almanac," New York.

Industrial Marketing, a monthly publication covering selling and advertising in business and industry, Advertising Publication, Inc., Chicago.

Modern Industry, New York, Vol. 18, No. 2, Aug. 15, 1949.

Printers' Ink, a weekly publication devoted to advertising, management, and sales, Printers' Ink Publishing Co., Inc., New York.

Sales Management, a monthly magazine of marketing, Sales Management, Inc., East Stroudsburg, Pa.

The Twentieth Century Fund, Inc., "Does Distribution Cost Too Much?" New York, 1939.

CHAPTER XXVII. ADVERTISING AND SALES PROMOTION

ANDERSON, CLARE WRIGHT, and IRA DENNIS ANDERSON: "Principles of Retailing," 2d ed., New York: McGraw-Hill Book Company, Inc., 1941.

BORDEN, NEIL H.: "Advertising in our Economy," Chicago: Richard D. Irwin, Inc., 1945.

BREWSTER, A. J., H. H. PALMER, and R. G. INGRAHAM: "Introduction to Advertising," New York: McGraw-Hill Book Company, Inc., 1947.

BRIDGE, H. P.: "Practical Advertising," New York: Rinehart & Company, Inc., 1949.

DOREMUS, W. L.: "Advertising for Profit: A Guide for Small Business," New York: Pitman Publishing Corp., 1947.

HECHERT, J. BROOKS: "The Analysis and Control of Distribution Costs," New York: The Ronald Press Company, 1940.

HEPNER, H. W.: "Effective Advertising," New York: McGraw-Hill Book Company, Inc., 1949.

MAYNARD, HAROLD H., and THEODORE N. BECKMAN: "Principles of Marketing," 4th ed., New York: The Ronald Press Company, 1946.

MAYTHAM, THOMAS E.: "Introduction to Advertising Principles and Practice," New York: Harper & Brothers, 1948.

NIXON, H. K.: "Principles of Selling," 2d ed., New York: McGraw-Hill Book Company, Inc., 1942.

PHILLIPS, CHARLES F., and DELBERT J. DUNCAN, "Marketing," Chicago: Richard D. Irwin, Inc., 1948.

POLIAK, SAUL: "Rebuilding the Sales Staff," New York: McGraw-Hill Book Company, Inc., 1947.

Printers' Ink Publishing Co., Inc., "Cutting Advertising and Printing Costs," New York: Funk & Wagnalls Company, 1948.

REED, VIRGIL D.: Recent Developments in Distribution, *Credit and Financial Management,* Philadelphia (National Association of Credit Men), Vol. 51, No. 8, pp. 7–31, August, 1949.

ROTH, CHARLES B.: "Stimulating Salesmen," New York: Prentice-Hall, Inc., 1948.

SANDAGE, C. H.: "Advertising: Theory and Practice," Chicago: Richard D. Irwin, Inc., 1948.

TOSDAL, HARRY R.: "Introduction to Sales Management," 2d ed., New York: McGraw-Hill Book Company, Inc., 1940.

YOUNG, J. O.: "Adventures in Advertising," New York: Harper & Brothers, 1949.

Periodicals:

Sales Management.
Industrial Marketing.
Printers' Ink.

CHAPTER XXVIII. OFFICE AND ACCOUNTING CONTROL

ANDERSON, DAVID R.: "Practical Controllership," Chicago: Richard D. Irwin, Inc., 1947.

BULLINGER, CLARENCE E.: "Engineering Economic Analysis," New York: McGraw-Hill Book Company, Inc., 1942.

CROXTON, FREDERICK E., and DUDLEY J. COWDEN: "Applied Statistics," New York: Prentice-Hall, Inc., 1942.

Factory Management and Maintenance, a monthly periodical, New York: McGraw-Hill Publishing Company, Inc.

LANG, THEODORE: "Cost Accountants' Handbook," New York: The Ronald Press Company, 1948.

LASSER, JACOB KAY: "Handbook of Accounting Methods," New York: D. Van Nostrand Company, Inc., 1943.

LAWRENCE, W. B.: "Cost Accounting," 3d ed., New York: Prentice-Hall, Inc., 1946.

LEFFINGWELL, W. H., and E. M. ROBINSON: "Textbook of Office Management," 2d ed., New York: McGraw-Hill Book Company, Inc., 1943.

LERNER, ABBA P., "The Economics of Control," New York: The Macmillan Company, 1947.

MACDONALD, JOHN H.: "Office Management," New York: Prentice-Hall, Inc., 1941.

———: "Controllership: Its Functions and Techniques," New York: Controllers Institute of America, 1940.

MARCH, JAMES H.: "Industrial Cost Accounting," New York: McGraw-Hill Book Company, Inc., 1949.

Mill & Factory, a monthly periodical devoted to management, production, and maintenance, New York.

PATON, W. A.: "The Accountants' Handbook," New York: The Ronald Press Company, 1947.

——— and E. F. GAY: "Essentials of Accounting," New York: The Macmillan Company, 1949.

RAUTENSTRAUCH, WALTER, and RAYMOND WILLERS: "The Economics of Industrial Management," New York: Funk & Wagnalls Company, 1949.

SCHLATTER, CHARLES F.: "Cost Accounting," New York: John Wiley & Sons, Inc., 1947.

TERRY, GEORGE R.: "Office Management and Control," Chicago: Richard D. Irwin, Inc.

CHAPTER XXIX. BUDGETARY CONTROL

GOETZ, BILLY E.: "Management Planning and Control," New York: McGraw-Hill Book Company, Inc., 1949.

HECHERT, J. BROOKS: "Business Budgeting and Control," New York: The Ronald Press Company, 1946.

MACDONALD, JOHN H.: "Practical Budget Procedure," New York: Prentice-Hall, Inc., 1939.

ROWLAND, F. H., and W. H. HARR: "Budgeting for Management Control," New York: Harper & Brothers, 1945.

WELLINGTON, C. O.: "A Primer on Budgeting," New York: D. Van Nostrand Company, Inc., 1949.

CHAPTER XXX. RECORDS AND REPORTS

GAUM, CARL G., HAROLD F. GARVES, and LYNE S. S. HOFFMANN: "Report Writing," New York: Prentice-Hall, Inc., 1946.

HERON, ALEXANDER: "Sharing Information with Employees," Stanford University, Calif.: Stanford University Press, 1942.

MACDONALD, JOHN H.: "Controllership: Its Functions and Technique," p. 99, Controllers Institute of America, 1940.

McCORMICK, CHARLES P.: "The Power of People," New York: Harper & Brothers, 1949.

National Industrial Conference Board, Inc., "Company Annual Reports," *Studies in Personnel Policy,* No. 47, New York, 1940.

NELSON, J. RALEIGH: "Writing the Technical Report," 2d. ed., New York: McGraw-Hill Book Company, Inc., 1947.

RUDOLPH, MODLEY: "How to Use Pictorial Statistics," New York: Harper & Brothers, 1937.

SAUNDERS, A. G., and C. R. ANDERSON: "Business Reports," New York: McGraw-Hill Book Company, Inc., 1940.

CHAPTER XXXI. COORDINATING THE ENTERPRISE

BARNARD, CHESTER I.: "The Functions of the Executive," Cambridge: Harvard University Press, 1938.

BRADY, ROBERT A.: "Business as a System of Power," New York: Columbia University Press, 1943.

DOOB, L. W.: "Public Opinion and Propaganda," New York: Henry Holt and Company, 1948.

HERON, ALEXANDER: "Sharing Information with Employees," Stanford University, Calif.: Stanford University Press, 1942.

————: "Why Men Work," Stanford University, Calif.: Stanford University Press, 1948.

LIVINGSTON, ROBERT TENIOT: "The Engineering of Organization and Management," New York: McGraw-Hill Book Company, Inc., 1949.

TRUNDLE, GEORGE T., JR. (Editor-in-Chief): "Managerial Control of Business," New York: John Wiley & Sons, Inc., 1948.

INDEX